# Rodale's
# LANDSCAPE
# PROBLEM SOLVER

# Rodale's
# LANDSCAPE
# PROBLEM SOLVER

## A Plant-by-Plant Guide
### by Jeff and Liz Ball

**Illustrations by Pamela and Walter Carroll and Robin Brickman**

**Photographs by Liz Ball and Rodale Press Photography Staff**

 Rodale Press, Emmaus, Pennsylvania

Printed in the United States of America on acid-free ∞, recycled ♻ paper

Book design: Denise Mirabello

**Library of Congress Cataloging-in-Publication Data**

Ball, Jeff.
    Rodale's landscape problem solver : a plant-by-plant guide / by
Jeff and Liz Ball ; illustrations by Pamela and Walter Carroll and
Robin Brickman ; photographs by Liz Ball and the Rodale Press
photography staff.
        p.    cm.
    Bibliography: p.
    Includes index.
    ISBN 0-87857-802-1
    1. Plants, Ornamental—Diseases and pests—Control—Handbooks,
manuals, etc. 2. Gardens—Management—Handbooks, manuals, etc.
3. Landscape gardening—Handbooks, manuals, etc.    I. Ball, Liz.
    II. Title.    III. Title: Landscape problem solver.
SB608.07B35    1989
635.9—dc 19                                                89-30190
                                                                CIP

**Distributed in the book trade by St. Martin's Press**

12    14    16    18    20    19    17    15    13

# Contents

# Acknowledgments

As with the first book in this problem-solving series (*Rodale's Garden Problem Solver*), we had to collect, sort, review, and then organize copious amounts of information. There are a number of key players in this data management process who made significant contributions for which we are very grateful.

The major task of sorting out the insects from the diseases for all the plants was shared by Mike Wisniewski and Pete Johnson. Their patience with our many style changes was notable. Jim Janczewski helped us with the complex task of checking horticultural nomenclature and verifying facts. Much of the valuable information about roses was offered by Jack Potter.

We also depended on many fine reference books for information on insect pests and diseases—their symptoms and life cycles—and for details about the various plants discussed in this book. Some of the most important sources we used were *Wyman's Gardening Encyclopedia* by Donald Wyman, *Diseases and Pests of Ornamental Plants* by Pascal Pirone, and Cynthia Wescott's *Gardener's Bug Book*.

For details about the trees described in this book, we referred to *The Gardener's Illustrated Encyclopedia of Trees and Shrubs* by Brian Davis, *Trees of North America and Europe* by Roger Phillips, and the *Taylor's Guide to Trees*. The *Taylor's Guide to Ground Covers, Vines, and Grasses* was an important source of information about the ground covers and vines we discussed. Barbara Barton's book *Gardening by Mail 2* provided much of the information for the source list. Publication facts for all these references are given in the Recommended Reading list at the back of this book. To all these authors, we owe our thanks.

A major source of information about safe techniques for pest control were the publications of the Bio-Integral Resource Center (BIRC). Helga and Bill Olkowlski and Sheila Daar performed a tremendous service to us all in pulling together such helpful information in a usable and readable form. We also are very much indebted to Niles Kinerk for his help and for the very informative catalog from his Natural Gardening Research Center. To all these folks, we give our thanks.

# Introduction

Scanning this book, you may be overwhelmed by all the problems of landscape plants you'll find listed. You may close the book, thinking that it's impossible to have a yard that isn't constantly under attack by insects, animals, diseases, and so forth. When all the information about landscape plant problems is gathered in one place, it can be intimidating. What you need to remember, though, is that this book will help free you and your yard from those problems. Furthermore, not all of these insects, diseases, and animal pests will show up in your landscape, and those that do certainly won't all strike at once. So take a deep breath and relax. With this book, we have armed you with what we believe to be the most complete, effective, and powerful guide to safe problem control on the market.

Another very important reason for owning this book is to learn that it is easier to prevent most of the problems that turn up in the landscape than it is to let everything go and wait for problems to appear. The surest way to have a healthy landscape is to locate your plants in the proper place with the right soil and the right amount of light, and then provide them with their basic food and water requirements. You'll find under each plant a description, along with details on how to plant and care for it. Healthy, vigorous plants are much less vulnerable to pest and disease problems, and they are better able to fight off any infections or infestations that do occur. Follow good garden cleanup practices; protect your plants from injury from wind, lawn mowers, and freezing temperatures; and keep your eye out for potential problems. Good problem prevention takes very little extra time over and above normal yard-care activities. So, while this book is dedicated to helping you identify and solve problems, its real story is about how to prevent those problems in the first place.

When problems do occur, you'll be able to solve them more quickly and effectively if you have the necessary tools. The following list includes some basic products for insect and disease control that you might want to consider gathering:

1. A generous pile of finished compost.

2. A bottle of seaweed or kelp extract (you'll need a fresh supply each year).

3. A bottle of liquid fertilizer, such as fish emulsion (this will keep for two to three years).

4. A bottle of insecticidal soap concentrate (this will last indefinitely).

5. A bottle of liquid Bt (*Bacillus thuringiensis;* you'll need a fresh supply each year).

6. A bottle of pyrethrum or a mix of pyrethrum and rotenone (this will keep for three to four years).

7. A bottle of flowable sulfur fungicide (this will keep for one year).

8. A bottle of copper-based fungicide (this will last indefinitely).

9. A bottle of dormant oil (this will last indefinitely).

10. A good sprayer with a capacity of at least 1 gallon.

11. At least one bird feeder to attract birds to your yard.

12. Sufficient organic mulching material to cover the area around plants that need mulch.

With these tools, you'll be able to face just about any problem that presents itself in your backyard; hopefully, there won't be too many.

# How to Use This Book

This book has been designed so that you can discover solutions to your landscape problems within seconds. Because it is so easy to use, you could sit down and figure it out yourself, but we'd like to save you even that bit of trouble. In addition, we'd like to direct you to some areas of general information that will help you use the text most effectively.

## FOR IMMEDIATE CONTROL OF PROBLEMS

If a problem develops on one of your landscape plants—holes in the blossoms or yellow spots on the leaves, for example—follow these steps to identify it and to find a quick solution.

1. Locate the entry for that plant in Part 1 of the book.

2. Scan that entry to find the symptom that matches the one you've discovered on your plant. Here you'll find the cause of the problem (insect, disease, or cultural deficiency), a more complete description of the symptoms, and the best method for immediate control.

## FOR GENERAL CONTROL AND PREVENTION

This book doesn't stop at the one quick solution to any given plant problem. Turn to Part 2 for an in-depth discussion of the control of insect pests, animal pests, and diseases. There you'll read about the best ways to use insecticides such as pyrethrum and rotenone, how to make pest-repellent sprays of garlic and other natural substances, how to set traps, and much more. You'll learn the details of disease control and how to keep animal pests away from your plants. Detailed descriptions of insects and diseases will help you identify these problems accurately, and prepare you to handle them more effectively.

Not only will you learn what to do once you find a problem in your backyard, but you'll discover techniques that will help you prevent insects, diseases, and animals from attacking your plants in the first place.

Part 3 discusses general environment and landscape management. You'll find details on caring for the soil, watering, fertilizing, pruning, weeding, and more. At the back of the book, you'll find a plant hardiness zone map so you can determine which varieties will grow in your part of the country. Give your plants the right environment from the start, and they'll give you a beautiful backyard that you can enjoy for years.

You probably already have a stock of tools, sprays, and dusts to help you fight the marauding insects and deadly diseases that show up in the landscape around your home. We've given you another powerful tool to help you manage a pest- and disease-free yard. So keep this book near the back door, where it's readily at hand. As the years go by, you'll need it less and less as you perfect your techniques for preventing plant problems . . . then you can move it to the bookshelf.

# PART 1

# *Plant Problems*

# CHAPTER 1

# *Trees*

Trees bring majesty and grace to the landscape. Their grandeur and permanence make them the true backbone of the backyard. Because they have probably been growing in the same place for years and years, it is easier to overlook them than a newly planted rosebush or your ever-increasing violets. But trees need care, too.

Unfortunately, large, mature trees are not so easy to care for. How do you prune a 70-foot oak tree all by yourself? If your oak has aphids, how do you spray all those leaves? The simple answer is, you don't. If you have any serious problems with any trees that are taller than 20 feet, seek the help of professional tree-care specialists. They know what needs to be done, they have the training and the skills, and they have the proper tools. Fortunately, mature trees have fewer problems than younger, smaller trees, and they survive insect and disease attack better.

So, this chapter focuses primarily on what you can do for the small and young trees in your landscape when they face insect or disease problems. Because young trees are more vulnerable, you should watch them carefully and attend to any problems as soon as you spot them.

You will also learn basic tree-care tasks that you can perform on trees of any size. You'll learn how to feed, water, and mulch around them. All of this care will go a long way to keeping insect infestation and disease to a minimum. A few preliminary suggestions: Prevent problems in the first place by being careful not to damage your trees with the lawn mower or the tractor. If you have several large trees on your property, bring in a professional tree-care specialist every three to five years to look at them. The specialist will prune your trees, treat any wounds, and nip in the bud any problems that may be developing.

Trees are tough. They'll weather a fair number of hardships. But if you want to keep them healthy and looking their best year after year, you must care for them well.

# Beech

*Fagus* spp.

## DESCRIPTION

A popular tree in the eastern part of the country, the majestic beech needs lots of space to grow and show off its handsome stature. Some cultivars, such as the weeping purple beech (*Fagus* 'Purpurea Pendula'),

have pendulous branches, which will sweep to the ground if permitted. Beeches grow quickly, and their beauty lasts through all the seasons. About eight species are hardy in the eastern United States. The American beech (*F. grandifolia*) and the European beech (*F. sylvatica*) are the two most commonly grown types. The American beech has a more upright habit, whereas the European is nearly as wide as it is tall. Both have gray bark and, when sheared, can be used in hedges. Because they require lots of room, they are not suited for planting along streets.

### Height

American beech (*F. grandifolia*), 90 feet
European beech (*F. sylvatica*), 90 feet

### Foliage

Deciduous trees, beeches have sharply toothed, ovate leaves. Those of the American beech have more veins. In both, the foliage is dense and dark green. However, the European beech can be distinguished by the glossy sheen of its leaves. In fall the foliage turns golden bronze.

## ENVIRONMENT

### Varieties by Zone

To zone 3, American beech
To zone 4, European beech

### Light Requirements

Full sun to partial shade.

# MOST COMMON INSECT PESTS

## Leaves Curled and Distorted

### Aphids

Aphids retard or distort tree growth by attacking foliage. The leaves of infested trees may turn yellow or brown, wilt under bright sunlight, or curl and pucker. You may see ants crawling on the tree; they are attracted to the honeydew secreted by aphids. Two species of aphids commonly attack beech trees. The beech aphid (*Phyllaphis fagi*) is dark green and covered with loose white flakes. The beech blight aphid (*Prociphilus imbricator*) is bluish and is covered with a white cottony substance. To control either of these species, spray the tree vigorously with water in the morning. Apply this technique three times, once every other day. For heavy infestations, spray with insecticidal soap every two to three days until the aphids are gone. As a last resort, use pyrethrum. Two applications made three to four days apart should finally eliminate this problem.

## Tiny Holes in Bark; Branches Girdled or Cankered

### Borers

Winding galleries in beech wood and tiny holes in its bark are typical signs of the brown wood borer (*Parandra brunnea*). The larvae are 1¼ inches long, with white bodies and black heads. Adults are ¾-inch-long shiny brown beetles. Another pest, the two-lined chestnut borer (*Agrilus bilineatus*), girdles branches of beech trees, taking off a ring of bark and cambium from the branches. The larvae of the leopard moth (*Zeuzera pyrina*) also bore into the trunks of beeches. These borers generally attack only those trees already weakened by some other injury. They work on the sunlit sides of branches, creating cankers of varying sizes.

To control borers in most situations, make a thorough examination of the tree before the spring season arrives and cut and burn any dying or unhealthy-looking twigs that may contain borers.

During the summer season, check to see if sawdust is being pushed from small borer holes. Such holes should be cut out with a sharp knife. If the tunnels are fairly straight, you can kill borers by probing with a flexible wire, or pull them out with a hooked wire and destroy them. If tunnels curve and wind, inject nicotine sulfate into each borer hole and plug the hole with putty.

By preventing any damage to beech tree bark and wood and treating any wounds, you can forestall most borer infestations.

## Holes in Leaves

### Caterpillars

Beeches can fall prey to any one of several caterpillars, including eastern tent, saddled prominent, walnut, and yellownecked caterpillars. All can be controlled in the same way. Pick off the caterpillars and any damaged leaves and destroy them; then spray the tree with Bt (*Bacillus thuringiensis*) every 10 to 14 days until the pests are gone. If the problem is very serious, spray the upper and lower surfaces of leaves with pyrethrum or a 1 percent rotenone solution. Usually two applications, 3 to 4 days apart, will take care of the caterpillars. Check your trees in fall and winter and scrape any egg masses off the leaves.

### Loopers

The cabbage looper (*Trichoplusia ni*), linden looper (*Erannis tilaria*), hemlock looper (*Lambdina fiscellaria*), omnivorous looper (*Sabulotes caberata*), and others consume foliage of beech trees. Adult loopers are small moths. The caterpillars are about 1½ inches long and have gained their notoriety by the way they walk. A looper arches its back as it walks by bringing up its rear toward its head and then jumping forward with its front legs.

Despite their entertaining movements across the surfaces of leaves, you won't enjoy the holes they chew in the foliage of your trees. So, stop their dancing by spraying infested trees with Bt (*Bacillus thuringiensis*) about every two weeks until these pests disappear.

## Leaves Consumed; Conspicuous, Tawny Egg Masses Present

### Gypsy Moths

Larvae of the gypsy moth (*Porthetria dispar*) gather in huge, hungry masses to devour foliage on trees like beeches. The tree may die after repeated defoliations. Newly hatched caterpillars are about 1/16 inch long and grow to about 2½ inches. Mature larvae have five pairs of blue spots and six pairs of red spots along the back. Adult male moths have a wingspan of 1½ inches. They are light tan to dark brown, with blackish wavy bands across the forewings. Female moths are larger and nearly white. Although they have a 2½-inch wingspan, they can barely fly. Both sexes have feathered antennae. Gypsy moths lay masses of 400 to 500 eggs. They are covered with velvety, buff-colored hairs. As with most caterpillar pests, Bt (*Bacillus thuringiensis*) is the weapon of choice. Spray trees every 10 to 14 days from late April, when eggs are beginning to hatch, until mid-June. If gypsy moth larvae are still a problem, wrap a piece of foot-wide burlap around the trunk of the tree, about chest high. Tie it around the center with heavy twine, letting the top fold over the twine. Gypsy moth larvae are night feeders and crawl down the tree each morning. When they reach the burlap, they will make themselves comfortable under the fold. In the late afternoon, put on garden gloves and sweep the caterpillars off into a container of detergent and water.

## Skeletonized Areas on Leaves

### Maple Leaf Cutters

Maple leaf cutters (*Paraclemensia acerifoliella*) can defoliate beech trees. These insects cut out small sections of the leaves and form cases, in which they hide while they feed. Leaf cutters often skeletonize the leaves in a circular path such that a section of leaf often drops to the ground. As soon as you spot these pests, spray the tree with Bt (*Bacillus thuringiensis*) at weekly intervals until leaf cutters are removed. In the fall, rake up and destroy all leaf litter, where the pupae hibernate.

## Leaves Discolored; Small Bumps on Leaves and Branches

### Scale

Discoloration of the upper leaf surface is the first sign of scale attack, followed by leaf drop, reduced growth of the tree, and twig dieback. Some scale species excrete honeydew, which coats the foliage, attracting ants and encouraging the growth of sooty mold. Beech scale (*Cryptococcus fagisuga*), black scale (*Saissetia oleae*), cottony-cushion scale (*Icerya purchasi*), and several other species attack beeches. These pests gather in groups and appear as small bumps or blisterlike outgrowths on stems and leaves. Scale insects have a round waxy covering, which protects them while they feed on the tree. These coverings may be white, yellow, or brown to black, and are about 1/10 to 2/5 inch in diameter.

If caught early on, before too many of these pests have discovered your tree, you can simply scrape them off with your fingernail or remove them with a cotton swab dipped in rubbing alcohol. For medium to heavy infestations, spray trees with a mixture of ½ cup alcohol and 1 quart insecticidal soap every three days for two weeks.

## MOST COMMON DISEASES

## Bleeding Lesions on Branches and Trunk

### Canker

Beeches infected with bleeding canker (*Phytophthora cactorum*) develop lesions that ooze either a watery light brown or a thick reddish brown liquid. No effective control measures are yet known. Some trees with mild cases of this disease have recovered. If your beech is severely infected, cut it down and destroy it to prevent the disease from spreading.

## Leaves Become Spotted, Turn Brown, and Fall Prematurely

### Leaf Spot

Leaf spot diseases, caused by the fungi *Gloeosporium fagi* and *Phyllosticta faginea*, develop on beeches and other trees late in the growing season. Gathering and destroying fallen leaves usually suffices for practical control. If your beeches continue to contract leaf spot year after year, spray them with a copper fungicide, following package directions, in late spring to prevent the disease from occurring again.

## White Powder on Leaves

### Powdery Mildew

Late in summer, you may find powdery mildew developing on the leaves of your beeches. This disease creates a thin white powdery film on the surface of plant foliage. It is caused by the fungi *Microsphaera* *alni* and *Phyllactinia corylea*. To control powdery mildew, spray all foliage thoroughly with wettable sulfur. Check leaves again in a week, and if it is still spreading, spray again.

## NOTES AND RESEARCH

Beeches have very shallow roots and feed near the surface of the soil. Other plants cannot compete successfully for soil nutrients within the dripline of a beech. This and the shade cast by the foliage make it impossible to grow grass or anything else under full-sized trees.

# TREE **Birch** *Betula* spp.

## DESCRIPTION

The English poet Coleridge called the birch the "lady of the woods." These trees have a graceful habit and peeling, textured bark. They are popular ornamental trees in the northern United States and in Canada. Most of us know the canoe birch (*Betula papyrifera*) for its white bark, which was used by Indians to make canoes and cover wigwams. The European birch (*B. pendula*) also has white bark and is noted for its pyramidal shape and pendulous branches. River birch (*B. nigra*) loves damp earth and grows well in lowlands and along stream banks. Both the European birch and river birch do well in California.

## Height

Canoe birch (*B. papyrifera*), 90 feet
Dahurian birch (*B. davurica*), 60 feet
European birch (*B. pendula*), 60 feet
River birch (*B. nigra*), 90 feet
Sweet birch (*B. lenta*), 75 feet

## Foliage

Birches are deciduous trees, with alternate, simple, toothed leaves. They turn bright yellow in autumn. Sweet birch is best for fall color.

## ENVIRONMENT

### Varieties by Zone

To zone 2, canoe birch and European birch
To zone 3, Dahurian birch and sweet birch
To zone 4, river birch

## Light Requirements

Birches prefer full sun, but will grow in partial shade.

# MOST COMMON CULTURAL PROBLEMS

## Tree Grows Poorly

### Shock of Transplanting; Improper Pruning

Birch trees can be difficult to transplant, so young trees should be planted where they are to grow permanently. Birches should be planted, or if necessary,

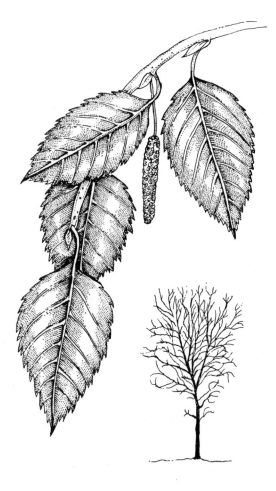

transplanted, in spring. Trees should be balled-and-burlapped or pot grown to minimize transplant stress.

Spring pruning can also be harmful to birches. Cuts made in late winter or spring, when the sap is running, will bleed excessively. They can be pruned at any other time of the year.

## Sudden Death

### Old Age

Birches aren't long-lived trees, and old trees sometimes just suddenly die for no apparent reason. Early death can also be due to wood-boring insects. Consult your local nursery for species best suited to your region and yard.

# MOST COMMON INSECT PESTS

## Leaves Curled and Distorted

### Aphids

Aphids retard or distort tree growth by attacking the foliage. The leaves of infected trees may turn yellow or brown and wilt under bright sunlight, or they may curl and pucker. Ants are attracted to the honeydew secreted by aphids. Birch aphids produce a lot of honeydew, which encourages the growth of sooty mold. The European birch aphid (*Euceraphis punctipennis*) is yellow and infests many birch varieties. If witch hazel grows anywhere near your birches, beware the witch hazel leaf gall aphid (*Hormaphis hamamelidis*). Although this pest primarily attacks witch hazel, it will migrate to birches in summer.

To control aphids, spray the tree vigorously with water in the morning and then twice again, every other day. For heavy infestations, spray with insecticidal soap every two to three days until the pests are gone. As a last resort, use pyrethrum in two applications, three to four days apart.

## Holes in Leaves

### Birch Skeletonizers

Brown, skeletonized leaves are the mark of the

birch skeletonizer. *Bucculatrix canadensisella* attacks in its larval form—a ¼-inch-long yellowish green worm. As an adult, the skeletonizer is a moth with white-lined brown wings that span ⅜ inch. If you notice only a few of the larvae on your tree, simply pick them off and destroy them; otherwise spray with Bt (*Bacillus thuringiensis*) every 14 days until they are gone. For serious infestations, spray with pyrethrum or a 1 percent rotenone solution. Two applications, 3 or 4 days apart, will usually take care of the problem.

### Loopers

The cabbage looper (*Trichoplusia ni*), linden looper (*Erannis tilaria*), hemlock looper (*Lambdina fiscellaria*), omnivorous looper (*Sabulotes caberata*), and others feed on the foliage of birch trees. Adults are small moths. Larvae are caterpillars, which grow to 1½ inches long. They are distinguished from other caterpillars by the way they loop when they walk, much as the inchworm humps its back as it crawls along a stem. Spray infested trees with Bt (*Bacillus thuringiensis*) about every two weeks until these pests disappear.

## Leaves Chewed; Rusty Red Patches on Bark; Trees Girdled

### Bronze Birch Borers

The bronze birch borer (*Agrilus anxius*) attacks birches on all fronts. The adult beetles feed on birch leaves for a while; then they lay their eggs in slits in the bark. The larvae that hatch are flat-headed, light-colored grubs, about ½ to 1 inch long. They tunnel through the bark to the sapwood, starting at the top of the tree and working downward. Telltale rusty red patches appear on the bark as they advance. Sometimes the top of the tree completely dies. Trees may eventually be completely girdled and die. The European birch is especially susceptible to the bronze birch borer.

To control borers in most situations, make a thorough examination of the tree before the spring season arrives and cut and burn any dying or unhealthy-looking twigs that may contain borers. During the summer season, check to see if sawdust

is being pushed from small borer holes. Such holes should be cut out with a sharp knife. If the tunnels are fairly straight, you can kill borers by probing with a flexible wire, or pull them out with a hooked wire and destroy them. If tunnels curve and wind, inject nicotine sulfate into each borer hole and plug the hole with putty.

## Leaves Skeletonized

### Cankerworms

These pests feed heavily on the foliage of birch trees, skeletonizing the leaves and sometimes defoliating the entire tree. You may know them as inchworms. They are about 1 inch long and may be brown or green with a yellow stripe. As soon as you discover them on your trees, begin spraying with Bt (*Bacillus thuringiensis*) every 10 to 14 days until the pests are gone. Early in spring, before the weather turns warm, place a sticky band on the trunks of vulnerable trees to catch the females as they climb the trees to lay their eggs.

## Leaves Consumed; Conspicuous, Tawny Egg Masses Present

### Gypsy Moths

Larvae of the gypsy moth (*Porthetria dispar*) gather in hungry masses and devour birch foliage. Trees may die after repeated defoliations. Newly hatched caterpillars are about ¹⁄₁₆ inch long and grow to about 2½ inches. Mature larvae have five pairs of blue spots and six pairs of red spots along their backs. The adult male moths have 1½-inch wing-spans. They are light tan to dark brown, with blackish wavy bands across their forewings. The white female moths are larger, with 2½-inch wings, but they can barely fly. Both male and female gypsy moths have feathered antennae. Gypsy moths lay masses of about 400 to 500 eggs. These masses are covered with velvety, buff-colored hairs.

As with most caterpillar pests, gypsy moth larvae are most effectively controlled with Bt (*Bacillus thuringiensis*). Spray trees every 10 to 14 days from late April, when eggs begin to hatch, until mid-June. If the larvae are still a problem, wrap a piece of foot-wide burlap around the trunk of the tree, about chest high. Tie it around the center with heavy twine, letting the top fold over the twine. Gypsy moth larvae are night feeders and crawl down the tree each morning. When they reach the burlap, they will make themselves comfortable under the fold. In the late afternoon, put on garden gloves and sweep the caterpillars off into a container of detergent and water.

## Brown Blotches on Leaves

### Leafminers

The larvae of the birch leafminer (*Fenusa pusilla*) attack gray (*B. alleghaniensis*), canoe, and European birches. These whitish larvae are only about ¼ inch long. They feed between the upper and lower surfaces of the leaves, causing the leaves to blister and turn brown. The adults are small black sawflies, ³/16 inch long, which overwinter in soil as pupae. They begin to lay their eggs on birch foliage in spring. The eggs hatch, and the first brood of larvae begin to feed anytime from very early to late May. These spring larvae cause the most damage because they attack the tender young foliage. Later broods cause less damage because they feed only on leaves of sucker growths and new leaves in tree crowns.

To control leafminers, remove the infested leaves. Spray with insecticidal soap to kill any adults that might lay eggs on your plants. If leafminers are a problem year after year, consider covering plants in spring with agricultural fleece.

## Galls on Branches

### Mites

You know mites have infested your birches if you find galls on the branches. The galls they create are about 1 inch in diameter. The seed mites (*Eriophyes betulae*) that cause these galls are about 1/50 inch in length. If you could see them, you'd find they have four pairs of legs (mites are not true insects) and piercing, sucking mouth parts. They can be yellow, green, red, or brown.

Usually simply spraying your trees with a forceful stream of water in the morning, three times,

once every other day, knocks these tiny pests off your trees for good. However, if this technique doesn't work, apply insecticidal soap every two to three days for two weeks.

## Holes in Leaves; Tents in Limbs

### Tent Caterpillars

The eastern tent caterpillar (*Malacosoma americanum*) and the forest tent caterpillar (*M. disstria*) are two of the most common species to attack birches. The silky tents they build in the limbs of trees clearly signal their presence. These striped, hairy caterpillars are about 3 inches long. They live in their tents while feeding on birch leaves. The adult moths have grayish or brown wings with a ½-inch span.

As soon as you see tents going up in your birches, spray with Bt (*Bacillus thuringiensis*) every five to seven days until the pests are gone. Pull down any established nests.

## MOST COMMON DISEASES

## Callused Stem Lesions Near Branch Forks

### Canker

Birches are susceptible to cankers caused by the fungus *Nectria galligena*. This fungus develops near the forks of branches, causing irregular swellings, which crack open and expose the wood. A thick callus develops at the border of the canker, which may eventually girdle and kill the tree. Save trees with cankers on their branches by pruning or cutting out and destroying the affected tissue; then sterilize the wound and paint it. Inspect plantings regularly and destroy any young diseased trees promptly. Feed, water, and prune your birches to keep them vigorous.

## Tumorlike Swellings on Roots, Trunk, or Branches

### Crown Gall

A bacterium, *Agrobacterium tumefaciens*, infects birch trees through wounds and stimulates cells to form tumorlike swellings, or galls, with irregular, rough surfaces. These may range in size from peas to large burls 1 to 2 feet in diameter. Tree growth may slow, the leaves often turn yellow, and branches or roots sometimes die. No control is known; all you can do is stop the spread of this disease to other birches by destroying affected trees and nursery stock.

## Upper Branches Die Back

### Dieback
A dieback disease caused by the fungus *Melanconium betulinum* kills the upper branches of birches. Trees weakened by drought or from attacks of the bronze birch borer are most susceptible. Prune affected branches back to sound wood and fertilize and water heavily to maintain tree vigor.

## Leaves Blistered and Curled

### Leaf Blister
Several fungi of the genus *Taphrina* produce blisters and curling of the leaves on many of the birch species. Gather and destroy all fallen leaves. Spray trees with lime sulfur just before buds open in the spring.

## Leaves Become Spotted, Turn Brown, and Fall Prematurely

### Leaf Spot
The fungi *Gloeosporium betularum* and *Cylindrosporium betulae* cause leaf spot disease in birches.

The former produces brown spots with a dark brown to black margin; the latter forms smaller spots with no definite margin. Leaf spot isn't serious. Simply gather and destroy fallen leaves to keep it from spreading. In late spring, spray your trees with a copper fungicide, following package directions.

## Powdery Pustules on Leaves

### Rust
A rust disease caused by the fungus *Melampsora betulinum* sometimes attacks birches. Easily identified by its bright reddish yellow pustules, it harms the leaves and may defoliate the tree. Gather and destroy fallen leaves and apply copper fungicide, following package directions, in late spring to control this disease.

## Shelflike Growths on Trunk

### Wood Rot
Several wood rot fungi attack birches. One, *Polyporus betulinus,* infects dying or dead birches and produces shelf- or hoof-shaped, gray, smooth, fruiting bodies along the trunk. In this case you should remove the tree to prevent spread of the disease.

Other wood rot fungi, such as *Torula* spp., *Fomes* spp., and *Poria* spp., infect living trees and cause their decay. You can prune rotted wood to slow the spread of this disease, but it's likely to take over your trees eventually and kill them. Keep trees healthy with regular watering, fertilizing, and pruning, and they will be less prone to infection.

# TREE **Crabapple**    *Malus* spp.

## DESCRIPTION

This group of trees includes apple and crabapple trees, all having five-petaled flowers and edible fruits. Those species that produce fruits less than 2 inches in diameter are considered crabapples. The fruits have a sour, bitter taste, so rather than plucking them off the tree and munching away, most people make crabapple preserves and jellies. In addition to bearing these tart little fruits, crabapples add beauty to the landscape. They look attractive in every season and are grown more often for this purpose than for their fruits.

Crabapples are small trees, most less than 50 feet tall; in fact, some seem more like shrubs than trees. They can be planted individually or in small groups, but are too difficult to care for in hedges or windbreaks. An added benefit of these trees is that they attract wildlife. Many hold their fruits all winter, providing food for birds. Crabapples are hardy trees and can be grown in the colder parts of the Midwest, where winter temperatures drop too low for the more commonly grown apples.

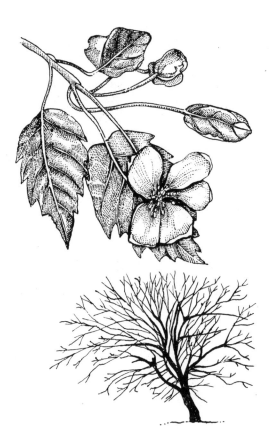

## Height

Japanese flowering crabapple (*Malus floribunda*), 30 feet

Siberian crabapple (*M. baccata*), 50 feet

Southern crabapple (*M. angustifolia*), 30 feet

Sweet crabapple (*M. coronaria*), 20 feet

## Blossoms

Crabapples bloom in the spring, in early May before the lilacs bloom. Some have fragrance, notably the Siberian crabapple. The blossoms are pink to white, the buds a lovely pink that gradually fades to white as the flower opens.

## Foliage

Crabapples are deciduous trees. Their alternate leaves are shorter and narrower than apple leaves, and their texture is finer. Most have green leaves, although some varieties show a subdued red-bronze color in summer. Those with a southwestern exposure may show some fall color.

# ENVIRONMENT

## Varieties by Zone

To zone 2, Siberian crabapple

To zone 4, Japanese flowering crabapple and sweet crabapple

To zone 6, southern crabapple

## Light Requirements

Crabapples prefer full sun.

# MOST COMMON CULTURAL PROBLEM

## Tree Produces Few Fruits

### Biennial Cycle

Actually, this is not a problem. If you begin to worry that your crabapple isn't producing many fruits, just be patient until next year. Like many woody plants, some species and varieties of crabapple bear large crops of flowers and fruits only every other year, whereas others bear annually.

# MOST COMMON INSECT PESTS

## Leaves Curled and Distorted

### Aphids

Apple aphids (*Aphis pomi*) cluster on the young growth of crabapples, especially the suckers, and as they feed, the leaves curl and pucker. Ants are attracted to the honeydew secreted by aphids. Aphids have soft, pear-shaped bodies, but that's difficult to see, since they are about the size of the head of a pin.

Light infestations of aphids are easily controlled by spraying the tree vigorously with water. Do this in the morning, three times, once every other day. If this doesn't remove aphids, use insecticidal soap every two to three days, until the pests are gone.

## Holes in Trunk

### Borers

The flat-headed apple tree borer (*Chrysobothris femorata*) and the round-headed borer drill their way into the inner bark and wood of crabapple trees, frequently girdling the trees. They may bore into tree trunks at or below ground level, often damaging young trees so badly that they can be easily pushed over. The damage they cause also renders trees vulnerable to disease. Inside, the tunnels they form may extend in all directions into the wood. If you were to cut into the tree, you would find it blackened. Infested trees can become badly disfigured.

To control borers in most situations, make a thorough examination of the tree before the spring season arrives and cut and burn any dying or unhealthy-looking twigs that may contain borers. During the summer season, check to see if sawdust is being pushed from small borer holes. Such holes should be cut out with a sharp knife. If the tunnels are fairly straight, you can kill borers by probing with a flexible wire, or pull them out with a hooked wire and destroy them. If tunnels curve and wind, inject nicotine sulfate into each borer hole and plug the hole with putty.

## Leaves Skeletonized

### Cankerworms

These pests feed heavily on the foliage of crabapple trees, skeletonizing the leaves and sometimes defoliating the entire tree. You may know them as inchworms. They are about 1 inch long and may be brown or green with a yellow stripe. As soon as you discover them on your trees, begin spraying with Bt (*Bacillus thuringiensis*) every 10 to 14 days until the pests are gone. Early in spring, before the weather turns warm, place a sticky band on the trunks of vulnerable trees to catch the females as they climb the trees to lay their eggs.

## Leaves Pale or Mottled

### Lace Bugs

Lace bugs suck sap from the undersides of leaves, causing them to turn pale or mottled. The adult insects have a squarish shape and rarely exceed $3/16$ inch in length. Their wings resemble lacework. If you find these pests on your crabapples, spray the undersides of the foliage with insecticidal soap. Two applications, a week or two apart, should solve the problem; if not, resort to spraying with nicotine sulfate or pyrethrum every seven to ten days until lace bugs are gone.

## Tunnels in or White to Brown Blotches on Leaves

### Leafminers

Several species of leafminer feed between the upper and lower surfaces of leaves, creating white to brown tunnels or blotches as they chew. Often you can see the larvae through the leaf tissue. Infested leaves eventually curl, turn brown, and die. The larvae are ½-inch-long yellow caterpillars.

To control leafminers, remove the infested leaves. Spray with insecticidal soap to kill any adults that might lay eggs on your plants. If leafminers are a problem year after year, consider covering plants in spring with agricultural fleece.

## Leaves Stippled Yellow or Red

### Mites

If the leaves of your crabapples are stippled with small yellow or red dots, suspect mites. Often the leaves and branches become distorted from curling and puckering. They may be covered in a fine webbing produced by the mites. Mites are about $1/50$ inch long, barely visible to the unaided eye. Not being true insects, they have four pairs of legs. They can be yellow, green, red, or brown.

As soon as you discover stippled leaves on your crabapples, spray them with a forceful stream of water. Do this in the morning. Three sprayings, once every other day, should knock all the mites off your trees; however, if they persist, spray with insecticidal soap every two to three days for two weeks.

## Leaves Yellowed; Small Bumps on Leaves and Branches

### Scale

Scale insects appear on leaves and branches, and don't look at all like insects, but little bumps or growths. These insects have rounded waxy shells, which protect them while they feed on the tree. They may be white, yellow, or brown to black and measure about $1/10$ to $2/5$ inch in diameter. Some scale species excrete honeydew, which coats foliage, attracting ants and encouraging the growth of sooty mold. The first sign of damage to your crabapple tree is yellowed leaves, followed by leaf drop and stunted growth. Heavy infestations can kill trees. The most common species to attack crabapples are the oystershell scale (*Lepidosaphes ulmi*), the San Jose scale (*Quadraspidiotis perniciosus*), and the Putnam scale (*Diaspidiotis ancylus*).

If you find only a few of these bumplike pests on your trees, simply scrape them off with your fingernail or a cotton swab dipped in rubbing alcohol. Medium to heavier infestations are more easily taken care of by spraying with a mixture of insecticidal soap and alcohol (½ cup of alcohol for every quart of soap). Apply once every three days for two weeks. In late winter, spray trees with dormant oil to suffocate overwintering adults and eggs.

# MOST COMMON DISEASES

## Swollen, Sunken Lesions on Branches and Trunk

### Canker

Two species of fungus, *Physalospora obtusa* and *Phoma mali*, can infect crabapples, causing cankers to develop on branches and trunks. These fungi usually enter the tree through wounds cut by lawn mowers or other sharp objects. Prevention is the best control. Increase the vigor and disease resistance of your trees by proper feeding and watering. Prune away and destroy all infected plant material.

## Flowers and Shoots Wilt Suddenly in Spring; Leaves Shriveled; Brown-Black Cankers on Bark

### Fire Blight

This disease is caused by a bacterium, *Erwinia amylovora*, and is spread by insects and rain. New shoots that appear in late spring may wilt suddenly, turn black or brown, and die. Prune diseased branches at least 3 inches below the infected area. When 25 percent of the blossoms have opened, begin spraying the tree with an antibiotic such as Agri-Strep. Continue spraying at five- to ten-day intervals during the bloom period. Fire blight is not a serious problem of flowering crabapples if pear and apple orchards are not nearby. Fire blight thrives in these orchards.

Don't feed your crabapples large amounts of nitrogen fertilizer; this encourages excessive growth, which ironically makes trees more susceptible to fire blight.

## Powdery Brown
## or Orange Spots on Leaves

### Rust

A rust disease caused by the fungus *Gymnosporangium juniperi-virginianae* may attack crabapples if your trees are within a mile of red cedar trees that are infected with cedar apple rust. On crabapples, the powdery brown or orange fungus appears on leaves, eventually causing defoliation. On cedars, the fungus causes bright orange, ball-like fungal growths called cedar apple galls. If you discover cedar apple galls on nearby cedars, begin spraying your crabapples with wettable sulfur. Four to five applications, one every seven to ten days, should protect your trees. Spray in dry weather for best results. If possible, prune away and destroy the cedar apple galls found on cedars.

## Olive Spots
## on Leaves and Fruit

### Scab

A fungus called *Venturia inaequalis* causes small, olive green spots on leaves and also attacks flowers, fruit, and twigs. The disease disfigures fruit and causes premature leaf drop. To control the problem, spray trees with a copper fungicide in early spring when the leaves have started to break. Repeat applications at ten-day intervals four or five times. Also gather up and destroy infected leaves. Susceptibility or resistance to scab varies from species to species and cultivar to cultivar. Plant breeders are always introducing new, disease-resistant cultivars, so consult your local nursery owner for a resistant selection recommended for your area. Cultivars with resistance to fire blight, rust, and scab are available.

# TREE **Dogwood** *Cornus* spp.

## DESCRIPTION
## AND ENVIRONMENT

Dogwoods flourish in every part of the United States except in the very hottest and most arid regions. They feature lovely flowers, distinctive fruits, and attractive fall foliage, making them ideal ornamental plants. They are easily grown and cared for, and species of all sizes exist. Most of us know the flowering dogwood (*Cornus florida*), which is native to the northern and eastern United States.

### Height

Alternate-leaved dogwood (*C. alternifolia*), 24 feet
Chinese dogwood (*C. kousa*), 21 feet
Flowering dogwood (*C. florida*), 40 feet
Giant dogwood (*C. controversa*), 60 feet
Pacific dogwood (*C. nuttallii*), 75 feet

### Blossoms

Most dogwoods bloom in mid- to late May, the Pacific dogwood showing earlier, in April, and the Chinese dogwood later, in mid-June. The "flowers" are technically bracts. Each bract has a characteristic notch at the top. The blossoms of most dogwoods are white or near white, and age to pink in some varieties; however, a pink cultivar of the flowering dogwood is quite common. The small flowers of the alternate-leaved dogwood are clustered, and resemble viburnums somewhat.

## Foliage

Dogwoods are deciduous. All but the alternate-leaved and the giant dogwood have opposite leaves. In fall, the leaves turn red to purplish.

## Varieties by Zone

To zone 4, alternate-leaved dogwood and flowering dogwood

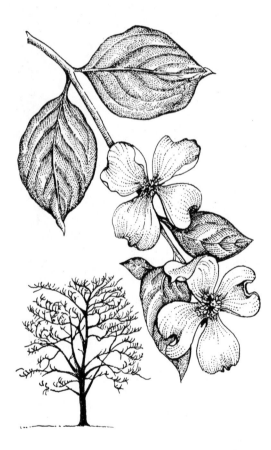

To zone 5, Chinese dogwood and giant dogwood
To zone 7, Pacific dogwood

## Light Requirements

Dogwoods will grow in full sun, but they like dappled light and will tolerate partial shade. Full shade may cause dogwoods to become leggy.

# MOST COMMON CULTURAL PROBLEMS

## Slow Growth

### Grass Growing Too Close to Tree

Dogwood trees can be inhibited by turf cover growing right up to the trunk. Under these conditions, they will grow more slowly and will be more vulnerable to insects and disease. For optimum growth, clear a circle 1 to 2 feet around the trunk of your tree and lay down mulch, keeping the mulch from touching the tree.

# MOST COMMON INSECT PESTS

## Leaves Curled and Distorted

### Aphids

As with any other tree, aphids attack the leaves of dogwoods, sucking the sap from them. The leaves become weak, turn yellow or brown, and often curl and pucker. In bright sunlight, they wilt. Ants are attracted to the honeydew secreted by aphids. The effects of aphids eventually will retard or distort tree growth. The melon aphid (*Aphis gossypii*) specifically likes dogwoods. It has a soft, pear-shaped body and is about the size of the head of a pin.

Aphids can often be easily controlled by spraying the tree vigorously with water. Do this in the morning, three times, once every other day. For heavy infestations, spray with insecticidal soap every two to three days until you don't see any more aphids. If you have a severe problem with these pests, you may have to resort to pyrethrum. Two applications made three to four days apart should finally eliminate this problem.

## Holes or Tunnels in Bark or Twigs; Branches Wilt, Die, or Break Off

### Borers

Several species of borer attack dogwoods by tunneling under the bark, often girdling the tree. Borers can kill or damage twig tips and branches, and will severely weaken or kill entire trees. Dogwoods infested with borers often have swollen, gall-like areas on the trunk either below or above the soil level. Sawdust at the base of the tree or emerging from wounds is another sign of borers. The flat-headed apple tree borer (*Chrysobothris femorata*) is a ½-inch-long, metallic gray or brown beetle that lays eggs on the bark; the white, 1-inch-long larvae tunnel under the bark and bore into the trunk to pupate. The adult phase of the dogwood borer (*Thamnosphecia scitula*) is a 1-inch-long moth with translucent, blue-black wings marked with yellow. The larva, a white caterpillar with a pale brown head, enters through wounds in the bark and tunnels under the bark. The dogwood twig borer (*Oberea tripunctata*) is a yellow beetle larva that bores through the twigs, which then wilt or break off completely. The pitted ambrosia beetle (*Corthylus punctatissimus*) is a brown or black, ⅛-inch-long beetle that bores into wood, causing infested stems to weaken, die, and break off. It is especially liable to attack heavily mulched plants.

Borers can be cut out of infested trees with a sharp knife, or can be killed by probing their tunnels with a flexible wire. Seal the wounds promptly and be sure to destroy all infested wood.

## Leaves Consumed; Conspicuous, Tawny Egg Masses Present

### Gypsy Moths

Larvae of the gypsy moth (*Porthetria dispar*) have a well-deserved reputation for devouring the foliage of trees. They will attack many species, including dogwoods. After repeated defoliations, a tree is likely to die. The larvae grow from about ¹⁄₁₆ inch to about 2½ inches. The mature caterpillars display five pairs of blue spots and six pairs of red spots along their backs. Adult male moths have a wingspan of 1½ inches. Their wings are light tan to dark brown, with blackish wavy bands across the forewings. The whitish females have wings that measure about 2½ inches; however, they can barely fly. Both sexes have feathered antennae. Gypsy moths lay masses of 400 to 500 eggs. These masses are covered with velvety, buff-colored hairs.

You can effectively control gypsy moths by destroying the larvae. Bt (*Bacillus thuringiensis*) is the weapon of choice. Spray trees every 10 to 14 days from mid-April, when eggs begin to hatch, until mid-June. If gypsy moth larvae are still a problem, wrap a piece of foot-wide burlap around the trunk of the tree, about chest high. Tie it around the center with heavy twine, letting the top fold over the twine. The caterpillars feed at night and then crawl down from the tree each morning. When they reach the burlap, they will make themselves comfortable under the fold. In the late afternoon, put on garden gloves and sweep the caterpillars off into a container of detergent and water.

## Blotches on Leaves

### Leafminers

Larvae of the locust leafminer (*Xenochalepus dorsalis*) occasionally attack dogwood leaves, raising blisterlike patches on their undersides. The adult beetles also feed on the undersides of leaves and skeletonize them.

To control leafminers, remove the infested leaves. Spray with insecticidal soap to kill any adults that might lay eggs on your plants. If leafminers are a problem year after year, consider covering plants in spring with agricultural fleece.

## Leaves Rolled and Bound with Silk Strands

### Leaf Rollers

Leaf rollers are easy to spot. These pests protect themselves while feeding on dogwood foliage by rolling leaves into tubes and binding them with strands or webs of silk. As the caterpillars feed, the leaves become skeletonized, then turn brown and die. The oblique-banded leaf roller (*Choristoneura rosaceana*) occasionally attacks dogwoods. The destructive larvae are ⅜ to 1¾ inches long and light to dark green or cream to yellow in color. The adult moths are brown or gray and measure only ¼ to ½ inch in length.

If only a few caterpillars have rolled themselves up in the leaves of your dogwood, simply pluck the leaves and destroy the pests. If leaf rollers are a common problem in your yard, spray vulnerable plants with Bt (*Bacillus thuringiensis*) before you expect the caterpillars to begin feeding.

## Galls on Limbs

### Midges

Adult midges are two-winged flies, 1/14 to 1/8 inch long, with long legs and antennae. The larvae of club gall midges burrow into small twigs, causing grayish tubular swellings, or galls, to form around them. Often several inches of the infested twigs die. Usually the fastest growing and most vigorous twigs become heavily infested, as do water sprouts or sucker growth nearest the ground. Most of the flower and leaf buds that develop on infested branches also die. Although serious infestations of club gall midges stunt the growth of dogwoods, a light infestation hardly affects development. Cut and destroy infested shoots as soon as they are detected. Then spray the plant with insecticidal soap every two to three days until the midges are gone.

## Leaves Discolored; Small Bumps on Leaves and Branches

### Scale

Discoloration of leaves is the first sign of a scale attack. This is closely followed by leaf drop, reduced growth, and eventually stunted trees. Heavy infestations kill dogwoods. Some species of scale excrete honeydew, which coats foliage, attracting ants and encouraging the growth of sooty mold. The scale species most likely to attack dogwoods include cottony-maple scale (*Pulvinaria innumerabilis*), dogwood scale (*Chionaspis corni*), obscure scale (*Melanaspis obscura*), oystershell scale (*Lepidosaphes ulmi*), and San Jose scale (*Quadraspidiotus perniciosus*). Scale insects form groups on dogwood stems and leaves. They look like little bumps, having concave waxy shells that protect them while they feed on the tree. The insects are 1/10 to 2/5 inch in diameter and their shells may be white, yellow, or brown to black.

If only a few of these insects have settled on your dogwoods, you can easily scrape them off with your fingernail or remove them with a cotton swab dipped in alcohol. For medium to heavy infestations, make a solution combining ½ cup alcohol and 1 quart insecticidal soap solution. Spray trees with this mixture every three days for two weeks. In late winter, apply dormant oil spray to smother overwintering adults and eggs.

# MOST COMMON DISEASES

## Sunken Black Spots on Leaves

### Anthracnose

This disease, caused by a few species of fungus, forms distinct lesions on leaves, which appear as moist, sunken black spots with fruiting bodies in the center. These leaf spots may run together in one irregular blotch. The dead areas follow the veins or are bounded by the larger veins of the leaves. Sometimes terminal shoots show blight down to several inches below the buds. Pustules containing pinkish spores appear. Severe cases of anthracnose cause dieback and defoliation.

Begin fighting this disease by cutting infected branches and gathering any fallen diseased leaves; destroy all this plant material. Spray the tree once with a copper fungicide, such as Bordeaux mixture. A strong dogwood is best prepared to fight off disease itself, so maintain the vigor of your trees by feeding and watering them well, especially during droughts.

## Flowers or Leaves Discolored; Cankers on Twigs

### Blight

Blights in dogwoods can be caused by any of several fungi, including *Botrytis cinerea*, *Myxosporium* spp., *Cryptostitis* spp., and *Sphaeropsis* spp. These fungi infect flowers, leaves, and growing twigs. The first symptom is discoloration, followed by wilting and death of affected parts. Cankers may erupt on twigs. Cut off any dead or infected twigs. Spray infected trees at least once with a copper fungicide during the flowering period. Keep your trees vigorous by feeding and watering them more heavily than usual.

## Leaves Small, Light Green; Swollen Growth on Lower Trunk or Roots

### Canker

Crown canker, caused by the fungus *Phytophthora cactorum*, primarily attacks transplanted dogwoods. Diseased trees produce leaves that are smaller and lighter green than normal, and they turn red earlier than normal in late summer. Twigs and even large branches die. Within a year or two, this disease spreads through the entire tree. A canker slowly develops on the lower trunk at or near the soil line or on the main roots. Eventually it girdles the tree and kills it.

Crown canker is incurable once the fungus has invaded most of the trunk base or root collar; however, you can control it if the infection is confined to a relatively small area at the base of the trunk. Remove a strip of healthy bark about 1 inch wide from around the edge of the canker. Gouge out all discolored bark and sapwood; then paint the wound edges with orange shellac and the center of the wound with tree paint.

## Leaves and Growing Tips Shriveled

### Dieback

The fungus *Botryosphaeria dothidea* causes die-back in dogwoods. Leaves become discolored at the tips or around the margins, and later, spots develop, which spread over the entire leaf. Leaf stalks and twigs also become infected. Prune out all diseased tips well below the infected parts. Bordeaux mixture or another copper fungicide, applied as new leaves emerge and again two weeks later, may help.

## Leaves Become Spotted and Turn Brown

### Leaf Spot

*Ascochyta* spp., *Cercospora* spp., and other fungi cause leaf spot in dogwoods. Yellow, brown, or black spots appear on leaves. These spots often merge to form large patches of dead tissue. Gathering and destroying fallen leaves controls this disease. If leaf spot is a continuing problem with your dogwoods, spray trees with a copper fungicide once a month, starting in April when the flower buds are in the cup stage, and continuing until new flower buds form in late summer.

## White Powder on Leaves

### Powdery Mildew

Powdery mildew, caused by the fungi *Microsphaera alni* and *Phyllactinia corylea*, shows up on dogwood leaves as a thin, white powdery substance. As soon as you discover this disease, spray your trees thoroughly with wettable sulfur once or twice at weekly intervals. In the fall, collect and destroy all fallen plant material from under your trees.

## NOTES AND RESEARCH

An alarming dogwood decline has been evident since 1977 in the area from Pennsylvania north to Connecticut and east to New Jersey. Numerous backyard dogwoods, as well as native flowering dogwoods in woodland areas, have become frail, showing signs of anthracnose, twig dieback, and trunk cankers. Progressive dieback in lower twigs signals advanced decline and is often accompanied by borer attacks.

Other opportunistic insects also move in on the vulnerable tree. As the tree struggles, it expends its energy reserves and sends out stem and branch water sprouts, which usually wither and die in the summer sun and heat. Usually a tree in this condition will die within two seasons.

The cause of this problem in these beloved dogwoods has been the subject of considerable debate, but a consensus has emerged that current environmental conditions are taking their toll on these trees. Climate patterns since the spring of 1975 in this region of the United States have been characterized by periods of excessive rain in spring, then summer drought, then cold winters. Such severe climatic fluctuations have stressed dogwoods, making them susceptible to insects and disease that they would normally resist.

To forestall this dogwood decline, boost the health and vigor of the trees on your property. Water faithfully during summer and fall dry spells. Dogwoods need at least 1 inch of water every ten days during their growing period to thrive, and to enable them to survive harsh winters. One inch of water for a normal mature dogwood tree represents about 50 gallons of water. Fertilize in the fall or early spring, but not in both seasons, and use a slow-release nitrogen product, so that the dogwood will not be stimulated to produce excess vegetation. Practice good hygiene in your yard by cleaning up organic debris, which might shelter disease and insects. And do not prune your trees when leaves or twigs are wet; water transmits disease very effectively.

Take preventive measures against disease. Spray trees with a copper fungicide to prevent the onset of fungal disease. Begin spraying when the buds begin to open. Repeat applications every seven to ten days while the trees leaf out. During a dry spring, a three-week spray program should suffice. If your area is experiencing a rainy spring, spray the dogwoods over a four- to five-week period.

When planting a new dogwood tree, ensure its health by placing it in a favorable location. Do not plant it in an unremittingly sunny, hot spot in the yard. Dogwoods are native to woodlands, so they appreciate dappled light or partial shade. Also, make sure they will get good air circulation. Plant them slightly less deep than they were previously. This facilitates root aeration and good drainage. And do not grow tight ground covers near the roots and trunk. In addition to aiding good air circulation, this helps to prevent root rot and rodent damage.

All these efforts may provide some measure of success in protecting against dogwood decline. The best solution may be to choose a tree that is not susceptible to dogwood decline. The Chinese dogwood, which is similar to the flowering dogwood, may serve just as well.

TREE **Elm** *Ulmus* spp.

## DESCRIPTION
## AND ENVIRONMENT

Traditionally, elms have been the standard shade tree in the United States, even though they are susceptible to several diseases. The American elm (*Ulmus americana*), native to the eastern half of the United States, is the most popular. But consider the Chinese elm (*U. parvifolia*): It grows fast and resists disease, and its peeling is attractive in the barren months of northern winters.

## Height

American elm (*U. americana*), 120 feet
Chinese elm (*U. parvifolia*), 90 feet
English elm (*U. procera*), 90 feet
Rock or cork elm (*U. thomasii*), 90 feet
Smooth-leaved elm (*U. carpinifolia*), 90 feet

## Foliage

Elms are deciduous trees with elliptical to oblong-ovate leaves that are 4 to 6 inches long and 1 to 3 inches wide. Their leaves turn yellow in fall except for those of the Chinese elm; some of its leaves turn glossy red.

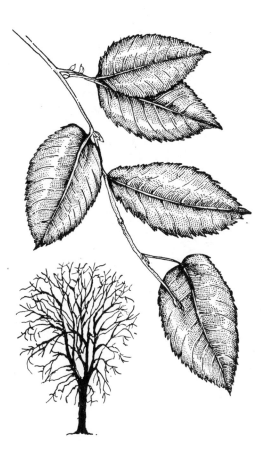

## Varieties by Zone

To zone 2, American elm and rock elm
To zone 4, smooth-leaved elm
To zone 5, Chinese elm and English elm

## Light Requirements

Elms will grow in full sun to light shade.

# MOST COMMON INSECT PESTS

## Galls on Leaves; Leaves Stunted or Curled

### Aphids
The elm cockscomb gall aphid (*Colopha ulmicola*) forms galls on elm leaves. Not surprisingly, these galls resemble a rooster's comb. The elm leaf curl aphid (*Eriosoma americanum*) and woolly apple aphid (*E. lanigerum*) also infest elms, stunting the growth of terminal leaves and causing them to curl. Several inches of the growing tips of branches may die. Ants are attracted to the honeydew secreted by aphids.

In general, aphids have soft, pear-shaped bodies about the size of the head of a pin. Aphids damage trees by sucking out the juices in the leaves. You can control light infestations easily by spraying the trees vigorously with water. Do this in the morning, three times, once every other day. If this doesn't rid your trees of aphids, spray with insecticidal soap every two to three days until the pests are gone. Use pyrethrum only as a last resort, making two applications three to four days apart.

## Bleeding Holes in Trunk; Sawdust on Trunk; Branches Girdled

### Borers
Elms are susceptible to attack from several borers. The larvae of elm borers (*Saperda tridentata*) and flat-headed apple tree borers (*Chrysobothris femorata*) are white grubs about ½ inch long. These insects drill their way into weak trees. Sap flow is

interrupted as the sap bleeds out of the elms through the holes created by the tunneling larvae. You can also spot the work of borers by the sawdust they push out of the holes as they gnaw their way into the wood.

The dogwood twig borer (*Oberea tripunctata*) is dull yellow and measures about ¾ inch in length. It sometimes girdles branches and kills twigs.

Leopard moth borers (*Zeuzera pyrina*) are whitish to light pink and marked with several dark spots. They are 2 to 3 inches long. They riddle twigs and branches with holes, sometimes girdling them.

As soon as you find borer holes in your elm trees, cut into them. Probe them with a hooked wire, and try to pull the grubs out. If the wire is unsuccessful, inject nicotine sulfate into the tunnel and plug the hole with putty. Cut and destroy infested twigs.

## Leaves Skeletonized

### Cankerworms

These pests feed heavily on the foliage of elm trees, skeletonizing the leaves and sometimes defoliating the entire tree. You may know them as inchworms. They are about 1 inch long and may be brown or green with a yellow stripe. As soon as you discover them on your trees, begin spraying with Bt (*Bacillus thuringiensis*) every 10 to 14 days until the pests are gone. Early in spring, before the weather turns warm, place a sticky band on the trunks of vulnerable trees to catch the females as they climb the trees to lay their eggs.

### Sawflies

Elm sawfly larvae (*Cimbex americana*) can skeletonize leaves of the elm tree, sometimes in just one night. Eventually they may defoliate a tree. Adults resemble wasps, but have thicker midsections. They are ⅝ to 1½ inches long, with two pairs of transparent wings. Their larvae are bluish black or olive green and are about ½ inch long.

As soon as you find the larvae on your trees, spray with insecticidal soap, pyrethrum, or rotenone. One application should get rid of these pests, but if a second generation appears, spray again.

## Angular Spots on Leaves; Leaves Turn Brown and Fall

### Casebearers

Elm casebearers (*Coleophora ulmifoliella*) work their way between the upper and lower surfaces of elm leaves and mine angular spots in the leaf tissue. The leaves eventually turn brown and drop from the tree. Casebearers produce cigar-shaped silken cases, which you can find hanging from the twigs of infested trees.

The larvae of casebearers measure about ⅕ to ¼ inch in length. They have black heads. The adult female moth has brown wings fringed with hairs.

Control casebearers with a dormant spray of lime sulfur before buds open in spring, or spray with pyrethrum or rotenone as soon as leaves are fully developed. Two applications made three to four days apart should finally eliminate this problem.

## Holes in Leaves

### Caterpillars

Many caterpillars chew elm leaves, including tent caterpillars, cankerworms, hemlock loopers, tussock moth larvae, mourning cloak butterfly larvae, and spiny elm caterpillars. Fortunately, they can all be controlled in the same way. If infestations are light, pick off the insects and destroy them, and spray your tree with Bt (*Bacillus thuringiensis*) every 10 to 14 days until the pests are gone. In the fall and winter, scrape off any egg masses you find.

### Japanese Beetles

Japanese beetles (*Popillia japonica*) are very destructive. They gather in large numbers and eventually skeletonize leaves. Their grubs sometimes attack the roots of elm trees. Adult beetles are ½ inch long, with shiny metallic green and copper-brown wing covers. The larvae are grayish white, with dark brown heads. Fully grown grubs are plump, ¾ to 1 inch long, and lie in the soil in a distinctive arc-shaped resting posture. It has been noted in the area around Philadelphia that where Siberian elms (*U. pumila*) and Chinese elms grow side by side, the beetles practically defoliated the former and hardly touched the latter.

If Japanese beetles have only just found your elms, you may be able to pick most of them off and destroy them. Set up pheromone beetle traps no closer than 50 feet from your trees. If you usually have trouble with Japanese beetles, set the traps a week before expected emergence in your area. The traps may not be able to control a heavy infestation. In that case, resort to pyrethrum. Spray trees as soon as you spot beetles. Two applications made three to four days apart should eliminate these pests.

## Rectangular Holes in Leaves; Leaves Skeletonized

### Elm Leaf Beetles

The elm leaf beetle (*Pyrrhalta luteola*) is ¼ inch long and brownish yellow. In spring, it feeds on new leaves and lays its eggs on the leaf undersides. Half-inch-long, yellow-and-black larvae hatch from these eggs, feed for several weeks, and then drop to the soil at the base of the tree to pupate. Soon after leaves unfurl in spring, adults chew out rectangular areas in the leaves. Later in the season, they skeletonize leaves, which then curl and dry up. In fall, they may migrate indoors, but they normally overwinter in tree bark and outbuildings.

Spray plants with a mixture of pyrethrum and isopropyl alcohol, which should be applied every three to five days for two weeks. Make this solution by combining two parts alcohol with one part water and adding pyrethrum in the concentration recommended on the bottle.

## Leaves Consumed; Conspicuous, Tawny Egg Masses Present

### Gypsy Moths

The notorious gypsy moth (*Porthetria dispar*) strikes elms as well as many other trees. Masses of larvae devour elm foliage and may kill the tree after repeated defoliations. At only ¹/₁₆ inch in length, the newly hatched larvae look rather harmless, but they grow to 2½-inch caterpillars with five pairs of blue spots and six pairs of red spots along their backs. Adult male moths have a wingspan of 1½ inches and are light tan to dark brown, with blackish wavy bands across the forewings. The whitish female moths have a 2½-inch wingspan, but can barely fly. Both sexes have feathered antennae. You might find gypsy moth egg masses on your trees; they are covered with velvety, buff-colored hairs, and contain 400 to 500 eggs.

Spray trees with Bt (*Bacillus thuringiensis*) every 10 to 14 days from mid-April, when eggs begin to hatch, until mid-June. If the larvae are still a problem, trap them with burlap. Wrap a piece of foot-wide burlap around the trunk of the tree, about chest high. Tie it around the center with heavy twine, letting the top fold over the twine. Gypsy moth larvae are night feeders and crawl down the tree each morning. When they reach the burlap, they will make themselves comfortable under the fold. In the late afternoon, put on garden gloves and sweep the caterpillars off into a container of detergent and water.

## Leaves Pale or Mottled

### Lace Bugs

Elm lace bugs (*Corythucha ulmi*) suck sap from the undersides of leaves, causing elm foliage to turn pale or mottled. The top leaf surfaces will look spotted, as if they had been sprinkled with white pepper. The undersides, though, will display a reddish orange discoloration, and you'll find black specks of excrement. The leaves eventually turn brown and die. This insect can damage elms considerably.

Adult lace bugs are small, measuring at most ¹/₁₆ inch. As their name implies, the wings have an elaborate lacey pattern. Because of the squarish shape of these wings, when they are folded over the back of the insect, the lace bug itself appears to have a square form. The nymphs are dark, spiny, and move with a strange sideways motion.

To remove these pests, spray your trees with insecticidal soap, and make a second application a week or two later. Heavy infestations may not be controlled by this method. If lace bugs continue to be a problem, spray with nicotine sulfate or pyrethrum every seven to ten days until symptoms disappear.

## Blotches on Leaves

### Leafminers

The larvae of the elm leafminer (*Fenusa ulmi*) attack elms in May and June. They feed between the upper and lower surfaces of leaves, producing unsightly blotches. Leaves turn brown, shrivel, and may drop prematurely. As many as 20 larvae may feast on a single leaf. The adult female, a shiny black fly, deposits eggs in slits in the upper leaf surfaces.

To control leafminers, remove the infested leaves. Spray with insecticidal soap to kill any adults that might lay eggs on your plants. If leafminers are a recurring problem, consider covering plants in spring with agricultural fleece.

## Leaves Prematurely Yellowed

### Mites

You'll recognize the attack of the four-spotted spider mite (*Tetranychus canadensis*) or the European red mite (*Panonychus ulmi*) by the premature yellowing of your elm leaves. And it's fortunate you can identify them by the damage they do, because you will have a difficult time seeing the pests themselves. Mites are about $1/50$ inch long, barely visible to the unaided eye. Not being true insects, they have four pairs of legs. They may be yellow, green, red, or brown.

At the first sign of mite damage, spray the trees in early morning with forceful streams of water. Do this three times, once every other day. If the problem continues, spray with insecticidal soap every two to three days for two weeks.

## Leaves Curled and Yellowed

### Root Aphids

Root aphids feed on elm leaves, buds, and roots, and on trunk wounds, and retard or distort tree growth. Affected leaves may turn yellow or brown,

wilt under bright sunlight, or sometimes curl and pucker. If you were to look at the roots, you would find them scarred and knotted. The woolly apple aphid (*Eriosoma lanigerum*) is a soft-bodied, pear-shaped sucking insect, the size of the head of a pin.

Ants are particularly fond of the honeydew secreted by aphids and will often round them up and herd them back to their nests. Often, these nests are located near the roots of your ornamental plants, so aphids have the perfect opportunity to infest your trees. The only effective way to control root aphids is to control the ants that shepherd them. Destroy the ant nest with its queen by digging into the nest and pouring a boiling water and hot pepper solution into it. Make this hot pepper solution by boiling ½ cup finely chopped hot peppers in 1 pint water. Take the solution directly from the stove out to the yard and pour it on the ants.

## Small Bumps on Leaves and Branches; Branches Yellowish

### Scale

The European elm scale (*Gossyparia spuria*) appear as little bumps on the undersides of elm branches and leaves in early summer. Scale insects have waxy shells that protect them while they feed. Females are oval, about $1/16$ inch long, reddish purple, and surrounded by a fringe of white, waxy secretions. Affected leaves become yellowed on lower branches in July. As the scale insects continue to feed on the tree, branches turn yellowish brown. With heavy infestations, the foliage turns gray-green and wilts. Eleven other scale species attack elms. They all form groups of small bumps or blisterlike outgrowths on tree stems and leaves. They may be white, yellow, or brown to black, and are about $1/10$ to $2/5$ inch in diameter.

If scale insects have only just begun to populate your elms, you can easily scrape them off with your fingernail or with a cotton swab dipped in alcohol. For medium to heavy infestations, make a mixture of insecticidal soap and alcohol, combining ½ cup alcohol with every quart of insecticidal soap. Spray your trees every three days for two weeks. In late winter, apply dormant oil to smother overwintering adults and eggs.

## Trees Weakened; Holes in Bark; Buds and Twigs Damaged

### Smaller European Elm Bark Beetles

The smaller European elm bark beetle (*Scolytus multistriatus*) is one of the principal carriers of the devastating Dutch elm disease fungus. These pests first attack elms weak from some other problem. The reddish black beetles are only $\frac{1}{10}$ inch long. They bore through the bark and excavate galleries in the sapwood, where they lay their eggs. Adults emerge through the bark, leaving tiny holes, and feed on buds and bark of twigs during the summer.

To control this pest, spray plants with a mixture of pyrethrum and isopropyl alcohol, which should be applied every three to five days for two weeks. Make this solution by combining two parts alcohol with one part water and adding pyrethrum in the concentration recommended on the bottle.

## Leaves Mottled

### Treehoppers

Buffalo treehoppers (*Stictocephala bubalus*), locust treehoppers (*Thelia bimaculata*), and others suck sap from elms and damage them further by puncturing stems to lay their eggs. This opens the way to disease. Adult treehoppers are compact, grotesquely humpbacked insects, ¼ to ⅜ inch long.

Remove treehoppers by spraying infested trees with pyrethrum or nicotine sulfate once a week until the pests are gone. If this doesn't seem to be controlling your particular problem, try dusting elms with a mixture of nine parts sulfur and one part pyrethrum. Apply this powder weekly until the treehoppers are gone.

## MOST COMMON DISEASES

## Swollen, Sunken Lesions on Branches and Trunk

### Canker

A variety of fungi cause cankers and dieback of twigs and branches of elms. Remove small cankers simply by cutting them out. Cuts should extend well beyond the visibly infected area to ensure complete removal of the diseased tissue. Next, protect the exposed area by brushing shellac on the edge of the wound and applying tree paint over the entire exposed surface. If the canker has completely girdled a branch, prune well below the affected area and destroy the branch. Mildly infected trees have been known to recover without any special treatments. However, once a tree becomes heavily infected, the disease cannot be cured; the tree must be destroyed.

## Leaves Wilted, Curled, and Yellowed; Branches Die

### Dutch Elm Disease

The fungus that causes Dutch elm disease, *Ceratocystis ulmi*, spreads from tree to tree by various bark beetles or by natural intergrafting of root systems. The most noticeable symptom of this disease is the wilting and yellowing of one or more branches of infected trees. Look for oval-shaped depressions at the crotches of one- or two-year-old twigs; these holes distinguish this disease from other wilts. In cross-section, affected wood shows brownish staining in the annual rings. This staining also shows up as discontinuous streaks or as black or brown dots in the wood, which can be seen when the bark is peeled away from the wood. The only way to be sure your tree has Dutch elm disease, though, is to have a plant pathologist perform tests.

There is no cure for this disease. Prevent its spread by repairing bark wounds promptly; remove dead, dying, and injured branches before they attract beetles. Prune out old and dying branches during the winter. Promptly remove diseased or dying elms before May, regardless of the cause of their problem. Isolate infected trees by trenching to sever any possible root connections with neighboring trees. (Root grafts can interconnect large elms 30 to 50 feet apart.) Keep surviving elms in vigorous growing condition. Feed with nitrogen fertilizers such as cottonseed meal or dried blood. Keep trees well watered.

## Leaves Drooping and Curled

### Elm Phloem Necrosis (Elm Yellows)

The leaves of elms infected by elm phloem necrosis droop, curl, yellow, and eventually turn brown and fall off. Usually this disease affects the entire tree all at once, but sometimes the symptoms develop branch by branch. A mycoplasmalike organism (MLO) is thought to cause localized epidemics of this disease among elms in the eastern central states. The organism attacks the phloem tissue of the inner bark. This tissue develops a butterscotch color and a distinctive wintergreen scent. Weak trees usually die, and tolerant ones become stunted and sometimes develop witches'-brooms—areas where lots of thin branches sprout and together resemble a broom. The phloem necrosis organism spreads from tree to tree through natural root grafts and by the white-banded elm leafhopper (*Scaphoideus luteolus*). It also overwinters in infected tree roots. Spray with rotenone or pyrethrum to control the insect factor. Even with nearly perfect control, only a few insects that are missed may spread the disease. Injections of tetracycline into trunks have halted the disease in many cases, but this method is too expensive except where valuable specimens are concerned. There isn't a known, complete cure for elm yellows.

## Leaves Become Spotted, Turn Brown, and Fall Prematurely

### Leaf Spot

Leaf spot diseases caused by fungi such as the *Cercospora* spp., *Gloeosporium* spp., *Phyllosticta* spp., and many others occur in elms. The leaves of elms infected with *Gnomonia ulmea,* a common leaf spot fungus, develop small white or yellow flecks on their upper surfaces. These specks enlarge and turn black in the center. If the disease spreads quickly throughout the tree, leaves may drop prematurely; however, this disease usually occurs in late fall when leaves normally drop, so little damage to the tree occurs. Gather and destroy the fallen leaves. The following year, spray with a copper fungicide. Begin when the leaves are half grown, and make three applications 10 to 12 days apart.

## White Powder on Leaves; Yellowish Spots Develop

### Powdery Mildew

Powdery mildew is caused by the fungi *Microsphaera alni, Phyllactinia corylea,* and *Uncinula macrospora.* You can easily identify this disease by the thin white covering of fungus on the leaves. Eventually, yellowish spots appear. As soon as you discover the telltale white growth, spray the tree thoroughly with wettable sulfur. Make a second application a week later. To keep the disease from spreading, collect and destroy all fallen twigs and leaves in autumn.

## Leaves Turn Yellow or Brown and Wilt

### Wilt

Elms are susceptible to a wilt disease caused by the soil-dwelling fungus *Verticillium albo-atrum.* The leaves on affected branches of infected trees suddenly wilt and die. Sapwood is discolored. Heavy feeding with a high-nitrogen fertilizer sometimes enables trees to produce a new ring of sapwood outside the infected area, and the trees may then recover. Prune and destroy dead branches. If your tree is badly infected, remove it, together with as many roots as possible, and destroy it. Since the soil may continue to harbor some of the fungi, replant with resistant trees such as most conifers, beech, birch, boxwood, dogwood, fruit trees, holly, locust, mulberry, oak, pecan, serviceberry, sweet gum, sycamore, walnut, or willow.

## Shelflike Growths on Trunk

### Wood Rot

Wood rot may be caused by any one of several fungi, including *Pleurotus* spp., *Phellinus* spp., *Coriolus* spp., and *Polyporus* spp. Infected elms develop shelflike growths on their trunks. The infection cannot be stopped once it has invaded large areas of the trunk, and the tree should be removed and destroyed. This disease can be prevented, though, by properly treating any injuries to the tree and by maintaining healthy trees through proper fertilizing and watering.

# TREE Magnolia *Magnolia* spp.

## DESCRIPTION

In spring, the large showy blossoms of the magnolia are a welcome sight. Some species produce flowers a foot in diameter. Often they bloom even before the leaves appear. An indication of how much these trees are loved is the fact that 22 species are recommended for their ornamental value. Although many people associate magnolias with the South, you can find a suitable species for all but the very coldest regions of the United States.

### Height

Big-leaved magnolia (*M. macrophylla*), 50 feet
Saucer magnolia (*M. ×soulangiana*), 20 to 30 feet
Southern magnolia (*M. grandiflora*), 90 feet
Star magnolia (*M. stellata*), 20 feet
Yulan magnolia (*M. denudata*), 45 feet

### Blossoms

Most magnolias bloom in early spring. In the South, some magnolias will bloom as early as February. Ironically, the southern magnolia itself is the exception. It blooms in late spring, June, or July, with occasional blooms appearing throughout summer and early autumn. All magnolias have a slightly scented flower; the star magnolia is very fragrant. Native magnolia species usually produce white flowers. Those species from the Orient, such as the yulan magnolia, have yellow, pink, red, or purplish flowers.

### Foliage

The leaves of most magnolias are fairly coarse. They vary in size from 4 to 30 inches, depending on the species. Southern magnolia's waxy leaves are evergreen, but all other species are deciduous. The star magnolia has long, finely textured, dark green leaves, which turn bronze to yellow in fall.

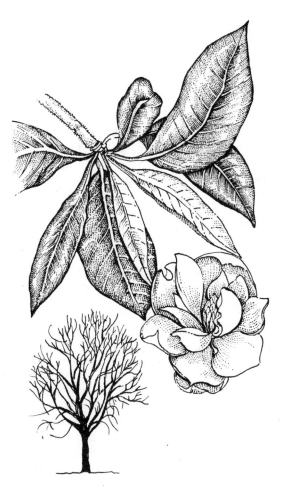

## ENVIRONMENT

### Varieties by Zone

To zone 5, big-leaved magnolia, saucer magnolia, star magnolia, and yulan magnolia.

To zone 7, southern magnolia. (The southern magnolia is precariously hardy up to Philadelphia and Harrisburg, but is safe up through zone 7.)

## Light Requirements

Magnolias prefer full sun, but they will tolerate light shade.

# MOST COMMON CULTURAL PROBLEM

## Stunted Growth

### Contact with Black Walnut Roots

Black walnuts have a reputation for harming all kinds of plants. A chemical substance produced by these trees has a negative effect on neighboring vegetables, flowers, and trees. This allelopathic reaction, as it is called, occurs in magnolias within a circle one and a half times the distance from the trunk of the magnolia to the tips of its outermost branches. The magnolia wilts, becomes stunted, and may die.

# MOST COMMON INSECT PESTS

## Holes in Leaves

### Caterpillars

Few caterpillars attack magnolias, but the omnivorous looper caterpillar and a few other loopers may chew some holes in the leaves. Handpicking solves the problem, if you find only a few caterpillars on your trees; otherwise use Bt (*Bacillus thuringiensis*). As soon as you see caterpillar damage, dust the top and bottom surfaces of the leaves, reapplying after every rain, until the pest is controlled. You can also apply Bt as a foliar spray, making applications every 10 to 14 days until the caterpillars are gone. If the infestation is so large that Bt doesn't take care of it, spray your trees with pyrethrum or a 1 percent solution of rotenone. Usually two applications, 3 to 4 days apart, are sufficient.

## Leaves Mottled

### Mealybugs

The comstock mealybug (*Pseudococcus comstocki*) sometimes infests magnolias. These small oval-shaped insects have a waxy covering. After hatching in late May, the young mealybugs crawl up the trunk to the leaves, where they suck out the juices and devitalize the tree. Control them by spraying the tree with an alcohol mixture. The mixture includes 1 cup alcohol and ½ teaspoon Volck oil in 1 quart water. The Volck oil can be replaced by insecticidal soap for equally effective results. Apply this spray every two days until the problem is solved. For large infestations, you may have to use insecticidal soap or pyrethrum. Spray three times, once every seven to ten days.

## Leaves Stippled Yellow or Red

### Mites

If the leaves of your magnolias show several small yellow or red dots, suspect mites. Mites usually attack the lowest leaves first. Leaves and stems are often distorted or swathed in fine webbing. Mites are barely visible to the unaided eye, since they are only ¹⁄₅₀ inch long. If you could see them, you'd find that they have four pairs of legs—they are not true insects—and piercing, sucking mouth parts. Mites may be yellow, green, red, or brown.

Simply spraying trees in the early morning with a forceful stream of water, three times, once every other day, will probably knock them off. If not, spray with insecticidal soap every two to three days for two weeks.

## Tree Weakened; Small Bumps on Leaves and Branches

### Scale

Scale insects don't look like insects at all, but rather like little bumps attached to leaves and branches. These pests have a concave shell-like covering, which hides them while they feed. About eleven species of scale attack magnolias. They all have the same effect and are controlled in the same way. The magnolia scale (*Neolecanium cornuparvum*) is covered by a brown, varnishlike hemispherical scale or cover. It is ½ inch in diameter (the largest American scale species). Scale insects appear in August and overwinter in the adult stage. Magnolias infested with scale produce underdeveloped leaves and become weak.

You can easily remove a few scale insects with your fingernail or a cotton swab dipped in alcohol. For even a light infestation, though, combine alcohol and insecticidal soap, mixing ½ cup alcohol with every quart of soap, and spray your magnolias every three days for two weeks. In late winter, apply dormant oil to smother overwintering adults and eggs.

## Holes in and Blotches on Leaves

### Weevils

The sassafras weevil (*Odontopus calceatus*) begins to feed on magnolias as soon as the buds break open and before the leaves have expanded. About ¼ inch long, these brown or black insects have a head that is elongated into a long, slender, downward-curved snout. They chew several holes in the leaves. Adult weevils lay eggs on the midribs of new leaves, and the larvae mine into the leaves, creating blotches as they feed on the plant tissue.

As soon as weevils appear, begin spraying weekly with pyrethrum mixed with isopropyl alcohol, making sure to cover all leaf surfaces. To make this solution, mix two parts alcohol with one part water and add pyrethrum according to package instructions.

## Leaves Pale

### Whiteflies

Magnolias are susceptible to attack specifically from citrus whiteflies (*Dialeurodes citri*). You can easily see these insects on dark green magnolia leaves. The adults are about ¹⁄₁₂ inch long and white, with four wings. Often they secrete a shiny, sticky honeydew, which encourages the growth of a black fungus. The leaves of magnolias infested with whiteflies turn yellow and die, and the trees themselves weaken.

Use a preventive insecticidal soap spray early in the season, and then use the soap spray again if there is any noticeable infestation. Several applications of the soap spray, two to three days apart, should control this pest. As a last resort, spray with pyrethrum every three days until the problem disappears.

# MOST COMMON DISEASES

## Swollen, Sunken Lesions on Stems and Trunk

### Canker

When the fungus *Nectria magnoliae* hits your trees, rounded to elongated, targetlike cankers develop on magnolia branches and trunks. Prune and destroy the cankered branches, and keep trees healthy by watering and feeding when necessary. If a tree is heavily infected, it will have to be destroyed.

## Fungal Threads Cover Leaves; Leaves Matted Together When Dead

### Leaf Blight

A leaf blight disease caused by the fungus *Pellicularia koleroga* develops on the undersides of leaves, where you'll find a mat of mycelium, or fungal threads. Leaves die and hang matted together. Eventually they drop. Spray trees two or three times with copper fungicide. Prune and destroy infected branches.

## Leaves Become Spotted, Turn Brown, and Fall Prematurely

### Leaf Spot

Leaf spot diseases in magnolias are caused by a number of fungi, including *Alternaria* spp., *Cladosporium* spp., *Mycosphaerella* spp., *Phyllosticta* spp., *Septoria* spp., and many others. Depending on the particular fungus that has infected your tree, you may find yellow, brown, or black blotches on the foliage. Often spots come together to form larger patches of dead tissue. Heavily infected leaves fall prematurely.

Leaf spot is rarely serious. Simply gather and destroy fallen leaves. If leaf spot is a continual problem in your backyard, spray trees once with a copper fungicide early in the spring.

## Leaves Turn Yellow
## or Brown and Collapse

### Wilt

A soil-dwelling fungus, *Verticillium albo-atrum*, attacks magnolias, causing the leaves to wilt, turn pale, and fall prematurely. In addition, one or more branches wilt suddenly and die. Sapwood is discolored. If you feed infected trees heavily with a high-nitrogen fertilizer, they may be able to put a new ring of sapwood outside the infected area, and the trees may then recover. Prune out dead branches.

If your trees are badly infected and nothing seems to be making them well, remove them, together with as many roots as possible. Do not replant that area with wilt-susceptible shrubs or trees, but replace magnolias with resistant trees such as most conifers, beech, birch, boxwood, dogwood, fruit trees, holly, locust, mulberry, oak, pecan, serviceberry, sweet gum, sycamore, walnut, and willow.

## Foliage Thins Out;
## Branches Die Back

### Wood Rot

A heart rot caused by the fungi *Fomes geotropus*

and *F. fasciatus* attacks magnolias, causing foliage and branches to die. In early stages, the rotted wood looks grayish black, with conspicuous black margins along the advancing edges of the decayed area. The mature rot is brown. Essentially a gangrene of trees, it cannot be stopped once it has invaded large areas of the trunk. Wood rot can, however, be prevented by avoiding bark injuries, by properly treating injuries that do occur, and by keeping the tree in good vigor by fertilizing and watering. Wounds should be treated promptly.

## NOTES AND RESEARCH

As a precaution against frost damage in the spring, plant your magnolia in a position where the shrub will not get early morning sun. This allows frozen flowers to thaw out slowly and incur less tissue damage and browning.

Big-leaved magnolia leaves are easily torn by whipping winds, so be careful to plant that species in a sheltered location.

# TREE Maple  *Acer* spp.

## DESCRIPTION

Maples offer some of the best shade to be found. This genus includes more than 100 species of trees of varied habit, rate of growth, size, and leaf character. All are noted for their autumn color and winged nuts. Although maples can be grown all across the United States, certain species are best suited for certain regions. The trident maple (*Acer buergera-*

*num*) is happiest in the central United States. The Rocky Mountain maple (*A. glabrum*) prefers, of course, the Rocky mountains, but also does well on the West Coast. The big-leaved maple (*A. macrophyllum*) grows best along the West Coast, and the box elder (*A. negundo*) is best suited to the Southwest and Great Plains. In the cold climates of the

Northeast, the sugar maple (*A. saccharum*) withstands ice and snow and produces a bounty of sap for maple syrup.

## Height

Box elder (*A. negundo*), 50 to 70 feet
Japanese maple (*A. palmatum*), 20 feet
Red maple (*A. rubrum*), 120 feet
Rocky mountain maple (*A. glabrum*), 20 to 30 feet
Silver maple (*A. saccharinum*), 120 feet
Small maple (*A. argutum*), 24 feet

Sugar maple (*A. saccharum*), 120 feet
Trident maple (*A. buergeranum*), 20 feet

## Blossoms

Inconspicuous.

## Foliage

Maples are deciduous trees. Some species have unlobed leaves; others produce leaves with three, five, or seven lobes, depending on the species. The foliage turns a brilliant red or yellow in autumn.

# ENVIRONMENT

## Varieties by Zone

To zone 3, red maple, silver maple, and sugar maple
To zone 5, Japanese maple and small maple
To zone 6, trident maple

## Light Requirements

Maples prefer full sun, but will tolerate light to medium shade.

# MOST COMMON CULTURAL PROBLEM

### Stunted Growth

**Contact with Black Walnut Roots**
Maple trees can suffer stunting, wilting, or even death when they come in contact with black walnut roots. Allelopathic reactions occur within a circle one and a half times the distance from the trunk of the maple to the outermost branches, or dripline. You must move the maple tree to solve this problem.

**Girdling Roots**
Look for a root encircling the trunk (or part of the trunk) at or just below the soil line. Cut away this root.

# MOST COMMON INSECT PESTS

## Leaves Wrinkled and Discolored

### Aphids

Aphids suck juices from maple leaves, causing them to turn yellow or brown. Affected leaves wilt under bright sunlight and sometimes curl and pucker. Defoliation may occur. Ants are attracted to the honeydew secreted by aphids. The common aphids of maples include Norway maple aphids (*Periphyllus lyropictus*), box elder aphids (*P. negundinis*), and painted maple aphids (*Drepanaphis acerifoliae*). All have soft, pear-shaped bodies and are no bigger than the head of a pin. The Norway maple aphid produces honeydew, which can be found on the ground underneath the tree.

To control aphids, spray trees vigorously with water. Do this in the morning, three times, once every other day. If aphids keep returning to your trees, spray with insecticidal soap every two to three days until the pests are gone. As a last resort, for serious infestations, apply pyrethrum twice, three to four days apart.

## Tree Defoliated; Twigs Girdled

### Bagworms

Bagworms (*Thyridopteryx ephemeraeformis*) feed on the leaves of maples and girdle the twigs. The adult males are black, clear-winged moths. Female moths have no wings. The bagworm caterpillar builds a silken cocoon and attaches bits and pieces of leaves for camouflage. The caterpillar itself is dark brown with a white or yellow head, and it carries its bag with it as it feeds.

Look for the bags, which are covered with leaves and twigs, and pick them off the tree; then spray with Bt (*Bacillus thuringiensis*) every week during the entire month of May. In August, set out pheromone traps designed to catch male bagworms, in the hope of reducing the population of these pests next year.

## Branches Girdled; Leaves Fall Prematurely; Trunk Scarred

### Borers

Several different species of borer attack maples. The larva of the maple leafstem borer, also known as the maple petiole borer (*Caulocampus acericaulis*), tunnels into twigs. The damage it does causes leaves to fall prematurely. The adult sawflies look like wasps with spiny hairs on the surfaces of their wings.

The flat-headed apple tree borer (*Chrysobothris femorata*) attacks weak trees. Larvae often girdle the tree. The adults are dark coppery brown beetles, ½ inch long.

The adult maple sesian, or maple callus borer (*Sylvora acerni*) is a clear-winged moth whose larvae bore into maple trees, especially in callused tissue around wounds.

The sugar maple borer (*Glycobius speciosus*) is the most destructive pest of sugar maple trees. The adults are black beetles with brilliant yellow decorations, including a W-shaped mark across the base of the wing covers. The larvae tunnel into the inner bark and sapwood and later cut large galleries in a spiral course upward and partly around the trunk. New growth over the wound forms a series of scars and ridges on the trunk.

Other, less common maple borers include the carpenter worm (*Prionoxystus robiniae*), the leopard moth borer (*Zeuzera pyrina*), and the pigeon tremex (*Tremex columba*), a horntail.

If you find holes of borers in your trees, cut them out with a sharp knife. If the tunnels are fairly straight, the borer can be killed by probing with a flexible wire, or it can be pulled out by means of a hooked wire to make certain it is destroyed. If the tunnels are not straight and chasing after borers with a wire seems impossible, inject nicotine sulfate into each hole and plug the hole with putty.

## Holes in Leaves

### Boxelder Bugs

Boxelder bugs (*Leptocoris trivittatus*) chew holes

in the flowers, fruit, and foliage of maple trees. Adult bugs are brownish black with red markings. They measure about ½ inch in length and resemble squash bugs. The nymphs are bright red. The adults frequently swarm in the fall around the bases of trees, fence posts, or walls.

Control boxelder bugs by spraying infected trees with insecticidal soap. Spray them two or three times at three- to five-day intervals.

### Caterpillars

In addition to the caterpillars of the major maple insect pests described in these pages, several minor caterpillars occasionally attack maple trees. These include the American dagger moth, brown tail moth, cabbage looper, cankerworm, maple leaf cutter, oriental moth, tent caterpillars, tussock moth larvae, and caterpillars of the saddled prominent moth. The green-striped maple worm prefers red and silver maples. Fortunately, most caterpillars can be controlled in the same way.

Handpicking takes care of very small infestations, but most often Bt (*Bacillus thuringiensis*) is the weapon of choice. Dust all parts of the leaves, especially the undersides, and dust again after rains. You can also use Bt as a foliar spray, applying it to infested plants every 10 to 14 days until the pests are gone. If caterpillars get out of control, spray both sides of the leaves with pyrethrum or with a 1 percent solution of rotenone, trying to spray the pest itself. Usually two applications, 3 to 4 days apart, are sufficient.

## Leaves Skeletonized

### Cankerworms

These pests feed heavily on the foliage of maple trees, skeletonizing the leaves and sometimes defoliating the entire tree. You may know them as inchworms. They are about 1 inch long and may be brown or green with a yellow stripe. As soon as you discover them on your trees, begin spraying with Bt (*Bacillus thuringiensis*) every 10 to 14 days until the pests are gone. Early in spring, before the weather turns

warm, place a sticky band on the trunks of vulnerable trees to catch the females as they climb the trees to lay their eggs.

## Brown Blotches with Yellow Margins on Leaves

### Japanese Leafhoppers

The leaves of maples infested with Japanese leafhoppers (*Orientus ishidae*) develop a distinctive brown blotching with a bright yellow margin, which merges with the green part of the leaf. You may also find swellings on the twigs where leafhoppers deposited eggs under young bark. Of all maples, the Norway maple is most vulnerable to attack from this pest and may become seriously infested with these yellowish leafhoppers. Use insecticidal soap laced with isopropyl alcohol to control any serious infestations. Make three applications about three to five days apart.

## Skeletonized Areas on Leaves

### Maple Leaf Cutters

Maple leaf cutters (*Paraclemensia acerfoliella*) can defoliate maple trees. These small, ¼-inch-long caterpillars cut out small sections of the leaves and form cases, in which they hide while they feed. Leaf cutters often skeletonize the leaves in a circular path such that a section of leaf often drops to the ground. As soon as you spot these pests, spray the tree with Bt (*Bacillus thuringiensis*) at weekly intervals until leaf cutters are removed. In the fall, rake up and destroy all leaf litter, where the pupae hibernate.

## Leaves Mottled

### Mealybugs

The comstock mealybug (*Pseudococcus comstocki*) is a small, elliptical, waxy insect. After hatching in late May, the larvae crawl up the trunk to the leaves, where they suck out the juices and devitalize the tree. Control mealybugs by spraying with insecticidal soap laced with alcohol (about 1 tablespoon alcohol to 1 pint soap mix), making three applications, one every seven to ten days. If the soap spray does not work, try pyrethrum, using three applications four days apart.

## Leaves Wilt and Turn Brown

### Midges

Trees infested by midges show wilted, deformed, and browned buds and foliage. Many species of midges also create galls on the trees, which protect their eggs and developing larvae. Adults are two-winged flies, $1/14$ to $1/8$ inch long, with long legs and antennae.

To control midges, pick and destroy infested leaves and gather and dispose of any fallen leaves; then spray the tree with insecticidal soap, using three applications at three- to five-day intervals. In late winter or early spring, spray with dormant oil to prevent any eggs from hatching.

## Numerous Galls on Leaves

### Mites

Maple bladder gall mites (*Vasates quadripedes*) cover the upper surfaces of maple leaves with small, green, wartlike galls, which later turn blood red. If the galls are very numerous, the leaves become deformed. Several other species of mites, including *Eriophyes* spp. and *Phyllocoptes* spp., produce brilliant purple, red, or pink blisterlike growths on leaves. In general, mites are about $1/50$ inch long, barely visible to the unaided eye. Not being true insects, they have four pairs of legs. Their piercing-sucking mouth parts allow them to suck juices from the leaves of plants. Depending on the species, they may be yellow, green, red, or brown.

As soon as you spot mite damage, spray trees in the early morning with a forceful stream of water to knock mites from leaf undersides. Repeat this procedure on three consecutive mornings. If you still find mites on your trees, spray with insecticidal soap. A spray of insecticidal soap mixed with light horticultural oil (1 tablespoon oil to 1 pint soap) works as a dormant spray if applied in late winter.

## Branches Wilt, Die, and Break Off

### Pitted Ambrosia Beetles

The pitted ambrosia beetle (*Corthylus punctatissimus*) is a dark reddish brown beetle, about $1/8$ inch long. Minute pits mark its body surface. The small, white larvae eat galleries in maple wood, causing branches to wilt, die, and break off. Adults overwinter in these galleries and emerge to feed on fungi in leaf litter.

As soon as you spot ambrosia beetles, begin handpicking. Try a mixture of pyrethrum and isopropyl alcohol applied every three to five days for two weeks.

## Small Bumps on Leaves and Branches

### Scale

Scale insects attach themselves to leaves and branches of trees and actually look like bumps. They protect themselves under a waxy, concave, shell-like covering. Silver maples are especially susceptible to attack from the cottony-maple scale (*Pulvinaria innumerabilis*). These insects are brown, about $1/8$ to $1/4$ inch in diameter, and create a cottony mass around them, which contains up to 500 eggs. The entire cottony mass is about $1/2$ inch in diameter. In June, the young move out and infest the leaves. Later they migrate to the branches, especially the undersides. Several other scale insects attack maples, including the maple phenacoccus (*Phenacoccus acericola*), the terrapin scale (*Lecanium nigrofasciatum*), the gloomy scale (*Melanaspis tenebricosa*), and the Japanese scale (*Leucaspis japonica*). Scale insects suck the sap from the leaves and branches of trees, causing the leaves to yellow and curl.

All scale insects are controlled in the same way. If caught early on, you can scrape them off the tree with your fingernail or a cotton swab dipped in rubbing alcohol; otherwise, spray with a mixture of alcohol and insecticidal soap every three days for two weeks. To make this mixture, combine $1/2$ cup of alcohol with every quart of insecticidal soap that you use.

## Many Twigs Break and Fall

### Twig Pruners

The twig pruner (*Elaphidionoides villosus*) attacks many shade trees, including maples, cutting off twigs, which fall to the ground. You will find larvae inside the fallen twigs in July. This pest is easily controlled simply by gathering and disposing of all fallen twigs; otherwise the larvae will overwinter in them and attack your trees again in the spring.

# MOST COMMON DISEASES

## Sunken Spots on Leaves

### Anthracnose

Maples infected with this fungal disease develop distinct lesions on their leaves, which appear as moist, sunken spots with fruiting bodies in the center. These leaf spots may run together, resembling a blotch or blight. The dead areas follow the veins or are bounded by larger veins. Sometimes the disease spreads down several inches below the buds on terminal shoots. Pustules containing pinkish spores appear. Twigs die back, and in severe cases, defoliation occurs. Gather and destroy diseased leaves when they fall, and prune diseased branches. Spray infected trees once with a copper fungicide such as Bordeaux mixture. Maintain the vigor of your maple by feeding and watering it well, especially during droughts.

## Swollen, Bleeding Lesions on Branches and Trunk

### Canker

Maples infected by the fungus *Phytophthora cactorum* develop cankers in their bark from which sap oozes. The leaves wilt, and branches die back. Mildly infected trees may recover without any special treatments. Once the tree is heavily diseased, it cannot be cured. Remove and destroy it. To prevent this fungus from infecting your trees, treat any frost cracks and wounds that appear near the base of the trunk with pruning paint, and feed and water trees as needed to maintain good vigor.

## Leaves Blistered and Curled

### Leaf Blister

Several fungi of the genus *Taphrina* produce circular or irregular blisters on the leaves of maples and cause the leaves to curl. Gather and destroy all fallen leaves, and spray trees with lime sulfur just before buds open in spring.

## Brown Spots on Leaves

### Leaf Spot

Maples infected by the fungus *Phyllosticta minima* show ¼-inch irregular spots on their leaves, which develop brownish centers and purplish margins. Fruiting bodies grow in the center of these spots. This disease is most severe on red, silver, and sugar maples, but also occurs on Japanese, Norway, and sycamore maples. Spray infected trees in spring with a copper fungicide three times at two-week intervals, starting when the leaves are unfolding from the buds.

Another fungus, *Rhytisma punctatum*, occurs more often on the Pacific coast than in the eastern states. Infected maples develop small black leaf spots. If your tree is badly infected, spray it in spring with copper fungicide when buds open and, in severe cases, repeat several times at two-week intervals. Rake up and destroy leaves in the fall.

## White Powder on Leaves

### Powdery Mildew

Powdery mildew caused by the fungi *Uncinula circinata* and *Phyllactinia corylea* is a common disease of maples. You can easily diagnose it from the whitish patches that cover the leaves of infected trees. If the disease is serious, spray the tree thoroughly with wettable sulfur once or twice at weekly intervals, starting as soon as the whitish coating of the fungus is visible. If the disease is mild, simply collect and discard all aboveground refuse in the fall.

## Mushrooms Sprout at Base of Tree; Stringlike Growths on Roots

### Shoestring Root Rot

If you find mushrooms growing around the base of your maple in late fall or early winter, look for other signs that shoestring root rot has infected the tree. The crowns of maples infected with shoestring root rot may gradually or suddenly die back. Foliage becomes scant, withers, turns yellow, and drops prematurely. Large white fans of fungal mycelium appear between the bark and the hardwood of the larger roots, and often, small, dark, shoestringlike strands cover the outside of the bark of infected roots.

Once the fungus becomes established, it is difficult to control. The fungus cannot exist under dry conditions. Because the fungus thrives in wet, heavy soils, improve drainage and avoid overwatering. Dig out and destroy seriously infected trees.

## Leaves Turn Yellow or Brown and Collapse

### Wilt

*Verticillium albo-atrum* is a soil-dwelling fungus that causes wilt in maples. Leaves of infected trees become pale and wilted and may fall prematurely. One or more branches wilt suddenly and die, often on only one side of the tree. Infected trees may die slowly, over a period of several years, or suddenly, within a few weeks. If you were to look at the sapwood, you would find it discolored.

Heavy feeding with a high-nitrogen fertilizer sometimes enables trees to produce a new ring of sapwood outside the infected area and the trees may then recover. Prune dead branches. Remove badly infected trees, together with as many roots as possible. Do not replant that area with wilt-susceptible shrubs or trees, but with resistant species, including most conifers, beech, birch, boxwood, dogwood, fruit trees, holly, locust, mulberry, oak, pecan, serviceberry, sweet gum, sycamore, walnut, and willow.

# TREE Oak *Quercus* spp.

## DESCRIPTION

Oaks have long been valued for their fine wood and for their grand stature as ornamental trees. They are generally large, long-lived trees, having a variety of leaf types, acorns, and, for those native to the United States, wonderful fall colors. Most oaks are not suitable for small properties, since they grow very tall and out of proportion to other plants. In a large landscape, though, they are stunning. The massive white oak (*Quercus alba*) is a good example, with dimensions up to 150 feet in height and 80 feet in spread. It holds its leaves through some of winter and with rounded profile and sturdy, thick horizontal branches looks impressive during this sometimes barren season. The red oak (*Q. borealis*) grows well along the street, and has a good tolerance for city conditions. The shingle oak (*Q. imbricaria*) can be clipped as a hedge, and makes an excellent windbreak. Some oaks have practical as well as ornamental value, such as the cork oak (*Q. suber*), identified by Thomas Jefferson as a potential source of cork. More than 100,000 of these trees are grown in the United States in California and in the South as far north as Baltimore.

## Height

Cork oak (*Q. suber*), 60 feet
Live oak (*Q. virginiana*), 60 feet
Pin oak (*Q. palustris*), 75 feet
Red oak (*Q. borealis*), 75 feet
Shingle oak (*Q. imbricaria*), 75 feet
White oak (*Q. alba*), 90 feet

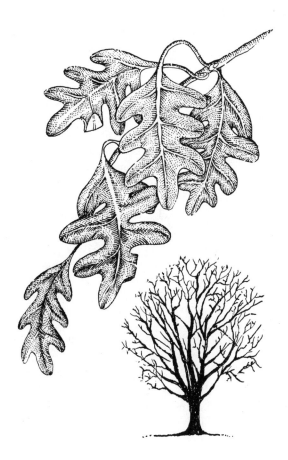

## Foliage

Most oaks are deciduous, though a very few, such as the live oak and the cork oak, which grow in the South, are evergreen. In general, oaks have lobed and leathery leaves. Most of the native American species turn red in fall; some turn yellow-bronze.

## ENVIRONMENT

### Varieties by Zone

To zone 3, red oak
To zone 4, white oak
To zone 5, pin oak and shingle oak
To zone 7, cork oak and live oak

### Light Requirements

Oaks will grow in full sun to light shade.

## MOST COMMON INSECT PESTS

### Trunk and Branches Girdled; Bark Discolored

#### Borers

Various species of borers attack oak trees. The two-lined chestnut borer (*Agrilus bilineatus*) is especially attracted to injured, weakened, or dying trees. The adults are slender greenish black beetles, ⅜ inch long, that appear in late June. It's the larvae, however, that do the damage. The leaves located above areas where borers are working turn brown and simply hang on the tree. The flat-headed apple tree borer (*Chrysobothris femorata*) also favors oaks that are not growing vigorously. The adults feed on leaves, and the larvae chew flattened galleries in the sapwood. Larval damage may girdle branches or entire trees. The bark overlying this damage becomes discolored.

Other borer pests of oaks include the carpenter worm (*Prionoxystus robiniae*), the leopard moth borer (*Zeuzera pyrina*), and the twig pruner (*Elaphidionoides villosus*).

To control borers in most situations, make a thorough examination of the tree before the spring season arrives and cut and burn any dying or unhealthy-looking twigs that may contain borers. During the summer season, check to see if sawdust is being pushed from small borer holes. Such holes should be cut out with a sharp knife. If the tunnels are fairly straight, you can kill borers by probing with a flexible wire, or pull them out with a hooked wire and destroy them. If tunnels curve and wind, inject nicotine sulfate into each borer hole and plug the hole with putty.

## Leaves Skeletonized

### Cankerworms

These pests feed heavily on the foliage of oak trees, skeletonizing the leaves and sometimes defoliating the entire tree. You may know them as inchworms. They are about 1 inch long and may be brown or green with a yellow stripe. As soon as you discover them on your trees, begin spraying with Bt (*Bacillus thuringiensis*) every 10 to 14 days until the pests are gone. Early in spring, before the weather turns warm, place a sticky band on the trunks of vulnerable trees to catch the females as they climb the trees to lay their eggs.

### Sawflies

Elm sawflies (*Cimbex americana*) skeletonize oak leaves as they feed. Trees may eventually become defoliated. Adults resemble wasps and have two pairs of transparent wings. They are about ⅝ to 1½ inches long. Their larvae resemble bluish black or olive green caterpillars and are about ½ inch long.

Handpick the larvae or spray infested trees with insecticidal soap, rotenone, or pyrethrum as soon as you spot these pests. One application should get rid of these pests, but if a second generation appears, spray again.

## Holes in Leaves

### Caterpillars

A number of different caterpillars eat holes in oak leaves. These include the tent caterpillar, the yellow-necked caterpillar, the larvae of the western tussock moth, the oak skeletonizer (*Bucculatrix ainsliella*), cankerworms, caterpillars of the io moth, the American dagger moth, the satin moth, and the saddleback caterpillar.

To control caterpillars, handpick them if you've found them before too many have found your tree; otherwise, use Bt (*Bacillus thuringiensis*). If you use the dust, apply it to all parts of the leaves, especially the undersides, and dust again after a rain. You can also make a foliar spray and apply it every 10 to 14 days until the caterpillars are gone. If the infestation is especially heavy, and Bt doesn't seem to be eliminating the pests, try pyrethrum or a 1 percent solution of rotenone. Usually two applications, 3 to 4 days apart, are sufficient.

## Leaves Consumed; Conspicuous, Tawny Egg Masses Present

### Gypsy Moths

The dreaded larvae of the gypsy moth (*Porthetria dispar*) gather in huge masses to devour foliage. The oak is the preferred host of the gypsy moth, which can defoliate an entire tree in two weeks. A tree is likely to die after repeated defoliations. Newly hatched caterpillars are about 1/16 inch long, and grow to about 2½ inches. As mature larvae they have five pairs of blue spots and six pairs of red spots along their backs. Adult male moths have a wingspan of 1½ inches. They are light tan to dark brown, with blackish wavy bands across their forewings. Female moths are nearly white in color and are much larger, with 2½-inch wings; however, they can barely fly. Both sexes have feathered antennae. Females lay about 500 eggs in masses covered with velvety, buff-colored hairs.

To control gypsy moths, spray trees with Bt (*Bacillus thuringiensis*) every 10 to 14 days from late April to mid-June. In June, when larvae are 1 inch long, they become night feeders and crawl down from the tree each morning. You can easily catch them in a burlap trap. Wrap a foot-wide piece of burlap around the tree trunk, about chest high. Tie it at the center with heavy twine, letting the top fold over the twine to form a skirt. Caterpillars on their way down the trunk of the tree will crawl under the burlap fold. In the late afternoon, put on garden gloves and sweep the caterpillars off into a container of detergent and water.

## Leaves Pale or Mottled

### Lace Bugs

Oak lace bugs (*Corythucha arcuata*) suck sap from the undersides of leaves, causing them to turn pale or become mottled. The leaves of many species of oaks, particularly the white oak, may turn whitish gray when heavily infested with this pest. Adult lace bugs are small, measuring at the most ³/₁₆ inch. They have a squarish shape and elaborately reticulated wings that resemble lacework.

As soon as you discover this pest on your oak tree, spray leaves, particularly the undersides, with insecticidal soap. Two applications a week or two apart should eliminate the problem. If not, spray with nicotine sulfate or pyrethrum every seven to ten days until symptoms disappear.

## Pale Blotches on Leaves

### Leafminers

The oak blotch leafminer (*Cameraria cincinnatiella*) mines between the upper and lower surfaces of white oak leaves, causing pale blotches to form. In any leaf blotch, you will see ten or more larvae. The adults are small moths.

To control leafminers, remove the infested leaves. Spray with insecticidal soap to kill any adults that might lay eggs on your plants. If leafminers are a problem year after year, consider covering plants in spring with agricultural fleece.

## Leaves Rolled and Bound with Silk Strands

### Leaf Rollers

It's easy to spot infestations of these pests: Just look for rolled leaves at the ends of branches. Leaf rollers protect themselves while feeding by rolling leaves into tubes around themselves and binding the leaves with strands or webs of silk. As these pests feed on oak foliage, the leaves become skeletonized, turn brown, and die. The oak leaf roller (*Argyrotoxa semipurpurana*) larvae are light to dark green or cream to yellow in color and ³/₈ to 1¾ inches long. The adult moths are brown or gray and ¼ to ½ inch long.

If you don't find too many leaf rollers on your trees, simply crush them in their rolled hideouts. Spray with Bt (*Bacillus thuringiensis*) before you expect the caterpillars to begin feeding in the spring, applying it again twice at five-day intervals.

## Leaves Discolored and Bound with Silk Strands

### Leaftiers

Oak leaftiers (*Croesia albicomana*) came up with the same idea that leaf rollers use. These pests protect themselves while feeding by binding leaf surfaces together with strands of silk. As they feed, the leaves become ragged and unsightly, turn brown, and die. The destructive larvae are light to dark green or cream to yellow in color and ³/₈ to ¾ inch long. Adult moths are brown or gray and ¼ to ½ inch long.

Control mild infestations of leaftiers by handpicking and crushing. Or spray with Bt (*Bacillus thuringiensis*) in early spring and repeat twice at five-day intervals.

## Leaves Mottled

### Mites

Oak mites (*Oligonychus bicolor*) suck on the juices of leaves, causing foliage to become mottled. Mites are about ¹/₅₀ inch long, and barely visible to the unaided eye. Not true insects, they have four pairs of legs. Their piercing-sucking mouth parts enable them to easily feed on leaf sap.

Start control measures as soon as you notice the first discoloration in the leaves. Spray plants in the early morning with a forceful stream of water to knock mites from leaf undersides. Repeat this procedure three times, once every other day. If that doesn't do the job, spray with insecticidal soap three times at three- to five-day intervals.

## Bark Pitted; Small Bumps on Leaves and Branches

### Scale

Scale insects look like small bumps when you find them on trees. As they feed on oaks, they make shallow pits in the bark. Infested trees have a ragged, untidy appearance. Young trees may be killed, the lower branches dying first. Various scale pests infest oaks. Golden oak scale (*Asterolecanium variolosum*) has a circular shape and measures about 1/16 inch in diameter. It is covered with greenish gold scales. Other scale pests include the oak gall scale (*Kermes pubescens*), lecanium scale (*Lecanium corni* and *L. quercifex*), the obscure scale (*Melanaspis obscura*), and the purple scale (*Lepidosaphes beckii*).

If caught early on, you can simply scrape these pests off your trees with your fingernail or remove them with a cotton swab dipped in rubbing alcohol. For any infestation too large to handle with handpicking, spray trees with a mixture of alcohol and insecticidal soap every three days for two weeks. To make this spray, mix ½ cup alcohol with each quart of insecticidal soap.

## Many Twigs Break and Fall

### Twig Pruners

The twig pruner (*Elaphidionoides villosus*) does exactly that: It prunes twigs off your oak trees. You'll know this pest has struck when you notice that small twigs constantly drop to the ground during late summer. Some twigs remain hanging, and the leaves dry upon them. The twig pruner grubs work under the bark and then tunnel along the pith in the center of the twig. Adult beetles emerge from the twigs the following summer. Gather and destroy fallen twigs in July, August, and early September; otherwise the larvae will overwinter in them and attack trees again next year.

## Galls

### Various Insects

Oaks are susceptible to hundreds of types of galls; so many that you will best be able to identify them using a special manual. An excellent book is *Plant Galls and Gall Makers*, by E. P. Felt. Most galls rarely affect the health of trees. Before growth starts in spring, spray your trees either with dormant strength lime sulfur or with a dormant miscible oil to destroy some of the pests overwintering on the branches. Prune and destroy heavily infested branches.

## Holes or Notches in Leaves

### Weevils

The adult Asiatic oak weevil (*Cyrtepistomus castaneus*) feeds on oak foliage, causing severe damage. This ¼-inch pest may be deep red or black, with scattered metallic green scales. The adult Japanese weevil (*Pseudocneorhinus bifasciatus*) also attacks oaks.

Control weevils by beating limbs of the infested tree and catching the startled insects in a drop cloth spread beneath the tree. Apply a sticky substance such as Tanglefoot around the trunks to prevent adults from climbing up and eating the leaves. In addition, spray trees weekly with pyrethrum mixed with isopropyl alcohol, covering all leaf surfaces. To make this mixture, combine two parts alcohol with one part water and add pyrethrum in the amounts indicated on the package directions.

# MOST COMMON DISEASES

## Sunken Spots on Leaves

### Anthracnose

You can recognize this disease by the distinct, moist, sunken spots that develop on leaves. Fruiting bodies grow in the center of these spots, and these diseased areas may run together, resembling a blotch or blight. The dead areas follow the veins of the leaves. Anthracnose affects the terminal shoots of trees, too, sometimes infecting an area that extends down several inches below the buds. Pustules containing pinkish spores appear. In severe cases, branches die back and defoliation occurs. Prune diseased branches and gather and destroy diseased leaves when they fall. As soon as you see the disease, spray your tree once with a copper fungicide such as Bordeaux mixture.

## Lesions on Twigs; Leaves Wilt and Die

### Blight

Oaks infected with blight caused by the fungus *Diplodia longispora* develop lesions or cankers on their twigs and small branches. If the tree is heavily diseased, branches die back and leaves wilt. During the summer, prune infected twigs and branches back to healthy wood. Cut to about 6 inches below the visibly infected area to ensure removal of all infected tissue. In severely weakened trees, the fungus may spread 2 or more feet down branches. Fertilize and water trees to maintain vigor. Control leaf-chewing insects with two applications of pyrethrum or rotenone, about three to four days apart, and spray with a copper fungicide.

## Swollen, Sunken Lesions on Stems and Trunk

### Canker

Oaks are susceptible to several types of fungi that cause cankers to form on the branches and trunk. These include *Fusarium* spp., *Botryodiplodia* spp., *Endothia* spp., *Polyporus* spp., and others. On young oaks, the cankers have a smooth surface and are slightly sunken. Cankers on older trees have a rough surface ridged with callus tissue. Those at the base of the tree may look simply like cracks in the bark, but underneath the bark you'll find dead wood that may girdle the tree. Prune any dying and dead branches and remove small cankers on the trunk using a clean, sharp knife. Fertilize and water the weakened trees to improve their vigor. If a tree becomes severely infected, it should be destroyed.

## Leaves Blistered and Curled

### Leaf Blister

During cool, wet springs, almost all species of oaks are subject to leaf blister caused by the fungus *Taphrina coerulescens*. Circular, raised yellowish white areas up to ½ inch in diameter appear scattered on upper leaf surfaces. If you turn over an infected leaf, you will see depressions where these blisters occur. Leaves continue to function and do not drop. A single application of lime sulfur at bud-swelling time is an effective control, but should be resorted to only if you have had this problem in the previous year.

## Brown or Yellow Spots on Leaves

### Leaf Spot

Many kinds of leaf spot fungi, including *Cylindrosporium* spp., *Dothiorella* spp., *Gloeosporium* spp., *Leptothyrium* spp., *Phyllosticta* spp., *Septoria* spp., and others attack oaks, but they rarely cause much damage, since they hit late in the growing season. Gathering and destroying fallen leaves usually is all that's needed to control these fungi in seasons of normal rainfall (roughly 1 inch of rainfall a week or less). If leaf spot has been a problem in the past, spray trees with copper fungicides at two-week intervals, starting in early spring when the leaves unfold.

## White Powder on Leaves

### Powdery Mildew

Powdery mildew in oaks is most often caused by the fungus *Sphaerotheca lanestris*. This fungus is especially common in the southern and western states. Infected trees have whitish patches on their leaves and growing tips. Other powdery mildew fungi affecting oaks include *Erysiphe trina*, *Microsphaera alni*, and *Phyllactinia corylea*. Fortunately, powdery mildew is not a fatal disease, although it makes plants look less attractive. If your oak suffers seriously from this disease, spray it the following spring with wettable sulfur once or twice, at weekly intervals, starting as soon as the whitish coating of the fungus is visible. This keeps the problem from becoming more serious.

## Mushrooms Sprout at Base of Tree; Stringlike Growths on Roots

### Shoestring Root Rot

If you find mushrooms growing up around the base of your oaks, your trees may be infected by root rot, caused by the fungus *Armillaria mellea*. Often, small, dark, shoestringlike strands cover the outside of the bark of infected roots, and large white fans of fungal mycelium appear between the bark and the hardwood of the larger roots. Shoestring root rot causes gradual to sudden dieback of tree crowns. Affected trees show a decline in vigor of all or part of the top of the tree. Foliage becomes scant, withers, turns yellow, and drops prematurely.

Once the fungus becomes established, it is difficult to control. Healthy plants are seldom attacked. The fungus cannot exist under dry conditions, so reduce mulch to dry out soil. Because the fungus thrives in wet, heavy soils, improve drainage and avoid overwatering. Dig out and destroy seriously infected trees and discard the surrounding soil.

## Leaves Turn Brown and Collapse

### Wilt

The fungus *Ceratocystis fagacearum* causes wilt in oaks. Affected trees have curled, drooping brown leaves, and sometimes the sapwood turns black or brown. Once trees become infected, wilt symptoms progress rapidly over the entire crown, affecting lower branches last. Death occurs within a few weeks to a year, depending on the size of the tree. This disease spreads via underground root grafts and several insects and related pests, including fruit flies, beetles, borers, mites, and squirrels. No effective control is known. Infected trees must be cut down and destroyed. Prune and destroy dead branches. If your tree is badly infected, remove it, together with as many roots as possible, and destroy it. Since the soil may continue to harbor some of the fungi, replant with resistant trees such as most conifers, beech, birch, boxwood, dogwood, fruit trees, holly, locust, mulberry, oak, pecan, serviceberry, sweet gum, sycamore, walnut, or willow.

## Shelflike Growths on Trunk

### Wood Rot

Wood rot diseases in oaks may be caused by several fungi, including *Stereum* spp., *Polyporus* spp., *Fomes* spp., and *Fistulina* spp. These usually attack near the soil line, where a variety of shelflike growths erupt perpendicularly from the trunks. Two types of rot, known as white heart rot and brown heart rot, generally result. Once wood rots have become established, having invaded large areas of the trunk, little can be done to stop the infection. Trees must be removed and destroyed. This disease can be prevented, though, by properly treating any injuries to the tree and by maintaining healthy trees through proper fertilizing and watering.

TREE **Pine**    *Pinus* spp.

## DESCRIPTION

In addition to being the most important lumber trees in the world, the pines are among the finest evergreen ornamentals. Most are trees, although this group includes a few shrubs. They can be grown all across North America, from the seashore all the way to timberline in the mountains. Pines are divided into groups according to the number of needles— five, three, or two—in each tuft of foliage on the branch. Also, they are often separated into soft and hard pine groups. So many pine species exist it is difficult to generalize about any of the characteristics below. Perhaps the most attractive of all is the eastern white pine (*Pinus strobus*), with its long, delicate, graceful foliage. Although it is the second tallest native pine, if judiciously pruned it can be restrained to the scale of the small property owner. It is a fine plant for backdrops, windbreaks, and specimen trees. As it ages, its density and pyramidal shape give way to a flatter topped, more open, picturesque shape.

## Height

Eastern white pine (*P. strobus*), 100 to 150 feet
Japanese red pine (*P. densiflora*), 100 feet
Shore pine (*P. contorta*), 30 feet

## Foliage

Pine foliage is evergreen. The needles vary according to species from less than 1½ inches to almost 1

foot in length. The eastern white pine has soft needles, five in a group; it keeps its good green color throughout the winter. Pines drop their three-year-old needles every year.

# ENVIRONMENT

## Varieties by Zone

To zone 3, eastern white pine
To zone 4, Japanese red pine
To zone 7, shore pine

## Light Requirements

Pine trees prefer full sun, but will tolerate partial shade.

# MOST COMMON INSECT PESTS

## Dry Twigs; Galls on Branches; Leaves Dwarfed

### Aphids

The pine bark aphid (*Pineus strobi*) attacks the undersides of pine limbs and the trunk from the ground up. These aphids may be detected by the white, cottony material that collects in patches wherever they are present. The white pine aphid (*Cinara strobi*) feeds on the smooth bark of the twigs, and during winter in cold regions of the country, these twigs dry out. The pine leaf chermid (*Pineus pinifoliae*) winters over on pines and then moves to spruces in the spring, where its infestation is marked by galls on the ends of branches. In summer, it moves again to white pines, where it attacks new shoots, dwarfing new leaves and even killing shoots. Ants are attracted to the honeydew secreted by aphids.

Light infestations are easily controlled by spraying trees vigorously with water. Do this in the early morning three times, once every other day. If aphids are still a problem, spray with insecticidal soap every two to three days until they are gone. As a last resort, use pyrethrum, making two applications, three to four days apart.

## Leaves Yellowish; Tunnels in Bark

### Beetles

Pines are susceptible to attack from a wide variety of beetles. The damage beetles do can be especially dangerous after a period of prolonged drought. Those of an overwintering brood emerge and attack trees in the spring. Weakened trees are prime victims. Beetles usually attack the midtrunk first and then work both up and down the tree. They bore through the outer bark and chew S-shaped crisscrossing tunnels throughout the inner bark. The earliest signs of infestation are numerous white, yellow, or red-brown pitch tubes scattered over the outer bark of the tree. Ten to 14 days after infestation, the needles turn yellowish. New broods often leave the trees when the foliage is only slightly faded or yellow. When the crown of the tree turns red, the beetles have usually left, except in the winter months. The pine beetle adult is a brown, ⅛-inch-long, short-legged, stout beetle. The young beetle is soft and yellow, but soon hardens and darkens to a dull brown. The larvae of the bark beetle (*Scolytidae* spp.) bore into the bark and mine their way through the sapwood. As the adult beetles emerge from the tree, they create tiny holes in the surface of the bark. These holes may be ¹/₂₀ to ⅓ inch in size, depending on the species.

Most beetles can be controlled by handpicking. If the infestation is large, spray infested pines with a mixture of pyrethrum and isopropyl alcohol every three to five days for two weeks. No effective control for bark beetles is known. Keep your trees in good condition with proper feeding and watering. Cut down severely infested trees and destroy them.

## Shoots Wilt and Die Back

### Borers

The white pine shoot borer (*Eucosma gloriola*) is a whitish caterpillar, about ½ inch long. This insect overwinters in the soil and emerges as a moth in spring. The caterpillars burrow into the centers of lateral shoots, causing them to wilt and die back several inches.

To control shoot borers in most situations, make a thorough examination of the tree before the spring season arrives and cut and burn any dying or unhealthy-looking twigs that may contain borers. During the summer season, check to see if sawdust is being pushed from small borer holes. Such holes should be cut out with a sharp knife. If the tunnels are fairly straight, you can kill borers by probing with a flexible wire, or pull them out with a hooked wire and destroy them. If tunnels curve and wind, inject nicotine sulfate into each borer hole and plug the hole with putty.

## New Growth Deformed and Wilted

### Budworms

If the new growth and terminal shoots of your pines appear wilted and deformed, suspect Jack pine budworms (*Choristoneura pinus*). The caterpillars are ½ to ¾ inch long, and mature to become small dull-colored moths. These caterpillars are most abundant in June and July.

Control budworms by handpicking or clipping and burning the infested shoots. Spray trees in spring with Bt (*Bacillus thuringiensis*) two or three times, once every three to five days, as buds burst. Because Bt washes off trees with rain, it should be renewed from time to time during the year.

## Needles Damaged

### Caterpillars

Several different kinds of caterpillars may infest your pines and cause problems. The larvae of the European pine shoot moth (*Rhyacionia buoliana*) are very serious pests of mugho pines and red pines. Austrian, Scots, and Japanese black pines also may be badly damaged. These caterpillars attack the tips of young shoots, which eventually become deformed and die. Often the lateral buds split open. Pine shoot moth caterpillars usually appear during May or the early part of June. If you find resin on your trees, it's a good sign that these pests are present. Adult moths emerge around June 15 and lay their eggs in August on new buds.

The greenish yellow larvae of pine tube moths (*Argyrotaenia pinatubana*) infest white pines in the eastern states and lodgepole and whitebark pines in the Rocky Mountain region. The caterpillars make tubes by tying the needles together and eating the ends of them.

Zimmerman pine moth larvae (*Dioryctria zimmermani*) bore into twigs and branches on many species of pines. Branch tips turn brown, and the entire tops of trees may break off if much damage is done. These caterpillars may be white to reddish yellow or green, and measure about ¾ inch in length. The adult moth is reddish gray and has a wingspan of 1 to 1½ inches.

All caterpillars can be controlled in basically the same way. Handpicking can eliminate all of them if you catch the infestation right away. If you don't, and your trees harbor more pests than you want to be collecting, dust with Bt (*Bacillus thuringiensis*), reapplying after rains. Bt can also be applied as a foliar spray; use it every 10 to 14 days until the pests are gone. If caterpillars get out of control, spray thoroughly with pyrethrum or a 1 percent solution of rotenone. Usually, two applications, 3 to 4 days apart, will eliminate the problem.

## Leaves Consumed; Conspicuous, Tawny Egg Masses Present

### Gypsy Moths

When gypsy moths (*Porthetria dispar*) infest trees, they lay eggs in masses, each containing 400 to 500 eggs, that are covered with velvety, buff-colored hairs. Numerous larvae hatch from these egg masses to devour pine needles. A tree may die after a single defoliation. Newly hatched caterpillars are about ¹⁄₁₆ inch long and grow to about 2½ inches. When mature, they have five pairs of blue spots and six pairs of red spots along their backs. Adult male moths have a wingspan of 1½ inches. Their wings are light tan to dark brown, with blackish wavy bands across the front. Females are nearly white

and larger, with 2½-inch wings; however, they can barely fly. Both sexes have feathered antennae.

To control gypsy moths, spray trees with Bt (*Bacillus thuringiensis*) every 10 to 14 days from late April to mid-June. In June, when larvae are 1 inch long, they become night feeders and crawl down from the tree each morning. You can easily catch them in a burlap trap. Wrap a foot-wide piece of burlap around the tree trunk, about chest high. Tie it at the center with heavy twine, letting the top fold over the twine to form a skirt. Caterpillars on their way down the trunk of the tree will crawl under the burlap fold. In the late afternoon, put on garden gloves and sweep the caterpillars off into a container of detergent and water.

## Needles Turn Gray or Brown

### Mites

Spruce spider mites (*Oligonychus ununguis*) attack pines as well as spruces. They spin webs in the branches and suck juices out of the needles, causing them to turn gray or brown. Spruce mites may be dull green to nearly black with a pale stripe.

To control mites, spray your trees vigorously with water in the early morning to knock mites from the branches; repeat this for three days. If mites are still a problem, spray with insecticidal soap. A spray of insecticidal soap mixed with light horticultural oil works as a dormant spray against eggs and newly hatched nymphs. Use about 1 tablespoon soap concentrate to 1 quart mixed oil, or combine equal parts of prepared soap mix and oil mix.

## Needles Disappear

### Sawflies

Several species of sawfly devour the needles of pine trees and can defoliate a tree. Adults of European pine sawfly (*Neodiprion sertifer*) are ⅝- to 1½-inch wasplike insects, with two pairs of transparent wings. Their bluish black or olive green larvae are about ½ inch long. Larvae generally begin attacking pines in spring or early summer.

If you find only a few caterpillars on your trees, handpicking will easily eliminate them; otherwise, spray with insecticidal soap, pyrethrum, or rotenone. Spray thoroughly when caterpillars are first sighted and watch for the second generation. Spray again if necessary.

## Small White Bumps or Cottony Masses on Branches or Needles

### Scale

If you see small bumps on the branches of your pines, you may be looking at scale insects. Scale insects suck the sap from needles and bark. The needles become yellowed and may drop and the trees lose their vigor. These pests have a concave waxy covering, which protects them while they feed. They may be white, yellow, or brown to black, depending on the species, and they have a diameter of $1/10$ to $2/5$ inch. They spin cottony webs on the undersides of pine branches, especially at branch axils. Some of the more common species to attack pines include the red pine scale (*Matsucoccus resiosae*), the pine tortoise scale (*Toumeyella numismaticum*), and the pine needle scale (*Phenacaspis pinifoliae*).

If caught early on, you can easily scrape the pests off your trees with your fingernail or remove them with a cotton swab dipped in rubbing alcohol. For any sizable infestation, though, spray with a mixture of alcohol and insecticidal soap every three days for two weeks. To make this mixture, combine ½ cup alcohol with each quart of insecticidal soap. In late winter, apply dormant oil spray to smother overwintering adults and eggs.

## Sticky Froth on Needles

### Spittlebugs

Sticky froth on the needles of your pines points to spittlebugs (*Aphrophora* spp.), also known as froghoppers. These are serious pests of pines. The nymphs suck sap from the branches of pines, causing stunting and distortion of the needles. They are yellowish in color and form unsightly masses of sticky froth, or "spittle," to protect themselves as they feed. Adults resemble small, drab leafhoppers and are about ¼ inch long. Control them by spraying with

insecticidal soap or rotenone. Try three applications every three to five days until the pests are gone.

## Brown Frass on Needles

### Webworms

The pine false webworm (*Acantholyda erythrocephala*) feeds on pine needles, and as it moves along the tree, it leaves little masses of excreta and leaf pieces tied together in loose balls. The larvae of this pest are about ¾ inch long and greenish to yellowish brown.

The pine webworm (*Tetralopa robustella*) is another species that attacks pines. The larva of this pest is a $4/5$-inch-long yellowish brown caterpillar, with a black stripe on each side of its body. It leaves masses of brown frass at the ends of twigs to mark its presence.

Control webworms by pulling down the loose balls and destroying them. Apply a sticky substance such as Tanglefoot to the trunks of trees to prevent night-feeding larvae from crawling up into the tree and feeding on the needles. Spray infested trees once with Bt (*Bacillus thuringiensis*) if the worms are small, and with pyrethrum or rotenone, in two applications, three to four days apart, if the worms are more mature. In winter, scrape off and destroy the eggs.

## Bark Damaged

### Weevils

Pines may become infested by any of a few different species of weevil. The pales weevil (*Hylobius pales*) is reddish brown to black and ⅓ inch long. It gnaws bark on the trunk and twigs of younger seedling pines and may girdle them completely. On older trees, these weevils tend to feed only on the lower branches.

Another weevil you might have to battle is the white pine weevil (*Pissodes strobi*). Adults are ¼ inch long, brownish, and mottled with light and dark scales. The larvae are pale yellowish grubs about ⅓ inch long. Usually the first evidence of damage is tiny drops of resin on the pine bark, a sign of feeding or egg laying. Larvae usually girdle the terminal branch, which then withers, bends over, and dies. The branches that grow out to replace the leader are distorted. Adult beetles emerge in July, leaving holes in the bark.

Control weevils by beating limbs of the infested tree and catching the startled insects in a drop cloth spread beneath. Apply a sticky substance such as Tanglefoot around the trunks of trees to keep adults from climbing up and eating the leaves. In addition, begin spraying trees weekly with pyrethrum mixed with isopropyl alcohol, making sure to cover all leaf surfaces, until the pest is under control. Concoct this mixture by combining two parts alcohol with one part water and adding pyrethrum according to package instructions.

## MOST COMMON DISEASES

### Needles Become Discolored and Drop Off; Twigs Die Back

#### Blight

Blight in pines is caused by various fungi, such as *Cenangium* spp., *Dothistroma* spp., and others. The needles of infested trees turn reddish and become distorted, and terminal buds die. Infection rarely spreads beyond the current season's growth. Severely affected trees show scanty foliage, resulting from premature needle drop. To control blight, simply prune affected branches to healthy wood. In severe cases, spray infected plants with a copper fungicide such as Bordeaux mixture in early spring and repeat three weeks later. Fertilize and water your trees thoroughly to increase their vigor.

### Swollen, Sunken Lesions on Branches and Trunk

#### Canker

At least nine species of canker-causing fungi attack pines. Typical pine cankers are elongated and may or may not have definite margins. Their centers are depressed, and after two or three years become rough and crack open. Weak, unhealthy pines are most susceptible to canker. Remove dead and weak branches, and destroy infected wood. Avoid injuring the bark and branches of trees to help prevent infection. Feed and water as needed to increase plant vigor.

### Needles Become Discolored and Fall Prematurely; Tree Appears Scorched

#### Needle Cast

Several kinds of fungi cause pine needles to turn yellow, then brown and to drop prematurely. Smaller trees may become defoliated. Collect and destroy fallen needles in late fall or winter to eliminate the most important source of disease spores. In the following spring, when needles are half grown, spray the infected tree with Bordeaux mixture or another copper fungicide, and repeat this application about two weeks later.

### Galls or Cankers on Trunks and Branches; Pustules on Needles

#### Rust

Pines are susceptible to a couple of different types of rust disease. When the fungi *Cronartium quercuum* and *C. comandrae*, commonly called blister rusts, infect trees, galls or cankers form on trunks and branches of pines. These growths may girdle and kill the trees. No effective means of controlling these fungi are known, so if your tree is seriously diseased, cut it down and destroy it.

Needle rust, caused by the fungus *Coleosporium asterum*, settles in the needles, where pustules filled with bright orange spores develop. Serious infection can defoliate the tree. Spray trees with wettable sulfur two or three times every ten days early in the season. Goldenrods and asters host rust, so remove these if they are growing near your pines.

### Branch Tips Die Back; Cankers Develop

#### Tip Blight

Cankers and dieback of branch tips in young pines are caused by the fungus *Diplodia pinea*. Rot develops in the tree, beginning at the collar below the surface of the soil and extending upward as the disease progresses. A deep red color appears on the bark and black streaks appear in the wood. This fungus also attacks the branches of older trees, causing them to die back. The new growth of such branches is stunted, needles turn brown, and the terminal buds exude an excessive amount of resin.

As soon as the blight appears, prune and destroy all infected needles, twigs, and cones. Do this when the branches are dry to minimize the spread of the disease. In early spring, spray your trees with a copper fungicide, starting when the buds open and making two more applications at weekly intervals until the needles break through the needle sheaths. Maintain tree vigor by fertilizing in fall or early spring.

## Shelflike Growths on Trunk

### Wood Rot

Because pine wood is highly resinous, wood rots are not so frequent as in some other evergreens; however, several fungi do infect pines, including *Stereum sanguinolentum, Fomes* spp., and *Polyporus* spp. *Stereum* commonly occurs when pruning wounds are not properly treated. The result of infection by any of these fungi is that shelflike growths develop on the trunk. Once wood rots have developed, little can be done to stop the infection. You can, however, try to prevent this disease by taking care not to injure your trees, by properly treating any injuries that do occur, and by keeping the tree in good health with proper feeding and watering.

TREE **Poplar** *Populus* spp.

## DESCRIPTION

The poplar family includes a variety of species, which are generally fast-growing, short-lived, and weak-wooded trees. In some areas of the country, particularly the Great Plains, where the climate is arid, cottonwoods and aspens are about the only deciduous trees that can be grown. Because poplars grow rapidly, they are a good choice when you need a screen for views, wind protection, or shade. The sexes are separate. If you plant male trees, you won't be bothered by fluffy, cottony seeds blowing all about your yard. Poplars have commercial value as a source of pulp for magazine paper, matches, and veneers.

### Height

Chinese poplar (*Populus adenopoda*), 75 feet

Quaking aspen (*P. tremuloides*), 90 feet

Simon poplar (*P. simonii*), 50 feet

White poplar (*P. alba*), 90 feet

### Foliage

The poplar is a deciduous tree. The quaking aspen has nearly round leaves, which are 1 to 3 inches in diameter. They have small rounded teeth, and are green above and silvery below. They turn a brilliant gold in fall. White poplars have coarsely toothed lobed leaves, 2 to 5 inches long. They are dark green on top, and white below. The foliage of the Simon poplar is similar to that of white poplars. Chinese poplars have 4-inch oval leaves that are pale green beneath.

# ENVIRONMENT

## Varieties by Zone

To zone 1, quaking aspen
To zone 2, Simon poplar
To zone 3, white poplar
To zone 5, Chinese poplar

## Light Requirements

Poplars need full sun.

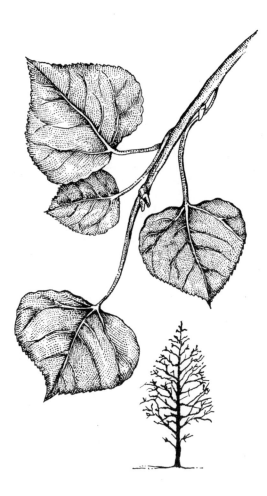

# MOST COMMON INSECT PESTS

## Galls on Leaf Stalks; Terminal Buds Distorted

### Aphids

Poplars are susceptible to infestation from a couple of species of aphids. If you find galls on the leaf stems, suspect the poplar petiole gall aphid (*Pemphigus populitransversus*). The poplar vagabond aphid (*Mordwilkoja vagabunda*) distorts terminal buds by sucking the juices out of the bud. Aphids have soft, pear-shaped bodies and are about the size of the head of a pin. Depending on the species, they may be green, brown, bluish, or pink. Ants are attracted to the honeydew secreted by aphids.

Light infestations are easily controlled by spraying the tree vigorously with water. Do this in the early morning, three times, once every other day. For medium to heavy infestations, spray with insecticidal soap every two to three days until aphids are gone. If the infestation is so serious that insecticidal soap doesn't control it, you will have to resort to pyrethrum. Make two applications, three to four days apart.

## Numerous Holes in Branches; Tops Die Back

### Borers

Shothole borers (*Scolytus rugulosus*) are white larvae that mine their way into branches of poplars, creating small holes as they go. Trees weakened by drought, winter injury, transplanting, mechanical injuries, or poor growing conditions are most vulnerable to infestation by these pests. The bronze birch borer (*Agrilus anxius*) also attacks poplars. Its white larvae are ½ to 1 inch long. Adult bronze-colored beetles, ¼ to ½ inch long, appear in June and feed on leaves for a short time. The larvae girdle branches, causing the upper parts of the tree to die back. Poplars also may be attacked by the poplar borer (*Saperda calcarata*) or the poplar and willow borer (*Cryptorhynchus lapathi*).

To control borers in most situations, make a thorough examination of the tree before the spring season arrives and cut and burn any dying or unhealthy-looking stems that may contain borers. During the summer season, check to see if sawdust is being pushed from small borer holes. Such holes should be cut out with a sharp knife. If the tunnels are fairly straight, you can kill borers by probing with a flexible wire, or pull them out with a hooked wire and destroy them. If tunnels curve and wind, inject nicotine sulfate into each borer hole and plug the hole with putty.

## Holes in Leaves

### Caterpillars

If you find holes in the leaves of your poplars, you can be fairly sure that some species of caterpillar has been dining there. Several different species like poplars, including the red-humped caterpillar, the poplar tent maker, the larvae of the satin moth, and eastern tent caterpillars.

All caterpillars can be controlled in the same way. You can quickly and easily remove all the pests by hand, if they have just begun to infest your trees. Once the population reaches a size such that handpicking would be a daunting task, dust the leaves, especially the undersides, with Bt (*Bacillus thuringiensis*). Reapply after rains. You can also make a foliar spray with Bt and apply it every 10 to 14 days until caterpillars are gone. If the problem is so serious that Bt can't control it, spray all sides of the leaves with pyrethrum or a 1 percent solution of rotenone. Usually, two applications, 3 to 4 days apart, are sufficient.

## Leaves Skeletonized

### Imported Willow Leaf Beetles

Skeletonized leaves are a sign of the imported willow leaf beetle (*Plagiodera versicolora*). The adult beetles are metallic blue and ⅛ inch long. The larvae are black and ¼ inch long. These larvae feed heavily on foliage, leaving only a network of veins.

Remove these pests by handpicking. You can also spray trees with a mixture of pyrethrum and isopropyl alcohol every three to five days for two weeks. For long-term control, apply milky spore disease (*Bacillus popilliae*) to your lawn, where many beetles lay their eggs. Cultivate nearby garden soil in the fall and again in the spring to expose eggs, larvae, and pupae to the weather and predator birds.

## Leaves Mottled

### Mealybugs

The comstock mealybug (*Pseudococcus comstocki*) is a small, elliptical, waxy insect that crawls up the trunks of poplars to suck juices from the leaves. Leaves become mottled, and the tree weakens.

Spray trees with an alcohol mixture made from 1 tablespoon alcohol and 1 cup water. For heavy infestations, use a strong spray of insecticidal soap or, as a last resort, pyrethrum. Make three applications, one every seven to ten days.

## Twigs Break Off

### Poplar Curculios

Adult curculios are small insects, usually less than ¼ inch long. They are generally distinguished by their long curved snouts. The grub of the poplar curculio burrows into poplar twigs and branches. Small scars are left at the spot where it enters, and twigs often break and drop off the tree. Prune and destroy all infested branches and twigs.

## Leaves Discolored; Small Bumps on Leaves and Branches

### Scale

If you spot small bumps on the leaves and branches of your poplars, look closely. These bumps may indeed be insects. Scale insects have circular, concave, waxy coverings, which protect them as they feed. Depending on the species, they may be ¹⁄₁₀ to ⅖ inch in diameter and white, yellow, or brown to black. Some species excrete honeydew, which coats foliage, attracting ants and encouraging the growth of sooty mold. The first symptom of damage is discoloration of the upper leaf surface, followed by leaf drop, reduced growth, and stunted trees. Heavy scale infestations kill trees. Many species of scale infest poplars: black scale (*Saissetia oleae*), cottony-maple scale (*Pulvinaria innumerabilis*), greedy scale (*Hemiberlesia rapax*), and willow scurfy scale (*Chionaspis salicis-nigrae*).

As with many pests, these can be easily removed by hand, if they are not too numerous. Simply scrape them off with your fingernail or remove them with a cotton swab dipped in rubbing alcohol. For medium to heavy infestations, spray trees with a mixture of alcohol and insecticidal soap every three days for two weeks. Make this mixture by combining ½ cup alcohol with every quart of insecticidal soap. In winter, apply dormant oil spray to smother overwintering eggs and adults.

# MOST COMMON DISEASES

## Swollen, Sunken Lesions on Branches and Trunk

### Canker

Various fungi produce cankers in poplars. These cankers are elongated, dark, and sunken. They can eventually girdle branches and trunks. Prune and destroy dead and dying branches. Weak trees are generally most vulnerable, so the most effective prevention is to keep trees healthy by feeding and watering them, controlling insects, and taking care not to injure your tree. Some diseases, such as hypoxylon canker, are highly contagious and destructive; infected trees should be cut down and destroyed.

## Leaves Blistered and Curled

### Leaf Blister

The fungus *Taphrina aurea* causes leaf blister disease in poplars. Leaves of infected trees develop brilliant yellow to brown blisters of varying sizes. These usually appear after extended periods of cool,

wet weather. Spray trees in early spring with lime sulfur two or three times at ten-day intervals.

## Brown Spots on Leaves; Leaves Fall Prematurely

### Leaf Spot

Many kinds of leaf spot fungi may infect your poplars. Of these, *Marssonina populi* is by far the most common. Leaves infected by this fungus develop brown spots with dark brown margins and they drop prematurely. *M. populi* also invades and kills the twigs. Collect and destroy fallen leaves. In spring, spray trees with Bordeaux mixture or any other copper fungicide. Make two or three applications, one week apart.

## White Powder on Leaves

### Powdery Mildew

Powdery mildew is easy to detect by the thin white powdery growth that spreads over both sides of poplar leaves. The fungus *Uncinula salicis* is responsible for this disease. Usually the damage is not serious. As soon as you spot the whitish coating of the fungus on your trees, spray them with wettable sulfur once or twice at weekly intervals.

## Powdery Orange Pustules on Leaf Undersides

### Rust

It's difficult to mistake the symptoms of rust. Yellowish orange pustules develop on the undersides of leaves in trees infected with this disease. The fungi *Melampsora medusae* and *M. abietis-canadensis* cause rusts in poplars. Little damage occurs and rarely are control measures required. If necessary, spray trees with wettable sulfur early in the season—two or three applications, one every ten days, should be sufficient. Larches and hemlocks are also vulnerable to rusts, so when planting, keep all these species at least 100 yards apart from each other.

 **Spruce** *Picea* spp.

## DESCRIPTION

Except for dwarf varieties, all spruces stand stiffly erect with a single trunk and symmetrical, pyramidal shape. All have hanging cones. Spruces are handsome additions to the landscape. Generally they do not blend nicely with other plants and are used best on their own. They handle extreme cold well and are good choices in harsh northern regions of North America. The Colorado or blue spruce (*Picea pungens*) is the most familiar species, with its striking bluish foliage. The oriental spruce (*P. orientalis*) has a compact and graceful form. The Serbian spruce (*P. omorika*) has a columnar habit; it is distinguished by its glossy needles. In addition to their ornamental value, spruces have commercial value as a source of paper pulp.

### Height

Colorado or blue spruce (*P. pungens*), 100 feet
Norway spruce (*P. abies*), 150 feet
Oriental spruce (*P. orientalis*), 150 feet
Serbian spruce (*P. omorika*), 90 feet

### Foliage

Spruces are evergreen trees with green to bluish needles. Most species have needles that are square when cut in cross section. This distinguishes them from hemlocks and firs, both of which have flat needles.

## ENVIRONMENT

### Varieties by Zone

Zone 7 to zone 3, Colorado spruce
Zone 8 to zone 3, Norway spruce
To zone 4, oriental spruce and Serbian spruce.

### Light Requirements

Spruces grow well in full sun to partial shade.

## MOST COMMON CULTURAL PROBLEM

### Tree Loses Its Uniform Habit

#### Old Age

Spruces do not age well, and many experts suggest replacing them after 20 years. They tend to lose their lower branches when they are crowded together. The top of a Norway spruce will thin as the tree ages because it usually needs more water than is available in the summer. Once this thinning begins, it cannot be reversed.

## MOST COMMON INSECT PESTS

### Galls on Shoots

#### Aphids

Galls on spruces signal aphid infestation. If you find galls measuring ½ to 2½ inches on the terminal shoots of your trees, the cooley spruce gall aphid (*Adelges cooley*) is at work. Cone-shaped, elongated galls under 1 inch in length develop when spruce gall aphids (*A. abietis*) infest trees. Heavy infestations can weaken and distort trees. The Norway spruce is most seriously affected; white, black, and red spruces show more resistance. Aphids are about the size of the head of a pin and have soft, pear-shaped bodies. Depending on the species, they may be green, brown, bluish, or pink. Ants are attracted to the honeydew secreted by aphids.

To control light infestations, simply spray your trees vigorously with water. Do this early in the morning, three times, once every other day. For medium to heavy infestations, spray with insecticidal soap every two to three days until aphids are gone.

### Tree Defoliated; Twigs Girdled

#### Bagworms

The bagworm (*Thyridopteryx ephemeraeformis*) disfigures spruce trees by feeding on needles and girdling twigs, removing a ring of bark and cambium. The name of this insect is quite appropriate. The wingless female adults and the dark brown larvae live in 2-inch-long bags of tough silk, camouflaged with bits of vegetation, which hang from the branches and somewhat resemble pine cones. Adult males are black, clear-winged moths.

Pick the bags from the tree and destroy the insects. Spray plants with Bt (*Bacillus thuringiensis*) once a week from May 1 to June 1. Seven to ten days later, if you still find bagworms on your trees, spray again. In August, set out pheromone traps designed to attract male bagworms in the hope of reducing populations next year.

### Tree Girdled

#### Borers

The larva of the destructive hemlock borer attacks spruce trees as well as hemlocks. It bores under the bark, chewing shallow, sinuous, winding galleries through the inner bark, eventually girdling the tree.

To control borers in most situations, make a thorough examination of the tree before the spring season arrives and cut and burn any dying or unhealthy-looking stems that may contain borers. During the summer season, check to see if sawdust is being pushed from small borer holes. Such holes should be cut out with a sharp knife. If the tunnels are fairly straight, you can kill the borer by probing with a flexible wire, or pull it out with a hooked wire and destroy it. If the tunnels wind around through the wood, inject nicotine sulfate into each hole and plug the hole with putty.

### New Growth Deformed and Wilted

#### Budworms

If the terminal shoots and new growth on your spruce trees are wilted and deformed, suspect the spruce budworm (*Choristoneura fumiferana*). These caterpillars are ½ to ¾ inch long, and they feed on terminal shoots and new growth. The adults are small, dull-colored moths. They are most abundant in June and July. As soon as you spot the caterpillars on your trees, spray them with Bt (*Bacillus thurin-*

*giensis*) two or three times, once every three to five days.

## Leaves Consumed; Conspicuous, Tawny Egg Masses Present

### Gypsy Moths

Gypsy moths prefer oaks and other trees to spruces, but if those trees aren't around, a spruce will do. Older larvae of the gypsy moth (*Porthetria dispar*) gather in huge masses to devour spruce foliage after their preferred food sources have been reduced. Spruces can die after a single defoliation. The mature caterpillars are about 2½ inches long. They have five pairs of blue spots and six pairs of red spots along their backs. Adult male moths have a wing-span of 1½ inches and are light tan to dark brown. Blackish wavy bands mark the forewings. Female moths are nearly white, and larger than males, with 2½-inch wings; however, they can barely fly. Both sexes have feathered antennae. Females lay masses of 400 to 500 eggs. These masses are covered with velvety, buff-colored hairs.

To control gypsy moths, spray trees with Bt (*Bacillus thuringiensis*) every 10 to 14 days from late April to mid-June. In June, when larvae are 1 inch long, they become night feeders and crawl down from the tree each morning. You can easily catch them in a burlap trap. Wrap a foot-wide piece of burlap around the tree trunk, about chest high. Tie it at the center with heavy twine, letting the top fold over the twine to form a skirt. Caterpillars on their way down the trunk of the tree will crawl under the burlap fold. In the late afternoon, put on garden gloves and sweep the caterpillars off into a container of detergent and water.

## Needles Yellowed

### Mites

Spruce spider mites (*Oligonychus ununguis*) are tiny pests, only 1/64 inch long. The young are pale green; the adult female is greenish black. Spruces infested with these pests have yellow needles, many of which are covered with a fine silken webbing produced by the mites.

As soon as you notice the needles of your spruces turning yellow, begin control measures. Often simply spraying trees vigorously with water will knock the pests off permanently. Do this in the early morning for three consecutive days. If mites are still a problem, spray with insecticidal soap. Insecticidal soap mixed with light horticultural oil works as a dormant spray against eggs and newly hatched nymphs. Use about 1 tablespoon of soap concentrate with each gallon of dormant oil spray.

## Tree Defoliated

### Sawflies

The larvae of sawflies (*Cimbex* spp.) devour needles of spruce trees, sometimes to the point of defoliating the entire tree. The bluish black or olive green larvae are about ½ inch long. The adults look like wasps, but have thicker midsections. They are ⅝ to 1½ inches long and have two pairs of transparent wings.

If only a few of the larvae have found your spruce trees, simply pick them off and destroy them. For medium to heavy infestations, spray with insecticidal soap. If sawflies continue to do damage, use pyrethrum or rotenone. Spray thoroughly when caterpillars are first sighted and watch for the second generation. Spray again if necessary.

## Needles Discolored; Small Bumps on Needles and Branches

### Scale

Scale insects don't look like insects at all, but rather like small bumps. These pests have a circular, waxy, concave covering, which protects them as they feed. The first symptom of scale attack is usually discoloration of the spruce needles, followed by needle drop, reduced growth, and stunted trees. Heavy infestations kill trees. Some scale species excrete honeydew, which coats the foliage, attracting ants and encouraging sooty mold growth. The spruce bud scale (*Physokermes piceae*) is an occasional pest. These are globular red scales, about ⅛ inch in diameter.

If caught early on, you can easily eliminate these pests simply by scraping them off with your fingernail or removing them with a cotton swab dipped in rubbing alcohol. For any sizable infestation, spray your trees with a mixture of alcohol and insecticidal soap every three days for two weeks. Make this mixture by combining ½ cup alcohol with each quart of insecticidal soap.

## Numerous Small Holes in Branches; Needles Discolored

### Spruce Beetles

Spruce beetles (*Dendroctonus rufipennis*) attack weak spruce trees, especially those a foot or more in diameter. As the beetles emerge from the tree in June and July, they create small round holes around which you will see gum and sawdust. Beetle damage to the tree results in a deficit of nutrients and fading of needles.

Control spruce beetles by handpicking, or spray infested trees with a mixture of pyrethrum and isopropyl alcohol every three to five days for two weeks. For long-term control, apply milky spore disease (*Bacillus popilliae*) to your lawn, where many beetles lay their eggs, or apply beneficial nematodes to soil near the vulnerable trees.

## Needles Webbed Together

### Spruce Needle Miners

If you see brown moths flying about your spruce trees, you may be in for a visit from the spruce needle miner. The moths lay their eggs early in summer and the hatched larvae (*Taniva* spp. and *Epinotia* spp.) bore into individual needles and web them together. The needles turn brown and are covered with webbing and frass. Infestation is usually heaviest on lower branches.

Adults are small, brown, fringed-winged moths. The greenish to brown larvae have black heads and are about 5/16 inch long.

Control miners by washing the dead needles off your trees with a garden hose; then collect and destroy them. Spray with pyrethrum in mid-May and again in mid-June.

## Leaders Turn Brown and Die; Tree Stunted

### Weevils

The white pine weevil (*Pissodes strobi*) not only attacks white pines, but oriental spruces and occasionally other spruces. Adults are ¼ inch long, brownish, and mottled with light and dark scales. The larvae are pale yellowish grubs about ⅓ inch long. They feed on the terminal shoots, causing sap to flow heavily from these shoots. Pine weevil larvae bore inside the terminal shoots. These shoots die, and tree growth is stunted.

As soon as weevils appear, begin spraying weekly with pyrethrum mixed with isopropyl alcohol. To make this spray, combine two parts alcohol to one part water; then add pyrethrum in the concentration called for in the package instructions.

# MOST COMMON DISEASES

## Needles and Twigs Curled and Withered

### Blight

Various fungi induce blight in spruces, including *Rehmiellopsis balsameae* and *Botrytis cinerea*. The needles of infected trees shrivel, especially in cool, wet weather. Spray your trees with a copper fungicide three times at 12-day intervals, starting when new growth begins to emerge from the buds in the spring. Improve air circulation around diseased plants to reduce humidity, which encourages the growth of fungi. Prune and burn affected branches.

## Branches Die Back; Needles Fall; Resinous Cankers Develop in Bark

### Canker

A destructive canker disease caused by the fungus *Cytospora* spp. infects Norway and Colorado blue spruce. The branches of diseased trees turn brown and die. Damage usually begins in branches nearest the ground and slowly progresses upward. Needles may drop immediately from infected branches or may persist for nearly a year. You may find white patches of pitch or resin along the bark of the dead or dying branches. Trees weakened by drought, winter injury, insects, fire, or mechanical injuries are more susceptible to this disease than healthy ones.

Prune and destroy diseased branches. Prune during dry weather; moisture helps to spread infection. In the spring, spray your trees three or four times with a copper fungicide.

## Whitish Blisters on Undersides of Needles; Needles Yellowed

### Rust

Rust disease in spruces attacks the undersides of needles, where whitish blisters appear. As the disease progresses, the needles turn yellow and may drop prematurely. Severe infection may defoliate the tree. In spruces, rust is caused by *Chrysomyxa* fungi. Spray with wettable sulfur two or three times at weekly intervals.

## Shelflike Growths on Trunk

### Wood Rot

Spruces are vulnerable to several fungi that cause wood rot. These include *Trametes pini, Polyporus schweinitzii, P. sulphureus,* and *Fomes pinicola.* Shelflike growths appear on the trunks of diseased trees. Once wood rot has taken hold of a tree, little can be done to stop it, and the spruce will eventually die. These diseases can be prevented by taking care not to injure trees in any way, by properly treating injuries that do occur, and by maintaining the health of your trees through proper fertilizing and watering.

TREE  *Salix* spp.

## DESCRIPTION

Of all the pendulous trees, willows are the most graceful and are therefore valued highly for ornamental use. Some are shrubby; others have colored twigs that add interest to winter landscapes. Some are ground covers, the use of which is limited to the most northern regions, and others have very long branches and are called weepers. Willows do not live long, but they are easy to grow and worth growing for their beauty. They thrive along banks of streams and help to limit soil erosion in those locations. They can be planted individually in the yard or in groups to make dense screens. The pussy willow (*Salix discolor*) is a well-known member of this clan. *S. babylonica,* the weeping willow, is the most familiar of the tree species.

### Height

Pussy willow (*S. discolor*), 20 feet

Weeping willow (*S. babylonica*), 30 to 50 feet
White willow (*S. alba*), 75 feet

### Foliage

Willows are deciduous. They have long, narrow, short-stemmed green leaves.

## ENVIRONMENT

### Varieties by Zone

To zone 2, pussy willow and white willow
To zone 6, weeping willow

### Light Requirements

Willows prefer full sun, but will grow in medium shade.

# MOST COMMON INSECT PESTS

## Leaves Curled and Distorted

### Aphids

Several species of aphids attack willows, and the damage they do may retard or distort tree growth. Willow leaves turn yellow or brown, wilt under bright sunlight, and curl and pucker. Ants are attracted to the honeydew secreted by aphids. The giant bark aphid (*Longistigma caryae*) is the species that most frequently attacks willow. Other pests include several species of willow aphids, which infest the bark of twigs. Aphids have soft pear-shaped bodies and

are about the size of the head of a pin. They may be green, brown, bluish, or pink, depending on the species.

For light infestations, spray trees vigorously with water in the early morning. Do this three times, once every other day. If this doesn't control aphids, use insecticidal soap every two to three days. As a last resort, spray with pyrethrum, making two applications, three to four days apart.

## Holes in Leaves; Twigs Girdled

### Bagworms

The bagworm (*Thyridopteryx ephemeraeformis*) feeds on the leaves and twigs of willow trees. Look on the branches for 2-inch bags of silk camouflaged with pieces of leaves. The wingless females and the dark brown larvae wrap themselves in these bags. The adult males are black, clear-winged moths.

Handpick the bags and destroy the insects. Spray trees with Bt (*Bacillus thuringiensis*) once a week for three weeks, from May 1 to June 1. If bagworms are still present seven to ten days later, spray again.

## Branches Swollen and Distorted; Holes, Sawdust, and Sap Stains at Base of Trunk

### Borers

The poplar and willow borer (*Cryptorhynchus lapathi*) bores into willow branches, causing rough, swollen, abnormal growth of the branches. This borer is about ½ inch long and works near the surface. The adult is a black beetle about ⅓ inch long. Willows are also susceptible to attack from the poplar borer (*Saperda calcarata*), which penetrates deeply into the wood at the base of the trunk and the roots. If you suspect borers have infested your willow, look for piles of sawdust and sap stains.

To control borers, make a thorough examination of the tree before the spring season arrives and cut and burn any dying or unhealthy-looking stems that may contain borers. During summer, check for borer holes and cut them with a sharp knife. If the tunnels are fairly straight, the borer can be killed by probing with a flexible wire, or pulled out with a hooked wire and destroyed. If the tunnels are rather crooked, inject nicotine sulfate into each hole and plug the hole with putty.

## Holes in Leaves

### Caterpillars

Various caterpillars will eat the foliage of the willow tree. These include the larvae of the orange tortrix, the red-humped caterpillar, loopers, tent caterpillars, the larvae of the western tussock moth, and the larvae of the satin moth.

Handpicking easily eliminates caterpillars, if they aren't too numerous. Any sizable infestation is easier to handle with Bt (*Bacillus thuringiensis*). Dust all parts of the leaves, especially the undersides, and reapply the dust after rains. You can also make a foliar spray with Bt. Follow package directions for doing so. Apply it to infested plants every 10 to 14 days until caterpillars are gone. If caterpillars get out of control and Bt doesn't seem to be working, spray all sides of the leaves with pyrethrum or a 1 percent solution of rotenone. Usually, two applications, 3 to 4 days apart, are sufficient.

## Leaves Consumed; Conspicuous, Tawny Egg Masses Present

### Gypsy Moths

Gypsy moth larvae (*Porthetria dispar*) seem to enjoy the foliage of most trees, including willows. They gather in huge masses to devour willow foliage. The tree may die after repeated defoliations. Newly hatched caterpillars are about 1/16 inch long, and grow to about 2½ inches. The mature larvae have five pairs of blue spots and six pairs of red spots along their backs. Adult males have a wingspan of 1½ inches. They are light tan to dark brown, with blackish wavy bands across their forewings. Female gypsy moths are nearly white and are larger than males, with 2½-inch wings; however, they can barely fly. Both sexes have feathered antennae. Females lay masses of 400 to 500 eggs. These masses are covered with velvety, buff-colored hairs.

To control gypsy moths, spray trees with Bt (*Bacillus thuringiensis*) every 10 to 14 days from late April to mid-June. In June, when larvae are 1 inch long, they become night feeders and crawl down from the tree each morning. You can easily catch them in a burlap trap. Wrap a foot-wide piece of burlap around the tree trunk, about chest high. Tie it at the center with heavy twine, letting the top fold over the twine to form a skirt. Caterpillars on their way down the trunk of the tree will crawl under the burlap fold. In the late afternoon, put on garden gloves and sweep the caterpillars off into a container of detergent and water.

## Undersides of Leaves Chewed

### Imported Willow Leaf Beetles

Grubs of the imported willow leaf beetle (*Plagiodera versicolora*) feed on the undersides of willow leaves, leaving only a network of veins. Adults are metallic blue beetles, about ⅛ inch long. They live through the winter under the bark scales and in the fallen leaves and branches around the tree. In early June, they emerge and lay eggs. The larvae are black and ¼ inch long. These larvae feed heavily on foliage, leaving only a network of veins. Adult beetles develop during July and produce a second brood in August.

Light infestations of beetles can easily be removed by handpicking. You can also spray trees with a mixture of pyrethrum and isopropyl alcohol every three to five days for two weeks. For long-term control, apply milky spore disease (*Bacillus popilliae*) to your lawn, where many beetles lay their eggs.

## Leaves Yellowed and Mottled

### Lace Bugs

Willow lace bugs (*Corythucha mollicula*) suck sap from willow leaves, causing them to become severely mottled and yellowed. Adults are square-shaped bugs, about 3/16 inch long, with elaborately reticulated wings that resemble lacework.

Spray trees, particularly the undersides of leaves, with insecticidal soap. Two applications made a week or two apart should eliminate these pests. If not, spray with nicotine sulfate or pyrethrum every seven to ten days until symptoms disappear.

## Leaves Wilt and Turn Brown

### Midges

If the buds and foliage of your willows wilt and turn brown, suspect the willow beaked gall midge (*Mayetiola rigidae*). Twigs may become distorted, and in many cases, galls containing eggs and developing larvae form. Adults are two-winged flies, $1/14$ to $1/8$ inch long, with long legs and antennae.

Handpick infested leaves and buds and spray the tree three times with insecticidal soap, once every three to five days. In early spring, spray trees with dormant oil.

## Leaves Distorted and Cupped

### Psyllids

Psyllids (*Psylla* spp.) suck juices from willow foliage. Leaves become discolored and distorted, taking on a cup-shaped form. The adults are about $1/10$ inch long and are commonly known as "jumping plant lice." They resemble tiny cicadas covered with whitish waxy filaments.

Control psyllids by spraying trees with insecticidal soap every three to five days for two weeks. In early spring, apply dormant oil to kill both adults and eggs.

## Leaves Skeletonized

### Sawflies

When the larvae of sawflies (*Cimbex* spp.) feed on the foliage of willows, they leave nothing but leaf skeletons. Some mine leaves as well. Trees may become defoliated. The adults look like wasps, but have thicker midsections. They are $5/8$ to $1\frac{1}{2}$ inches long and have two pairs of transparent wings. Their larvae resemble caterpillars, and are about $\frac{1}{2}$ inch long.

Handpick the larvae if they are not too numerous; otherwise apply insecticidal soap, pyrethrum, or rotenone. Spray thoroughly when caterpillars are first sighted and watch to see if a second generation develops. Spray again if necessary.

## Small Bumps on Leaves and Branches

### Scale

All scale insects have a circular, convex, waxy covering, which protects them as they feed on plants. They look like small bumps on leaves and branches. They may be white, yellow, or brown to black, depending on the species. Scale insects are only about $1/10$ to $2/5$ inch in diameter. They suck sap from the leaves and bark of trees. Leaves turn yellow and may become distorted and drop. The infested tree loses its vigor. Branches and even small trees may be killed by heavy infestations of willow scurfy scale (*Chionaspis salicis-nigrae*). Eggs of this species overwinter on trees, protected under the shell-like covering of the adult female. Several other species of scale may infest your willows. These include black scale (*Saissetia oleae*), California red scale (*Aonidiella aurantii*), cottony-cushion scale (*Icerya purchasi*), greedy scale (*Hemiberlesia rapax*), and the terrapin scale (*Lecanium nigrofasciatum*).

If caught early on, you can simply scrape the pests off plant surfaces with your fingernail or remove them with a cotton swab dipped in rubbing alcohol. Medium to heavy infestations can be controlled by spraying trees with a mixture of alcohol and insecticidal soap every three days for two weeks. To make this mixture, combine ½ cup alcohol with each quart of insecticidal soap. In late winter, apply dormant oil to trees to smother overwintering adults and eggs.

## Leaves Discolored

### Thrips

Thrips rasp at leaf surfaces to break open plant cells so they can suck the juices. Their feeding results in flecked and whitened leaves. Leaf tips eventually wither, curl, and die. If you turn leaves over you will find tiny black specks of excrement on the undersides. Pear thrips (*Taeniothrips inconsequens*) and citrus thrips (*Scirtothrips citri*) are pests of willows. Adults are slender insects, $1/25$ inch long. They have four long, narrow wings fringed with long hairs. Their legs are very short. The larvae of thrips are usually wingless. A spray of insecticidal soap every three days for two weeks controls most infestations.

## Leaves Mined and Discolored

### Weevils

The adult willow flea weevil (*Rhynchaenus rufipes*) emerges in mid-April and attacks the foliage of willows in late May, excavating a circular mine on the undersides of leaves. There it lays its eggs; then it turns to feeding on foliage, which becomes brown and dry. The larvae begin mining through leaves in mid-June. By the end of July, heavily infested trees look as if they've been scorched with fire.

As soon as weevils appear, begin spraying trees weekly with a solution of pyrethrum and isopropyl alcohol. To make this spray, combine two parts alcohol to one part water; then add pyrethrum in the concentration called for in the package instructions. Be sure to spray this over all leaf surfaces.

# MOST COMMON DISEASES

## Leaves Wilted and Discolored; Cankers on Branches

### Bacterial Blight

A blight caused by the bacterium *Pseudomonas saliciperda* causes willow leaves to turn brown and wilt. Blighted branches die back. These bacteria overwinter in cankers on the trees and infect young leaves as soon as they emerge. Seriously infected trees may be defoliated.

Prune and destroy infected branches. In spring, when leaves begin to emerge, spray three or four times, once every ten days, with a copper fungicide.

## Spots on Leaves; Cankers on Twigs

### Canker

Several fungi cause cankers in willows. Willows infected by the fungus *Physalospora miyabeana* develop dark brown spots with concentric markings on the upper surfaces of their leaves. Next, whitish to gray elliptical cankers with black borders appear on twigs and leaf stalks. Clusters of minute fruiting bodies grow in the stem lesions. Successive attacks over two or three years usually kill the tree. Prune and discard infected twigs and branches and keep trees vigorous by feeding and watering them, and by controlling insects and disease.

## Galls on Roots, Trunk, or Branches

### Crown Gall

The bacterium *Erwinia tumefaciens* infects willow trees through wounds and stimulates cells to form galls (tumorlike swellings) with irregular rough surfaces. These may range in size from peas to large burls 1 to 2 feet in diameter. Tree growth may slow, leaves often turn yellow, and branches or roots sometimes die. The only way to control this disease is to destroy affected trees.

## Leaves Wilt and Blacken; Cankers Sometimes Form

### Leaf Blight

The fungus *Venturia saliciperda* causes a leaf blight, which can seriously damage willows. In spring, the leaves wilt and blacken, appearing scorched. Twig cankers may develop after leaves become infected. After it rains, olive-colored fruiting bodies appear on leaf undersides. Collect and destroy all fallen debris. Spray three or four times with a copper fungicide when leaves begin to emerge in the spring. Some resistant willow species include bay-leaved (*S. pentandra*), purple osier (*S. purpurea*), weeping, and pussy willows. The crack willow (*S. fragilis*) and heart-leaved willow (*S. cordata*), however, are particularly susceptible to leaf blight.

## Yellow, Brown, or Black Spots on Leaves

### Leaf Spot

Leaf spots on willows can be caused by any of several fungi, including *Ascochyta* spp., *Asteroma* spp., *Cercospora* spp., *Cylindrosporium* spp., *Marssonina* spp., and *Phyllosticta* spp. Depending on the species, these spots may be yellow, brown, or black. Often these spots merge to form larger patches of dead tissue. Certain leaf spot fungi cause premature defoliation.

In all cases, gather and destroy fallen leaves. If a considerable amount of defoliation occurs, spray trees with copper fungicide two or three times at weekly intervals.

## White Powder on Leaves

### Powdery Mildew

A thin white powdery growth on the upper surfaces of the leaves of willows is a sure sign of powdery mildew, caused by the fungus *Uncinula salicis*. If the mildew is serious, the following spring spray trees with wettable sulfur once or twice at weekly intervals, starting as soon as you notice the whitish coating of the fungus. In fall, collect and destroy all plant debris around the trees.

## Yellowish Spots and Dark Pustules on Leaf Undersides

### Rust

Willows infected with rust disease caused by *Melampsora* fungi develop lemon yellow spots on leaf undersides, which later become spore-bearing pustules. Usually rust infections are not serious. In severe cases, leaves drop from the trees; young trees may become defoliated. Prune infected branches and collect and destroy fallen leaves. Spray with a copper fungicide two or three times at weekly intervals.

# CHAPTER 2

# *Shrubs*

There's something that seems blasé about shrubs. Trees, ground covers, vines—their names sound a bit more sophisticated, but shrubs? Yet consider some of the members of this class of plants. The rhododendron stands quite elegantly with its deep green, leathery foliage and clusters of trumpetlike flowers. The lilac sweetly announces spring with its fragrant lavender blossoms. And the rose, what plant commands more respect and love than the rose?

Far too often we take for granted the year-round color, texture, and appeal that shrubs add to the landscape. Shrubs serve many purposes; in fact, their use is restricted only by the imagination. Evergreen shrubs such as juniper, holly, and arborvitae add warmth to the winter garden, protection from howling winds, and shelter for birds and other wild-life. 'Blue Rug' juniper (*Juniperus horizontalis* 'Blue Rug') is an inches-high selection that serves as a ground cover. Many shrubs are grown individually so that we can enjoy their brilliant blossoms, colorful fruit, or autumn foliage. Others, such as arborvitae, privet, shrub roses, and holly, make fine hedges along the edge of a yard to create a living privacy screen. Some shrubs, such as euonymus, can be trained against walls to resemble vines. Gardeners with small spaces will find that shrubs can provide height where trees would simply be too large. In fact, several shrubs, including some hydrangeas and viburnums, can be used as small trees or clumps of trees. So take good care of these medium-size landscape plants: They play a grand-size role in your backyard.

# Arborvitae

*Thuja* spp. and *Platycladus* spp.

## DESCRIPTION

Arborvitae make attractive hedges and foundation plantings. They look especially striking when grown in groups. You can choose from numerous species of different colors and textures. Anyone living anywhere in the United States can grow these shrubs; they tolerate heat, cold, and air pollution. Arborvitae have evergreen foliage and grow slowly to moderately. Three species are particularly popular:

the oriental arborvitae (*Platycladus orientalis*) thrives in the southern United States; the American or eastern arborvitae, sometimes called white cedar (*Thuja occidentalis*), includes cultivars that are best for northern gardens; and the western red cedar (*T. plicata*) is perhaps the most beautiful of the arborvitae and is native to the Pacific Northwest.

### Height

American arborvitae (*T. occidentalis*), 50 feet
Oriental arborvitae (*P. orientalis*), 18 to 25 feet
Western red cedar (*T. plicata*), 50 to 70 feet

### Spread

American arborvitae, 10 to 15 feet
Oriental arborvitae, 10 to 12 feet
Western red cedar, 15 to 25 feet

### Foliage

Arborvitae are evergreen shrubs with soft, scalelike needles arranged in flat sprays. Most species have medium to dark green foliage. The oriental arborvitae, though, is bright green. Some cultivars, such as the American arborvitae 'Golden', produce dramatic yellow foliage that brightens in winter. In the North, the foliage of many arborvitaes turns brownish from fall to winter.

## ENVIRONMENT

### Hardiness

Arborvitae are best adapted to the southern parts of the United States. In northern areas, they should be protected from severe, cold, strong winds, which tend to burn the needles.

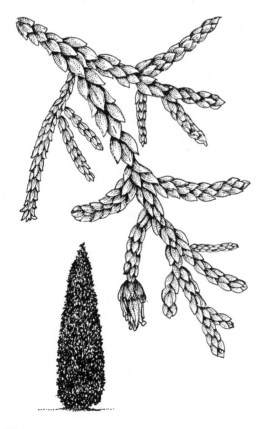

## Varieties by Zone

Zone 3 to zone 7, American arborvitae
Zone 4 to zone 7, western red cedar
Zone 6 to zone 8, oriental arborvitae

## Light Requirements

Arborvitae thrive in full sun. They will tolerate some light shade, which actually reduces scorch in zones 3 and 4, but in prolonged shade, they become ragged. Varieties with yellow foliage need sun all day in order to develop and retain their bright color.

## Soil Requirements

Arborvitae like deep, moist, well-drained soil. They will tolerate either acidic or alkaline soil.

# PLANTING AND PROPAGATION

## Planting

You can plant these shrubs in spring or fall; however, fall is best. Arborvitae root easily.

## Propagation

Propagate arborvitae in late spring from softwood or hardwood cuttings.

## Container Gardening

Arborvitae grow well in containers that are 24 inches deep or larger.

# PLANT MANAGEMENT

## Water Requirements

Arborvitae need about 1 inch of water a week, and they prefer humid conditions.

## Feeding Requirements

Give arborvitae a single application of slow-release nitrogen fertilizer in the fall. Spread the fertilizer no closer than 2 inches from the trunk out to a foot beyond the dripline of the branches. In spring, add 1 inch of compost to the soil.

## Winterizing

In northern states, especially when the plant is young, wrap it in burlap, agricultural fleece, or some other material that will protect it from wind. An antitranspirant spray, applied around the date of the first frost time, will help protect its foliage from wind burn.

# MOST COMMON CULTURAL PROBLEMS

## Foliage Turns Brown in Early Spring

### Exposure to Wind and Sun

Overexposure to drying winds and hot sun increases the rate of evaporation of moisture from the needles faster than roots can bring water into the plant. This causes needles to turn brown. Shrubs that have been recently transplanted are most severely affected. You can minimize damage by mulching around plants and thoroughly soaking the ground around them before it freezes. Spray foliage with an antitranspirant in the fall.

## Needles Turn Brown and Drop Off

### Normal Foliage Loss

All evergreens drop some of their foliage every year, usually in the fall, but it can occur in the spring as well. Don't panic when you see some dead needles on your shrubs. This usually occurs on the inside of the tree near the trunk. You may find it every year or every second or third year. If the foliage browns or develops spots during the summer, investigate the cause; it may be a sign of spider mites or an environmental problem (see below).

## Twigs and Needles Turn Brown

### Twig Browning

Arborvitaes suffer when grown in dry soil. Twigs turn brown and shed their needles. Eventually, whole branches drop. Shrubs located on lawns or along streets probably will require watering during the hot months of summer. Soak the soil to a depth of about 2 feet. Applying the water slowly with a porous hose or with sprinklers is best. Do not water more often than at two-week intervals to allow for aeration of the soil between waterings.

# MOST COMMON INSECT PESTS

## Needles Yellowed and Distorted

### Aphids

The arborvitae aphid (*Cinara tujafilina*) feeds on stems and foliage from spring to fall, and on roots the rest of the year. It is reddish brown and has a soft pear-shaped body about the size of the head of a pin. As aphids feed, foliage becomes distorted and may turn yellow or brown or wilt under bright sunlight. Eventually the growth of the entire shrub is retarded. Ants are attracted to the honeydew secreted by aphids.

For light infestations, spray the undersides of the leaves vigorously with water three times, once every other day. Do this in the early morning. For medium to heavy infestations, spray with insecticidal soap every two to three days until aphids disappear. As a last resort, if the problem is very serious, use pyrethrum spray two or three times every three to five days.

## Pine-Conelike Bags Hanging from Branches

### Bagworms

If you find small spindle-shaped bags resembling pine cones hanging from the branches of your arborvitae, bagworms are present. The adult males are black, clear-winged moths. Female moths have no wings. The bagworm caterpillar builds a silken cocoon and attaches bits and pieces of leaves for camouflage. The caterpillar itself is dark brown with a white or

yellow head, and it carries its bag with it as it feeds. These bags eventually reach a size of about 2 inches. In fall, the bagworm lays up to 1,000 eggs in this sack. These eggs will hatch in May or June of the following year. As bagworms feed, shrubs weaken and become sickly; in sufficient numbers, bagworms can kill an arborvitae.

During winter, pick the bags from your shrubs and burn them. In late spring and early summer, after caterpillars have emerged, spray the shrub with Bt (*Bacillus thuringiensis*) every ten days through mid-July; then in August set out pheromone traps to catch male bagworm moths to reduce the population next year.

## Shrub Grows Poorly

### Cedar Tree Borers

A mass of gummy sawdust, called frass, at the base of an injured arborvitae shrub signals the presence of borers. These pests chew the inner bark of the lower trunk and often girdle plants. The shrub weakens and becomes less resistant to heat, drought, and disease. The cedar tree borer (*Semanotis ligneus*) is the specific pest of arborvitaes. The adult is a ½-inch-long black beetle with orange or red markings.

To control these borers, examine your shrub thoroughly before spring arrives and cut and burn any dying or sickly branches that may contain borers. During the summer, look for borer holes surrounded by frass. Cut out any borers you find with a sharp knife. If the tunnels are fairly straight, probe with a flexible wire. Try to hook the borer with the wire, pull it out, and destroy it. If tunnels are not straight, you can kill borers with nicotine sulfate. Make a solution from one part nicotine sulfate and four parts water. Dip a piece of cotton or soft cloth into this solution and stuff it into the borer's hole.

## Leaves Blistered, Curled, and Brown at Tips

### Leafminers

Arborvitae leaves under attack from leafminers become blistered and curled, turn brown, and die. Some leafmining insects carry blackleg and soft rot diseases. Arborvitae leafminers (*Argyresthia thuiella*) are small greenish larvae with black heads. They eat out galleries between the upper and lower surfaces of leaves and overwinter there. Adults are gray moths with a wingspan of ⅓ inch. Pluck and destroy infested leaves. If the shrub is heavily infested, prune back branches to healthy growth.

Larvae can sometimes be repelled by insecticidal soap. Spray trees in late June or early July, making two or three applications every three to five days.

## Needles Turn Gray or Brown

### Mites

Spruce spider mites (*Oligonychus ununguis*) and red spider mites feed on the needles of arborvitae, causing them to turn gray or brown. These mites can be detected by the webs that they spin over the branches. The spruce spider mites are dull green to nearly black with pink legs and spines on the back. About ¹⁄₅₀ inch long, you can barely see them without a magnifying glass. Not true insects, they have four pairs of legs. Their piercing-sucking mouth parts enable them to suck the juice from the foliage of plants.

As soon as you have determined that your arborvitae are infested with these pests, start control measures. Light infestations can easily be taken care of simply by spraying plants with a forceful stream of water. Do this every day for three days. If mites continue to be a problem, spray with insecticidal soap every three to five days for two weeks.

## Leaves Discolored; Small Bumps on Leaves and Branches

### Scale

Scale insects look like small bumps when you find them on your shrubs. These insects have a waxy, circular, rounded covering that protects them while they feed. Scale may be white, yellow, or brown to black, and are about ¹⁄₁₀ to ⅖ inch in diameter. Some species excrete honeydew, which coats foliage, attracting ants and encouraging the growth of sooty mold. The leaves of infested plants become discolored and drop, and overall growth of the shrub becomes stunted. Heavy infestations of scale can kill arborvitae. Some of the species that attack arborvitae include European fruit lecanium (*Lecanium corni*), Fletcher scale (*L. fletcheri*), juniper scale (*Carulaspis juniperi*), and San Jose scale (*Quadraspidiotus perniciosus*). Plants that have undergone stress from adverse environmental conditions such as too much or too little water are more susceptible to scale attacks. Overuse of nitrogen fertilizer also encourages the growth of scale populations. Avoid this by using a slow-release nitrogen fertilizer.

If only a few scale insects have found your arborvitae, you can simply scrape them off with your fingernail or remove them with a cotton swab dipped in rubbing alcohol. Any sizable infestation is more easily controlled by spraying infested plants with a mixture of alcohol and insecticidal soap every three days for two weeks. To make this mixture, combine 1 cup isopropyl alcohol and 1 tablespoon insecticidal soap concentrate in 1 quart water. If your insecticidal soap is already mixed with water, simply add 1 tablespoon alcohol to 1 pint of this soap spray. In late winter or early spring, spray plants with dormant oil to smother overwintering adults and eggs.

## Holes in Leaves

### Weevils

If you find holes along the margins of arborvitae leaves, your plants are probably infested with arborvitae weevils (*Phyllobius intruscus*). These insects are small and black. Their body and wings are covered with metallic green scales and fine short hairs. The larvae are white to pink, with brown heads. They feed on the roots of arborvitae and may attack anytime from June or July to midwinter or the following spring.

Adult weevils emerge from the soil to feed on aboveground plant parts from May to July. The adults usually feed at night and hide in soil and trash during the day. Adult weevils will play dead when disturbed, folding their legs and dropping off plants to the ground. Turn this trait to advantage when fighting this pest. Gently beat the branches of an infested arborvitae and catch the startled insects in a drop cloth spread beneath the shrub. Apply a sticky substance such as Tanglefoot to the trunks of the shrub to prevent adults from climbing up and eating the leaves.

Another means of control is to spray shrubs once a week with a solution of pyrethrum mixed with isopropyl alcohol. Combine 1 tablespoon alcohol with 1 pint pyrethrum mix and apply at night, when weevils are active, making sure to cover all leaf surfaces.

# MOST COMMON DISEASES

## Tips of Twigs
## Turn Brown and Die Back

### Blight

If the needles of your arborvitae are turning brown only at the ends of branches, your shrubs probably have tip blight. This disease is most often caused by the fungus *Coryneum berckmanii*, but *Cercospora* fungi, *Pestalotia* fungi, or *Phacidium* fungi may also be the culprits. This disease occurs in late spring or early summer. If you look closely at infected needles, you'll see tiny black spore-bearing bodies on the surfaces.

Once you have determined that your shrubs have blight, spray them with a copper fungicide,

making two or three applications at weekly intervals. This will discolor the needles, but new foliage will cover up the damaged needles. Prune and destroy diseased twigs and branches.

## Needles Appear Scorched
## and Fall Prematurely

### Leaf Blight

The fungus *Fabrella thujina* causes leaf blight in arborvitae. This disease is most troublesome in giant arborvitae in the northwestern United States. Irregular circular brown to black spots appear on foliage in late spring. Needles later turn brown and drop prematurely. Spray infected shrubs several times with Bordeaux mixture or another copper fungicide in midsummer and early autumn.

## Needles Turn Yellow
## and Fall Prematurely

### Leaf Spot

Leaf spot in arborvitae can be brought on by any of a number of fungi: *Macrophoma candollei, Phyllosticta auerswaldii, Fusarium buxicola,* or members of the *Collectotrichum* spp. The needles of infected shrubs turn straw yellow or brown and are thickly dotted with small black fruiting bodies. Leaf spot usually occurs in shrubs already weakened by some other cause.

Control leaf spot by shaking out all fallen and diseased needles from the center of the bush and destroying them. Prune and destroy dead branches in the center of the bush to allow better aeration. The following spring, before growth starts, spray shrubs with copper fungicide, making two or three applications at weekly intervals. This will discolor the needles, but new foliage will cover up the damaged needles. Enrich the soil and ensure good drainage around the shrub.

# SHRUB *Azalea and Rhododendron*

*Rhododendron* spp.

## DESCRIPTION

The genus *Rhododendron* includes more than 900 species and thousands of cultivars. Although azaleas are included in this genus, they are still treated separately by most nurserymen. Here they are grouped together because they have the same cultural, pest, and disease problems. One basic difference between azaleas and rhododendrons is the location of the buds. Azaleas have lateral axillary buds as well as terminal buds. Rhododendrons bloom only at the ends of branches. Also, most rhododendrons are evergreen, whereas most azaleas are deciduous.

Azaleas and rhododendrons are easy to hybridize. Plant breeders have developed numerous cultivars with outstanding foliage, flower color, habit, and hardiness. Some popular azaleas include Exbury hybrids, gable hybrids, torch azaleas, mollis hybrid azaleas, kurume azaleas, royal azaleas, and glendale hybrids. Rhododendrons and azaleas have inestimable landscape value, serving in shrub borders, groups and mass plantings, and foundation plantings.

### Height

Azaleas grow from 3 to 8 feet, depending on the variety. Dwarf rhododendrons reach only 3 feet at maturity, whereas the tall species grow to more than 15 feet in height.

### Spread

Azaleas can spread to 9 feet. Rhododendrons spread from 6 to 13 feet, with the dwarf varieties reaching 3 to 5 feet.

### Blossoms

Most azaleas bloom in mid- to late spring, although the swamp azalea (*Rhododendron viscosum*) flowers in late June to July. They have showy funnel-shaped flowers in many colors, including white through primrose, yellow, gold, pink, apricot, orange-flame, and dark red. Some native species such as sweet azalea (*R. arborescens*) and swamp azalea have a light scent, but most do not.

Rhododendrons bloom in mid-spring to early summer. Like azaleas, they produce showy blossoms. These bell-shaped flowers bloom in clusters at the ends of branches. They have some fragrance. Colors range from white through pink, to rosy purple.

## Foliage

Some azaleas are evergreen, but most are deciduous. The leaves are oblong or elliptical in shape and have a deep green color. They are usually ¾ inch to

3 inches long, and in some species may be even longer. With most azaleas, the foliage is glossy and may have pale undersides. The leaves of the pink-shell azalea (*R. vaseyi*) and the royal azalea (*R. schlippenbachii*) turn red in the fall.

Most rhododendrons have smooth evergreen leaves, which are 3 to 6 inches long, elliptical in shape, and have a deep green color. The foliage of the PJM hybrids turns purplish in the fall.

## ENVIRONMENT

Azaleas and rhododendrons grow best in a cool climate with high humidity, and they prefer an acidic soil. If you live in the central United States or in the dry desert areas of the West and Southwest, you may have difficulty growing them. In the mid-Atlantic, northeastern, and Pacific Northwest states, these shrubs thrive.

Azaleas and rhododendrons are sensitive to excess calcium. So, if possible, you should avoid placing them too close to a stucco or brick wall, since splashing rain may wash small amounts of calcium into the soil. Plant them at least 12, preferably 18, inches away.

### Azalea Varieties by Zone

To zone 5, Exbury hybrids, royal azalea, and torch hybrids

To zone 6, gable hybrids, Glen Dale Hybrids, kurume azalea, and mollis hybrids

### Rhododendron Varieties by Zone

To zone 3, rosebay rhododendron (*R. maximum*)

To zone 5, catawba rhododendron (*R. catawbiense*); Dexter hybrids; Korean rhododendron (*R. mucronulatum*); PJM hybrids; and Yako rhododendron (*R. yakusimanum*)

### Light Requirements

Azaleas and rhododendrons prefer light shade, but will tolerate either full sun or medium shade.

The best site for azaleas and rhododendrons is in the filtered shade of high tree branches or on the eastern side of a sheltering structure. In general, azaleas will grow in sunnier locations than rhododendrons.

## Soil Requirements

Azaleas and rhododendrons prefer a cool, well-drained soil. When planting these shrubs, add a mixture of one part soil, two parts organic material, such as peat, leaf mold, or composted pine chips, and one part coarse sand to the hole. If your soil is heavy and not well drained, build raised beds for your plants.

Both azaleas and rhododendrons prefer an acidic soil with a pH of 4.5 to 6.5. They cannot handle alkaline conditions at all, so do not use bonemeal or wood ashes around them. Azaleas and rhododendrons are also extremely sensitive to saline soils.

# PLANTING AND PROPAGATION

## Planting

Plant balled-and-burlapped or container-grown plants that have reached a planting height of about 18 to 30 inches. Azaleas and rhododendrons have very shallow roots, which require careful placement in the soil. Place the plant in the hole so that the soil level is the same as it was in the pot. You can set them in the ground slightly higher than pot level and then mulch them. If azaleas or rhododendrons are planted too deeply, they may die. Place rhododendrons about 5 feet apart and azaleas about 3 feet apart, and plan to eventually remove every other one to new sites as they mature.

## Transplanting

Azaleas and rhododendrons can be transplanted easily either in the spring or the fall, but fall is the best time. Get a good-sized root ball when you dig them up.

## Propagation

Propagate evergreen azaleas from semiripe cuttings taken in late spring to early summer. Wait until midsummer to cut deciduous azaleas. Rhododendrons are best propagated by grafting or layering.

## Container Gardening

Some azaleas can be grown in containers as houseplants if kept pruned. They also make good bonsai. Plant them in tubs no less than 18 inches in diameter. Rhododendrons can also be grown in containers, but tend to be too large to be brought indoors. The yako rhododendron, with its compact habit, is the exception.

# PLANT MANAGEMENT

## Water Requirements

Neither azaleas nor rhododendrons will tolerate drought for long. They need to be watered regularly, but are unhappy in soggy soil. Make sure they receive about 1 inch of water each week, increasing this amount to 1½ inches during the hot summer. Judicious restraint in watering from late August to mid-October will prevent excessive fall growth, which might be susceptible to winterkill. Resume normal watering in late fall, and soak plants well prior to the first hard freeze. This last good drench prevents these shallow-rooted shrubs from suffering water deficiency in frozen winter grounds.

## Feeding Requirements

Azaleas and rhododendrons need only one application of slow-release fertilizer, such as compost. Apply it in spring immediately after the blooms have faded. These shrubs also benefit from a monthly spray of dilute liquid fertilizer, such as fish emulsion, mixed with dilute seaweed extract. In cool climates, stop all fertilizing two months before the first frost to allow your plants to harden off for the winter.

## Mulching

Azaleas and rhododendrons do best when they have a 2- to 4-inch layer of organic mulch surrounding them all season long. Use chopped leaves, peat moss, pine needles, or wood chips. Do not use leaves that have not been chopped, because they mat together and prevent water from getting into the soil. Mulch keeps the soil cool, reduces weed problems, and will slowly add humus to the soil. Weed control is guaranteed if you first lay down some geotextile mulch (a synthetic fabric that allows water to pass through while preventing weeds from growing) and then cover that with organic material.

## Weeding

Mulch should take care of any weeds. If you do not mulch, weed by hand; the fibrous, shallow root systems of azaleas and rhododendrons are easily damaged when the soil around them is cultivated with tools.

## Pruning

Azaleas and rhododendrons need grooming more than pruning. Removing spent flowers will stimulate the growth of new buds for the next season. Pinch the tips of azaleas immediately after flowering to encourage bushy plants. If azaleas and rhododendrons have become leggy with age, prune them lightly. Because buds are produced all along the branches on azaleas, you can prune anywhere along the branch and a stem will grow. On rhododendrons, cut down to the first live rosette of leaves. If there aren't any rosettes, cut out the whole branch. Prune older branches by cutting them off at the base of the plant to encourage new, vigorous branches.

While it is best to do any pruning right after the plant has finished blooming, radical pruning, to 6 inches, must be done in early spring to ensure sufficient recovery time before winter. Approach radical pruning on a mature rhododendron over a period of a few years to avoid irreparable harm to the plant. When radically pruning azaleas, never cut more than a third of the plant each year.

## Winterizing

In northern states, both azaleas and rhododendrons appreciate protection from winter sun and wind. This is especially important for evergreen species of the rhododendron family. Because their shallow root systems usually do not penetrate the frost line, these shrubs cannot take up water when the ground is frozen; however, their leaves continue to transpire water through the winter. Consequently, the leaves may become dry. To prevent this, spray the leaves of all evergreen rhododendrons thoroughly with an antitranspirant in late fall, and give each plant a good, deep watering to a depth of 18 inches every two weeks for about a month prior to the first hard freeze. Do not water plants again until spring. Then, when the ground has frozen, lay down a 4- to 6-inch layer of organic mulch. If you've already mulched your plants for summer, remove this to the compost pile. It may be harboring insect pests that like to overwinter there. If your azaleas or rhododendrons are located in an open site, wrap them with burlap or create a wind screen from burlap, laths, or agricultural fleece to protect the flower buds from damage by severe wind chill. Do not use plastic screens; they block air flow, and heat builds up inside them around the shrub. After a month or two, spray again with an antitranspirant.

## Cutting Fresh Flowers

Cut blossoms for indoor display just as the buds are about to break open.

# MOST COMMON CULTURAL PROBLEMS

## Leaves Turn Yellow

### Iron Deficiency

If the leaves of your azaleas or rhododendrons begin to yellow, your plants may be suffering from an iron deficiency. The leaf margins and the tissue between the veins turn light in color, while the veins themselves may remain dark green. This yellowing can progress to the point where the leaves become very pale and turn brown at the tips. Iron deficiencies can occur under any of a number of circumstances: roots damaged by tilling or by dry soil; sandy soil with insufficient organic matter; an overabundance of hard coal ash in the soil; poor soil drainage; or alkaline soil caused by too much lime or by setting plants near cement walls. Also, if roots have been damaged by tilling or by drying out, they become less able to take up nutrients from the soil.

To quickly remedy an iron deficiency, apply an iron chelate, adding it to the soil or spraying it on the foliage. Check the soil pH and correct it if necessary. To permanently solve an iron deficiency, improve soil by adding 1 to 2 inches of compost each year.

Chlorosis also results from winter injury. When more water is lost from the leaf surface than the roots can absorb, areas between the veins of leaves turn yellow, while the tissue immediately adjacent to the veins remains green. So, first determine if your plants have been damaged by winter weather before you treat them for an iron deficiency.

## Plant Looks Weak

### Root Injury

Root injury may result from hoeing or cultivating the soil too close to the azalea or rhododendron. The roots of these plants remain very near the surface of the ground and spread to a point a bit beyond the dripline. Try not to disturb the soil around the azaleas or rhododendrons.

## Edges of Leaves Turn Brown; Bark May Split

### Winterkill

Dramatic changes in temperature can damage azaleas and rhododendrons. During winter, these plants are dormant, and transpiration—the taking up of water through the roots and releasing of it from the leaves—has slowed. A sunny, warm day in midwinter may stimulate the leaves to increase their winter transpiration rate even though the roots in the frozen ground cannot take up water to replace the moisture lost from the leaves. Brisk winds exacerbate this problem by helping the process of evaporation. As the shrubs lose water, the edges of the leaves turn brown, and bark may split. To prevent winterkill, simply follow the steps for winterizing your plants given earlier.

## MOST COMMON INSECT PESTS

## Leaves Yellowed and Curled

### Aphids

Aphids suck the leaves and stems of azaleas and rhododendrons, causing the foliage to wilt under bright sunlight, and sometimes curl, pucker, and yellow. If you ignore aphids, they will reduce the plant's vigor, making it more vulnerable to disease. Many aphids secrete honeydew, which attracts ants, so you may find them wandering over your aphid-infested shrubs. If you notice any of these symptoms, check the undersides of leaves for small groups of rhododendron aphids (*Macrosiphum rhododendri*). These aphids are about the size of the head of a pin and pale pink and green in color. They have soft, pear-shaped bodies.

Light infestations may be simply knocked off your plants by vigorously spraying them with water. Do this in the early morning three times, once every other day. If this doesn't work, spray with insecticidal soap every two to three days until aphids are gone. As a last resort, use pyrethrum. Make two applications, three to four days apart.

## Holes in Leaves; Leaves and Flowers Skeletonized

### Beetles

Both Japanese beetles (*Popillia japonica*) and Asiatic garden beetles (*Maladera castanea*) attack the younger leaves on azaleas or rhododendrons and lay their eggs in the soil at the base of the plants. Their grubs feed on the roots and on the base of young stems. Beetles can skeletonize leaves. Adult Japanese beetles are ½ inch long, with shiny metallic green and copper-brown wing covers. They feed during the day. The larvae are grayish white, with dark brown heads. Fully grown grubs are plump, ¾ to 1 inch long, and lie in the soil in a distinctive arc-shaped resting posture. Adult Asiatic garden beetles work at night, feeding on leaves and flowers until they are skeletonized. The adults somewhat resemble Japanese beetles. They are nearly ½ inch long, velvety, and chestnut brown. They lay their eggs in the soil at the base of the plants. These larvae are grayish, ¾ inch long, and bent in the shape of a C.

Handpick the beetles and drop them into a pail of soapy water. Set up pheromone traps for Japanese beetles, making sure traps are no closer than 50 feet to your shrubs. Handpick stragglers not caught by the traps. If the traps cannot handle the infestation, spray your plants with a mixture of pyrethrum and isopropyl alcohol as needed. To make this solution, add 1 tablespoon alcohol to each pint of pyrethrum. You can also use a solution made from 1 tablespoon alcohol mixed with a pint of pyrethrum combined with rotenone. Spray your plants every three to five days for two weeks.

For long-term control, apply milky spore disease (*Bacillus popilliae*) to the soil. In the spring, carefully cultivate the soil around the azaleas and rhododendrons, without hurting the roots, to expose the eggs, larvae, and pupae to the weather and to predator birds.

## Holes in Stems

### Borers

Soon after bloom time, borers drill their way into the tips of stems and twigs. As these pests get larger, they move into the woody part of the shrub, pushing out fine sawdust as they go. Ugly scars mark the branches, and sometimes branches die. The specific borers of azaleas and rhododendrons are the azalea stem borer (*Oberea myops*) and the rhododendron borer (*Synanthedon rhododendri*). Both these stem borers are about ½ inch long and yellowish. They overwinter in their stem burrows as partly

grown larvae; then in June, adults emerge and lay eggs on leaves, new twigs, or the rough bark of the main stem. Adults sometimes girdle branches when laying their eggs. This causes the tips to die back and break off.

In June, crush any eggs that you find. An effective but time-consuming remedy against both of these borers is to shove a wire into each hole to crush or remove the borer. You can also inject nicotine sulfate into each hole. The most complete control is to prune and burn affected stems. Coat wounds with tree paint or paraffin. A blacklight trap may prove effective against the adult borer, if used in May or June when the insect is in the moth stage. This trap uses black light to attract insects. A fan sucks the pests into a sticky container, where they are trapped.

## Ragged Holes in Leaf Margins

### Weevils

Ragged holes along the margins of leaves are a sign that the fuller rose beetle (*Pantomorus cervinus*) is at work. Despite its name, this pest is actually a weevil. In addition to foliage, fuller rose beetles feed on roots and girdle stems of azaleas and rhododendrons. Infested shrubs turn yellow and may eventually die. The adults are grayish brown with short, broad snouts and white diagonal stripes across their wing covers. The larvae are yellowish with brown heads and measure about ⅓ inch in length.

Black vine and strawberry root weevils (*Otiorhyncus sulcatus* and *O. ovatus*) also feed on azalea and rhododendron leaves at night, cutting holes along their edges. These weevils sometimes devour the whole leaf except for the midribs and large veins. Their grubs attack shrub roots and bark around the base of the plant, often endangering the life of the plant. The Japanese weevil (*Pseudocneorhinus bifasciatus*) also attacks azaleas and rhododendrons, producing similar damage. This pest feeds by day. Weevils are sometimes called snout beetles because their heads are elongated, forming a long, slender, downward-curved snout. The insect's mouth parts are at the end of this snout. Most adult weevils are either brown or black, with a tear-shaped, hard-shelled body, which may be $\frac{1}{10}$ to $\frac{1}{4}$ inch long. They commonly live under tree bark or in other plant tissues.

If these pests have only just discovered your shrubs, you can easily eliminate them simply by picking them off and destroying them. Many species of weevil play dead when disturbed, folding their legs and dropping from plants to the ground. You can turn this trait to advantage when trying to control weevils. Gently beat the branches of the infested bush and catch the startled insects in a drop cloth spread beneath. Smear a sticky substance such as Tanglefoot on the trunks of your azaleas or rhododendrons to prevent the adults from climbing up and eating the leaves. As soon as weevils appear, begin spraying weekly with a solution made from pyrethrum and isopropyl alcohol. Mix 1 tablespoon alcohol with a pint of pyrethrum solution. Apply this spray at night at least two hours after dark. Cover all leaf surfaces so you will hit the weevils that have not dropped to the ground. Spray your plants every three to five days for two weeks.

## Leaves Pale or Mottled

### Lace Bugs

A variety of lace bugs may attack your azaleas or rhododendrons. These include the azalea lace bug (*Stephanitis pyrioides*) and the rhododendron lace bug (*S. rhododendri*). These pests suck sap from the undersides of leaves, causing them to turn pale or mottled. The adults are small square-shaped bugs, $\frac{3}{16}$ inch long or less, with elaborately reticulated wings that resemble lacework. Lace bugs appear in late May or early June and spend the summer on the undersides of the leaves of azaleas and on rhododendrons.

For small infestations, simply crush the bugs. Control medium to large infestations by spraying the undersides of leaves with insecticidal soap, a nicotine spray, or a pyrethrum spray. Make three applications, one every three to five days.

## Leaves Mined and Rolled

### Leafminers

Leafminers burrow their way in between the upper and lower surfaces of leaves. They create tunnels or blotches, which appear yellow or white to brown. You can often see the larvae in these tunnels. Leaves may later blister or curl, turn brown, and die. The specific leafminer of azaleas and rhododendrons is azalea leafminer (*Gracilaria azaleella.*) The larvae are yellow caterpillars, $\frac{1}{2}$ inch long. After feeding inside the leaves, the larvae emerge, roll leaves, and continue feeding inside the rolls. The adult moths have a wingspan of $\frac{3}{8}$ inch. They are garden pests in southern states and greenhouse pests in northern areas.

As soon as you discover infested leaves, trim and destroy them. If necessary, prune branches to healthy growth. Larvae can sometimes be repelled by spraying trees with an insecticidal soap solution in late June or early July.

## Leaves Discolored and Bound with Silk Strands

### Leaftiers

You can suspect leaftier insects when the leaves of your azaleas or rhododendrons become discolored, and you notice that some of the leaves are tied together with a silklike material. The larvae of leaftiers protect themselves while feeding by binding leaves around them with strands of silk. The specific pest of azaleas and rhododendrons is the azalea leaftier (*Archips argyrospilus*). As these insects feed, foliage becomes ragged and unsightly, turns brown, and dies. Larvae are pale green with brown heads. Adult moths have a wingspan of $\frac{3}{4}$ inch and are brown with gold markings.

If only a few caterpillars have settled comfortably in the leaves of your shrubs, simply crush them in their rolled hideouts; however, if these pests are too numerous, spray infested azaleas and rhododendrons with Bt (*Bacillus thuringiensis*) three times over a three-week period. If leaftiers are a recurring problem, spray your azaleas and rhododendrons with Bt before you expect the caterpillars to begin feeding, remembering when you first saw them last year.

## Leaf Edges and Buds Turn Brown

### Midges

If the foliage and buds on your azaleas or rhododendrons turns brown, suspect midges. Rhododendron tip midge (*Giardomyia rhododendri*) is the most common species on rhodendrons and azaleas. As they feed, they roll the edges of young leaves and cause leaf edges to turn brown. Shrubs wilt and buds and foliage turn brown and become deformed. Many species also produce galls where eggs are stored and larvae develop. Adults are two-winged flies, $1/14$ to $1/8$ inch long, with long legs and antennae.

Pick off and destroy affected leaves and buds and spray the whole plant with insecticidal soap. Some gardeners mix tobacco dust with the soil around bases of affected plants to kill the larvae. In early spring, spray plants with dormant oil to kill eggs and overwintering nymphs.

## Leaves Stippled Yellow or Red and Puckered

### Mites

Several species of spider mite infest azaleas and rhododendrons. Watch the lowest leaves on your azaleas or rhododendrons for two-spotted spider mites (*Tetranychus telarius*). Azalea mites (*Aculus atlantazaleae*) infest the tips of branches. If these pests have infested your shrubs, the upper surfaces of the lower leaves will be stippled with small yellow dots or red spots. The leaves, stalks, and adjacent stems often become distorted and are swathed in fine webbing. Mites are about $1/50$ inch long, barely visible to the unaided eye. They may be yellow, green, red, or brown.

Start control measures as soon as you notice the first stippling on the leaves. Spray the plants in the early morning with a forceful water spray to knock mites from leaf undersides. Repeat this procedure daily for three days. If mites are still present,

spray with insecticidal soap every three to five days for two weeks.

## Shrub Sickly, Wilted, or Stunted

### Nematodes

Nematodes attack plants at the roots, so you won't find any mechanical signs of damage on the foliage or branches of infested shrubs. Instead, the overall health of the plant slowly declines. Foliage becomes yellowed or bronzed and eventually the shrub dies. If you were to look at the root system, you would find it poorly developed and even partially decayed. Knots or galls appear on the roots. The effects of nematode activity are most apparent in hot weather, when the plants recover poorly from the heat. In Florida, leaf nematodes (*Aphelenchoides fragariae*) may attack azaleas, causing leaf lesions and possibly stunting. Stunt nematodes (*Tylenchorhynchus claytoni*), stubby root nematodes (*Trichodorus christiei*), and spiral nematodes (*Helicotylenchus nannus*) also attack azaleas and rhododendrons. Nematodes are whitish, translucent, wormlike creatures, $1/50$ to $1/10$ inch long.

To control these pests, add lots of compost, especially leaf mold, to the soil around shrubs to encourage beneficial fungi. Fertilize with liquid fish emulsion poured into the soil as a drench; it is toxic or repellent to nematodes. Also, plant French marigolds among your azaleas and rhododendrons; these plants repel nematodes.

## Stems Wilt and Break Off Near Ground

### Pitted Ambrosia Beetles

The pitted ambrosia beetle (*Corthylus punctatissimus*) is about $1/8$ inch long, dark reddish brown, and marked with several tiny pits. Its small white larvae eat galleries in woody azalea or rhododendron stems, causing them to wilt, die, and break. They usually infect stems near the ground. Adults overwinter in the chambers created by the larvae and emerge to feed on fungi in mulch.

Pick pitted ambrosia beetles off your shrubs

and introduce beneficial nematodes to the soil. For long-term control, apply milky spore disease (*Bacillus popilliae*) to the soil. When spring arrives, carefully cultivate the soil around the azaleas and rhododendrons, without hurting the roots, to expose the beetle eggs, larvae, and pupae to the weather and to predator birds.

## Leaves Yellowish; Small Bumps or Cottony Masses on Branches

### Scale
Several species of scale attack rhododendrons and azaleas. Soft azalea scale (*Pulvinaria ericicola*) usually appear in the crotches of branches or close to the buds. You also may find sooty mold on leaves and branches growing on honeydew secreted by the scale. Look for the insects themselves, which resemble small bumps and appear in clusters. Scale insects have a rounded covering, which protects them while they feed on plants. They are somewhat flattened, waxy, reddish gray or brown, and just a bit bigger than the head of a pin. As these pests feed, shrubs weaken and often fail to produce healthy flowers. Leaves turn yellowish and plants may die if severely infested.

The azalea bark scale, also called azalea mealybug (*Ericoccus azaleae*) feeds by sucking sap from branches and twigs. Adults are oval, flattened, and ⅕ to ⅓ inch long. Although their outer shells are red-brown, they are concealed under a white, cottony covering. Peony scale (*Pseudaonidia paeoniae*) forms clusters of unobtrusive brown bumps on twigs. Soft azalea scale (*Pulvinaria ericicola*) somewhat resembles azalea bark scale. For light infestations, scrape them off plant surfaces with your fingernail or a cotton swab dipped in rubbing alcohol. If your shrubs are heavily infested, spray them with a mixture of alcohol and insecticidal soap every three days for two weeks. To make this solution, combine 1 cup isopropyl alcohol and 1 tablespoon insecticidal soap concentrate in 1 quart water. If you already have insecticidal soap mixed with water, simply add 1 tablespoon alcohol to a pint of this solution. In late winter or early spring, spray plants with dormant oil to smother overwintering adults and eggs.

## Ragged Holes in Leaves

### Slugs or Snails
Large ragged holes in leaves are sure signs of slug or snail attack. Slugs are slimy creatures, usually 1 to 2 inches long, although a few species grow up to 8 inches. Their color may be white, gray, yellow, or brown-black. Moist, well-mulched gardens and acidic soil are the perfect conditions for slugs—these are also perfect conditions for azaleas and rhododendrons. These pests are always most destructive in shaded gardens and during rainy spells. Slugs feed at night, rasping holes in leaves with their filelike tongues. During the day, they hide in the darkness under boards or leaf litter.

Snails are land-dwelling mollusks that are soft-bodied and covered with sticky slime. Their eyes protrude on retractable, flexible stalks. They are protected by coiled shells, the markings of which are quite variable.

The best way to control slugs and snails is with traps. You can buy traps or make them at home using a shallow container and filling it with beer. The yeast in the beer attracts slugs; they climb in and drown. Begin trapping within the first three to four weeks after the last frost. As soon as you find the first slug in the trap, increase the number of traps. Try to catch them before they can lay eggs and multiply beyond control.

## Leaves Yellowed; Plant Weakened

### Whiteflies
The azalea whitefly (*Pealius azaleae*) and the rhododendron whitefly (*Dialeurodes chittendeni*) suck juices from the leaves of azaleas and rhododendrons, creating a yellowish mottling on the upper sides of leaves. Once you spot the yellowish mottling, look for the pests themselves to make a certain diagnosis that whiteflies are the problem. The adults are clearly visible on the undersides of leaves. They are white-winged mothlike insects about the size of a pinhead.

When a plant is bumped or brushed, they fly up in clouds. Both nymphs and adults suck juices from plant leaves, buds, and stems, gradually weakening the plant. The oval pupae are greenish white and are present in large numbers on the undersides of leaves. The sooty mold fungus develops on the honeydew secreted by these immature whiteflies.

Control whiteflies with insecticidal soap. Spray your shrubs every three to five days for two weeks. If that does not work, apply pyrethrum every five days for two weeks.

# MOST COMMON DISEASES

## Spots or Blotches on Flowers, Buds, and Twigs

### Blight

Several different types of fungi produce blights in azaleas and rhododendron: *Ovulinia* spp., *Briosia* spp., *Pestalotia* spp., *Monilinea* spp., and others. The flowers, buds, and growing shoots of infected shrubs become spotted, blotched, and discolored. In addition, they may be covered with powdery fungal spores or a thin mat of fungal strands. Azalea petal blight (*Ovulinia azaleae*), also known as azalea flower spot and Ovulinia flower blight, is a common disease of azaleas in the southeastern states. It first appears as small pale spots on the inner surfaces of the petals of colored flowers and as brown spots on white flowers. These spots rapidly enlarge until the whole flower collapses. Small dark resting bodies of the fungus overwinter on dead flowers and in the soil.

Prune and destroy infected branch tips, leaves, and flowers. The fungi that cause blight overwinter on the ground in dead flowers and other debris, so gather and destroy diseased plant material promptly. To prevent the disease from spreading, avoid overhead watering while the plants are in flower. Plant azaleas or rhododendrons where they will be protected from sunscald and winter injury, which makes shrubs more susceptible to blight.

## Spots and Roughened Lesions on Leaves and Twigs

### Canker

Azaleas and rhododendrons infected with canker caused by the fungus *Botryosphaeria dothidea* develop spots on their leaves and branches. These spots then develop into roughened lesions or cankers. The tips and margins of leaves are first affected, followed by branches, which may die. Remove the diseased growth, cutting about 2 inches below the canker. Spray plants once a month or so with a copper fungicide.

## Galls on Stems

### Crown Gall

If you find swollen growths of various shapes and sizes on the crowns, roots, and stems of your azaleas or rhododendrons, your plants probably have crown gall. This disease occurs worldwide and is caused by the bacterium *Agrobacterium tumefaciens*. Unlike other plant galls, these are malignant. Crown gall is a form of plant cancer. Gall bacteria enter susceptible plants through wounds and are easily transmitted on tools, in soil water, and by splashing rain. Prune and destroy the diseased stems. Destroy heavily infected plants.

## Leaves and Growing Tips Shriveled

### Dieback

Dieback in azaleas and rhododendrons can be caused by a couple different fungi. First the tips and margins of leaves become discolored; then spots appear, which spread over the entire leaf. Leaf stalks and twigs also become infected.

The fungus *Phytophthora cactorum* causes terminal buds and leaves to turn brown, roll up, and droop as though in a winter condition. The stem shrivels and a canker forms, which encircles the twig. All parts above the canker soon die. This fungus also infects lilacs; they should therefore be planted far away from azaleas and rhododendrons.

To control dieback, prune all diseased tips well below the infection and destroy them. When new leaves emerge, spray with Bordeaux mixture or another copper fungicide. Spray again two weeks later; hopefully this will prevent dieback from reoccurring.

## Leaves Become Spotted, Turn Brown, and Fall Prematurely

### Leaf Spot

Azaleas and rhododendrons are susceptible to all kinds of leaf spot produced by all kinds of fungi. Spots may be yellow, brown, or black. The bothersome fungi include members of the *Cercospora* spp., *Coryneospora* spp., *Diplodina* spp., *Gloeosporium* spp., *Mycosphaerella* spp., *Phyllosticta* spp., *Septoria* spp., *Venturia* spp., and others. Often the spots come together to form larger patches of dead tissue. Fortunately, the control practices are the same for all, so you don't have to determine exactly which fungus has infected your shrubs. Simply gather and destroy all fallen leaves. In late spring of the following year, spray with a copper fungicide to prevent the disease from recurring.

## White Powder on Leaves

### Powdery Mildew

A thin, white, powdery coating on leaves is the telltale mark of powdery mildew. This disease is caused by the fungus *Microsphaera alni*. As it progresses, shrubs wilt and die. Once you spot the white coating of fungus, spray plants with wettable sulfur once or twice at weekly intervals. Prevent future attacks of powdery mildew by collecting and destroying all plant debris around your shrubs in the fall.

## Powdery Pustules on Leaf Undersides

### Rust

You can easily diagnose rust by the pustules that develop on the undersides of leaves. Golden or brownish spores erupt from these pustules. The fungus *Pucciniastrum vacinii* is responsible for causing rust in azaleas and rhododendrons. Once shrubs are weakened by rust, they become vulnerable to infection by other fungi.

Avoid planting azaleas near hemlocks, which are also vulnerable to rust. Spray infected shrubs with a wettable sulfur fungicide every ten days through July and August. Prune and destroy all infected foliage.

## Mushrooms Sprout at Base of Shrub

### Shoestring Root Rot

Shoestring root rot is so named because dark, shoestringlike strands cover the bark of roots of infected shrubs. In addition, large white "fans" of fungal mycelium develop between the bark and the hardwood of the crown and larger roots. The most obvious sign of root rot, though, is the growth of mushrooms around the base of infected shrubs in late fall or early winter. The guilty fungus is *Armillaria mellea*.

Once the fungus becomes established, it is difficult to control. Expose the crowns of infected shrubs to air. The fungus cannot exist under dry conditions. Because the fungus thrives in wet, heavy soils, improve drainage and avoid overwatering. Plant resistant azalea. Dig out and destroy seriously infected shrubs and discard the surrounding soil.

## Leaves Yellowed and Wilted

### Wilt

Wilt in azaleas and rhododendrons is caused by the soil-dwelling fungus *Phytophthora cinnamomi*. It usually infects young azaleas or rhododendrons in their first two or three years; therefore it is most commonly found in nurseries. Wilt is more likely to attack plants recently transplanted. The fungus enters roots and spreads to the crown. Young leaves become yellowish and wilt.

Proper care of azaleas and rhododendrons will prevent infection. Do not overwater; this kills the roots and encourages the fungus. Mulch to keep soil temperatures low and increase soil acidity by adding aluminum sulfate or sulfur.

## NOTES AND RESEARCH

Many gardeners overfeed azaleas. These shrubs are sensitive to excess levels of nitrogen and are more prone to insect attack and disease if fed too well. Fertilize only once in the spring. Do not treat plants with anything more than a dilute foliar spray, and apply this only once a month until two months before first frost.

SHRUB **Barberry** *Berberis* spp.

## DESCRIPTION

The barberry belongs to a genus of almost 500 species of evergreen and deciduous shrubs commonly used as hedges and barrier plantings. They can be grown throughout the United States. These shrubs add interest to the landscape through all the seasons. The paleleaf barberry (*Berberis candidula*) is prized for its bright green foliage. It withstands pruning so well it can be used as a ground cover. The mentor barberry (*B. ×mentorensis*) makes an impenetrable hedge because it is so thorny. The vigorous Japanese barberry (*B. thunbergii*) is one of the best deciduous shrubs of all because it grows easily and requires little care. All barberries have three spines located at most of the leaf axils. Deciduous barberries turn bright red in the autumn.

### Height

Darwin barberry (*B. darwinii*), 10 feet
Japanese barberry (*B. thunbergii*), 2 to 7 feet
Korean barberry (*B. koreana*), 6 feet
Mentor barberry (*B. ×mentorensis*), 7 feet
Paleleaf barberry (*B. candidula*), 2 feet
Warty barberry (*B. verruculosa*), 4 feet
Wilson barberry (*B. wilsoniae*), 4 feet
Wintergreen barberry (*B. julianae*), 13 feet

## Spread

Darwin barberry, 10 feet
Japanese barberry, 10 feet
Wilson barberry, 8 feet
Wintergreen barberry, 13 feet

## Blossoms

Small yellow or orange waxlike flowers bloom profusely over barberries in mid-spring to early summer. These flowers are gathered in long racemes or in clusters. In fall they are replaced by bright red or bluish black berries, which attract both people and birds.

## Foliage

Most barberries are deciduous. Their simple leaves appear in small clusters at the ends of short spurs. At the base of these leaves, along the branches, you will find spines on most varieties. The cultivar 'Crimson Pygmy', a dwarf Japanese barberry, has purplish leaves (if it gets enough sun), but the foliage of most is green and turns a brilliant scarlet, orange, or yellow in the fall.

# ENVIRONMENT

## Varieties by Zone

To zone 3, Korean barberry
To zone 4, Japanese barberry
To zone 5, mentor barberry
To zone 6, paleleaf barberry, warty barberry, and wintergreen barberry
To zone 7, Darwin barberry

## Light Requirements

Most types of barberry can handle either full sun or light shade, but they prefer part sun. The Japanese barberry cultivar 'Crimson Pygmy' likes full sun.

## Soil Requirements

Most barberries prefer average, well-drained soil; however, the Japanese barberry is famous for its ability to grow in poor, dry soils. Barberries are tolerant of a pH range of 6 to 7.5.

# PLANTING AND PROPAGATION

## Planting

You can plant bare-rooted or container-grown plants in the spring or fall, although fall is the best time if you have a choice. Barberry establishes itself slowly after being transplanted and is vulnerable to major changes in water availability from drought to excess moisture. Consequently, it is important to incorporate a significant amount of organic material such as compost, peat moss, or well-aged sawdust in the hole before setting in the plant. That organic material, with its water-holding capacity, will serve to buffer the swings in the availability of water during the plant's first year in its new location.

## Propagation

You can propagate barberry from cuttings taken in late spring.

# PLANT MANAGEMENT

## Water Requirements

One inch of water a week will keep barberries happy and healthy. Usually normal rainfall suffices and you do not need to water, except in the hottest summer months.

## Feeding Requirements

One application in the fall or early spring of a slow-release nitrogen fertilizer provides sufficient nutrients. In the spring, lay down a 1-inch layer of compost to give the plant great vigor and improved disease and insect resistance.

## Mulching

A 2- to 4-inch layer of organic mulch all season long helps keep soil moisture levels constant and eliminates weed problems. During the winter, mulch helps protect barberry from losing moisture. Chopped leaves, aged sawdust, or wood chips make good mulch.

## Pruning

Most barberries tolerate severe pruning well. You can rejuvenate mature plants by pruning them to 3 or 4 feet from ground level each spring. Wintergreen barberry is slow to become established and does not require pruning.

## Winterizing

Some protection from drying winter winds in northern areas helps to ensure healthy barberry shrubs. Use a wind screen, a snow fence, or some other device to shield the shrub from the wind. Spraying shrubs with an antitranspirant in late fall also helps to protect the plant during the drying winter months.

# MOST COMMON
# CULTURAL PROBLEMS

## Plant Dies during Summer

### Root Damage
Sections of shrubs or entire barberry plants may die very suddenly in the summer. This may be due to root damage caused by fluctuations in the moisture around the roots—dry or waterlogged. Mulching around shrubs with 2 to 4 inches of organic matter helps to prevent this problem.

# MOST COMMON INSECT PESTS

## Leaves Yellowed and Curled

### Aphids
Barberry aphids (*Liosomaphis berberidis*) suck the juices of the leaves and stems of barberry, causing the foliage to curl, pucker, and yellow. Eventually, the entire plant loses vigor. Ants crawling over your shrubs are also a sign of aphids. Ants are attracted to the honeydew secreted by aphids. Check the undersides of leaves for small groups of aphids. These soft, pear-shaped, greenish yellow insects are not much bigger than the head of a pin.

Light infestations can easily be controlled by spraying the undersides of the barberry vigorously with water three times, once every other day. Do this in the early morning. If aphids are still present, spray with insecticidal soap every two to three days. As a last resort, use pyrethrum. Make two applications, three to four days apart.

## Plant Stunted; Leaves Yellowed

### Nematodes
Diagnosing nematode infestation is a little bit difficult, because these tiny creatures work underground. The symptoms resemble those of disease. Nematode-infested plants look sickly, wilted, and stunted. Their leaves turn yellow or bronze, and their root systems are poorly developed and may even be partially decayed. The shrub declines slowly and eventually dies.

Northern root knot nematode (*Meloidogyne hapla*) attacks barberries in the northern United States. Nematodes are not insects, but slender, unsegmented roundworms. Most are soil-dwellers, less than 1/20 inch long. Once you've determined that nematodes are responsible for the waning of your barberries, add lots of compost, especially leaf mold, to the soil around the plants to encourage beneficial fungi. In addition, apply liquid fish emulsion as a drench to repel nematodes.

## Leaf Surface Discolored;
## Small Bumps on Leaves

### Scale
The first sign of a scale attack is often discoloration of the upper leaf surface, followed by leaf drop, reduced growth, and stunted plants. Heavy infestations of this pest kill plants. Other signs of scale include the presence of ants and the growth of

sooty mold. Both are attracted to the honeydew secreted by some species of scale. White, cottony or woolly masses appear on twigs, usually in the crotches or close to the buds. Barberry scale (*Lecaniodiaspis* spp.) look like bumps. They have a convex reddish brown covering. Florida wax scale (*Ceroplastes floridensis*) have a red or purplish brown shell covered with a thick, waxy, white coating.

If you catch scale early on, you can scrape them off plant surfaces with your fingernail or a cotton swab dipped in rubbing alcohol. Medium to heavy infestations are more easily controlled by spraying the infested plants with a mixture of alcohol and insecticidal soap every three days for two weeks. To make this solution, combine 1 cup isopropyl alcohol and 1 tablespoon insecticidal soap concentrate in 1 quart water. If your insecticidal soap is already mixed with water, simply add 1 tablespoon alcohol to a pint of the pre-mixed soap spray. In late winter, apply dormant oil to smother these pests.

## Leaves and Twigs Bound with Webbing

### Webworms
The barberry webworm (*Omphalocera dentosa*) is a blackish caterpillar with white spots that is nearly 1½ inches long when full grown. The worm ties together leaves and twigs, forming a nest within which it feeds. This webbing usually starts after midsummer, and the nests remain on the bushes during the winter. The webworm is prevalent in the southwestern United States. It attacks both the common and the Japanese barberry.

You can easily handpick the nests of webworms to eliminate them, if they are not too numerous. To effectively control large webworm infestations, spray with Bt (*Bacillus thuringiensis*), making three applications over a three-week period. If webworms are still a problem, try a spray or dust of pyrethrum. Make two applications, three to four days apart.

## Holes in Leaves

### Weevils
The Japanese weevil (*Pseudocneorhinus bifasciatus*) chews on barberry leaves, beginning at the leaf margins and sometimes devouring the whole leaf, except for the midribs and large veins. Weevil grubs may attack the roots, often endangering the life of the shrubs. The adults are about ¼ inch long and dark brown. They cannot fly. Sometimes called snout beetles, their heads are elongated into long, slender, downward-curved snouts. Most adult weevils have a tear-shaped, hard-shelled body. They commonly live under tree bark or in other plant tissues. Many species play dead when disturbed, folding their legs and dropping to the ground.

Remove weevils by spreading a cloth beneath the infested shrub; then gently beat the branches. Startled beetles will drop onto the cloth. Apply a sticky substance such as Tanglefoot to the trunks of your shrubs to prevent the adults from climbing up and eating the leaves. In addition, begin spraying weekly with pyrethrum mixed with isopropyl alcohol, combining 1 tablespoon alcohol with each pint of pyrethrum required.

# MOST COMMON DISEASES

## Sunken Spots on Leaves

### Anthracnose
If you find moist, sunken spots on the leaves of your barberries, on which fruiting bodies are growing, anthracnose (*Colletotrichum* spp. or *Gloeosporium* spp.) has struck. These leaf spots may run together, resembling a blotch or blight. The dead areas follow the veins or are bounded by larger veins. This disease may progress down the terminal shoots to several inches below the buds. Pustules containing pinkish spores appear on the lesions. In severe cases, dieback and defoliation may occur.

Gather and destroy diseased leaves when they fall and prune infected branches. Spray with a copper fungicide such as Bordeaux mixture. Two or three applications at weekly intervals should take care of the problem. Maintain the vigor of your shrubs by feeding and watering well, especially during droughts.

## Orange Powdery Spots on Leaves

### Rust

Bright orange powdery spots on foliage is a sure sign of rust. This disease is caused by the fungus *Puccinia graminis*. It is rarely something to fret over; only heavy infections cause leaf loss. However, rust on common barberry threatens nearby fields of wheat, oats, rye, barley, or other cereal crops. Some states require that common barberry be destroyed, and interstate shipment of certain barberries is banned. Consult your state department of agriculture or County Extension agent. If a susceptible variety of barberry is growing on your property, destroy it. Japanese barberries are immune to the disease. The other varieties mentioned on page 80 are also resistant to black stem rust.

## Leaves Turn Brown or Reddish and Fall Prematurely

### Wilt

Wilt in barberries is caused by a soil-dwelling fungus *Verticillium albo-atrum*. This disease infects the water-conducting tissues of barberries. The leaves turn brown or reddish, shrivel, and finally fall. Eventually, the entire plant may die. Remove and destroy infected shrubs and discard the soil immediately surrounding them in an area 3 feet square and 1 foot deep. Replace with clean soil and replant with healthy stock.

# SHRUB Boxwood *Buxus* spp.

## DESCRIPTION

Of the 30 known species of boxwood, only 2 are commonly grown: little-leaved boxwood (*Buxus microphylla*) and common boxwood (*B. sempervirens*). Common boxwood is also known as English boxwood or American boxwood. Some have described it as man's oldest garden ornamental shrub. The Romans were the first to appreciate the fine qualities of this shrub, and today it is still used for hedges and topiary. There are many different cultivars of common boxwood, including selections dwarf to those the size of a tree. They may have weeping, pyramidal, globe-shaped, or treelike forms. Some have variegated foliage. Use boxwood as a border for a walkway, to delineate a boundry, accent a space, surround a space, or form a screen. It can be grown in containers and used as a background for other plants or for topiary. The cultivar 'Suffrutiosa' is a dwarf form of common boxwood and has been used for centuries to edge formal gardens like knot gardens. Little-leaved boxwood is a smaller shrub and has a more open form.

### Height

Common boxwood (*B. sempervirens*), from dwarf cultivars to 20 feet
Little-leaved boxwood (*B. microphylla*), 6 feet

### Spread

Common boxwood, 3 to 13 feet

### Blossoms

Boxwood produces inconspicuous sulfur yellow blossoms in the spring.

## Foliage

Boxwoods are evergreen. The leaves are opposite each other on the stem. They are ¾ to 1½ inches in length, rounded, and slightly notched at the tip. Both sides are a lustrous green, but the upper leaf surfaces are slightly darker. Rub the foliage, and you'll find it has a papery texture. Boxwoods can have a somewhat unpleasant odor. Little-leaved boxwoods turn an unattractive yellow or brown in winter.

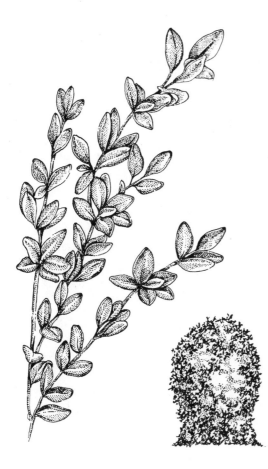

# ENVIRONMENT

Place boxwoods where there is some protection from winter wind and cold. The first year after transplanting, they should be shaded from direct hot sun in the summer. Boxwoods do have invasive roots, so watch that they do not overwhelm a neighboring plant.

## Hardiness

The best region for growing boxwood is the eastern seaboard, Chesapeake Bay area, although it does well throughout the southern United States. Boxwoods like mild maritime climates; however, if their cultural needs are met, many varieties and cultivars will withstand temperatures as low as −20°F. These shrubs tolerate cold better than unseasonal temperature fluctuations, which trigger the breaking of dormancy.

## Varieties by Zone

To zone 5, common boxwood
To zone 6, little-leaved boxwood

## Light Requirements

Boxwoods can be grown under nearly any light conditions, from full sun to deep shade; however, leaves lose their luster in heavy shade, and the coloring of variegated and golden varieties becomes less attractive. In northern states, plant boxwoods where they will get light shade during the winter to prevent sunscald.

## Soil Requirements

As adaptable as boxwoods are to different light conditions, they are adaptable to a wide range of soil types. These shrubs tolerate almost any soil, but prefer a fertile, well-drained earth. Their least favorite are heavy clay soils. The roots like cool soil, so it is wise to mulch. Boxwoods will tolerate a pH range between 6 and 7.5.

# PLANTING AND PROPAGATION

## Planting

First find a site with an exposure to the north, northeast, south, or southeast. Avoid a western or southwestern orientation. Plant balled or burlapped boxwoods in spring or early summer. They should be at least three years old. Container-grown shrubs can be planted anytime from spring through early fall. Do not set plants deeper in the hole than they were in their containers. Their roots benefit from the looser, more aerated soil near the surface. Boxwood roots are naturally close to the surface, so cover them with mulch to prevent weeds from growing in among them and to hold moisture.

Avoid crowding these shrubs. Space medium to large plants (3½ to 6 feet in height) 5 feet apart. Plant dwarf or small shrubs about 3 feet apart. For a low hedge, space small plants 15 to 18 inches apart, and for a taller hedge, 2 feet apart.

Do not plant ground covers beneath boxwoods. They will compete with the shallow roots of your shrubs for soil nutrients.

## Propagation

Propagate boxwoods from semiripe cuttings taken from new growth in early to mid-summer.

## Container Gardening

Boxwoods can be grown in containers. The best container for boxwood has a diameter of 1 to 2 feet. Use a soil mix that is friable and has a soft texture. Boxwoods are perfect for topiary.

# PLANT MANAGEMENT

## Water Requirements

Boxwoods thrive on about 1 inch of water a week. If normal rainfall isn't sufficient and you need to water, hose out the interior of the shrub and soak the root area. Judiciously reduce watering from mid-August to mid-October to discourage excessive fall growth, which might be susceptible to winterkill. Resume generous watering late in fall and soak the ground well before it freezes. With their shallow root systems, boxwoods can dry out in winter if they do not get that last good drenching before freeze sets in.

## Feeding Requirements

Boxwoods are heavy feeders. In spring, enrich the soil with a slow-release nitrogen fertilizer such as compost. Then, once a month during the growing season, give it a snack of a dilute solution of liquid fertilizer mixed with a dilute solution of seaweed extract.

## Mulching

A 2- to 4-inch layer of compost or shredded leaves keeps the shallow roots of boxwood cool during the growing season. In winter, protect the roots with 4 to 6 inches of mulch.

## Weeding

Pull weeds by hand rather than cultivating around boxwoods; tools might damage the shallow roots.

## Pruning

Boxwoods don't require pruning, but they take well to it, which is why they are often used in hedges and topiary. Boxwoods naturally have an attractive habit, so unless you need to trim them for some specific purpose, such as topiary or hedges, leave them to grow and spread as they like.

Plants can be sheared in late winter to encourage denser foliage and to shape plants. If winter damage occurs, you can drastically cut back your shrubs, but do it in stages, taking off no more than a third of the height or breadth of a plant in any one year. Remove all dead twigs and debris, especially from the center, where fungus disease can start. Do not prune after midsummer, so new growth can harden before winter.

## Winterizing

Boxwoods tolerate normal winds, but they can be harmed when exposed to constant or hard winds. If your boxwood is exposed to the winter wind, screen or cover it, but do not block the air circulation. Spraying shrubs with an antitranspirant helps protect them from winter winds and cold damage.

# MOST COMMON CULTURAL PROBLEMS

## Shrub Grows Poorly

### Salt in Soil

Boxwoods cannot tolerate salt, so keep them away from roads and walks that might get salted in the winter. By the time your shrubs show symptoms of poor growth, the salt has probably already damaged the roots, and nothing can be done to reverse the damage.

## Bark Splits

### Winterkill

If unseasonal warm temperatures break the dormancy of boxwood during the winter months, sap will rise through the stems and tender new growth develops. When frigid temperatures return, the sap in the limbs freezes and the bark splits. In addition, any new growth freezes. Remove severely damaged stems or branches. Protect your shrubs from exposure to wind, and spray with an antitranspirant in fall when freezing begins to set in. Avoid fertilizing in fall, to discourage a growth spurt.

# MOST COMMON INSECT PESTS

## Dark Blotches on Leaves

### Leafminers

The boxwood leafminer (*Monarthropalpus buxi*) is the most serious insect enemy of boxwoods in the United States. This pest weakens shrubs by feeding on leaves. Foliage turns yellowish, new growth is stunted, and twigs may die. It's the larvae that are to be feared. These ⅛-inch-long yellowish maggots burrow between the upper and lower surfaces of leaves, where they feed on plant tissue. Oval, water-soaked swellings appear on the undersides of leaves. You can often see the maggots inside these swellings. Leaves may later blister or curl, turn brown, and die. The adults are small two-winged flies (midges), which emerge in April or May, mate within 24 hours, lay eggs, and die.

Trim and destroy the infested leaves as soon as you discover them. Rake up and destroy any fallen leaves. In early spring, prune back succulent new growth, especially water sprouts, which are vulnerable to attack. If damage is severe, prune back branches to healthy tissue. When the adult midges emerge (about the time the weigelas are in full bloom) spray your boxwoods with an insecticidal soap solution. Repeated applications two or three days apart may help control this pest.

## Cottony Masses on Shrub; Shrub Grows Poorly

### Mealybugs

Boxwoods infested with mealybugs tend to look unsightly, do not grow well, and may die if heavily infested. The insects gather in cottony white masses on boxwood roots, stems, branches, and leaves. They suck sap from the plant, thus reducing its vigor. As they feed, they secrete honeydew, which encourages the growth of mold and attracts ants. The comstock mealybug (*Pseudococcus comstocki*) is one of two mealybugs that attacks boxwoods. This is one of the few insect species that can withstand exposure to harsh winters. It is a small (⅕ to ⅓ inch), flattened, oval, waxy insect, with short, soft spines around its edges. After hatching in late May, the young crawl up the trunk to the leaves, where they suck out the juices and debilitate the shrub. The telltale cottony tufts they build contain eggs. The ground mealybug or root mealybug (*Rhizoecus falcifer*) feeds on the roots of boxwood. It produces the same symptoms in boxwoods as the comstock mealybug.

Control mealybugs by spraying them with an alcohol-based spray every two to three days until they are gone. Make this spray from 1 cup isopropyl alcohol and ½ teaspoon Volck oil in 1 quart water. You can substitute 1 tablespoon insecticidal soap concentrate for the Volck oil and get equally effective results. In late winter or early spring, spray your boxwoods with dormant oil to smother overwintering adults and eggs.

## Leaves Bronzed

### Mites

Watch the lowest leaves on your boxwoods for mites. When they attack, the leaves become bronzed or grayish, wither, and sometimes drop to the ground, leaving the plant looking scraggly. Boxwood mites (*Eurytetranychus buxi*) are about $\frac{1}{64}$ inch long when full grown and are yellow-green to reddish brown in color. Eggs hatch in April, and the young mites immediately begin to suck the juices of boxwood leaves. By June or July, considerable damage may have been done.

Start control measures as soon as you notice the first discoloration of the lower leaves. Spray infested shrubs in the early morning with a forceful stream of water to knock the mites from leaf undersides. Repeat this for three days. If mites are still present, use insecticidal soap, spraying every three to five days for two weeks. In late winter or early spring, spray susceptible plants with light horticultural oil, before growth starts. This spray will destroy many overwintering mites.

## Leaves Bronzed; Growth Stunted; Lack of Vigor

### Nematodes

Southern root knot nematodes (*Meloidogyne incognita*), ring nematodes (*Criconema* spp.), spiral nematodes (*Helicotylenchus* spp.), and meadow nematodes (*Pratylenchus pratensis*) attack boxwoods. The leaves of infested shrubs turn bronze, growth becomes stunted, and the general vigor of the plant declines. Nematodes attack at the roots, so you won't find these pests crawling on leaves or along branches. The roots develop galls and die. As new roots form, they, too, become infested. Eventually the entire root system becomes stunted. Even heavy rains may fail to wet the densely woven, witches'-broom-like root-bundles. The effects of nematode

activity are most apparent in hot weather, when the plants recover poorly from the heat.

Most nematodes are barely visible to the unaided eye, being $\frac{1}{50}$ to $\frac{1}{10}$ inch long, but if you could see them, you'd find they are whitish, translucent, wormlike creatures. Add lots of compost, especially leaf mold, to the soil around boxwoods to encourage beneficial fungi. Water infested plants thoroughly during dry spells. Fertilize with liquid fish emulsion by pouring it into the soil as a drench; it repels nematodes and will encourage root growth.

## Leaves Yellowed

### Psyllids

Psyllids are also commonly known as jumping plant lice. They are about $\frac{1}{10}$ inch long and look like tiny cicadas covered with whitish waxy filaments. They suck the juices of leaves, which causes discoloration and cupping. Boxwood psyllids (*Psylla buxi*), laurel psyllids (*Trioza alacris*), willow psyllids (*T. maura*), and other species attack boxwoods. Control them by spraying infested shrubs with insecticidal soap every three to five days for two weeks. In late winter or early spring, apply dormant oil to smother overwintering adults, larvae, and eggs.

## Leaves and Twigs Bound with Webbing

### Webworms

Boxwood webworms (*Galasa nigrinodis*) build nests in shrubs by binding together foliage and twigs with webs. They reside in these nests while they feed on your shrubs.

The full-grown webworm is a yellow-green caterpillar, about 1 inch long, whose back and sides are covered with numerous black spots. You can remove the nests and destroy them, but to control webworms more effectively, spray with Bt (*Bacillus thuringiensis*) as soon as you spot small caterpillars out on the leaves feeding. Apply Bt three times over a three-week period. If webworms are still a problem, use pyrethrum. Make two applications, three to four days apart.

# MOST COMMON DISEASES

## Leaves and Twigs Die Back

### Blight

If the leaves and twigs of your boxwoods are dying, your plants might have blight. This disease can be caused by the fungi *Phoma conidiogena* or *Hyponectria buxi*. Prune and destroy the infected branches and spray the entire shrub with a copper fungicide or lime sulfur. Make four applications: first, after you have removed dead leaves and branches and before plant growth starts in the spring; second, when spring growth is half completed; third, once spring growth is complete; and fourth, after fall growth stops.

## Leaves Pale; Lesions on Leaves and Stems

### Canker

The fungus *Pseudonectria rousseliana* causes a serious canker disease in boxwoods. The foliage on infected boxwoods turns light green, then tan, and then curls upward, lying close to the stem rather than spreading out. You will find small, rose-colored, waxy pustules on the leaves of your plants. Bark at the base of the branches peels off readily, and you will notice that the wood underneath is discolored. Infected shrubs may delay their production of new growth in the spring and when new shoots and foliage do appear, they may be smaller and weaker than usual.

Remove any dead branches and leaves as soon as you notice them. Spray your boxwoods with a copper fungicide or lime sulfur. Make four applications: the first, after you have removed the dead leaves and dying branches and before plant growth starts in the spring; the second, when spring growth is half complete; the third, after spring growth is complete; and the fourth, after fall growth is complete. Proper watering and fertilizing of your shrubs will keep them healthy, and they will be more resistant to disease.

## Leaves Turn Yellow and Fall Prematurely; Branches Die

### Leaf Spot

Several different fungi are responsible for causing leaf spot in boxwoods. These include *Macrophoma candollei, Phyllosticta auerswaldii, Fusarium buxicola,* and members of the *Collectotrichum* spp. The leaves of infected shrubs turn yellow or brown and may be spotted with small black fruiting bodies. These diseases usually strike plants already weakened by some other disease or injury.

The fungus *Macrophoma candollei* can cause branches to die, especially following winter injury or on shrubs growing in poorly drained soil. In spring, infected foliage changes from dark green to gray-green or bronze and then to a yellowish straw color. New shoots are weak, and old leaves drop prematurely. Entire branches die, especially in the middle or top of the plant. Sunken areas or cankers may appear on the trunk just above the soil line or in crotches where dead leaves and debris accumulate.

Control leaf spot by shaking all fallen and diseased leaves from the bush and destroying them. Prune and destroy dead branches in the center of the bush to allow better aeration. Prune severely diseased branches back to healthy wood several inches below the cankers. Paint all wounds with shellac and, when they dry, cover them with tree paint. In the spring, apply copper fungicide before growth starts. This spray will discolor the foliage but new leaves will soon hide the damaged ones. Enrich the soil and ensure good drainage to maintain the vigor of your boxwoods.

## Shrub Wilted

### Root Rot

The symptoms of root rot appear in the leaves. The foliage becomes dull, wilts, and loses color. The *Phytophthora* fungus is responsible for root rot in boxwoods. Infected plants cannot be saved. Remove them and destroy them. Before you replant that site, solarize the soil. You can try to prevent root rot with careful soil preparation, good drainage, and by planting shrubs at the proper depth.

# SHRUB *Euonymus* *Euonymus* spp.

## DESCRIPTION

Noted for their showy fruits and evergreen foliage, the shrubs, vines, and trees in this genus, sometimes called the spindletrees, are highly prized in the yard and garden landscape. Wintercreeper (*Euonymus fortunei*) is an evergreen vine or prostrate shrub that is tough and ubiquitous in North America, except the desert. It is often used as a ground cover, but can climb to 20 feet or more. When well established, it forms a dense mass that weeds cannot penetrate. Both evergreen and deciduous forms of euonymus are serviceable as hedges and specimens. All add interest and color to the landscape.

### Height

European spindletree (*E. europaea*), 20 feet

Evergreen euonymus (*E. japonica*), 15 feet

Spreading euonymus (*E. kiautschovica*), 6 to 10 feet

Winged euonymus (*E. alata*), 9 feet

Wintercreeper (*E. fortunei*, vine or ground cover), 2 feet; to 20 feet, with support

### Spread

European spindletree, 20 feet

Evergreen euonymus, 12 feet

Winged euonymus, 13 feet

Wintercreeper, 10 feet

### Blossoms

Euonymus have greenish, white, or yellowish inconspicuous flowers that bloom in the spring. The fruit appears in midsummer and lasts to frost time. Most euonymus produce small pink to red hanging fruit.

### Foliage

Euonymus are evergreen or deciduous, with opposite, stalked leaves that are nearly always smooth. Most species have green foliage, but some are variegated. The leaves of the winged euonymus turn red in the fall. Some varieties of wintercreeper turn purplish, including the cultivar 'Coloratus'.

## ENVIRONMENT

### Varieties by Zone

Zones 3 or 4 to zone 8, winged euonymus

Zone 5 to zone 9, wintercreeper and wahoo (*E. atropurpurea)*

Zone 7 to zone 9, evergreen euonymus and spreading euonymus

## Light Requirements

Most euonymus tolerate a wide range of light conditions, from full sun to very deep shade; however, variegated forms may lose their variegation if located in the shade.

## Soil Requirements

Euonymus do well in most any soil. Wintercreeper and evergreen euonymus tolerate all soils with a pH range of 6 to 7.5. The European spindletree prefers an alkaline soil (7 to 7.8).

# PLANTING AND PROPAGATION

## Planting

Euonymus can be planted in the spring or fall, but fall is the best time if you have a choice. Plant euonymus so that the root ball fits snugly into the hole while being even with the surface of the soil.

## Propagation

Propagate euonymus from softwood or semi-hardwood cuttings taken in the spring.

# PLANT MANAGEMENT

## Water Requirements

Euonymus need about 1 inch of water each week, with an increase to 1½ inches a week during the hot summer months. From late August to mid-October, judiciously refrain from watering to discourage excessive fall growth that might be susceptible to winterkill. Resume normal watering in the late fall. Soak all shrubs well before the ground freezes solid. Euonymus have relatively shallow root systems and can suffer moisture deficiency in the late winter without that last good drenching before the hard freeze sets in.

## Feeding Requirements

In the fall, apply compost to the soil around your shrubs. A spring application of 1 inch of compost ensures good growing conditions.

## Pruning

Euonymus needs no pruning to maintain its attractive appearance in the landscape. Specimens that grow too large can be pruned in winter, when they are dormant.

# MOST COMMON CULTURAL PROBLEMS

## Foliage Damaged in Winter

### Wind Chill Effect

A very severe wind chill may damage the foliage during winter, but the shrub usually regenerates itself the following spring. Some variegated forms, especially the golden varieties, may revert to green if they experience a severe wind chill. This problem can be controlled somewhat by pruning the plant in the late fall and surrounding it with some kind of protective material such as burlap or agricultural fleece. If this is an annual problem, move the plant to a more protected location.

# MOST COMMON INSECT PESTS

Many of the euonymus shrubs attract ladybugs and serve as an excellent nectar plant for other beneficials as well.

## Leaves Yellowed and Curled

### Aphids

Aphids suck juices from the leaves and stems of euonymus, causing the foliage to curl, pucker, and yellow. Eventually, the plant loses its vigor. You may find ants wandering over infested shrubs. They are attracted to the honeydew secreted by aphids. If you suspect an aphid infestation, check the undersides of leaves for these pests. They have soft, pear-shaped bodies, not much bigger than the head of a pin. Depending on the species, they may be green, brown, black, or pinkish. Euonymus are vulnerable to bean (*Aphis fabae*), green peach (*Myzus persicae*), and ivy (*Aphis hederae*) aphids.

You can easily control light infestations simply by spraying the undersides of leaves vigorously with water to knock the pests off. Do this early in the morning, three times, once every other day. If aphids are still present, spray your shrubs with insecticidal soap every two to three days until the pests are gone. As a last resort, use pyrethrum. Make two applications, three to four days apart.

## Small Bumps on Branches; Cottony Masses on Twigs

### . Scale

Euonymus are bothered by many different scale insects, including greedy scale (*Hemiberlesia rapax*) and San Jose scale (*Quadraspitiotus perniciosus*); however, the euonymus scale (*Unaspis euonymi*), is perhaps the most serious pest, often killing entire branches. All scale insects have a convex covering, which protects them while they feed and gives them the appearance of small bumps on branches and leaves. The female euonymus scale are dark brown and shaped like oyster shells; the males are smaller, narrower, and whitish. Both are just a bit bigger than the head of a pin. These pests cover leaves and stem tips. You may also find black sooty mold on the leaves and branches. It grows on the honeydew secreted by scale insects. Wintercreeper, the climber, is extremely susceptible to scale, and the winged euonymus is least susceptible.

If you find only a small number of scale on your shrubs, simply scrape them off with your fingernail or with a cotton swab dipped in rubbing alcohol. To control heavy infestations, cut and destroy all infested and injured branches; then spray the plants with a mixture of alcohol and insecticidal soap every three days for two weeks. To make this spray, mix 1 cup isopropyl alcohol and 1 tablespoon commercial insecticidal soap concentrate in 1 quart water. If you already have insecticidal soap mixed with water, add 1 tablespoon alcohol to a pint of this diluted soap. In late winter or early spring, spray susceptible plants with light horticultural oil, before growth starts.

## Leaves Flecked and Whitened

### Thrips

Thrips (*Heliothrips haemorrhoidalis*) are not common pests of euonymus, but when they do attack, they rasp at leaf surfaces to break plant cells and feed on the juice. As a result, leaves become flecked and whitened. The tips wither, curl, and die. If you turn leaves over, you'll find the tiny black specks of excrement. Adult thrips are tiny, slender insects, $1/25$ inch long, and colored pale yellowish, black, or brown.

Since thrips burrow into leaves, early identification and control is necessary. Set out yellow sticky traps and apply a spray of insecticidal soap every three days for two weeks. Commercially available predatory mites, lacewings, ladybugs, and beneficial nematodes are effective backups to the soap spray.

# MOST COMMON DISEASES

## Sunken Spots on Leaves

### Anthracnose

Anthracnose (*Colletotrichum* spp. and *Gloeosporium* spp.) shows up on euonymus leaves as moist, sunken spots with fruiting bodies growing in the center. These spots may run together, resembling a blotch or blight. The dead areas follow along the veins. This disease can progress down terminal shoots to several inches below the buds. Pustules containing pinkish spores develop on the lesions. In severe cases, dieback and defoliation may occur.

Gather and destroy diseased leaves when they fall, and cut off any diseased branches. Spray the entire shrub with a copper fungicide such as Bordeaux mixture. Maintain plant vigor by feeding and watering well, especially during droughts.

## Tumorlike Swellings on Roots, Trunk, or Branches

### Crown Gall

The bacterium *Agrobacterium tumefaciens* infects euonymus through wounds and stimulates the production of cells, which form tumorlike swellings, or galls, with irregular rough surfaces on roots and stems. If only a few galls are present, cut off and destroy the affected stems. Sterilize pruning shears afterward in 70 percent denatured alcohol to prevent the spread of the disease. Destroy heavily infected plants.

## Leaves Become Spotted, Turn Brown, and Fall Prematurely

### Leaf Spot

Leaf spot diseases come in all sizes and colors and may be caused by any one of a number of fungi:

*Cercospora* spp., *Exosporium* spp., *Phyllosticta* spp., *Septoria* spp., and others. Spots may be yellow, brown, or black. Often they merge to form larger patches of dead tissue. Gathering and destroying fallen leaves usually provides sufficient control. If the disease continues to spread, spray with a copper fungicide, making several applications at weekly intervals until the disease is controlled.

## White Powder on Leaves

### Powdery Mildew

The distinguishing mark of this disease is a thin, powdery, whitish coating that covers leaves. The fungi responsible for producing it are *Oidium euonymijaponici* and *Microsphaera alni*. Powdery mildew is more common in euonymus grown in southern states and along the Pacific coast.

As soon as you see the whitish coating creeping across the foliage of your shrubs, spray them thoroughly with wettable sulfur once or twice at weekly intervals. Collect and destroy all plant debris around euonymus in the fall.

# SHRUB **Firethorn** *Pyracantha* spp.

## DESCRIPTION

As the name suggests, the firethorns are exciting landscape plants with their fine foliage, thorns, and bright red or orange berries. This genus is a small group of Asiatic evergreen shrubs, which are closely related to cotoneasters and hawthorns. The scarlet firethorn (*Pyracantha coccinea*) can be trained against a wall as an espaliered plant.

### Height

Chinese firethorn (*P. fortuneana*), 10 to 15 feet

Formosa firethorn (*P. koidzumii*), 10 to 12 feet
Scarlet firethorn (*P. coccinea*), 6 to 15 feet

### Spread

10 feet for all species

### Blossoms

The white, musty-scented flowers bloom in good-sized clusters in early spring. Bright red or orange berries are produced in the fall and last through most of the winter.

## Foliage

Firethorn is an evergreen with oval leaves, 1 to 3 inches long. Some species, such as the scarlet firethorn, have leaves that are long and toothed, while other varieties have leaves that have smooth edges.

# ENVIRONMENT

## Varieties by Zone

To zone 2, alder firethorn (*P. frangula*) and dahurian firethorn (*P. davurica*)

To zone 4, scarlet firethorn ('Mohave', 'Teton')
To zone 6, Chinese firethorn ('Graberi', 'Rosedale')
To zone 8, formosa firethorn

## Light Requirements

Firethorns grow best in full sun, but will tolerate deep shade. They produce fewer berries in the deep shade and their form tends to be more open.

## Soil Requirements

Firethorns grow well in most soils, but prefer an average, well-drained soil, and the soil pH should be between 6 and 7. Firethorns become distressed in very alkaline soils with a pH above 7.5.

# PLANTING AND PROPAGATION

## Planting

You can plant balled-and-burlapped or container-grown firethorns in the spring or fall, but fall is best if you have a choice.

## Propagation

Propagate firethorns from semiripe cuttings taken in early summer.

# PLANT MANAGEMENT

## Water Requirements

Firethorns need about 1 inch of water each week, with an increase to 1½ inches a week during hot summer months. Don't water your plants from late August to mid-October. This discourages excessive fall growth, which might be susceptible to winterkill. Resume watering in late fall and soak the ground well before it freezes. Firethorns have fairly shallow root systems, which will not be able to take up water from the frozen earth, and they may suffer moisture deficiency in the late winter.

## Feeding Requirements

You only need to feed firethorns once a year, applying compost in the spring or the fall. However, your firethorns will look best if you spray them once a month for three months after the last frost with a dilute liquid fertilizer mixed with dilute seaweed extract. Stop all fertilizing two months before the first expected frost in your area to encourage hardening off for winter. If you live in a frost-free region, you can continue feeding firethorns year round.

## Pruning

Firethorns don't require pruning, but some gardeners like to shape their shrubs somewhat. If you want to prune your firethorns, the best time is in late winter or early spring. Firethorn needs good air circulation to avoid blight and scab.

## Winterizing

Winter winds can damage firethorns. If you live in an area where winters are particularly harsh or if your shrubs are located in a very open windy area, set up wind barriers around your plants to protect them.

# MOST COMMON INSECT PESTS

## Pale or Yellow Spots on Leaves

### Aphids

Firethorns are vulnerable to both the foxglove aphid (*Acyrthosiphon solani*) and the apple aphid (*Aphis pomi*). These pests feed on leaves, sucking out the juices. Pale or yellow spots develop and the leaves eventually become distorted. You may find ants crawling over infested shrubs; they are attracted by the honeydew that aphids secrete. If you suspect aphids, look for small groups of them on leaf undersides. Just a little bigger than the head of a pin, they have soft, pear-shaped bodies and may be green, brown, black, or pinkish.

Light infestations can easily be washed away simply by spraying shrubs vigorously with water. Do this in the morning three times, once every other day. For medium to heavy infestations, spray with insecticidal soap every two to three days. As a last resort, use pyrethrum. Make two applications, three to four days apart.

## Leaves Pale or Mottled

### Lace Bugs

Like aphids, hawthorn lace bugs (*Corythucha cydoniae*) suck sap from the undersides of firethorn leaves, causing the foliage to turn pale or mottled. Adult lace bugs are square-shaped bugs, 3/16 inch long or less, with elaborately reticulated wings that resemble lacework. In the South, they appear as early as April and continue feeding through autumn.

If only a few of these pests have found your firethorns, simply pick them off and crush them. Control larger infestations by spraying the undersides of leaves with insecticidal soap, nicotine spray, or pyrethrum spray. Make three applications, once every three to five days.

## Holes in Flowers; Leaves Rolled and Bound with Silk Strands

### Leaf Rollers

If you find holes in the flowers of your firethorns, suspect leaf rollers. The caterpillars gorge themselves on flower buds and foliage, often skeletonizing leaves, which turn brown and drop in late summer. After they've had their fill, they roll themselves up in leaves and bind them shut with strands of silk. There, they pupate.

Leaf rollers are caterpillars of various moths that gorge themselves on foliage and then pupate within the protection of rolled up leaves. Adult are brown or gray moths, ¼ to ½ inch long. The larvae are dark to light green or cream to yellow, ⅜ to 1¾ inches long. In many cases, two generations of this pest occur every year—one in spring and the other in late summer.

If only a few leaf rollers have found your shrubs, simply crush them; otherwise, spray infested shrubs with Bt (*Bacillus thuringiensis*) two or three times at three- to five-day intervals until the pests are gone. If leaf rollers attack your shrubs year after year, begin spraying with Bt before you expect the caterpillars to begin feeding.

## Leaves Stippled, Puckered, and Distorted

### Mites

Watch the lowest leaves on your firethorn plants for mites. The foliage of infested plants becomes stippled with small yellow or red spots and often becomes puckered. You may see a fine webbing stretching over leaves and branches.

Mites are only about $1/50$ inch long, barely visible to the unaided eye. They may be yellow, green, red, or brown. Start control measures as soon as you notice the first stippling on the leaves. Spray the plants in the early morning with a forceful stream of water to knock mites from leaf undersides. Repeat this daily for three days. If mites continue to be a problem, spray with insecticidal soap every three to five days for two weeks.

## Leaves Yellowed; Small Bumps on Leaves and Stems

### Scale

The first sign of scale attack on firethorns is yellowing of the upper surfaces of leaves, followed by leaf drop, reduced growth, and stunted shrubs. Heavy infestations can kill plants. Some scale species excrete honeydew, which attracts ants and encourages the growth of sooty mold. Firethorns are vulnerable to greedy scale (*Hemiberlesia rapax*) and olive scale (*Parlatoria oleae*). Aptly named, scale insects look like small rounded bumps when you find them on plants. They have waxy convex coverings that protect them as they feed. They may be colored white, yellow, or brown to black, and are about $1/10$ to $2/5$ inch in diameter.

If you catch the infestation early on, you can simply scrape scale off leaves and branches with your fingernail or a cotton swab dipped in rubbing alcohol. If the number of insects is large enough that this task seems formidable, spray shrubs with a mixture of alcohol and insecticidal soap every three days for two weeks. To make this solution, mix 1 cup isopropyl alcohol and 1 tablespoon commercial insecticidal soap concentrate in 1 quart water. If your insecticidal soap is already diluted with water, simply add 1 tablespoon alcohol to a pint of the soap solution. In late winter or early spring, smother overwintering adults and eggs.

## Holes in Leaves and Stems; Leaves and Branches Bound with Webbing

### Webworms

Webworms are a major pest of firethorns, particularly in the southwestern United States. They eat holes in the leaves and stems of these shrubs. The full-grown webworm is a yellow-green caterpillar, about 1 inch long, whose back and sides are covered with numerous black spots. It protects itself inside a thin silken web that it spins about the host shrub, webbing together both leaves and twigs.

Handpick the nests of webworms and destroy them, and spray shrubs with Bt (*Bacillus thuringiensis*) three times at three- to five-day intervals. For very heavy infestations that might not be controlled by Bt, try a spray or dust of pyrethrum, applied twice, with a two- to three-day interval.

## MOST COMMON DISEASES

## Leaves Die

### Blight

Sometimes a blight fungus infects firethorns, killing all the foliage. There is no control. Remove and destroy affected shrubs.

## Flowers and Shoots Wilt Suddenly in Spring

### Fire Blight

Fire blight is caused by the bacterium *Erwinia amylovora*, which insects and rain transmit to plants.

The new shoots of infected shrubs wilt suddenly in late spring, turn black or brown, and eventually die.

Between November and March, cut diseased branches to at least 3 inches below the affected area. When a fourth of the blossoms are open, spray the entire shrub with an antibiotic such as Agri-Strep, repeating this every five to ten days during bloom. Destroy any nearby diseased and neglected pear, quince, or apple trees, since they, too, harbor the fire blight organism. *P. coccinea* var. *lalandii* and *P. fortuneana* are both resistant to fire blight.

## Scabby Lesions on Leaves and Fruit

### Scab

The fungus *Fusicladium pyracanthae* infects fire-thorns, causing dark, scabby blotches to develop on the leaves and berries. The foliage turns yellow and then brown as the disease progresses, and eventually the leaves drop to the ground. The best way to control scab is with proper watering and fertilizing. Healthy firethorns show good resistance to this disease and are better able to fight off any infection that might occur. Spray with a copper fungicide in spring when buds break, and repeat twice, ten days apart.

SHRUB # Forsythia *Forsythia* spp.

## DESCRIPTION

Of spring-blooming plants, forsythias make one of the boldest statements of spring's arrival, with their flamboyant flowing branches covered with bright yellow blossoms. These shrubs are of Asiatic origin and were introduced to North America about 100 years ago. They belong to the olive family. Forsythias bloom just prior to the emergence of leaves, and their branches have an arching or spreading habit. Forsythias look spectacular when massed in hedges or clumps against an evergreen background and make good landscape plants for cities because they tolerate the urban environment better than most decorative shrubs. The Korean forsythia (*Forsythia ovata*) is the hardiest and earliest to bloom. The border forsythia (*F. ×intermedia*) produces the most flowers. If given proper care, a forsythia can live for 50 to 60 years.

### Height

Border forsythia (*F. ×intermedia*), 10 feet

Bronx greenstem forsythia (*F. viridissima* 'Bronxensis'), 2 feet

Korean forsythia (*F. ovata*), 4 feet

Weeping forsythia (*F. suspensa*), 10 feet

### Spread

6 to 12 feet for all species

### Blossoms

Forsythias produce lemon yellow to golden yellow flowers, which appear in early to mid-spring. Some forsythias, such as the cultivar 'Arnold Dwarf', have small greenish yellow blossoms and are not planted for their blossoms, but instead are used as woody ground covers.

## Foliage

Deciduous shrubs, forsythias have green, oval-oblong, toothed leaves, which are opposite each other on the stem.

# ENVIRONMENT

## Varieties by Zone

To zone 5, border forsythia, Bronx greenstem forsythia, Korean forsythia, and weeping forsythia.

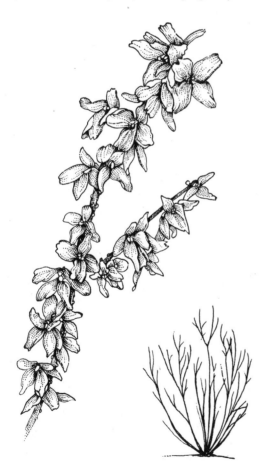

## Light Requirements

Forsythias grow well in full sun to light shade, but bloom best in full sun.

## Soil Requirements

Few shrubs are as forgiving of such a wide variety of soil conditions as the forsythia. It tolerates almost anything except poor drainage, and prefers a range in pH from 6 to 7.5.

# PLANTING AND PROPAGATION

## Planting

You can plant balled-and-burlapped, bare-root, or container-grown forsythias in the early fall or late spring, but fall is best if you have a choice. Forsythias grow vigorously, so allow room for them to expand. If you are creating a border for a lawn or walkway, plant them 8 to 10 feet from the edge.

## Propagation

Propagate forsythias from semiripe cuttings. Forsythias root themselves where the ends of their arching branches touch the ground, so they are good candidates for propagation by layering as well.

## Container Gardening

Forsythias can be grown in containers. Use one with a 5- to 10-gallon capacity.

# PLANT MANAGEMENT

## Water Requirements

Like most shrubs, forsythias need about an inch of water each week, with an increase to 1½ inches a week during hot summer months. Stop watering from late August to mid-October to discourage excessive fall growth, which might be susceptible to winterkill. Resume watering in late fall and soak the ground well before it freezes solid. With their shallow root systems, shrubs can suffer from moisture deficiency in the late winter without a last good drenching before the first hard freeze.

## Feeding Requirements

Forsythias need only one application of compost in the spring or the fall; however, they will also benefit from monthly sprays of dilute liquid fertilizer mixed with dilute seaweed extract. Apply this in spring during the first three months after the last frost. In fall, encourage hardening off for winter by stopping any feeding two months before first frost.

## Pruning

Prune forsythias very soon after they flower, otherwise you are likely to cut off next year's buds. Take out dead canes and those that are more than three years old from the center of the clump. Prune them to ground level. Forsythias have a graceful arching natural habit, so do not attempt formal shearing. You can cut them into hedges, but you sacrifice heavy flowering if you do so.

If your shrubs have become overgrown due to neglect, prune them ruthlessly to within 6 inches of the ground. Similarly, cut old, overgrown bushes back to the ground to rejuvenate them. Your shrubs will recover, although the following year's bloom may not be as full as usual.

## MOST COMMON INSECT PESTS

### Yellow Stippling on Leaves; Leaves Puckered

#### Mites

Spider mites attack the lowest leaves on shrubs first. Their feeding leaves foliage stippled with small yellow dots or red spots. Leaves, their stalks, and adjacent stems may be distorted or swathed in fine webbing. The culprit, the two-spotted spider mite (*Tetranychus telarius*), is about $1/50$ inch long, barely visible to the unaided eye. It may be yellow, green, red, or brown.

Start control measures as soon as you notice the first stippling on the forsythia leaves. Spray the plants in the early morning with a forceful water spray to knock the mites from the leaf undersides. Repeat the water spray daily for three days. If that does not do the job, spray with insecticidal soap every three to five days for two weeks.

## Plant Sickly

#### Nematodes

A forsythia infested with nematodes looks sickly, wilted, or stunted. Its foliage turns yellow or bronze, and it declines slowly and dies. Nematodes dwell in the soil and feed on the roots of plants. If you were to take a look at the root system of an infested forsythia, you would find it to be poorly developed, disfigured by galls, and even partially decayed. The effects of nematode activity are most apparent in hot weather, when the plants recover poorly from the heat. Northern root knot nematodes (*Meloidogyne hapla*) attack forsythia. They are whitish, translucent, wormlike creatures, anywhere from $1/50$ to $1/10$ inch long.

Add lots of compost, especially leaf mold, to the soil around infested plants to encourage beneficial fungi. Fertilize with liquid fish emulsion, applying it as a drench. Fish emulsion repels nematodes.

## Holes in Leaves

#### Weevils

If you find holes in the leaves of your forsythias, Japanese weevils (*Pseudocneorhinus bifasciatus*) are probably at work. They feed during the day along the edges of leaves, sometimes eating them down to the bare ribs and veins. These beetles are about ¼ inch long and may be light to dark brown, with striated wing covers. They usually have a tear-shaped, hard-shelled body. They are sometimes called snout beetles because their heads are elongated into a long, slender, downward-curved snout, at the end of which are the insect's mouth parts. They commonly live under tree bark or in other plant tissues. The grubs of weevils attack the roots of forsythia, and the damage they cause can endanger the life of a shrub.

Many weevil species play dead when disturbed, folding their legs and dropping off plants to the ground. Turn this trait to an advantage when controlling these pests. Spread a cloth beneath an infested forsythia; then gently beat the branches. The startled insects will drop onto the cloth; simply gather them up. Apply a sticky substance such as Tanglefoot around the base of the stem of the forsythia near the soil to prevent the adults from climbing up and eating the leaves. As soon as weevils appear, begin spraying shrubs weekly with pyrethrum mixed with isopropyl alcohol (mix 1 tablespoon alcohol with each pint of pyrethrum). Apply this solution at night, at least two hours after dark. Spray all leaf surfaces in order to get all the weevils that have not dropped to the ground.

## MOST COMMON DISEASES

### Tumorlike Swellings on Stems

#### Crown Gall
The bacterium *Agrobacterium tumefaciens* causes crown gall in forsythias. It infects these shrubs through wounds. Infected shrubs develop tumorlike

swellings, called galls, along the stems. A serious infection causes branches to die back. Prune and destroy all branches that bear galls.

### Flowers and Twigs Shriveled

#### Dieback
A dieback disease in forsythias is caused by the fungus *Sclerotinia sclerotiorum*. This fungus infects blossoms and flower stalks, then spreads to twigs, killing them. The fruiting bodies of this fungus are black and develop on the surface of or inside the infected twigs. Prune away and destroy all dead twigs and stems.

### Leaves Become Spotted, Turn Brown, and Fall Prematurely

#### Leaf Spot
Forsythias can become infected with any one of several leaf spot fungi, including members of the *Alternaria* spp., *Phyllosticta* spp., and others. You may find yellow or black dead blotches on the leaves. Often spots come together to form larger patches of dead tissue. Gathering and destroying fallen leaves usually controls this disease. If it doesn't, spray with a copper fungicide two or three times at weekly intervals.

SHRUB **Holly** *Ilex* spp.

## DESCRIPTION

Hollies conjure up thoughts of Christmas and seasonal decorations, but these festive shrubs and trees beautify the landscape outside your home as well as the rooms inside your home. About 400 species of holly are known and can be found in both temperate and tropical regions of the world. Hollies have attractive leaves, bright berries, and pleasant shapes. Most

are slow-growing evergreens. There are some deciduous kinds of holly, which are easy to grow and transplant. You can prune hollies into hedges, let them grow freely, or train them to be espalier, topiary, or bonsai plants. Some varieties can be used as screens, foundation plantings, edges, or specimens. The sexes of most hollies are borne on separate plants, so male and female plants must be located near each other to ensure the production of berries.

English holly (*Ilex aquifolium*) and American holly (*I. opaca*) are widely grown. At first glance, they appear to be very similar, but English holly has glossier leaves and bears its fruit on the current year's growth. Common winterberry (*I. verticillata*) is deciduous and produces more fruit than any other holly, fruit that lasts almost all winter. If you are looking for a plant with dark blue-green leaves, consider one of the blue hollies, such as 'Blue Princess' (*I. ×meserveae*). Blue hollies are the best evergreen shrub

hollies for northern areas, where they grow well with little care. Japanese holly (*I. crenata*) is a boxwood-like plant and produces unusual black berries.

## Height

American holly (*I. opaca*, evergreen), 15 to 50 feet
Chinese holly (*I. cornuta*, evergreen), 8 to 15 feet
English holly (*I. aquifolium*, evergreen), 10 to 70 feet
Inkberry (*I. glabra*, evergreen), 3 to 10 feet
Japanese holly (*I. crenata*, evergreen), 5 to 15 feet
Meserve holly (*I. ×meserveae*, evergreen), 8 to 12 feet
Possum haw (*I. decidua*, deciduous), 10 to 30 feet
Winterberry (*I. verticillata*, deciduous), 5 to 15 feet

## Spread

Blue holly, 12 feet
English holly, 12 feet
Japanese holly, 5 feet
Winterberry, 13 feet

## Blossoms

Most hollies produce inconspicuous white or greenish flowers in late spring or early summer. Male and female flowers appear on separate plants. The berries appear in fall and are either red or black.

## Foliage

Most hollies are evergreen, but some are deciduous. The leaves are borne alternately on the stem. Evergreen varieties have spiny, stiff foliage. Colors range from green to dark green to blue-green, depending on the variety, and undersides are usually paler than the upper surfaces. Some variegated hollies include *I. aquifolium* 'Argenteo Marginata', *I. aquifolium* 'Golden Milkboy', *I. aquifolium* 'Silver Milkboy', *I. aquifolium* 'Ferox Argentea', and *I. crenata* 'Aureovariegata'.

## ENVIRONMENT

### Hardiness

Most evergreen hollies are hardy to at least −5°F; deciduous species are generally hardier. English holly requires a moist atmosphere and won't survive hot, dry conditions. It is best grown on the Eastern Seaboard or in the Pacific Northwest.

### Varieties by Zone

Zone 3 to zone 9, inkberry and winterberry
To zone 5, blue hollies and possum haw
To zone 6, American holly
To zone 7, Chinese holly and English holly

### Light Requirements

Evergreen hollies can be grown in full sun to medium shade. The deciduous hollies prefer partial shade.

### Soil Requirements

Hollies prefer well-drained loam that is fairly light and sandy. Many varieties will tolerate dry soil. As for pH, they will do well in a neutral to slightly acid environment (pH of 5.8 to 7). Winterberry likes an acid soil with a pH of 5 to 6.5.

Many hollies, especially the inkberry, tolerate urban conditions and can even withstand road salt splashed on them in winter.

## PLANTING AND PROPAGATION

### Planting

Remember, if you want your hollies to produce berries, plant male and female shrubs relatively close to each other—within several hundred feet is fine. One male per four or five females is a fine ratio.

As with most shrubs, you can plant root-balled or container-grown hollies in the early fall or late spring; however, fall is best. Locate your plant at a distance equal to half its mature spread from other permanent plants.

### Propagation

Propagate hollies from stem cuttings. Dip the cuttings in rooting hormones and plant them in sand. Deciduous hollies are difficult to propagate, which is one reason they are less commonly found in nurseries.

## PLANT MANAGEMENT

### Water Requirements

Hollies need about 1 inch of water each week until the hot summer months, when they do best with 1½ inches a week. From late August to mid-October, stop watering to discourage excessive fall growth that might be susceptible to winterkill. Resume watering in the late fall and soak the ground well before it freezes solid. Hollies have shallow root systems, which will not be able to take up water once the winter freeze has set in. As a result, they can suffer from moisture deficiency in the late winter.

### Feeding Requirements

Hollies need only one main feeding of compost in early spring or late fall, but they will benefit from a monthly spray of dilute liquid fertilizer mixed with dilute seaweed extract. Apply this spray just during the first three months after the last frost in spring. In cold climates, encourage hardening off for winter by stopping any feeding two months before first frost.

### Mulching

Hollies do best when they have a 2- to 4-inch layer of organic mulch over their roots all season long. Spread it to cover an area that begins 6 to 12 inches from the trunk and extends out beyond the tips of the branches. Mulch placed too near your shrubs encourages decay and rodent damage. Use chopped leaves, peat moss, pine needles, or wood chips. Do not use unchopped leaves because they mat together and prevent water from getting into the soil. For guaranteed weed control, first lay some geotextile mulch and then cover that with organic matter.

## Weeding

Mulching, as described on the preceding page, is the best way to control weeds around hollies. If you don't use mulch, be careful with weeding tools. The fibrous and shallow root systems of hollies are easily damaged when the soil around them is cultivated. To be safe, pull weeds by hand.

## Pruning

Hollies do not require pruning, but they can be cut if you want to train or shape the shrub. When pruning, cut back to a bud; new growth will appear and grow in the direction the bud is aiming. Many gardeners prefer to trim the bottom branches off trees to expose the trunk. Prune hollies when they are dormant. Christmas is an excellent time; then you can bring the trimmings indoors.

## Winterizing

Severe winter conditions can cause sunscald and purple spot on the leaves of evergreen hollies. Punctures occur when harsh winds blow the spiny leaves together and they poke holes in each other. To prevent this damage, erect a wind barrier around shrubs growing in an exposed location. Spray the leaves with an antitranspirant to protect them from the drying winter sun and wind.

# MOST COMMON CULTURAL PROBLEMS

## Leaves Turn Yellow or White

### Malnutrition

If hollies are underfed, the leaves will turn yellow or even white in the spring when the new growth starts and again in the late summer after berries have formed. Feed your shrubs properly as described on the preceding page.

# Plant Fails to Produce Berries

### Problems of Pollination

All hollies except the Chinese holly need pollination to produce berries. If your plant does not produce berries, the cause may be any of the following: the plant is male; it is too young; the plant is female but no male plant is nearby; flowers were injured by late spring frosts or cold; or rainy weather hindered the spread of pollen by insects.

# MOST COMMON INSECT PESTS

## Berries Do Not Turn Red

### Berry Midges

If the berries on your holly bushes do not turn red in the fall, your plants are probably infested by berry midges (*Asphondylia ilicicola*). The larvae sometimes infest holly berries and prevent them from ripening. Adults are two-winged flies, $\frac{1}{14}$ to $\frac{1}{8}$ inch long, with long legs and antennae.

If the infestation is light or only a few shrubs or trees are involved, handpick the insects and destroy infested berries. For heavier infestations, spray the whole plant with insecticidal soap. Some gardeners mix tobacco dust into the soil around the bases of plants to kill the larvae. In early spring, before new growth starts, apply dormant oil.

## Holes in Leaves

### Black Blister Beetles

A couple of pests could be responsible for the holes in the leaves of your hollies—the blister beetle, *Epicauta pennsylvanica,* is one of those pests. It only occasionally attacks hollies. The adult beetle is $\frac{1}{2}$ to $\frac{3}{4}$ inch long, slender, and entirely black. It has soft, flexible wing covers. The larvae don't bother plants at all; they feed on grasshopper eggs in the soil.

To control the adults, pick them off your shrubs and destroy them. Wear gloves, because a chemical in the beetles will blister skin if the insects are crushed. Apply beneficial nematodes to the soil to eliminate the larvae. For long-term control, add milky spore disease (*Bacillus popilliae*) to the soil.

### Japanese Beetles

Japanese beetles (*Popillia japonica*) occasionally attack the new foliage on hollies. They lay their eggs in the soil at the base of shrubs. Grubs hatch and feed on the roots and on the base of young stems. The adult beetles eat the foliage and can skeletonize holly leaves. They are ½ inch long, with shiny metallic green and brown wing covers. The larvae are grayish, with dark brown heads. Fully grown, they are plump, ¾ to 1 inch long, and lie in the soil in a distinctive arc-shaped resting posture.

Handpick the beetles from the holly plants and drop them into a pail of soapy water. Set up pheromone beetle traps, placing them no closer than 50 feet from the holly or any other plant vulnerable to beetle attack, such as azaleas and roses. Handpick stragglers not caught by the trap. If this doesn't control the infestation, spray your shrubs with a solution of pyrethrum and isopropyl alcohol twice, with a two- to three-day interval. To make this solution, mix 1 tablespoon alcohol with 1 pint pyrethrum mixture.

## Leaves Turn Brown

### Holly Bud Moths

The caterpillars of holly bud moths attack new foliage of hollies as leaves unfold in spring. They tie the leaves together with webs and feed on them, causing them to eventually turn brown or black. The holly bud moth (*Rhopobota naevana ilicifoliana*) has grayish wings mottled with brown. Its wingspan is ½ inch. It lays eggs in July and August on the leaves and twigs of hollies. The larvae, which hatch in the spring, are yellowish to greenish gray ½-inch-long caterpillars. Bud moths are serious pests of hollies in the Pacific Northwest.

Handpick any infested leaves, and clean up plant debris around the base of the tree or shrub. In late March of the following season, spray the undersides of holly leaves with a light horticultural oil before eggs hatch. Eliminate any caterpillars that do hatch by spraying with Bt (*Bacillus thuringiensis*). Make three applications ten days apart. The larvae

pupate in the leaves on the ground, so fallen leaves must be raked and destroyed.

## Leaves Mined

### Leafminers

Of all the insect pests that might attack your hollies, the only one to really worry about is the leafminer. Although the maggots begin feeding on leaves in June, leaf injury does not become evident until mid-August, when small, irregular, linear, serpentine ridges appear on the surfaces of leaves. Each irregular ridge indicates a maggot mining through leaf tissue beneath the surface. At first, the ridges are a darker green than the leaf itself. Later they take on a reddish or reddish brown tinge. By mid-September the mines increase in size, with one end shaped like a blotch. If left uncontrolled, eventually the entire upper surfaces of the leaves will be covered with coalesced mines, giving the leaves a blistered appearance.

The holly leafminer (*Phytomyza ilicis*) is a small, yellowish white maggot, ⅙ inch long. The adult is a small black fly, which emerges from the leaves in April or early May and makes slits in the lower leaf surfaces, where it deposits eggs. Another species that attacks hollies is the native leafminer (*P. ilicicola*). This insect chews very slender mines through leaves. It may occur on the same tree or shrub that holly leafminers have infested.

To control leafminers, remove and burn all infested leaves. If the infestation is severe, prune back branches to healthy tissue. Severely damaged bushes should be removed and destroyed. Adults may be repelled by several applications of insecticidal soap when they emerge. Spray three times on alternate days.

## Cottony Tufts on Shrub; Leaves Yellowish

### Mealybugs

The comstock mealybug (*Pseudococcus comstocki*) occasionally becomes a pest of hollies. These insects are ⅕ to ⅓ inch long, oval, and flattened. White waxy powder covers their bodies, and short soft spines protrude from the edges. They build cottony, tuftlike egg sacks, which can be seen on roots and branches. Honeydew secreted by the adult insects encourages the growth of mold and attracts ants. Mealybugs suck sap from plants. Leaves turn yellowish, and the entire plant eventually loses its vigor. A heavily infested plant may die.

To control mealybugs, make a solution from 1 cup isopropyl alcohol and ½ teaspoon Volck oil in 1 quart water. You can substitute 1 tablespoon insecticidal soap concentrate for the Volck oil. Spray this on shrubs every two to three days until the pests are gone. In late winter or early spring, just before new growth starts, apply dormant oil to kill overwintering eggs.

## Leaves Discolored and Deformed

### Mites

Watch the lowest leaves on your holly shrub. If mites discover your plants, the upper leaf surfaces will become stippled with small yellow dots or red spots. Leaves, stalks, and adjacent stems often become distorted or may be swathed in fine webbing. The southern red mite (*Oligonchus ilicis*) has become a serious pest of holly, and makes its attack in spring and fall. These mites are about ¹⁄₅₀ inch long, with piercing-sucking mouth parts. Not being true insects, they have four pairs of legs.

Spray your affected holly in the early morning with a forceful stream of water to knock mites from leaf undersides. Repeat this daily for three days. If mites are still a problem, spray with insecticidal soap every three to five days for two weeks. In late winter or early spring, before new growth starts, apply dormant oil to destroy overwintering mites.

## Tiny Holes in Leaves; Roots Damaged

### Potato Flea Beetles

Lots of tiny holes in holly leaves signal flea beetles. It's the potato flea beetle (*Epitrix cucumeris*) that specifically attacks hollies; fortunately, it is only an occasional pest. These insects can destroy small holly plants rapidly with their feeding. The adults

are ¹⁄₁₆ inch long, winged, shiny black, and jump like fleas when startled, hence their name. They lay their eggs near the bases of holly plants. These hatch in about 1 week, and the larvae feed on roots for two to three weeks before pupating and emerging as adults to attack foliage.

Spray infested shrubs with pyrethrum or rotenone every three to five days for two weeks. Use beneficial nematodes to control the larvae.

## Yellow Spots on Leaves; Small Bumps on Leaves and Branches

### Scale

Yellow spotting of the leaves on hollies is a symptom of scale infestation. In addition, you might find sooty mold growing on leaves where honeydew was secreted by the scale. Shrubs eventually lose their vigor. If you notice these symptoms, look for the pests themselves. Holly scale (*Dynaspidiotus britannicus*) usually gather on leaf undersides, but will also infest twigs and berries. They resemble small bumps, having a rounded covering, which protects them as they feed. The covering is oval, light brown to tan in color, and extremely small. The insect itself and its eggs are lemon yellow. These scale overwinter in a partially grown condition. They begin to feed in the latter part of March or early April, and lay eggs in June and July. Only one generation occurs each year. Although holly scale is most common, 11 other species of scale insects attack hollies. These include black, California red, greedy, holly, lecanium, oleander, oystershell, peach, pit-making, soft, and tea scale.

If you catch these pests before too many of them have gathered on your shrubs, simply scrape them off plant surfaces with your fingernail or a cotton swab dipped in rubbing alcohol. Spray heavily infested plants with a mixture of alcohol and insecticidal soap every three days for two weeks. Make this mixture by combining 1 cup isopropyl alcohol and 1 tablespoon commercial insecticidal soap concentrate with 1 quart water. If you are using insecticidal soap already mixed with water, add 1 tablespoon alcohol to a pint of the diluted soap. If scale insects have consistently been a problem, try spraying hollies in late winter or early spring with a 3 percent dormant oil to smother overwintering scale and keep them from getting a good start.

## Leaves Notched

### Weevils

Japanese weevils (*Pseudocneorhinus bifasciatus*) chew at the edges of leaves, giving them the appearance of being notched. If they're really hungry, though, they may devour the entire leaf except for the midribs and large veins. Weevil grubs attack holly roots, and the damage they cause often endangers the life of the shrub. The adult beetles are about ¼ inch long. They may be light or dark brown in color, with striated wing covers. They feed by day and live under tree bark or in other plant tissues at night. When disturbed, they play dead, folding their legs and dropping off plants to the ground. Turn this trait to your advantage when trying to control these pests. Spread a cloth beneath the infested shrub and beat the branches gently. Startled weevils will drop to the cloth, and you can easily gather them up and destroy them. To remove any that haven't dropped from the shrub, spray weekly with a solution made from pyrethrum and isopropyl alcohol. Make this solution by combining 1 tablespoon alcohol with each pint of pyrethrum. Apply a sticky substance such as Tanglefoot to the trunk to prevent the adults from climbing up and eating the leaves.

## Leaves Mottled Yellow; Shrub Weakened

### Whiteflies

Hollies are vulnerable to infestation from both citrus and mulberry whiteflies (various species). Both the nymphs and adults of these pests suck the juices from leaves, buds, and stems, causing leaves to turn yellowish, and eventually weakening the entire shrub. You also often find sooty mold growing on leaves where the insects have secreted honeydew. If you suspect whiteflies, look for them on the undersides of leaves. These white-winged mothlike insects are about the size of a pinhead. When you bump or brush an infested shrub, they fly up, looking somewhat like flying dandruff. The greenish white, oval pupae also appear in large numbers on the undersides of the leaves. Control whiteflies with insecticidal soap. Spray infested shrubs every three to five days for two weeks. If the infestation is so serious that insecticidal soap doesn't work, try pyrethrum every five days for two weeks.

# MOST COMMON DISEASES

## Sunken Spots on Leaves

### Anthracnose

On the leaves of anthracnose-infected hollies, you will see distinct sunken spots with fruiting bodies in the center. These leaf spots may run together, resembling a blotch or blight. The dead areas follow the veins of the leaves. This disease sometimes extends down several inches below the buds. Pustules containing pinkish spores appear. In severe cases, dieback and defoliation may occur.

Gather and destroy diseased leaves when they fall and prune infected branches. Spray the entire shrub with a copper fungicide such as Bordeaux mixture, and maintain the plant's vigor by feeding and watering it well, especially during droughts.

## Leaves and Shoots Scorched and Wilted

### Bacterial Blight

The bacterium *Corynebacterium ilicis* causes bacterial blight in hollies. Leaves and new shoots wilt and look scorched. The infection spreads to the previous year's growth, where the leaves turn black. Control this disease by spraying your shrubs with copper fungicide every five to seven days until symptoms disappear. Excessive nitrogen fertilization and cultivation beneath shrubs increase the risk of infection.

## Water Spots on Flower Clusters

### Blight

Hollies are susceptible to a blight disease caused by the fungus *Botrytis cinerea*. The flowers of infected shrubs develop tan water-soaked spots. Entire flower clusters may be affected, and in some cases, during humid weather, twigs die back.

Leaf spotting and twig cankers signal another type of blight, caused by *Phytophthora* spp. Prune to remove affected parts and increase air circulation around shrubs. Spray with a copper fungicide every five to seven days until the symptoms disappear.

## Swollen, Sunken Lesions on Branches and Trunk

### Canker

Canker can be caused by one of several kinds of fungi: *Diaporthe* spp., *Nectria* spp., *Physalospora* spp., *Phomopsis* spp., and others. Sunken areas form on branches and stems. These areas may eventually girdle stems or branches. Prune and burn diseased branches and spray the entire shrub with copper fungicide several times in late spring.

## Spots on Leaves; Cankers on Branches

### Dieback

The dieback-causing fungus *Phytophthora ilicis* infects hollies in the Pacific Northwest. Black cankers form on stems, and black spots appear on leaves. In autumn, at the onset of cool rainy weather, spray your shrubs with Bordeaux mixture.

## Cankers on Twigs

### Fusarium Dieback

Fusarium dieback, caused by *Fusarium* fungi, is primarily a problem of hollies grown in the eastern United States. Cankers develop in the bark, and they can cause new twigs to die back, but usually only slight damage occurs. This problem is easily solved simply by cutting and destroying damaged parts.

## Spots on Leaves

### Leaf Spot

Yellow, tan, brown, or black leaf spots on holly leaves may be caused by any of the following fungi: *Cercospora* spp., *Gloeosporium* spp., *Phyllosticta* spp., *Septoria* spp., *Phacidium* spp., and others. These fungi usually attack in early spring or summer. The leaf spots are often covered with tiny black fruiting bodies. The tar spot fungus, *Phacidium curtisii*, causes yellow spots on holly foliage in spring. The spots, which can also occur on berries, turn red-brown, then black, by autumn. This disease is especially a problem with hollies grown in southern states. It usually strikes plants during prolonged wet weather.

Pick off and destroy infected leaves and maintain the vigor of your shrubs by gently incorporating oak leaf mold or cottonseed meal into the soil around them. Water well, especially during droughts. Spray infected shrubs thoroughly with wettable sulfur or a copper fungicide once or twice at weekly intervals, starting as soon as the spots of the fungus are visible on the leaves. A late summer or fall application of copper fungicide will also help prevent leaf spot. Copper fungicides may damage foliage of hollies, and will leave unattractive residue.

## White Powder on Leaves

### Powdery Mildew

A thin white powdery coating on leaves is a sure sign of powdery mildew. Either of the fungi *Phyllactinia corylea* or *Microsphaera alni* can cause this disease in hollies. Spray infected shrubs thoroughly with wettable sulfur once or twice at weekly intervals, starting as soon as you see the white coating of the fungus. In fall, collect and destroy plant debris.

# NOTES AND RESEARCH

Hollies attract several different birds, including bluebirds, catbirds, cedar waxwings, brown thrashers, flickers, thrushes, robins, and mockingbirds.

# Hydrangea

*Hydrangea* spp.

## DESCRIPTION

Gardeners value members of this group of garden shrubs and woody vines for their showy blossoms, which bloom in dense, flat or rounded clusters. Most ornamental hydrangeas are from Asia or North America. They are well suited to natural landscape settings. They combine well with rhododendrons and azaleas, and will bloom after these shrubs have faded. Residents of mid-Atlantic states would recognize big-leaved hydrangea (*Hydrangea macro-*

*phylla*) as the seashore hydrangea with big, brilliant blue, lavender, or white flowers. The most common hydrangea, however, is the panicle hydrangea (*H. paniculata*), which is grown almost universally. The climbing hydrangea (*H. anomala* subsp. *petiolaris*) is a vine ideal for northern sides of houses.

### Height

Big-leaved hydrangea (*H. macrophylla,* hortensia varieties), 10 feet
Climbing hydrangea (*H. anomala* subsp. *petiolaris*), 50 feet
Oak-leaved hydrangea (*H. quercifolia*), 6 feet
Panicle hydrangea (*H. paniculata*), 30 feet
Rough-leaved hydrangea (*H. aspera*), 6 feet
Smooth hydrangea (*H. arborescens*), 4 feet

### Spread

Big-leaved hydrangea, 10 feet
Oak-leaved hydrangea, 8 feet
Panicle hydrangea, 13 feet
Rough-leaved hydrangea, 12 feet
Smooth hydrangea, 12 feet

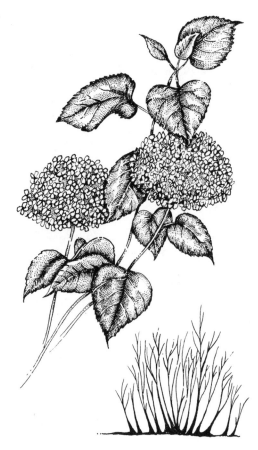

### Blossoms

Hydrangeas bloom from summer to autumn, depending on the variety, and a few are grown indoors as pot plants and bloom throughout the winter. Most varieties have white flowers. Soil pH determines the color of the blooms of big-leaved hydrangea. Plants grown in acid soil have violet or blue flowers; those grown in neutral or slightly alkaline soil have pink flowers. Acid soil promotes blues and violets, and alkaline soil encourages pinks. In addition, the more acidic the soil, the paler the colors. The flower heads of hydrangeas are usually quite large, often between 4 and 10 inches across, depending on the variety. The oak-leaved hydrangea produces flower clusters up to 10 inches long.

## Foliage

Hydrangeas are deciduous. Their large, somewhat oval, toothed green leaves sit opposite each other on the stem. The undersides of the foliage on oak-leaved hydrangeas feel like felt. Oak-leaved and climbing hydrangeas also have distinctive reddish bark.

# ENVIRONMENT

## Varieties by Zone

To zone 4, panicle hydrangea and smooth hydrangea
To zone 5, oak-leaved hydrangea
To zone 6, big-leaved hydrangea

## Light Requirements

Hydrangeas prefer light to medium shade, though the big-leaved hydrangea can handle almost full sun.

## Soil Requirements

Hydrangeas like well-drained, loamy soil, but will do well in most soil conditions. Big-leaved hydrangeas can stand a dry soil. Hydrangeas are comfortable in woodland conditions. They can stand a range of pH from quite acid, 5, to somewhat alkaline, 8.

# PLANTING AND PROPAGATION

## Planting

Plant balled-and-burlapped or container-grown hydrangeas in the early fall or late spring, although fall is the best planting time. To sway your big-leaved hydrangea into blue tones, create an acidic soil by adding plenty of peat moss. For pink blossoms, make the soil alkaline by adding ground limestone. Locate each hydrangea so that it stands a distance of half its spread from the nearest permanent plant.

## Propagation

Propagate hydrangeas by layering or by taking semiripe cuttings in early summer.

# PLANT MANAGEMENT

## Water Requirements

Hydrangeas like to be kept moist, and grow best with about 1½ inches of water each week, with an increase to 2 inches a week in the hot summer. Ease up on water from late August to mid-October to discourage excessive fall growth, which might be susceptible to winterkill. Resume watering in late fall, and soak the ground well just before it freezes solid. The shallow roots of shrubs are unable to take up moisture from frozen winter soils and can suffer from lack of moisture late in winter.

## Feeding Requirements

One main feeding of compost, either in early spring or late fall, is all that hydrangeas require.

Although hydrangeas only require one main feeding, they do benefit from a monthly spray of dilute liquid fertilizer mixed with dilute seaweed extract. Apply this solution for just the first three months after the last frost. If you fertilize your shrubs in the fall, stop two months before the first frost to encourage hardening off for winter. If you live in a frost-free climate, spray your plants with seaweed extract, beginning late in spring and making no more than three applications during the growing season.

## Pruning

On big-leaved hydrangeas, flowers bloom from buds formed the previous year, so hold off pruning your shrubs until after flowering. Each year, thin about a third of the weakest growth of mature plants. In very cold climates, do this thinning in the early spring. You can ensure new growth and improved flowering of panicle hydrangeas by cutting the plant back hard each spring.

# MOST COMMON CULTURAL PROBLEMS

## Leaves Yellowed

### Alkaline Soil

Big-leaved hydrangeas like an acid environment with a pH of 5.5 to 6.5. Yellowing leaves may be a sign that the soil is too alkaline. If this is indeed the problem, apply ammonium sulfate to acidify the soil. A new way to cure chlorosis (yellowing of the leaves) is to use iron chelates either as foliage sprays or in the soil. Yellowing foliage can also be related to very high levels of nitrates and calcium, so if none of your efforts seem to be alleviating the problem, have a soil test done.

# MOST COMMON INSECT PESTS

## Leaves Yellowed, Curled, and Distorted

### Aphids

Aphids suck the sap from leaves, causing them to turn yellow or brown and wilt under bright sunlight. Sometimes the foliage curls and puckers, and eventually plant growth becomes retarded. Ants crawling on the plants are attracted to honeydew secreted by the aphids. Hydrangeas are vulnerable to attack from green peach aphids (*Myzus persicae*), crescent-marked lily aphids (*Neomyzus circumflexus*), and melon aphids (*Aphis gossypii*). All of these species have soft, pear-shaped bodies and are about the size of the head of a pin.

If you suspect aphids, look for them on the undersides of leaves, where they gather in groups. Light infestations are easily washed away by spraying shrubs vigorously with water. Do this in the early morning, three times, once every other day. For medium to heavy infestations, spray with insecticidal soap every two to three days. As a last resort, use pyrethrum. Make two applications, three to four days apart.

## Leaves Discolored and Bound with Silk Strands

### Leaftiers

You can suspect leaftier insects when the hydrangea leaves become discolored, and you notice that some of the leaves are tied together with silklike threads. The larvae of these pests protect themselves while feeding by binding leaf surfaces together with strands of silk. As they feed, the foliage becomes ragged and unsightly, turns brown, and dies. Hydrangea leaftier larvae (*Exartema ferriferanum*) are green caterpillars, ½ inch long, with dark brown heads. Spray infested plants with Bt (*Bacillus thuringiensis*) two or three times at three- to five-day intervals. Light infestations are easily controlled by simply crushing the larvae inside their rolled leaves.

## Leaf Margins Look Burned

### Mites

Two-spotted spider mites (*Tetranychus telarius*) cause damage resembling sunscald. The leaves look burned, especially along their margins. These insects are about 1/50 inch long, barely visible to the unaided eye. They may be yellow, green, red, or brown. As soon as you notice symptoms of mite damage, spray your shrubs vigorously with water to knock them from the leaves. Do this in the morning, once every day for three days. This should completely eliminate a light infestation. If mites are still present, spray with insecticidal soap every three to five days for two weeks. In late winter or early spring, before the leaves begin to come out, spray shrubs with dormant oil to destroy any overwintering mites.

## Stems Swollen and Split; Shrub Sickly

### Nematodes

Hydrangeas are vulnerable to both stem nematodes and root nematodes. When infested with stem nematodes (*Ditylenchus dipsaci*) the stems become swollen and split, and the leaves drop off. Root knot nematodes (*Meloidogyne incognita* and *M. hapla*) attack the roots, of course. The entire shrub becomes sickly, wilted, and stunted, with yellow or bronze foliage. It declines slowly and dies. If you look at the roots, you'll find that they are poorly developed and may be even partially decayed.

Nematodes are not insects, but slender, unsegmented roundworms. Most live in the soil and are $\frac{1}{50}$ to $\frac{1}{10}$ inch long. Add lots of compost, especially leaf mold, to the soil around infested hydrangeas to encourage beneficial fungi. Fertilize with liquid fish emulsion, pouring it into the soil as a drench; it repels nematodes.

## Leaves Skeletonized; Flowers Damaged

### Rose Chafers

The rose chafer (*Macrodactylus subspinosus*) occasionally attacks hydrangeas. It is rarely a problem for suburban gardeners and is more likely to be found in rural areas where hydrangeas might be grown close to fallow fields. Rose chafers feed on both leaves and petals, skeletonizing foliage and damaging flowers. The adult is a beetle, readily distinguished from other beetles by the grayish or fawn color of its ½-inch, elongated body and by its sluggish movements. This pest appears suddenly, feeds on plants for four to six weeks, then abruptly disappears.

Control rose chafers by handpicking. If you know when to expect the rose chafer, cover the plants with cheesecloth or fleece a week or so before

expected pest arrival time. For long-term control, scratch milky spore disease (*Bacillus popilliae*) into the soil to kill grubs.

## Leaves Yellowed; Small Bumps on Leaves and Stems

### Scale

The first sign of a scale attack is yellowing of the upper leaf surfaces, followed by leaf drop, reduced growth, and stunted shrubs. Hydrangeas are vulnerable to several types of scale, including the oystershell scale (*Lepidosaphes ulmi*). They usually appear on the upper ends of the stems, looking like small bumps rather than insects. Aptly named, scale have rounded, waxy coverings, which protect them while they feed. They may be white, yellow, or brown to black, and are $\frac{1}{10}$ to $\frac{2}{5}$ inch in diameter.

If you spot them early, before too many have taken up residence on your hydrangeas, you can simply scrape them off plant surfaces with your fingernail or a cotton swab dipped in rubbing alcohol. Heavy infestations are easier to control by spraying shrubs with a solution of alcohol and insecticidal soap every three days for two weeks. Make this solution by combining 1 cup isopropyl alcohol and 1 tablespoon commercial insecticidal soap concentrate with 1 quart water. If you already have soap mixed with water, add 1 tablespoon alcohol to a pint of this diluted soap spray.

## MOST COMMON DISEASES

## Buds and Flowers Become Spotted and Deteriorate

### Blight

The fungus *Botrytis cinerea* causes a blight disease that can wreak havoc on your hydrangeas. It strikes the flower clusters during wet weather. Spots develop, which later merge into blotches. The flowers deteriorate badly. When symptoms first appear, spray shrubs with a copper fungicide. Apply the fungicide every ten days in wet seasons. Increase air circulation around the plants by pruning and avoid overhead watering.

## White Powder on Leaf Undersides

### Powdery Mildew

The distinctive thin, white, powdery fungus *Erysiphe polygoni* that causes powdery mildew grows on the undersides of hydrangea leaves. The upper surfaces of the infected leaves may stay green or turn purplish brown. Buds and new growth may also be attacked with the powdery coating.

As soon as you discover the white, powdery coating on hydrangea leaves, spray your diseased shrubs thoroughly with a wettable sulfur fungicide

once or twice at weekly intervals. Collect and discard all plant debris in the fall.

## Powdery Brown Pustules on Leaves; Leaves Shriveled

### Rust

Rust, caused by the fungus *Pucciniastrum hydrageae*, is easy to diagnose. The leaves of infected plants become brittle and spotted with many yellowish to rusty brown pustules, especially on the undersides. Prune out and destroy any affected branches and spray the entire shrub with wettable sulfur at weekly intervals until the symptoms disappear.

---

SHRUB **Juniper** *Juniperus* spp.

## DESCRIPTION

The many varieties of juniper trees and shrubs are extremely versatile and adaptable, making them valuable landscape plants. Some are used as foreground cover, others as foundation plantings, shrubs in groupings, or specimen trees. Like hollies, the sexes are usually separate, and only the female bears the tiny bluish or reddish brown cones, often called juniper berries. Common juniper (*Juniperus communis*) is a sprawling shrub that grows in most regions of the United States. Many varieties of common juniper are used as ornamentals. The eastern red cedar (*J. virginiana*) is grown widely throughout the northeastern and midwestern United States.

### Height

Chinese juniper (*J. chinensis*), 50 to 60 feet
Common juniper (*J. communis*), 12 to 35 feet
Creeping juniper (*J. horizontalis*), 1 foot

Eastern red cedar (*J. virginiana*), 90 feet
Savin juniper (*J. sabina*), 15 feet
Shore juniper (*J. conferta*), 1 foot
Singleseed juniper (*J. squamata*), 3 feet

### Spread

Junipers vary from creeping spreading ground covers that may spread several feet in all directions to shrubs to upright trees that spread to 13 to 20 feet across.

### Foliage

Junipers are evergreen. Their foliage is scalelike with overlapping branchlets. Generally, young leaves are more sharply pointed than older ones. They are green or blue-green, with a needlelike texture.

## ENVIRONMENT

### Varieties by Zone

To zone 3, common juniper, creeping juniper, and red cedar

To zone 4, Chinese juniper and savin juniper

To zone 5, singleseed juniper

To zone 6, shore juniper

### Light Requirements

Junipers prefer full sun and open exposure, but they can handle anything except deep shade. As shade increases, junipers become loose and spindly.

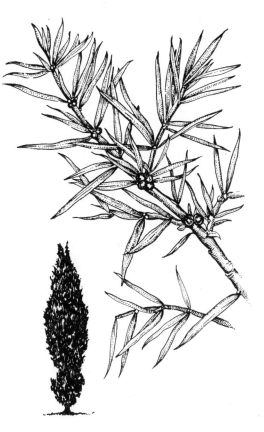

### Soil Requirements

Junipers like a sandy, well-drained loam best, but can tolerate almost any soil except one that is water-logged. Many types will do well in dry, rocky soils. Junipers can withstand alkalinity, but thrive in soil with a pH range between 6 and 7. The shore juniper, as might be expected, tolerates salt well.

## PLANTING AND PROPAGATION

### Planting

You can plant balled-and-burlapped or container-grown junipers in the early fall or late spring, but fall is best. Place the shrub at a distance of half its spread from the nearest permanent plant.

### Propagation

Propagate juniper from seed or cuttings of nearly ripe wood in the autumn.

### Container Gardening

Junipers make excellent bonsai plants.

## PLANT MANAGEMENT

### Water Requirements

Junipers need about an inch of water each week throughout the season. They are vulnerable to overwatering, so don't place them near lawn sprinklers or wet areas on your property. Stop watering from late August to mid-October to prevent excessive fall growth, which might be susceptible to winterkill. Resume normal watering in late fall and soak the ground around junipers well just before the ground freezes solid. The shallow root systems of junipers cannot take up water from frozen ground, and plants may suffer from moisture deficiency in the late winter.

### Feeding Requirements

Junipers need only one application of compost each year in early spring or late fall. Although not necessary, a monthly spray of dilute seaweed extract and dilute liquid fertilizer applied just the first three months after the last frost helps to increase disease resistance in junipers.

## Pruning

Most junipers respond well to pruning and can be sheared into attractive hedges.

# MOST COMMON INSECT PESTS

## Leaves Yellowed and Curled

### Aphids

If the foliage of your junipers begins to turn yellow, check the undersides of branches for aphids. The Rocky Mountain juniper aphid (*Cinara sabinae*) is not much bigger than the head of a pin. It has a soft, pear-shaped body and is yellowish brown marked with black. Aphids suck juices from the leaves and stems of junipers. The foliage turns yellow, and the plant loses vigor. The branches of heavily infested shrubs stop growing. Aphids secrete honeydew, which attracts ants and creates a good environment for sooty mold fungus. Its growth further weakens shrubs.

If the infestation is light, it can easily be taken care of by spraying junipers vigorously with water. Do this in the morning three times, once every other day. If you continue to find aphids, spray with insecticidal soap every two to three days. As a last resort, use pyrethrum, making two applications, three to four days apart. In April, an application of dormant oil will suffocate any eggs that have overwintered on your plants.

## Pine-Conelike Bags Hanging from Branches; Shrub Sickly

### Bagworms

Bagworms (*Thyridopteryx ephemeraeformis*) build small spindle-shaped bags from silk and pieces of the host plant. A completed bag somewhat resembles a pine cone, may be about 2 inches long, and can contain up to 1,000 eggs. Eggs are laid in fall and hatch in May or June of the following year. The bagworm carries its bag with it as it feeds on your shrub. The caterpillar is dark brown with a white or yellow head. Bagworms can kill a juniper if not kept in check. Red cedars are among the most susceptible of the junipers to the attacks of the bagworm.

Handpick the bags and burn them. In late spring and early summer, as soon as the caterpillars have emerged, spray infested shrubs every ten days with Bt (*Bacillus thuringiensis*). Continue through mid-July. In August, set out pheromone traps designed to catch male bagworm moths in the hopes of reducing the population next year.

## Leaves Yellowish

### Juniper Mealybugs

Yellowish foliage may mean any of a number of problems, including infestation by the juniper mealybug (*Pseudococcus juniperi*). This insect is a pest of junipers in the midwest. The leaves of infested plants turn yellowish, and the entire shrub grows poorly and looks unsightly. A severe infestation can kill a juniper plant. Juniper mealybugs are $1/5$ to $1/3$ inch long, oval, flattened, dark red in color, and covered with white waxy powder. They have short, soft spines around their margins. These insects gather in cottony white masses on roots, stems, branches, and leaves. They suck sap from the plant, reducing its vigor. Honeydew secretions encourage the growth of mold and attract ants to the shrub. The cottony tufts on leaves are their egg sacks.

Control mealybugs by spraying infested shrubs with an alcohol-based solution every two to three days until the problem is solved. To make this solution, mix 1 cup isopropyl alcohol and ½ teaspoon Volck oil in 1 quart water. You can substitute 1 tablespoon insecticidal soap concentrate for the Volck oil and obtain equally effective results. In late winter or early spring before growth begins, spray plants with dormant oil to smother overwintering adults and eggs.

### Mites

Yellowed foliage might also mean mites. Look for them on the undersides of branches. In very severe infestations, you'll find a fine silken webbing over the foliage. The specific pests of junipers are the spruce spider mite (*Oligonychus ununguis*) and the two-spotted mite (*Tetranychus telarius*). They are only about ¹⁄₅₀ inch long and may be green, yellow, or red.

As soon as you have determined that your junipers have mites, begin control measures. Spray shrubs in the early morning with a forceful stream of water to knock the mites from leaf undersides. Repeat the water spray every morning for three days. If you continue to find mites on your plants, spray affected shrubs with insecticidal soap every three to five days for two weeks. In spring, apply dormant oil to kill any mites that overwintered on your junipers.

## Leaf Tips Die

### Midges

Blisters at the bases of juniper needles and death of leaf tips indicate the presence of the juniper midge (*Contarinia juniperina*). The tiny yellow maggots of this small fly cause all the damage. Control them by pruning and destroying the affected plant parts; then spray the entire shrub with insecticidal soap. Some gardeners mix tobacco dust with soil around the bases of plants to kill the larvae. In early spring, one application of dormant oil should kill eggs and overwintering nymphs.

## Galleries in Bark; Girdled Twig Tips

### Red Cedar Bark Beetles

The cedar bark beetle (*Phloeosinus dentatus*) is about ¹⁄₁₆ inch long. It lays its eggs in narrow, 1- or 2-inch-long tunnels in the trunk. As the grubs hatch, they bore out of the bark, making galleries as they go. They also will bore and girdle twigs. The cedar bark beetle is more apt to attack trees recently transplanted or those that are suffering from lack of water. Handpick the beetles and drop them into a pail of soapy water. Spray infested shrubs with a solution of pyrethrum and isopropyl alcohol; mix 1 tablespoon alcohol in each pint of pyrethrum and make two applications, three to four days apart.

## Leaves and Twigs Bound with Webbing

### Webworms

Juniper webworms (*Dichomeris marginella*) spin webs around the foliage and branches on which they feed. You'll find their webs in early summer and again in the fall. The twigs and needles turn brown and may eventually die. The juniper webworm is a ½-inch-long, brown larva with longitudinal reddish brown stripes. The adult female moth has a wingspan of ⅗ inch. She appears in June or July to deposit eggs, which hatch in two weeks. Webworms pass the winter in the immature larval stage.

Remove webworm nests and destroy them. For a more effective control, spray the entire shrub with Bt (*Bacillus thuringiensis*) as soon as you spot the small worms. Apply it three times over a three-week period. If webworms are still present, try pyrethrum, making two applications, three to four days apart.

## Leaves Gray or Yellowish; Tiny White Dots on Needles

### White Juniper Scale

If the needles of your junipers are turning yellow and looking unhealthy, and you find clusters of tiny white or gray bumps on needles and branches, your plants probably are infested with juniper scale (*Calrulaspis juniperi*). Black sooty mold is another sign of scale. It grows on honeydew secreted by scale. Juniper scale look like tiny bumps. They have circular rounded coverings, which are at first white, then turn gray or black.

Simply scrape these pests off branches with your fingernail or a cotton swab dipped in rubbing alcohol. If the number of insects is large enough that this seems a formidable task, spray the shrub with a solution of alcohol and insecticidal soap every three days for two weeks. To make this solution, mix 1 cup isopropyl alcohol and 1 tablespoon insecticidal soap concentrate in 1 quart water. If your insecticidal soap is already mixed with water, add 1 tablespoon alcohol to a pint of this diluted soap spray. An application of dormant oil in late winter or very early in spring also helps to control this pest.

# MOST COMMON DISEASES

## Branch Tips Turn Brown and Die Back

### Blight

The fungus *Phomopsis juniperovora* causes the tip of a juniper branch to turn brown, then die back until the entire branch is killed. If left untended, the whole shrub may die. This disease usually strikes seedlings and nursery stock, but may infect larger trees. Any shrub or tree older than five years, though, is not seriously affected.

In late winter, when the trees are dry, prune and burn affected twigs and branches. Avoid this disease altogether by planting resistant varieties.

## Galls on Branches

### Rust

If you find galls on the branches of your junipers, it is a sure sign of rust. Junipers are susceptible to three different types: cedar apple, cedar hawthorn, and cedar quince rust. The fungus *Gymnosporangium juniperi-virginianae* causes cedar apple rust, a disease that infects apple or crabapple trees and red cedars. Infected red cedars develop galls an inch or more in diameter. The second spring after infection, the galls form many long, yellow, tonguelike outgrowths, especially during warm, rainy weather. Infected branch tips may die, but generally, red cedars suffer little damage unless several hundred galls develop. Common juniper is harmed by a similar rust fungus, *G. clavariaeforme*, which causes cankers in branches and bark, and witches'-brooms.

Cut out the galls in early April before the tonguelike growths develop. Spray nearby apple trees with wettable sulfur, beginning when leaves first emerge. Six applications, one every ten days, should take care of the problem. Avoid growing susceptible cedars within a mile of alternate hosts.

---

SHRUB **Lilac** *Syringa* spp.

---

# DESCRIPTION

Lilacs make up a large group of Old World decorative shrubs and trees, noted for their showy clusters of fragrant blossoms. The common lilac (*Syringa vulgaris*) is the best known species in the United States. These shrubs stand out in the spring, when their lilac blossoms grace the landscape and their fragrance fills the air. The rest of the year they serve as background foliage or as a screen or a border for your property. Most lilacs grow too large for use next to one-story buildings; however, the Chinese lilac (*S.* ×*chinensis*) works well in these instances. It combines height and the heavy flowering of the common lilac with a denser habit and a desirable fullness at the base. Some excellent old hybrids of the common lilac include 'President Lincoln' (pale blue), 'Ellen Willmott' (double white), and 'Katherine Havemeyer' (double pink).

## Height

Chinese lilac (*S.* ×*chinensis*), 6 to 15 feet
Common lilac (*S. vulgaris*), 20 feet

Late lilac (*S. villosa*), 10 feet
Little-leaved lilac (*S. microphylla*), 6 feet
Meyer lilac (*S. meyeri*), 4 to 8 feet
Persian lilac (*S. ×persica*), 5 to 6 feet

## Spread

Chinese lilac, 10 feet
Common lilac, 20 feet
Little-leaved lilac, 3 feet
Meyer lilac, 4 feet
Persian lilac, 8 feet

## Blossoms

Lilacs bloom in late spring to early summer (early May to late June). Most bloom around the third week of May. All lilacs have fragrant flowers. Colors include blue, lilac, pink, red, purple, white, and yellow, and some bicolored forms exist.

## Foliage

Although lilacs are best known for their flowers, their foliage is attractive, too. The green leaves are oval or elliptical in shape, with no lobes. Usually their surfaces are smooth, but some are hairy beneath.

# ENVIRONMENT

## Varieties by Zone

To zone 2, late lilac
To zone 3, Chinese lilac and common lilac
To zone 4, little-leaved lilac, Meyer lilac, and
   Persian lilac

## Light Requirements

Lilacs can live in full sun to medium shade, but they bloom best when grown in full sun.

## Soil Requirements

Lilacs grow in most soils, but prefer a loamy, well-drained soil. In general, the pH should not go below 4.5 and can go as high as 7.5.

# PLANTING AND PROPAGATION

## Planting Requirements

You can plant bare-root or container-grown plants in the spring or fall, but fall is best.

## Propagation

Lilacs are most easily propagated by division. Simply dig up the young shoots that come up near the mature bush and replant them. However, many hybrid lilacs are grown on common lilac or privet as understock, and suckers and young shoots from these plants should be discouraged, for they will not be true to form. Lilacs can also be raised from semiripe cuttings taken from spring to midsummer.

## PLANT MANAGEMENT

### Water Requirements

Lilacs need about an inch of water each week, with an increase to 1½ inches a week in the hot summer. Don't water your shrubs from late August to mid-October. This deprivation discourages the production of excessive fall growth, which might be susceptible to winterkill. Resume normal watering in late fall, and soak the ground beneath your shrubs well just before it freezes solid. Their shallow root systems cannot take up water from frozen ground, so lilacs can suffer from moisture deficiency in late winter.

### Feeding Requirements

Feed lilacs every two years. Use compost or another fertilizer that releases nitrogen slowly. Your lilacs will look best if you spray them with a mixture of dilute liquid fertilizer and dilute seaweed extract once a month for just the first three months after the last frost. Do not feed lilacs for two months prior to the first frost. This allows them to harden off for winter.

### Pruning

Remove the spent flower heads each year to encourage flower production next spring. Lilacs need to be pruned at least every three years to develop a regular bloom sequence. Prune just after flowering, since they bloom on the previous season's wood. Cut out all dead or diseased wood when it appears. When you prune lilacs, you want to remove some canes to let more air and light in to the center of the plant. If a shrub has become so tall that the blooms are above sight lines, cut back a few branches to a more reasonable height each year to force the lower branches to fill out. Remove all suckers on grafted lilacs; otherwise the common lilac or privet understock will assert itself and quickly overwhelm the grafted hybrid.

### Cutting Fresh Flowers

Lilac blooms make wonderfully fragrant bouquets. Cut stems in the morning when the blossoms are just barely opening.

## MOST COMMON CULTURAL PROBLEMS

### Plant Fails to Bloom Well

#### Maintenance Practices

Like many woody plants, lilacs have the habit of perfect bloom only every other year. For best bloom every year, fertilize as described earlier. If your soil is very acidic, occasionally add limestone to it. When pruning, cut out most of the suckers at the base of the shrub, leaving the healthier, sturdier ones to develop into flowering branches. Remove the dead flower clusters right after the bloom period to forestall seed formation. If the vegetative parts of the plant grow too profusely, cut back on the fertilizer.

### Leaves Turn Yellow

#### Soil Too Alkaline

Yellowed leaves may be a sign that the soil is too alkaline for the lilacs. Test the pH and if it is indeed too high, you need to bring it down below 7.5. (See chapter 9 for techniques on making soil more acidic.)

## MOST COMMON INSECT PESTS

### Leaves Yellowed, Curled, and Distorted

#### Aphids

Aphids suck the juices from foliage. Leaves turn yellow or brown, wilt under bright sunlight, and sometimes curl and pucker. Ants are attracted to the honeydew secreted by aphids. Of the many aphids known, the melon aphid (*Aphis gossypii*) is the one that infests lilacs. Like its relatives, it has a soft, pear-shaped body no bigger than the head of a pin.

You can easily eliminate light infestations simply by spraying the undersides of the leaves vigorously with water. Do this in the morning, three times, once every other day. For medium to heavy infestations, spray shrubs with insecticidal soap every two to three days. As a last resort, use pyrethrum, making two applications, three to four days apart.

## Holes in Branches and Trunk; Branches Wilted

### Borers

Borers leave holes in branches and trunks of lilacs. Infested branches wilt and are frequently so weakened that they break. Borers literally open the way for the wood-destroying fungus *Polyporus versicolor* to infect shrubs. Roughened scars showing the old borer holes may occur on larger stems at places where the borers have worked for several seasons.

The lilac borer (*Podosesia syringae*) is a brown-headed, creamy colored caterpillar, which grows to a length of ¾ inch. It overwinters in the tunnels it mines in lilac stems. The adult, a clear-winged, wasp-like moth, emerges in spring and usually lays its eggs on the roughened or wounded places on the bark.

The leopard moth borer (*Zeuzera pyringa*) also attacks lilacs. This borer invades the heartwood, tunneling up and down for some distance. Its tunnel is much larger and more regular than that of the lilac borer. As it bores into your shrubs, it pushes damp sawdustlike frass out of the opening and onto the ground. These little piles of sawdust give away the presence of this borer. The larvae are pale yellow or cream colored and are marked with numerous black spots. The adult moth has white wings marked with black, somewhat resembling the markings of a leopard, hence its name. These moths don't move like leopards. Feeble flyers, they are also sluggish and can often be seen hanging around on the trunks of trees.

To control either type of borer, thoroughly examine your lilac in early spring and cut and burn any dying or unhealthy stems that might contain borers. Swollen areas with cracked bark mark these sites. You'll also see numerous holes in the bark and wood. If you find borer holes in summer, cut them out with a sharp knife and examine the tunnels. If they look fairly straight, you can kill the borer by probing with a flexible wire. To be sure of destroying the pest, though, use a hooked wire and pull the caterpillar out. If the tunnel is not straight, inject a preparation that contains nicotine sulfate, then plug the holes with chewing gum or putty.

## Dark Blotches on Leaves; Leaves Covered with Webs

### Leafminers

The larvae of lilac leafminers (*Gracillaria syringella*) burrow between the upper and lower surfaces of leaves, forming unsightly blotches in the leaves. Heavily infested shrubs look scorched. From three to eight larvae inhabit one leaf. Once they are full grown, they emerge, spin webs around the leaves, and continue to feed until the leaves are skeletonized. Lilac leafminers make cocoons, which they cover with plant debris. They spend the winter in these cocoons on the ground under plants. Two or three generations occur a year, the last one in September. The adult moth of the lilac leafminer has brown forewings mottled with silver, and two silvery bands across its middle. It spends winter in debris-covered cocoons in the ground under the plants. The moths usually emerge during May, and the larvae mature in July.

To control lilac leafminers, remove any rolled leaves and burn them. If the infestation is very heavy and much damage has been done, cut back branches to healthy growth. In July, before the insect grows out of the larval stage, spray the entire shrub with a strong insecticidal soap solution.

## Leaves Rolled and Bound with Silk Strands

### Leaf Rollers

The obvious symptom of a leaf roller infestation is, of course, rolled leaves. The larvae of this insect protect themselves while feeding by rolling leaves into tubes and binding them with strands or webs of silk. The pests feed from inside, until leaves are skeletonized, turn brown, and die. The oblique-banded leaf roller (*Choristoneura rosaceana*) attacks lilacs, and arrives in late spring to do so. The caterpillars are dark to light green or cream to yellow and are ⅜ to 1¾ inches long. The adult moths are brown or gray and ¼ to ½ inch long. If only a few caterpillars have found your shrubs, simply crush them in their rolled residences; otherwise, spray with Bt (*Bacillus thuringiensis*) two or three times at three- to five-day intervals.

## Leaves Discolored; Small Bumps on Leaves and Branches

### Scale
The first sign of a scale attack is discoloration of the leaves, followed by leaf drop, reduced growth, and stunted shrubs. Heavy infestations kill plants. If you see these symptoms occurring on your lilacs, look for the pests themselves. Scale don't look like insects at all, but rather like small bumps. They have a convex covering, which protects them as they feed. Eight species of scale infest lilacs. The oyster-shell scale (*Lepidosaphes ulmi*) attacks lilacs more often than the others. It is about ⅛ inch in diameter with a gray to black shell. As its name suggests, it looks like masses of small oyster shells attached to branches. Some species excrete honeydew, which attracts ants and encourages sooty mold growth.

You can easily remove a minor scale infestation by scraping the insects off with your fingernail or a cotton swab dipped in rubbing alcohol. Spray heavily infested plants with a mixture of alcohol and insecticidal soap every three days for two weeks. To make this solution, mix 1 cup isopropyl alcohol and 1 tablespoon commercial insecticidal soap concentrate in 1 quart water. If your insecticidal soap is already mixed with water, add 1 tablespoon alcohol to a pint of this dilute soap. In late winter or early spring, spray plants with a dormant oil to smother overwintering adults and eggs.

## Leaves Notched

### Weevils
If the leaves of your lilacs look chewed around the edges, they may well have been tasted by the Japanese weevil (*Pseudocneorhinus bifasciatus*). Sometimes they do more than taste, devouring the whole leaf except for the midribs and large veins. Weevils are tear-shaped beetles about ¼ inch long. They may be light to dark brown in color, with striated wing covers. They feed by day and live under tree bark and under debris on the ground at night. These weevils are sometimes called snout beetles because their heads are elongated, with a slender downward-curved snout, which terminates with the insect's mouth parts.

Weevils play dead when disturbed, folding their legs and dropping from plants to the ground. Turn this trait to advantage when you are trying to control them. Spread a cloth beneath infested lilacs; then gently beat the branches. The startled weevils will drop onto the cloth, and you can gather them up and destroy them. To remove any that might be left, spray your bushes weekly with a solution of pyrethrum and isopropyl alcohol (add 1 tablespoon alcohol to a pint of pyrethrum mixture). Smear a sticky substance such as Tanglefoot around the trunks of the lilac shrubs to prevent the adults from climbing up and eating the leaves.

# MOST COMMON DISEASES

## Leaves Spotted or Shriveled; Shoots Blackened; Flowers Blasted

### Bacterial or Fungal Blight
Bacterial blight caused by *Pseudomonas syringae* affects every part of the shrub it infects. Brown to black spots form on leaves, which eventually turn completely black and dry on the branches. Shoots develop black stripes or turn black at the ends. Flowers become limp and turn dark brown. Blight is most severe during moist, mild weather, and infects the developing young shoots. The bacteria may enter

twigs directly or through blighted leaves. They overwinter in diseased twigs. White-flowered cultivars seem most susceptible to this disease.

The fungus *Phytophthora cactorum* causes a similar disease in lilacs. Terminal buds and leaves turn brown instead of black, roll up, and droop. Stems are often killed to the ground. This fungus also causes dieback of azaleas, so if you grow both of these plants, place them far apart.

For bacterial blight, prune and destroy diseased shoots, sterilizing your tools between each cut. Spray the entire bush with a copper fungicide. To prevent this disease, avoid overfeeding your plants, and promote good air circulation by proper pruning.

For fungal blight, prune the diseased tips well below the infection. In spring, as new leaves emerge, spray the entire shrub with Bordeaux mixture or another copper fungicide. Spray again two weeks later.

## Swollen Growths on Crowns and Stems

### Crown Gall

If you find swollen growths of various shapes and sizes on the crowns, roots, and stems of your lilacs, suspect crown gall. This disease is caused by the bacterium *Agrobacterium tumefaciens*. Unlike any other plant galls, the growths formed by this bacterium are malignant; they are tumorlike swellings. Contaminated tools, water, and splashing rain carry the bacteria to lilacs, where they enter the plants through wounds. Prune and destroy infected canes, twigs, and stems. Destroy heavily infected plants.

## Brown Spots and Holes in Leaves

### Leaf Blight

Leaf blight in lilacs is caused by the fungi *Cladosporium herbarum* and *Heterosporium syringae*. These two fungi often occur together, creating large brown spots on leaves that later dry out and fall away, leaving an irregular shot-hole appearance. Spray lilac foliage every week or two with a copper fungicide, beginning about mid-June in the northeastern United States. Spray right through to first frost. In rainy weather, one or two applications at weekly intervals should be sufficient.

## Brown Spots on Leaves

### Leaf Spot

Several kinds of fungi may be responsible for causing leaf spot disease in your lilacs. These include members of the *Cercospora* spp., *Macrophoma* spp., *Phyllosticta* spp., and *Pleospora* spp., among others. The leaves of infected shrubs show brown or black spots. Spray plants with a copper fungicide two or three times, at weekly intervals. Prune and destroy severely diseased branches.

## White Powder on Leaves

### Powdery Mildew

Powdery mildew, caused by the fungus *Microsphaera alni*, commonly infects lilacs, especially in the humid southern states. It is easily diagnosed from the thin, powdery whitish growth that covers leaves. This fungus does little permanent damage other than causing the plant to weaken and look unattractive. Leaves may fall prematurely. Spray shrubs thoroughly with wettable sulfur once or twice at weekly intervals, starting as soon as you see the whitish coating of the fungus. In the fall, collect and destroy all plant material on the ground under your shrubs.

## Leaves Turn Yellow or Brown and Wilt

### Wilt

Wilt disease in lilacs is caused by the soil-dwelling fungus *Verticillium albo-atrum*. The leaves of infected shrubs lose their glossiness, turn pale, and wilt. They fall prematurely, leaving the branches bare toward the end of the season. The branches themselves wilt suddenly and die, and if you were to look at the sapwood, you would find it discolored. Heavy feeding with a high-nitrogen fertilizer sometimes enables shrubs to produce a new ring of sapwood outside the infected area; the shrubs may then recover. Prune dead branches. Remove badly infected shrubs, together with as many roots as possible. Do not replant with wilt-susceptible shrubs or trees in the same location, but replace the lilacs with resistant species such as most conifers, beech, birch, boxwood, dogwood, fruit trees, holly, locust, mulberry, oak, pecan, serviceberry, sweet gum, sycamore, walnut, and willow.

## Shoots Branch Freely; Plant Produces Small Leaves

### Witches'-Broom

A peculiar disease, witches'-broom is caused by a virus. On infected lilacs, two to six or more slender shoots branch freely, and they bear leaves only one-fourth the normal size. This disease may spread by means of grafts. No controls are known, other than pruning and burning the affected shoots.

SHRUB **Privet** *Ligustrum* spp.

## DESCRIPTION

Privets make excellent hedge plants. They are hardy and vigorous, and they tolerate pruning, wind, drought, and pollution. The genus includes both evergreen and semievergreen species. You can use them to fill shady spaces, provide screening, or act as foundation plantings. Their foliage blends well with other plants. Good shrubs for wildlife gardens, their flowers attract honeybees, and their inconspicuous fruit, if left unpruned, sustains birds in many areas through the winter.

The European or common privet (*Ligustrum vulgare*) is, not surprisingly, the most common variety grown in the United States, but many gardeners plant the California privet (*L. ovalifolium*) for its lustrous leaves. The extremely graceful Chinese privet (*L. sinense*) features drooping flowers and is one of the oldest varieties in the country. In the southern United States, most growers plant Japanese privet (*L. japonicum*) or glossy privet (*L. lucidum*).

### Height

Amur privet (*L. amurense*), 10 to 15 feet

Border privet (*L. obtusifolium*), 8 to 12 feet
California privet (*L. ovalifolium*), 15 feet
Chinese privet (*L. sinense*), 20 feet
European privet (*L. vulgare*), 15 feet
Glossy privet (*L. lucidum*), 30 feet
Japanese privet (*L. japonicum*), 6 to 18 feet

### Spread

California privet, 15 feet
Chinese privet, 26 feet
European privet, 16 feet
Glossy privet, 26 feet

### Blossoms

Privets bloom in late spring to midsummer. Their musty-scented white or cream blossoms appear in small spikes or pyramidal clusters.

### Foliage

Privets are evergreen or semievergreen. Their leaves

are oval with smooth edges, generally 1½ to 2½ inches long.

## ENVIRONMENT

### Varieties by Zone

To zone 4, amur privet and border privet

To zone 5, European or common privet

To zone 6, California privet

To zone 7, Chinese privet, glossy privet, and
Japanese privet

### Light Requirements

Privets grow well in full sun to partial shade.

### Soil Requirements

Privets will grow in most soils, but do not tolerate very wet soils.

## PLANTING AND PROPAGATION

### Planting

As with most shrubs, you can plant privets in spring or fall, but fall is best.

### Propagation

Both softwood and hardwood cuttings root easily. Semiripe cuttings taken in early summer to mid-summer will also root successively.

## PLANT MANAGEMENT

### Water Requirements

Most varieties of privet need about an inch of water each week, with an increase to 1½ inches a week in the hot summer. Don't water from late August to mid-October. This is to prevent excessive fall growth, which might be susceptible to winterkill. Resume watering in late fall and soak the ground well just before it freezes hard. Because of their generally shallow root systems, shrubs cannot take up water from winter ground and may suffer moisture deficiency in late winter. Japanese privet and glossy privet dislike extremely dry or extremely wet soils.

### Feeding Requirements

Privets need only one main application of fertilizer each year. Use compost or another fertilizer that releases nitrogen slowly. Although not required, a spray made from dilute liquid fertilizer and dilute seaweed extract, applied once each month for three months after the last frost, will keep privets looking their best. In cold climates, do not give these shrubs any fertilizer during the two months prior to the first frost. This allows the plants to harden off for winter.

## Mulching

Privets benefit from a 2- to 4-inch layer of organic mulch. Use chopped leaves, peat moss, pine needles, or wood chips. Do not use unchopped leaves, because they mat together and prevent water from getting into the soil. Weed control is guaranteed if you first lay some geotextile mulch and then cover that with the organic material.

## Pruning

For general maintenance, shear privets three or four times a year. This encourages dense growth. When training a privet into a hedge, clip it often during the summer to build up a strong, wide base. Periodically remove the oldest wood from the base. Do any major cutting in the early spring, before new growth begins.

# MOST COMMON CULTURAL PROBLEMS

## Hedge Becomes Thin at the Base

### Neglect
If you neglect your privet hedges, they become thin at the base as they get older, and begin to look unsightly. If you care to save your shrubs, prune the hedge down so that just a few inches of foliage remain above the bare base. Do this in early spring, before the plant begins to grow again. Apply 2 to 4 inches of compost around your plants and spray them with liquid fertilizer every month during the growing season. It may take several years for the base to begin to fill in again. Improper pruning can also cause branches at the base of the plant to die. Hedges should be pruned so the base is several inches wider than the top. This allows light to reach lower branches.

# MOST COMMON INSECT PESTS

## Leaves Curled and Distorted

### Aphids
The privet aphid (*Myzus ligustri*) sucks juices from leaves, causing them to tighten and curl. Like all aphids, it has a soft, pear-shaped body, about the size of the head of a pin.

For light infestations, spray shrubs vigorously with water to knock the pests off. Do this in the morning, three times, once every other day. If the infestation is large enough that this control doesn't work, spray with insecticidal soap every two to three days until the pests are gone. As a last resort, use pyrethrum, making two applications, three to four days apart.

## White, Yellow, or Brown Tunnels in or Blotches on Leaves

### Leafminers
If you find white, yellow, or brown tunnels or blotches in the leaves of your privets, leafminers are probably present. These pests get between the upper and lower surfaces of leaves and mine their way through leaf tissue. You can often see the larvae under the surface of the leaf. Leaves may later blister or curl, turn brown, and die.

Privets are vulnerable to both the lilac leafminer (*Gracillaria syringella*) and the privet leafminer (*G. cuculipennella*). Trim and destroy the infested leaves as soon as you spot them. If any branches are severely affected, prune them back to healthy growth.

## Small Yellow or Red Spots on Leaves

### Mites
Mites attack the lowest leaves on shrubs first. The upper surfaces become stippled with small yellow dots or red spots. As the infestation worsens, leaves and stems often become distorted, and the mites swath them in fine webbing. Privets are vulnerable to citrus flat mites (*Brevipalpus lewisi*), privet mites (*B. obovatus*), and tuckerellid mites (*Tuckerella*

*pavoniformis*). They are so tiny, you can barely see them. If you could see them, you'd find that they have four pairs of legs (they are not true insects), piercing-sucking mouth parts, and very compact bodies. They may be yellow, green, red, or brown.

Start control measures as soon as you notice the first stippling on the leaves. Spray shrubs in the early morning with a forceful stream of water to knock the mites from the leaf undersides. Repeat this procedure once daily for three days. If you still find mites on your shrubs, spray with insecticidal soap every three to five days for two weeks. To destroy many overwintering mites, spray shrubs with a solution made from one part flowable sulfur fungicide and ten parts superior-type dormant oil before growth begins in late winter or early spring.

## Leaves Yellowed; Plant Stunted

### Nematodes

The foliage of nematode-infested privets turns yellow or bronze, and the entire shrub looks sickly, wilted, and stunted. You won't find nematodes on the leaves or branches; they feed on roots. As a result, root systems are poorly developed, even partially decayed. Shrubs decline slowly and die.

Privets are susceptible to attack from southern root knot nematodes (*Meloidogyne incognita*) and a leaf nematode (*Aphelenchoides* spp.) Nematodes are not insects, but rather slender, unsegmented roundworms. Most are soil-dwellers, less than $1/20$ inch long.

To control these pests, add lots of compost (especially leaf mold) to the soil around infested shrubs to encourage beneficial fungi. Fertilize with liquid fish emulsion, applying it as a drench; it repels nematodes.

## Leaves Discolored; Small Bumps on Leaves and Branches

### Scale

The first sign of a scale attack is usually discoloration of the upper leaf surface, followed by leaf drop, reduced growth, and stunted plants. Heavy infesta-tions of scale kill privets. Some species excrete honey-dew onto foliage, which attracts ants and encourages sooty mold growth. If you find these symptoms developing on your privets, look for the pests themselves. Scale look like small bumps on leaves, branches, and twigs. They have a rounded waxy covering, which protects them while they feed, and their diameter measures somewhere from $1/10$ to $2/5$ inch. Depending on the species, they may be white, yellow, or brown to black. Many scale species infest privets, including black scale (*Saissetia oleae*), Japanese scale (*Leucaspis japonica*), mining scale (*Howardia biclavus*), and San Jose scale (*Quadraspidiotus perniciosus*). Mealybugs, which are soft, scalelike insects with white, cottony coverings, also infest privets, causing similar symptoms.

If you find only a few pests, simply scrape them off with your fingernail or a cotton swab dipped in rubbing alcohol; otherwise, spray your shrubs with a solution of alcohol and insecticidal soap every three days for two weeks. To make this solution, mix 1 cup isopropyl alcohol and 1 tablespoon insecticidal soap concentrate in 1 quart water. If you have insecticidal soap already mixed with water, add 1 tablespoon alcohol to a pint of this diluted soap. In late winter or early spring, spray with a dormant oil to smother overwintering adults and eggs.

## Leaves Flecked and Whitened

### Thrips

Thrips rasp at plant cells to break them open and feed on the juices. As a result, leaf surfaces become flecked and whitened; leaf tips wither, curl up, and die. On the undersides of leaves, you will find tiny black specks of excrement. A privet that is heavily infested will have a gray or dusty appearance. Privet thrips (*Dendrothrips ornatus*) are dark brown to black with a bright red band. They have narrow, fringed wings and are only about $1/50$ inch long. Their larvae are yellow and spindle shaped.

Since thrips burrow deep between petals of flowers, the sooner you start to control them, the better will be your chances of solving this problem. Spray infested plants with insecticidal soap every three days for two weeks. Commercially available predatory mites, lacewings, ladybugs, and beneficial nematodes are effective backups to the soap spray. Thrips prefer a dry environment, so be certain to water plants adequately.

## Leaves Notched; New Growth Damaged

### Weevils

Privet hedges can be badly damaged by weevils. These pests feed on the tender new shoots. They begin by nibbling on leaf edges, giving them a notched appearance, but their voracious appetite drives them to gorge on leaves until nothing is left but the midribs and large veins. Japanese weevils (*Pseudocneorhinus bifasciatus*) are ¼-inch-long tear-shaped insects, which may be light brown to dark brown in color with striated wing covers. Also called snout beetles, they have a relatively long, slender, downward-curved snout. They feed by day and crawl under tree bark or inside other plant tissues at night.

Japanese weevils play dead when disturbed, folding their legs and dropping from plants to the ground. Take advantage of this when trying to remove these pests from your shrubs. Spread a cloth beneath an infested privet. Gently beat the branches. The startled insects will drop to the cloth, where you can gather them up. To remove any weevils that might not have dropped, spray the shrub weekly with a pyrethrum and isopropyl alcohol solution made from 1 tablespoon alcohol to a pint of pyrethrum. Smear a sticky substance such as Tanglefoot around the main stems of the shrubs to prevent the adult weevils from climbing up and eating the leaves. To stop the reproduction of weevils, introduce predatory nematodes to the soil.

## MOST COMMON DISEASES

## Sunken Spots on Leaves

### Anthracnose, Twig Blight

In privet, anthracnose and twig blight are caused by the fungus *Glomerella cingulata*. The fungus causes leaf spot, and eventually the entire leaf dries out and hangs from the stem. Twigs are killed, and cankers spotted with pinkish pustules form at the base of the stems. Entire stems die when cankers encircle the stems.

Gather and destroy diseased leaves when they fall, and prune and destroy infected branches. Spray infected plants with a copper fungicide such as Bordeaux mixture. Two or three applications at weekly intervals should suffice. Maintain the shrub's vigor by feeding and watering it well, especially during droughts. Of all the species, common privet is most susceptible to anthracnose. Resistant varieties include amur, California, ibota, and regal privet.

## Leaves Become Spotted, Turn Brown, Fall Prematurely

### Leaf Spot

Several different leaf spot fungi infect privets, including *Cercospora adusta, C. lingustri, C. lilacis,* and *Phyllosticta ovalifolii*. Leaves become spotted, turn brown, and fall prematurely. The disease becomes a problem only during very rainy seasons and in overcrowded, poorly aerated plantings. Increase air circulation by pruning dense growth and maintaining the vigor of your plants with proper feeding and watering, especially during droughts. If the disease persists, spray privets with a copper fungicide. Prune out and burn severely affected branches and foliage.

## White Powder on Leaves

### Powdery Mildew

The powdery mildew fungus, *Microsphaera alni*, grows on the upper surfaces of privet leaves and appears as thin, white, powdery coating. Spray the shrub thoroughly with wettable sulfur once or twice at weekly intervals, starting as soon as the whitish coating of the fungus is visible. Collect and destroy plant debris around your privets.

# SHRUB **Spirea** *Spiraea* spp.

## DESCRIPTION

Spireas have a graceful arching habit, and lovely flowers cover their many thin branches in spring. Several species are native to North America. They are vigorous shrubs. Most spireas are deciduous and have fibrous roots, making them easy to move. The billiard spirea (*Spiraea ×billiardii*) is particularly suited for planting in masses on steep banks, for it quickly spreads by underground stems to form a thick clump. Others make good hedges. While their glory days are limited to a brief period in the spring or early summer, spireas make excellent fillers in shrub borders during the rest of the growing season.

### Height

Billiard spirea (*S. ×billiardii*), 6 feet
Bridal wreath (*S. prunifolia*), 9 feet
Bumald spirea (*S. ×bumalda*), 3 feet
Garland spirea (*S. ×arguta*), 5 to 6 feet
Japanese white spirea (*S. albiflora*), 1½ feet
Reeve's spirea (*S. cantoniensis*), 6 to 10 feet
Snow garland (*S. ×multiflora*), 5 feet
Vanhoutte spirea (*S. ×vanhouttei*), 4 feet

### Spread

Mature spireas are from 5 to 8 feet wide, depending on the species.

### Blossoms

Spireas produce showy blossoms in white, purple, rose, or pink, which appear in flat clusters along the length of an arching branch. Many species start blooming in early May. Some, like Japanese white spirea, bloom as late as July.

### Foliage

The leaves are small (about 1 inch in length) and oblong or elliptical, with toothed ends. Most are deciduous, but Reeve's spirea keeps its foliage all year in parts of California.

## ENVIRONMENT

Most of the spirea species are hardy in zones 5 and south and will suffer winter damage in colder areas.

### Varieties by Zone

To zone 5, bridal wreath, bumald spirea, garland spirea, Japanese white spirea, and vanhoutte spirea (vanhoutte spirea tolerates city conditions well)

To zone 7, Reeve's spirea

### Light Requirements

Spireas will take full sun to medium shade, but produce more flowers under full sun.

### Soil Requirements

Spireas are not too particular about the type of soil they occupy. They dislike highly alkaline soil, and may show signs of yellowing if planted in such soil. The pH should be no higher than 6 to 6.5.

## PLANTING AND PROPAGATION

### Planting

You can plant spireas in the spring or fall, but fall is the best time for planting if you have a choice. Spireas are easily transplanted.

### Propagation

Propagate spireas from semiripe cuttings taken in the early summer.

## PLANT MANAGEMENT

### Water Requirements

Spireas dislike extremely dry soil and need about an inch of water each week, with an increase to 1½ inches a week in the hot summer. Cut back somewhat on supplemental watering from late August to mid-October to prevent excessive fall growth, which might be susceptible to winterkill. Resume watering in the late fall and soak spireas thoroughly before the ground freezes hard. Their shallow root systems cannot take up water in frozen soils, and these shrubs may suffer moisture deficiency in the late winter without that last good drenching.

### Feeding Requirements

One application of compost every year in the late fall or early spring is all spireas need. Spireas look their best if sprayed with a solution of dilute liquid fertilizer mixed with dilute seaweed extract once a month for just the first three months after the last frost. Do not fertilize at all during the two months prior to the first frost. This allows shrubs to harden off for winter.

### Pruning

Although not essential, spireas will be healthier and will look their best if pruned annually. The method of pruning depends on the life cycle of the particular species. Spring-flowering spireas bloom on the previous year's wood, so prune those varieties just after flowering. Prune them hard, cutting up to one-third of the oldest growth right down to ground level. Summer-flowering spireas bloom on the current year's wood, so prune those shrubs in the early spring, before plant growth starts.

## MOST COMMON INSECT PESTS

### Leaves Yellowed and Curled

#### Aphids

Aphids suck leaves and stems of spireas, causing the foliage to yellow, curl, and pucker. The spirea aphid (*Aphis spiraecola*) infests tender shoot tips up to and including the flower cluster. Gradually, the entire shrub loses its vigor. You may find ants crawling all over your shrubs. They are attracted by the honeydew that these aphids secrete. If you suspect aphids, look for small groups of them on the undersides of leaves. They are soft, pear-shaped insects just a little bigger than the head of a pin. They may be green, brown, black, or pinkish.

For light infestations, spray the undersides of the spirea leaves vigorously with water. Do this in the morning. Make three applications, once every other day. For medium to heavy infestations, spray shrubs with insecticidal soap every two to three days until aphids are gone. As a last resort, use pyrethrum, making two applications, three to four days apart.

## Leaves Rolled and Bound with Silk Strands

### Leaf Rollers

As their name implies, leaf rollers roll leaves into tubes and bind them with silken strands. They crawl inside for protection while they feed. Leaf rollers have a fair appetite, often skeletonizing leaves, which then turn brown and die. The oblique-banded leaf roller (*Choristoneura rosaceana*) favors spireas. Adult leaf roller moths are brown or gray, ¼ to ½ inch long; larvae are dark to light green or cream to yellow, ⅜ to 1¾ inches long.

If the infestation is light, you can simply crush the caterpillars in their rolled leaves. Spray spireas with Bt (*Bacillus thuringiensis*) three times, once every three to five days.

## Leaves Yellowed or Bronzed; Shrub Sickly

### Nematodes

Spireas infested with nematodes look sickly, wilted, or stunted. Their foliage turns yellow or bronze. Then they decline slowly and die. All these symptoms result from the attack of the nematodes on the roots of the plants. Upon inspection, you can see that the root systems are poorly developed, and even partially decayed. The roots have knots or galls on them. The effects of nematode activity are most apparent in hot weather, when the plants recover poorly from the heat.

The southern root knot nematodes (*Meloidogyne incognita*) attack spireas. Nematodes are whitish, translucent, wormlike creatures, ¹⁄₅₀ to ¹⁄₁₀ inch long.

To control these pests, add about 1 inch of compost to the soil around your plants. Leaf mold is especially effective. This encourages beneficial fungi. Fertilize your shrubs with liquid fish emulsion, pouring it into the soil as a drench; it repels nematodes.

## Leaves Yellowed; Small Bumps on Leaves and Branches

### Scale

The first sign of a scale attack is yellowing of the leaves, followed by leaf drop, reduced growth, and stunting. Heavy infestations kill plants. Some species of scale excrete honeydew, which attracts ants and encourages the growth of sooty mold. If you notice any of these symptoms, look for the scale themselves. They resemble bumps, having rounded waxy shells, which protect them while they feed on your plants. Some of the species that infect spireas are cottony-maple scale (*Pulvinaria innumerabilis*), oystershell scale (*Lepidosaphes ulmi*), and spirea scale (*Eriococcus borealis*). They have a diameter of ¹⁄₁₀ to ⅖ inch and may be white, yellow, or brown to black.

Early on in the infestation, you can simply scrape the pests off your plants with your fingernail or a cotton swab dipped in rubbing alcohol. Once the number of pests becomes too large to control this way, spray the entire shrub with a solution of alcohol and insecticidal soap every three days for two weeks. To make this solution, mix 1 cup of isopropyl alcohol and 1 tablespoon of insecticidal soap concentrate in 1 quart of water. If your insecticidal soap is already mixed with water, add 1 tablespoon of alcohol to a pint of the diluted soap. In late winter or early spring, spray plants with a dormant oil to smother overwintering adults and eggs.

## MOST COMMON DISEASES

### Leaves and Twigs Die

#### Fire Blight

Caused by the bacterium *Erwinia amylovora*, fire blight is a particularly destructive disease of spireas. It is a blight of young twigs and limbs. Leaves on affected shoots die, hang downward, and cling to the blighted twigs. Dying branches, which appear scorched, are very conspicuous during the summer and detract greatly from the beauty of the shrubs. Rain and insects spread this disease.

Prune infected branches, cutting well below blighted areas. Spray shrubs with the antibiotic Agri-strep. Be careful not to overfeed spireas; this makes them more prone to blight.

### Dead Blotches on Leaves

#### Leaf Spot

Any of several fungi may be responsible for leaf spot on your spireas. The spots may be yellow, brown, or black and they frequently run together, forming larger dead blotches. Severely infected leaves turn yellow or brown and fall prematurely. Some fungal spots are surrounded by flecks or black dots, which are the spore-bearing fruiting bodies.

You can easily distinguish leaf spot diseases from spots caused by unfavorable environmental conditions. Examine the leaves with a magnifying glass, and you will see the tiny black fruiting bodies of the fungus embedded in the discolored leaf tissues. Environmental spots are caused by winter injury and ice that focuses sunlight so that it burns the leaves.

In the spring, fungal spores germinate and grow into the leaf. Some leaf spot fungi produce summer spores, which are scattered by rain, spreading the disease even farther. Cool, moist weather favors these diseases, especially when new leaves are developing. The fungi of leaf spot overwinter in dead leaves on the ground.

To control leaf spot, pick off and destroy infected leaves. Shake out all fallen and diseased leaves caught in the center of the shrub and destroy them, and prune all dead branches from the center of shrubs to enable air to circulate more freely. Spray the entire shrub every seven to ten days with a sulfur or copper fungicide, particularly in rainy seasons. Remove fallen plant debris promptly to reduce overwintering spore populations. Mulching helps prevent water from splashing up on plants, bringing with it fungal spores. Cut down and destroy any seriously infected shrubs, together with the soil ball.

### White Powder on Leaves

#### Powdery Mildew

Powdery mildew in spireas is caused by a variety of fungi. The fungi create a thin white powdery coating on the upper surfaces of leaves. Spray plants thoroughly with wettable sulfur once or twice at weekly intervals until the problem is controlled. Collect and destroy all plant debris around your shrubs.

## NOTES AND RESEARCH

Bumald spirea is relatively free of pests, but is also most sensitive to a high soil pH.

## SHRUB *Viburnum*    *Viburnum* spp.

### DESCRIPTION

Viburnums boast attractive flowers, showy berries, and interesting foliage, and they are very easy to grow. This diverse group includes about 225 species of valuable shrubs and small trees. They have an ornamental role during every season, blooming in spring and producing red, yellow, blue, or black berries in the fall. Use them in a shrub border, with broad-leaved evergreens, or as groupings or screens.

## Height

Arrowwood (*Viburnum dentatum*), 10 to 15 feet
Burkwood viburnum (*V. ×burkwoodii*), 6 feet
European cranberrybush (*V. opulus*), 12 feet
Fragrant snowball (*V. ×carlcephalum*), 9 feet
Hobblebush (*V. alnifolium*), 10 feet
Japanese snowball (*V. plicatum*), 9 feet
Judd viburnum (*V. ×juddii*), 8 feet
Koreanspice (*V. carlesii*), 5 feet
Leatherleaf (*V. rhytidophyllum*), 10 feet
Linden (*V. dilatatum*), 9 feet

Mapleleaf viburnum (*V. acerifolium*), 6 feet
Nannyberry (*V. lentago*), 30 feet
Siebold viburnum (*V. sieboldii*), 30 feet
Wayfaring tree (*V. lantana*), 15 feet
Withe-rod viburnum (*V. cassinoides*), 6 feet

## Spread

Viburnums will spread to a width of 3 to 12 feet, depending on the species.

## Blossoms

The pink or white flowers of viburnums bloom in early to mid-spring. Viburnums display their blossoms in one of three forms: in clusters shaped like snowballs; in flat clusters; or in flat, tight clusters with sterile flowers around the outside and fertile flowers near the inside. Most have a pleasant scent, with the fragrant viburnum giving off the most fragrance of all. In fall, attractive berries replace the fertile flowers.

## Foliage

Most viburnums are deciduous, although a few are evergreen or partly evergreen (Burkwood viburnum, David viburnum [*V. davidii*], leatherleaf viburnum, and Sandankwa [*V. suspensum*], among others). Foliage varies considerably from shrub to shrub. It may be green, dark green, or even bluish green, sometimes with pale or hairy undersides. The leaves fall opposite each other on the stem and are 2 to 3 inches long. Some have a leathery texture, some are wrinkled, some are deeply veined, and some are waxy and glossy.

## ENVIRONMENT

### Varieties by Zone

To zone 3, arrowwood, European cranberry bush, and nannyberry

To zone 4, Burkwood, hobblebush, mapleleaf viburnum, Siebold viburnum, witherod viburnum, and wayfaring tree

To zone 5, fragrant snowball, Japanese snowball, Judd viburnum, Koreanspice, leatherleaf viburnum, and linden

To zone 8, David viburnum

To zone 9, Sandankwa

## Light Requirements

Most viburnums live in full sun to medium shade. Mapleleaf, hobblebush, and withe-rod viburnums can be grown in shade, but must have moist soil.

## Soil Requirements

Viburnums will tolerate almost any soil. Their preference is for a slightly moist, well-drained soil that is slightly acid (pH range 6 to 7.5).

# PLANTING AND PROPAGATION

## Planting

Fall is the best planting time for viburnums, but they may also be planted in spring.

## Propagation

Propagate viburnums from semiripe cuttings taken in the early summer, June to July.

# PLANT MANAGEMENT

Viburnums vary in their needs, sometimes greatly, depending on the species.

## Water Requirements

Viburnums need about an inch of water each week, increasing to 1½ inches a week in the hot summer. Stop watering from late August to mid-October to prevent excessive fall growth, which might be susceptible to winterkill. Resume any necessary supplemental watering in the late fall and soak the ground before it freezes solid. Viburnums have relatively shallow root systems, which cannot take up water from frozen ground. Without one last good drenching, your shrubs might suffer moisture deficiency in the late winter.

## Feeding Requirements

One main application of compost every year in the late fall or early spring is all that viburnums need for good, healthy growth. Although supplemental feedings aren't necessary, viburnums will look their best if you spray them with a solution of dilute liquid fertilizer mixed with dilute seaweed extract. Apply this supplement once a month for just the first three months after the last frost. If you live in a cold climate, stop all feeding two months prior to the first frost to help plants harden off for winter.

## Pruning

After four to five years, remove one-third of the oldest flowering growth on your viburnums in the winter, and prune every two or three years thereafter. If you want to shape your viburnums, prune them after they flower.

## Cutting Fresh Flowers

Bring viburnum flowers indoors to enjoy their fragrance. Cut them just as they begin to open.

# MOST COMMON INSECT PESTS

## Leaves Curled, Discolored, and Distorted

### Aphids

Viburnums are vulnerable to attack from several species of aphid: viburnum aphids (*Aphis viburniphila*), snowball aphids (*Neoceruraphis viburnicola*), foxglove aphids (*Acyrthosiphon solani*), bean aphids (*Aphis fabae*), and currant aphids (*Cryptomyzus ribis*). All have generally the same effect. As they feed on foliage, leaves become discolored, curled, and distorted. Ants are attracted to the honeydew secreted by aphids. If you suspect aphids, look for them on the undersides of leaves. They have soft, pear-shaped bodies just a little bigger than the head of a pin, and they may be green, brown, black, or pinkish.

Knock aphids from your shrubs by spraying the undersides of the viburnum leaves vigorously with water. Do this in the early morning, three times, once every other day. You can control medium to heavy infestations more effectively if you spray shrubs with insecticidal soap every two to three days until aphids are gone. As a last resort, use pyrethrum, making two applications, three to four days apart.

## Leaves and Flowers Skeletonized

### Asiatic Garden Beetles

If the flowers and leaves of your viburnums are simply being devoured, especially near the base of the plant, suspect the Asiatic garden beetle (*Maladera castanea*). The adults cause most of the damage, but the larvae feed on plant roots. Larvae are ¾ inch long, grayish, and bent in a C-shape like Japanese beetle grubs. Adult Asiatic beetles feed at night and with their voracious appetites they skeletonize foliage and flowers. These beetles are ½ inch long, velvety, and chestnut brown; they resemble Japanese beetles. They lay their eggs in the soil at the base of plants.

As soon as you discover them on your shrubs, apply beneficial nematodes to the soil. For long-term control, apply milky spore disease (*Bacillus popilliae*). In the spring, carefully cultivate the soil around the viburnum to expose the eggs, larvae, and pupae to the weather and to predator birds. Take care not to harm the roots.

## Holes in Twigs

### Borers

Viburnums are susceptible to attack from the dogwood twig borer (*Oberea tripunctata*). These pests bore into the tips of stems and twigs soon after bloom time. As they get larger, they move into the woody part of the viburnum, pushing out fine sawdust as they go. Twigs may break off as the larvae bore through them, and sometimes large branches

die. Borer grubs are about ¾ inch long and dull yellow in color. They overwinter in the twigs of the viburnum. Adult beetles appear in the spring. In spring, crush any eggs that you can find.

Prune and burn infested stems, if this won't mean deforming your shrub. Coat wounds with tree paint or paraffin. If borer holes seem fairly straight, poke a wire inside to kill the borer. Actually, a hooked wire is best because it allows you to pull the grub out and dispose of it. If the tunnels wind around or if you find too many of them, inject nicotine sulfate into the holes and plug them up with putty.

## Leaves Discolored; Shrubs Sickly, Wilted, and Stunted

### Nematodes

You won't see nematodes on your viburnums, but they'll be sure to let you know they are there. Plants infested with nematodes look sickly, wilted, and stunted. Their leaves turn yellow or bronze, and they decline slowly and die. Nematodes attack at the roots of a plant. An examination shows that infested root systems are poorly developed, even partially decayed. The southern root knot nematode (*Meloidogynes incognita*) is the culprit in infested viburnums. Nematodes are not insects, but slender, unsegmented roundworms. Most are soil-dwellers, less than 1/20 inch long.

To control nematodes, add lots of compost—especially leaf mold—to the soil around the plant to encourage beneficial fungi. Fertilize with liquid fish emulsion poured into the soil as a drench; it repels nematodes.

## Leaves Discolored; Small Bumps on Leaves and Branches

### Scale

Discolored leaves, followed by leaf drop, reduced growth, and stunted shrubs, make up the progression of a scale infestation. You may also see ants and sooty mold on shrubs. They are attracted by the honeydew that some species of scale secrete. Heavy infestations kill viburnums. Any one of several species of scale may attack your plants. These include cottony-cushion scale (*Icerya purchasi*), oystershell scale (*Lepidosaphes ulmi*), chaff scale (*Parlatoria pergandii*), and San Jose scale (*Quadraspidiotus perniciosus*). If your plants show the symptoms described above, look for the insects themselves. Scale look like small bumps with their rounded waxy covering, which protects them while they feed. They range from $1/10$ to $2/5$ inch in diameter and may be white, yellow, or brown to black.

If you catch the infestation early on, you can simply scrape these pests off your shrubs with your fingernail or a cotton swab dipped in rubbing alcohol. Any sizable number of scale is more easily controlled by spraying shrubs with a mixture of alcohol and insecticidal soap every three days for two weeks. Make this solution by combining 1 cup isopropyl alcohol and 1 tablespoon insecticidal soap concentrate in 1 quart water. If your insecticidal soap is already mixed with water, add 1 tablespoon alcohol to a pint of the diluted soap. In late winter or early spring, spray plants with dormant oil to smother overwintering adults and eggs.

## Leaves Flecked and Whitened

### Thrips

Thrips feed on plants by rasping at plant cells to break them and then sucking the juices. As a result, leaf surfaces become flecked and whitened, and leaf tips wither, curl up, and die. Turn the leaves over and you will see tiny black specks of excrement. Both flower thrips (*Frankliniella tritici*) and greenhouse thrips (*Heliothrips haemorrhoidalis*) attack viburnums. Adult thrips are tiny, slender insects, $1/25$ inch long. They may be yellow, black, or brown. They have four relatively long and narrow wings fringed with hairs. The yellowish nymphs are wingless.

Since thrips burrow deep between flower petals, start control measures as soon as possible. As soon as you discover thrip damage, spray shrubs with insecticidal soap every three days for two weeks. Commercially available predatory mites, lacewings,

ladybugs, and beneficial nematodes are effective backups to the soap spray.

# MOST COMMON DISEASES

*Note:* Sulfur-based fungicides can be harmful to certain species of viburnum, but not to all. If they are recommended as the best control for a particular disease, test the sensitivity of your viburnum. Spritz some sulfur fungicide on one branch and watch it for a few days to see if any negative reaction occurs. If nothing looks awry after three days, you can use sulfur on that plant.

## Sunken Spots on Leaves

### Anthracnose

Anthracnose may be caused by any one of several fungi in the *Colletotrichum* spp. or *Gloeosporium* spp. Moist, dark brown, sunken spots with fruiting bodies develop on the leaves of anthracnose-infected shrubs. These leaf spots may run together, resembling a blotch or blight. The dead areas follow the veins of the leaves. Sometimes the disease extends down to several inches below the buds. Pustules containing pinkish spores develop on the lesions. In severe cases, dieback and defoliation occur.

Gather and destroy diseased leaves when they fall, and prune infected branches. Spray the entire shrub with a copper fungicide, such as Bordeaux mixture. To increase the resistance of your shrubs to this disease, maintain their vigor by feeding and watering them well, especially during droughts.

## Spots on Buds and Flowers; Blotches on Leaves

### Blight

The fungus *Botrytis cinerea* attacks dense flower clusters of viburnums during wet weather. The blight also attacks and kills shoot tips. Spots develop on flowers and foliage, and merge to form blotches as the disease progresses. Entire flowers deteriorate.

Leaves develop grayish brown decayed patches.

As soon as you discover these symptoms, prune away and destroy all infected growth and spray the infected plants with copper fungicide. Repeat applications every ten days in wet seasons. Increase air circulation around plants by pruning. Avoid overhead watering, which creates the conditions that this disease favors.

## Tumorlike Swellings on Stems

### Crown Gall

Galls with rough, irregular surfaces develop on the stems of viburnums infected with crown gall. The bacterium *Agrobacterium tumefaciens* causes this disease in viburnums. A serious infection causes branches to die back. Prune and destroy all branches that bear galls.

## Dead Blotches on Leaves

### Leaf Spot

Several species of fungi cause leaf spot in viburnums: *Cercospora* spp., *Phyllosticta* spp., *Septoria* spp., and many others. Depending on the fungus, spots may be yellow, brown, or black. Some are surrounded by flecks or black dots—the spore-bearing fruiting bodies. Frequently the spots run together, forming larger blotches. Heavily infected leaves turn yellow or brown and fall prematurely. Cool, moist weather favors leaf spot diseases, especially when new leaves are developing.

Spots caused by leaf spot are easily distinguished from those caused by unfavorable environmental conditions. Examine leaves with a magnifying glass, and if your plants are diseased, you will see the telltale tiny black fruiting bodies of the fungus embedded in the discolored leaf tissues.

Pick off and discard infected leaves and shake out all fallen leaves from the shrub and destroy them. Cut out dead branches from the center of plants to allow better aeration. Remove dead plant debris promptly from around viburnums to reduce overwintering spore populations. Finally, spray the entire shrub every seven to ten days with either a sulfur or copper fungicide, particularly in rainy seasons. Cut down and discard seriously infected shrubs, together with the soil ball. Mulching helps prevent water carrying fungal spores from splashing up onto your shrubs.

## White Powder on Leaves

### Powdery Mildew

This disease is easily identifiable by the thin, white, powdery growth of the fungus *Microsphaera alni* that spreads across the upper surfaces of viburnum leaves. In late summer, bushes in shady spots may be badly infected. Spray plants thoroughly with wettable sulfur once or twice at weekly intervals, starting as soon as the whitish coating of the fungus is visible. In the fall, collect and destroy all plant debris around your viburnums.

## Rust-Colored Spots on Leaves

### Rust

Rust is one of the more colorful diseases of viburnums. The leaves of infected shrubs develop raised powdery spots that are rust-colored, orange, yellow, or white. Several fungi can cause rust in viburnums. These include members of the *Puccinia* spp., *Melampsora* spp., *Cronartium* spp., and others. Infected leaves wilt and wither, and the entire plant may be stunted.

Fortunately, rust is seldom a serious problem on viburnums. Remove diseased leaves as soon as possible. Collect and destroy all plant debris around your viburnums in fall.

# CHAPTER 3

# *Roses*

**A**h, roses...Who doesn't love roses? Who hasn't loved roses? Their blossoms radiate beauty, mean beauty, create beauty. For centuries people have given roses in bouquets of love, bathed in rose water, perfumed their bodies and homes with rose oil, scattered rose petals around rooms, awarded roses for achievement, planted rose gardens. This queen of flowers graces the mind, the home, and the landscape.

## DESCRIPTION

Roses have almost as many forms as they have uses, and are classified accordingly. Roses are classified into a variety of classes and sub-classes according to origin, bloom type, and habit. These groups include species, shrub, climbing, old garden, and miniature roses, as well as the familiar hybrid teas, grandifloras, and floribundas. Each group has characteristics that suit it for specific landscape uses.

Hybrid tea, floribunda, and grandiflora roses produce spectacular blooms. These roses are best planted in masses, where they create grand splashes of color in the landscape. The grandifloras are taller than floribundas and produce fairly long-stemmed roses, making them ideal plants for a background border.

Shrub roses combine both a pleasing form and beautiful flowers. They have a more informal growth habit than hybrid teas, floribundas, or grandifloras, and so can be, and often are, planted individually in the landscape. They are very durable plants. Old garden roses have begun regaining much-deserved popularity among gardeners. Both shrub and old garden roses are further divided into many different classes based on flower form and origin, and both

groups include many valuable landscape plants.

Miniature roses are ideal for edgings and container plantings.

Climbing roses have long arching canes that reach 6 feet or more in length. This group is divided

A floribunda

137

ypes, including large-flowered climbers, edium or large blooms in small clusters, hybrid teas, which are climbing forms of hybrid teas. Both have thick, somewhat stiff canes and an upright habit. Rambling roses have flexible, thinner canes and thick clusters of smaller blossoms. Climbing roses have no tendrils with which to hold onto trellises or arbors, so you will have to fasten the canes loosely to these structures.

The blossom of a hybrid tea rose

Roses can be used as hedges, in beds, as boundary plantings, in front of evergreens, with or among other shrubs, and along fences. When planting a rose bed, greater impact is achieved when roses are planted in groups with three plants of the same variety in each group. Consider, too, bordering the roses with low annuals.

## Height

Floribundas, 3 feet
Hybrid teas, 4 to 5 feet
Grandifloras, up to 6 feet

### Shrub and Old Garden Roses
Most varieties, 2 to 8 feet; some 12 feet or more

### Miniature Roses
Most varieties, 6 to 18 inches

### Climbing Roses
Large-flower type, 10 to 15 feet
Rambling type, 10 to 20 feet

## Spread

Roses usually spread about two-thirds the height of the plant. Generally, roses will grow larger and wider the warmer the climate. A particular hybrid tea rose might have a spread of 2 feet in Boston but 4 feet in Seattle, where growing conditions are better. Climbing roses will spread as they are permitted, reaching coverage of up to 20 feet if unpruned.

## Blossoms

It's the hybrid tea rose that most of us picture when we think of roses. This group has been bred specifically for large, spectacular blossoms, which burst forth from the ends of long, straight, sturdy stems. The flowers of floribundas bloom in large clusters on these compact plants.

Roses come in many colors—red, pink, orange to gold, white to cream, burgundy, and even lavender. Some roses have a classic scent, though many of the modern hybrids, bred for beautiful blossoms, have lost the strong familiar rose fragrance of their ancestors. Some roses bloom from early summer steadily into late fall. Others bloom in early summer and again in fall. Still others bloom only in late spring or early summer. Some roses produce red or orange "hips" that are valued for their ornamental usefulness.

## Foliage

Roses are deciduous. The leaves are green and have a smooth texture. Some varieties have shiny leaves, while others have leaves with more of a matte surface.

# ENVIRONMENT

Roses thrive in a place with good sun and good air movement, which helps the dew and the rain to dry quickly, discouraging disease problems. Too much wind, however, can damage the foliage in summer and the canes in winter. If you live in a windy area, plant roses where they will get some protection, such as near a wall, fence, windbreak, or hedge.

## Hardiness

Most shrub roses and some old garden roses can survive the cruelest winters, while only a few of the hybrid teas, grandifloras, and floribundas do. These are only generalizations; within each group, hardiness changes from cultivar to cultivar. Experts disagree on what rose is hardy where. Consequently, hardiness zones have not been assigned to specific cultivars.

## Light Requirements

Roses need bright sun at least five to six hours a day. Most roses will tolerate filtered shade, but too much shade reduces the number of blossoms, encourages legginess, and invites rust and mildew problems. If you have a choice, locate your roses so that they receive sunlight early in the day. Roses prefer some shade in the afternoon to the scorching summer sun.

## Soil Requirements

A well-drained but moist soil provides the best environment for rose roots. When planting roses, place them in a soil that contains at least 25 percent organic matter. The ideal mix consists of five parts loamy soil, four parts organic matter (compost, leaf mold, peat moss, and so forth), and one part builder's sand. Roses like a slightly acid environment with a pH of 6 to 6.5, but will tolerate soils with a pH as high as 7.5 or as low as 6.

A climbing rose

# PLANTING AND PROPAGATION

Unlike most shrubs, roses are a bit more precise in their planting requirements. In the end, of course, if you place them in good soil and provide them with the proper environment, your planting techniques become secondary. Nevertheless, you will enjoy healthier, more vigorous roses if you plant them correctly.

## Planting

Most roses are sold bare root rather than in containers. They are usually two-year-old, field-grown plants, which arrive at your home in the mail or are shipped to nurseries in the early spring. You are likely to have more success with bare-root plants than container-grown ones. The roots of roses that have been grown in containers may be cramped, and as a result these plants may have difficulty becoming established.

In most parts of the country, bare-root and container roses are planted in the early spring before the green buds begin to show. You can, though, plant them just about any time of year as long as you water them well. You will be taking a risk if you plant bare-root roses during hot summer months, but again, if you take care to water them well, they'll survive. Get bare-root plants into the ground as soon as you receive them. If you cannot, keep them dormant by dampening the roots and storing them in a cool, dark place where they can remain for up to two weeks. You can plant either bare-root or container roses any time during their dormant season, provided, of course, the soil is not frozen. In the South and Southwest, and on the West Coast, this can be in January or February. Container roses can be planted almost any time during the growing season. Soak bare-root roses in water for 6 to 24 hours before planting.

In general, the technique for planting roses is the same as that for other shrubs, but you should keep some specific details in mind. Rose roots eventually grow to a length of 16 to 18 inches, so try to mix organic material that deep into the soil. Plant-ing depth varies with your climatic zone. Determine it by the level of the bud union—the bulbous or swollen area just above the roots where the flowering stock was grafted to the root stock. In the South, plant bush, shrub, and climbing roses so the bud union is even with the surface of the soil. In the North, place the plant so the bud union is 2 to 4 inches below the surface of the soil to protect it from winter cold. In the middle latitudes of the United States, place the bud union about an inch below the surface of the soil. When digging the hole for your roses, remove any rocks to give the roots more room to spread.

Miniature roses have no graft or bud union, so they can be set slightly deeper in the soil than they were in the container in which they originally grew.

If the plant is still dormant when you plant it in the early spring, mound at least 6 inches of soil around and over it. This prevents canes from drying out and protects the roots from any quick cold spells. When the weather warms and buds do begin to sprout, gradually remove the soil mound over a period of a week or two. Loosen the wire holding the name tag so it does not constrict the cane to which it is attached.

About a month after the buds begin to pop, you should notice vigorous growth. Fertilize your plants according to the feeding instructions given later. *Do not add fertilizer to the planting mix;* doing so delays growth and can injure the developing roots.

### Spacing

The distance between plants depends on which type of rose you are growing.

**Hybrid Teas and Grandifloras.** Hybrid teas and grandifloras are a little sensitive to the amount of space around them. In northern and central states, set them 24 to 30 inches apart. Increase this to 36 inches if you live in the South, Southwest, or West. In frost-free areas such as the Gulf Coast and southern California, roses do not have a dormant period and will grow larger than in other parts of North America. In these regions, allow 48 inches between plants. If you want a little extra room for working around roses without being stabbed or scratched by thorns, add a foot or so to the planting distance.

**Floribundas.** These roses are usually grouped for mass effect. Plant them 24 inches apart in cold climates and 30 inches apart in mild climates.

**Shrub Roses.** Because of their large, sprawling, informal growth habit, these roses look great planted individually in the landscape. If you do plant them in groups, space them 4 to 10 feet apart, using the spread of the particular plants you are growing as your guide.

**Miniature Roses.** Set them in the ground 10 to 12 inches from each other and from larger plants that could deny them soil nutrients, sunshine, and moisture.

## Propagation

The easiest way to propagate roses is from softwood cuttings taken during the blooming season. You can also propagate them by budding, or grow them from seed.

## Container Gardening

Some of the smaller hybrid roses can be grown in containers, and should be planted in pots that are at least 14 inches deep and 18 inches wide. Miniature roses make fine container plants. They require pots 6 to 10 inches in diameter. Miniature roses can be set outdoors on decks or patios, and they grow very well indoors, too. When raising them indoors, use commercial soil mixes to avoid fungal disease, which might be carried in soil from your yard. They need at least four to five hours of sunshine a day. Do not let them dry out. Container-grown roses that decorate the outside of your home need to be moved to unheated shelters when the temperature falls below 28°F.

# PLANT MANAGEMENT

Roses are not low-maintenance plants. They require a fair amount of care in order to look their best, but they're worth it.

## Water Requirements

Roses are thirsty plants and need a steady flow of moisture for peak performance. Do not let them dry out. In most soils and regions, about an inch of water a week suffices. In very sandy soil or in the South, roses may need as much as 2 inches of water every week. You want to keep roots moist but not wet throughout the growing season. Water must penetrate 16 to 18 inches to reach the full depth of the roots of mature plants. That is why the best soil drains easily but also retains moisture. You can water roses in their dormant season if the ground is not frozen, but on a more limited schedule, about ½ to 1 inch every two weeks. Watering is only necessary during the dormant season, though, if conditions have been unusually dry.

The best system for watering roses uses drip irrigation placed under a layer of organic mulch. This puts water right into the soil and prevents any from splashing up to the plants and bringing with it any fungal spores that might be on the soil surface. Whatever method you use, water your roses in the morning so the plants can dry off by evening, when fungal diseases thrive.

## Feeding Requirements

In most regions, roses require only one major feeding in the early spring after pruning. However, because these plants work hard producing blossoms for a long season, they do best with more than one application of fertilizer each year. Spray them with a dilute liquid fertilizer every three to four weeks throughout the season, until six weeks before the last bloom cycle. Prepare the liquid fertilizer at half the strength recommended on the bottle for these foliar feedings. You can add diluted seaweed extract (1 tablespoon extract in a gallon of water) to the foliar spray to improve the plant's ability to use nutrients. (See chapter 10 for more information on the use of seaweed extract.) If you live in the South or if your roses are growing in fast-draining sandy soil, give them a second major feeding about halfway between the time flower buds appear and eight weeks before the first expected frost.

Some rosarians give their roses a dose of brewer's yeast to overcome the midseason blahs that sometimes occur. Mix 1 or 2 tablespoons dry brewer's yeast with a gallon of water and spray the mixture over the entire plant. Rosarians report that this tonic produces greener foliage, sturdier growth, and improved bloom.

One cautionary note: You can overfertilize your roses. Too much nitrogen generates frequent flushes of lush, weak growth that is very susceptible to attack by powdery mildew, black spot, and rust. Don't feed them any more than is recommended above, and stay away from fertilizers that release nitrogen quickly.

## Mulching

Roses benefit enormously from mulching. While it keeps weeds down, its greatest value is in reducing evaporation. It helps maintain moisture levels and keeps the soil cooler in the summer, when roses are vulnerable to heat stress. A thick organic mulch, freshly applied in early spring while the plant is still dormant, also helps to reduce fungal disease problems. It does this simply by covering infected soil and preventing any spores from being bounced up onto plants with splashing rain.

At least a month before the expected last frost in spring, spread 2 to 4 inches of organic mulch around the stem of the rose bush, starting 2 inches away from the stem. Although the soil around the roses will warm up more slowly, you will have fewer fungal disease problems to deal with later in the season. Use wood chips, shredded bark, pine needles, cottonseed or cocoa bean hulls, chopped leaves, ground corn cobs, or peat nuggets for mulch. Geotextile material makes an excellent first layer for mulching around roses. Lay the textile on the soil and then cover it with organic matter for a more attractive look.

## Deadheading

Roses will bloom profusely if you cut faded blossoms.

This encourages plants to put nutrients and energy into producing more leaves and flowers rather than into producing seeds. Dead flowers also provide a desirable environment for disease.

To properly deadhead roses, cut the stem back to an out-facing bud or leaflet. This encourages strong new growth away from the center of the plant. Try to avoid removing any more leaves than you have to. The leaves are the plant's food factory and are essential to the regrowth of new leaves and blossoms. At the same time, don't be so prudent that you snip off only the blossoms, because that favors the production of smaller leaf stems or buds.

Deadhead climbing roses as well. After blossoms have passed their prime, cut the stem back to a leaflet or a bud with five leaves, making the cut just above the bud.

## Fall Cleanup

A thorough fall cleanup every year is essential to keep roses healthy. Remove any leaves that remain on the plant, and rake up and discard all old leaves, prunings, and any other debris on the ground or around the bases of the plants. This removes any insect eggs or disease spores that overwinter on plant debris. After cleaning the bed, water the soil thoroughly; the roots of roses remain active long after winter begins.

## Winterizing

How well your roses survive winter depends on which species or hybrids you are growing—some are hardier than others—and also the health and vigor of the plants. But you can take measures to increase a plant's chances of passing through this sometimes harsh season completely unharmed.

Icy temperatures, vast fluctuations in temperature, and whipping winds are the three threats of winter. To protect your roses, your goals are to prevent the temperature around plants from dropping below a certain point; to steady that temperature so that alternate freezing and thawing does not occur; and to keep branches from being thrashed by winds that loosen the entire plant from the ground. Work to keep roses sufficiently cold so that they are dormant at a fairly constant temperature—ideally within a range of 15°F to 25°F—and buffer them from the wind.

The techniques of winter protection generally apply to all roses grown in all regions of the country. The extent of protection varies according to just how cold winters get. Timing also varies from region to region, but begin winterizing your plants just before hard freezing weather sets in, which usually occurs about a month or two after the first frost.

Roses growing in an area where winter temperatures do not drop below 20°F really don't require winter protection, although it doesn't hurt to spray them with an antitranspirant to minimize water loss during the cool months. If your plants are located in a site that is exposed to drying winter winds, wrap the plants or build a wind barrier with burlap or agricultural fleece. These materials allow air to get to the plant, but protect it from the drying effects of the wind. Another option is to shield plants with a permanent fence or hedge; leave 10 feet between the fence and the rose bushes.

In areas where winter temperatures drop as low as 10°F to 15°F for a two-week period or more, begin winterizing roses after the first hard frost. Mound fresh, loose soil or compost 6 to 8 inches high around the base of each plant. Do not pull up soil from the rose bed, but bring it in from another part of the garden just in case any rose-infecting diseases lie in the ground beneath your shrubs. Prune the plants back only enough to prevent the canes from whipping about in the wind and to allow them to fit under a protective covering (in particularly harsh areas, this might mean pruning back to 12- to 18-inch canes). Spray the bushes with an antitranspirant spray, and then lay 8 to 10 inches of organic mulch over the entire bed. You can wrap rose bushes with burlap or agricultural fleece to limit the movement of the canes in winter winds and to keep the plants from drying out. Some gardeners surround their plants with a cylinder of chicken wire or netting to keep the mulch from blowing away in the wind.

If you live where temperatures dip to −15°F or lower, follow all of the steps mentioned earlier and enclose the entire plant under a protective shield such as a peach basket, tar paper cone, or some commercially available rose cap or cone designed to protect roses in winter.

When spring arrives, don't be too eager to remove this winter covering. As the mounds around the base of your roses thaw, gradually remove soil over a period of two to three weeks. Do this carefully to avoid breaking any stems that may have already begun to grow. Tender new growth can be easily killed by even a light freeze, so keep some straw or agricultural fleece handy to spread around plants in the event of a late frost.

Climbing roses require a slightly different method of winter protection. If you live in an area where winter temperatures drop below −5°F, detach your large-flowered, repeat-blooming climbers from their support and lay them on the ground. Carefully bunch the canes together and peg them to the soil with wooden or wire hoops of some kind. Finally, completely cover them with 4 to 6 inches of well-drained soil, compost, or organic mulch.

## Pruning

Prune roses to give them good form; to encourage new growth; to remove any diseased, damaged, or dead wood; and to generate larger blossoms.

Get your pruning shears out in early spring after the last frost, just before your roses break dormancy. You should be as certain as you can that freezing temperatures won't strike again. You don't want a late frost to damage the new growth that forms after pruning. In warm climates, you may begin as early as January. Where winters are severe, you may have to wait until April. The blooming of forsythia is a reliable signal that it is time to prune.

The pruning of roses is a precise technique, the guidelines for which are the same for all forms of roses. First, remove any dead wood down to the nearest healthy, dormant bud eye. A bud eye is a small bulge on the stem that has what looks like a tiny eye with a horizontal crease underneath it.

Once dormancy has broken, or it has been stimulated by pruning, the bud eye will develop into a new shoot. Notice the direction in which bud eyes point. After pruning, the top bud on each cane should be facing away from the interior of the plant so that new canes don't all grow into the center, where they will tangle and compete for sunlight. Position your shears so that the cutting blade is on the lower end of the cut to ensure a clean cut. Make the cut at a 45 degree angle, at least 1 inch below the dead wood and about ¼ inch above the outward-facing bud. If cuts are made too high above the bud, the wood above the bud will die, providing a haven for pests and disease. If the cane that you are pruning has no buds, remove the entire branch down to the union with the stem. Also completely remove any old thick and woody canes; they produce a profusion of twigs rather than strong stems.

After pruning the dead canes, remove all diseased wood. Cut any sickly canes down to a plump, healthy bud, at least 1 inch below the infected area.

Next, remove all undesirable wood—the weak, spindly, and deformed growth; the doglegs, canes that grow straight out and then curve upward. Cut canes that are growing toward the center of the bush. If two branches cross, remove the weaker one.

Finally, remove all suckers or reversion growth (undersized shoots that come from the rootstock below the bud union). When cutting them out, take the entire base of the sucker from the crown area, along with a piece of the crown if necessary.

After you've finished pruning, consider spraying your plants with Bordeaux mixture or a flowable sulfur fungicide to prevent the early onset of fungal diseases. Then spray with dormant oil as a final obstacle to insect eggs and disease spores that may have remained on the plant through winter. This must be done before green leaves begin to emerge.

### Pruning Specific Types of Roses

Although, as said, the technique and purposes of pruning are the same for all roses, consider specific methods for specific types to bring the best form, health, and vigor to the particular roses you are growing.

**Hybrid Teas and Grandifloras.** The degree to which you prune these roses depends on the effect you want to achieve, as well as the state of your plants. In general, more pruning produces fewer but showier blossoms on smaller shrubs.

If you want to produce a few very showy blooms, or if your plants have become weak and need to be rejuvenated, remove all but three or four canes and cut those down to a height of 6 to 10 inches. This degree of pruning also reduces the chances for recurrence of any serious fungal diseases your roses had last year.

If you want to create a larger, well-shaped bush with smaller but more numerous blossoms, prune moderately. Leave 5 to 12 canes and cut them down to 18 to 24 inches. Light pruning means that less than one-third of the plant is cut back, a practice that will produce an even larger bush covered with a profusion of short-stemmed flowers. The moderate approach produces the best look for most gardens.

**Floribundas.** Floribundas are not pruned as severely as hybrid teas, but you do need to remove all the dead and undesirable wood each year. Cut all the longer canes down to about half their former height to maintain the plant's good form. For healthier, more vigorous roses, cut the canes of the floribunda every two to three years to within 6 inches of the ground.

**Shrub Roses.** It is not true that shrub roses need no pruning. They do require far less pruning than bush roses, but you'll get more vigorous, healthy shrub roses if you give the plants some light attention with the pruning shears in the early spring.

Take a long-term approach when pruning shrub roses. You want to encourage strong new shoots to grow from the base of the plant by removing older, less vigorous wood that shades new growth. This is a process of gradual renewal rather than radical removal. After the second growing season, cut back the overly long vigorous shoots about 25 percent. During the third and subsequent dormant seasons, routinely remove one or two of the oldest shoots to favor the strong new canes. Trim growth to maintain the open, upright shape and cut back any excessively long shoots.

**Miniature Roses.** If you want to keep a miniature rose compact, prune it back severely every year, cutting canes to 6 to 8 inches. Otherwise, prune lightly as you would a floribunda rose.

**Climbing Roses.** During the first two years, do not prune large-flowered climbers except to remove dead wood. Climbing roses produce better flowers on canes that grow horizontally rather than vertically. So the trick to managing a climbing rose is to thin out the oldest wood from time to time, keeping the total number of canes constant, and securing the canes to the trellis so that they tend toward a more horizontal position. Do this major pruning in the winter, when the plant is dormant.

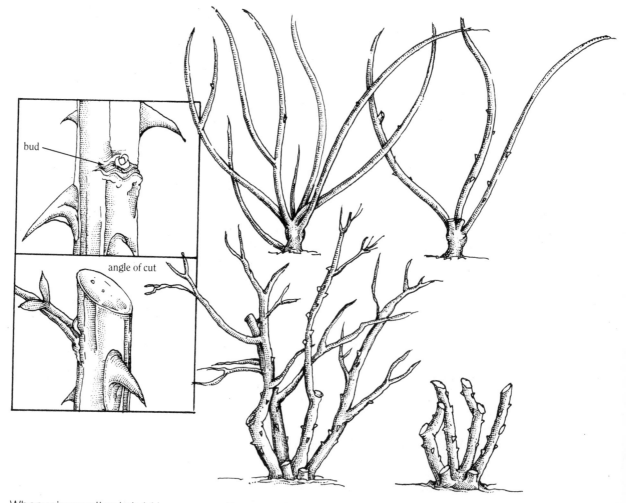

When rejuvenating hybrid tea roses, or if you want to encourage them to produce a few very showy blossoms, remove all but three or four canes and cut those to a height of 6 to 10 inches (*bottom*). Climbing roses that are beginning to outgrow their trellis should be pruned to just a few main canes (*top*). When pruning roses, cut the stems at a 45-degree angle ¼ inch above an outward-facing bud.

Prune the newer canes with some restraint in order to keep young shoots appearing throughout the bush. Cut them back 6 to 8 inches, leaving three or four bud eyes on each stem. This pruning will allow your plants to produce more blossoms. Remember to guide those young canes to grow horizontally whenever possible. As the climber fills the space you have allotted it, you will want to do some pruning each spring, just after the bush begins to put out new growth.

When climbers become old and begin to outgrow their trellises, prune them vigorously, cutting back old canes to the ground.

**Rambling Roses.** Though you prune climbers during dormancy, you must prune ramblers immediately after flowering. You prune to remove dead, diseased, or unsightly wood and to keep the plant under control. Since ramblers produce so many flowers along their stems, you do not need to be so concerned with finding buds against which to prune. Prune branches that stick out of the general shape of the plant and prune branches deep inside that are clearly dead or producing few leaves or flowers. Ramblers can be cut back severely to just a foot or two immediately after flowering and will come charging back if fed and watered properly. They are not as delicate and fragile as some of the tea roses might be.

## Cutting Fresh Flowers

How uplifting and cheerful the sight of roses in a vase on the table; how sad to see them wilted and dropping petals. We all want our cut roses to last as long as possible. With a few tricks, you can add days to the life of the blooms you bring indoors.

Cut blossoms when the air is cool, preferably at dusk, but early morning will do. Roses cut during the heat of the day wilt quickly. Bring with you to the rose bed not only your sharp knife or shears, but a bucket full of tepid water for immersing cut stems. Select those flowers that are only partially opened. Single blooms will last longest if picked when they are barely starting to unfold.

When cutting flowers, leave at least two leaves above the main stem. Using a sharp knife or shears, make the cut at a 45 degree angle, just above a leaf. New growth will originate from the base of this leaf, so choose a leaf that faces toward the outside of the plant. Immediately after you cut a stem, plunge the entire stem to the base of the blossom into the bucket of water.

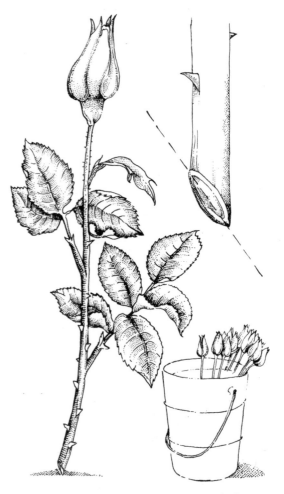

When cutting fresh blossoms to bring indoors, make the cut at a 45-degree angle.

Keep cut flowers in water in a cool place out of drafts until you are ready to arrange them; you can keep them in water in the refrigerator to retard the opening of buds.

## Arranging Flowers

When cutting flowers for arrangements, select several in various stages of early blooming to give your arrangement a less uniform and more interesting appearance. Remove thorns and foliage that will be below the surface of the water in the vase, but don't scrape the stem with a knife. At ½ inch or more above the end of each stem, make a fresh cut at a sharp angle to expose as much of the cut surface to water as possible. Then plunge stems deeply into hot water (about 120°F). Leave the roses there for about 30 minutes, until the water cools; then set them, still in the water, in a cool place. Revive wilted roses with the same procedure.

Fill your vase with fresh water and add 7-Up or Sprite, about a tablespoon to a quart of water (the citric acid in these beverages prolongs the life of the blossom). Then arrange your roses. Keep the arrangement out of drafts and move it to a cool spot at night. Many gardeners feel it's worth the extra effort to change the water daily and make a new cut in the bottom of the stem every couple of days.

## Drying Roses

Dried rose petals are a staple of traditional potpourri. Pick rose blossoms after the morning dew is gone, but early enough so that the essential oils remain. For a moist potpourri, pull the petals from the blooms, spread them on a drying rack, and place them away from the light for a few days until they are limp. For a dry potpourri, leave the petals for four days to two weeks, or until they dry completely.

You can dry rose petals in the oven. Set the oven temperature to warm and place the petals on a cookie sheet in the oven, leaving the door ajar to allow moisture to escape. Stir the petals occasionally for even drying. This technique is faster, but the petals will lose the intensity of their color.

# MOST COMMON CULTURAL PROBLEMS

## Climbing Rose Only Blossoms on Ends of Canes

### Improper Growing Habit

If your climbing rose produces blossoms only at the ends of the canes and not along their length, examine its growing habit. Climbing roses produce more blossoms when they are growing horizontally or within a 45 degree angle to the ground. If the canes are growing vertically, the flowers will bloom only at the ends. Reposition your canes and secure them so that most of them have a more horizontal orientation.

## Canes Damaged by Fall Freezes

### Lack of Winter Protection

Sudden changes in temperature in the fall, before the plant has hardened off for the winter, can be disastrous. Early freezes kill more canes than even colder winter temperatures. Damage occurs most often on tender new shoots, so avoid late summer feedings of nitrogen and hold back on water, which encourages new growth. If a very early cold spell is expected, cover the rose bush with agricultural fleece over night to give it some protection.

## Bush Does Not Grow Uniformly in Spring

### Mild Winter

Sometimes after a very mild or warm winter, the branch tips may not produce leaves or the side buds on some canes will fail to grow because they were not chilled enough to induce normal growth. Prune out such canes.

## Plants Are Leggy and Do Not Produce Flowers

### Not Enough Sun

If roses don't get five to six hours of full sun each day, they will become leggy and may not produce any blossoms at all. The only solution is to move the plant to a better location.

## Blossoms Do Not Open Fully

### Overexposure to Cool Temperatures and Dampness

Cool nights or dark, damp days can cause balling—that's when blossoms open halfway and then stop. Cut off these blooms; when weather conditions improve, good growth will begin again. If you live in an area where cool or foggy summers are common, select rose varieties that have fewer petals, and balling will occur less often.

## Plant Wilts

### Overexposure to Heat

Very hot weather fatigues a rose plant. At temperatures above 90°F, the plant uses food faster than the leaves can manufacture it. In hot climates, don't overprune roses. If the season is particularly hot and sunny, cover part of the rose garden with a lath to give some shade during the hottest part of the day. Move container-grown roses to partially shaded locations.

## New Foliage Dies

### Over-Fertilizing

If the new foliage of your roses dies or is stunted and off-color, the soil may contain excessive salts from too much fertilizing. Water the plant heavily to put the excessive salts into suspension. A day later, again water heavily to leach those salts from the soil.

## New Roses Grow Slowly

### Plants Dried Out

New roses cannot be allowed to dry out either before or after you plant them or they will grow poorly. Soak bare-root plants 6 to 24 hours before planting. Water them very well when you plant them, and if it is unusually hot, protect the plants from drying out by shading them with some moist burlap or agricultural fleece. Leave the material on the plants until the weather cools or the plants become established.

## New Foliage Dies

### Soil Too Alkaline

Roses prefer a slightly acid soil. If the soil has a pH over 7.5, the foliage will turn yellow or brown and eventually die. Apply a dose of soil sulfur according to package instructions and then add about 3 inches of peat moss to the soil around the plant.

# MOST COMMON INSECT PESTS

## Leaves Curled, Discolored, and Distorted

### Aphids

Aphids feed on the foliage and flowers of plants, sucking out the juices. The leaves turn yellow or brown, wilt under bright sunlight, and eventually curl and pucker. Flowers, too, can become malformed. You may find honeydew secreted by the aphids on the surfaces, which will attract ants.

Melon aphids (*Aphis gossypii*), green peach aphids (*Myzus persicae*), potato aphids (*Macrosiphum euphorbiae*), and rose aphids (*Macrosiphum rosae*) are among the species that attack plants in the rose family. They feed on the undersides of leaves. These insects are about the size of a pinhead and have soft, pear-shaped bodies. Most are green, but some species are pink or reddish. You will usually see them on buds and leaves of garden roses in May and June, and they are common pests in greenhouses. Aphids multiply so rapidly that infested flower buds and stalks become covered with them.

Wipe the pests off by hand. This won't kill all of them, because they reproduce so quickly, but it slows them down until you get time to take other actions. To control light infestations, spray flower buds and the undersides of the leaves vigorously with water. Do this in the early morning, once every other day, for three days. For medium to heavy infestations, spray with insecticidal soap every two to three days until aphids are gone. If these pests become a very serious problem, make two applications of pyrethrum, three to five days apart.

# Holes in Leaves, Flowers, or Buds

A variety of insect pests chew or bore holes in rose foliage and flowers.

## Beetles

Beetles eat leaves or flowers of roses, leaving obvious holes. In large numbers, they can completely skeletonize leaves and destroy flowers. Sometimes the grubs of beetles attack the roots of roses. You won't see any immediate obvious symptoms, but rather a general weakening of the plant. Some of the more troublesome pests of roses include fuller rose beetles, goldsmith beetles, Japanese beetles, rose chafer beetles, rose curculios, and rose leaf beetles.

**Japanese Beetles.** These ubiquitous pests (*Popillia japonica*) are familiar to most gardeners. The adult beetles are ½ inch long, with shiny metallic green and brown wing covers. The larvae are grayish white grubs with dark brown heads. Fully grown, these plump pests measure ¾ to 1 inch long. They lie in the soil in a distinctive arc-shaped resting position.

**Rose Chafer Beetles.** Also known as the rose bug or rose beetle (*Macrodactylus subspinosus*), this pest is tan, has long legs, and measures about ¼ inch long. It skeletonizes foliage and damages flowers. Rose chafer beetles are common in the northeastern states and as far west as Colorado.

**Rose Curculios.** The rose curculio (*Rhynchites bicolor*) is a curious-looking pest—a red beetle with a long, black snout. Adults eat holes in the buds of roses, which often prevents them from opening. The white larvae feed on flowers and seeds. This pest occurs throughout most of the United States, but is most common in the northern states. Collect and burn the dried, infested buds before larvae have a chance to complete their development.

**Rose Leaf Beetles.** These small, oval, metallic-looking insects bore into buds and partially opened flowers. When abundant, the beetles also may eat shot holes in flowers at any stage of development. Larvae sometimes damage the roots of roses.

## Controlling Beetles

For the most part, all beetles are controlled the same way. First, pick them off the plants and drop them into a pail of soapy water. If the infestation is light, this is all you will need to do; otherwise, move on to additional control measures. Spray infested roses with a solution of pyrethrum and isopropyl alcohol, mixing 1 tablespoon alcohol with every pint of pyrethrum mixture. Apply this solution every three to five days until the problem is corrected. You can kill the larvae of most of these beetles using milky spore disease (*Bacillus popilliae;* see chapter 6 for details on using milky spore disease).

You have a couple more options when trying to control Japanese beetles. Set up pheromone traps a week before you expect the beetles to emerge in your area, making sure traps are no closer than 50 feet from your plants. Handpick stragglers not caught by the trap. A combined program that uses traps and milky spore disease, implemented for three to five years, permanently reduces the population of Japanese beetles on your property.

## Caterpillars

If the leaves or buds of your roses are chewed, it's very likely that some type of caterpillar has done the damage. Some common caterpillar pests of roses include the bristly rose slug, the fall webworm, and the rose budworm.

**Bristly Roseslugs.** You wouldn't want to meet up with this insect in the middle of a dark night. Contrary to its name, the bristly roseslug (family Noctuidae) isn't a slug at all, but a ½-inch-long, hairy, slimy larva of a sawfly. The larvae chew on the undersides of rose leaves, skeletonizing them, and then eat holes clear through. This pest is active primarily at night. The adults eat entire leaves. If you handpick them, wear gloves, because their bristles irritate the skin.

**Fall Webworms.** These pale yellow or green caterpillars (*Hyphantria cunea*) are 1 inch long. The adult moth has white to brown spotted wings, with a spread of 1½ inches. Caterpillars attack in August, when you'll find their webbed nests among the foliage. Inside the nests, you'll see leaves skeletonized from webworm feeding. Cut out or remove well-established nests. As soon as you spot webs forming, spray the entire rose bush with Bt (*Bacillus thuringiensis*), making two or three applications every three to five days.

**Rose Budworms.** Two types of budworm have been known to infest roses. One is whitish orange, about ⅛ inch long; and the other is green, about ¾ inch long. They feed on rose buds and leaves.

## Controlling Caterpillars

Pick off caterpillars and their nests and destroy the infested buds, leaves, or stems. Then, spray the plant weekly with Bt (*Bacillus thuringiensis*) until the symptoms and the caterpillars disappear. Repeated applications of insecticidal soap can be used to control bristly roseslugs.

## Slugs and Snails

Large, ragged holes in the leaves of your roses are sure signs of slug and/or snail attack. These creatures are particularly attracted to damaged plants. They begin feeding at the bottom and work their way up. A moist, well-mulched garden with acidic soil is heaven to them. They're active at night, rasping holes in rose leaves with their filelike tongues. After a night of debauchery, they hide under boards or leaf litter during the day. Slugs and snails are always most destructive during rainy spells.

The best way to control slugs and snails is to trap them. You can buy commercial traps or make one at home. Simply pour some beer into a pie plate or other shallow dish and leave it out for them. The pests head straight for the beer, climb in, and drown. If slugs and snails are a constant problem in your yard, begin trapping them within the first three to four weeks after the last frost, setting out just one trap to start. As soon as a slug or snail is caught, increase the number of traps to catch them before they can lay eggs and multiply beyond control.

## Weevils

Japanese weevils (*Pseudocneorhinus bifasciatus*) chew along the margins of rose leaves, giving them a notched appearance. If abundant, they can defoliate plants. The beetles are about ¼ inch long and light to dark brown in color, with striated wing covers. They feed at night and hide in soil and plant debris during the day. The larva of Japanese weevils bore into the roots and stems of roses. Fuller rose beetles are gray-brown weevils found mostly in the South and California. They have cream-colored strips on each side and are about ⅓ inch long. Adults feed at night, chewing ragged edges around rose leaves. During the day, they rest on twigs or in foliage and can be handpicked. The yellowish, brown-headed larvae feed on roots of roses.

Weevils play dead when disturbed, folding their legs and dropping to the ground. You can turn this to your advantage when trying to remove these pests from your roses. Spread a cloth on the ground beneath infested plants; then gently shake the limbs of the plant. Startled weevils will drop onto the cloth, and you can easily gather them up and destroy them. As soon as you find weevils on your roses, begin spraying weekly with a pyrethrum-alcohol solution. Make this solution by combining 1 tablespoon alcohol with a pint of pyrethrum mix. Apply the mixture at night, at least two hours after dark. For further control, apply a sticky substance such as Tanglefoot around the main stem of the rose to prevent adults from climbing up and eating the leaves. Introduce predatory nematodes to the soil to stop the reproduction of weevils.

# Canes Girdled, Die Back; Leaves Wilt

## Borers

Borers are the larvae of various insects. As their name implies, they bore into the canes of roses, causing new growth to wilt suddenly.

**Carpenter Bee Larvae.** Carpenter bees (*Ceratina* spp.) are ⅓-inch black or metallic-colored bees that lay eggs in rose canes. Their larvae will bore out the pith of rose canes, which causes serious wilting.

**Raspberry Cane Borers.** The adults of this pest (*Oberea maculata*) are slender beetles, striped black and yellow, about ½ inch long. The larvae make holes in canes and bore down through the cane to the crown below the ground, where they pupate. This takes them from one to two seasons. They attack uninjured canes at a point 6 to 8 inches below the ends of the tips, causing them to droop and the leaves to wilt.

**Rose Stem Girdlers.** Girdler larvae (*Agrilus aurichalceus*) mine the canes of roses, traveling in a spiral up the stems as they go. The stems swell up, split, and often die. The adults are metallic green beetles, ¼ inch long; they appear in June and July.

**Rose Stem Sawflies.** This wasplike insect (*Hartigia trimaculata*) has transparent wings. Its larvae are yellowish white worms with brown heads, which grow to ⅗ inch in length. They bore into the canes, causing them to wilt and die back.

### Controlling Borers

As soon as you discover borer damage, prune the canes below the infested section. To keep the larvae from entering cut canes, insert a flat-headed tack in the end or plug the hole with grafting wax, putty, or paraffin. Some gardeners paint the end of a pruned cane with shellac or tree wound paint.

## Leaves Stippled White

### Leafhoppers

The nymphs and adults of leafhoppers suck juices from the leaves, buds, and stems of roses, leaving tiny white spots on the surfaces of the plant. Eventually, the leaves shrivel and drop off. You may also find secretions of honeydew on your plants, which fosters the growth of sooty mold.

Rose leafhoppers (*Edwardsiana rosae*) are ¼- to ⅓-inch-long, wedge-shaped insects. They carry their wings in a rooflike position above their bodies. They're very active, and, true to their name, they hop suddenly or move sideways when disturbed. Their eggs hatch in May, and young insects feed on leaf undersides. Potato leafhoppers (*Empoasca fabae*) also sometimes infest roses.

Spray infested plants with a solution of insecti-cidal soap and isopropyl alcohol, mixing 1 table-spoon alcohol with each pint of soap mixture. You may need to make two applications, three to five days apart. If leafhoppers are a common problem in your backyard, consider covering your roses with agricultural fleece in early spring to deny them access. Take the fleece off when the air temperature under it exceeds 85°F.

## Leaves Rolled and Bound with Silk Strands

### Leaf Rollers

The caterpillars of these insects protect themselves while feeding on roses by rolling leaves into tubes around themselves and binding them with strands or webs of silk. The leaves become skeletonized, turn brown, and die.

Roses are vulnerable to attack from a few different species, including fruit tree leaf rollers (*Archips argyrospilus*), oblique-banded leaf rollers (*Choristoneura rosaceana*), and red-banded leaf rollers (*Argyrotaenia velutinana*). The caterpillars may be light to dark green or cream to yellow in color, and ⅜ to 1¾ inches long. Adult moths are brown or gray and ¼ to ½ inch long.

Handpick the rolled leaves and destroy the caterpillars. To prevent problems with leaf rollers, spray roses with Bt (*Bacillus thuringiensis*) just as the flower buds begin to emerge on the rose bush. This removes any young caterpillars before they begin feeding. A dormant oil spray applied in very early spring while your plants are dormant also reduces leaf-roller problems.

## Leaves Stippled and Distorted

### Mites

Yellow stippling on rose foliage is a sign of mite infestation. Several species of spider mite attack roses. They spin webs across leaf surfaces and on new growth. As they continue to feed, leaves become spotted red, yellow, or brown; then they curl and eventually drop off. Some floribunda roses are so susceptible to mites that they lose their leaves prematurely. You'll find mites on the undersides of leaves. They are about $1/50$ inch long, the size of a grain of pepper, and may be yellow, green, red, or brown.

As soon as you discover stippled leaves on your roses and have determined mites are the cause, begin control measures. Spray plants in the early morning with a forceful stream of water to knock mites from the leaves. Repeat this once a day for three days. If mites are still present, spray with insecticidal soap every three to five days for two weeks.

## Leaves Yellowed; Plant Stunted

### Nematodes

Nematodes feed at the roots of plants. As a result, infested roses look sickly, wilted, or stunted, and their foliage is yellowed or bronzed. They decline slowly and die. Root systems are poorly developed, even partially decayed, and have galls. The effects of nematode activity are most apparent in hot weather, when plants recover poorly from the heat.

The root knot nematodes *Meloidogyne hapla* and *M. incognita* attack roses. The former infests roses grown outdoors in the northern states; the latter is a common pest of greenhouse roses in the North and outdoor roses in the South. Nematodes are not insects, but slender, unsegmented roundworms, $1/50$ to $1/10$ inch long.

Control these pests by adding lots of compost—especially leaf mold—to the soil around your roses. This encourages beneficial fungi, which attack nematodes. Fertilize your plants with a drench of fish emulsion to repel nematodes.

## Leaves Yellowed; Plant Grows Poorly

### Root Aphids

Root aphids, *Eriosoma lanigerum*, attack the roots of roses. The damage they cause interferes with the flow of water and nutrients, which eventually retards or distorts plant growth and is most severe in young rose plants recently placed in the garden. Early symptoms of root-aphid damage include yellow or brown leaves, which may wilt under bright sunlight.

If you were to look at the roots, you would find them scarred or knotted. Often you will see ants going into holes in the soil around the base of the rose plant. They may be herding root aphids, as they do aphids above the ground. Like all aphids, root aphids have soft, pear-shaped bodies no bigger than the head of a pin.

Once root aphids have become established in the soil around your roses, there is no environmentally safe method for dealing with them. You can reduce their impact by spraying your roses and all nearby deciduous shrubs with dormant oil to smother their eggs and halt reproduction. Controlling the ants that accompany these aphids will also help to keep the populations down. (See the entry on ants in chapter 6.)

## Buds and Leaves Turn Black and Die

### Rose Midges

Midges (*Dasineura rhodophaga*) might be microscopic insects, but they can blacken and kill rose buds and leaves. It's the whitish maggots that are destructive. They hatch usually after the first bloom cycle and rasp tender plant tissue as they feed. Leaves and blossoms blacken and shrivel. Unchecked, a heavy midge infestation can eliminate all bloom from late spring through early fall. After feeding, the larvae drop to the soil where they pupate and emerge as reddish or yellowish brown flies within a week.

As soon as you spot midge damage, remove and destroy all the infected flower buds.

## Leaves Discolored; Small Bumps on Leaves and Canes

### Scale

The first sign of a scale attack is wilting and darkening of the leaves. This is followed by leaf drop, reduced growth, and stunted plants. Heavy infestations of scale can kill a plant. Some species excrete honeydew, which coats the foliage, attracting ants and encouraging the growth of sooty mold. If you suspect scale, look for the pests themselves. Scale insects have rounded waxy coverings, $1/10$ to $2/5$ inch in diameter, giving them the appearance of small bumps. You can find them on leaves and canes. Depending on the species, they may be white, yellow, brown, or black. The most common species to attack roses is the rose scale (*Aulacaspis rosae*). It is gray or brown, and thickly infests older canes. Other species include San Jose scale (*Quadraspidiotus perniciosus*), black scale (*Saissetia oleae*), cottony-maple scale (*Pulvinaria innumerabilis*), and oyster-shell scale (*Lepidosaphes ulmi*). Scale outbreaks can be triggered by environmental stresses such as too much or too little water. Overfeeding roses with nitrogen also encourages scale populations by accelerating the growth of plants. Scales are attracted by the new, succulent, sugary shoots.

If you've caught the problem before many scale have infested your plants, simply scrape them off with your fingernail or with a cotton swab dipped in rubbing alcohol. For heavier infestations, spray plants with a mixture of alcohol and insecticidal soap every three days for two weeks. Make this mixture by combining 1 cup isopropyl alcohol and 1 tablespoon insecticidal soap concentrate in 1 quart water. If your insecticidal soap is already mixed with water, take a pint of it and add 1 tablespoon alcohol.

## Brown Edges on Blossoms

### Thrips

If you see brown edges on your rose blossoms, and the buds only partially open or don't open at all, suspect thrips. These insects attack buds in their early stages, working among the unfurled petals. The buds become deformed and fail to open properly, and the damaged petals turn brown and dry. New growth also may be damaged, in the same way.

Roses are vulnerable to flower thrips (*Frankliniella tritici*) and tobacco thrips (*F. fusca*). The adults are tiny, slender insects, $1/15$ inch long, and may be pale yellow, black, or brown. They have four narrow wings fringed with long hairs, and their legs are very short.

Since thrips burrow deeply between the petals, early identification and control is important. Set out yellow sticky traps about four weeks after the last frost. As soon as you spot thrips on the traps, spray your roses with insecticidal soap every three days for two weeks. Commercially available predatory mites, lacewings, ladybugs, and beneficial nematodes are effective backups to the soap spray. Thrips prefer a dry environment, so make sure plants are adequately watered.

## GENERAL DISEASE PROTECTION

Black spot, powdery mildew, and rust are the major threats to roses. However, most rose growers will face only two of these, because whereas mildew occurs across the country, rust and black spot territories seldom overlap. You can prevent disease in your roses with some careful planning and care. Good air circulation reduces disease by eliminating warm, moist conditions that favor the growth of fungi and bacteria, so avoid planting roses in walled or crowded areas, and prune to keep the centers of the plants open. Water plants before noon, and try not to splatter the foliage. Water that splashes up from the ground can carry to the plant any disease spores that might be lying around in the soil. Spreading organic mulch also helps keep fungal spores off your roses simply by covering soil that might be infected.

### An Annual Spray Program

Your roses will have an excellent chance of avoiding disease altogether if you implement the following preventive spray program. This program is safe to the environment, to you, and to your roses. If you have the proper spray equipment, it takes little time to follow. All of the products last for years in storage, so buy everything you need for the whole year. The basic requirements are an antidesiccant spray, flowable sulfur fungicide, and a bottle of dormant oil. The sulfur fungicide protects against the three most common fungal diseases (black spot, powdery mildew, and rust) and controls mites, thrips, and aphids. If you can't find flowable sulfur, other sulfur-based or copper-based fungicides can be substituted.

Do not use this program with rugosa roses; sulfur damages them. Besides, they are immune to fungal diseases anyway.

To implement the spray program, follow these steps:

1. In late fall or early winter, at the end of the growing season, after fall cleanup and before the hard freeze sets in, spray each of your rose bushes thoroughly with an antidesiccant. This protects plants from drying out in winter, but also presents a barrier to any spores that might land on your roses during warm spells.

2. Early in spring, when you finish your spring pruning and while the plants are still dormant, spray them with the flowable sulfur fungicide and then cover them completely with dormant oil. The fungicide kills most of the spores; then the dormant oil suffocates any that remain. The oil also presents a barrier to airborne spores.

3. From the time when leaves first emerge, and every seven days thereafter until July 4, spray each plant again with a flowable sulfur fungicide. Remember, sulfur sprays should not be applied in hot sun or when temperatures exceed 85°F.

4. Continue to spray with the sulfur fungicide from July 4 until the first frost, now making applications every ten days.

## MOST COMMON DISEASES

### Black Spots on Leaves

#### Black Spot
Not surprisingly, the disease black spot (*Diplocarpon rosae*) produces black spots on the leaves of infected plants. These spots are surrounded with yellow. Eventually, leaves turn yellowish pink and fall off. In severe cases, this disease can defoliate a rose bush by midsummer.

Black spot prefers roses with light-colored blossoms; red roses are less susceptible. It thrives in moist environments and is most common in north-eastern and southeastern states, and in some Midwestern states where summers are warm and moist. Black spot begins to appear when the air temperatures approach 65°F and rain is abundant or humidity high. Infection begins on leaves low to the ground. Young leaves, 6 to 14 days old, are the first to go.

To control this disease, prune and destroy all the affected leaves immediately and begin a weekly application of a flowable sulfur spray, continuing applications throughout the season.

### Buds Fail to Open

#### Blight
If the buds on your roses don't open, but turn brown and decay instead, your plants have been infected with botrytis blight (*Botrytis cinerea, B. allii*). The fungus that causes this disease resides in old blooms and in winter-killed canes, so pick off and destroy the faded blooms. Spray shrubs weekly with a sulfur- or copper-based fungicide.

### Plant Grows Poorly; Tumorlike Growth on Roots

#### Crown Gall
If your roses look a little sickly, inspect them closely. You may find a rough, tumorlike growth near the soil or on the roots. Such a growth signals crown gall. This bacterial disease (*Agrobacterium tumefaciens*) often gains entry to a plant through wounds made by cultivating. The galls should be pruned off and the wound sealed with landscape paint or putty. Disinfect the knife between cuts.

### White, Powdery Mold on Leaves and Buds

#### Powdery Mildew
Powdery mildew is easily recognized by the thin, white, powdery growth of fungus (*Spaerotheca pannosa*) that grows on leaves and canes. This disease infects young leaves first. Raised, blisterlike areas develop, which cause the leaves to curl; then the infected leaves become covered with grayish

white powdery fungus. This disease hits flowers, too, and you may find the unopened flower buds of infected plants white with mildew. The buds may not open at all.

Mildew prefers young, succulent growth. The mature tissue on the plant is usually not affected. The disease usually occurs during periods of cool nights, humid days, and no rain, and is severe only in coastal areas, like the Pacific coast, where temperatures are moderate, high cloud cover or fog is common, and summer rainfall is minimal.

As soon as you discover this disease on your roses, prune off the infected leaves or tips and spray the plant weekly with flowable sulfur. If powdery mildew is a common problem in your yard, take preventive measures and begin spraying roses in early spring while they are still dormant. Use the spray schedule described at the beginning of the rose disease section. Keep an eye on your roses when temperatures reach around 65°F and it hasn't rained in a while: These conditions favor the growth of the powdery mildew fungus.

## Raised Red-Orange or Yellow Spots on Leaves

### Rust
Small red-orange or yellow pustules on the leaves or canes of your roses indicate rust (*Phraqmidium* spp.). These spots usually develop on the undersides of leaves first and may be inconspicuous. Later, they pop up on the upper leaf surfaces and stems. Rose rust is primarily a problem in the western United States. Some cultivars will drop the infested leaves.

When you find rust spots, prune infected leaves and begin spraying your plants weekly with flowable sulfur, using the spray schedule described at the beginning of this section. If this disease commonly occurs on your roses, try to prevent it by spraying plants with flowable sulfur in early spring, when temperatures optimal for rust coincide with heavy dew, rain, or periods of cloudcover or fog.

## Canes Swollen and Discolored

### Stem Canker
Swollen and discolored dead areas on rose canes can mean that the soft tissue just under the canes' surface is infected. Canes commonly split open, exposing underlying tissues and sometimes bleeding a gummy exudate. The cause is common canker or stem canker, which occurs in wounds on canes, and in the cut ends of pruned canes, especially if the cut was not made close to a bud. Prompt pruning of infected canes is the best control.

# CHAPTER 4

# Ground Covers, Vines, and Plants for Foliage

**A** well-dressed landscape combines lawn, flower gardens, trees, and shrubs in a pleasing combination. But just as accessories—scarves, ties, jewelry—add interesting touches to our everyday attire, so ground covers, vines, and plants grown for foliage bring highlights and accents to the yard.

Dress up your landscape with these plants. Send English ivy racing across a bare patch of ground. Wind clematis up a trellis or let wisteria cascade from porch roofs. Brighten a monochrome expanse with the reddish purple accents of coleus. Cushion an area under trees with lush, feathery ferns. Spark up flower beds or borders with the striking foliage of variegated hostas or liriope. These plants have many wonderful uses in the backyard: Let your imagination wander.

Because many of these plants are used as accents, they'll catch your eye quickly, and as with all the plants in your landscape, you'll want them to look their best. Of course, this means not only

planting, feeding, and watering them properly, but taking care of pests and diseases as soon as possible to keep your vines and leaves free of unsightly spots, holes, and wilting foliage.

Fortunately, most of these plants don't require much care. They seem to be full of life, many of them climbing and scrambling everywhere if left uncontrolled. For the most part, basic care keeps them lush and healthy. Because many of the plants described in this chapter are grown in groups or used as ground covers, you'll want to pay some attention to spacing. Crowding creates a humid environment perfect for infectious bacteria and fungi.

Many of these plants, however, are virtually free of disease and pests—another good reason to grow them in your backyard. They'll offer beauty without a lot of bother. Give them a little water and some compost, touch them up by pruning, and sit back and enjoy them.

# Ajuga *Ajuga* spp.

## DESCRIPTION

Also called bugleweed for its buglelike flowers, this perennial is a member of the mint family. Ajuga is most commonly used in the landscape as a ground cover. Of all the species, carpet bugle (*Ajuga reptans*) is the best choice. Its roots spread rapidly so that it quickly forms a dense mat close to the ground. It has interesting foliage, which it keeps throughout the winter. With its rapidly spreading habit, it discourages weeds, and it isn't bothered by pests. Ajuga looks best in borders and rock gardens and can be planted between stepping stones and anywhere that grass won't grow.

### Height

*A. pyramidalis,* 1 foot
Carpet bugle (*A. reptans*), up to 6 inches
Geneva bugleweed (*A. genevensis*), 8 to 12 inches

### Spread

Carpet bugle spreads by underground runners, so it can be invasive. Other species of ajuga tend to form clumps about 1 foot across.

### Blossoms

Ajuga has irregular two-lipped flowers, which look like bugles and bloom on upright spikes in the spring or early summer. They may be white, blue, or reddish purple.

### Foliage

Ajuga produces lustrous evergreen leaves that are oval in shape and measure about 2½ inches long. They may have either smooth or toothed edges. *A. reptans* 'Bronze Beauty' produces bronze foliage, and 'Burgandy Glow' has foliage marked with green, white, dark pink, or purple foliage.

## ENVIRONMENT

### Varieties by Zone

To zone 3, *A. pyramidalis,* carpet bugle, and Geneva bugleweed

### Light Requirements

Ajuga prefers partial sun to light shade.

## Soil Requirements

Bugleweed grows best in normal, well-drained soils, but will grow in poor soils. It tolerates acid soil to a pH of 5.5, an acidity that grass cannot tolerate.

## PLANTING AND PROPAGATION

### Planting

Plant sets of ajuga in the spring. Place plants 1 to 2 inches deep in the soil and about 6 to 8 inches apart. Sets can be transplanted in the fall as well.

### Propagation

Mature ajuga can be divided in the spring or fall. You can also root stems in damp sand or perlite.

## PLANT MANAGEMENT

### Water Requirements

Ajuga grows well with ½ to 1 inch of water each week. Do not let it dry out.

### Feeding Requirements

One application of compost in the spring is all ajuga needs for the year. Excessive fertilizing encourages fungal disease.

### Pruning

Rejuvenate ajuga by pruning or mowing it to a height of 3 or 4 inches. Do this after the flowers have finished blooming.

### Deadheading

Remove the flower stalks after the blooming period to encourage another crop of flowers later in the season. Thin out ajuga plants when the bed becomes overcrowded.

## MOST COMMON DISEASES

### Crown and Roots Rot

#### Crown Rot

The only common disease of ajuga, crown rot is caused by soil-dwelling *Pellicularia* fungi. Crowded conditions encourage the growth and spread of this disease. The fungi enter the plant through the roots and travel into the crown and up the stem. At first only a few spots appear on the crown of the plant. Eventually, the entire crown rots. If the ajuga is in leaf, the lower leaves rot and young shoots wilt. Meanwhile, the roots blacken with rot and become covered with white fungal threads. The whole plant dies within a few days.

No cure for this disease is known. Remove and discard any infected plants and the soil immediately surrounding them. Do not compost the infected plants. Before replanting ajuga in the same place, pasteurize the soil or enrich it with compost, which has fungus-fighting qualities. Thoroughly cultivating around plants encourages the soil to dry out and hinders the spread of the fungus. Because the disease overwinters on plant debris, clean your garden well in the fall.

# GROUND COVER *English Ivy* *Hedera helix*

## DESCRIPTION

These evergreen vines climb or spread by rootlets that attach themselves to walls or rocks. You can choose from 50 to 100 cultivars of English ivy, depending on where you live. This ivy is a favorite among gardeners and landscapers for its versatility. It grows well outdoors year round in both the North and the

South, and it can also be used as a houseplant. It remains evergreen all year and so brings color to the winter garden. It is perfect for wooded lots because it forms an excellent ground cover in shade where grass can't survive. In addition, its deep roots retard soil erosion. Planted in bulb beds, its foliage sets off spring bulbs, then masks their dying foliage. You can plant it in hanging baskets or rock gardens, use it as edging for patios, or train it on a trellis to create a privacy screen.

## Height

When used as a ground cover, ivies grow to a height of about 1 foot.

## Spread

Ivies will spread as permitted and can climb to 50 feet on a wall or a tree. They can become rampant in the landscape, and must be controlled by pruning.

## Blossoms

Only mature English ivy has blossoms. These inconspicuous greenish white flowers appear in September or October.

## Foliage

The evergreen foliage of ivy is coarsely toothed with alternate lobes. The leaves are dark green and veined and have a leathery texture. Many variegated cultivars of English and Algerian ivy are available.

# ENVIRONMENT

## Hardiness

English ivy is hardy to −25°F, though ivy in the far northern regions needs a snow cover to survive the winter. Trellised ivy in exposed areas can be damaged by winter temperatures in zone 5 and farther north.

## Varieties by Zone

To zone 5, English ivy (*H. helix*)
To zone 7, Algerian ivy (*H. canariensis*)

## Light Requirements

In most areas, ivy will cope with anything from heavy shade to full sun (it will only take full sun, however, if well watered). Its preference is for partial shade, and it doesn't like continuous sun in the winter. In parts of the country where English ivy doesn't do well when trained upright, it thrives when grown on the ground. It is happy under maples and beeches, where few other plants do well. If ivy is used as a vine, it prefers northern or eastern exposure.

## Soil Requirements

Ivy prefers a rich, loamy soil that stays slightly moist.

It grows well in an environment with a pH range of 6 to 7.5.

# PLANTING AND PROPAGATION

## Planting

Plant ivy in spring or fall. Set it 2 to 4 inches deep, spacing plants 6 to 18 inches apart, depending on how fast you want it to cover the ground. If you are planting a slope, stagger the plants at 6-inch intervals and form a shallow basin around each plant to hold water. To help plants become established quickly, mulch them with 2 to 4 inches of organic mulch. If you plant ivy in the fall, get it into the ground before the soil temperature falls below 40°F.

If using ivy as a climbing vine, do not plant it against the wall of your house. Ivy climbs with its rootlets, which fix themselves in cracks in the wall, and it will hasten the deterioration of a brick or masonry wall. Plant ivy against a trellis instead. While ivy will anchor itself on masonry or wood, it has no tendrils for twining, so it cannot climb on a wire trellis without some help. Ivy does best on a north- or east-facing trellis.

## Propagation

Cuttings of ivy root easily in water or damp sand or perlite. Take sections that have already developed climbing roots at the leaf nodes. You can propagate ivies at any time during the year.

## Container Gardening

Ivy grows well indoors and doesn't require much sun. It looks great in window boxes and in hanging baskets.

# PLANT MANAGEMENT

## Water Requirements

Ivy thrives on ½ to 1 inch of water each week. Its moderately to deeply rooted plants do not compete with tree roots for water.

## Feeding Requirements

Feed newly planted ivy several times during the first growing season; then don't fertilize it unless the soil is so poor that some supplemental feeding is essential for basic growth. Excess fertilizer tends to make the ivy grow too quickly and encourages fungal disease.

## Pruning

Beds of ivy look ragged and dull after two or three years of being on their own. To encourage dense, rich growth, prune or shear the plants back to 3 to 4 inches in March. The ivy will look pretty terrible for a few weeks, but it will rebound quickly with lush, healthy foliage. The easiest way to prune ivy is by mowing it with your lawn mower adjusted to the highest setting.

If your ivy grows on a trellis, regular pruning is especially important to keep it looking its best. Cut off dangling or torn pieces, and prune to control spread.

# MOST COMMON CULTURAL PROBLEMS

## Leaves Scorched or Burned

### Scorch or Heat Burn

Heat burn can occur in the summer or winter. When ivy grows in the full summer sun without enough water, its leaves dry out. Similar injury occurs in the winter, when plants growing in sunny southern or western exposures lose water through their leaves but cannot take it up from the frozen ground. Ivies growing near a light-colored wall can also be scorched by the heat and light reflected off the wall.

If your ivies suffer from scorch, water them and remove any discolored leaves. To prevent winter burn, give plants a good soaking before the ground freezes. If winter burn is a serious problem, you might cover the ivy bed during the winter with agricultural fleece.

# MOST COMMON INSECT PESTS

## Leaves Yellowed and Curled

### Ivy Aphids

Ivy or nasturtium aphids suck the juices from the leaves and stems of ivy, causing the foliage to curl, pucker, and yellow, and reducing the plant's vigor. You'll often find ants wandering over the plants. They are attracted by the honeydew that aphids secrete. Check the undersides of leaves for small groups of aphids. They are not much bigger than the head of a pin, and they have soft, pear-shaped bodies. They may be green, brown, black, or pink.

You can easily eliminate a light infestation of aphids by spraying the plant vigorously with water. Do this in the early morning, three times, once every other day. For heavier infestations, use insecticidal soap every two to three days until aphids are gone. If aphids are still a problem, you might have to resort to pyrethrum. Make two applications three to four days apart.

## Plant Grows Poorly; Cottony Masses on Roots, Stems, and Leaves

### Mealybugs

Ivy infested with mealybugs (*Pseudococcus* spp.) looks unsightly and does not grow well. The insects gather in cottony white masses on the roots, stems, and leaves, sucking sap and reducing plant vigor. They secrete honeydew as they feed, which attracts ants and encourages the growth of mold.

Mealybugs are ⅕ to ⅓ inch long, oval, flattened, covered with white waxy powder and adorned with short, soft spines around their margins. The telltale cottony tufts on the ivy leaves and stems are their egg sacks. Control mealybugs by spraying them with an alcohol-based spray every two to three days until the pests are gone. To make this spray, mix 1

cup isopropyl alcohol and ½ teaspoon horticultural oil in 1 quart water. You may substitute 1 tablespoon insecticidal soap concentrate for the oil and get equally effective results.

## Leaves Stippled Yellow or Red

### Mites

If your ivy has two-spotted spider mites (*Tetranychus telarius*), the upper surfaces of its leaves will be stippled with small yellow dots or red spots. Eventually, these leaves turn gray and dry. You also may see a fine webbing around the leaves and stems.

Mites are barely visible to the unaided eye. They may be yellow, green, red, or brown. Start control measures as soon as you first notice the stippling on the leaves. Spray infested plants in the early morning with a forceful stream of water to knock mites from the leaves. Repeat this procedure for three days. If you still find these pests on your plants, spray with insecticidal soap every three to five days for two weeks.

## Leaves Yellowed

### Scale

If your ivy leaves turn yellow and start to drop, your plants may be infested with scale. Scale appear in clusters. They look like little bumps, having waxy shells that cover them while they feed. Ivy scale may be reddish gray or brown.

Light infestations can be controlled simply by scraping scale off plants with your fingernail or with a cotton swab dipped in rubbing alcohol. Spray heavily infested plants with a mixture of alcohol and insecticidal soap every three days for two weeks. To make this mixture, combine 1 cup isopropyl alcohol and 1 tablespoon commercial insecticidal soap concentrate in 1 quart water. If your insecticidal soap is already mixed with water, simply add 1 tablespoon alcohol to a pint of this diluted soap spray. A commercially available parasitic wasp, the golden chalcid (*Aphytis melinus*), will help control scale on ivy grown outdoors.

# MOST COMMON DISEASES

## Water-Soaked Spots on Leaves

### Bacterial Leaf Spot

Blisterlike transparent brown or black spots on ivy leaves are a sign of bacterial leaf spot. The bacterium *Xanthomonas hederae* causes this disease. It thrives in moist conditions, so this disease occurs more often in humid climates than in dry. Leaf spot usually first appears on lower or inside leaves of densely crowded ivy foliage. Often the spots come together to form larger patches of dead tissue. Ruptured spots release a bacterial ooze. Serious infections will defoliate ivy, and the whole plant may eventually collapse. Unlike fungal leaf spot (discussed later in this section), bacterial leaf spot moves quickly and can infect a series of plants in a matter of days.

Remove and discard affected leaves as soon as suspicious spots appear. Remove heavily infected plants and surrounding soil and destroy; do not compost this material. Spray nearby plants weekly during rainy spells with a copper-based fungicide to stop the spread of this disease. Increase air circulation by spacing ivy plants more widely apart, and remove the lower 4 to 6 inches of foliage to prevent its contact with wet soil. Be sure to control insects, such as aphids, that may spread the disease organisms.

## Swollen Bumps on Stems

### Canker

Canker in ivy can be caused either by fungi or bacteria. Cankers are swollen, discolored, dead areas that develop on stems from an infection that occurs in the soft tissue just under the stem's surface. They commonly split open, exposing underlying tissues, and they sometimes bleed a gummy exudate. The fungi and bacteria that cause canker are easily transmitted by rain, by handling plants, or on contaminated tools. Plants weakened from wounds, nutrient deficiencies, harsh winters, or pest infestations are most vulnerable to canker.

Prompt pruning of infected ivy is the best control. Remove and destroy infected plants or plant parts as soon as you notice them. Cut the ivy back several inches beyond the cankers. In the fall, gather and destroy all plant debris. A spray with Bordeaux mixture may give some control and possibly reduce the spread of the disease to adjacent plants.

## Tan to Brown Spots or Blotches on Leaves

### Fungal Leaf Spot

Several species of fungi cause leaf spot in ivy, producing tan to brown spots on the leaves. These blotches may be surrounded by black dots of the fungal fruiting bodies. These black dots distinguish fungal leaf spot from bacterial leaf spot, above. Often the spots come together to form larger patches of dead tissue.

Pick off and discard the infected leaves, and dig up and discard seriously infected plants, along with the soil around the roots. Spray affected plants every seven to ten days with a flowable sulfur spray to minimize the spread of the fungus. When watering infected plants, avoid wetting the foliage.

## Leaves Covered with White Powder

### Powdery Mildew

A thin whitish powdery coating on the leaves of ivy signals powdery mildew (*Erysiphe* spp.). These fungi frequently occur on plants that are very crowded. They thrive in either humid or dry conditions. Badly infected leaves become discolored, distorted, and eventually drop off.

As soon as you discover this disease on your plants, spray them thoroughly with wettable sulfur once or twice at weekly intervals. Prune to allow air to circulate within the ivy. Be sure to collect and discard all plant debris in the fall.

# NOTES AND RESEARCH

Ivies are sometimes attacked by a parasitic weed called dodder (*Cuscuta* spp.). Dodder clutches onto ivy, wrapping itself around ivy stems. This weed looks like orange strings. Its small clusters of white flowers produce seed in April or May. When the seeds germinate, the dodder climbs up the nearest vine stem, sends little suckers into the tissue of the ivy, and lives on the ivy's sap. The dodder roots are dropped as soon as this attachment is made, and the plant becomes a true parasite. Once this weed has taken hold, it is nearly impossible to detach. You'll have to dig up and destroy the parasitized ivies.

GROUND COVER **Lily of the Valley**

*Convallaria* spp.

## DESCRIPTION

Lily of the valley makes a delightful little ground cover for the landscape. Its waxy, nodding, bell-shaped flowers give way to orange berries nestled among handsome green foliage. It looks lovely planted alone or interplanted among ferns. You can plant it beneath trees, near walls, or between shrubs. It does tend to be invasive, however, and can take over a perennial bed, so it is best to plant lily of the valley in more informal areas. This plant is tough and requires little attention.

### Height

8 inches

### Spread

Lily of the valley will spread as far and wide as permitted.

### Blossoms

The very fragrant, waxy, bell-shaped white flowers bloom along upright spikes. They appear in late spring (early May to mid-June) for a week or two. The *Convallaria majalis* cultivar 'Rosea' has purplish pink flowers.

### Foliage

Lily of the valley is deciduous. The deep green oval leaves rise from the base of the plant and may be 4 to 8 inches long. The *C. majalis* cultivar 'Aureo-variegata' has yellow-striped leaves.

# ENVIRONMENT

## Varieties by Zone

Zone 2 to Zone 7, *C. majalis* (in zones 6 and 7, grow this plant in shade only)

Zone 4 to Zone 7, 'Rosea' and 'Aureo-variegata'

## Light Requirements

Lily of the valley can handle full sun, but prefers filtered sun or partial shade. It can live in full shade, but deep shade forestalls flower production.

## Soil Requirements

The best soil for lily of the valley is moist and fertile, with plenty of organic matter. Lily of the valley thrives in a deep, sandy humus, but will grow well in ordinary soil as long as it is well drained and slightly acidic, with a pH of 5.5 to 6.5.

# PLANTING AND PROPAGATION

## Planting

Plant lily of the valley in the spring. The roots are shallow, so set plants 1 to 2 inches deep and place them 8 to 12 inches apart. Take care not to break the pips, which are the little bulblike buds attached to the roots.

Some gardeners use a random method of planting lily of the valley for a natural effect. To do this, scatter pips randomly over the area you are planting; then adjust them for uniform distance from each other and plant them where they have fallen.

## Propagation

Divide lily of the valley in the spring. Lift a clump with a spade, garden fork, or trowel and gently separate the plants. Replant the original clump and relocate the divided ones.

# PLANT MANAGEMENT

## Water Requirements

Lily of the valley needs about 1 inch of water a week.

## Feeding Requirements

Enrich the soil around these plants with compost. One application every fall suffices.

# MOST COMMON CULTURAL PROBLEMS

## Few Blossoms

### Needs Thinning
When lily of the valley gets overcrowded, the flowers become sparse. Simply divide or thin the plants, and next year more blossoms will appear.

## Leaves Yellowed

### Summer Dieback
Don't fret when, in late summer, the leaves of your plants turn yellow and begin to look a little sickly. The foliage of lily of the valley dies back every year. Keeping the bed well watered through the hot summer months delays this natural process a bit.

# MOST COMMON INSECT PESTS

## Leaves Yellowed; Plant Sickly

### Nematodes
Occasionally, nematodes will infest lily of the valley. Both the root knot nematode (*Meloidogyne* spp.) and the meadow nematode (*Pratylenchus pratensis*) attack this plant. Nematodes are not insects, but slender unsegmented roundworms. Most are soil-dwellers and are $1/50$ to $1/10$ inch long. They attack the roots of plants. Infested plants become wilted and stunted, and their foliage turns yellow or bronze. The root systems show poor development, and they decay partially. Eventually, the plant dies.

To control nematodes, add lots of compost, especially leaf mold, to the soil around your plants. Compost attracts beneficial fungi, which attack nematodes. Fertilize with a fish emulsion drench, which repels nematodes.

## Leaves Notched

### Weevils

Weevils chew leaves along the edges, giving them the appearance of being notched. They usually don't attack lily of the valley until well after flowering time. Weevils have a very distinctive long snout. Most are between ⅛ and ½ inch long. They have hard bodies and are usually brown or black. They are active at night and hide in soil and debris during the day.

As soon as you discover that these pests are chewing away on your lily of the valley, dust your plants with sabadilla. Be sure to dust both sides of the leaves, and reapply sabadilla after a rain. For long-term control, introduce beneficial predatory nematodes to the soil around the plants to stop the reproduction of the weevils.

# MOST COMMON DISEASES

## Dead Areas on Leaves and Flowers

### Botrytis Blight

When botrytis gray mold infects lily of the valley, the leaves and flowers develop brown areas that eventually die. Pick off and discard all of the diseased plant parts and destroy any badly infected plants. Spray the plants with a copper or sulfur-based fungicide twice, five days apart.

## Leaves and Stems Die Back; Roots Rot

### Crown Rot

Crown rot is caused by a soil-dwelling fungus that occasionally attacks lily of the valley at the soil line. The leaves are discolored as they emerge, and the young shoots wilt. Roots blacken, rot, and become covered with white fungal threads. The whole plant dies in a few days.

There is no cure for this disease. Remove and discard the infected plants and the surrounding soil. Do not compost infected plants. Before replanting the same area, pasteurize the soil or enrich it with compost or other organic matter to attract organisms antagonistic to this disease.

## Brown Spots on Leaves

### Fungal Leaf Spot

Leaf spot in lily of the valley can be caused by any of several fungi. The leaves of infected plants develop circular brown spots. Pick off and discard these leaves, and spray plants with a sulfur-based fungicide every seven to ten days until symptoms begin to disappear. Remove dead plant debris promptly from the garden to reduce overwintering spore populations, and remove and discard seriously infected plants, together with the surrounding soil.

## Yellow or Gray Spots on Leaves; Stem Bases Rotted

### Stem Rot

A fungal stem rot infects lily of the valley growing in very humid conditions. At first, the leaves develop yellowish or grayish specks, which later turn into dark brown sunken spots. The disease spreads downward into the lower parts of the plant to the crown, which rots.

Remove and discard infected plants, or cut away affected plant parts with a clean, sharp knife or razor blade. To reduce moisture around plants, lighten heavy soil by adding perlite, vermiculite, or peat moss to provide good drainage. Avoid overwatering. Space plants farther apart to prevent crowding.

# NOTES AND RESEARCH

All parts of lily of the valley are poisonous.

# Pachysandra

*Pachysandra* spp.

## DESCRIPTION

Although not the most striking plant to be found, pachysandra is an excellent choice for a ground cover. It forms a thick carpet of foliage in shady areas. The southern species, Alleghany spurge (*Pachysandra procumbens*), is native to the southeastern states and is evergreen there. In the North, its leaves die back to the ground. Japanese spurge (*P. terminalis*) keeps its foliage year round and is undoubtedly the best ground cover in the North, certainly for shaded areas. Plant pachysandra under shallow-rooted shrubs like azaleas and rhododendrons to protect their roots. Use it on banks to retard soil erosion.

### Height

Both Alleghany spurge and Japanese spurge grow to a height of 8 to 10 inches.

### Spread

Pachysandra spreads rapidly by way of underground runners, and it will spread as far as you let it.

### Blossoms

The blossoms of pachysandra are white and bloom on spikes in April or May.

### Foliage

Pachysandra has evergreen, spoon-shaped leaves with toothed edges. They are arranged in whorls on the plant. New leaves will be yellowish green, changing to dark green as the plant matures. The leaves of the Alleghany spurge have an interesting gray mottling. An attractive variegated cultivar of the Japanese spurge is 'Silver Edge', which has cream-colored leaf margins.

## ENVIRONMENT

### Varieties by Zone

To zone 5, Alleghany spurge and Japanese spurge

### Light Requirements

Alleghany spurge requires shade; its leaves will turn yellow in full sun. Japanese spurge prefers part sun to part shade, but will endure deep shade.

167

## Soil Requirements

Pachysandra likes some humus around its roots and prefers a somewhat acidic soil, with a pH of 5.5 to 6.5.

# PLANTING AND PROPAGATION

## Planting

You can plant pachysandra almost anytime during the growing season. Set the plants 12 inches apart, and in two years the area will be covered; however, you can plant them more closely together if you are eager for the area to fill in.

## Propagation

Pachysandra is easily started from cuttings taken in the summer. Snip the stem at least 2 inches up from the lowest leaves on the plant to get the newest growth. You can root cuttings directly in rich soil if you keep the soil moist.

Pachysandra can also be propagated by division almost anytime during the growing season. Take a section of the bed by cutting down 2 to 3 inches deep under the plants and shearing off the roots. Roll up the mat of plants just as sections of sod are rolled; then simply lay the pachysandra rug in freshly worked soil and water it frequently for two weeks.

# PLANT MANAGEMENT

## Water Requirements

Pachysandra does best with about 1 inch of water a week; however, once established, this tough plant can stand neglect all season except during the hottest summer periods when you must give it some water.

## Feeding Requirements

Add compost to the soil in the spring. This one feeding is all that pachysandra needs.

## Pruning

Like many ground covers, pachysandra responds to spring shearing by spreading and thickening. Cut or pinch back individual plants or mow the entire bed with the lawn mower adjusted to the highest setting. You want to cut back about 25 percent of the plant's height.

# MOST COMMON INSECT PESTS

## Leaves Discolored and Bound with Silk Strands

### Leaftiers

The larvae of leaftiers protect themselves while feeding by binding leaves together with strands of silk. As they feed, the foliage becomes ragged and unsightly, turns brown, and dies. Larvae are ¾-inch-long olive green worms with two prominent black spots near the head. If you find only a few of them in your pachysandra bed, simply crush them; otherwise, spray infested plants with Bt (*Bacillus thuringiensis*). If the leaftier is an annual pest in your landscape, spray the pachysandra bed with Bt in late spring, just before the caterpillars begin to feed.

## Leaves Stippled Yellow or Red

### Mites

If the leaves of your pachysandra are stippled with small yellow dots or red spots, your plants are probably infested with two-spotted spider mites (*Tetranychus telarius*). These pests suck the sap from leaves and stems. Often they produce a fine webbing, which covers leaves and stems. Mites are barely visible to the unaided eye. They may be yellow, green, red, or brown.

Start control measures as soon as you notice the first stippling on the leaves. Spray your plants in the early morning with a forceful stream of water to knock mites off the leaves. Repeat this procedure for two more mornings. If you continue to find mites on your pachysandra, spray the bed with insecticidal soap every three to five days for two weeks.

## Leaves Yellowed; Plant Sickly

### Nematodes

Northern root knot nematodes (*Meloidogyne* spp.) attack pachysandra at the roots, which develop galls and decay. Above the ground, the infested plant wilts and becomes stunted. Foliage turns yellow or bronze and eventually the plant dies. Effects of nematode activity are most apparent in hot weather, when infested plants recover slowly from the heat.

Nematodes are whitish, translucent, wormlike creatures, $1/50$ to $1/10$ inch long. To control them, add lots of compost (especially leaf mold) to the soil in your pachysandra bed. Compost attracts beneficial fungi, which attack nematodes. You can also fertilize around the plants with a fish emulsion drench, which repels nematodes.

## Leaves Yellowed; Small Bumps on Leaves and Stems; Growth Stunted

### Scale

Scale insects look like small bumps. These pests have a circular, waxy shell, which covers them while they feed on plants. An early sign of scale infestation is yellowing of the leaves, and you may find honeydew secreted by these pests. Euonymus scale (*Unaspis euonymi*), oystershell scale (*Lepidosaphes ulmi*), and San Jose scale (*Quadraspidiotus perniciosus*) attack pachysandra.

If you catch them early, before too many of them have populated your plants, you can scrape them off plant surfaces with your fingernail or a cotton swab dipped in rubbing alcohol. If scale insects are too numerous for this control, spray infested plants with a mixture of alcohol and insec-

ticidal soap every three days for two weeks. To make this mixture, combine 1 cup isopropyl alcohol and 1 tablespoon commercial insecticidal soap concentrate in 1 quart water. If your insecticidal soap is already diluted with water, simply add 1 tablespoon alcohol to a pint of the soap. The golden chalcid (*Aphytis melinus*), a parasitic wasp, will hold scale in check.

## MOST COMMON DISEASES

## Gray Spots on Leaves and Stems

### Botrytis Blight

Pachysandra plants infected with botrytis blight show ashy gray spots on their bud scales and stems. The plants may die down several nodes from the top. If an infected plant is not too far gone, remove the old flowers and diseased leaves. Dig up and destroy any seriously damaged plants. Do not compost plant parts.

## Leaves Turn Brown and Shrivel; Dark Spots on Stems

### Canker

Pachysandra plants are susceptible to infection by the fungus *Volutella pachysandrae*. When this disease hits, brown to black blotches appear on the leaves, eventually coming together and covering the whole leaf. Similar dark spots develop on the stems as well. Masses of pink spores can sometimes be seen on the stem cankers.

Remove and destroy infected leaves and stems as soon as you notice them, cutting the pachysandra back to several inches below the infected area. Thin overcrowded plants, and spray with Bordeaux mixture for added control and to prevent the spread of this disease to adjacent plants.

# Periwinkle

*Vinca* spp.

## DESCRIPTION

Tough and tolerant, with simple but pretty flowers and foliage that colors the landscape year round, periwinkle is a popular landscape plant. About 12 species of this perennial are known. The most common species are common periwinkle, or myrtle (*Vinca minor*), and big periwinkle (*V. major*). Big periwinkle is grown outdoors in the South and indoors in the North. Common periwinkle is widely grown outdoors in the North. Both are slow-growing, trailing vines with wiry stems. They do not climb, but rather crawl along the ground, rooting every so often.

Periwinkle is very easy to care for. The plants have no problems with pests, and they tolerate air pollution, making them good city plants. They can be planted on a hill to help control erosion. Ornamentally, they form an attractive ground cover under the filtered light of tall hardwood trees. Periwinkle plants are good partners for bulbs, especially yellow daffodils. Because they keep their foliage, they beautify the landscape in winter.

### Height

Big periwinkle (*V. major*), 18 inches
Common periwinkle (*V. minor*), 10 inches

### Spread

4 to 5 feet

### Blossoms

The flowers of this plant have five lobes and may be white or blue. They appear in late April.

### Foliage

Periwinkle plants are evergreen. Their simple leaves are oval, shiny, deeply veined, and leathery. The leaves of the big periwinkle cultivar 'Variegata' have yellowish white margins. Certain cultivars of common periwinkle are also variegated.

## ENVIRONMENT

### Varieties by Zone

To zone 5, common periwinkle
To zone 7, big periwinkle

## Light Requirements

Periwinkle tolerates sun, but prefers light shade. It produces fewer blossoms in shaded areas.

## Soil Requirements

Both types of periwinkle grow well in moderately fertile soils with a pH range of 6 to 7.

# PLANTING AND PROPAGATION

## Planting

Spring is the best time for planting periwinkle sets from the nursery, but you can also put them in the ground in early fall. Periwinkle has shallow roots, so plant it only 1 to 2 inches deep. Leave about 12 inches between plants.

## Propagation

Propagate periwinkle by division or by rooting stem cuttings in the summer. It roots quite easily.

## Container Gardening

An excellent plant for growing in containers, periwinkle looks great in hanging baskets or window boxes and will hang down 18 to 24 inches. In the North, big periwinkle can only be grown in containers indoors or in sunspaces.

# PLANT MANAGEMENT

## Water Requirements

Avoid overwatering periwinkle seedlings. These plants do not require frequent watering; ½ to 1 inch a week is sufficient. However, in the hottest part of summer, keep the bed reasonably moist.

## Feeding Requirements

Periwinkle needs only one application of compost in the spring. Avoid excessive fertilizing, which encourages fungal disease.

## Pruning

Pinch off the tips of periwinkle stems to encourage fullness.

# MOST COMMON DISEASES

## Shoots Turn Black and Die Back to Ground

### Canker

Canker, also known as dieback, is caused by the fungi *Phomopsis livella* and *Phoma exigua*. The tips of shoots of infected periwinkle plants turn dark brown to black, wilt, and die back to the soil. This disease occurs most often during rainy weather. Prune and destroy infected shoots and spray with Bordeaux mixture. Any plants that are severely damaged should be removed and destroyed.

## Spots or Blotches on Leaves

### Fungal Leaf Spot

Periwinkle is susceptible to many kinds of leaf spots caused by many different types of fungi. These fungi thrive on moist leaf surfaces. The spots they produce are usually brown to black, but may be yellow, red, or gray. Often they come together to form larger patches of dead tissue. Sometimes the tiny black fruiting bodies of the fungus surround the spots.

Spray your spotted periwinkle with a flowable sulfur spray every seven to ten days. Pull out and discard any seriously diseased plants, along with the surrounding soil. When watering your periwinkle, avoid wetting the foliage; this will help to prevent the spread of the disease.

## Roots and Stems Decayed

### Root Rot

The root rot fungus (*Pellicularia filamentosa*) attacks the roots and stems of periwinkle. The disease resembles canker disease because both plant roots and stems become decayed. Cut away infected stems and destroy them. Remove and discard any seriously infected plants. Avoid overwatering, and space plants farther apart to allow air to circulate among them.

## NOTES AND RESEARCH

You might some day walk into your backyard and find thin orange strands twirling around your periwinkle plants. This is dodder, a parasitic seed plant (*Cuscuta* spp.) related to morning glory. Its thin leafless stems wind around a host plant and it feeds entirely off that plant by means of tiny suckers. Dodder cannot be controlled by hand-pulling or cultivation. Infested plants must be destroyed. If you notice the dodder before its seeds form (April to October), cut out any affected plant parts and destroy them, along with the dodder. Cultivate the bare ground repeatedly over several weeks to allow any remaining dodder seeds to sprout and die.

## GROUND COVER Sedum *Sedum* spp.

## DESCRIPTION

Sedum is also called stonecrop, and this name suits it well: The succulent leaves and compact habit work well in rock gardens, in the nooks and crannies of stone walls, and along walkways. This is a large genus of some 600 perennials and some annuals. The various types of sedum have diverse habits. Some creep, some are tufted, some grow in rosettes, and some stand upright. They grow throughout the temperate and colder regions of the northern hemisphere. Members of this group make excellent ground covers.

### Height

Goldmoss stonecrop (*Sedum acre*), 2 inches
Lydian stonecrop (*S. lydium*), 3 to 6 inches
Showy sedum (*S. spectabile*), 18 inches
Stringy stonecrop (*S. sarmentosum*), 6 inches
Two-row stonecrop (*S. spurium*), 2 to 3 inches

### Spread

Sedum will spread as far as permitted.

## Blossoms

The pretty star-shaped flowers of sedum bloom in terminal clusters during the months of July and August, though some types bloom through October. The flowers may be white, yellow, pink, red, or purplish, depending on the species and cultivar.

## Foliage

Most sedum plants are evergreen. The leaves are fleshy and usually cylindrical. The length varies from as small as ⅛ inch to 2 inches, depending on the species. Most types turn reddish in the fall.

# ENVIRONMENT

## Varieties by Zone

To zone 3, goldmoss stonecrop, lydian stonecrop, showy sedum, stringy stonecrop, and two-row stonecrop

## Light Requirements

Sedum prefers full sun, but will tolerate light shade.

## Soil Requirements

Sedum actually thrives in a dry, well-drained, poor, sandy soil. If plants fail to do well, the soil might be too rich. Do not fertilize sedum that is growing in rich soils.

# PLANTING AND PROPAGATION

## Planting

Plant sedum in the spring. The distance between plants varies with the variety or species. When using sedum as a ground cover, place the plants only a few inches apart.

## Propagation

Sedum cuttings root easily in sand. Even broken leaves will root. You can also propagate these plants by division in spring or summer.

# PLANT MANAGEMENT

## Water Requirements

Sedum is best adapted to warm, dry climates where its water-storing ability enables it to go long periods without irrigation. The plants need only light watering through the growing season. Avoid getting them too wet, and do not use organic mulch around them. Organic mulch holds moisture and may encourage rot. Sometimes adding sand or gravel to the soil around the plants makes them happier.

## Feeding Requirements

Since these plants prefer poor soils, you only need to feed them once every two years with compost.

## Pruning

Sedum used for a ground cover doesn't require pruning. Sedum planted in the flower garden can be pinched back early in the season to encourage bushiness and dense growth.

# MOST COMMON CULTURAL PROBLEMS

## Plants Fail to Flourish

### Soil Too Rich

Since sedum prefers sandy, relatively poor soil, soil that is too rich or that has been over-fertilized may encourage excessive development of the foliage, resulting in lank, top-heavy plants with few flowers. If this is happening to your sedum, do not add any fertilizer to the soil. Better yet, try to move plants to a location with a poorer soil.

## MOST COMMON INSECT PESTS

### Leaves Yellowed and Distorted

#### Aphids

Aphids suck the sap from the foliage of sedum, causing discoloration and distortion. The foliage may turn yellow or brown, and will wilt under bright sunlight. Ants are attracted to a sticky honeydew secreted by aphids. Melon aphids (*Aphis gossypii*), green peach aphids (*Myzus persicae*), and sedum aphids all attack sedum. These soft-bodied, pear-shaped insects are about the size of the head of a pin. They may be green, brown, or pink.

You can easily remove a light infestation by spraying the leaves of infested sedum vigorously with water. Do this early in the morning for three consecutive days. If this doesn't solve the problem, spray your plants with insecticidal soap every two to three days for two weeks. As a last resort, use pyrethrum spray in two applications, three to four days apart.

### Plant Stunted; Leaves Yellowed

#### Nematodes

Occasionally, southern root knot nematodes (*Meloidogyne* spp.) infest sedum. Nematodes are not insects; they are slender, unsegmented roundworms, $1/50$ to $1/10$ inch long. They attack the roots of plants, causing them to develop poorly and decay. On the whole, infested plants wilt, and their growth becomes stunted. Foliage turns yellow or bronze.

Add a seaweed extract drench to the soil around plants to attract beneficial fungi, which attack nematodes. If all else fails, pull the plants and solarize the soil before replacing them with new nursery stock.

## MOST COMMON DISEASES

### Dead Blotches on Leaves and Blossoms

#### Botrytis Blight

Botrytis gray mold attacks sedum leaves and flowers, causing blotches to form. Eventually, the leaves and flowers become brown and die. Leaf blotch causes round, dark circles on leaves, which quickly drop. Cut off and discard all diseased plant parts and destroy entirely any badly infected plants. Spray infected plants with a copper- or sulfur-based fungicide, making two applications five days apart.

### Stems Rot at Soil Line

#### Crown Rot

Crown rot caused by *Pellicularia rolfsii* causes sedum to decay at the soil line. You'll probably find the white fibers of the fungus near the bases of your plants. There is no permanent cure for crown rot. Remove and discard infected plants and the soil around them. Do not compost the plants. Before replanting in the same place, pasteurize the soil or enrich it with compost or other organic matter to encourage the growth of soil organisms antagonistic to this disease. Thoroughly cultivating around the plants allows the soil to dry out and helps prevent the spread of the fungus.

### Powdery Spots on Leaves

#### Rust

Powdery spots on the undersides of sedum leaves signal rust. This fungal disease may be caused by *Puccinia rydbergii* or *P. umbilici*. Rust seldom harms the plant, but it looks unsightly. Remove and destroy infected leaves. If the infestation is serious, remove and destroy diseased plants and all debris before growth starts in the spring. Control weeds in and around the garden, as they can contribute to rust problems.

If your sedum frequently becomes infected with rust, you can take measures to prevent it from recurring. Beginning several weeks before you expect this disease to appear, spray plants periodically with wettable sulfur. Space plants widely to allow air to circulate among them, and avoid wetting their foliage when you water.

# Sweet Woodruff

*Galium odoratum*

## DESCRIPTION

This gentle, low-growing perennial is a favorite of many gardeners. In the spring it produces small white flowers that nestle in a soft foliage. It makes a lovely ground cover, especially in combination with English ivy, and it can be used as an accent in the front of the perennial bed. It is particularly suited to growing around shallow-rooted rhododendrons, as it likes the shade there, and it protects the shrubs' shallow roots. The leaves of sweet woodruff are used to flavor May wine.

### Height

6 to 8 inches

### Spread

Sweet woodruff spreads far and wide rather quickly.

### Blossoms

The dainty four-petaled flowers look like white stars. They are about ¼ inch across and bloom from May through June.

### Foliage

Sweet woodruff has delicate, medium green, deciduous foliage. The leaves have an elliptical shape, are about 1 inch long, and grow in whorls, and they have a pleasing sweet fragrance, even when dried.

## ENVIRONMENT

### Hardiness

Sweet woodruff is hardy to zone 5.

### Light Requirements

This plant prefers partial shade, but can handle some morning sun.

### Soil Requirements

Moist, humusy, well-drained soil provides the best environment for woodruff's roots.

175

## PLANTING AND PROPAGATION

### Planting

You can plant sweet woodruff in the spring or the fall. Set plants 6 to 12 inches apart.

### Propagation

This plant is easily propagated by division either in the spring or fall, or you can take stem cuttings to root.

### Container Gardening

Sweet woodruff grows well indoors in pots.

## PLANT MANAGEMENT

### Water Requirements

Sweet woodruff needs regular watering, especially if it is not in a shaded woodland setting where the soil is humusy and moist. Make sure it gets about 1 inch of water a week.

### Feeding Requirements

Work some compost into the soil around woodruff in the spring, and your plants will be happy for the year.

## NOTES AND RESEARCH

Sweet woodruff doesn't suffer from any problems with pests or disease—another good reason to plant this perennial in your landscape. The foliage can turn messy brown, and the stems flatten and die back toward late summer, but that is normal in the plant's life cycle. The beauty sweet woodruff adds to the landscape in spring and summer more than compensate for this short period of homeliness. Watering your plants in the heat of the summer can delay this period somewhat.

# VINE *Bittersweet*   *Celastrus* spp.

## DESCRIPTION

It's the brilliant orange berries of bittersweet that make this a delightful plant. They appear in fall to add another burst of color to the burning yellows, oranges, and reds of this season. Oriental bittersweet (*Celastrus orbiculatus*) is a species from China and Japan that is becoming naturalized in this country. The native American bittersweet (*C. scandens*) grows wild along roadsides and in woods in the eastern parts of North America. You can use these vines against low walls and on trellises or fences. Neither should be permitted to twine around live shrubs or trees because they can smother them.

### Height

American bittersweet (*C. scandens*), 20 feet
Oriental bittersweet (*C. orbiculatus*), 36 feet

### Spread

Bittersweet can spread rampantly and is controlled by pruning.

### Blossoms

In most cases, male and female flowers are produced on separate plants, but occasionally both appear on the same vine. These small greenish flowers won't knock you off your feet, but the clusters of red-orange fruits they turn into just might. These fruits develop on female plants. Each is a yellow capsule that splits open to display the red-orange seed inside.

## Foliage

The fruits aren't the only asset of this vine. Bittersweet foliage is attractive, too. The leaves are green and oblong-oval in shape, with tapered tips.

# ENVIRONMENT

## Varieties by Zone

To zone 2, American bittersweet
To zone 4, oriental bittersweet

## Light Requirements

Bittersweet can handle shade, but sun encourages more generous fruiting.

## Soil Requirements
Ordinary soil is just fine for bittersweet.

# PLANTING AND PROPAGATION

## Planting

Buy bittersweet in the fall when the fruit is produced so you can be sure to buy both a male and a female plant, or buy from a nursery that offers sexed plants. Both are required for fruiting. Plant bittersweet plants within several yards of one another to promote pollination.

## Propagation

Bittersweet can be grown from seed. Sow it as soon as it is ripe, or stratify it for three months at 40°F and plant it later. You can also propagate bittersweet easily from root cuttings and from hardwood and softwood stem cuttings.

# PLANT MANAGEMENT

## Water Requirements

Bittersweet grows well with ½ to 1 inch of water each week.

## Feeding Requirements

One application of compost a year, worked into the soil in the spring, is all the feeding bittersweet requires.

## Pruning

Prune bittersweet regularly every winter. Remove branches with spent berries. If the vine has a tendency to tangle or to retain too many old branches, cut it all the way back to the ground in the wintertime; it will sprout anew in the spring.

# MOST COMMON CULTURAL PROBLEMS

## Failure to Yield Fruit

### Need Plants of Opposite Sex

The male and female flowers of bittersweet are produced on separate plants. Both male and female plants are needed for fruiting. If you do have plants of both sexes and still no berries appear in fall, your plants are probably too far apart. Move them closer together.

# MOST COMMON INSECT PESTS

## Leaves Yellowed; Bumps on Leaves and Stems

### Scale

If you notice the leaves of your bittersweet turning yellow, look for scale insects. The most common species to infest bittersweet is the euonymus scale (*Unaspis euonymi*). They gather in clusters on the leaves and stems and look like small bumps. The males are white and elongated; the females, brown and oval. The leaves of infested plants may drop.

If you catch an infestation early on, you can simply scrape the scale off plants with your fingernail or a cotton swab dipped in rubbing alcohol. When scale insects become too numerous for handpicking, cut out infested growth and spray plants with a mixture of alcohol and insecticidal soap every three days for two weeks. Make this solution by combining 1 cup isopropyl alcohol and 1 tablespoon commercial insecticidal soap concentrate in

1 quart water. If you already have diluted insecticidal soap, add 1 tablespoon alcohol to a pint of the soap. The golden chalcid (*Aphytis melinus*) is a parasitic wasp available commercially that helps control scale.

## Sticky Froth on Stems and Leaves

### Two-Spotted Treehoppers

Spots of white froth on the stems and leaves of bittersweet signals the presence of the female two-spotted treehopper (family Membracidae). The adult treehopper looks like a tiny black thorn about ¼ inch high, sitting on the stem of the bittersweet. The female lays her eggs on the plant and covers them with a frothy substance that in itself does no harm. But once these eggs hatch, the emerging nymphs suck the sap of new leaves around them, and then the adults move around freely, also sucking foliage sap. Treehoppers are only a problem on bittersweet when their numbers become high.

To control these pests, spray your infested vines in late winter with a dormant oil spray to smother the eggs. When spring arrives, look for nymphs. They are less than ¼ inch long and spiny, and they jump when disturbed. If you find them, spray with pyrethrum every three to five days for three weeks.

# MOST COMMON DISEASES

## Leaves Covered with White Powder

### Powdery Mildew

A whitish, powdery dust on the leaves of your plants is a sure sign of powdery mildew. This is a fungal disease, and in bittersweet may be caused by *Microsphaera alni* or *Phyllactinia corylea*. These fungi thrive in humid or dry conditions. Badly infected leaves become discolored and distorted, and drop off.

Spray infected plants thoroughly with wettable sulfur once or twice a week until the problem subsides. Prune your vines to allow good air circulation in and around the plant, and collect and discard all aboveground plant debris in the fall.

# ― VINE **Clematis** *Clematis* spp.

## DESCRIPTION

The large, starry blossoms of clematis make this perennial vine a beautiful landscape plant. The leafstalks act as tendrils and fasten this vine to its supporting structure. Clematis clings readily to trellises, fences, walls, stumps, or lightposts. Its flowers and fluffy seed clusters attract birds, who also like to take shelter among the leaves. You must be patient with this plant; it takes up to seven years for clematis to reach dense flowering maturity. However, the beauty is worth the wait, and these vines live for years and are easy to care for.

### Height

Anemone clematis (*Clematis montana*), 20 feet

Armand clematis (*C. armandii*), 20 feet

Curly clematis (*C. crispa*), 9 feet

Durand clematis (*C. ×durandii*), 6 to 8 feet

Golden clematis (*C. tangutica*), 9 feet

Hybrid clematis (*C. ×jackmanii* and related hybrids), 12 feet

Scarlet clematis (*C. texensis*), 6 feet

Sweet autumn clematis (*C. paniculata*), 30 feet

### Spread

Most clematis vines will spread laterally as they are trained. Armand clematis can spread 50 or even 100 feet if it is grown in the Pacific Northwest.

### Blossoms

The flowers of clematis may be solitary or clustered, flat and open or bell shaped, depending on the species or hybrid. Most gardeners grow the showy hybrids such as *C. ×jackmanii,* the blossoms of which can be 4 to 5 inches across. You can choose from white, yellow, pink, red, and purple shades, and most have some fragrance. Clematis will bloom from June to September, again depending on the species or hybrid.

### Foliage

The leaves of clematis are compound, usually having three to five leaflets. Most species have smooth green foliage, but not all.

# ENVIRONMENT

## Varieties by Zone

To zone 4, golden clematis

To zone 5, anemone clematis, curly clematis, durand clematis, hybrid clematis, scarlet clematis, and sweet autumn clematis

To zone 7, armand clematis

## Light Requirements

Clematis can take full sun to some shade. They are especially happy in a location where the base of the plant is shaded by shrubbery, while the top is in the sun.

## Soil Requirements

Clematis likes a moist, fertile, well-drained soil. One with lots of humus—more than 5 percent—is best. Most species prefer neutral to slightly alkaline soil. If your clematis are growing near concrete walls or foundations, watch that your soil doesn't become too alkaline with lime that may leach into the soil from the walls and foundations.

# PLANTING AND PROPAGATION

## Planting

Plant clematis about 24 inches apart, even though they are slow to fill in.

## Propagation

You can propagate clematis from softwood cuttings taken in late spring.

# PLANT MANAGEMENT

## Water Requirements

Clematis likes a moist soil, so water regularly, especially in the summer, to keep roots cool. Make sure it receives about 1 inch a week.

## Feeding Requirements

One application of compost in the spring is all clematis needs for the year. For exceptional performance, give your clematis a supplemental light feeding, applying a side-dressing or foliar spray once a month throughout the growing season.

## Pruning

After it grows to a height of 2 feet, clematis can be pinched and trained. Spring-blooming clematis produce their flowers on last year's growth, so delay pruning until after the bloom period; then cut off any damaged stems and shape the vine. Summer-flowering types, which include the large-flowered hybrids, must be pruned in late winter or very early spring, because their flowers bloom on the current year's wood.

## Mulching

Because clematis grows best when its roots are cool, mulch plants during the summer. Use 2 to 4 inches of organic mulch and spread it so that it is close to the plant but does not touch the main stem.

## Staking

Clematis vines need a fence, trellis, or some other kind of supporting structure. Set up the structure you desire when you plant your vines, or the vines won't grow well. Keep in mind that clematis tends to grow straight up 8 to 10 feet before generating much side growth.

## General Care

Protect the lower stems of clematis from injury and breakage. A wounded vine is very vulnerable to infection from disease. Many gardeners circle the base of their plants with a wire cage or fence that is about 3 feet high. A ring of annuals or low shrubs can also serve to protect the exposed lower stems.

## Drying

Clematis air dries well. For a natural look, curl the

stems around a string stretched horizontally. The seedpods are often used in decorative displays. Dried naturally, the seed heads are fluffy, white, and fragile. You can dip them in a very thin varnish to make them last.

# MOST COMMON CULTURAL PROBLEMS

## Vine Stems Break Frequently

### Lack of Support
Clematis vines break easily, especially in windy or rainy conditions. Give them firm support as they climb, and protect the lower parts of the stem with mulch or underplantings.

# MOST COMMON INSECT PESTS

## Leaves and Flowers Eaten

### Blister Beetles
Black blister beetle (*Epicauta pennsylvanica*) chews the flowers and leaves of clematis. Swarms of this pest will devour almost everything in sight. The blister beetle is about ¾ inch long and slender, with soft, flexible wing covers. It is gray with a yellowish tinge.

The best quick defense is to handpick the insects. Wear gloves: True to their name, these beetles secrete a substance that painfully blisters the skin. If a heavy population has infested your plants, spray weekly with a solution of pyrethrum and isopropyl alcohol, mixing 1 tablespoon alcohol in a pint of pyrethrum.

## Vines Stunted

### Clematis Borers
In midsummer, clematis vines may become stunted and their branches may die. This is probably the work of the clematis borer (*Alcathoe caudata*), which hollows out stems and tunnels through the crown and roots of the plant. This borer, the larva of a clear-winged moth, is a dull white worm with a brown head, about ⅔ inch long. It spends the winter in the roots of the plant.

Controlling this pest is difficult. There is little to do but to immediately cut out and burn the infested stems. Remove the soil carefully from around the crown of the plant and dig out any larvae you see.

## Leaves Yellowed; Plant Sickly

### Nematodes
Nematode-infested clematis become sickly, wilted, or stunted. Their foliage turns yellow and bronze, and the roots become malformed and decay. Eventually, the plant dies. Knots on the roots are a definite sign that nematodes have attacked. The effects of nematode activity are most apparent in hot weather, when the plants recover poorly from the heat.

Nematodes are whitish, translucent, wormlike creatures, ¹⁄₅₀ to ¹⁄₁₀ inch long. All the damage they do results from their assault on the roots of plants. To control them, add lots of compost, especially leaf mold, to the soil. This encourages beneficial fungi, which will discourage nematodes. You may also fertilize around your vines with a fish emulsion drench, which repels nematodes.

## Leaves Yellowed

### Soft Scale
If your clematis leaves begin to turn yellow, suspect scale. Both brown soft scale (*Coccus hesperidum*) and oystershell scale (*Lepidosaphes ulmi*) attack clematis. These insects look like small bumps, having waxy shells that protect them while they feed. They are very flat, oval in shape, and vary from greenish to brown in color.

If you spot these pests before too many of them have covered your clematis vines, simply scrape them off with your fingernail or a cotton swab dipped in rubbing alcohol. Heavy infestations are more easily controlled by spraying plants with a mixture of alcohol and insecticidal soap every three days for two weeks. To make this solution, combine 1 cup isopropyl alcohol and 1 tablespoon commercial insecticidal soap concentrate in 1 quart water. If you already have some diluted insecticidal soap, add 1 tablespoon alcohol to a pint of the soap. In addition, the golden chalcid (*Aphytis melinus*) is a commercially available parasitic wasp, which attacks scale and helps to control the pests.

## Holes in Leaves

### Weevils

Adult weevils eat holes in clematis leaves or chew notches along the edges. If abundant, they may defoliate an entire plant. Weevil larvae chew zigzag paths into clematis roots or stems, which causes the plant to wilt. A clematis that has been damaged by larvae can be pulled out of the ground easily.

Adult weevils are either gray or black, with a tear-shaped, hard-shelled body, $1/10$ to $1/4$ inch long. The larvae are fleshy, white, legless grubs. Both adults and larvae feed during the night and curl up under bark or other plant tissue during the day.

Weevils will play dead when disturbed, folding their legs and dropping off plants to the ground. Turn this trait to advantage when controlling these pests. Spread a cloth underneath your plants; then gently shake the vines. The startled weevils will drop to the cloth, where you can gather them up and destroy them. In addition to trying this procedure,

spray your clematis weekly with a solution of pyrethrum and isopropyl alcohol. Make this solution using 1 tablespoon alcohol per pint of pyrethrum. Introduce predatory nematodes to stop the reproduction of weevils.

## MOST COMMON DISEASES

### Brown to Black Spots or Blotches on Leaves

#### Leaf Spot

Any of several kinds of fungi may cause leaf spot in clematis. Usually the spots are brown to black, and often they come together to form large patches of dead tissue. You might see the tiny black dots of the fruiting bodies surrounding these spots. Some species of fungus can spread from the leaves to the stems, eventually girdling the stems and causing the vines above the point of infection to wilt and die.

Pick off and discard the infected leaves, and remove and discard seriously infected plants, together with the soil around them. Spray vines with a flowable sulfur spray every seven to ten days until symptoms subside. Since leaf spot fungi thrive in moist conditions, avoid wetting the foliage when watering plants.

# VINE *Climbing Hydrangea*

*Hydrangea anomala*

## DESCRIPTION

Most of us know the billowy, showy flower clusters of hydrangea shrubs. The climbing hydrangea also produces pretty flower heads to perk up the landscape. This vine is one of the most popular ornamental

vines in the world. Once established, it will climb with gusto up walls or the trunks of tall trees. You can use it to soften harsh architectural lines, hide utilities, or decorate a neglected north wall.

## Height

Unrestrained, climbing hydrangea will grow up to 75 feet.

## Spread

Laterally, these vines can spread as much as 30 feet.

## Blossoms

The white flowers are small, but together form dense flat-topped or globe-shaped clusters, 6 to 8 inches across. They bloom in mid-June.

## Foliage

Climbing hydrangea is deciduous. Its lustrous green leaves are heart-shaped or oval, and usually toothed.

# ENVIRONMENT

## Hardiness

Climbing hydrangea is hardy to zone 4.

## Light Requirements

These vines grow best in light to medium shade, but will tolerate full sun.

## Soil Requirements

Climbing hydrangea prefers good, well-drained loam, but will do well in most types of soil. It likes a somewhat acid soil, with a pH between 5.8 and 6.5.

# PLANTING AND PROPAGATION

## Planting

You can plant climbing hydrangea in either spring or fall.

## Propagation

Climbing hydrangea is easy to grow from seed, but is notorious for its slowness in becoming established. The plants are best propagated by layering or from semiripe cuttings taken in the early summer. Newly transplanted vines take a year or two to start major growth.

# PLANT MANAGEMENT

## Water Requirements

Make sure your plants get 1 inch of water every week.

## Feeding Requirements

One application of compost in the spring supplies climbing hydrangea with all its basic nutrient needs for the year. If you want exceptional performance from your vines, give them light supplemental feedings (side-dressings or foliar spray) every month throughout the growing season.

## Pruning

Climbing hydrangea is brittle and easily damaged, making it vulnerable to disease. Prune damaged or broken stems early in summer, immediately after blooming.

# MOST COMMON CULTURAL PROBLEMS

## Leaves Yellowed

### Alkaline Soil

If the pH of the soil exceeds 7 by too much, the leaves of climbing hydrangea will turn yellow, and the plants will not grow very well. To correct this problem, add powdered sulfur to the soil. Mulch the plants each year with peat moss, which lends a little acidity to the soil. (See chapter 9 for more information on correcting an alkaline soil.)

# MOST COMMON INSECT PESTS

## Leaves Yellowed, Curled, and Distorted

### Aphids

If the leaves of your climbing hydrangea are yellowed and curled, suspect aphids. These insects suck the juices from the leaves of plants, causing them to turn yellow or brown and curl. Eventually, growth of the plant is slowed. Ants are attracted to the sticky honeydew secreted by aphids. Green peach aphids (*Myzus persicae*) and melon aphids (*Aphis gossypii*) are the two most common pests of climbing hydrangea. They are not much bigger than the head of a pin and have soft, pear-shaped bodies.

Light infestations are easily removed simply by spraying infested plants vigorously with water. Do this early in the morning, three times, once every other day. For medium to heavy infestations, spray vines with insecticidal soap every two to three days until aphids are gone. As a last resort, use pyrethrum, making two applications, three to four days apart.

## Leaves Discolored and Bound with Silk Bands

### Leaftiers

If the foliage of your climbing hydrangea is covered with silken threads, your plants are probably infested with hydrangea leaftiers (*Exartema ferriferanum*). Leaftiers are moths, the larvae of which attack your plants. The larvae are ½ inch long and green with dark brown heads. They bind the leaves of hydrangea together and crawl inside them to feed. These leaves become ragged and unsightly, and eventually turn brown and die.

Crush the larvae in the leaves if there are not too many; otherwise, spray infested plants with Bt (*Bacillus thuringiensis*), making three applications, seven days apart.

## Leaf Margins Appear Burned

### Mites

Two-spotted spider mites (*Tetranychus telarius*) cause damage in climbing hydrangea that resembles sunscald. The leaves look as though they've been burned along their margins. If you find such damage on your plants, look for mites. These pests are barely visible to the unaided eye. They may be yellow, green, red, or brown. To control mites, spray infested vines with insecticidal soap every three to five days for two weeks.

## Leaves Fall; Plant Stunted

### Nematodes

Root knot nematodes (*Meloidogyne incognita* and *M. hapla*) and bulb and stem nematodes (*Ditylenchus dipsaci*) will infest climbing hydrangea if given the chance. They attack at the roots of plants, and affect the plants' ability to develop normally. Roots themselves will be poorly developed, knotted, and may be partially decayed. Above the ground, the vine wilts and appears stunted. Foliage turns yellow or bronze. The bulb and stem nematodes cause stems to swell and split. Leaves drop off as a result. Eventually, the plant dies.

Nematodes are not insects, but slender, unsegmented roundworms. They are $\frac{1}{50}$ to $\frac{1}{10}$ inch long. To combat them, add lots of compost, especially leaf mold, to the soil around the affected vine. This attracts fungi, which attack nematodes. You might try fertilizing your vine with a drench of fish emulsion, which repels nematodes.

## Leaves Discolored; Small Bumps on New Growth

### Scale

The first sign of a scale attack in climbing hydrangea is discoloration of the tops of leaves. This is usually followed by leaf drop, reduced growth, and stunted plants. When these things start happening to your plants, look for the scale pests themselves. They'll appear as small bumps on the new growth of the vine. The oystershell scale (*Lepidosaphes ulmi*) is the species that most often infests climbing hydrangea. Aptly named, these insects have an oyster-shaped shell, which covers them while they feed on your plants. They are about ⅛ inch long and may be gray or brown.

If you discover them before too many have clustered on your vines, simply scrape them off with your fingernail or a cotton swab dipped in rubbing alcohol. Medium to heavy infestations are more easily controlled by spraying plants with a mixture of alcohol and insecticidal soap every three days for two weeks. To make this solution, combine 1 tablespoon isopropyl alcohol and 1 cup insecticidal soap concentrate with 1 quart water. If your insecticidal soap is already mixed with water, add 1 tablespoon alcohol to a pint of this soap spray.

## MOST COMMON DISEASES

## Concentric Rings on Leaves

### Hydrangea Ring-Spot Virus

If you see concentric rings on your climbing hydrangea's leaves, alternating in color from dark green to light green, your plants have hydrangea ring-spot virus. You also may find small spots of dead tissue on the foliage. There is no cure for plant viruses, so remove infected plants promptly and destroy them. If the infection is mild and doesn't seem to be harming the overall performance of the plant, you can simply learn to live with annual leaf spots. Do not take cuttings from infected plants, for they will be infected, and disinfect pruning shears after each cut to avoid spreading the virus.

## Brown to Black Spots or Blotches on Leaves

### Leaf Spot

Climbing hydrangea is susceptible to many kinds of leaf spots, caused by many kinds of fungi. Spots are usually brown to black and often come together to form large patches of dead tissue. Sometimes you will see the tiny black specks of spore-bearing fruiting bodies surrounding these spots.

Pick off and discard the infected leaves, and spray infected plants with flowable sulfur every seven to ten days until symptoms subside. When watering your climbing hydrangea, avoid wetting the foliage. Mulching will help reduce splash-borne infection.

# VINE *Creeper* *Parthenocissus* spp.

## DESCRIPTION

These vines are members of the grape family, so you can imagine the impact of their deep green foliage splashing over walls, stretching along fences, and climbing up trellises. Virginia creeper (*Parthenocissus quinquefolia*) is a particularly good climber, and drapes attractively over walls and trellises and along fences. Boston ivy (*P. tricuspidata*) has a denser habit, and is noted for its ability to climb on stone, and is an especially fine plant for urban areas. All creepers have excellent fall color, and their small blue berries attract birds to the garden.

## Height

Boston ivy (*P. tricuspidata*), 60 feet
Silver-vein creeper (*P. henryana)*, 20 feet
Virginia creeper (*P. quinquefolia*), 50 feet

## Spread

Creepers will spread as permitted.

## Blossoms

You won't grow creeper for its flowers—they are small and inconspicuous. Blue-black fruit replaces them in fall.

## Foliage

Creepers produce outstanding foliage. The leaves have three or five leaflets and turn scarlet in the fall. Silver-vein creeper has variegated foliage that is purplish underneath and striped along the top mid-vein. Boston ivy leaves are shiny on both sides.

# ENVIRONMENT

## Varieties by Zone

To zone 4, Virginia creeper
To zone 5, Boston ivy
To zone 8, Silver-vein creeper

## Light Requirements

Creepers like sun, but will grow in light shade. Silver-vein creeper looks best in the shade, where its foliage color becomes more developed.

## Soil Requirements

Creepers appreciate fairly moist, loamy soil, although they will tolerate most soils.

# PLANTING AND PROPAGATION

## Planting

Plant the vine about 12 inches from its intended support to give the roots room to spread. Once it is planted, identify the three or four strongest shoots and cut them halfway back to encourage new growth and to invigorate the other shoots.

## Propagation

You can propagate creepers by seeds or cuttings, or by layering. If you are starting them from seed, first stratify the seed at 40°F for three months, then sow it. Cuttings will root easily. Suckers, readily found on older plants, also root easily.

## PLANT MANAGEMENT

### Water Requirements

Creepers need 1 inch of water every week.

### Feeding Requirements

One application of compost in the spring will meet this vine's basic needs for a season. If you want your plants to look their very best, give them light supplemental feedings (side-dressings or foliar spray) monthly throughout the growing season.

### Pruning

Virginia creeper can handle lots of shearing. Any part that has been torn from its support must be pruned, because it won't reattach itself. Always cut away any broken or diseased stems.

## MOST COMMON INSECT PESTS

### Plant Defoliated

#### Caterpillars
The striped caterpillar of the eight-spotted forester moth can strip the creeper leaves rapidly, especially in the late summer, when the second generation appears. Spray your plants with Bt (*Bacillus thuringiensis*) as soon as you spot the caterpillars. Two applications five days apart should remove these pests.

### Holes in Leaves

#### Japanese Beetles
Japanese beetles (*Popillia japonica*) love Boston ivy and Virginia creeper and can skeletonize a plant's leaves. The adults are ½ inch long, with shiny metallic green and brown wing covers. If you catch them early, handpick the beetles from the plants and

drop them into a pail of soapy water. If beetles are too numerous for handpicking alone to be effective, set up pheromone beetle traps, making sure the traps are no closer than 50 feet to the creeper or any other plant vulnerable to beetle attack, such as roses. Handpick stragglers not caught by the traps. If the traps cannot handle the infestation, spray infested vines with a solution of pyrethrum and isopropyl alcohol. Make this solution from 1 tablespoon alcohol and 1 pint diluted pyrethrum.

### Leaves Yellowed

#### Scale
If the leaves of your Boston ivy turn yellow and drop, suspect a scale infestation, and look for these pests on your plants. Brown soft scale (*Coccus hesperidum*) is the species that most commonly infests creepers. These insects don't look like insects at all, but rather like small bumps. Scale insects have concave shells, which protect them while they feed. They gather in clusters on plants. They are oval, flatish, and greenish to brownish in color.

If you catch an infestation early enough, you can scrape scale off plants with your fingernail or a cotton swab dipped in rubbing alcohol. Dense populations are more easily controlled by spraying plants with a mixture of alcohol and insecticidal soap every three days for two weeks. This solution is made from 1 cup isopropyl alcohol and 1 tablespoon commercial insecticidal soap concentrate in 1 quart water. If you already have some diluted insecticidal soap, simply add 1 tablespoon alcohol to a pint of it.

## MOST COMMON DISEASES

### Brown to Black Spots or Blotches on Leaves

#### Leaf Spot
Leaf spot diseases in creepers are caused by any of several fungi that thrive on moist leaf surfaces. Brown to black spots develop on the leaves of infected plants. These spots often come together to form larger patches of dead tissue. Sometimes you will

see flecks or black dots around the spots. These are the spore-bearing fruiting bodies of the fungus.

Pick off and discard the infected leaves, and spray the plants every seven to ten days with a flowable sulfur spray. Avoid wetting the foliage while watering your vines. Mulching around plants helps prevent fungi from being splashed up from the ground by rain or when you are watering.

## Leaves Covered with White Powder

### Powdery Mildew

Powdery mildew (*Uncinula necator*) appears as a distinctive white powdery coating on the leaves of the plants it infects. This fungus can occur during either very hot, dry or very humid conditions. Where vines are crowded and air does not circulate freely among them, the environment is even more favorable for powdery mildew. Badly infected leaves become discolored, distorted, and drop. As soon as you notice the whitish bloom of fungi on your plants, spray them with wettable sulfur once or twice, a week apart.

VINE **Honeysuckle** *Lonicera* spp.

## DESCRIPTION

For many, the sweet, heady fragrance of honeysuckle recalls childhood memories of gently pulling off a delicate blossom to squeeze from it one sugary drop. This group of plants includes both shrubs and vines that are full of foliage. Blossoms burst out all over, and in the fall, brightly colored berries take their place. Honeysuckle vines do not cling to masonry or to a wooden wall, so train them along a fence or up a trellis. They like to sprawl over a bank, too. Use this vine to soften architectural lines, conceal utilities, or provide greenery in a wooded setting. Birds love honeysuckle berries.

### Height

Everblooming honeysuckle (*Lonicera* ×*heckrottii*), 12 feet
Japanese honeysuckle (*L. japonica*), 20 to 30 feet
Trumpet honeysuckle (*L. sempervirens*), 50 feet
Woodbine (*L. periclymenum*), 15 feet

### Spread

Honeysuckle will spread as far as you let it. Japanese honeysuckle tends to take over an area if it is not pruned yearly.

### Blossoms

Most honeysuckle types are spring and summer bloomers and produce lots of showy, fragrant blossoms. The Japanese honeysuckle blooms from May or June through the whole summer. The flowers are about 2 inches long and may be shaped either like trumpets or bells, depending on the species. They usually bloom in clusters at the tips of branches, and may be white, yellow, or orange. Sometimes they are tinged with red or pink. The flowers of the trumpet honeysuckle are not fragrant, but do attract hummingbirds, as do their scarlet berries. The Japanese honeysuckle produces black berries.

## Foliage

Honeysuckle leaves are oval to oblong and about 2 inches long. They have bluish green undersides, which are also downy in the case of woodbine and trumpet honeysuckle. Sometimes the leaves are evergreen. In the North, the leaves sometimes take on a purplish color.

# ENVIRONMENT

## Hardiness

The trumpet honeysuckle is the hardiest of the recommended species. It is evergreen in mild climates.

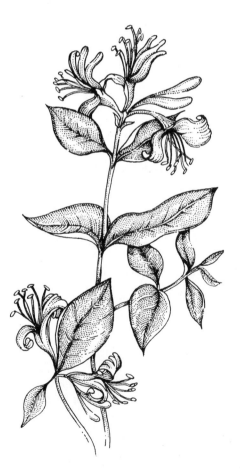

## Varieties by Zone

To zone 4, everblooming honeysuckle and trumpet honeysuckle

To zone 5, Japanese honeysuckle and woodbine

## Light Requirements

Most honeysuckle types thrive in full sun to partial shade. Woodbine prefers partial shade.

## Soil Requirements

Honeysuckle will grow in any soil; however, it does best in a loamy soil that is reasonably moist.

# PLANTING AND PROPAGATION

## Planting

You can plant honeysuckle in either the spring or fall.

## Propagation

The best way to propagate honeysuckle vines is from cuttings of ripe wood. Divide large shrub honeysuckle plants by cutting into the mass of roots with a sharp spade.

# PLANT MANAGEMENT

## Water Requirements

Most honeysuckle types like moist soil; however, Japanese honeysuckle tolerates dry conditions very well. See that your plants get 1 inch of water every week.

## Feeding Requirements

A spring feeding with compost is all these plants need to stay lush and healthy throughout the year.

Any more fertilizing than this will stimulate too much growth.

## Pruning

Honeysuckle takes well to pruning, and since it grows rampantly, you'll want to cut the plants back some to keep them under control. You can do some light pruning to shape them after they've finished flowering, but do any major pruning while the plant is dormant. To prevent an overabundance of foliage, clip off all suckers and crowded stems. Cut them back to the trunk. In general, shorten the previous year's growth to one or two nodes. Never cut the vine back to the ground or shorten the trunk except when major rejuvenation efforts are needed. If you do, you will have to retrain the vine every year.

## MOST COMMON INSECT PESTS

### Leaves Yellowed and Curled; Witches'-Brooms Develop

#### Aphids

Honeysuckle and parsnip aphids (*Hyadaphis foeniculi*) and woolly honeysuckle aphids (*Prociphilus xylostei*) feed on vines in the spring, when the tender young leaves and stems are bursting forth. They suck juices from plants, causing the foliage to curl, pucker, and yellow. The infested stems die, creating tufts of dead branches or witches'-brooms. Eventually, this damage reduces the plant's vigor, and if left unchecked, aphids will stop the vine from blooming. Ants are attracted to the sticky honeydew secreted by the aphids.

If you suspect that your honeysuckle might be infested with these pests, look for them inside the curled leaves. Aphids are not much bigger than the head of a pin and have soft, pear-shaped bodies, which may be green, brown, black, or pink. Woolly honeysuckle aphids, as their name suggests, have a woolly covering. If you find only small numbers of these pests, spray the undersides of the leaves vigorously with water. Do this in the morning, three

times, once every other day. Heavy infestations of aphids are more easily controlled with insecticidal soap. Spray plants every two to three days. As a last resort, use pyrethrum, making two applications, three to four days apart.

### Leaves Stippled, Puckered, and Distorted

#### Mites

Mites attack honeysuckle only when vines are exposed to the reflected heat of a south-facing wall, usually in midsummer. Leaves will appear stippled with yellow or red dots. Often you'll find fine webbing on plants, and the leaves and stems may become distorted. Mites are not true insects, being members of the spider family. They are barely visible to the eye and may be yellow, green, red, or brown. Spray infested plants with insecticidal soap every three to five days for two weeks to control these pests.

## MOST COMMON DISEASES

### Swollen Bumps on Stems

#### Canker

Swollen, discolored areas on the stems of honeysuckle plants are cankers, which can be caused by fungi or bacteria that have infected the soft tissue just under the bark. Cankers commonly split open, exposing underlying tissues and bleeding a gummy substance. The infecting bacteria or fungi are transmitted by rain, contaminated tools, or by handling plants. They usually work their way into a plant through a wound.

Remove and destroy the infected stems, cutting them back several inches from the site of the cankers. If a plant is severely diseased, remove it entirely. A spray with Bordeaux mixture may help control canker. It also may inhibit the spread of the disease to adjacent plants. In the fall, gather and destroy all fallen plant debris to reduce overwintering populations of the fungi or bacteria.

## Leaves Covered with White Powder

### Powdery Mildew

Powdery mildew in honeysuckle is caused by the fungi *Microsphaera alni* and *Erysiphe polygoni*. A characteristic powdery white dust appears on leaves and flowers of infected plants. Powdery mildew can occur in either hot, dry weather or humid conditions.

It occurs more often on vines grown very close together. Badly infected leaves become discolored and distorted, and then drop off.

Spray diseased plants thoroughly with wettable sulfur once or twice at weekly intervals until symptoms subside. Collect and discard all plant debris in the fall.

# VINE *Morning Glory*   *Ipomoea* spp.

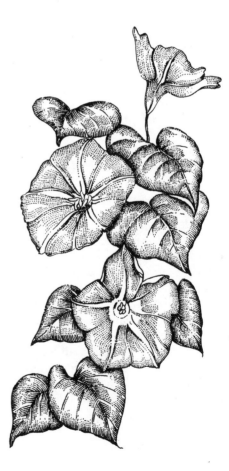

## DESCRIPTION

Once only showing its glory in the morning, the modern cultivated varieties of the annual morning glory tolerate bright light and heat well and stay open all day. These tender, twining vines with simple trumpetlike flowers will wind gently along porch railings and fences, climb trellises, and wander over steep hills.

### Height

This vine will grow to a height of 8 to 10 feet.

### Spread

Morning glory does not spread broadly. You will need to grow several plants if you want a fair amount of width and fullness.

### Blossoms

The blossoms are trumpet shaped and vary in color from white to purple to sky blue to scarlet; some cultivars have stripes. The flowers are 3 to 5 inches across, and appear from midsummer to frost. Modern varieties of morning glory and common morning glory, which tolerate bright light and heat well, stay open all day.

## Foliage

The dark green, heart-shaped leaves present a good contrast to the pale blossoms.

# ENVIRONMENT

## Hardiness

Common morning glory is a hardy annual. The other species are tender perennials grown as annuals.

## Light Requirements

This vine loves full sun, but appreciates some protection from harsh summer sun at noontime. It will grow well with less than full sun, but needs at least half a day of sunlight.

## Soil Requirements

As evidenced by the fact that you can find this plant growing all over the eastern seaboard, morning glory grows easily in any soil, even poor, dry soil. It does best in well-drained earth of moderate fertility.

# PLANTING AND PROPAGATION

## Planting

Sow seeds in early spring directly in the garden outdoors. To ensure good germination, nick each seed with a knife and then soak them overnight in warm water before you plant them. If you are impatient and want early blooms, you can start plants indoors, sowing seed in March. Morning glories can be difficult to transplant, so sow seed in individual peat pots for minimal disturbance when moving them to the garden. Set out seedlings after frost is past. Place each vine near a support on which it can twine. Do not enrich the soil when planting or the vines will produce nothing but leaves.

## Propagation

Propagate morning glory from seed.

# PLANT MANAGEMENT

## Water Requirements

See to it that your plants get 1 inch of water a week.

## Feeding Requirements

The basic nutrient needs of morning glory are easily satisfied simply by adding a slow-release nitrogen fertilizer to the soil in spring. For exceptionally lush and healthy vines, give them light supplemental feedings (side-dressings or foliar spray) monthly throughout the growing season.

## Pruning

In zone 8 and farther south, where most morning glories are perennials, cut vines to the ground when winter arrives and retrain the vines in the spring.

# MOST COMMON INSECT PESTS

## Leaves Wilted

### Leaf Cutters

Morning glory leaf cutters (*Loxostege obliteralis*) work at night and cut the leaf stalks, causing the leaves to wilt. You may also find holes eaten in the leaves. The adults are yellowish moths with light brown markings. The destructive larvae are greenish caterpillars that hide in rolled, wilted leaves during the day.

Remove rolled, wilted leaves and crush larvae hiding in them. Spray infested vines with Bt (*Bacillus thuringiensis*). Two applications three to five days apart should take care of leaf cutters. Throughout the growing season, clean up any debris under the plant, where caterpillars might hide during the day.

## Blotches on Leaves

### Leafminers

The larvae of morning glory leafminer (*Bedellia somnolentella*) bore their way between the upper and lower surfaces of leaves, making threadlike tunnels, which later become blotches, through the leaves. When the larvae mature, they build their slender cocoons, which hang from the leaves by a silk thread. In a few days, small gray moths emerge. To control these pests, handpick the infested leaves and cocoons.

## Holes in Leaves

**Tortoise Beetles**
The larvae of tortoise beetles (family Chrysomelidae) look like spiny slugs. They love morning glory, and eat holes in the leaves. The adult beetle is somewhat turtle shaped and about ¼ inch long, with spots or stripes. Handpick the larvae and spray plants with insecticidal soap. Two applications three to five days apart should eliminate this pest.

# VINE *Wisteria* *Wisteria* spp.

## DESCRIPTION

Wisteria is truly one of the most beautiful of the woody vines. The Chinese and Japanese species earn the highest acclaim from many gardeners for their profuse, fragrant blossoms. Some gardeners encourage these vines to grow like trees by rigidly staking and training the stem upright, forcing it to become trunklike, while severely pruning the tops over several years. More commonly, wisteria is left to ramble over porch roofs, up trellises, and along walls. Some gardeners allow the vines to crawl on the ground to form a ground cover. Don't let wisteria climb and wind around a tree or it will eventually strangle the tree.

In addition to being a simply enchanting landscape plant, wisteria is nearly problem-free. No insects or diseases bother these vines.

## Height

These vines will climb to 40 feet.

## Spread

Wisteria spreads as wide as is permitted.

## Blossoms

The flowers of wisteria are borne in drooping clusters on the vines. These clusters are usually 8 to 18 inches long; however, those of the Japanese wisteria (*Wisteria floribunda*) can reach a length of 36 inches. The flowers themselves are usually lavender or lilac in color, but may be pink or white. Their bloom can last up to four or five weeks in spring. Most forms of Japanese wisteria have a wonderful fragrance. All plants bloom, but some take 10 to 15 years to produce their first flowers.

## Foliage

The leaves are compound with many leaflets, 2 to 4 inches long, arranged in a featherlike fashion. The foliage of the Japanese wisteria turns yellow in autumn.

# ENVIRONMENT

## Varieties by Zone

To zone 5, Chinese wisteria (*W. sinensis*) and
   Japanese wisteria (*W. floribunda*)

## Light Requirements

Wisteria flowers best in full sun, but will tolerate some shade.

## Soil Requirements

Wisteria needs well-drained soil, but that characteristic is the only one that has been determined. Experts are not sure what kind of soil promotes the best blooming. It seems that wisteria grown in light, sandy soil produces flowers sooner, but the vegetative growth of the plant as a whole is less vigorous. Rich soil fosters strong vegetative growth, but is not necessarily conducive to heavy flowering.

# PLANTING AND PROPAGATION

## Planting

You can plant wisteria in the spring or fall, but fall is best. Before setting the plants in the ground, work compost 2 to 3 feet down into the soil so that it makes up 30 percent of the soil mix.

## Propagation

Propagate these vines by layering or by hardwood or softwood cuttings taken in the late summer.

# PLANT MANAGEMENT

## Water Requirements

Wisteria will manage fine with a normal watering of about 1 inch a week. Some evidence from Japan, where wisteria thrives, suggests that growing the vines near an unlimited supply of water, such as a pond, encourages optimal growth and flowering.

## Feeding Requirements

Feed young plants generously, as they are slow to become established. As the plant matures, a single application of compost in the spring will take care of the plant's nutrient needs for the year. For the most profuse blossoms, do not give your vines supplemental feedings.

## Pruning

Prune wisteria very severely each year, after the blooming season and before the growth of new wood. During the summer, prune any vines that failed to blossom. Cut them back to within six or seven buds, and they should flower the next spring.

## Mulching

Wisteria likes cool roots, so spread a thick organic mulch around the vines.

## Winter Protection

Chinese wisteria is not quite as hardy as other species, and some gardeners in the northern states and Canada lay the vines on the ground during the fall and cover them with soil to protect the flower buds from the cold of winter.

## MOST COMMON CULTURAL PROBLEMS

## Vine Does Not Flower

### Plant Not Established

Wisteria has a reputation for taking its time about blooming. Young vines may not bloom for years. To prompt mature vines to set buds, try root pruning extraneous vigorous young shoots in late spring. Insert a shovel straight down into the soil about 15 inches away from the main stem. This cuts off some of the roots. Do this at two or three points around the plant. Also heavily prune any vigorous growth to promote blooming. Apply rock phosphate powders in the fall to be sure your plants are getting enough phosphorus to produce blossoms.

## Excessive Vegetative Growth

### Too Much Nitrogen in Soil

Although newly planted vines need a rich soil, you want to keep nitrogen from mature plants. Excess nitrogen causes the plant to put most of its energy into producing leaves and little energy into blossoming.

FOLIAGE PLANT # Artemisia *Artemisia* spp.

## DESCRIPTION

Artemisia offers some of the most interesting foliage of any plant. It complements most flowers and is often used to separate groups of strong-colored flowers in the garden. Artemisia is tough and tolerant, and looks good throughout the growing season. Most types die back each winter. Satiny wormwood (*Artemisia schmidtiana*) forms a soft, compact mound; its cultivar 'Silver Mound' is particularly good for rock gardens. Dusty miller (*A. stellerana*) makes attractive borders, and is especially suited to seashore gardens. Silver king artemisia (*A. ludoviciana* var. *albula*) has striking silvery, feathery leaves. It is enormously popular in northern gardens.

## Height

Dusty miller (*A. stellerana*), 2½ feet
Satiny wormwood (*A. schmidtiana*), 2 feet
Silver king (*A. ludoviciana* var. *albula*), 3½ feet
White mugwort (*A. lactiflora*), 4 to 5 feet

## Spread

Artemisia grows to a width of about 18 inches.

## Blossoms

White mugwort is the only artemisia grown for its flowers, which are grayish yellow. Other types have inconspicuous yellow or white flowers that bloom in clusters.

## Foliage

The foliage is characteristically gray-green or silverish, and has a lacy texture. The deeply cut leaves give this plant its lacy look. Some species, like dusty miller, have fuzzy leaves. Reflecting their herb heritage, the foliage of many types of artemisia is fragrant.

# ENVIRONMENT

## Varieties by Zone

To zone 3, dusty miller, satiny wormwood, silver king artemisia, and white mugwort

## Light Requirements

For best growth, artemisia needs full sun. It will, however, tolerate a half-day of filtered sun.

## Soil Requirements

Artemisia thrives in normal soil, as long as it has good drainage. It tolerates dry soil extremely well and won't survive winter with wet feet. Actually, these plants do better in poorer soils and become spindly in ground that is rich.

# PLANTING AND PROPAGATION

## Planting

Spring is the best time to plant artemisia. Space plants 12 inches apart.

## Propagation

You can easily propagate artemisia by division. These plants grow from underground rhizomes and root readily. Artemisia can also be propagated by stem cuttings. In late spring or late summer, cut 3- to 4-inch pieces from nonflowering stems, and root them.

# PLANT MANAGEMENT

## Water Requirements

One-half to 1 inch of water a week is all that artemisia needs.

## Feeding Requirements

Work some compost into the soil in the spring, and your plants will have enough food to last them the year. Remember, do not overfertilize artemisia or it will become spindly.

## Pruning

Summer pruning discourages flowering and promotes a denser, bushier form. Cut the plant back by one-third its height just before it begins to flower.

### Drying

Many garden crafts, such as wreaths, are made from dried artemisia. Cut stems in late August. Strip off any soiled or dead leaves at the bottom of each stem, and hang them in bunches upside down in a dry place.

## MOST COMMON CULTURAL PROBLEMS

### Center Dies Back

#### Natural Dieback

With many species of artemisia, the center of the plant dies back. 'Silver Mound', for example, forms compact mounds or clumps; however, in the middle of the summer, the center may die, leaving the plant looking rather unsightly. You can combat this by cutting the whole clump back to a height of about 1 inch. The plant will produce new growth, which will fill in the center as well as the sides.

## MOST COMMON DISEASES

### Rust-Colored Patches on Leaves

#### Rust

Not surprisingly, powdery, rust-colored spots on the leaves of your plants are a sign of rust disease. This disease is caused by fungi. The foliage will wilt and wither. Remove the infected leaves as soon as possible. If spotting continues, remove and destroy the entire plant.

If rust becomes a yearly occurrence in your yard, you can prevent it with periodic applications of wettable sulfur spray. Begin treatment two to three weeks before rust normally appears—in late spring or early summer. In addition, keep plants spaced widely apart to allow air to circulate among them.

## NOTES AND RESEARCH

The aromatic oils these plants produce repel most insects.

**FOLIAGE PLANT** Coleus *Coleus*

## DESCRIPTION

Coleus can brighten any landscape with its striking colored foliage. It grows well in shade. You can use it as an accent in flower beds, as edging in flower borders, or in window boxes or containers. Although actually a perennial, common coleus (*Coleus blumei*) is grown as an annual in most parts of the United States. These plants make handsome houseplants as well.

### Height

As an annual, coleus grows to a height of 1 to 2 feet.

## Spread

Its width is about 1 foot.

## Blossoms

Coleus produces small blue, lilac, or white flowers in clusters of six or more on a stem.

## Foliage

It's the foliage that attracts most gardeners to this plant. Its showy, multicolored leaves may be fringed or deeply cut. The leaves may be variegated with shades of green, yellow, orange, reddish purple, or white. Most have a smooth texture, but some look almost velvety.

# ENVIRONMENT

## Hardiness

Coleus cannot tolerate frost or cold at all, which is why it is grown as an annual in most parts of the country.

## Light Requirements

Coleus can handle full sun, but its colors are more vivid when it is placed in partial shade.

## Soil Requirements

An average, well-drained garden soil suits this plant best.

# PLANTING AND PROPAGATION

## Planting

Coleus is easy to grow from seed. Do not cover seeds with soil; they need light to germinate. For best results, sow seeds indoors four to six weeks before the last expected frost. Put out transplants after all danger of frost is past, spacing them 12 to 20 inches apart.

## Propagation

Coleus roots easily from stem cuttings, and this is an easy way to repeat a desired color pattern. Cut 3- to 4-inch pieces from the tips of the stems and remove the leaves from the bottom 3 inches. Take some cuttings in September, before frost hits. Once they develop roots, pot them up for the winter and then plant them outside in the spring. Follow this practice every fall, and you'll have coleus plants year after year.

## Container Gardening

Coleus readily adapts to container gardening. You can plant it in window boxes or in containers to be set on a deck or patio. Use a light, well-drained potting mix. Coleus grown outdoors can easily be potted and brought indoors for the winter. Pinch back plants often to encourage dense, bushy growth.

## PLANT MANAGEMENT

### Water Requirements

Coleus needs about 1 inch of water each week. During dry periods in the hottest part of summer, plants will need a little more water, about 1½ inches a week.

### Feeding Requirements

Work compost into the soil in the spring, and your coleus will be happy for the year. For more intense colors, spray plants with seaweed extract in late spring and once again in early summer.

### Pruning

To keep your coleus in top form, pinch the stems that shoot up outside the general shape of the plant. Nip them just above a leaf node. Also, remove flower spikes to encourage bushiness.

## MOST COMMON CULTURAL PROBLEMS

### Plant Leggy

#### Needs Pruning or Pinching

Coleus will get leggy and top heavy if allowed to produce flowers. Pinch off the flower stems to encourage a bushy, low-growing plant.

## MOST COMMON INSECT PESTS

### Plant Grows Poorly

#### Mealybugs

Plants infested with mealybugs (*Pseudococcus* spp.) look unsightly and do not grow well. Their leaves are limp and may have cottony tufts on them. Mealybugs gather in cottony white masses on roots, stems,

branches, and leaves of coleus to suck the sap. As they feed, they secrete honeydew, which encourages the growth of mold and attracts ants. Mealybugs are ⅕ to ⅓ inch long, oval, flattened, and covered with white waxy powder. Short, soft spines protrude from their sides.

Control mealybugs by spraying them with an alcohol-based spray every two to three days until they are gone. Make this spray by combining 1 cup isopropyl alcohol and ½ teaspoon insecticidal soap in 1 quart water.

### Leaves Stippled, Puckered, and Distorted

#### Mites

If you find yellow stippling on the leaves of your coleus, it's not part of the beautiful variegated coloring of this plant: It's probably a sign of mites. These pests suck the sap from plants, leaving the foliage discolored and often puckered and distorted. You can also diagnose mite presence from the fine webbing that they weave around leaves and stems. The mites themselves are barely visible to the unaided eye, but you'll find them on the undersides of leaves. They may be yellow, green, red, or brown.

Start control measures as soon as you notice the first stippling of the leaves. Spray your coleus plants in the early morning with a forceful stream of water to knock mites from the leaf undersides. Repeat this daily for three days. If mites are still present, spray plants with insecticidal soap every three to five days for two weeks.

### Galls on Roots; Brown Areas on Leaves

#### Nematodes

If your coleus looks somewhat sickly but doesn't seem to be infested with any insects or infected with any disease, consider nematodes. Southern root knot nematodes (*Meloidogyne* spp.) attack coleus at the roots, causing swellings or galls to form. Brown patches on leaves are signs of fern leaf nematodes. Because these pests attack the root system, the whole plant is affected and becomes wilted and sickly.

Nematodes are not insects, but slender, unsegmented roundworms, $\frac{1}{50}$ to $\frac{1}{10}$ inch long. Most are soil-dwellers. To control them, add lots of compost, especially leaf mold, to the soil. This attracts beneficial fungi, which attack nematodes. You can also try fertilizing infested plants once a month with a dilute fish emulsion drench; make a solution one-half the strength specified on the label. Fish emulsion seems to repel nematodes, as do French marigolds, which you can plant among your coleus plants if they fit your landscape design.

## Leaves Yellowed; Small Bumps on Leaves and Stems

### Scale
The first sign of a scale attack is often the yellowing of the leaves, followed by leaf drop, reduced growth, and stunted plants. You may see secretions of honeydew on the leaves, and sometimes white, cottony masses. The scale insects look like clusters of somewhat flattened, waxy, reddish gray or brown bumps a bit bigger than the head of a pin. These insects have a shell that protects them while they feed.

If you catch the problem early, before too many pests have found your plants, simply scrape them off leaves and stems with your fingernail or remove them with a cotton swab dipped in rubbing alcohol. Control medium to heavy infestations by spraying plants with a mixture of alcohol and insecticidal soap every three days for two weeks. Make this spray by combining 1 cup isopropyl alcohol and 1 tablespoon insecticidal soap concentrate in 1 quart water. If you already have some diluted insecticidal soap, add 1 tablespoon alcohol to a pint of the soap.

## Leaves Yellowed; Plant Weakened

### Whiteflies
Small plants that display poor coloring may be infested with whiteflies (*Trialeurodes vaporariorum*). Look for these white insects on the undersides of coleus leaves. They show up clearly on the purple leaf surfaces of most varieties. Adult whiteflies are white-winged, mothlike insects about the size of the head of a pin. When a plant is bumped or brushed, they fly up, looking like flying dandruff. Both nymphs and adults suck juices from the plant's leaves, buds, and stems, eventually weakening the plant. The undersides of the leaves may also be covered with honeydew secreted by the whiteflies. This honeydew provides the perfect environment for the growth of fungi. As the infestation worsens, the entire plant weakens, and the leaves turn yellow and die.

Control whiteflies by spraying infested plants with insecticidal soap spray every three to five days for two weeks. If that doesn't work, try pyrethrum every five days for two weeks.

# MOST COMMON DISEASES

## Seedlings Rot at Base and Fall Over

### Damping-Off
If your coleus seedlings suddenly drop to the ground one day, they've probably been struck by damping-off. This disease is caused by any of several soil-dwelling fungi that attack germinating seeds before they emerge from the soil or shortly after. A soft, blackened area develops on the stem at the soil line, and the stem collapses.

Obviously, once your plants have collapsed, you can't do anything to save them, but if damping-off is a common problem in your garden, you can take measures to prevent it. Start your seeds and cuttings in a sterile growing medium. Keep the medium on the dry side and space plants so that air can circulate among them and remove any excess moisture. Soil out in the garden should be sterilized before replanting.

## Brown to Black Spots or Blotches on Leaves

### Leaf Spot
Several species of fungi cause leaf spot on coleus. Usually the spots are brown to black and they often

come together to form larger patches of dead tissue. Sometimes you will see the tiny black dots of the spore-bearing fruiting bodies around these spots.

Pick off and discard the infected leaves, and remove and discard any seriously infected plants, together with their soil ball. Spray the infected and surrounding plants with a flowable sulfur spray every seven to ten days until symptoms subside. Since leaf spot fungi thrive in moist conditions, avoid wetting the foliage when watering plants.

# FOLIAGE PLANT **Fern**

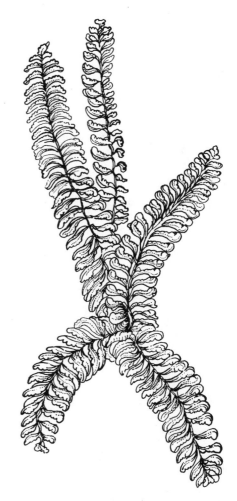

## DESCRIPTION

Ferns are one of the most useful plants in the perennial garden. Their foliage is lush and exquisite. Ferns mix well with other plants. They soften landscape borders and fill sparse areas, and tall species offer handsome backgrounds for flowers and low shrubs. Plant them with bulbs and they'll mask the foliage once it dies down.

### Height

Christmas fern (*Polystichum acrostichoides*), 2 to 3 feet

Cinnamon fern (*Osmunda cinnamomea*), 3 to 5 feet

Common maidenhair fern (*Adiantum pedatum*), 18 to 24 inches

Common polypody fern (*Polypodium vulgare*), 10 inches

Crested wood fern (*Dryopteris cristata*), 30 inches

Goldie's fern (*Dryopteris goldiana*), 4 feet

Hay-scented fern (*Dennstaedtia punctilobula*), 30 inches

Interrupted fern (*Osmunda claytoniana*), 4 to 5 feet

Japanese holly fern (*Cyrtomium falcatum*), 30 inches

Lady fern (*Athyrium filix-femina*), 2 to 4 feet

Marginal shield fern (*Dryopteris marginalis*), 20 inches

New York fern (*Thelypteris noveboracensis*), 2 feet

Ostrich fern (*Matteuccia pensylvanica*), 5 feet

Royal fern (*Osmunda regalis*), 6 feet

Sensitive fern (*Onoclea sensibilis*), 12 to 30 inches

Spinulose wood fern (*Dryopteris austriaca* var. *spinulosa*), 3 feet

Virginia chain fern (*Woodwardia virginica*), 2 feet

## Spread

Most ferns spread 1 or 2 feet.

## Foliage

Foliage varies from fern to fern, but in general these plants produce light to dark green to gray-green lacy fronds. Some species are evergreen and others deciduous. Ferns grow in a unique manner, uncurling from tight fiddleheads as they mature.

## Environment

Ferns like moist, woody places, as well as some other habitats, such as along roadsides. For most, the best site is under deciduous trees.

## Hardiness

Many ferns are hardy.

## Varieties by Zone

To zone 3, Christmas fern, cinnamon fern, common maidenhair fern, common polypody, crested wood fern, Goldie's fern, hay-scented fern, interrupted fern, lady fern, marginal shield fern, New York fern, ostrich fern, sensitive fern, royal fern, and spinulose wood fern

To zone 5, virginia chain fern

To zone 9, Japanese holly fern

## Light Requirements

The following ferns prefer full sun: hay-scented fern, interrupted fern, lady fern, ostrich fern, sensitive fern, and virginia chain fern. Some ferns that thrive in full shade: American maidenhair fern, Christmas fern, common polypody, crested wood fern, Goldie's fern, New York fern, royal fern, and the spinulose wood fern.

## Soil Requirements

Having come from a woodland environment, most ferns need a rich, humusy earth that is constantly moist but well-drained. The pH should be somewhat acidic, between 5 and 6. When preparing a site for ferns in your yard, mix normal garden soil with enough compost for a 50–50 mix. Then, every fall after the ferns have died back, add at least 2 to 3 inches of compost to the bed.

# PLANTING AND PROPAGATION

## Planting

Ferns may be sold bare root or in pots by the garden center or nursery. Plant bare-root plants as soon as possible. Keep their roots moist until planting by wrapping them with damp paper towels or newspaper; then place them in a plastic bag and store them in a cool place.

When you are ready to plant your ferns, cut off any broken fronds. If the roots are skimpy, cut the fronds back one-third to minimize water loss from leaf surfaces. Dig a hole slightly larger and deeper than the root ball and add leaf mold or compost. Rhizomatous varieties have shallow roots and are planted only about 1 inch deep in a trench. Lay the rhizomes in the hole so they are level and horizontal as they are naturally oriented. Plant them just below the soil surface, and keep the crown of the plant slightly above the soil. Tamp the soil gently but firmly and dress around the plant with compost. Place large ferns, like the ostrich fern, 3 feet apart;

most ferns can be spaced at 12- to 18-inch intervals. Give shade-loving ferns a little more space than those grown in sunny areas.

## Propagation

Most ferns can be propagated by division in the spring. Gently lift the plant mass up from the soil with a spade. Shake off excess soil to expose the roots, then carefully pull them apart. Tightly tangled roots may have to be cut apart with a sharp knife. Disturb the fronds as little as possible. Plant the separate ferns carefully, as described above.

## Container Gardening

Some ferns grow well in containers. Choose low, fairly shallow pots—3 to 6 inches deep is best. Good drainage is essential, so any container you use should have holes in it or pebbles placed on the bottom. Make a soil mix from equal parts of compost, rich soil, peat, and sand. A soilless medium also works with ferns. Pack the soil gently, water well, and place the plant in a shaded, humid place for a few days. To maintain some humidity around the plant, place a plastic bag over it during these few days. Grow them in strong indirect light.

# PLANT MANAGEMENT

## Water Requirements

Ferns need at least 1 inch of rain a week for most of the year and 1½ inches a week in the heat of summer. If your ferns are located under trees, the leaf canopy may prevent light rain from getting to your plants, so watch these ferns and give them extra water as needed. Soaker systems, which drip directly into the soil while keeping the fronds dry, are excellent devices in the fern bed.

## Feeding Requirements

Ferns grown in the shade need regular feeding because nearby tree roots often usurp nutrients from the soil in and around the ferns. One major application of compost in the fall or spring supplies most of a plant's needs, but to keep ferns looking their best, spray them with liquid fertilizer once a month throughout the growing season.

## Mulching

Ferns benefit greatly from mulch. Spread 3 to 4 inches of organic mulch, such as chopped leaves or chopped straw, around your plants late in the spring to keep roots cool. This will also discourage weeds and help keep soil moist. Remove the mulch in the fall after the fronds have died back. Then, after the ground has frozen solid, lay a 2-inch layer of organic mulch to protect the roots from winter heaving. Remove this mulch in the spring, about four weeks before the last expected frost, so the soil can warm up faster.

## Drying

Ferns can be dried and used in various crafts or arrangements, especially the tougher ones like Christmas fern. The hay-scented fern turns gold in fall and can be dried or pressed. Most ferns can be pressed and used in pressed flower pictures.

## Cutting Fresh Foliage

Fresh fern fronds make an excellent accent in flower arrangements.

# MOST COMMON CULTURAL PROBLEMS

## Plants Grow Poorly

### Crowding

If you've been doing everything right, and your ferns simply aren't growing well, they are probably crowded. When plants are grown too close together, air cannot circulate easily among them. This is often a problem in shaded areas, especially in the sultry summer, when the humidity hangs over the plants and causes mildew problems. Dig out any excess plants, or at least prune the outside fronds to improve circulation.

# MOST COMMON INSECT PESTS

## Leaves Yellowed and Curled

### Aphids

Aphids suck the juices from the leaves and stems of ferns, causing them to turn yellow, curl, and pucker. As a whole, the plant loses its vigor. Ants are attracted to the sticky honeydew secreted by aphids. Look for aphids on the undersides of leaves. These insects aren't much bigger than the head of a pin. They have soft, pear-shaped bodies.

Light infestations are easily controlled by spraying plants vigorously with water. Do this early in the morning, three times, once every other day. For medium to heavy infestations, spray infested ferns with insecticidal soap every two to three days until aphids are gone.

## Holes in Fronds

### Japanese Beetles

Japanese beetles (*Popillia japonica*) occasionally attack ferns, chewing holes in the fronds and sometimes skeletonizing them. The adult beetles are ½ inch long, with shiny metallic green and brown wing covers. Handpick them and drop them into a pail of soapy water. Set up pheromone beetle traps no closer than 50 feet to the fern bed. If handpicking and trapping don't take care of the problem, spray your plants with a mixture of pyrethrum and isopropyl alcohol. Make this solution by combining 1 tablespoon alcohol and 1 pint diluted pyrethrum.

## Reddish Brown or Blackish Spots on Fronds

### Nematodes

Ferns are susceptible to leaf nematodes (*Aphelenchoides fragariae*). Infested plants have reddish brown or blackish bands or spots on their fronds. In the bird's nest fern (*Asplenium nidus*), the base of the frond is affected first; then brown discoloration extends upward to cover more than half the leaf. If all the fronds in a cluster are attacked by nematodes, the plant usually dies.

Nematodes are not insects, but are slender, unsegmented roundworms. Most are soil-dwellers and are $1/50$ to $1/10$ inch long. To control them, add lots of compost, especially leaf mold, to the soil. Ferns will benefit in two ways. They'll get a boost of nutrients, which they like, and the compost encourages certain fungi that attack nematodes. You can also fertilize the fern bed with dilute liquid fish emulsion applied as a drench to the soil. Fish emulsion repels nematodes.

## Fronds Yellowed; Small Bumps on Fronds

### Scale

Yellowed fronds are the first sign of scale attack. Look for fern scale (*Pinnaspis aspidistrae*) on your plants. These insects resemble little bumps, having an oval-shaped shell that covers them while they feed. Heavy infestations can kill ferns.

If you catch them early, you can scrape them off the fronds with your fingernail or with a cotton swab dipped in rubbing alcohol. Spray heavily infested plants every three days for two weeks with a solution of isopropyl alcohol and insecticidal soap. To make this solution, mix 1 cup isopropyl alcohol and 1 tablespoon commercial insecticidal soap concentrate in 1 quart water. If you already have diluted insecticidal soap on hand, add 1 tablespoon alcohol to a pint of the soap. Some ferns are very tender and may not tolerate the alcohol in this solution, so test this mix on one plant or a portion of a plant to be sure it does no harm. If the plant wilts or changes color, use the soap spray without the alcohol.

## Ragged Holes in Fern Fronds

### Slugs and Snails

Slugs and snails do enjoy dining on fern fronds and

eat good portions of them, leaving large, ragged holes. They find young ferns and weak or wounded plants especially tasty. Slugs have soft, sticky, slimy bodies that are not coiled into protective shells. They are usually 1 to 2 inches long, but some species reach a length of 8 inches. Their coloration runs the gamut, including white, gray, yellow, and brown-black. Snails are land-dwelling molluscs. They have soft, sticky, slimy bodies coiled into protective shells. Slugs and snails are active at night, rasping holes in foliage with their filelike tongues. Although you won't see the pests themselves during the day, you will find their silvery slime trails on fern fronds.

The best way to control slugs and snails is to trap them. Either homemade or commercial traps work very well. Simply set out shallow dishes of beer. The pests are attracted to the yeast in the beer; they climb in and drown. If slugs are regular visitors to your yard each year, try to catch them early. Set out a few traps three to four weeks after the last frost. As soon you catch a slug, set out more traps to catch as many as possible before they become too numerous.

## Fronds Flecked and Whitened; Fronds Wilt and Turn Brown

### Thrips

Thrips rasp at plant cells to break them and suck the sap. The surfaces of fronds first become flecked and whitened and the tips wither, curl up, and die. On the undersides of the foliage, you'll find tiny black specks of excrement. Heavy infestations of thrips can turn the fronds brown.

Adults are tiny, slender insects, $1/25$ inch long, and may be yellowish, black, or brown. Spray infested ferns with insecticidal soap every three days for two weeks. Predatory mites, lacewings, ladybugs, and beneficial nematodes can be introduced into the environment to help control these pests. If thrips are an annual problem in your fern bed, try to catch them as early as possible by setting out yellow sticky traps about four weeks after the last frost. As soon as you find thrips on the traps, begin spraying with insecticidal soap. Thrips prefer a dry environment,

so make sure plants are adequately misted and/or watered.

## Fern Rhizomes Damaged; Holes in Fronds; Plants Wilted

### Weevils

Black vine weevils (*Brachyrhinus sulcatus*) attack ferns on all fronts. The larvae feed on the rhizomes of ferns, causing the plants to wilt. Damaged plants can be pulled out of the soil with little effort. Adult weevils feed on the fronds at night, as evidenced by the holes they leave. In sufficient numbers these weevils can rapidly defoliate an entire fern.

Black vine weevils have a tear-shaped, hard-shelled body, about $1/10$ inch long. They play dead when disturbed, folding their legs and dropping to the ground. Turn this trait to your advantage when trying to control these pests. Spread a cloth beneath your ferns and gently tap the fronds. The startled weevils will drop onto the cloth. Simply gather them up and destroy them. In addition to scaring them off your plants, spray infested ferns once a week in the evenings with pyrethrum mixed with isopropyl alcohol. Add 1 tablespoon alcohol to a pint of pyrethrum. Predatory nematodes will help stop the reproduction of weevils.

# MOST COMMON DISEASES

## Rotten Spots on Fronds; Odor Present

### Bacterial Soft Rot

Small water-soaked lesions on the fronds of your ferns are a sign of soft rot caused by the bacterium *Erwinia carotovora*. This disease enters ferns through wounds. Small brown lesions appear on fronds near the stems. These enlarge and become soft and mushy. The diseased tissue usually gives off a foul odor. Plants become stunted, wilt, and die. Soft rot cannot be cured. Dig up and destroy infected fern plants.

## Gray Spots on Leaves

### Botrytis Blight

The botrytis blight shows up on ferns as ashy gray spots. The fronds of infected plants may die back several inches. Remove and destroy any infected fronds or shoots, and dig up any severely diseased plants. Do not compost them. Spray all remaining ferns with a sulfur-based fungicide, making two applications five days apart.

## Young Ferns Rot at Base and Collapse

### Damping-Off

If in spring your new ferns simply collapse, they most likely have been struck by damping-off. This disease can be caused by any one of several soil-dwelling fungi. It strikes seedlings and new plants in the spring. The tissue around the base of plants turns dark and becomes soft, and the entire plant simply falls over.

While you can't do anything to bring back plants once they've been infected, you can prevent this disease from occurring in the first place. Poor air circulation and excess moisture around ferns pro-

vide perfect conditions for damping-off fungi, so grow ferns in well-drained soils. Although ferns like a moist soil, keep it a little on the dry side in the spring when danger of damping-off is greatest. Do not allow ferns to become too crowded; otherwise air will not circulate among them easily. Sterilize the soil in any bed that has been infected with this disease before replanting.

## Spots along Margins of Ferns

### Leaf Spot

Several species of fungi cause leaf spot in ferns. Infected plants have circular or oblong brown spots along the margins of their fronds. Pick off and discard infected fronds and completely remove any plants that show serious damage, along with the soil surrounding them. Promptly remove any plant debris from the garden to prevent this disease from spreading or from overwintering. If leaf spot is a frequent problem in your yard, take measures to prevent it. Avoid wetting your plants when watering them, and spread mulch under them, which helps prevent spores from being splashed up onto plants from the ground. Spray ferns with a sulfur-based fungicide every seven to ten days.

FOLIAGE PLANT # *Hosta*    *Hosta* spp.

## DESCRIPTION

Hostas have a very bold, handsome foliage. They are popular landscape plants, and a wide range of species and cultivars exist, from those with variegated leaves to those with a deep blue-green color. The flowers, although not as ornamental as the foliage, add a pretty touch of color in late summer, nodding from upright stalks. Hostas can be planted in partially shady areas as border plants, ground covers, or specimen plants. They hold the soil well and are good for areas that are sloped or difficult to

reach. They also do well in open borders or in flower gardens. Plant hostas among spring bulbs. When the bulbs finish flowering, emerging hosta foliage will hide the withering bulb leaves.

### Height

Hostas grow 1 to 3 feet tall, depending on the species. Their flower stalks usually are 12 to 18 inches above their leaves.

## Spread

Undivided, healthy, mature plants can spread to 5 feet, but most gardeners divide their hostas once they have reached half that width.

## Blossoms

Most hostas bloom in midsummer. The flowers are tubular and may be white or lilac. They bloom along stalks that rise up from the base of the plant and usually rise above leaves. The only species with fragrant flowers is appropriately named the fragrant

plantain-lily (*Hosta plantaginea*). Its scent is strong and sweet, and it is the best choice if you want good flowers.

## Foliage

The leaves of most hostas are oval or sword shaped. Depending on the variety, they might be as short as 1 inch or as long as 1½ feet. Most are deeply ribbed. They come in bold greens, though some varieties are almost yellow and others are variegated in green and creamy white. Still others, such as *H. sieboldiana* 'Elegans', have blue-gray leaves.

# ENVIRONMENT

## Hardiness

Hostas are fairly hardy. Most will stand winter temperatures down to −30°F, or zone 4.

## Light Requirements

Most hostas prefer partial shade, although a few cultivars will take full sun and hot summers. Full sun can burn many species. Under shady conditions, hostas may produce fewer leaves, but they will be larger.

## Soil Requirements

Hostas like moist, damp locations, and produce their best foliage in such an environment. Provide them with soil rich in humus (more than 5 percent). Most hostas prefer a slightly acidic soil, with a pH of 6 to 6.5.

# PLANTING AND PROPAGATION

## Planting

Hostas can be raised from seed, but you'll have to wait three years for them to flower. If you decide to raise them from purchased plants, plant pot-grown specimens in spring or early summer. Bare-root crowns should be planted in late fall or early spring. Set plants in the ground so the crowns are level with the surface of the ground. Space them 12 to 15 inches apart for best growth, depending on the species or cultivar selected. If you want to fill an area with plants immediately, you can place them closer, but you'll have to transplant some in a few years to avoid crowding.

## Propagation

The best way to propagate hostas is by division in the spring. There is no particular time period within which these plants must be divided. Some may grow for 30 or more years before they need to be dug and separated. Small divisions will reach full size in 3 to 5 years.

## Container Gardening

Hostas don't make the best container plants. They can be raised in large tubs, though.

## PLANT MANAGEMENT

### Water Requirements

Hostas require ½ to 1 inch of water a week. They can tolerate some dry periods.

### Feeding Requirements

Work compost into the soil in the spring, and your hostas will have enough nutrients to meet their needs. If they are located in a shady spot near trees, they will appreciate a midsummer feeding, since nearby trees tend to suck up most of the available nutrients in the soil. For great-looking plants, spray them with dilute seaweed extract in late spring and again in early summer.

### Mulching

Give hostas a little protection through their first winter by spreading a 2- to 4-inch layer of organic mulch around them. Don't cover the crowns, though;

the moist conditions under mulch can encourage crown rot. Hostas get tougher with age and won't require mulching after their first year.

## Deadheading

The flower stalks tend to look unsightly once the blossoms are spent, so remove them after the blooming period.

## MOST COMMON INSECT PESTS

### Ragged Holes in Leaves

#### Slugs and Snails

Hostas are particularly vulnerable to slugs and snails. These ravenous creatures devour good-sized pieces of foliage, leaving large ragged holes. Slugs find wounded plants especially delicious. They begin feeding at the bottom of a plant and work their way up.

Slugs are essentially snails without shells. Most are 1 to 2 inches long, but some have been known to reach a length of 8 inches. They may be white, gray, yellow, or brown-black. Snails are land-dwelling molluscs. They have soft, sticky, slimy bodies, which are curled inside protective shells. Their markings vary, depending on the particular species.

Moist, well-mulched gardens with acidic soil present the ideal environment for these pests; they love rainy days and will cavort and chew their way through your plants during wet spells. Slugs and snails curl up under plant debris during the day and head out at night to rasp at hosta leaves with their filelike tongues.

The best way to control slugs and snails is to trap them with either homemade or commercial traps. Simply take a pie plate or some other shallow container and fill it with beer. True to their rowdy nature, they'll dive right in and drown. If slugs frequent your yard every year, try to catch them early. Set out a few traps three to four weeks after the last frost. As soon as you catch the first slug, increase the number of traps to catch others before they get out of hand. Two cultivars of hosta, 'Invincible' and 'Sum and Substance', are reported to be resistant to slug attack.

## MOST COMMON DISEASES

Hostas with any physical damage are vulnerable to disease, because infectious fungi and bacteria can enter the plant through those wounds. Prune damaged foliage. Waterlogged soil, which prevents air from getting to the roots, also encourages disease in hostas, and heavily packed mulch can encourage problems as well. Your plants will suffer from fewer diseases if you make sure that the soil in which they are growing is well drained.

### Crowns and Roots Rot; Odor Present

#### Crown and Root Rot
Crown and root rot, caused by soil-dwelling fungi (*Botrytis cinerea, Sclerotium rolfsii,* and *Rhizoctonia solani*) and bacteria, is the most common disease of hostas. The bacteria attack first, causing a few spots and eventually turning the crowns to mush. Infected plants will have an unpleasant odor. The diseased crown then becomes a victim of fungal colonies. Infected plants will not produce shoots in spring. If the hosta is already in leaf when this disease strikes, the lower leaves become discolored,

and the young shoots begin to wilt. The roots blacken and rot and are covered with white fungal threads. They have a bad odor. In a few days, the whole plant dies.

There is no cure for this disease. Immediately remove and destroy any infected plants and the soil around them. Before replanting hostas in the same place, pasteurize the soil and enrich it with compost, which has fungus-fighting qualities.

Crown and root rot usually strikes during the late winter thaw, when dead leaves decompose on the ground and harbor bacteria and fungi. Keep winter mulch away from the crowns of your hostas to prevent infectious organisms from reaching them. Check your plants often to catch disease early.

### Spots on Leaves and Stems

#### Leaf Spot
The stems and leaves of hostas are sometimes disfigured by leaf spots, usually caused by *Alternaria* fungi or *Phyllosticta* fungi. Pick and discard the infected leaves. Remove and discard any seriously infected plants, together with their surrounding soil. In addition, spray your hostas every seven to ten days with a sulfur- or copper-based fungicide. Mulch helps to prevent fungi from splashing up off the ground with the rain, but remember to keep mulch about an inch away from the crown of the plant.

---

**FOLIAGE PLANT** # Lamb's Ears *Stachys byzantina*

## DESCRIPTION

Few plants delight us more than lamb's ears. The leaves of this perennial do indeed look like the soft little ears of lambs. With their white, woolly hairs, they call out to be stroked. The flowers can some-

times be attractive, and the foliage can look striking. Plant lamb's ears as ground covers, use them as accents in the landscape, or edge a sunny perennial border with them. Left to ramble, they will spill over walls or onto paths. Lamb's ears are easy to grow and suffer few problems.

## Height

Considering the foliage alone, these plants grow to about 6 to 8 inches. The flower spikes, however, can reach a height of 18 inches.

## Spread

Lamb's ears spread quickly. Usually, gardeners control their clumps at widths of 1 to 2 feet.

## Blossoms

The tiny purplish to pink blossoms appear on tall, thick spikes in the early summer. 'Silver Carpet' does not flower at all.

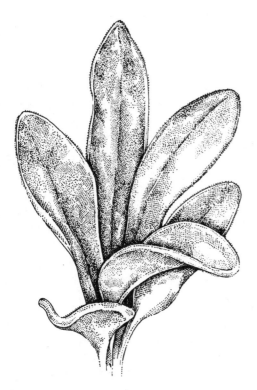

## Foliage

The silver-green leaves are 4 to 6 inches long and invitingly fuzzy.

# ENVIRONMENT

## Hardiness

Lamb's ears can withstand winter temperatures down to −20°F.

## Light Requirements

These plants grow best in full sun.

## Soil Requirements

Lamb's ears aren't too fussy about the ground they grow in—an average soil will do, and they don't mind an occasional dry spell. They tolerate a wide pH range, from 5.5 to 7.5. All they ask for is excellent drainage.

# PLANTING AND PROPAGATION

## Planting

Plant seeds indoors in pots or flats in the early spring. When seedlings appear, thin them to 12 inches apart. You can also purchase plants from a nursery or garden center. Plant these at 12-inch intervals.

## Propagation

Lamb's ears will need to be divided once about every four years, or when a clump spreads so wide that it intrudes on neighboring plants. Divide the plants in early spring or in early fall.

## Container Gardening

You can grow lamb's ears in containers if you provide good drainage.

## PLANT MANAGEMENT

### Water Requirements

One inch of water each week is all this plant requires.

### Feeding Requirements

In the spring, work some compost into the soil around your lamb's ears; then they'll have all the nutrients they need for the growing season.

### Deadheading

Since the flower stalks of lamb's ears detract from their appearance, most gardeners cut them off immediately.

## MOST COMMON CULTURAL PROBLEMS

### Rotting Foliage

#### Too Much Moisture

This plant really is very easy to care for and requires little but a well-drained soil to grow in. If drainage is not good, or if water accumulates after heavy rains or in crowded conditions, the foliage in the center of the plant may become matted and rot. Gently clean out the damaged foliage, and if plants are crowded, move them apart to improve air circulation. If the problem is a poorly drained soil, you'll have to improve drainage by adding organic matter to the soil.

FOLIAGE PLANT **Liriope**   *Liriope* spp.

## DESCRIPTION

Liriope is an Asiatic perennial herb with striking grasslike foliage. The plants spread quickly and make excellent ground covers. You can also plant them as accents in flower beds. You can substitute liriope for lawn grass, but it does not handle foot traffic as well. Blue lily-turf (*Liriope muscari*) grows in clumps; creeping lily-turf (*L. spicata*) is stoloniferous, and indeed creeps through the landscape, sometimes making a nuisance of itself and intruding on other plants. You can grow liriope on hills to control soil erosion. It makes an excellent border along paths, and looks stunning under trees or in rock gardens. Reportedly, liriope also withstands salt spray.

### Height

Blue lily-turf (*L. muscari*), 18 inches
Creeping lily-turf (*L. spicata*), 10 inches

### Spread

Blue lily-turf tends to stay in clumps that are 10 to 15 inches across, whereas creeping lily-turf has rhizomatic roots and will spread as widely as permitted.

### Blossoms

The flowers of liriope bloom in clusters on spikes. They may be blue, violet, or white. Blue lily-turf flowers in August and September. Creeping liriope blooms somewhat earlier—July through August.

### Foliage

Liriope is evergreen. The leaves are grasslike blades, ¼ to ¾ inch wide and 10 to 15 inches long. Blue lily-turf forms clumps of arching, strap-shaped leaves. The blue lily-turf cultivar 'Variegata' has striking green foliage edged in white or yellow. The leaves of creeping lily-turf have tiny teeth along their margins. Liriope foliage is best suited for warm regions. Although evergreen, leaves may turn brown during northern winters. If it is to be used as a ground cover, liriope is best grown in the South.

# ENVIRONMENT

## Hardiness

To zone 5, creeping lily-turf
To zone 6, blue lily-turf

# Light Requirements

Liriope can be grown in either shade or sun.

## Soil Requirements

The best soil for this plant is fertile and moist, with a pH range of 6 to 7, but it will grow in a dry soil, with a pH as low as 5.5.

# PLANTING AND PROPAGATION

## Planting

Plant blue lily-turf in the spring, setting the plants about 12 inches apart. If you are growing them in the shade, space them a little farther apart, about 15 inches, to permit adequate air circulation and prevent overly humid conditions. Creeping lily-turf plants can be planted within a few inches of each other. In either case, set liriope plants deep enough so that their roots are completely covered with soil.

## Propagation

Divide liriope in the spring.

# PLANT MANAGEMENT

## Water Requirements

Liriope needs ½ to 1 inch of water each week.

## Feeding Requirements

Normally, liriope only needs one feeding of compost in the spring, and it will be satisfied for the year; however, if it is growing under or near trees, it will benefit from another light feeding in the early summer. Trees tend to hog all the nutrients in the soil around them.

## Pruning

Liriope do not require pruning, but to keep plants looking their best, cut back dead leaves to about 2 inches in the early spring, before new growth starts. If you are growing liriope as a ground cover, you can simply set the lawn mower to its highest setting and mow right over it.

# MOST COMMON CULTURAL PROBLEMS

## Bed Is Weedy

### Crabgrass

Crabgrass tends to encroach on creeping lily-turf. Try to prevent this weed from taking hold, because it is extremely difficult to remove once it has become established within the liriope bed. Attack it with spot treatments of SharpShooter, a soap-based herbicide.

# MOST COMMON INSECT PESTS

## Ragged Holes in Leaves

### Slugs and Snails

Liriope plants are virtually problem-free, but slugs and snails can make pests of themselves among blue lily-turf plants. These bothersome creatures feed ravenously on plants, chewing ragged sections out of leaves.

Slugs are usually 1 to 2 inches long, although some species can grow to a length of 8 inches. They may be white, gray, yellow, or brown-black. They have fleshy, slimy bodies, and no shells. Snails are land-dwelling molluscs. Their soft, slimy bodies are protected inside shells, which vary in coloration from species to species.

Moist, well-mulched gardens and acidic soil offer a veritable haven to these pests. Slugs and snails will lounge under plant debris during the day and rise for a night of debauchery when darkness falls. They seek out lush foliage and rasp at it with their coarse tongues. Apparently invigorated by water, these pests are always most destructive during rainy spells.

The best way to control slugs and snails is to catch them with commercial or homemade traps. Simply fill a pie plate or other shallow dish with beer and set it in the garden. Attracted to the yeast in the beer, slugs and snails will climb in and drown. If these pests are a constant problem in your yard, begin catching them as early in the season as possible. Set out traps three to four weeks after the last frost in spring. When you catch your first slug or snail, increase the number of traps to catch others before they get out of control.

# CHAPTER 5

# *Lawns*

**W**ith hardly a thought, we walk on it day after day. It's felt the spike of heels, the tread of boots, the rubber of running shoes. In its often endless expanse, how easily we take it for granted. But the lawn is not to be forgotten. It is the fabric of the landscape. It is the piece on which everything is rooted—trees, shrubs, and flowers. It stretches from path to garden, from porch to street, from back step to woods edge.

Since it is such an integral part of the home landscape, you'll want your lawn looking its best. A little watering, feeding, and grooming will help keep grass green and lush. Watch for pests, weeds, and disease. They don't take your lawn for granted. Chubby little grubs love to chew on the roots of grass. Moles merrily maraud their way through the yard, and, given the chance, weeds are happy to choke out tender blades of grass and sink their roots in for a permanent place in your backyard.

The exact care and maintenance your lawn requires depends on where you live. Certain grasses grow better in the cool North, and others are best for southern lawns. The line dividing the North and South occurs along the northern borders of North Carolina, Tennessee, Arkansas, Oklahoma, and Texas, through New Mexico and Arizona and the lower part of California. Problems with insects, disease, and weeds are generally the same throughout the country; you'll find information about controlling them in the second half of the chapter.

## DESCRIPTION OF NORTHERN GRASSES

Grasses that are suitable for northern lawns are so because they grow during the North's cool seasons of spring and fall. Following are descriptions of the most common types of northern (also called cool-season) lawn grasses.

### Kentucky Bluegrass (*Poa pratensis*)

Kentucky bluegrass is one of the most desirable of all turf grasses. It spreads quickly from runners to form deep green sod with a fine texture. It grows best in areas with mild summers and ample water, and it produces a beautiful lawn in cold regions as well as the middle South. It does not, however, like the excess heat of the deep South; its growth stops when *soil* temperatures exceed 85°F to 90°F.

**Light Requirements**
This grass thrives under full sun. Powdery mildew frequently infects Kentucky bluegrass grown in shady locations where air circulation is poor.

**Water Requirements**
It likes regular watering and will turn brown in drought periods.

215

## Soil Requirements

Soil should be fertile and well drained, with a pH near neutral, between 5.8 and 7.5.

## Propagation

You can propagate Kentucky bluegrass from runners, tillers (plantlets on a stem), or from seed. Use at least two Kentucky bluegrass varieties if you are establishing a lawn. This reduces the chance that a disease or insect pest will wipe out the entire lawn. Use 1½ to 2 pounds of seed for every 1,000 square feet. It will germinate in 20 to 28 days.

## Varieties

Popular varieties include 'Estate', 'Fylking', 'Glade', 'Merit', 'Nassau', and 'Sydsport'. 'Adelphi' is resistant to leaf spot, 'Majestic' resists stripe smut, and if fusarium blight is common in your area, consider planting 'Merion'.

# Red Fescue or Fine-Bladed Fescue (*Festuca rubra*)

As its name blatantly suggests, fine-bladed fescue produces a lawn with fine blades of grass. It is often grown in combination with Kentucky bluegrass. Having lower nitrogen requirements and vigorous growth, which effectively chokes out weeds, it complements Kentucky bluegrass. It rarely suffers from any disease or insect problems. You can renovate a poor, worn lawn by overseeding with red fescue. In the South, sow it over bermudagrasses during the winter months, when these lawns lose their vitality.

## Light Requirements

This grass likes partial shade. It does not grow well in full sun.

## Water Requirements

The roots of red fescue reach deep into the soil, allowing it to find water during droughts.

## Soil Requirements

Red fescue tolerates almost any kind of soil with a pH range of 5.6 to 6.8.

## Propagation

Sow 3 to 4 pounds of seed for every 1,000 square feet of lawn. Red fescue germinates in 10 to 14 days.

## Varieties

Popular varieties include 'Falcon', 'Finelawn', 'Jamestown', and 'Jaguar'. 'Pennlawn' is less susceptible to leafspot than others.

# Tall Fescue (*Festuca arundinacea*)

If traffic is heavy over your lawn—perhaps you have a play area for your children—consider growing tall fescue. This is a tough grass that easily withstands the hammering of little feet. It grows well in the shade in both northern and southern lawns. It's a good choice for lawns that border the North and South. Not surprisingly, given the character of this grass, it has a coarse texture.

## Light Requirements

Tall fescue likes partial shade. It is often used as shade grass in the South.

## Water Requirements

With its fast-growing, deep roots, tall fescue tolerates drought better than any other northern grass, and it is quite resistant to insects and disease.

## Soil Requirements

Poor soil with a pH in the range of 5.5 to 7 is just fine for tall fescue.

## Propagation

Tall fescue does not spread by underground runners and therefore does not form thatch (a layer of dried grass clippings, roots, stolons, and rhizomes that lies on the soil down in among the healthy blades of grass in your lawn). It's best not to combine it with other grasses unless it makes up more than 80 percent of the total mixture. Sow 5 to 6 pounds of seed over every 1,000 square feet of lawn. It will germinate in six to seven days.

## Varieties

The toughness of this plant is well reflected in the names of a few of the most popular varieties: 'Houndog', 'Arid', and 'Rebel II'.

## Perennial Ryegrass
## (*Lolium perenne*)

If you want to get your lawn off to a quick start, grow perennial rye. It germinates and establishes itself quickly. You can also overseed an old, worn lawn with this grass to give it a burst of color. Planted with Kentucky bluegrass, it will eventually be overtaken by the prettier bluegrass, but it can dominate if you sow too much of it. If you mix the two together, keep the quantity of rye around 20 percent to be sure the bluegrass gets a foothold and is able to spread easily. Perennial rye has high resistance to insect pests and disease. It produces very little thatch.

### Light Requirements
Prefers full sun, but tolerates part shade.

### Water Requirements
Perennial ryegrass likes regular watering, but is moderately tolerant of drought conditions.

### Soil Requirements
This grass grows well in almost any kind of soil, and prefers a pH level of 5.8 to 7.4.

### Propagation
Use 4 to 8 pounds of seed to cover 1,000 square feet of ground. It should germinate in three to five days.

### Varieties
Popular varieties include 'All Star', 'Pennant', 'Derby', 'Elka', 'Gator', and 'Regal'.

## Colonial Bentgrass
## (*Agrostis tenuis*)

Once considered a very fine grass for lawns, colonial bentgrass really has little place in the backyard. Although it is an attractive, fine-textured grass, it produces perhaps the ultimate high-maintenance lawn. It is slow to become established and requires watering and mowing almost constantly. A bentgrass lawn is rather fragile, too. It cannot tolerate drought or traffic and is quite vulnerable to pest and disease problems. (One situation it *can* tolerate is an acid soil, and so it may be useful in such circumstances.)

Whereas you would probably never plant an entire lawn of colonial bentgrass, it can be mixed in with other seed. But do use it in small quantities, for as feeble as this grass may be, it can overtake other species.

### Light Requirements
Bentgrass does tolerate shade well.

### Water Requirements
Frequent watering is needed to keep this grass looking good.

### Soil Requirements
Bentgrass needs a nitrogen-rich, well-drained soil. It can withstand acid soils and can be grown in areas too acidic for Kentucky bluegrass.

### Propagation
One-half pound of bentgrass seed will fill 1,000 square feet of lawn. The seed should germinate in 7 to 12 days.

# DESCRIPTION
# OF SOUTHERN GRASSES

Southern grasses, also called warm-season grasses, are most active during the summer months. They slow down and turn brown in the fall. Warm-season grasses grow very well at temperatures between 80°F and 95°F, and so are well suited to hot climates. Most types are very efficient at taking up water from the soil and storing it. Studies have shown that two of the southern grasses, bermudagrass and buffalograss, require 20 percent less water than their northern counterparts, bluegrass and fescue. The following are the most popular grasses for southern lawns.

## Bermudagrass
## (*Cynodon dactylon*)

Whenever you find yourself gazing over a southern lawn, you're probably looking at bermudagrass. It is one of the most commonly grown of the warm-season grasses. Many varieties exist. Textures range from fine to medium, and color from light to deep green. The grass spreads rapidly from stolons or rhizomes and is so aggressive that it can become a nuisance by invading areas it shouldn't. The advantage to its growing habit, though, is that it becomes established quickly and snuffs out weeds. It holds up well under foot traffic, but its greatest virtue is that it tolerates heat and needs less water than most lawn grasses. It can be mowed to 1 inch, and thatch must be removed once a year. At the approach of frost, the lawn slows in growth and changes color, eventually becoming brown. Bermudagrasses do especially well throughout the upper South, from middle Georgia to eastern Oklahoma, and throughout lower elevations of the Southwest.

## Light Requirements
It thrives under full sun and does not tolerate shade very well.

## Water Requirements
Bermudagrass will thrive on less water than most grasses need.

## Soil Requirements
A good choice for poor soils, bermudagrass will grow in anything from heavy clay to deep sand, but it does require regular feedings of nitrogen.

## Propagation
Plant bermudagrass by sod or sprigs. You can tear enough sprigs from 1 square yard of sod to create 1,000 square feet of lawn. This grass spreads rapidly.

## Varieties
Two of the most widely used hybrid forms of bermudagrass are 'Tifway' and 'Midiron'. They are less invasive than common bermuda.

# St. Augustinegrass (*Stenotaphrum secundatum*)

St. Augustinegrass is a coarse-textured subtropical grass with pointed blades. It spreads at a moderate rate by both stolons and runners, crowding out other grasses and weeds as it forms a dense lawn.

This is a tough plant, enduring shade better than any other southern grass, and it tolerates salt fairly well, making it a good grass for lawns by the sea; however, it does not make for a low-maintenance lawn. It requires a fair amount of water and fertilizer throughout the year and frequent mowing, and you must remove thatch once a year. In addition, it's vulnerable to chinch bugs. It will survive in the higher, drier, colder environments north to the Piedmont and Little Rock and west to Dallas, but it does not grow as well in the deep South.

## Light Requirements
If you have a shaded yard, give some serious thought to growing this grass. It endures shade better than any other southern grass.

## Water Requirements
St. Augustinegrass needs regular watering throughout the year.

## Soil Requirements
St. Augustinegrass needs a rich, well-drained soil with a pH of 6 to 7.

## Propagation
Plant St. Augustinegrass in the spring or early summer from sod, stolons, or plugs. One and a half to 2 square yards of sod yields enough sprigs for 1,000 square feet of lawn. Plant the sprigs 12 inches apart in rows 12 inches apart.

## Varieties
'Roselawn' is one of the more popular varieties, but consider 'Floratam'; it is resistant to chinch bugs.

# Zoysia (*Zoysia* spp.)

If you are looking for a low-maintenance lawn, consider zoysia. Depending on the species, its texture may be fine or coarse. Zoysia spreads slowly and lowly by stolons and rhizomes. It may take two to three years to fill in, but it forms a thicker, more resilient cover than just about any other grass variety. Since it grows slowly, it doesn't need mowing as often, nor does it require much fertilizing. Thatch must be removed once a year, though, and because it has shallow roots, it must be watered regularly in dry climates. Zoysia rarely has problems with insect pests or disease, though chinch bugs may invade.

Zoysia needs warm nights for best growth, and turns light brown during its dormant period. Obviously, the shorter the growing season, the longer your lawn will be brown. It's not the best choice for that area where the North ends and the South begins. In the mid-latitudes, zoysia is dormant from October until April. In the same locations, cool-season grasses are usually dormant for about two months, and would probably be a better choice.

Since it's such a bully and will run any other plant off of its ground, it does not mix well with other grass varieties and shouldn't be planted with them.

### Light Requirements
Zoysia will tolerate shade better than bermudagrass.

### Water Requirements
In dry climates, it will need regular watering.

### Soil Requirements
Zoysia adapts to any soil conditions with a pH range of 5.5 to 7.

### Propagation
Plant zoysia from plugs or sprigs. You will get enough sprigs from 1½ square yards of sod to fill 1,000 square feet of lawn. Plant the sprigs 6 inches apart in rows that are also 6 inches apart. If you choose to grow zoysia from plugs, you will need 3 square yards of sod.

### Varieties
'Emerald' is a superior variety. It has a fine texture and a dark green color, and it grows thickly.

# WHICH GRASS TO GROW

When planting a new lawn or renovating an existing one, choosing the right grass is essential to producing a great-looking lawn that won't require hours and hours of maintenance. The wrong choice can leave you with a yard full of problems. A mixture of grasses produces an attractive lawn that is highly resistant to insect pests and disease.

## Northeast and Northern Midwest

A good seed mixture for lawns in zone 6 or colder contains 50 percent Kentucky bluegrass, 30 to 40 percent red fescue, and 10 to 20 percent perennial ryegrass. Unless your yard is used very heavily, avoid the tall fescues. Each type of grass contributes its particular assets to the lawn. Bluegrass brings its attractive deep green blades to the yard. The fescues add some toughness and durability, and they are a little more tolerant of shade and drought than bluegrass. The perennial ryegrass provides quick green cover and prevents erosion, while the slower-germinating bluegrass and fescue come in underneath.

## Northern Plains and Mountain Areas

In the northern Plains states, where land is not irrigated, a mixture of crested wheatgrass and red fescue produces a good drought-tolerant lawn. If you water your lawn regularly, you can combine Kentucky bluegrass, red fescue, and perennial ryegrass as described above for the Northeast and Northern Midwest.

## Coastal Northwest

A good lawn for the Pacific Northwest can be grown from a combination of 50 percent Kentucky bluegrass, 30 to 40 percent red fescue, and 10 to 20 percent colonial bentgrass. The bluegrass lends its beauty; red fescue makes the lawn more durable; and colonial bentgrass will grow well in the slightly acid soils of the northwest.

## The Transitional Area

There isn't a simple dividing line between the North and the South, above which only certain grasses can be grown and below which others are best suited. Rather, a fuzzy transitional band extends across the country, along the northern borders of North Carolina, Tennessee, Arkansas, Oklahoma, and Texas, through New Mexico and Arizona to the Pacific, in which either the northern grasses or the southern grasses will grow well. One guideline offers a little help when deciding which grass to grow. Cool-season varieties are better suited for mountainous areas and warm-season for lower elevations.

## The Humid South

Bermudagrass, St. Augustinegrass, or zoysia grow well in humid southern climates. St. Augustinegrass is particularly good for shady areas.

# EVALUATING YOUR LAWN

You probably already have a lawn, or you've just moved into a new home and are becoming acquainted with a new yard. Take a little time to get to know your lawn, and you'll be able to care for it more easily and more successfully. Following are some easy tests for evaluating the condition of your yard.

## Visual Inspection

There's a lot you can learn about the condition of your lawn simply by looking at it carefully. Take into account its color and physical characteristics, and you'll be able to make a fair diagnosis of your lawn's health.

### Color

A healthy lawn has a deep, rich green color; however, an excessively brilliant green color and rapid growth suggest that you are overfeeding your grass. Over-fertilization causes shallow roots to develop and makes grass more vulnerable to insects and disease. If this is the case, simply fertilize the lawn less often.

### Clippings

Do the grass clippings disappear quickly? At least within a week? If they don't, check to see if thatch is building up in your lawn.

### Water Run-Off

Does water run off the lawn, or is it immediately absorbed by the soil? If it runs off, the soil needs aeration and a supplement of organic material. First use an aerating tool or machine to pull narrow plugs of soil out of the lawn, then go back and spread compost lightly on the lawn. Much of it will get down into the soil through the holes you've punched and should begin to improve drainage.

### Discolored Spots

Do you see brown circles anywhere in the lawn? If so, your grass may be infected with a disease. (See the section on disease later in this chapter.)

### Weeds

If weeds have invaded about half of your lawn, and the other half of your lawn is marred by bare patches, your grass is probably struggling in soil that is either infertile, poorly drained, or both. A lawn growing on infertile, poorly drained soil may have to be completely renovated.

## Physical Tests

Once you've examined the surface of the lawn, look beneath it for more information about the lawn's condition. This is most easily done after a heavy rain, when the ground is more pliable. With a strong knife, cut out a triangular core of sod 3 to 4 inches deep and examine it for its physical characteristics.

### Moisture Penetration

The sod core should be moist all the way through. If it isn't, examine the thatch. A layer ¼ inch or more thick may prevent water from penetrating the soil. If the thatch is not heavy, the soil is too compact.

### Depth of Roots

Look at the roots of the grass. If they are 6 inches or more in length, your grass is in good shape. Roots that reach 4 to 6 inches down into the soil indicate that you are overwatering or overfertilizing the lawn and that the grass should be mowed a little higher —2½ to 3 inches. If roots are shorter than 4 inches, the lawn needs aerating and you should cut back on fertilizer.

### Thickness of Thatch Layer

Next, examine the thatch. A layer less than ¼ inch thick will not harm your lawn. Any thicker, though, and the thatch must be removed. You can remove most of the thatch by raking stiffly with an ordinary wire rake, but a cavex rake will do a better job. If your layer is too thick for even the cavex rake to remove, you can rent special dethatching machines called verticutters or vertimowers. These will cut the thatch and lift it off the ground. Afterward, rake up the thatch and compost it.

## Chemical Test

To complete your examination of the lawn, test the pH of the soil. (See chapter 9 for instructions on how to do this.) Most grasses flourish in an environment with an acidity range of 6.8 to 7, but they'll also do well enough in soils having a pH of 6.5 to 7.2. If the soil is too acidic, apply limestone (see table 1 for the amount of limestone to use). When establishing a lawn in soil that is too acidic, apply lime before seeding and mix it 5 to 6 inches deep. Add limestone to the soil in late fall, winter, or very early spring. It takes about four to six months for lime to begin to have its impact.

If your soil is too alkaline (soil pH is above 8), elemental sulfur will lower the pH. Spread 3 to 5 pounds over every 1,000 square feet.

## RENOVATING A LAWN

If your lawn has become thin, damaged, or weedy, it's time to renovate. Do any major lawn renovation in the early fall, late August, or early September so the new grass has time to get established. If you cannot renovate your lawn in the fall, then do so just as early in the spring as possible, after the last frost. By the time lilacs have bloomed in your area, it is too late to begin any major work on your lawn. You can take one of two approaches to renovation: overseeding existing lawn or killing all weeds and old grass and reseeding the lawn.

### Renovation by Overseeding

If more than 50 percent of your lawn is in good shape, you don't have to dig up the whole lawn and create a new one; overseeding will work just fine. Through this method of renovation, you can breathe new life into your lawn, as well as bring in a new grass that you'd like to see growing there. The best time to overseed northern lawns is in the fall, six weeks before the first frost. In the South, overseed in the spring. Simply follow these steps:

1. Mow your lawn down to about ¼ to ½ inch to remove as much foliage as possible.

2. Vigorously rake the lawn to pull out the thatch. Removing it allows the new seed to come in

TABLE 1.

| Adding Limestone to Lawns | | | |
|---|---|---|---|
| Soil pH | Sandy Soil (lb/1,000 sq ft) | Loam (lb/1,000 sq ft) | Clay Soil (lb/1,000 sq ft) |
| Under 5.0 | 40 to 50 | 105 to 135 | 155 to 195 |
| 5.0 to 6.0 | 30 to 40 | 80 to 105 | 110 to 155 |
| 6.0 | 15 | 40 | 55 |

contact with the soil. For large lawns, you can rent machines called power rakes, turf thinners, dethatchers, or vertical mowers to make this job easier. These tools tear out weeds and thatch, but leave the grass intact. At the same time, they cut shallow grooves in the soil that will catch newly sown seed and facilitate its germination. This also aerates the soil. The machines are easy to use, and save a lot of labor. You can find them at most rental agencies.

3.  Pull out all weeds and rake the lawn one more time.

4.  Spread compost over the lawn and sow the grass seed. Use one and a half times the amount recommended on the package for making new

A cyclone seeder spreads lawn seed evenly and quickly.

lawns. You can sow grass seed by hand, although the best sowing tool is a cyclone seeder. If you are sowing by hand, take only an ounce or two of seed in your hand at a time and cast it to cover as much area as possible. Go over the area several times in different directions for even coverage.

5.  Lightly rake over the lawn surface to bring the seed into contact with the top ⅛ inch of soil for successful germination. For best results, spread a thin layer of topsoil over the seed. One and a half cubic feet of topsoil will be enough to cover 1,000 square feet of lawn.

6.  While it is not essential, it helps to firm the seedbed by going over the area once with a lawn roller filled with water. Seed does not germinate and grow as well in loosely packed soil, which dries out quickly.

7.  After sowing, a thorough gentle watering is essential. Follow up with frequent sprinklings—daily or more often—to keep the top layer of soil moist until the young grass plants are established.

8.  A very light mulch of straw or hay protects the seeds. Mulch so lightly that you can see the soil through the mulch, so that the grass seedlings will receive sunlight. One bale of straw or hay should be enough to cover 1,000 square feet. Mulch retains moisture and breaks the fall of raindrops, encouraging the water to sink into the soil rather than form little brooklets, which wash the seed away and erode the soil. You won't have to remove the mulch later, so take your time placing it lightly and evenly over the lawn. Avoid laying it in bunches that will obstruct the lawn mower or shade seedlings. Your first mowing will simply turn the mulch into finer mulch, which will eventually break down into humus.

You also can mulch with a layer of spunbound floating row covers. Leave these woven mulches on until the grass is 1 inch high.

## Spot Seeding

Perhaps your lawn is beginning to show a few bare patches or weedy spots. It doesn't need a complete overhaul, but you would like to patch it and perk it up. First, you need to determine why the bare spots have occurred. Did you spill too much fertilizer in those spots? Are they located in a common walkway in your yard? Does the soil drain poorly in that area? Once you've figured out what has caused the problem, solve it before you reseed. Try to divert traffic from the area if that is the problem. Add organic matter to the soil if drainage is poor; then you can renovate. Perhaps the bare patches are caused by a disease or insect pest. See later in this chapter for solutions to these problems.

In the North, spot-seed during the fall, six weeks before the first frost. In the South, seed in spring or early summer, anytime from March until June. If the soil is compacted, dig it up and rake it; then give the ground about an inch of water. Seed the patch and cover it with a thin layer of topsoil. Cover the seed with a thin layer of mulch and keep it moist until it germinates.

## Complete Lawn Renovation

If weeds have overtaken half of your lawn and the grass on the other half is looking weak, with perhaps a few bare patches showing up, remove the lawn entirely and start a new one either by seeding, laying sod, or planting plugs or sprigs of grass. The following section provides details on these different techniques.

There are several ways to remove a lawn. The easiest and fastest is to remove the lawn by strips with a sod stripper, which you can rent. The disadvantage to this method is that you lose valuable topsoil with the sod. You can plow the grass under, but buried sod takes a long time to decompose. A rotary tiller breaks the sod into smaller pieces and mixes it with the soil for faster decomposition. You still must wait about a month in warm climates to a year in cool climates, however, for all the grass, weeds, and thatch to break down. You can speed up this process by adding high-nitrogen material to the soil. If you are going to till the lawn in, follow these steps:

1. Let your grass grow to a height of 5 to 6 inches.

2. Mow it as close to the ground as possible and remove the clippings.

3. Till in the sod.

4. Spread the grass clippings over the ground and till them into the soil. Grass clippings are high in nitrogen and will speed up the decomposition of the soil.

5. Finally, work a thin layer of blood meal or a thick layer of manure into the soil to aid in the decomposition process.

## PLANTING GRASS

Whether you're completely redoing a lawn or starting a new lawn around a new house, you want to get your grass off to a good start. The first step in doing so is to plant the grass at the right time of year. Cool-season grasses germinate best in cooler temperatures, which means spring or fall. Because in the North annual weeds finish their life cycles in the fall, this is the best time to plant grass, because it won't have to compete for food and water. You can plant in spring, but do so as soon as you can work the ground. In the South, weeds get going in the fall. So the best time to plant warm-season grasses is in the spring and early summer.

You can start lawns from seed, sod, plugs, or sprigs. Bermudagrass, zoysia, and St. Augustine-grass are usually grown from plugs or sprigs rather than seed.

### Seeding

Before you begin to seed, whip your soil into tip-top shape. Correct any drainage problems. Check the soil's fertility and pH and add any necessary amendments; then you're ready to begin. Simply follow these steps:

1. Rake the soil smooth.

2. Divide your seed in half and spread one batch over the entire area with a seeder or by hand, working in one direction.

3. Spread the second half of the seed, working perpendicular to your first pass.

4.  Rake the ground lightly to cover the seed, and firm the area with a lawn roller, which you can rent if necessary, or the back of a rake.

5.  Spread a thin layer of straw over the ground to keep the ground moist and also to prevent rain from washing the seed away. You can also mulch with spunbound floating row covers. Remove them once the grass has grown 1 inch.

6.  Water the seed and keep the ground moist until the grass reaches a height of 2 inches.

7.  You can mow your new lawn once it has grown 3 inches.

## Sodding

Roll out the sod and presto—new lawn! Well, it's not as simple as that, although this method does estab-

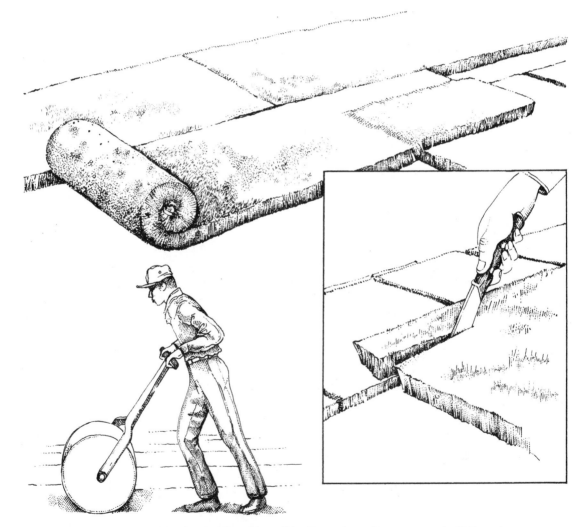

When planting sod, lay strips in a brick pattern. Trim the edges, if necessary, to fit the pieces closely against any walkways in your yard. Once all the sod has been placed, firm it to the ground with a lawn roller.

lish a lawn quickly. Sod should be no thicker than 1 inch—¾ inch works best. Prepare the soil for sod just as you would for seeding and follow these steps:

1. Water soil to a depth of 6 inches.

2. Lay the first strips of sod against a walkway, if you have one, or against a 2-by-4 placed on the ground or some other straight boundary.

3. Lay remaining strips in a brick pattern so that the top and bottom edges are staggered

rather than lining up. Place them as close together as possible.

4. Use a lawn roller to firm the sod into place.

5. Spread a thin layer of soil over the sod, working it into the cracks between the pieces.

6. Keep the lawn moist until the grass has rooted into the ground.

## Plugs

Grass plugs are small blocks of sod about 2 inches square and about 2 to 3 inches thick. To plant them, dig holes just a little bit larger than the plugs and 1 foot apart, and simply insert the plugs.

## Sprigs

Sprigs are stolons (shoots) or rhizomes that root when planted in the soil. They are produced by shredding sod into individual stems 4 to 8 inches long. Bermudagrass, St. Augustinegrass, and zoysia all can be grown from sprigs. Look under the descriptions of these grasses on pages 217 to 219 for specific information on planting distances.

To start a lawn from plugs of sod, simply dig holes slightly larger than the plugs and drop in the little hunks of sod.

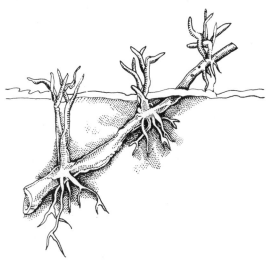

Lawns can be planted from individual sprigs or stolons. Use pieces that are 4 to 8 inches long, and bury the lowermost joint of the sprig in the soil.

## Winter Overseeding in the South

Because most southern grasses turn brown during the winter, you might want to overseed your lawn with a northern grass that will keep the lawn green through this season. In addition, weeds commonly pop up in southern lawns during the winter months, and the fresh growth of a cool-season grass will help to keep them out, as well as improving the appearance of the lawn.

Overseed in late August or September with bluegrass, annual ryegrass, or perennial ryegrass, following these steps:

1. Mow the grass as low as possible.

2. Rake it with a steel rake and sow the seed, using 1½ times more seed than you would if you were starting a new lawn.

3. Water the ground and keep it moist until the seed germinates.

4. Mow the winter grass to a height of 2 inches throughout the winter.

# LAWN MANAGEMENT

Once you've selected and planted or replanted the right grass, a little watering, feeding, and mowing will make your lawn a lush, green space—the perfect ground for the landscape around your home.

## Water Requirements

Proper watering keeps your lawn healthy and helps to prevent problems with insect pests and disease. Northern lawns rarely need to be watered. They usually get enough rain during the growing season, and if they don't, they'll go into a semi-dormant period. Even if the grass begins to brown a little during a dry period, it'll green up quickly with the next rain. Once the grass looks dull and grayish and does not spring back when you walk on it, the lawn has wilted—it's time to water.

When you water, give the lawn a good drenching. Fewer deep waterings are better than frequent light sprinklings. Light daily watering keeps grass green, but does not encourage roots to grow deeply. Over-watering encourages rapid growth of the blades above the ground. The lawn will need mowing more often and will be more vulnerable to disease. In addition, Japanese beetles prefer to lay their eggs in lawns that are constantly moist, and their larvae will burrow through the soil and chew the luscious roots of your lawn.

Water in the morning, after the dew has dried. To be effective, each watering must be generous enough to ensure that moisture is absorbed by the lawn to a depth of at least 6 to 8 inches. Most lawns will use 1½ to 2 inches of water a week. How much you water, though, depends on the type of soil your grass grows in. One-half to 1 inch of water is sufficient for sandy soil. At least 1 inch will serve for loamy soil. Clay soil requires 1 to 2 inches of water.

Southern lawns will need watering a little more often during the hot summer months. Most need 1 to 2 inches of water a week in normal weather and 3 inches a week when the weather is very hot and dry.

## Feeding Requirements

As with watering, overdoing the fertilizer is more harmful than helpful. The healthiest lawns are fed prudently. Too much fertilizer, especially in the spring, encourages excess growth of the grass aboveground. The lawn will need to be watered and mowed more often, and it will be more vulnerable to attack from insect pests and disease. In addition, gluttonous grass that has been overfed becomes lazy. The roots have no need to stretch in search of food. They'll remain shallow, and if drought hits, they will not be able to pull up water from the depths of the soil.

To avoid all these problems, fertilize the lawn once. Fall is the best time to feed northern lawns. At this time of year, cool-season grasses are still engaged in photosynthesis, but top growth has slowed, so grasses don't lose control when given a boost of fertilizer. The best fertilizers to use are organic fertilizers because they release nutrients slowly to plants and do not upset the chemical balance of the soil. Choose dried cow manure, dried poultry manure, blood meal, cottonseed meal, fish emulsion, or mixed organic products. (See table 2 for details on the amount of fertilizer to use.) You can use any method of fertilizer application you want, but a drop spreader is one of the best tools for spreading it evenly.

When it comes to clippings, many homeowners have been raking their lawns promptly after mowing, but in fact, the lawn will benefit from clippings. Research has found that grass clippings begin to decompose almost immediately after being cut. Grass is a great source of nitrogen and can supply up to 50 percent of a lawn's nitrogen requirements for the year. In addition, researchers have found that clippings help to suppress the growth of weeds. No more need for raking—what a relief! After pushing the mower around, put it away, sit back, and relax. Isn't this how we'd all like life to be—less work providing more benefits?

**TABLE 2.**

## Natural Nitrogen Numbers

Amount of organic fertilizer needed to provide 1 pound of nitrogen per 1,000 square feet of lawn.

| Fertilizer | Amount (lb/1,000 sq ft) |
|---|---|
| Alfalfa meal | 10 |
| Blood meal (10-0-0) | 10 |
| Castor pomace (5-1-1) | 20 |
| Cottonseed meal (7-2-1) | 15 |
| Erth-Rite (3-2-2) | 34 |
| Milorganite (6-2-0) | 17 |
| Mix 1 (4-5-4) | 25 |
| 2 parts dried blood | |
| 1 part rock phosphate | |
| 4 parts wood ashes | |
| Mix 2 (2-4-2) | 50 |
| 4 parts coffee grounds | |
| 1 part bonemeal | |
| 1 part wood ashes | |
| Nitro-10 (10-0-0) | 10 |
| Poultry manure (4-4-2) | 25 |

(Reprinted with permission from *The Chemical Free Lawn*, Rodale Press, 1988.)

Although one fall feeding is all that's needed, a little seaweed extract can also help maintain the health of your lawn. Seaweed extract has been found to increase the drought resistance and insect and disease resistance of grass, and it improves the appearance of lawns. Make a dilution from 7½ ounces of extract in 100 gallons of water and spray it over the lawn. Three applications a year, once in early spring, once in midsummer, and once in late summer, will strengthen and brighten your lawn, and keep it looking great.

Southern grasses grow most vigorously during spring and summer, so that's the time to fertilize. Do not feed them in the fall. It will encourage new growth in these cold-sensitive grasses, which may then be injured during the winter months.

## Mowing the Lawn

Mowing not only keeps your yard looking neat, but actually produces a lusher, denser lawn. Mowing prevents grass from setting seed, so it will spread through its rhizomes and create a lush, thick carpet of green. Cutting is stressful for grass, however. It opens plants to infection from disease, and any time grass is cut, the root system is weakened slightly. Nevertheless, if you follow good mowing practices, your lawn can only benefit from it.

The key is mowing the grass to the right height. The depth that grass roots reach corresponds to the height of the top growth. Letting the grass grow up lets the roots grow down. Grass with deep roots is better able to withstand drought. Tall grass also helps shade the soil, which cools the crowns of the grass plants and reduces soil drying.

Small changes in mowing height make a big difference in lawn health and vigor. Increasing the height of the cut only ⅛ inch results in about 300 square feet more leaf surface for each 1,000 square feet of lawn. Since the leaf blade is the food factory of the grass plant, the more surface available to receive light, the more efficient its metabolism, and the better it grows. Tests show that cutting off about a third of the blades produces the best results; deeper mowing damages the grass.

The height to which you mow also depends on the type of grass you have and the time of year. In general, cut cool-season grasses shorter during the cool seasons, when they are more active. Grass under shade grows better when clipped a little shorter. For the final mowing of the season, lower your mower blades and trim the lawn a little closer than you would normally. (See table 3 for precise mowing heights of different grasses.) If you live in the Southwest, mow your lawn about ¼ inch shorter than the recommended height.

The following tips will perfect your mowing technique:

• Keep the blades of your mower sharp. This provides a nice clean cut rather than a tear, and thus makes the grass less vulnerable to disease.

• Don't cut grass when it's wet or mowing will be uneven. In addition, wet clippings form clumps that block light from the grass.

• Alternate mowing patterns for even wear on the lawn. Mowing in the same direction every time tends to compact the soil and causes wear patterns.

A beautiful lawn doesn't require hours of labor. It's simply a matter of timing and proper technique. Do the right thing at the right time, and you'll have a lush, healthy lawn with little trouble.

A healthy lawn will have few problems with insect pests, weeds, or disease, but there, too, the right control at the right moment will keep your yard looking great.

# MOST COMMON CULTURAL PROBLEMS

## Small Dead Spots Ringed in Green

### Dog Urine
The urine of female dogs kills grass. The dead spots on your lawn are likely to be surrounded by a ring of very green grass, distinguishing this problem from disease or some other cause. Soak the spots with water, and grass should begin to grow again. If it does not, reseed the spots.

## Lawn Turns Brown

### Excessive Thatch Buildup
Grass clippings mat together on your lawn to form thatch. As discussed earlier, clippings do break down and enrich the soil, but if they don't break down quickly enough, they can cause more harm than good. The use of chemicals on the lawn, overwatering, compaction, and improper mowing can increase the buildup of thatch while slowing its decomposition, thus leaving you with a layer that's just too

TABLE 3.

## How Low to Go—Mowing Heights of Grasses

| Grass | Height in Cool Months (in.) | Height in Hot Months (in.) | Height of Final Mow (in.) |
|-------|-----------------------------|----------------------------|---------------------------|
| Bermudagrass | ½ | 1 | ½ |
| Fine fescue | 1½ | 2½ | 1 |
| Kentucky bluegrass | 2½ | 3 | 2 |
| Perennial ryegrass | 1½ | 2½ | 1 |
| St. Augustinegrass | 2 | 3 | 1½ |
| Tall fescue | 2½ | 4 | 2 |
| Zoysia | ½ | 1 | ½ |

thick. The soil underneath a thick layer of thatch becomes more compacted and cannot absorb water. In addition, air cannot circulate near the soil to remove any excess moisture, and the thatch may become a haven for various diseases and pest insects.

If your lawn is looking brown and drought is not the cause, measure the thatch layer. One-fourth inch or less poses no threat to the lawn. It is a sign that the clippings are decomposing at a good rate. A thatch layer thicker than ¼ inch will cause problems and will need to be removed. You can do this with a simple leaf rake if the layer is not too thick or compacted. Heavier jobs will require a power rake or a dethatching tool. An alternative to physically removing thatch is to speed up its decomposition with the product Ringer's Lawn Rx, available at garden centers and nurseries. This product contains microorganisms that break down thatch.

If the soil beneath the thatch is compacted, aerate it with a core cultivator or an aeration machine. Experts say that to appreciably improve grass rooting, you must punch aeration holes at least 8 inches deep.

To prevent thatch buildup, simply follow good care techniques. Do not overfertilize or overwater your lawn, and mow lightly and frequently.

## Weed Takeover

### Improper Lawn Care

Excessive weeds are a signal that something is amiss. A healthy lawn grows vigorously enough to crowd out most of the weeds. When soil becomes poor and the grass weakens, weeds will take advantage of the situation and move right in and all over your yard.

Inevitably, some weeds will invade your lawn, so you need to establish your "weed tolerance level" and then control these pests to that level. Decide which weeds you'll tolerate in small numbers and which ones you absolutely cannot have in your lawn.

Very often, an outbreak of a particular variety of weed indicates a problem. For example, a burst of prostrate knotweed (*Polygonum aviculare*) in the lawn means the ground is probably dry and compacted, whereas yellow nutsedge (*Cyperus escu-*

*lentus*) indicates waterlogged soil. If all types of weeds have invaded your yard, you may have overfertilized the lawn. Too much fertilizer can upset the balance of the soil environment: The grass blades will become weak and weeds will move into their territory.

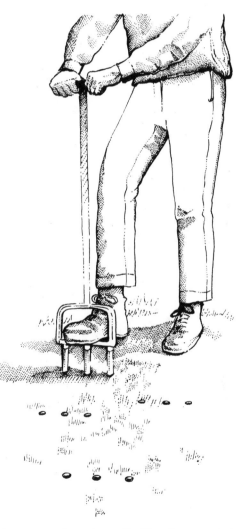

You can revive a lawn that has been growing in dense, compacted soil by creating holes in it with an aerating tool or machine.

Of course, hand pulling is still the safest way to remove weeds from the lawn. However, one product, SharpShooter, widely available at garden centers and nurseries, will remove weeds with ease. This is a soap-based material that dries up plants quickly on contact. It will kill any plant, including grass, so be sure to shield neighboring plants and direct the spray or paint only onto the weeds. (You can spray this product on carefully or paint it on individual plants, but don't spray it on a windy day.) Sharp-Shooter is most effective when the air temperature is higher than 70°F. If removing weeds leaves a bare spot, reseed that area so new weeds don't move into it.

## Grass Yellowed and Pale

### Lack of Food
Grass that isn't getting enough nitrogen turns pale green or yellow. It grows slowly and becomes thin. Don't immediately dump fertilizer all over the lawn. Follow the feeding guidelines given earlier in this chapter and the emerald hue of your grass will return.

## Grass Dull Gray-Green Color

### Lack of Water
When grass doesn't get enough water, its color changes from fresh green to a dull, gray-green. In addition, the lawn lacks springiness; when you walk across it, the blades don't bounce back up quickly, and your footprints will remain for more than just a few seconds. On close inspection, you'll find that some blades are completely brown. To correct this problem, follow the watering guidelines outlined earlier in the chapter.

## Grass Grows Poorly and Becomes Thin

### Soil Compaction
If you're watering, fertilizing, and mowing correctly, but the lawn still looks thin and sickly, the soil might be so compacted that your efforts are going to waste. Test the soil by pushing a screwdriver into it. If the soil is easily penetrated, compaction is not the problem. If there is much resistance, the soil is packed too tightly. Compacted soil can easily be loosened with aerating tools. You can rent power aerating machines or buy a simple manual aerating tool. Both work by pushing tines into the ground that actually pull out narrow plugs of soil from

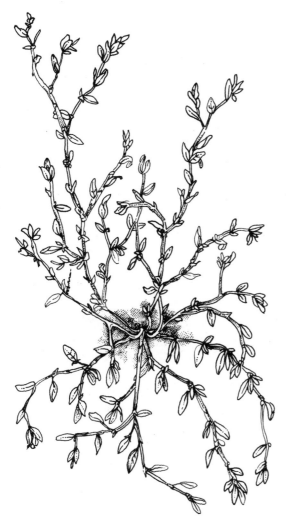

If you find lots of prostrate knotweed growing in your lawn, it may be a sign that the soil is dry and compacted.

Yellow nutsedge may indicate that the ground is waterlogged.

find these velvety mounds growing in your yard, your soil is suffering from these problems. Power raking will correct all of these conditions. To take care of the moss, apply Safer's Moss Killer, widely available at garden centers and nurseries. This is a soap-based product that will not harm the environment. In extremely wet, cool seasons, moss will grow even in unshaded lawns.

# MOST COMMON INSECT PESTS ABOVE GROUND

The symptoms of insect infestation can look like the symptoms of disease or improper lawn care. If you suspect that insects indeed are the cause of your problems, but you haven't seen any little pests around, follow this simple procedure to bring them out in the open. Mix 1 teaspoon liquid detergent or insecticidal soap in 1 quart water. Pour the mixture over about 1 square foot of lawn. Test several spots around the yard this way, and look very closely for gray worms or caterpillars that will wriggle to the surface within 10 minutes. Each pest does leave its own particular mark on your lawn, and each requires a specific control as discussed on the following pages. This particular test only makes visible those insects that are in the thatch and not those in the soil.

## Grass Yellow-Orange

### Aphids
Aphids, also called greenbugs (*Toxoptera graminum*), suck the sap out of blades of grass, causing them to turn yellow-orange and lose their vigor. Aphid damage occurs most often during hot, dry spells or after a mild winter and a cool spring. Areas under trees are usually infested. Look for the aphids themselves amidst the yellow-orange grass. They aren't much bigger than the head of a pin. They have soft, pear-shaped bodies that may be green, brown, black, or pink.

Mow the lawn, and spray the grass with insecticidal soap once every two to three days for a total of

about 4 inches deep, allowing air to move into the ground. This, in turn, stimulates the microbiological activity necessary to keep soil healthy.

## Moss Grows in Bare Spots

### Various Soil Problems
Shade, soil compaction, low fertility, and a low pH all create a perfect environment for moss, so if you

three applications. If the aphids persist, spray your lawn with pyrethrum twice, five days apart.

## Bare Areas

### Armyworms

Irregular bare patches in the lawn may be a sign of armyworms (*Pseudaletia unipuncta*). The damage they cause looks very similar to that caused by sod webworms. If armyworms have infected your lawn, symptoms usually appear in late summer or fall. In significant numbers, they can eat the grass down to the soil level. These pests feed at night and can be found under brown or dead sod during the day. They are about 1½ inches long and have a brown, somewhat hairy body and a black head. Three yellowish white lines stretch down the back from head to tail, and on each side you'll see a dark stripe with a yellow wavy line splotched with red beneath it. A prominent white V or Y marks the head.

Apply Bt (*Bacillus thuringiensis*) to the area where the worms are at work, thoroughly covering the grass. If you use Bt in liquid form, spray the lawn every 10 to 14 days until the pest is gone. Reapply Bt after it rains. Beneficial nematodes that are specifically used to control armyworms are now available commercially. You also can use milky spore disease (*Bacillus popilliae*) to control armyworm, but it takes three to five years to be completely effective. Sabadilla dust may be effective as well.

## Yellow Circular Patches

### Chinch Bugs

Large circular patches of yellow grass may be a sign of chinch bugs (*Blissus leucopterus*). These patches turn brown, and the grass eventually dies. Chinch bugs are sun lovers, usually appearing during hot dry spells when temperatures are in the high 70s or even warmer, and they seek out the warm, sunny areas of the lawn. Often you'll find them at the edge of the lawn, where the grass has been warmed by the reflected heat of sidewalks and streets. They soon spread outward into healthy turf. Chinch bugs congregate down in the leaves and stems of the grass and suck the plant juices. Adult chinch bugs

have a black body that measures about ⅕ inch long. They sport a black triangular pad between their white, folded wings. Lawns weakened by excess thatch, lack of water, or lack of nitrogen are prime targets for these pests. Chinch bugs find St. Augustinegrass particularly tasty.

If you suspect chinch bugs, use the soap test described on page 231 to root them out. If you find that your lawn is indeed infested with these pests, spray it with insecticidal soap laced with isopropyl alcohol every three to five days for two weeks. Make the soap-alcohol solution by combining 1 tablespoon isopropyl alcohol with each quart of insecticidal soap needed. The fungus *Beauvaria bassiana* has also been found to effectively control chinch bugs. The St. Augustinegrass cultivar 'Floratam' is resistant to these pests.

## Small Dead Spots

### Cutworms

Cutworms create dead spots 1 or 2 inches in diameter in the lawn. They chew blades of grass below the mowing level, so look for patches of closely cut grass stubble. Cutworm damage occurs during warmer months. They feed mostly at night and bury themselves in the soil during the day. The cutworm is a plump, soft-bodied, dull grayish or brownish caterpillar that measures 1 to 2 inches long. When startled, it curls up.

To control cutworms on your lawn, sprinkle cornmeal or bran meal lightly around the affected spots. The cutworms will eat the meal and die. Juvenile nematodes are also excellent cutworm control agents.

### Sod Webworms

In late spring, check your lawn for small dead patches 1 to 2 inches in diameter. By midsummer, thanks to sod webworms (*Crambus* spp.), these may be large dead patches. The most severe damage usually occurs in July and August. Sod webworms chew grass blades off just above the thatch line and pull the blades into a silken tunnel in the ground to eat them. As several worms work your lawn, these small patches become larger and begin to overlap, forming large, irregular dead patches. Sod webworms feed at night, but you can find them during the day by carefully breaking apart the damaged areas of the lawn with your fingers. If you notice that lots of birds have been feeding on your lawn, it's a good sign that sod webworms have arrived.

The adult webworm is a buff-colored moth with a wingspan of about 1 inch. It flies in the early morning or late evening in a jerky, zigzag pattern, just a few feet above the lawn. The moths themselves don't damage the lawn, but they drop eggs into the grass that, upon hatching, produce very hungry caterpillars. These larvae hatch in six to ten days and start feeding on grass blades and building silk-lined tunnels in the thatch and debris on the soil surface. They are ¾ to 1 inch long, and are a dull tannish brown with brown-black spots along the sides and back. Stiff hairs protrude from these spots. Their heads are shiny and dark brown.

To make an accurate diagnosis of the problem, use the soap drench test described on page 231 to expose the pesky larvae inhabiting your lawn. If more than 15 webworms are present, spray your lawn with Bt (*Bacillus thuringiensis*) every three to five days for two weeks. If Bt doesn't control the problem, plant resistant grass varieties. You can also try introducing predatory nematodes, which are available commercially. (See the source list at the back of the book for suppliers.)

## Holes in Grass Blades

### Earwigs

Earwigs (*Forficula auricularia*) sometimes eat holes in the blades of lawn grass, but they are seldom a serious problem. More often the earwig is an ally, feeding on aphids and other pests by night. Adults are reddish brown and 1 inch long, with distinctive pincers protruding from the tip of the abdomen.

If the infestation is heavy, spray the lawn with insecticidal soap laced with isopropyl alcohol every two to three days for two weeks. To make this solution, add 1 tablespoon alcohol to each quart of soap spray you use. You can also trap earwigs in pieces of old hose or in rolled-up newspapers set around the lawn, then shake the insects into a bucket of soapy water.

## Grass Chewed

### Grasshoppers

Grasshoppers don't usually cause too much trouble unless your grass has become dry. If you spot a few bouncing around the lawn, don't worry about them, but if several are munching away on the grass, take action. Handpick them early in the morning, before they've warmed up and become active. If grasshoppers make an appearance in your yard year after year, try controlling them with the disease *Nosema locusta*. Mix it with bran, which acts as bait, and sprinkle it on the lawn in the spring. Young larvae will eat the bran and will either become sick and die or pass this disease to the next generation. Use 1 to 2 pounds of this bran mixture for each acre.

## Lawn Looks Bleached

### Leafhoppers

Leafhoppers (*Empoasca fabae*) usually create trouble on newly seeded lawns. They pierce blades of grass and suck the sap, removing chlorophyll from the cells. The grass plants weaken and turn pale. New lawns grow poorly and may die. A mature lawn hit by a large number of leafhoppers will look bleached and unhealthy.

Leafhoppers may be green, brown, or yellow, and often have colorful markings. They hold their wedge-shaped wings in a rooflike position over their ¼- to ⅓-inch-long bodies. To control them, spray the lawn with insecticidal soap laced with isopropyl alcohol every three to five days for two weeks. To make this solution, add 1 tablespoon isopropyl alcohol to 1 quart soap. The alcohol helps the soap penetrate the bug's outer shell. You can also use pyrethrum on lawns infested with leafhoppers. Make two applications, three to four days apart.

## Grass Yellowed

### Mites

Like aphids, mites suck the sap from blades of grass, turning them yellow. A heavy infestation can kill grass, causing the lawn to become thin and brown. Mites are members of the spider family. They are so tiny, you can barely see them. They usually attack during hot, dry weather. Spray your lawn repeatedly with insecticidal soap until the grass recovers.

## Grass Withered and Dead; Small Bumps on Blades

### Scale

If your grass withers and dies, it might be infested with scale. Look for these insects on individual blades. They resemble small bumps, having protective rounded, waxy shells. They are only ⅛ inch in diameter and are purple-brown in color. Scale insects attack grass at its crowns, causing it to wither and die. Spray infested areas of the lawn with insecticidal soap until symptoms disappear.

## Blades of Grass Ragged

### Snails and Slugs

Snails and slugs are notorious for their ravages over all kinds of plants. They devour large portions of grass at once, leaving blades looking quite ragged. They are most active in dark, wet conditions, commonly attacking shady areas under trees and feeding on plants during the night. During the day, you'll find them curled up under boards or plant debris.

Snails and slugs are land-dwelling molluscs. They have soft, chubby little bodies covered with sticky slime. Snails wear protective coiled shells, and their markings vary considerably. Slugs, on the other hand, wander around with their slick bodies exposed to the world. They may be white, gray, yellow, or brown-black. Most species are 1 to 2 inches long, but certain species can reach 8 inches in length.

The best way to control these pests is to trap them. You can buy a commercial trap or make one at home by filling a pie plate or other shallow container with beer. The yeast in the beer lures these pests; they jump in and drown. If snails and slugs are a problem in your yard year after year, begin trapping within the first three to four weeks after the last frost. As soon as you catch one pest, increase the number of traps to catch the others before they get out of control.

## Wilted Patches

### Wireworms

Wireworms feed on the roots of grass, causing it to wilt. Usually, these pests don't cause enough trouble to warrant your attention; however, if you find lots of them in wilted patches on your lawn, begin taking steps to eliminate them. The larvae of click beetles, wireworms have brown, hard-shelled bodies and are ⅓ to ½ inch long. The adults are about ½ inch long and black to gray or brown, with dark spots on their heads.

Watch for the emergence of the beetles in spring and handpick them from your lawn. To control the larvae, trap them: Cut several potatoes in half, pierce them with sticks, and bury them in the top 3 inches of soil. In three or four days, pull out the potato pieces, along with the wireworms they have attracted. Continue trapping until the pests are gone.

# MOST COMMON INSECT PESTS BELOW GROUND

If the grass in your lawn is loose and pulls up easily, its likely that insect pests are attacking from underneath. When you see spots of damage in your lawn, test for underground pests by pulling gently on the grass in that area. See the following pages for a description of some possible culprits.

## Yellow or Brown Patches

### Billbug Grubs

A small and distinct circular pattern of grass that becomes yellowish or brown may indicate a possible billbug grub attack. Affected grass pulls up in mats, and you'll see a light brown, sawdustlike material around the roots. Adult billbugs have a large snout or "bill." They vary in color from cream to brown to almost black and are ¼ to ½ inch long. You may see them strolling along sidewalks or driveways early in the spring. Billbugs are generally residents of the South, though they are moving northward. Bermudagrass and zoysia are particularly vulnerable to this pest.

It's the larvae that cause all the trouble. These legless worms are ¼ to ⅜ inch long and mostly white, with a black blotch on their backs. They have bright orange-brown heads. If you find more than one billbug grub in 1 square foot of lawn, treat the area with beneficial nematodes or rotenone for quick short-range control. Apply milky spore disease (*Bacillus popilliae*) to the lawn for long-term control.

## Irregular Streaks of Brown Grass through the Lawn

### Mole Crickets

Appropriately named, mole crickets tunnel under the lawn, eating grass roots as they go. Above the ground, grass wilts and turns brown, and you'll see irregular brown streaks over your lawn. In newly planted lawns, mole crickets will completely uproot grass seedlings and sever young grass blades from their roots. One cricket can ravage several yards of lawn in a single night.

Mole crickets are common in newly seeded areas. They are prevalent in the southern part of the United States from the Atlantic coast to Texas. Look for damage from April to October in the South. Mole crickets look much like the common cricket, except that their heads and their front legs, used for digging, are notably large. They are 1½ to 2 inches long and are brown or grayish brown. Bt (*Bacillus thuringiensis*) and predatory nematodes are both effective controls for these pests.

## Grass Sickly

### Nematodes

If your lawn grows slowly, looks thin and yellow, and wilts easily during dry periods in the summer, the soil under it is probably infested with nematodes.

These pests attack at the roots. Pull up a clump of grass, and if nematodes have infested it, you'll find galls on the roots. They may be partially decayed. Effects of nematode activity are most apparent in hot weather, when plants recover poorly from the heat. St. Augustinegrass and zoysia are vulnerable to nematode attack, and in the Southeast, bermudagrass is a major target.

You can barely see nematodes. These tiny wormlike creatures are whitish and translucent, and are ¹⁄₅₀ to ¹⁄₁₀ inch long. Spread some compost over the lawn in fall or spring. This will encourage certain fungi that discourage nematodes. In the spring, fertilize the lawn with fish emulsion, which repels nematodes.

## Irregular, Brown, Dead Patches

### White Grubs

Grub-damaged sections of lawn appear burned and can be lifted up with ease to expose the culprits. These burned sections are brown and irregular in shape. Damage most often occurs in late summer to early fall, especially during dry spells.

Grubs chew away at the roots of your grass. They have fat, whitish bodies, ¾ to 1½ inches long, and may be the larvae of any one of several beetles, including Japanese beetles, May beetles, and Asiatic garden beetles. Fortunately, all are controlled in the same way. Introduce beneficial nematodes to the lawn. For long-term results, apply milky spore disease (*Bacillus popilliae*), using 4 ounces for every 1,000 square feet. (See chapter 6 for more information on milky spore disease.) Handpicking beetles also reduces the populations of grubs that will develop in your lawn.

## MOST COMMON DISEASES

Unlike insect-damaged lawns, grass that has died from disease remains firmly attached to the ground. The exception is leaf spot, also known as root and crown rot, which softens the grass so that it pulls up easily.

## Brown Circular Patches

### Brown Patch

Brown patch, also called summer patch (*Rhizoctonia solani*), kills circular areas of grass up to 2 feet in diameter. The infected areas change color and develop a likeness to frog's eyes, having a circular spot surrounded by a discolored ring of grass. Grass in these patches will probably be thin. The problem-causing fungus flourishes in the warm temperatures and damp conditions caused by thatch, and it is encouraged by excessive nitrogen fertilization and poor drainage. St. Augustinegrass is particularly vulnerable to brown patch.

Apply a flowable sulfur fungicide to infected areas every three to five days until symptoms disappear. Remove thatch with a rake or dethatcher, or apply Ringer's Lawn Rx, available at garden centers and nurseries, to break it down. Avoid applying heavy doses of nitrogen fertilizer to your lawn, and if drainage needs improving, top-dress the lawn with organic matter.

## Small, White, Circular Patches That Turn Brown

### Dollar Spot

So named because it creates tan or straw-colored spots in your lawn the size of silver dollars, the dollar spot fungus (*Sclerotinia homeocarpa*) thrives on dry, undernourished lawns. Infected lawns show small, white, cobwebby spots in the morning that turn brown later in the day. These patches will grow together to form larger patches.

Apply flowable sulfur fungicide to the infected areas every three to five days until the symptoms disappear. Frequent light applications of nitrogen will help your lawn recover, and regular mowing cuts off the infected tips of the grass. Since dollar spot fungi prefer dry conditions, water the lawn deeply. Also, recent studies have shown that regular applications of seaweed extract help control this fungus.

## Green Spots Outlined with Brown

### Fairy Ring

If you look out on your lawn and see bright green circular areas that look like they're growing more rapidly than the rest of your lawn, the grass is probably infected with the fairy ring fungus (*Marasmius oreades*). This disease might have an enchanting name, but you won't find it charming at all. A ring of grass around these bright green spots turns brown, and eventually the overgrown patches of grass decline, too. A circle of mushrooms usually develops around the edge of the infected area.

Fairy ring often occurs following an extended rainy period, when moisture builds up on the lawn. It is usually only a problem in the Pacific Northwest. To remove the fungus, dig out the infected areas of the lawn to a depth of 2 feet and extending 1 foot all the way around the diseased patch. Then fill in and replant those places.

## Reddish Brown, Tan, or Yellow Patches

### Fusarium Blight

Reddish brown spots 2 to 6 inches in diameter are the first symptom of fusarium blight (*Fusarium tricinctum*). These turn tan and finally yellow. They occur in areas of the lawn where grass is stressed. If you suspect fusarium blight, further confirmation can be obtained by looking at the roots and crowns of the grass blades. If this disease is the problem, they will show rot and may be covered with pink fungal threads. Fusarium thrives under heat and humidity and can ruin an entire lawn under such conditions.

To control the disease, mow the grass high and discard clippings. Remove thatch and refrain from fertilizing the lawn in late spring or early summer.

## Grass Pale Green and Stunted

### Leaf Smut

An overall pale green appearance and stunted growth are signs of leaf smut (*Ustilago* spp. and *Urocystis* spp.). On individual blades, black stripes develop, which rupture and expose masses of spores. The blades curl, tear easily, and look shredded. Leaf smuts are active in spring and fall. They thrive under cool, moist conditions.

Leaf smut can be controlled by mowing the lawn frequently to cut off the infected tips of grass and removing the clippings from the lawn. Follow proper watering and fertilizing practices to boost the strength of the grass and prevent further infection.

## Dark Spots on Blades of Grass

### Leaf Spot

Reddish brown to purplish black spots on grass are caused by leaf spot fungi (*Drechslera* spp.). Eventually, the blades shrivel, crowns and roots rot, and irregular patches of thin grass develop over the lawn. Leaf spot occurs most often when weather is cool and moist.

Spray the lawn with flowable sulfur fungicide every three to five days until symptoms disappear. To bring your lawn back to its peak health and to prevent disease from occurring in the future, make sure drainage and aeration are adequate, and follow proper lawn-care practices.

## Brown Rings; Blades of Grass Tattered

### Necrotic Ring Spot

Promoted by thatch buildup and poor air circulation near the soil, necrotic ring spot (*Leptosphaeria korrae*) causes grass to look tattered. Brown rings develop over the lawn. They usually hit suddenly, appearing in grass that very recently seemed perfectly healthy. To control ring spot, remove thatch, mow the grass high, and continue proper watering and feeding to reduce stress to the grass.

## White, Powdery Substance on Grass

### Powdery Mildew

A thin white powdery coating on your grass is a sure sign of powdery mildew (*Erysiphe graminis*). It often hits shaded areas when nights are cool. If this disease infects your lawn heavily, the grass will turn yellow and die. Spray the lawn with flowable sulfur fungicide every three to five days until symptoms disappear. Do not overwater or overfertilize your lawn.

## Grass Blackened and Water-Soaked

### Pythium Blight

Pythium blight is also known as cottony blight or grease spot. Caused by *Pythium* fungi, it will kill spots or streaks of grass if it infects a newly established lawn. The first sign of its arrival is a blackened, water-soaked appearance of patches of grass in your lawn. During humid weather, you may also see a cottony growth on the grass. An area as small as a few inches or as large as several feet in diameter can be affected; however, you'll most likely see spots about 2 inches across. Infected grass lies flat on the ground.

This blight frequently develops on closely cut lawns. It will infect northern lawns when they have been watered in the evenings during hot, humid weather. This disease is virtually impossible to stop once it has infected your lawn. Try to prevent it by following proper watering, fertilizing, and mowing practices.

## Circular, Scorched Patches or Pink, Gelatinous Masses

### Red Thread or Pink Patch

If your lawn has developed circular patches of scorched grass, look closer. If you find red or rusty threads on the blades, red thread (*Laetisaria fuciforme*) has infected your lawn. Pink, gelatinous masses indicate pink patch (*Limonomyces roseipellis*). These fungi are related and occur most often in the Northeast and the Pacific states. They thrive under cool, damp conditions.

Control these diseases with regular watering and feeding. Mowing cuts off the infected blade tips.

## Rust-Colored Tinge to Grass

### Rust

If your lawn or sections of it have an overall rust-colored hue, look more closely at the grass. If you find yellow-orange or red-brown powdery pustules on the blades, rust (*Puccinia* spp.) has hit. Rust occurs usually in late summer and in the fall during warm, dry weather. It can be especially damaging to 'Merion K' bluegrass.

Spray your lawn with flowable sulfur fungicide every three to five days until symptoms disappear. Fertilize with a foliar spray and mow more frequently, catching and discarding the clippings.

## Matted Grass Covered with White, Gray, or Pink Fungus in Spring

### Snow Mold

Snow mold is so named because these diseases can occur under the cover of snow. Two different fungi are responsible for the problem. *Typhula* spp. produces typhula blight or gray snow mold, which is most common on lawns that have been covered by heavy snow throughout the winter. When the snow finally does melt in spring, you'll see patches up to 2 feet in diameter covered with the white or gray fungus.

Fusarium patch (*Fusarium nivale*) produces similar symptoms. In spring, white or pink dead patches of matted grass 1 foot across or larger mar the lawn. Fusarium patch can occur even if it doesn't snow. Under these circumstances, the spots will be smaller, 1 to 2 inches in diameter. They change from purple to tan to white, and may develop pink mold.

Apply flowable sulfur fungicide to the infected areas every three to five days until the symptoms disappear. Aerate the soil and improve its drainage. Avoid excessive nitrogen fertilizing in the fall, and remove thatch if necessary.

# MOST COMMON ANIMAL PESTS

## Tunnels in the Lawn

### Gophers or Moles

The two most troublesome animal pests of the lawn are gophers and moles. Gopher tunnels are distinguished from mole tunnels by the crescent-shaped mound of soil around the entrance hole. Neither of these pests are interested in eating your grass, but the tunnels they plow through your yard definitely detract from its appearance. (See chapter 7 for more information about gophers and moles and how to control them.)

# PART 2

# *Pests and Diseases*

# CHAPTER 6

# *Insects*

Insect pests can wreak havoc on the landscape around your home, chewing holes in flowers and leaves, boring tunnels in wood, stripping rings of bark around trunks. The damage they do can weaken, even kill your plants. Although many homeowners are quick to pull out the chemical warfare and spray the little pests to death, pesticides can upset the balance in the environment of the landscape. Most people aren't too keen on handling these dusts and sprays either. Who knows what they're doing to our health?

Today more than ever, the homeowner has a choice. Safe and effective means of controlling insect pests in the backyard are continually being researched and tried. New techniques are known. New products that don't harm the environment or the people who use them are available. Some methods have still to be tested, but the homeowner can turn to a host of potential insect controls to find out what works best in his or her backyard.

Of course, many of the pest problems you face in the landscape can be prevented by following good gardening practices and giving your plants the care they need. Remember, your plants don't want to be eaten. The healthier they are, the better able they will be to fend off intruders themselves.

Remember, too, that you don't have to eradicate all insects. Some are beneficial to your yard. You don't even have to kill off the last pest insect. The good and bad insects tend to keep each other under control.

The best approach to insect pest control in the landscape is a well-rounded one that includes general good garden practices, prevention, and when needed, safe controls. With such an approach, your landscape can be beautiful and healthy year after year.

## IDENTIFYING THE PEST

Obviously, one of the most important steps in controlling and preventing insect pests is identification.

Voracious little pests, weevils can chew rhododendron leaves down to their bare bones.

241

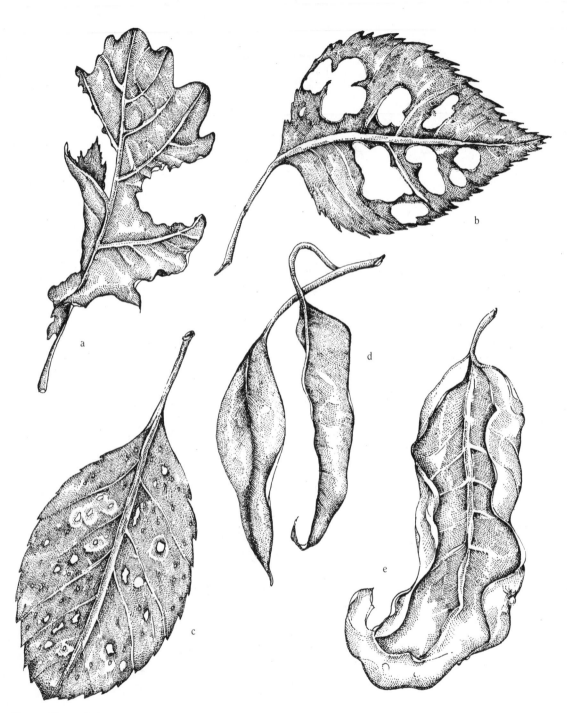

Signs of insect damage on leaves include (*a*) chewed sections, (*b*) holes, (*c*) spots, (*d*) wilting, (*e*) curling.

Once you spot a symptom that makes you suspect an insect pest problem, start looking for the culprits themselves. In most cases, insect pests attack the plant's youngest and newest growth. So, as you walk through your landscape, randomly check the newest growth of each group of plants, first looking at the upper leaf surfaces, then the undersides of the leaves (where most insects and their eggs are located), and finally check the point where leaves

From roses to rags—Japanese beetles can tear up these beautiful blossoms.

When you find a problem on a landscape plant, you will need to know what has caused it before you'll be able to effectively control the culprit.

## Look for Symptoms

Learn to recognize the signs of insect attack. The symptoms sometimes can look like those of disease. Some of the most common symptoms of insect pest attack include the following:

- Leaves chewed from the outside edge
- Holes chewed in the leaves
- Complete defoliation
- Wilting and discoloring of the leaves
- Discolored speckles on the leaves
- Leaves curled

Aphids can congregate in great numbers on the stems and leaves of landscape plants.

attach themselves to the stem. Although pests can also strike roots, and many pests work at night, this daytime search will reveal most problems.

There are a number of good books for identifying pest insects. *Rodale's Color Handbook of Garden Insects, Rodale's Garden Insect, Disease and Weed Identification Guide,* and *The Golden Guide to Insect Pests* are particularly easy to use.

### Colored Sticky Traps

These attract pests with color and hold them with a sticky material, such as Tanglefoot or motor oil. Yellow traps are good for catching aphids. Spherical red traps catch codling moths. White 8-by-10-inch sticky panels, hung from an outer branch of a holly bush, 1 to 2 feet off the ground, will let you know when flea beetles are around. Place these traps

These traps might not look too sexy, but they do emit pheromones, specifically insect sex hormones, to lure pests inside.

around your landscape two to three weeks before you expect the insects to emerge. Do not leave these traps out for more than three or four weeks after they have started attracting pests, or beneficial insects may be trapped as well.

### Pheromone Traps

Some insect pests can be caught and monitored with pheromone traps. These devices release an odor, based on the insect's sex hormones. The insects are lured into a bag or a sticky trap. Place pheromone traps in the landscape two to three weeks before the expected emergence of the target pests and keep your eye on them. When using such a trap, be careful not to rub any other strong scent such as perfume or bug spray on it. As soon as you've caught the pest you're after, begin control measures.

There are pheromone lures available now for more than 30 species of insects. By the way, you might be interested to know that scientists at the U.S. Department of Agriculture's (USDA) Agricultural Research Center, in Beltsville, Maryland, are using pheromones without traps to attract beneficial insects to prey on pests. Watch for new developments in this area.

In both cases, trap placement is very important. Put it near the plant you want to protect. If you are trying to catch a pest with color, try to keep an area 12 to 18 inches around the trap clear. Don't place traps above the plant; many pests do not look up for color. Hanging the traps on the south side of each tree or group of plants often will catch the first arrivals.

## CONTROLLING INSECT PESTS

Once you detect the presence of an insect pest, you have several options for controlling that pest before it causes any serious harm to the landscape. You want to remove or kill as many of the pests as you can so their population never gets out of control.

## Use Early Warning Devices

The sooner you note the presence of an insect pest in your landscape, the easier it will be to control it. You can expect a much higher rate of success if you begin controlling pests when populations are small. If a particular pest visits your landscape year after year, but you aren't exactly sure when the infestation starts, set up a trap to catch them a couple of weeks before expected emergence. Keep an eye on the trap, and as soon as you see some of the culprits in question, immediately begin control measures. You can choose from a number of different kinds of early warning devices.

## Traps and Manual Control Techniques

Before you reach for any sprays or dusts, even though they might be natural or safe, consider trapping or some other physical means of removing insect pests from plants. Often these solutions to the problem are the safest, surest, and least expensive.

### Cover Traps

Some pests seek protection from the hot sun during daylight hours. A simple piece of board or a length of empty garden hose can provide just the right shelter for these shade-loving insects. Slugs happily crawl under boards, and earwigs readily crawl into a piece of garden hose. Check these traps twice a day and deposit any inhabitants in a can of water containing a little kerosene.

### Handpicking

Perhaps the oldest method of safe and effective insect control, handpicking can be very effective, especially in the early stages of infestation. It is an easy way to make a sizable dent in the pest population immediately, and it can prevent a population explosion. Pick off bugs and squash them between your fingers, if you feel so mean, or just drop them in a can of kerosene or soapy water. Wear tight-fitting rubber gloves if you don't like the idea of handling insects.

Handpicking can be slow, especially if you must hunt for the little buggers. One way to bring the pests into sight is to spray water on the plants. Then wait for the pests to crawl from their wet hiding places to the tops of the plants, where you can just snatch them right up.

Oh, and don't leave behind any eggs. Look for them on the undersides of leaves, on stems, and on the bark of trees, and scrape them off.

### Sticky Traps

Sticky traps can be used to control insects as well as tell of their arrival in your yard. You can purchase them or make your own. To make a trap for aphids and whiteflies, take a 10-by-10-inch piece of Masonite or other sturdy material that is colored school-bus yellow and cover it with something sticky such as Tack Trap, motor oil, or petroleum jelly. Hang the trap in your landscape so that it is adjacent to, but not above, susceptible plants. These traps can catch enormous numbers of whiteflies and aphids, reducing their population long enough for natural predators to exert control. As said earlier, do not leave these traps out for more than three or four weeks, or beneficial insects, as well as pests, may be trapped.

### Water Spray

Certain insects can be taken care of by bombarding infested plants with a forceful spray of water. Don't forget to hit the undersides of leaves where many insects and their eggs reside. Aphids, mealybugs, and spider mites can all be controlled this way. Spraying plants with water several days in succession will disrupt the pests' breeding and hatching cycle and can eliminate the population altogether.

When spraying plants, do it in the early morning. Use a hose with a nozzle that will give you a fine spray of water. Turn the water on high and thoroughly spray the infested plant. You must perform this little routine at least three times, either three days in a row or every other day. Besides washing off the pests that are already feeding on your plants, you want to eliminate those that will hatch from eggs laid before you began spraying.

# Natural Sprays and Dusts

If handpicking and mechanical controls don't work, you can try a spray or dust to get rid of insect pests. Most products can be applied in either form, but sprays are a little easier to use and generally provide more thorough and even coverage than dusts. You can use virtually any type of sprayer, from a plastic hand-held bottle to a large garden sprayer, depending on the size of the plant or the area of yard you need to cover. (See the source list at the back of this book for a number of companies that produce quality sprayers.) Following are several different types of sprays and dusts, with details on how to use them.

## Bug Juice

Bug juice is a spray made from crushed insect pests and applied to the infested plants. Research has not proven that bug juice is effective, but some gardeners have reported success with it. Bug juice may indeed be a good control, because grinding up the insects could release their "alarm pheromone," or warning scent, which would frighten other insects away. Another possibility is that a few diseased bugs, when ground up and sprayed on plants, spread disease to live pests. Or, natural predators of the insect pest may be attracted by the smell of the spray.

To make bug juice, collect ½ cup of the problem insect and liquefy in a blender with 2 cups warm water. (Don't use your household blender! If you don't have an old blender jar, mash the insects with a mortar and pestle, add water, and proceed.) Strain the liquid through cheesecloth or a fine strainer. Dilute ¼ cup of the strained liquid with 1 or 2 cups water in a small hand sprayer. Spray stems and both sides of an infested plant's leaves. Respray after rains. Leftover liquid can be frozen for a year or longer.

## Insecticidal Soap

Don't confuse insecticidal soap with homemade kitchen soap sprays. The commercial product has been specially formulated to kill certain insects, while not harming beneficial insects. It is biode-gradable and breaks down within 7 to 14 days so it does not harm plants or the environment. And, it is safe to use around animals and people. While homemade brews might be effective, only commercial soap spray is recommended for uniform performance. It is easy to use and is effective against many insect pests, including aphids, mites, and whiteflies.

When dealing with a heavy infestation, spray plants every two to three days for two weeks. Set the sprayer for medium droplet size and strong pressure to thoroughly wet all surfaces of the plant from top to bottom. Insecticidal soap is a contact insecticide, so it must directly contact the insect to be effective. Don't forget to spray the undersides of leaves, where you will find most of the pests.

## Insecticidal Soap and Alcohol

You can increase the effectiveness of insecticidal soap by mixing it with isopropyl alcohol. Combine about ½ cup alcohol with each quart of soap. Alcohol alone can burn plants, but diluted in the soap spray, it penetrates the insect's waxy protective coating and carries the pesticide with it, bringing it in direct contact with the insect's body.

## Garlic Spray

We're all cautious about eating anything with garlic or onions when we're in the company of others, fearful that those we're talking with will turn and walk away at the smell of garlic breath. Well, apparently, garlic has that effect in the landscape. Homemade sprays from garlic, onions, or chives have been found to effectively repel certain insect pests. To make the spray, mix ½ cup finely chopped garlic cloves, onions, or chives with 1 pint water; then strain out the particles. Make two or three applications, one per week, repeating a spray after rain.

Researchers are working on a more potent brew made by soaking 10 to 15 finely minced garlic cloves in a pint of mineral oil for at least 24 hours. The oil is then strained. Two teaspoons of the oil are mixed with a quart of insecticidal soap spray and applied to infested plants. In some tests, the soap spray's effectiveness has been greatly improved by the garlic oil, even on pests not normally killed by the soap alone, but the full effectiveness of this spray is still unknown.

## Horticultural Oil Sprays

Horticultural oils work by smothering insect pests and their eggs. There are two grades of horticultural oil—the traditional heavier grade oil, which is often used as a preventive spray on fruit trees in early spring, and the newer light horticultural oils, which are very effective insect controls because they can be used on foliage without harming trees, even in the summer months.

The heavy horticultural oils have a viscosity of 100 to 200. If used indiscriminately on foliage, they can clog the pores of leaves and buds, cutting off respiration and killing the plant. These dormant oil sprays are designed to be used from fall through early spring on deciduous trees and shrubs. They should be applied when temperatures are above 40°F. Why spray plants in the winter when most insects are dormant themselves? Because the oil smothers insect eggs and overwintering adults and larvae hidden in the bark and foliage of trees and shrubs.

A newer type of oil, called superior horticultural spray oil, is lighter and less viscous (60 to 70) than heavy oil, and it evaporates much more quickly from leaves and stems. Any woody ornamental plant can tolerate a 2 percent solution of this oil, as long as the plant is healthy, soil moisture is adequate, and the relative humidity is low enough so that the oil will evaporate fairly rapidly. Two to 3 percent solutions can be very effective against mites and other soft-bodied sucking insects, and they have minimal impact on beneficial insects.

Light horticultural oil also suffocates insects. Use a lower concentration of oil on plants with hairy leaves. If you are uncertain about using the oil on a particular plant, test it on a few leaves first. Check the leaves in several days; if the tips and margins have turned yellow, do not use oil on that plant. Light horticultural oils may be used in spring, summer, or winter. Never spray a plant in full leaf when the soil around it is dry.

Horticultural oils do not remain on plants very long and are extremely low in toxicity to man, pets, and wildlife. They pose little threat to any of the natural enemies of your target pests.

## Horticultural Oils and Alcohol

Just as with insecticidal soap, when you add isopropyl alcohol to a horticultural oil mixture, you increase its effectiveness. To make such a solution, combine 1 cup alcohol and ½ teaspoon horticultural oil in 1 quart water. The alcohol kills the insects on contact, and the Volck oil stays on the plant to smother unseen young and eggs. This mixture can be sprayed every day or every two days until the pest population is reduced to a nondestructive level.

## Hot Pepper Spray

Another home concoction, hot pepper spray can be an effective insect control. Mix ½ cup finely chopped or ground hot peppers with 1 pint water. Strain the mixture to form a clear solution; then use this solution on your plants. Protect your eyes when mixing and using this solution. It can burn.

## New Developments in Sprays

A number of new products, which are still being researched, hold some promise of being effective pest controls someday. Watch gardening magazines for their introduction in the next few years.

**Antifeedant Sprays.** Antifeedants are chemicals produced by plants that, when sprayed on another plant, deter insects from eating that plant. Researchers have begun extracting antifeedants by distilling, boiling, or grinding plants and applying the liquid to infested plants. Many plants contain antifeedant substances: Peppermint contains a substance that seems to be effective against Colorado potato beetles. The Japanese flower glory-bower (*Clerodendron tricotomum*) apparently inhibits feeding of European corn borers, oriental tussock moth caterpillars, and tobacco cutworms, and certain chemicals in common sagebrush (*Artemisia tridentata*) repel Colorado potato beetles and southern armyworms. Seed of the neem tree (*Azardirachta indica*) contains a powerful antifeedant that scientists are now testing. Neem extract promises to be useful on a wide range of insects, and can be used as a spray, soil drench, or systemic insecticide.

Current research probably will lead to the introduction of a number of commercial antifeedant products in the next few years. One product already available is Green Ban, which is made in Australia from kelp, English ivy, sage, garlic, and eucalyptus. You can obtain this product from Gardener's Supply Company. (See the source list in the back of this book for the address.)

**Caffeine.** Many of us know that caffeine affects our behavior; research is beginning to show that caffeine also disrupts the behavior of numerous insects, from tobacco budworms to mosquitoes. When exposed to caffeine, mosquito larvae cannot swim, mealworms cannot reproduce, and tobacco budworms lose their appetites, develop tremors, and die. When combined with other insecticides, caffeine multiplies their strength many times. Researchers found that when given a choice, most insects will avoid foods treated with caffeine. One of the drawbacks to using caffeine is that it is only effective in large quantities. Home gardeners eager to make their own insecticide must brew up coffee that is five to ten times stronger than normal, let it cool, and then either spray it as is, or mix it with insecticidal soap or light horticultural oil.

**Citrus Peel.** Research has also determined that citrus peels have insecticidal qualities. The effective substance is called limonene and is concentrated in the outer part of the peel. It can damage leaves and is used in very low concentrations. Researchers are testing limonene as a contact insecticide and a fumigant. Watch for new insect control products with citrus peel in them.

## Biological Controls

You can recruit a few volunteers to help you in the battle against insect pests. A variety of beneficial insects, bacteria, and viruses are willing to take arms against the insect pests that are ruining your landscape, and they may already be at work in the yard. Perhaps the best known of the biological controls are the predatory and parasitic insects, which attack and destroy pests. They are discussed a little later in this chapter. Below you'll find the microscopic creatures—the viruses and bacteria—that are

more than willing to ambush the troublesome insects in your yard.

### Bt (*Bacillus Thuringiensis*)

Bt is a parasitic bacterium usually used against leaf-eating caterpillars. It invades their digestive system and kills them. You can purchase Bt under a number of trade names, including Bactur, Biotrol, Dipel, Safer, and Thuricide. It comes in powder form and can be applied as a dust or diluted with water and sprayed on plants.

The timing of Bt applications is critical. It must be eaten by the caterpillars to be effective, so you want to apply it when the larvae are actually present. Generally, caterpillars are most active in the spring and late summer. Observe your plants closely during these times, and as soon as you see worms or caterpillars beginning to feed, spray or dust them with Bt. Thoroughly cover all parts of the plant leaves, especially the undersides. When using the powdered form of Bt, wet plants before you dust them. Dusting the undersurfaces as well as the top surfaces of leaves keeps Bt active longer, because the bacteria survive longer when not hit by direct sunlight. Reapply the dust after rain.

To make a foliar spray from powdered Bt, follow the directions on the container. Spray infested plants every 10 to 14 days until the pest is under control. To help the diluted powder adhere to plant leaves, add 1 tablespoon fish emulsion to each gallon of spray. A little commercial insecticidal soap or light horticultural oil also works as an adherent. The liquid concentrate formulation of Bt adheres well to plants.

Keep in mind that Bt breaks down in sunlight. The powdered form remains viable for only seven days after application, and the liquid spray for just 24 hours. Bt does not reproduce or overwinter in nature, so you must apply it each year as the pest caterpillar emerges. Stored in the container in a cool, dark place, the dry form will last at least three years. Once it has been mixed with water, it lasts just one year. If you store it at temperatures of 40°F to 50°F, you can use it indefinitely.

### Milky Spore Disease (*Bacillus Popilliae*)

Milky spore is a disease of insects caused by the

bacterium *Bacillus popilliae*. It often infects white grubs and can be used to control their populations in your yard. It infects more than 40 species of white grubs, but is most effective against and used almost exclusively to stop Japanese beetles. It is sold as a dust or wettable powder under the trade names Doom, Japidemic, or Grub Attack. You must apply the spores to large areas of the soil for it to be effective. Although it acts much more slowly than chemical pesticides, milky spore eventually reduces the beetle population and remains viable in the soil for many years. Do not use it in areas treated with insecticides.

### Grasshopper Spore Disease

Obviously this disease is used to control grasshoppers, but it is also effective against many species of cricket. It comes in powder form. Grasshoppers won't just gobble this up raw. It must first be mixed with flaked wheat bran. The grasshoppers will feed on the bran, and once inside, this spore disease reproduces and kills the pest. Grasshoppers will feed on their dead relatives, further spreading the spores through the population. Apply this spore disease in early summer, when grasshoppers are no more than ¾ inch long.

### New Developments in Biological Controls

Avermectin Insecticides. Avermectin insecticides, such as abamectic (Avid), are fermentation products of a soil-inhabiting streptomyces organism. They are very potent against mites, thrips, loopers, beetles, and other insects.

Viral Insecticides. MicroGeneSys has developed Preserve, a viral insecticide that infects the European sawfly. It is a naturally occurring virus, grown in the larvae of the European pine sawfly. More of these types of products will be appearing on the market in the coming years.

## The Last Resort— Botanical Poisons

If the traps, sprays, or parasites discussed above do not effectively solve a particular pest problem in your landscape, you may need to bring in the big guns—the botanical poisons. This sounds serious, and it is. These poisons have been extracted from various plants, and include pyrethrum, ryania, rotenone, and sabadilla. Although natural substances, they are deadly. They will kill off many of the insect pests that infest your plants, as well as beneficial insects, including honeybees. And you'll want to handle them carefully, too. There are some situations where botanical poisons are necessary, but use them as a last resort. (These products do break down fairly quickly, though, and so don't pose a great threat to the environment.)

You can minimize the impact of botanical poisons by using them carefully. If a botanical poison must be used while honeybees are pollinating, use pyrethrum rather than rotenone, and spray at dusk, when bees are least active. Even though it's more toxic to bees, pyrethrum breaks down more quickly—within six hours if the temperature is 55°F or higher. Foliar sprays of either pyrethrum or ryania are less toxic to bees than dusts. If a heavy dew is predicted, do not spray; the insecticide will not break down before the bees begin feeding in the morning.

### Nicotine Sulfate

Nicotine sulfate is a deadly poison. Use it with extreme care, if you must use it at all. It can be used to control aphids, borers, lace bugs, and treehoppers. Mix ¼ teaspoon nicotine sulfate with 5 cups water. Immediately before applying it, add a handful of soap flakes to the mixture.

### Pyrethrum

Made from the crushed dried flowers of the painted daisy, pyrethrum paralyzes many insects on contact. It acts quickly, passing directly through the skin of the insect and disrupting its nerve centers. The insect becomes disoriented and stunned. However, if an insect receives less than a lethal dose, it will revive completely. Pyrethrum residues do not persist in the environment, and their impact on pests lasts only six hours. It must contact the insect directly to be effective. Usually, two applications to the threatened plant, three to four days apart, will successfully control a pest problem.

Do not confuse this botanical insecticide with synthetic pyrethrins, like allethrin, or with the synthetic pyrethroids, which are altogether more complex and persistent types of chemicals, and have a much more devastating effect on beneficial insects and the environment.

**Pyrethrum Plus Alcohol.** We've already seen that alcohol boosts insecticidal soaps and other products; it can also make pyrethrum more effective. Again, it penetrates an insect's waxy protective coating, allowing the pyrethrum to move right on in and kill the pest. To make this solution, mix two parts alcohol with one part water, then add the pyrethrum in the concentration called for on the bottle. Do not get this mixture on your skin. If you do, wash with soap and water.

**Pyrethrum Blends.** In crisis situations, when the life of an important plant is seriously threatened by insect infestation and no other control has worked, you can raise the ante even higher. Potent blends of poisons are available that combine pyrethrum with rotenone, ryania, or both. In a typical blend, the pyrethrum serves as the immediate "knockdown" agent, while the rotenone or the ryania kill insects over a longer period. Apply these blends at dusk, after honeybees have returned to the hive.

**Timed-Release Pyrethrum.** You can now purchase pyrethrum that has been encapsulated so that it functions as a timed-release insecticide when sprayed onto plants. It adheres to the leaves of plants and remains potent for up to a week. Look for X-clude, by Whitmire Research Laboratory. (See the source list at the back of the book for the address.)

### Rotenone

Rotenone is refined from the roots of several tropical plants, including derris, cube barbasco, and timbo. When used properly, it doesn't harm humans, wildlife, or pets, but it is a very powerful insecticide and should be used with respect. It will kill beneficial insects, including ladybugs and honeybees, as well as pests. You can apply rotenone as a dust; however, less is needed if you dilute it with water and spray it on plants. Use it only at dusk, after the bees have returned to the hive. A 1 percent solution will take care of most insects. If you are dealing with Japanese beetles or weevils, or if the 1 percent

solution doesn't seem to be effective, increase the concentration to 5 percent. Rotenone remains potent for two or three days. If after ten days you do not see results, reapply. Because it is very toxic to fish, do not spray it around bodies of water.

### Ryania

Ryania is a mildly alkaline insecticide made from a resin (ryanodine) that is extracted from the ground stems of a shrub native to Trinidad. When insects ingest ryania along with their leafy lunch, they become fatally ill. To use this poison, mix ⅓ to ½ tablespoon ryania in 1 gallon water. Usually, two sprays, ten days apart, will be sufficient. Ryania is also available in combination with pyrethrum or diatomaceous earth. If stored in a cool, dry place, ryania can be used for years.

### Sabadilla

A Caribbean lily is the source of sabadilla. One of the safer of the poisons, it has little effect on mammals but is toxic to bees. It is available only as a dust. Apply it weekly on the undersides of the leaves of infested plants until pests are under control. Sabadilla isn't easy to find, but you can purchase it through mail-order catalogs.

## Insect Predators and Parasites

You are not alone in your battle against invading pest insects in your landscape. You have allies already in residence in your yard and garden. Songbirds and toads are constantly feasting on plant-eating insects. In addition, many species of resident beneficial insects devour thousands of insects each day. Learn to recognize these "good" insects and how to make them welcome in your landscape.

Many beneficial insects emerge later in the season than the enemy insects do. Consequently, homeowners may notice more pest problems early in the season than they do later, when the beneficials have arrived. Try not to succumb to the temptation to eradicate all insect pests immediately. To do so would be to deny the beneficial insects their food supply, and they will only stay in your yard and police it if there is something for them to eat. Your goal should be to maintain a balance of "good" and "bad" insects, so use pesticides sparingly early in the season before beneficials come on the scene.

## Create the Best Environment

While you can buy beneficial insects and introduce them to your landscape, it is far cheaper and probably more effective to simply encourage the beneficial species native to your area. Create the kind of environment they like. The more diverse the plantings in and around your yard and garden, the more attractive it will be to a wide variety of helpful insects. The more permanent plantings you have around the landscape—perennial beds, woodland gardens, groupings of shrubs—the more stable the habitat you offer for beneficials to reside in year after year. Some homeowners go so far as to set aside a special nursery, or insectary patch, where weeds, brambles, and wildflowers are encouraged to thrive, providing a haven for good bugs. These special plantings are most effective within 25 to 50 feet of the plants you are trying to protect, but they are effective up to 150 feet away. Hedgerows, windbreaks, and wooded patches also serve as nurseries for beneficials.

As for specific plants, parasitic wasps are especially fond of Queen Anne's lace and other members of the carrot family. Daisies, related flowers, and some evergreens provide a haven for all sorts of helpful insects.

Clyde Robin Seed Company (see the source list at the back of the book for the address) offers a wildflower mixture specially designed to attract and support beneficial insects. This mix produces an attractive wildflower garden with a secret agenda of supporting a beneficial insect population in your landscape. It contains seeds for evening primrose, wild buckwheat, baby blue eyes, candytuft, bishop's flower, blackeyed susan, strawflowers, nasturtiums, angelica, and yarrow.

Entomologist Linda Gilkeson has observed in her research that water is as important to maintaining a beneficial insect population as is food and shelter. Consider placing two birdbaths in the yard. To make one of them attractive to insects, stack several piles of small stones in it to allow the insects to drink water without the danger of drowning. Place this bath in among the flowers where birds are less likely to land. You don't want them eating the insects you are trying to attract. Put the birdbath out in the open where birds prefer to land so they can spot cats and other predators. This makes water available to both the good birds and the good bugs, while preventing the birds from gobbling up too many beneficials.

Following are descriptions of some of the predators and parasites that already might be lurking around your landscape, looking for some insect pest to pounce on. Get to know them so that you can provide the conditions that will make them happy residents in your yard, and they'll help keep pests in line.

## Assassin Bugs

How appropriate to employ the assassin bug in your army of pest controllers. Assassin bugs move rather clumsily and fly slowly—hard to imagine them being very helpful at catching and killing insect pests, but they do have lightning-fast front legs with which to snatch their victims. With their powerful beaks they pierce their catch and inject a paralyzing venom before devouring them completely. (This insect is also called the "kissing bug"!!) Assassin bugs will kill aphids, various caterpillars, Colorado potato beetles, Japanese beetles, leafhoppers, and Mexican bean beetles. They will also catch bees and butterflies.

Several species exist. Most are brown or black and range from ⅜ to 2 inches long. They have slender heads with protruding eyes and legs armed with sharp spines. They feed mostly on larvae and lay their eggs in the soil. Assassin bugs overwinter as adults, nymphs, or eggs. During the rest of the year you'll find them on alfalfa, camphorweed, plants in the carrot family, goldenrod, Mexican tea, and oleander. Do not pick them up; their bite stings.

## Bigeyed Bugs

Found in western North America, this insect preys on aphids, chinch bugs, leafhoppers, spider mites, and most immature insects. It has huge eyes and is grayish, with tiny black spots on its head and thorax. The adults hibernate in garden trash for the winter. Several generations are produced each year. Attract them to your yard with alfalfa, plants in the carrot family, goldenrod, Mexican tea, and oleander.

## Damsel Bugs

These damsels won't find themselves in distress, but any aphids, leafhoppers, or small caterpillars that cross their paths are likely to suffer distress as they become a meal for these beneficials. Damsel bugs may be black or yellowish, and are rather flat. They have front legs modified for grasping and fitted with fine spines for catching their prey.

## Damselflies

The damselfly has a small, slender body about ⅜ inch long. It likes to hide in flowers, but prowls over the rest of a plant as well. It attacks several insect pests, including aphids, leafhoppers, treehoppers, and many caterpillars and other immature insects. Attract damselflies by planting wildflowers. This insect is common throughout North America.

## European Earwigs

Although it can be a pest in its own right, some species of earwig are beneficial predators. Earwigs are about ¾ inch long and reddish brown, with short, leathery forewings and pincers on the tip of their abdomens. One to two generations occur each year.

Earwigs will help you control the common aphid as well as *Aphis pomi*, the aphid that attacks apples, plums, pears, spirea, dogwoods, flowering crabapples, and flowering quinces, among other plants. They are widespread throughout North America. Grow some wild plants in your landscape to attract them.

## Fireflies

Fireflies are well known for the summer light show they put on, but these insects have even more to offer. Both the adults and larvae eat insect pests, though the larvae are better predators than their parents. The larvae look like flat beetles with jaws. They emerge from eggs laid in the soil and will feed on slugs, mites, and small crawling insects.

## Ground Beetles

There are many different species of ground beetle. Most are about 1 inch long and black to purplish in color. They have hard shells and long legs. Adults overwinter in the soil, and only one generation is produced each year. Ground beetles feed at night on caterpillars, grubs, and slugs. They also eat the eggs or larvae of ants, aphids, Colorado potato beetles, flea beetles, gypsy moths, nematodes, spider mites, and thrips. Frisky little creatures, they will chase prey in trees and will pursue armyworms and tent caterpillars. Occasionally, they may dine on some other beneficial insect. Ground beetles like the shade of low vegetation. Attract them with camphorweed, evening primrose, pigweed, or any low-growing plants.

## Robber Flies

Found throughout North America, the adults and larvae of the robber fly will attack bees, beetles, flies, grasshoppers, grubs, leafhoppers, and wasps. The adult is ¼ to 1⅛ inches long and gray, with long legs and a hairy mouth. Some species have slender, tapering abdomens; others are so stocky they look like bumblebees. Robber flies overwinter in the soil as larvae.

## Rove Beetles

You can find rove beetles roaming around decaying plant and animal material, including piles of manure and compost. Various species are scattered throughout North America. The adults are ⅛ to 1¼ inch long. They have unusually slender bodies and extremely short wing covers. They may overwinter as larvae, pupae, or adults, and produce several generations each year. They eat mites, beetle larvae, aphids, and small worms.

## Soldier Beetles

Another insect you want protecting your landscape, the soldier beetle will attack aphids, various small beetles and caterpillars, grasshopper eggs, and spider mites. Soldier beetles are found throughout most of North America. Adult beetles are ½ inch long and black with a white thorax and head. They resemble fireflies, but they don't light up. In a year, one or two generations may occur. They overwinter in the soil as mature larvae. You can lure these soldiers to your yard with wild lettuce, milkweed, hydrangea, and goldenrod.

## Spiders

Spiders aren't insects, but they're close enough.

There are all sorts of species, and they eat all sorts of pest insects. Some adult spiders will hibernate through the winter, but it's usually the eggs that pass the winter months. Spiders are one of the first predators to emerge in the spring. Any insect can be a target for spiders. You are likely to find some spiders in your yard no matter what's growing out there, but if you plant camphorweed, goldenrod, or asters, spiders will build webs in them and catch many insect pests for you.

### Syrphid Flies

Syrphid flies, also called flower flies or hover flies, resemble small wasps. Like hummingbirds, they appear to be motionless in flight even though they are spinning their wings like crazy. The adult is ½ inch long with short antennae and one pair of wings. The larva is a sightless green or brown maggot. Syrphids spend the winter as larvae. Adults feed on nectar and other sweet fluids and are important pollinators. It's the larvae that are the predators, eating aphids, leafhoppers, thrips, and a number of other soft-bodied pests. Plant coreopsis, baby blue eyes, candytuft, morning glory, or oleander to host these beneficials.

### Tachinid Flies

The tachinid is the most beneficial of all flies. The adult is often mistaken for a housefly, but it is larger, nearly ½ inch long. Their yellow larvae parasitize adult beetles, grasshoppers, caterpillars, armyworms, sawflies, and various other insects.

### Tiger Beetles

Tiger beetles make good predators. Their larvae trap and eat ants, aphids, caterpillars, and other crawling insects. Adult tiger beetles are ⅜ to ⅞ inch long, with big eyes, long antennae, and long, thin legs for running swiftly. They are metallically colored, from green, blue, and purple to black and bronze. Tiger beetles will pass the winter as either adults or larvae.

## Beneficial Insects and Organisms Available Commercially

You may not want to plant a wildflower patch or set up a birdbath to attract beneficials. They just might

Although soldier beetles may already be present in your yard, they are also available commercially. Release them in your backyard to help control aphids, small beetles and caterpillars, grasshoppers, and spider mites.

not fit in with the landscape design around your home. You can purchase beneficial insects and release them in your backyard. This isn't easy, though. You might let a bunch of bugs loose into the environment, only to see them all fly away, and you'll see all the money you spent flying away with them. But if you are willing to make the effort to determine the right time to release these pest-fighters and follow the technique correctly, commercial beneficial insects can help you.

Timing is critical. You want to introduce predatory and parasitic insects before pests get out of hand, but when there are sufficient numbers of them to keep the beneficials busy and well fed. Unless they find insects to eat and the right plants to shelter them, they will go elsewhere. If you plan to buy beneficials, consider the type of environment they need. If your backyard doesn't provide suitable living conditions, you'll have to make it more comfortable for the insects you want to bring in. Following are descriptions of the various predators and parasites that might be able to help you control the insect pests in your landscape, along with information on how to introduce them to your backyard and keep them there.

### Aphid Midges

If you are having serious problems with aphids, consider recruiting the assistance of aphid midges. These North American natives are hardy little insects. The small orange larvae have a voracious appetite for many species of aphids. Midges are sold in the pupal stages. When the adults emerge, each female will go looking for aphids on which to lay her eggs. She will lay about 250 eggs. The larvae that hatch will then eat the aphids. The entire life cycle of aphid midges lasts only about three weeks in the summer, and they increase quickly.

### Beneficial Fungi

Certain fungi attack harmful root knot nematodes. One fungus forms rings that close around nematodes when they pass through the opening of the rings. Another fungus is a parasite of nematode eggs. The third attacks nematodes that are already within plant roots. Beneficial fungi are sold by the pound, and are available from Natural Garden Company and Necessary Trading Company. (See the source list at the back of the book for the addresses.) Three pounds will cover 100 square feet of garden; 10 pounds covers 350 square feet.

### Beneficial Nematodes

Not all nematodes are nasty. Certain species will help you control pests. These soil-dwelling worms burrow inside maggots of pests and reproduce. They release bacteria, which then kill the maggots.

The nematode *Neoaplectana carpocapsae* attacks black vine weevils, chinch bugs, cutworms, Japanese beetle grubs, pine weevils, sod webworms, strawberry weevils, wireworms, and the larvae of cucumber beetles, flea beetles, gypsy moths, and squash vine borers. It will not harm beneficial insects or earthworms.

Beneficial nematodes are sold in packages of 1,000,000 to 10,000,000. They look like powder and can be stored in your refrigerator for up to three months. Mix them with water and use a sprayer or sprinkling can to introduce them into the soil. If you are trying to control borers or other pests that dwell deep in the soil, apply the nematode solution with a syringe to ensure that it gets deep enough into the ground. To treat container-grown plants, apply 5,000 nematodes to each gallon of soil. In the landscape, use 50,000 around each large plant, such as an azalea. Water the nematodes into the soil around the base of your plants in the early spring. You should see an effect within five days, but allow two months for maximum control.

Nematodes will overwinter in the soil as far north as Minnesota, but their survival rate is not high enough to provide effective insect control the following season. Only the infective juvenile stage of the nematode is functional as an insect control.

### Green Lacewing Larvae

Of all the beneficial insects you can buy through the mail, green lacewings (*Chrysopa carnea*) are probably the most effective. Various species occur throughout North America, but all have a slender body and delicate long green wings. They are ½ to ¾ inch long. The adults eat pollen, nectar, and honeydew. It's the larvae that feed on pest insects. They are yellowish gray with brown marks and tufts of long hair, and they grow to about ⅜ inch long. Their most distinctive feature is a pair of long, thin jaws, which curve together like ice tongs. Three to four generations are produced each year. Lacewings pass the winter in the pupal stage in cocoons.

The insects they attack include aphids, mealybugs, mites, scale insects, whiteflies, and the eggs of caterpillars, mites, thrips, and other small pests. Ravenous little creatures, they can eat up to 60 aphids an hour. By boosting your landscape's natural lacewing population in the early summer, you can get a jump on these insect pests. Lacewings cannot bear the cold, so wait until the average air temperature is at least 70°F.

You can purchase lacewings in egg or larval form. Eggs are harder to handle. Purchase approximately 1,000 lacewing larvae to cover an area of about 1,000 square feet. They like to eat each other, so release them as soon as you receive them, simply placing them in different areas of the yard.

If you've ordered eggs, don't be surprised to find some larvae in the container; the eggs may have hatched in shipment. As mentioned, a little more care and effort is required to place them in your landscape. If possible, lodge them gently in crevices, in spaces between petals, or in flowers. If you really want to be careful about placing them, take a 1-by-1½-inch square piece of facial tissue and fold it to make a small sling for the egg; then tape or pin it to infested plants.

You will probably not see evidence of the larvae's work immediately, as you would with a chemical insecticide. These insects do most of their hunting in their last larval phase, just before adulthood. Expect the younger, smaller larvae to attack the younger, smaller pests, and the larger, older larvae to attack the larger, older pests.

To keep your lacewings happy and to keep them in your yard, you can offer them a few bonuses for staying. Place Wheast around the yard and garden. This is a sweetened dairy product sold as food for beneficial insects. Lacewing adults also eat a mixture made from one part sugar and one part brewer's yeast in water. Set this mixture near plants that are vulnerable to the pests you want lacewings to control. Finally, if they suit your landscape design, plant some wild carrot, yarrow, or oleander, and lacewings will feel right at home.

## Ladybugs

When we think of beneficial insects, the first to come to mind are the ladybugs, and how nice it is that these rather endearing little orange-colored beetles with black spots are friends of the homeowner rather than foes. Both the larvae and the adults eat small insects. They can eat up to 40 aphids an hour and will also make meals of thrips, mealybugs, various small larvae, beetle grubs, scale insects, spider mites, whiteflies, and other soft-bodied pests, as well as insect eggs.

Ladybugs reverse their coloring from larval to adult stage. The beetles are orange with black spots and the grubs black with orange spots. The larvae are about ½ inch long and are usually covered with spines. The eggs are yellow. Only one generation occurs each year. In the East and Midwest, ladybugs

When releasing ladybugs in your yard, don't simply let them fly off into the air. Place groups of them at the base of plants, or gently set them on the leaves.

overwinter in weedy areas or garden trash.

You'll need 3,000 ladybugs, or about 2 ounces, to control aphids in 1 acre of landscape. For 5,000 to 7,000 square feet, 500 ladybugs will suffice. Do not release them too early in the season; they'll leave your yard quickly if the food supply is low. If you're not sure whether the pest population in your yard will support all the ladybugs you've bought, release only some of them and store the rest in the refrigerator, where they'll last for up to three weeks. Release them late in the evening when dew has settled on the grass. If the ground is dry, lightly water the yard and garden. When releasing ladybugs, don't simply toss them into the air. Gently place handfuls of beetles at the base of your pest-ridden plants and immediately cover them with straw or hay. They should climb the plant and begin to hunt for food. Walk 20 to 30 paces and release another handful near another group of infested plants. Handle ladybugs gently so as not to excite them into flight. Under normal conditions, they will mate within 48 hours and produce offspring in two weeks.

To encourage ladybugs to stay in your yard, grow pollen and nectar plants such as yarrow, evergreen euonymus, coffeeberry, angelica, alfalfa, goldenrod, Mexican tea, morning glory, and oleander.

## Parasitic Wasps

Wasps—just hearing that name should scare pests off your landscape. Hearing it also scares homeowners, who fear the painful sting, but these parasitic wasps do not sting. They aren't interested in you, but they are interested in the insects you have in your backyard. A few different types are available commercially. Planting weeds and wildflowers, particularly those in the daisy and carrot families, will encourage wasps to remain in your yard. All of the wasps listed below are sold commercially as eggs. (See the source list at the back of the book for suppliers.)

Braconid Wasp. This wasp lays its eggs in the bodies of grubs and caterpillars. The larvae hatch and grow inside their hosts, weakening and often killing them; then they pupate on the backs of the hosts. Braconids attack aphids, cucumber beetles, cutworms, gypsy moths, tent caterpillars, and various other larvae.

Braconid wasps are sold commercially as eggs. The adults are just 1/16 to 5/8 inch long. They prefer humid, warm conditions with temperatures above 59°F.

Chalcid Wasp. Chalcid wasps seek out aphids, asparagus beetles, leafhoppers, scale insects, whiteflies, and various caterpillars and beetles. They lay their eggs in or on the pest. The larvae grow inside the pest, weakening and eventually killing it. Some adults also feed directly on the host. The adult chalcid is just 1/16 to 3/8 inch long, so you'll probably not see them unless you take pains to do so. Chalcid wasps are found throughout North America.

Ichneumonid Wasp. The ichneumonid ranges in size from 1/8 to 3 inches long. Adults lay eggs in eastern tent caterpillars, cutworms, fall webworms, sawflies, European corn borers, and other larvae. Release these wasps when there are plenty of pest eggs around, but before any or many of them have hatched.

Trichogramma Wasp. The tiny trichogramma wasp kills the eggs of insect pests. The female wasp lays her eggs in the pest egg, and when the trichogramma egg hatches into a larva, it consumes its host. The release of trichogramma wasps is more effective when coupled with a spray of Bt (*Bacillus thuringiensis*) on infested plant leaves, and a sequence of three smaller releases is preferable to just one large release. It is important to make the three releases at two-week intervals in order to catch pests in the most vulnerable stages of their life cycle.

Among the pests which trichogramma wasps parasitize are aphids, armyworms, loopers, fall webworms, leaf rollers, gypsy moths, mealybugs, scale insects, whiteflies, and various beetle larvae.

Adult trichogramma parasites feed on nectar, which they obtain from weeds and wildflowers, particularly those in the daisy and carrot families. By planting some of these in your yard, you will encourage trichogramma wasps to stay.

## Praying Mantids

These insects are quite distinguished, with their long, slender bodies. Various species are found throughout North America. They may be green or brownish and are about 2 inches long. They have papery wings and enlarged front legs adapted for grasping. Mantids overwinter in the egg stage. They deposit their eggs on twigs and grass stems in an egg case that looks like it was made from papier-mâché. Each case contains 200 or more eggs. One generation of mantids occurs each year.

When you buy praying mantid egg cases, you may get more than you bargained for. Unlike most of the other beneficials, the mantids prey on all insects, including each other. Each egg case may produce a couple hundred hungry little mantids, but they will probably eat each other before they start working on your pest problem. The few that do survive will establish territories and drive off others of their kind. No matter how many egg cases you set out, by midsummer, you will probably find only two or three mantids in a 20-by-40-foot garden. At this rate, those mantids will have cost you a couple dollars each, and you probably already have some occurring naturally in your backyard anyway.

If this hasn't discouraged you, and you still

want to purchase mantids, try about three egg cases for 2,000 to 3,000 square feet of garden. To increase the young mantids' survival rate, put the egg cases in a screen-covered box. Check them every day after the trees begin to leaf out. Provide them with water, and after two days separate the newborns before they start eyeing one another. Scatter them around the garden, orchard, and flower beds. They will still drive off many of their brothers and sisters, but coverage should still be fairly good, and you may even have a generation that will reproduce for next year.

### Predatory Mites
Predatory mites will attack Mexican bean beetles, spider mites, and greenhouse mites. Package instructions will suggest appropriate quantities of mites to release. One release per season should be adequate. After control is gained, some predatory mites will remain to provide continued assistance throughout the growing season. Mites flourish in warm weather with temperatures averaging between 68°F and 86°F. If daytime temperatures are too low, their reproductive rate slows. If dry conditions occur, mist plants to provide necessary moisture for these mites.

## Animal Predators

In addition to the little army of soldier beetles, assassin bugs, and other insects that will police your yard for pests, you can enlist the aid of some big guys—birds, bats, and lizards, for example. A number of animals eagerly gobble up grubs or binge on beetles. Of course, these animals can make pests of themselves. The skunk is a voracious eater of grubs and larvae, but it can also tear up your seedlings while looking for them. So you'll have to keep an eye on these animals and decide which ones you are happy to have in your yard keeping down the insect pests and which ones aren't worth the trouble.

### Bats
Bats bring to our minds images of vampires, fangs, and bites in the neck. We fear them because they sometimes carry rabies. Their erratic flying patterns do seem a little crazed, but these maligned little mammals do not bother humans unless they are cornered or provoked. They aren't interested in biting your neck, either. They'd much rather make a meal of insects, including many of the pests that cause problems in your yard and garden. A single bat will eat over 1,000 mosquitoes a night. So, welcome their frantic flight around your home in the early evening.

### Birds
Songbirds are seldom credited for all their help in controlling landscape pests. Although many adult songbirds eat seeds, baby birds cannot digest seeds and must be fed fresh insects. Increase your yard's bird population and you'll reduce the pest population.

Many people feed birds during the winter months, and that is certainly an important step toward maintaining a good-sized bird population in your area. However, if you want to keep those birds around during the gardening season, don't stop feeding them when spring arrives. Put out less food, less often. This will encourage them to stay around without making them entirely dependent on the feeder.

The best backyard for birds will have plants that offer tasty berries and trees and shrubs where birds can take shelter and hide from the neighbor-

---

## Common Birds and the Insects They Eat

**Bluejays.** Cutworms

**Blackbirds.** Cutworms

**Chickadees.** Aphids, Colorado potato beetles, flea beetles, and leafminers

**Robins.** Colorado potato beetles, cutworms, leafminers, loopers, and slugs

**Sparrows.** Cabbage loopers, cucumber beetles, cutworms, and leafhoppers

**Starlings.** Cabbage loopers and Japanese beetles

**Warblers.** Aphids, cucumber beetles, and flea beetles

**Wrens.** Cutworms and leafhoppers

hood cats. Another very important feature for making the yard suitable for birds is water. You should have a supply of water all year long, even in the middle of winter. Sometimes water can be more important than food. Finally, for a landscape that birds will find truly luxuriant, build birdhouses and nesting platforms; then you'll be certain to have many parent birds flitting about collecting insects for their young.

Some of the best pest patrollers are the house wren, Baltimore oriole, and chickadee, but many other birds will help you control insect pests. Even the lowly starling and the pugnacious English sparrow devour literally thousands of pest insects or insect larvae each season.

### Frogs and Toads

Frogs and toads are princes when it comes to pest control. Well, maybe this is a bit of an exaggeration, but they do eat insects. Unfortunately, they don't discriminate between pests and beneficial insects. If presented with a large number of cutworms or potato beetles, they'll happily gobble them up, but they're just as likely to eat helpful spiders or beneficial insects. Frogs do happen to be particularly fond of sow bugs, and toads will devour ants, aphids, caterpillars, cutworms, slugs, spiders, and squash bugs, but in general, what they eat depends on what happens to be in your yard.

### Lizards

If you live in southern or western states, the lizards you see lolling about on some sunny rock or warm patch of ground will help keep the insect population down once they warm up and get moving. Lizards prefer stony, open terrain. Vertical surfaces like trees, fences, and walls of abandoned buildings are favorite haunts.

### Skunks

Skunks eat a wide variety of food, including yellow jackets, snakes, and mice, but their favorite fare is plant-eating insects and larvae. They are particularly good at rooting out grubs and cutworms. Of course, they also love fruit, but they usually gather pieces that have fallen to the ground. So, if you see a skunk waddling across the lawn, don't chase it, especially since it will probably spray you with a fragrance you won't enjoy wearing.

### Snakes

Stories about the paralyzing venom of rattlers, the bone-crushing grip of boa constrictors, and the deadly bite of slithering water moccasins are told all the time. No wonder the moment we see something slither through the grass we jump back. Most snakes that find their way into your backyard are completely harmless . . . at least to humans. They will swallow rodents and snap up bugs and beetles. Don't chase them away. You can surely bear their presence for the good they'll do in controlling insect and animal pests around your home.

When you begin to add up the very impressive number of pest insects consumed each day by the collection of insects and animals found in a balanced, active ecosystem, it gives you one more very good reason for not using garden chemicals that might harm these friends of the garden. If you attract and encourage beneficial insects and predatory animals, you will find that most of your insect problems will be reduced considerably. The process may take a few years, but the results will be worth the effort. And once you have achieved a landscape that balances a variety of plants, insects, and animals, no pest problem should get out of control. Remember, too, that when you have a system in which all the elements are balancing and controlling each other, you'll have less work to do.

## PREVENTING INSECT PESTS

Of course, the best way to control insects is to prevent them. By simply following good gardening and landscaping practices and taking a few precautionary steps to protect your plants in the first place, you can ward off most of the pests that want to chew away on the leaves and buds of your flowers, trees, and shrubs. Remember, just a little more effort up front saves hours of labor later on.

## Yard and Garden Cleanup

Perhaps the most important step you can take to maintain a pest-free and disease-free landscape is to keep the yard and garden neat and clean. Fallen decaying leaves and twigs make nice little shelters for slugs, snails, and other pests that hide out during the day, and they offer cozy spots where pests can settle down for the winter and wait for the warm spring, when they'll begin hunting for tasty young leaves and flower buds. Keeping your yard free of clutter and plant debris is essential to keeping down populations of insect pests.

## Fall Cleanup

Do your major garden cleanup in the fall. This is the time when the landscape is undressing from summer and getting ready for the cooler months of winter. Leaves and twigs have dropped to the ground and summer flowers have withered. Collect all the fallen matter and compost it, providing none of it has come from diseased plants. You should even gather up any organic mulch you've used, in case it harbors any insect pests or disease spores. Completely bare the soil in all your gardens where annuals have been, around perennials, and under all shrubs. That means no blades of straw, no stems or roots left in the ground to decompose—no exceptions.

Once your garden soil is cleared, cultivate it thoroughly, down 6 to 8 inches if possible. In perennial beds and close around shrubs, cultivate only an inch or two to avoid damaging the shallow root systems. This fall cultivation buries those insects that normally overwinter on the surface of the soil and brings to the surface those that prefer to snuggle a little deeper in the earth. The former suffocate and the latter will be eaten by birds.

This is also a good time to add any amendments to the soil. Work in any lime or compost that the landscape needs.

About two to three weeks after that first deep cultivation, shallowly rake any empty gardens or bare areas. This exposes more larvae to birds and other predators. Then, just leave the soil bare until it freezes hard. In those areas of the South where there is no freeze, leave the soil bare for at least a month before mulching it.

Once the soil has frozen hard, lay a 2- to 6-inch layer of organic mulch over all the bare soil in the garden and around the shrubs. Chopped leaves are ideal material for this task. For one thing, you'll have a good supply of them, but more importantly, they make excellent composting material next spring when the mulch comes off.

## Spring Cleanup

Having done a major cleanup in the fall, all you need to do in spring is remove the winter mulch from any areas containing spring bulbs and perennials that will be popping up just after the last frost time. You can leave the mulch around the shrubs and simply supplement it later in the season.

# Preventive Sprays

Fruit tree growers automatically spray their trees with dormant oil in the very early spring to help prevent insect problems. You should consider spraying ornamental trees, too. This is a valuable first line of defense against the coming season's insect pests.

## Horticultural Oil and Flowable Sulfur

Spraying deciduous shrubs or trees with oil will smother many of the eggs and larvae that may have overwintered in the bark. Do this in late winter or very early spring, before any leaf buds open—oil can damage foliage. For a more potent spring spray, combine horticultural oil (also called dormant oil) with a flowable sulfur fungicide. This combination spray controls many sucking and chewing insects, such as aphids, mealybugs, thrips, and whiteflies, as well as various forms of scale and red spider mites. At the same time, it destroys the eggs of many moths and assorted leaf rollers. Cover the entire surface of the bark with the oil, as high as you can reach. Remember, use this oil only on deciduous trees when they are leafless. Do not spray evergreen shrubs such as rhododendrons, azaleas, or hollies. You can, however, use *light* horticultural oil mixed with flowable sulfur fungicide on these plants.

# Setting up Barriers

Another way to prevent insects from getting to your ornamental plants is to deny them access with some kind of barrier.

## Bands for Trees

To discourage insects from climbing trees, consider placing bands around the trunks. Cotton quilt batting effectively prevents gypsy moths and other pests from scaling a trunk. You can also make a sticky barrier with Tanglefoot or some other sticky material. First tack or wire a strip of paper or cloth around the trunk, then smear the sticky substance on that so as not to damage the bark. Put up these barriers at the end of September to thwart the tree-climbing pests that overwinter in your trees.

## Diatomaceous Earth (D.E.)

D.E. acts as a barrier in the same way that hot coals would prevent most people from walking up to something. It actually consists of powdered diatoms—microscopic sea creatures composed primarily of silica (glass). The granules of this fine powder are very sharp; they scratch the bodies of soft-bodied pests such as caterpillars as they crawl toward a plant. The insect eventually dries up and dies. D.E. only works against larvae, grubs, and maggots. It does not harm earthworms.

You can trap gypsy moth larvae with a folded band like this one. When the caterpillars crawl down from the tree during the day, they'll take refuge in the dark, comforting fold, but only until you gather them from this hiding place and destroy them.

To apply D.E., dust it around the base of plants in the late evening, ideally after a light rain or after plants have been sprayed with a fine mist of water. Dust progressively upward from the ground, covering stems and leaves, especially the undersides of leaves. You can also spray it on plants. Put ¼ pound D.E. in a 5-gallon sprayer. Add 1 teaspoon of flax soap (available from paint supply stores) or insecticidal soap concentrate in a quart of warm water; then add more water, enough to make 5 gallons. Mix the solution well. Reapply it after rainstorms.

You can paint the trunks of shrubs and small trees with this mixture to protect them from caterpillar attack. Also, sprinkle a liberal amount of the dust on the ground around the trunks.

A D.E. barrier is worth trying against aphids, loopers, Colorado potato beetles, cutworms, slugs, snails, and thrips.

## Mulch

Among its other benefits, mulch can block some insect pests from reaching your plants, especially

This sticky band stops insects in their tracks as they climb the tree to feed on lush foliage.

those that overwinter just under the surface of the soil. At the very least, it controls weeds, which may harbor pests. Black plastic mulch or any of the new geotextile mulches laid on bare soil will prevent many larvae from emerging from the soil. Geotextile mulch can be particularly effective at keeping weevils away from azaleas. Cut a circle of material wide enough so that it extends half again wider than the width of the shrub all the way around. Fit the geotextile mulch snugly around the stem of the plant and fasten it firmly to the soil. Weevils will be unable to emerge from the soil to attack your azalea.

### Netting or Fleece

Nylon netting, fine screening, or agricultural fleece are all effective barriers, allowing sun, air, and rain to get through while keeping out insects. Cover transplants or newly seeded areas with the preferred material immediately to prevent insect egg laying and damage. Lay the barrier material directly on the plants and seal all the edges to the ground. Provide lots of extra material so that when the plants grow larger they don't strain against the covering.

### Resistant Plant Cultivars

One of the best ways to prevent pest problems is to grow plants that simply aren't bothered by insects. Over the years, researchers have developed many hybrids that are resistant to specific insect pests. Researchers are actively developing disease- and insect-resistant ornamental plants, as well as identifying species that naturally have these characteristics. Keep your eye on the market for new developments, and check seed catalogs for the resistant varieties that will grow best in your area.

### Learn Insect Emergence Times

One of the real keys to insect pest control is learning just when these little creatures will show up in your yard. Timing is crucial. If you are there at the right time with the right control, you can zap a problem before it has even begun. Each species of insect has its own fairly predictable pattern of birth, feeding, maturity, reproduction, wintering, and death. If you can learn these patterns and how they coincide with your yard and garden calendar, you'll be able to predict when problems might arise. It is especially important to know when overwintering pests emerge in your landscape to facilitate prevention measures.

The emergence times of insects vary from region to region, even neighborhood to neighborhood. Air temperature, moisture, and the availability of food all affect an insect's schedule. Check with your County Extension agent for a rough idea of when the problem insect typically appears, and then record these times. More importantly, observe the landscape yourself and mark down the date when you begin to see pests arrive. To make these emergence times easier to remember, connect them with some other event that happens in your yard, such as the budding or blooming of lilacs in the spring.

# Guide to Insect Pests

There are hundreds of insects that cause damage to flowers, trees, and shrubs. It would take years of studying to know all of them and their habits.

Fortunately, most of them won't do any serious damage to your landscape. A few exotic creatures may on occasion present themselves in your backyard and baffle you, but for the most part, a relatively small group of insects commonly occur on ornamental plants.

The following pest profiles will tell you a lot about the looks and lifestyles of these common insect pests. You'll find tips on the best methods of control, as well as several other suggestions for removing these pests or preventing their attack. The recommended control might not be the best one for your particular situation. You may have to try others to find which works best in your yard. At least you will be armed with an arsenal of weapons in your fight against the injurious insects of your backyard.

## INSECT Ant

## DESCRIPTION

The family of ants includes a wide variety of members. They may be black, brown, or reddish and can range in size from a mere $\frac{1}{16}$ inch to 1 inch long. The most distinctive physical feature of the ant is the very thin waist between the abdomen and thorax. Ants have elbowed antennae. They form colonies or nests in the ground where the queens reside and produce thousands of ant eggs. Most species have only one queen, and she may reign from 1 to 15 years.

fire ants

cornfield ants

## MOST OBVIOUS SYMPTOMS

Ants themselves don't do a lot of damage to plants, but they are indirectly responsible for certain problems in your landscape. Ants love sweets and are particularly fond of the honeydew produced by aphids. In order to keep themselves in constant supply, some species will go out and round up some corn root aphids and keep a herd of them near their nests. These aphids will then attack your plants. So, if you control the ants, you will control the aphids.

## BEST CONTROL STRATEGY

To control ants, destroy their nest and the queen. The best method is to make a hot pepper drench and pour it over as many ants as possible while digging up the nest. Make this hot pepper solution by boiling ½ cup finely chopped hot peppers in 1 pint water. Take the solution directly from the stove out to the yard and pour it on the ants.

# OPTIONS FOR CONTROLLING ANTS

## Traps and Mechanical Controls

### Sugar and Sponge Trap
Small infestations of ants might be handled easily by soaking a large-pored sponge with a thick sugar solution and setting it as a trap near the entrance of the nest. Ants should come running to it. Collect the sponge each day and rinse it out in a bucket with water and insecticidal soap. Clean the sponge with clear water and recharge it with the sugar solution for another round of ant trapping.

## Botanical Poisons

See the beginning of the chapter for more information on pyrethrum.

### Boric Acid
Boric acid poisons ants and can harm humans, too, if ingested, so be sure to keep it away from children and pets. Make a drench by mixing 3 cups water with 1 cup sugar and 4 teaspoons boric acid. Pour this mixture into the entrance of the ant colony. The ants will be attracted to the sugar and take the solution back into the colony to feed the queen. If this technique does not work the first time, add another ½ cup sugar and another teaspoon boric acid to the recipe and try again.

### Pyrethrum
Pyrethrum paralyzes ants on contact, but it is more effective if it is mixed with isopropyl alcohol, which helps the pyrethrum penetrate the ant's hard outer skin. Add 1 tablespoon alcohol to 1 pint prepared pyrethrum. This mix must come in direct contact with the ants to work, so you must dig up the colony and stir it around while spraying or pouring the drench right on the ants. With luck, one of those that gets drenched will be the queen.

# PREVENTING ANTS

## Fall Cleanup

Good garden sanitation will help cut down on both aphid and ant populations. A thorough spading of ant nests in the fall will not only disturb and possibly destroy the ant colony, but may destroy caches of aphid eggs that the ants have hidden in their nest.

## Barriers

### Chalk Dust
A circle of chalk dust around vulnerable plants can prevent ants from crossing the ground to get to plants. Replenish the chalk dust every few days when you see aphids on your plants.

### Diatomaceous Earth
Dust diatomaceous earth around the base of vulnerable plants to prevent ants and aphids from getting to those plants. Reapply after each rain.

## Animal Predators

Yellow-shafted flickers love to eat ants.

## Insect Predators Found in the Garden

Ground beetles and humpback flies attack ants.

# NOTES AND RESEARCH

Certain parasitic nematodes are being researched for their potential ability to control ant colonies. They may be available to consumers in the near future. The nematodes are mixed in with a sugar bait, which the ants carry into the nest. The bait, along with the nematodes, will be eaten by the ants, hopefully including the queen, and once ingested, the nematodes will kill the ants.

# Aphid

## DESCRIPTION

It's likely you'll get to know what these insects look like even though they are quite tiny. They'll pop up on almost any plant anywhere in the United States. Aphids are less than $1/10$ inch long. They have soft,

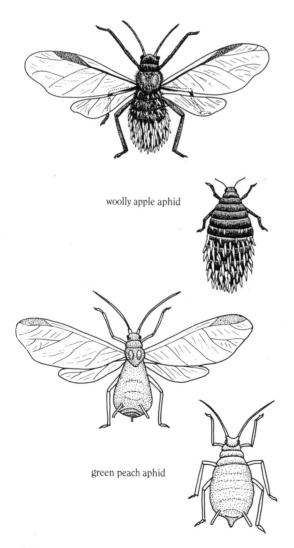

woolly apple aphid

green peach aphid

pear-shaped bodies, and depending on the exact species may be green, brown, black, or pink. They have long antennae and two tubelike projections at the rear of the abdomen, and may or may not have wings. They overwinter as eggs.

Aphid problems may be a symptom of too much nitrogen fertilizer, excessive pruning of trees and shrubs (which causes succulent sucker growth), or extravagant use of pesticides that kill off aphid predators and parasites. Switching to organic slow-release fertilizers and nontoxic pesticides and encouraging the natural enemies of aphids are important steps in reducing aphid problems.

## MOST OBVIOUS SYMPTOMS

Aphids suck the juice from leaves, fruit, and stems. The foliage of infested plants will curl, pucker, and yellow, and the plants' vigor will decline. Of great concern is the fact that aphids carry many viral diseases, such as mosaic. In addition, they excrete honeydew, which supports the growth of black sooty mold and attracts ants. They can do a lot of damage to seedlings and young trees. Check the undersides of leaves for small groups of aphids and you may find them clustered on the new buds, stems, and young leaves of your ornamentals. Aphids often spin cottony masses on the trunks and twigs of trees and shrubs.

Certain species, such as the corn root aphid, live in the soil and attack roots, bulbs, and corms. If you suspect this soil-dwelling form, the only way to verify it is to examine the roots of your plants for knots caused by the aphids. Ants often bring these soil-dwelling aphids to your plants. They will carry young aphids through their tunnels to plant roots, and will nurse aphids' eggs through the winter.

Besides the knotted roots, plants infested with root aphids show the same symptoms as those attacked by aboveground aphids—curled, yellowed foliage.

# BEST CONTROL STRATEGY

Light infestations of aphids are easy to control. Simply spray infested plants vigorously with water three times, once every other day, in the early morning. If this doesn't take care of them, use insecticidal soap every two to three days for two weeks. As a last resort, spray with pyrethrum.

If your plants are infested with root aphids, the only way to effectively control them is by controlling the ants that herd them. (See the entry on ants on page 262.) Thorough spading in fall disturbs ant nests and any caches of aphid eggs in them.

# MONITORING APHIDS

## Emergence Time

In warmer climates, aphids reproduce continually. In the North, the eggs overwinter on bark or in ground litter and the larvae emerge at the end of May or early June. Look for them on the undersides of leaves. If you see ants crawling on or around your plants, watch them to see if they are herding groups of aphids.

## Early Warning Devices

### Sticky Trap
You can buy or make a yellow sticky trap, which will attract aphids and let you know when they have arrived. Place them on or near vulnerable plants a week or two before you expect aphids to appear.

### Trap Crop
Nasturtiums can be used as a trap crop to spot early infestations of aphids, provided they fit in with your landscape design. Grow them in the garden, or within 10 to 15 feet of it. Aphids are attracted to nasturtiums, so if these pests are in your yard, they'll show up on the nasturtiums, which you can then destroy.

# OPTIONS FOR CONTROLLING APHIDS

## Natural Sprays

A variety of natural pesticides can be used against aphids. See the beginning of the chapter for more information on making and using the following list of sprays.

### Bug Juice
Crush some of the pests, mix them with water, and spray the strained liquid on infested plants.

### Garlic
Homemade sprays made of garlic have been found to effectively repel aphids. To make the spray, mix ½ cup finely chopped garlic cloves, onions, or chives with 1 pint water; then strain out the particles.

### Horticultural Oil
If aphids are a persistent problem on your shrubs, coat them entirely and evenly with a heavy horticultural spray during the dormant season. This will smother the eggs. The lighter, less viscous (60 to 70) oil, called superior horticultural spray oil, can be used during the growing season to control aphids.

### Hot Pepper
Hot pepper spray can be an effective insect control. Mix ½ cup finely chopped or ground hot peppers with 1 pint water. Strain the mixture to form a clear solution; then use this solution on your plants.

### Insecticidal Soap
Commercial insecticidal soap effectively controls aphids. Spray infested plants every two to three days for two weeks.

## Traps and Mechanical Controls

### Sticky Trap
If you don't mind the look of yellow sticky traps hanging around the yard, they can provide another effective means of controlling aphids.

### Handpicking

Handpicking will help reduce the aphid population. Simply squeeze the little pests in your fingers. Try to destroy the first generation, before eggs are laid.

## Botanical Poisons

See the beginning of the chapter for more information on nicotine sulfate, pyrethrum, and rotenone.

### Nicotine Sulfate

Mix ¼ teaspoon nicotine sulfate with 5 cups water. Immediately before applying it, add a handful of soap flakes.

### Pyrethrum

Pyrethrum is most effective if it is mixed with isopropyl alcohol, which helps the pyrethrum penetrate the aphid's skin. Add 1 tablespoon alcohol to 1 pint prepared pyrethrum. This mix must come in direct contact with the aphids to work.

### Rotenone

Rotenone can be sprayed or dusted on plants; a 1 percent concentration should kill aphids.

## Insect Predators and Parasites Available Commercially

You can bring either green lacewings, ladybugs, or braconid or chalcid wasps into your yard to feed on aphids.

## PREVENTING APHIDS

## Fall Cleanup

A thorough cleaning of the yard in fall eliminates any eggs that might be overwintering on leaf litter or twigs of trees and shrubs. It is an important step in preventing future infestations of aphids.

## Preventive Spray Programs

See the beginning of the chapter for more information on horticultural oil.

### Horticultural Oil

In late winter, before any leaf buds open, spray heavy horticultural oil on the bark of trees and shrubs to suffocate any overwintering eggs. Cover the entire surface of the plant.

### Seaweed

During the growing season, treat gardens with liquid seaweed extract to minimize aphid damage. Spray plants at transplant time and every four weeks after that.

## Barriers

### Diatomaceous Earth

If aphids are repeated visitors to certain plants in your yard, dust the whole plant with diatomaceous earth.

### Flour or Baking Powder

You might be able to slow down aphids by dusting the undersides of leaves with flour or baking powder. Dust the leaves frequently and reapply after rain.

## Animal Predators

Winter songbirds eagerly root through the bark of trees and gobble up as many aphid eggs as they can find. These birds include chickadees, nuthatches, purple finches, warblers, and chipping sparrows. During the summer, toads are good aphid-eaters.

## Insect Predators Found in the Garden

Assassin bugs, bigeyed bugs, chalcid wasps, damselflies, dance flies, the sluglike larvae of flower flies, ground beetles, hoverflies, the orange larvae of predatory midges, minute pirate bugs, predatory thrips, soldier beetles, and spiders all help to keep populations of aphids down.

## Other Preventive Steps

Make sure the air can circulate around vulnerable plants. Stagnant air around plants creates a more attractive environment for aphids.

## NOTES AND RESEARCH

Greenhouse growers have been reporting success with a small fly, *Aphidoletes aphidimyza*, as a bio-control for aphids on greenhouse crops such as carnations and chrysanthemums. Watch for developments of this control in the next few years.

INSECT # Armyworm

## DESCRIPTION

The fall armyworm is the caterpillar of a gray mottled moth. The armyworm is about 1½ inches long and has a somewhat hairy body. It is usually brown, but may be green or black, and has a black head. Three yellowish white hairlines stretch down its back from head to tail. You'll find a dark stripe along either side, and below that a wavy yellow line splotched with red. A white V or Y marks its head. The eggs are covered with hair and are laid in clusters of 50 to 150. As many as six generations can occur during a southern summer. Fall armyworms are found throughout most of North America, except the far north.

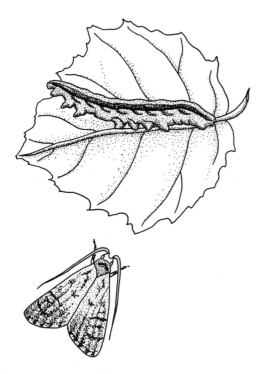

## MOST OBVIOUS SYMPTOMS

Armyworms cause problems in lawns. They sometimes travel in large groups, and usually feed at night. Their work on your lawn shows up as round, bare areas. In large numbers, they will eat the grass right down to the soil. The damage they do resembles that caused by sod webworms. If you lift up the dead sod in these areas, you'll find armyworms in the soil.

## BEST CONTROL STRATEGY

Spray the infested lawn or plants with Bt (*Bacillus thuringiensis*) every 10 to 14 days until the worms are under control. Reapply Bt after rain.

## MONITORING FALL ARMYWORMS

### Emergence Time

The fall armyworm is a tropical insect. Its primary residence in North America is in southern Florida and along the Gulf Coast, where it is active all year long. In the spring, swarms of moths fly North and lay eggs, and the caterpillars begin their devastation in the fall. In the deep South, they'll show up in midsummer, possibly even in early spring. Only one generation occurs each year in the North, but five to ten may develop in the South.

## OPTIONS FOR CONTROLLING FALL ARMYWORMS

### Insect Predators and Parasites Available Commercially

Trichogramma and braconid wasps and the nema-tode *Neoaplectana carpocapsae* parasitize fall armyworms.

## PREVENTING FALL ARMYWORMS

### Animal Predators

Various songbirds, skunks, and toads will eat the fall armyworms in your yard.

### Insect Predators Found in the Garden

Tachinid flies and ground beetles attack fall armyworms.

# INSECT *Asiatic Garden Beetle*

## DESCRIPTION

Asiatic garden beetles resemble Japanese beetles in shape. They are about ½ inch long, velvety, and chestnut-brown in color. They lay their eggs in the soil at the base of plants, and when the larvae hatch, they begin to feed on the plants. The grayish larvae are ¾ inch long, and curled in the shape of a C.

## MOST OBVIOUS SYMPTOMS

Both adults and larvae feed on ornamentals. The grubs attack at the roots. They are in the soil. The adults dine at night, and with their ravenous appetites can skeletonize leaves and flowers.

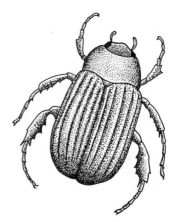

## BEST CONTROL STRATEGY

Handpick beetles and introduce beneficial nematodes to the soil. For long-range control, use milky spore disease (*Bacillus popilliae*). In the spring, carefully cultivate the soil around the affected plants to expose eggs, larvae, and pupae to the weather and to predator birds.

<u>INSECT</u> **Bagworm**

### DESCRIPTION

Bagworms are the larvae of moths. They spin silken bags around themselves, to which they attach pieces of the leaves they are eating. Full-grown, they measure 1 to 1¼ inches. Their bodies are brown with that portion inside the bag lighter than the rest. The adult male moths have black wings, and the females are wingless. The females lay their eggs in fall, and the eggs hatch the following May or June.

### MOST OBVIOUS SYMPTOMS

The foliage of infested trees is stripped or very ragged. You'll know the bagworm is at work when you see its leaf-covered pouches on your trees or shrubs.

### BEST CONTROL STRATEGY

The best way to remove these pests from plants is to simply handpick the bags with the insects and destroy them. Spray plants with Bt (*Bacillus thuringiensis*) from May 1 to June 1. Spray once, and repeat seven to ten days later if live bagworms are still present.

Pheromone traps that attract male bagworms and prevent them from finding females are also available. Put them up in August to reduce future populations.

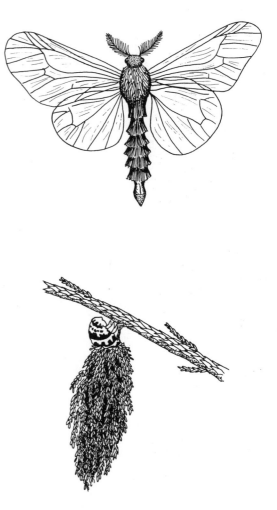

# INSECT Beetles

The world is full of all kinds of beetles that could do damage to your plants: the Asiatic garden beetle, the blister beetle, the Japanese beetle, and many, many others. There are so many, in fact, that one could write a whole book about them, so the author has chosen to focus only on those that are most likely to be found in your backyard. For the occasional exotic beetle insect that might wander over one of your plants, some general suggestions for control follow.

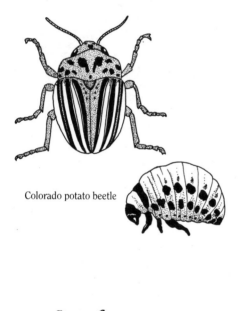

Colorado potato beetle

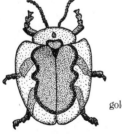

golden tortoise beetle

## DESCRIPTION

Beetles make up 40 percent of all insects. They come in a variety of colors, shapes, and sizes, but in general, all have hard, opaque wing covers that meet in a straight line down the middle of their backs. This characteristic gives beetles an armored appearance.

## MOST OBVIOUS SYMPTOMS

Beetles will eat leaves, stalks, and flowers. You may find damage ranging from small holes in the leaves of infested plants to large chunks ripped off the edges of leaves to defoliation of the entire plant.

## BEST CONTROL STRATEGY

Handpicking will immediately eliminate a lot if not all the insects from an infested plant. You can also try spraying plants with a mixture of pyrethrum and isopropyl alcohol, which should be applied every three to five days for two weeks. Make this solution by combining two parts alcohol with one part water and adding pyrethrum in the concentration recommended on the bottle.

Milky spore disease (*Bacillus popilliae*) also controls many beetles when spread over the lawn where the beetles lay their eggs, but it takes a few years to be completely effective. Cultivate your garden soil in the fall and again in the spring to expose beetle eggs, larvae, and pupae to the weather and to predator birds.

## NATURAL PREDATORS

Many songbirds, toads, rodents, and spiders like to snack on beetles.

## INSECT *Blister Beetle*

## DESCRIPTION

Blister beetles are very active and frequently appear in large numbers in the latter part of June and through July. They are slender and about ¾ inch long, with soft, flexible wing covers. The entire body is black or dark gray, and the wing covers may be marked with white stripes or margins. The adult chews foliage and fruit. It is a poisonous beetle, and its venom causes blisters if you happen to get it on your hand. The larvae feed on grasshopper eggs.

## MOST OBVIOUS SYMPTOMS

Rarely do blister beetles cause problems in the landscape; more often they will solve problems by preying on other insect pests. Every now and then, though, they can gather in swarms and defoliate a plant or seriously damage its blossoms.

## BEST CONTROL STRATEGY

First try handpicking and destroying these pests,

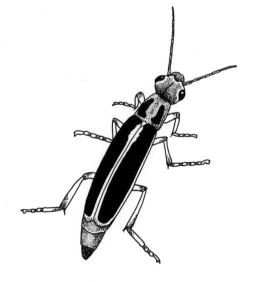

wearing gloves for protection. If the infestation is simply too large to control this way, spray plants with pyrethrum. This will paralyze blister beetles on contact. Usually, two applications made three to four days apart will remove them from your plants.

## MONITORING BLISTER BEETLES

### Emergence Time

The pupae of blister beetles overwinter in soil, and adults emerge in midsummer.

## OPTIONS FOR CONTROLLING BLISTER BEETLES

### Natural Sprays

#### Lime and Flour
Some homeowners have had success at controlling these pests by dusting infested plants with a mixture of equal parts of lime and flour. Apply this dust during the warmest time of day.

### Botanical Poisons

See the beginning of the chapter for more information on pyrethrum, rotenone, and sabadilla.

#### Pyrethrum
Pyrethrum is most effective if it is mixed with isopropyl alcohol, which helps the pyrethrum penetrate the beetle's skin. Add 1 tablespoon alcohol to 1 pint prepared pyrethrum. This mix must come in direct contact with the beetles to work.

#### Rotenone
You can apply rotenone as a dust; however, less is needed if you dilute it with water and spray it on

plants. A 1 percent solution will take care of most insects.

### Sabadilla
Apply sabadilla weekly on the undersides of the leaves of infested plants.

## PREVENTING BLISTER BEETLES

### Barriers

#### Coffee Grounds
Coffee grounds repel blister beetles. If it can be done discreetly, scatter some over the soil around each infested plant.

### Animal Predators

Baltimore orioles, bluebirds, and chickadees lunch on blister beetles.

# INSECT *Borers*

Just as there are zillions of beetles that could potentially chew the leaves off your landscape plants, there are many borers that tunnel into the trunks of trees and shrubs. These include the stalk borer, the cedar tree borer, the ash borer, the azalea stem borer, the maple borer, the poplar borer, and many, many others. Some of the more common species are discussed separately later on, but general information to help you control most borers follows.

## DESCRIPTION

Borers are the larvae of many different kinds of beetles and moths. They range in length from ½ inch to more than 2 inches. Usually they are white or pink with brown heads.

## MOST OBVIOUS SYMPTOMS

When borers tunnel their way into the soft stem of an herbaceous plant, they weaken the stem and often break it. If you notice that certain plants are bent over, or that they have wilted suddenly, check

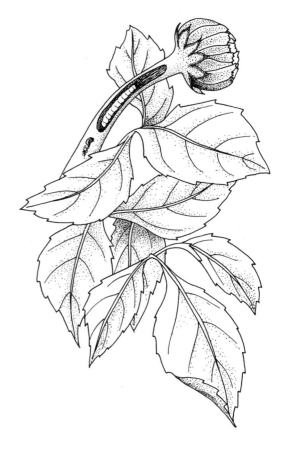

the stems for small holes, which might have been drilled by borers. Around the edge of the holes you will often see frass (excrement) or sap that has been pushed out by the insect.

In trees and shrubs, you will find holes in the trunk, often surrounded by sawdust. The tunnels inside the trunk may be straight, or they may wind around in all directions. The wood turns black. Some borers attack trees and shrubs near the ground, weakening them so much that they can be pushed over easily. The damage borers do makes trees vulnerable to disease.

# BEST CONTROL STRATEGY

To control borers in most situations, make a thorough examination of the shrub or tree before the spring season arrives, and cut and burn any dying or unhealthy-looking stems or branches that may contain borers. During the summer, check for borer holes and cut into them with a sharp knife. If the tunnels are fairly straight, you can kill borers by probing the hole with a flexible wire. By using a hooked wired, you can catch the worms and pull them out. If you find that the tunnels wind all over inside the trunk and you simply won't be able to track down borers with a wire, inject nicotine sulfate into each borer hole and plug the hole with chewing gum or putty.

# MONITORING BORERS

## Emergence Time

Look for borers in the spring.

# OPTIONS FOR CONTROLLING BORERS

## Mechanical Controls

### Cutting Infested Parts
Since the partly grown larvae pass the winter in the stems of shrubs or trees, prune infested branches and destroy them before the pest begins working in the spring. These branches are often marked by swollen areas with cracked bark that has broken away from the wood. You'll see numerous holes in the bark and wood.

If borers have infested your herbaceous plants, slit the stems in the area of the borer hole. Remove the insect and bind the stems together with green twine, available from garden centers and nurseries.

## Botanical Poisons

See the beginning of the chapter for more information on nicotine sulfate.

### Nicotine Sulfate
Many borers can be killed by nicotine sulfate. Make a solution from one part nicotine sulfate and four parts water. You can purchase a special garden syringe to inject this solution into borer tunnels, or you can dip a piece of cotton or soft cloth into the nicotine sulfate and stuff it into the hole. Seal the hole with gum or putty.

# PREVENTING BORERS

Although you do have good options for controlling borers, control is difficult, so try to prevent these pests from working their way into your trees and shrubs. Stressed trees and shrubs are most vulnerable. Maintain the vigor of your trees and shrubs with proper fertilization, watering, mulching, and pruning. Immediately coat any wounds that the tree or shrub suffers with tree paint or paraffin.

## Fall Cleanup

Keep your yard clean by gathering and destroying weeds and any stems or branches that might harbor eggs through the winter.

## Barriers

### Tree Wrap
New transplants are more vulnerable to attack than mature trees. To keep borers out of them, wrap

them with commercial borer wrap or paper and keep them wrapped for two years or until the trees are well established. Remove the wrap once a year to be sure no borers are active underneath; then rewrap.

### Other Preventive Steps

The best remedy of all is to discourage local borers before they get a chance to cause trouble. Many infestations in trees and shrubs can be prevented by avoiding mechanical injuries to bark and wood and by treating open wounds promptly.

## INSECT *Boxelder Bug*

### DESCRIPTION

Boxelder bugs look like squash bugs. They are brownish black with red markings and measure about ½ inch in length. The nymphs are bright red, and in fall you will often find them swarming around the bases of trees, fence posts, or walls.

### MOST OBVIOUS SYMPTOMS

Holes in the leaves, flowers, or fruit of your trees might mean boxelder bugs. These pests will infest maples and ashes and sometimes invade houses in large numbers.

### BEST CONTROL STRATEGY

Control boxelders by handpicking or by spraying infested plants with insecticidal soap, rotenone, or pyrethrum.

## INSECT *Bud Moth*

### DESCRIPTION

The overwintering eggs of bud moths begin hatching late in March, and small greenish white to gray-green caterpillars appear between the terminal leaves of young shoots in late April or early May. When fully grown, these caterpillars are a little more than ⅜ inch long. They build shelters for themselves by binding together leaves with their silk. When disturbed, they wiggle out of these hiding places and drop to the ground. Many of the larvae leave the shelters when fully grown and spin loose cocoons among the dead leaves or rubbish on the ground. Others pupate within the shelters used by the larvae. Bud moths are serious pests in the Pacific Northwest. Two common species are the holly bud moth (*Rhopobota naevana ilicifoliana*) and the verbena bud moth (*Endothenia hebesana*).

## MOST OBVIOUS SYMPTOMS

You'll notice that bud moths have infested your trees and shrubs when you see the leaves at the ends of branches bound together with silk. Bud moth larvae arrive about the middle of May. The caterpillars feed within these shelters, eating back the shoot so that the mass of leaves spun together dies and turns black. This blackened, chewed foliage usually does not drop until it has been pushed off by subsequent growth.

## BEST CONTROL STRATEGY

Control bud moth caterpillars by picking the infested leaves where the pests reside and destroying them. If you continue to find larvae crawling around on your plants, spray them with Bt (*Bacillus thuringiensis*). Make three applications, each ten days apart.

## PREVENTING BUD MOTHS

Clean up all plant debris in your yard in the fall and spray the undersides of leaves with *light* horticultural oil in March to smother any overwintering eggs.

## INSECT *Budworm*

## DESCRIPTION

The common spruce budworm is a caterpillar ½ to ¾ inch long and dark brown. Its parents are brown moths marked with gray spots. They arrive in the yard in June and July, when females lay clusters of flat, pale green eggs on the needles of trees. In ten days the eggs hatch. One generation of budworms occurs each year. A few of the most common species include the spruce budworm (*Choristoneura fumiferana*), the Jack pine budworm (*C. pinus*), and the Western spruce budworm (*C. occidentalis*).

## MOST OBVIOUS SYMPTOMS

One of the most destructive pests of evergreens, budworms chew the opening buds and needles of trees and shrubs, including Douglas fir, pine, larch, and hemlock. They usually web the needles together with their silk while they feed. Trees wilt and terminal shoots and new growth become deformed. Plants may be so weakened that they become prime targets for other insect pests.

## BEST CONTROL STRATEGY

Control budworms by handpicking or by pruning and destroying infested shoots. Spray infested trees with Bt (*Bacillus thuringiensis*) as the buds burst in spring. Tests in eastern Canadian forests showed an 80 percent mortality rate of spruce budworms in trees sprayed with Bt. Remember to reapply Bt after rains.

## PREVENTING BUDWORMS

### Animal Predators

Red squirrels eat budworms, as do birds. Encourage birds by providing birdhouses and alternate sources of food.

### Insect Predators Found in the Garden

Various wasp predators, spiders, spider mites, and trichogramma wasps are probably already out there hunting down any budworms that might be in your yard.

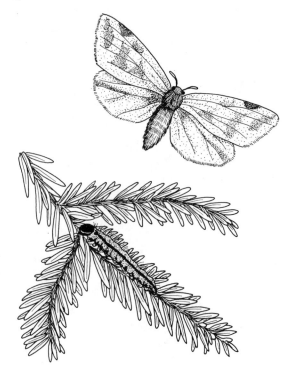

# INSECT *Cankerworm*

## DESCRIPTION

Also known as inchworms, these are striped brown and green worms about 1 inch long. You may have bumped into them at times when walking under a tree. They often drop from branches on fine silken threads. Some species attempt to mimic a twig by remaining stiff and motionless when disturbed. The adult males are grayish moths; adult females are wingless moths.

The fall cankerworm lays eggs in late fall, after frost, in compact masses on tree trunks or branches. These eggs are shaped like flowerpots and are brown or gray in color. Spring cankerworm eggs are brownish purple and can be found in clusters beneath the bark of trees in very early spring. Both fall and spring cankerworms can be found throughout most of North America.

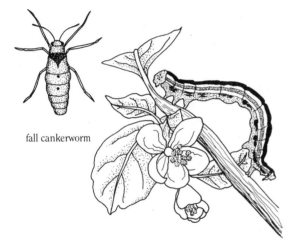

fall cankerworm

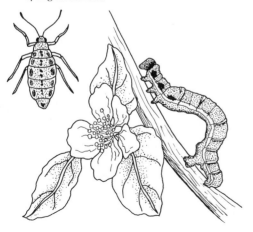

spring cankerworm

## MOST OBVIOUS SYMPTOMS

Cankerworms feed heavily on the foliage of plants and will skeletonize the leaves. Infested trees weaken each year. Not much fruit will mature. Cankerworms can defoliate a tree and kill it.

## BEST CONTROL STRATEGY

As soon as you find cankerworms on your trees, spray them with Bt (*Bacillus thuringiensis*) every 10 to 14 days until the pests are gone. If your trees are infested with eggs, begin spraying them once the flowers have finished blooming. Apply the Bt every two weeks for a month.

The best way to control cankerworms, though, is to prevent them. The following procedures will help you keep these insects off your plants.

## MONITORING CANKERWORMS

### Emergence Time

Larvae of the fall cankerworm emerge in the spring from the eggs laid the previous fall; then they begin to feed on new foliage. The spring cankerworm lays its eggs anytime between February and the end of April. These will hatch within a month's time, and the larvae will begin to eat.

## OPTIONS FOR CONTROLLING CANKERWORMS

### Insect Predators and Parasites Available Commercially

Chalcid and trichogramma wasps will help you control cankerworms.

## PREVENTING CANKERWORMS

### Fall Cleanup

The pupae of fall cankerworms lie in the soil during autumn. The adults emerge to lay eggs after the frost. So, till the soil around susceptible plants in the fall. This will bring cankerworms to the surface, where predators can more easily find them.

### Preventive Spray Programs

See the beginning of the chapter for more information on horticultural oil.

#### Horticultural Oil

Before the leaves begin to show in spring, spray trees with a heavy dormant oil to suffocate any overwintering eggs.

### Barriers

#### Sticky Band

Create a sticky band and place it around the trunk of vulnerable trees to catch the wingless females that must crawl up to lay their eggs. Wrap a band of cotton batting or heavy paper around each tree trunk and coat it with Tanglefoot or some other sticky material. Place them on trees from mid-October to December and again in February until late May.

### Animal Predators

Bluebirds, chickadees, nuthatches, tufted titmice, and other birds are terrific controls for cankerworm because they eat the eggs in the bark.

### Insect Predators Found in the Garden

Among the naturally occurring beneficial insects that kill cankerworms are the predatory beetles (such as ground beetles and soldier beetles), stinkbugs, tachinid flies, and a predatory mite, *Nothrus ovivorus*.

## INSECT *Casebearer*

### DESCRIPTION

Casebearers are the larvae of a brown moth. They make cigar-shaped cases, in which they reside for the winter. You will see these cases hanging from the branches of infested trees. The larvae are ⅕ to ¼ inch long with black heads. The adult female moth has a wingspan of about ⅖ inch. Her brown wings are fringed with hairs. This group of insects includes the elm casebearer (*Coleophora ulmifoliella*), the larch casebearer (*C. laricella*), and the pecan cigar casebearer (*C. laticornella*).

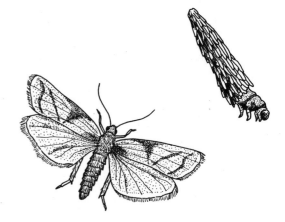

## MOST OBVIOUS SYMPTOMS

Casebearers attack foliage, mining inside leaves. The leaves turn brown and fall. The leaves of infested deciduous trees will have small holes in them and angular spots mined between the veins.

## BEST CONTROL STRATEGY

Control these pests by spraying trees with a dormant spray of lime sulfur before the buds open in spring, or you can spray them with pyrethrum or rotenone as soon as the leaves are fully developed. Encourage predator birds such as chickadees, nuthatches, and titmice.

# INSECT *Caterpillars*

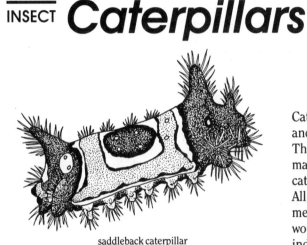

saddleback caterpillar
(poisonous hairs)

red-humped caterpillar

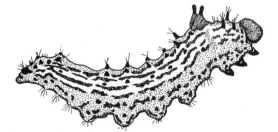

Caterpillars come in all shapes, sizes, and colors, and they can be found anywhere in North America. There are diamondback caterpillars, green-striped maple worms, hornworms, woolly bears, red-humped caterpillars, and hickory-horned devil caterpillars. All of these and many more are happy to make a meal of the leaves on your landscape plants. It would take pages and pages to discuss each one individually. Fortunately, the methods for controlling caterpillars are basically the same for all species. You'll find those methods in the following text. Still, some of the more common species are discussed in detail throughout this chapter.

## DESCRIPTION

Caterpillars are the wormlike larvae of moths and butterflies. They may be only ¼ inch long or more than 2 inches long. Some are fuzzy; others are smooth. Many are either green or brown, but others are brightly colored and have beautiful markings.

## MOST OBVIOUS SYMPTOMS

Caterpillars will eat the foliage and stems of just about any plant in your landscape. Holes in leaves and chunks taken from along their edges are typical signs of caterpillar attack. In a very short period of time, caterpillars can defoliate a plant.

## BEST CONTROL STRATEGY

Handpicking most caterpillars (use protection with poisonous types) can keep them from getting out of hand if you catch the infestation right away. Bt (*Bacillus thuringiensis*) kills most leaf-eating caterpillars. Dust all parts of the leaves, especially the undersides, reapplying the dust after rains. You can also make a foliar spray of Bt and apply it to infested plants every 10 to 14 days until the caterpillars are gone.

If the infestation gets out of control, spray all sides of the leaves with pyrethrum or a 1 percent solution of rotenone. Usually, two applications, three to four days apart, will solve the problem.

# INSECT **Chinch Bug**

## DESCRIPTION

Chinch bugs are so small and inconspicuous that they can destroy a lawn right under your eyes without being noticed. An adult is only about ⅕ inch long, with a black body. A black triangular pad

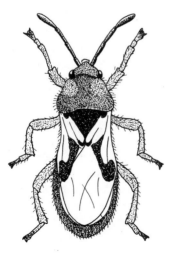

separates white, folded wings. Chinch bugs gather and accumulate down in lawns and suck the juices from grass. They thrive in hot, dry weather and become active when temperatures are in the high 70s. Chinch bugs occur throughout most of the country, but are worst in the Midwest, East, and South. The southern chinch bug (*Blissue insularis*) is the particular pest of the South. The hairy chinch bug (*B. hirtus*) infests lawns in the Northeast. Chinch bugs are encouraged by excess thatch, too little irrigation, and too much or too little nitrogen.

## MOST OBVIOUS SYMPTOMS

Suspect chinch bugs when you see large, distinct, circular patches, primarily in the sunny areas of your lawn, that turn yellow, then brown, and then die. These patches often first appear near sidewalks and streets, where heat is reflected onto the lawn, but soon they spread outward into the rest of the lawn. The yellowish spots show the greatest damage at their centers. Chinch bugs can do a lot of damage to lawns composed of St. Augustinegrass, but they'll also infest Kentucky bluegrass lawns and creeping bentgrass.

# BEST CONTROL STRATEGY

Monitor to catch the chinch bug infestation as soon as possible. If you've discovered the pests early, before too many of them have infested your lawn, remove them with a white cloth trap (at right, you'll find information on making and using this trap). Control heavy infestations with insecticidal soap. Spray the affected area of your lawn every two to three days for two weeks.

# MONITORING CHINCH BUGS

## Emergence Time

Overwintering bugs hibernate in the thatch and upper parts of the soil. They begin to become active in March. In southern climates, the chinch bug may continue to remain partially active throughout the winter.

In spring, check four or five different spots in the lawn each month during the season. Spread the grass apart with your hands and look at the surface of the soil. If you see small black or red bugs with white markings scurrying around the soil surface, your lawn is infested with chinch bugs.

## Early Warning Devices

### Can Trap

To check for chinch bugs, cut the bottom from a can, push it a few inches into the soil where grass is beginning to turn yellow, and fill it with warm water. If abundant, chinch bugs will float to the surface within a few minutes.

# OPTIONS FOR CONTROLLING CHINCH BUGS

## Traps and Mechanical Controls

### White Cloth Trap

In late spring, mark off two or three sections of lawn 2 feet square in both damaged and undamaged areas. Mix 2 tablespoons liquid detergent (or 1 tablespoon pyrethrum) into 1 gallon water and pour it evenly on each area with a sprinkling can. The soap irritates the chinch bugs, causing them to crawl up to the surface of the grass in 5 to 10 minutes. After wetting the spot, lay a piece of white cloth (flannel or agricultural fleece are best for this) over the area treated with the soapy water. Wait about 15 to 20 minutes, then look under the cloth to see if chinch bugs have crawled onto the white surface in order to escape the soap. Scrape the trapped bugs into a bucket with water and insecticidal soap. Where thatch layers are thick, you may need to pour several more gallons of soap solution on the test area to be sure to saturate the thatch and reach the chinch bugs. If your lawn is in good condition, 10 to 15 chinch bugs per square foot probably will not cause any problems, but chinch bugs can do more damage to a lawn under stress from compaction, poor irrigation or fertilization, or heavy thatch.

## Biological Controls

### Beauvaria Bassiana

A fungus, *Beauvaria bassiana*, causes disease in chinch bugs. You can purchase commercial forms of this fungus to apply to the soil, but its impact will not be seen until the following year.

# PREVENTING CHINCH BUGS

Keep your lawn healthy with proper watering and fertilizing and aerate the soil when it becomes compacted. If you grow St. Augustinegrass, plant 'Floratam'; it is resistant to chinch bugs.

Bigeyed bugs prey on chinch bugs. Encourage them to come stay in your yard.

# INSECT Cutworm

## DESCRIPTION

Several different species of cutworm are known. They occur throughout North America. These pests are plump, soft-bodied, dull grayish or brownish caterpillars, 1 to 2 inches long. You'll usually find them in a curled position—that is, if you find them; they feed at night and hide in the soil during the day. Cutworms develop into moths. The females lay their eggs in the soil. Cutworms overwinter either in the larval or pupal stage. Up to five generations can occur in one year.

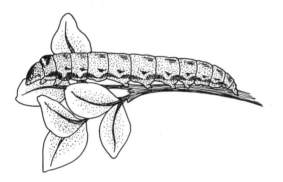

## MOST OBVIOUS SYMPTOMS

Cutworms work quickly and invisibly. Cutworms generally attack seedlings, severing the stems at or below the level of the soil. They work at night, so you won't catch them in the act of hacking down your landscape plants. Examine any toppled plants closely. If they look like they've been mowed, cutworms have probably been at work. If the cut is angled, rabbits might be the culprits. Sometimes cutworms attack plants from below the soil, damaging the root system and causing the plant to wilt and collapse.

## BEST CONTROL STRATEGY

You can't save seedlings once they've been attacked, so if cutworms are an annual problem in your yard, use a barrier to deny them access to your seedlings. Several different methods work well and are easy to use. You'll find details about them in the following text.

## MONITORING CUTWORMS

### Emergence Time

Most cutworms attack plants in early spring; however, many species produce new generations throughout the growing season. In the North, most cutworms overwinter as larvae and in the South, most overwinter as pupae.

## OPTIONS FOR CONTROLLING CUTWORMS

### Traps and Mechanical Controls

#### Cornmeal or Bran Trap

After putting out transplants, sprinkle ½ teaspoon

cornmeal or bran meal around each plant. Apply it in a circle leading away from the stem of the plant. Cutworms will eat the meal, which will swell inside them and kill them.

### Molasses Trap

Immobilize cutworms with molasses. Mix equal parts of hardwood sawdust and bran. Add enough molasses to make the mixture sticky and enough water to moisten it. Scatter a few spoonfuls around each plant at dusk. Thinking this is a treat, the cutworms will get caught in the sticky molasses, which will harden on their bodies and render them helpless.

### Handpicking

You can handpick cutworms at night. Look for them near the base of plants and just under the soil surface.

## Biological Controls

Bt (*Bacillus thuringiensis*) effectively controls some species. Dust seedlings and transplants at the soil level.

## Insect Predators and Parasites Available Commercially

Beneficial nematodes can be used to control cutworms. Apply them to the ground around your seedlings or transplants, using 50,000 around each plant. Braconid and trichogramma wasps also prey on cutworms.

## PREVENTING CUTWORMS

## Fall Cleanup

The adult moths lay eggs in the fall in weeds and grass, and the larvae or pupae overwinter in the soil. Clearing the yard of weeds in the fall is an important step in preventing cutworms from appearing next spring.

## Barriers

Using barriers to keep cutworms away from plants while they are young is perhaps the best way to control cutworm damage. One method that doesn't work is placing matchsticks or toothpicks around the stems of seedlings. The thought was that cutworms must curl their bodies around stems to cut through them and that the matchsticks would prevent this. Well, apparently the premise was incorrect; a ring of toothpicks won't keep cutworms from getting to seedlings and knocking them down. The various methods described here, though, are effective.

### Diatomaceous Earth

Dust diatomaceous earth around the base of your plants. It will scratch the bellies of cutworms and keep them from reaching your seedlings.

### Milk Carton

To protect vulnerable seedlings, plant them in half-gallon paper milk cartons. When you transplant them outside, merely cut out the bottom of the carton and plant the whole carton, leaving its edge sticking out of the soil about an inch. Cutworms will be unable to get to the plants.

### Paper Collar

Protect individual plants by putting a 3-inch collar made from stiff paper or plastic around them. Push the collar 1 to 2 inches into the ground.

### Paper Cup

Cut a hole in the bottom of a paper cup, then cut a radial slit and fit the cup upside down into the soil and around the stem of the plant you want to protect. Be sure to push the rim of the cup 1 to 2 inches deep in the soil.

### Wood Ashes

Sprinkle two handfuls of wood ashes around the base of each transplant after you put them in the ground, keeping the ashes from touching the plant. You can also make a trench around each plant, 3 to 4 inches wide and a few inches deep, and fill it with wood ashes. Cutworms don't like to crawl over them.

## Animal Predators

Swallows and bats eat the adult moths. The worms provide a fine meal for blackbirds, bluejays, brown thrashers, meadowlarks, chickens, robins, sparrows, and wrens, as well as moles, shrews, snakes, and toads.

## Insect Predators Found in the Garden

Any of the caterpillar-eaters prey upon cutworms. These include ground beetles, fireflies, soldier beetles, stinkbugs, and tachinid flies.

# INSECT *Flea Beetle*

## DESCRIPTION

Flea beetles are shiny, black beetles, about the size of a pinhead. Some species have yellow or white markings. They are very active and jump like fleas when disturbed. Females lay eggs near the bases of plants. These hatch in about one week, and the larvae feed on the roots of plants for two to three weeks before pupating and emerging as winged adults to attack foliage. Flea beetles transmit viral and bacterial diseases, including early blight and bacterial wilt. These insect pests are found throughout the United States.

## MOST OBVIOUS SYMPTOMS

Lots of tiny holes in leaves are a sign of flea beetles. These insects can destroy small plants rapidly. Flea beetle larvae also weaken plants by feeding on the roots.

## BEST CONTROL STRATEGY

Control flea beetles by spraying infested plants with pyrethrum. Two applications three to four days apart should solve the problem. If not, spray plants with a 5 percent rotenone solution. Beneficial nematodes introduced to the soil will take care of the larvae.

## MONITORING FLEA BEETLES

### Emergence Time

Adults overwinter in the soil and in garden debris and emerge in early spring.

## Early Warning Devices

### Sticky Trap
White sticky traps provide early warning of flea beetle infestation.

## Natural Sprays

See the beginning of the chapter for information on garlic and hot pepper sprays.

### Garlic and Hot Pepper
Garlic sprays and hot pepper sprays can be used to repel flea beetles.

# OPTIONS FOR CONTROLLING FLEA BEETLES

## Traps and Mechanical Controls

### Sticky Trap
White sticky traps, often used to tell of the arrival of flea beetles, will also reduce their numbers in your yard.

## Insect Predators and Parasites Available Commercially

Beneficial nematodes will control flea beetle larvae in the soil.

# PREVENTING FLEA BEETLES

## Barriers

### Diatomaceous Earth
Sprinkle diatomaceous earth around the base of vulnerable plants to keep flea beetles away, or dust the whole plant with the earth.

### Netting or Fleece
To protect vulnerable seedlings in the spring, you might want to cover them with netting, agricultural fleece, cheesecloth, or some similar material as soon as you plant them. These materials prevent the flea beetles from getting to the plant. When the plants have grown some and become well established, remove the cover.

### Other Barriers
Other materials used by gardeners to repel flea beetles include lime and coffee grounds. Spread them in a circle around each plant.

## Animal Predators

Chickadees, purple finches, titmice, vireos, warblers, and toads eat flea beetles or their larvae and pupae.

## Insect Predators Found in the Garden

Beneficial insects that prey on flea beetles include ground beetles and parasitic wasps.

## Other Preventive Steps

Flea beetles like it hot and dry, so make the microclimate around the vulnerable plants somewhat cool and moist. Sprinkle the plants during the hottest part of the day. Space plants close together so that the leaves touch; this will create a more humid environment.

# INSECT *Fuller Rose Beetle*

## DESCRIPTION

This nocturnal insect is a weevil that is about ⅓ inch long and has a cream-colored stripe on each side. Its larvae are yellowish with brown heads. Fuller rose beetles occur outdoors in the South and in Cal-

ifornia. They are serious greenhouse pests in the North, where they are most abundant in December.

## MOST OBVIOUS SYMPTOMS

The larvae feed on roots and girdle stems, while the adults chew on the edges of leaves at night, making them ragged. Plants turn yellow and die.

## BEST CONTROL STRATEGY

The beetles hide on twigs and in foliage during the day. Hunt them out and handpick them. For heavy infestations, spray with pyrethrum or rotenone laced with isopropyl alcohol every three to five days until they are gone. A band of sticky material such as Tanglefoot will prevent adults from climbing plants.

# INSECT *Goldsmith Beetle*

## DESCRIPTION

The goldsmith beetle is a cousin of the June bug. It is quite large (about 1 inch long), with a hairy, lemon-yellow body. The larvae resemble grubs and attack the roots of roses, chrysanthemums, canna lilies, and other ornamental plants. These pests are common in eastern states and the Southwest.

## MOST OBVIOUS SYMPTOMS

Goldsmith beetles chew holes in the leaves of plants.

## BEST CONTROL STRATEGY

Handpick the beetles or spray infested plants with pyrethrum or rotenone laced with isopropyl alcohol every three to five days until the beetles are controlled.

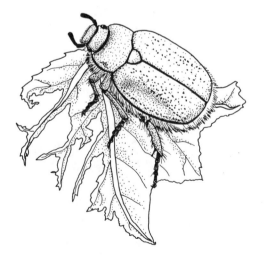

# INSECT *Grasshopper*

## DESCRIPTION

Grasshoppers may be green, brown, yellow, black, gray, or even reddish. They are 1 to 2 inches long and have a tough armor on their bodies. They have short antennae and large hind legs designed for spectacular jumping. Females lay their eggs in the soil or on weeds. Grasshoppers feed during the day. Only one generation occurs each year.

## MOST OBVIOUS SYMPTOMS

Grasshoppers will chew any part of a plant that sticks up above the ground. They can do a lot of damage, eating a plant right down to its bare bones.

## BEST CONTROL STRATEGY

Control grasshoppers by handpicking them or trapping them. To make a trap, combine one part molas-

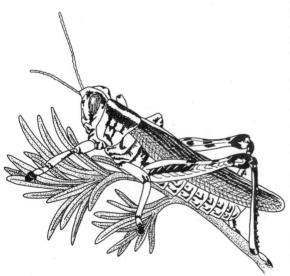

ses with ten parts water. Pour this solution in a jar and bury it in the soil to its rim, leaving the top open. The grasshoppers will dive into the sweet solution and drown.

## MONITORING GRASSHOPPERS

### Emergence Time

The eggs overwinter in the soil and hatch in late spring.

## OPTIONS FOR CONTROLLING GRASSHOPPERS

### Natural Sprays

See the beginning of the chapter for more information on insecticidal soap.

#### Insecticidal Soap

For heavy infestations, spray infested areas with insecticidal soap every two to three days for two weeks.

### Biological Controls

#### Grasshopper Spore Disease (*Nosema Locustae*)

A spore disease, *Nosema locustae*, infects grasshoppers specifically and disrupts their circulation, excretion, and reproduction, eventually killing them. This pathogen is available commercially. Apply it in early summer, when grasshoppers are no more than ¾ inch long. This disease is known to infect 58 species of grasshopper, the Mormon cricket (*Anabrus simplex*), a black field cricket (*Gryllus* spp.), and a species of pygmy locust (*Tetrigidae* spp.). Infected eggs carry the disease from one generation to the next. You can purchase *Nosema locustae* from Colorado Insectary or Reuter Laboratories (see the source list at the back of the book for addresses).

## Botanical Poisons

See the beginning of the chapter for more information on sabadilla.

### Sabadilla
Another option for controlling grasshoppers is to dust plants with sabadilla. Apply this poison weekly, dusting under the leaves of plants wet with dew, or moist from showers. You'll get best results if you hit pests directly. Sabadilla is available only as a dust.

## PREVENTING GRASSHOPPERS

### Fall Cleanup

Because the eggs overwinter in the soil, the fall cleanup is important to preventing problems with grasshoppers.

### Barriers

#### Cheesecloth or Fleece
If grasshoppers are a serious problem in your yard, consider covering your young seedlings in spring with cheesecloth or fleece as soon as you plant them outdoors. These materials prevent grasshoppers from getting to the plant; in addition, grasshoppers simply don't like the shady conditions under these covers. Later in the season, as the plants get larger and become well established, remove the cover.

## Animal Predators

Many garden animals take delight in munching on grasshoppers. Baltimore orioles, bluebirds, crows, starlings, sparrows, mockingbirds, catbirds, meadowlarks, hawks, and brown thrashers eat them. Grasshoppers have been enjoyed by chickens, guinea fowl, skunks, snakes, toads, and spiders. Ground squirrels, field mice, and other rodents eat the adults and also dig for their eggs.

## Insect Predators Found in the Garden

Blister beetles, grasshopper beeflies, ground beetles, and red grasshopper mites attack the eggs of grasshoppers. Flesh flies, tangle-veined flies, hairworms, robber flies, nematodes, and tachinid flies will eat nymphs and adult grasshoppers.

## NOTES AND RESEARCH

Grasshoppers are sometimes affected by the growth hormones in the plants they eat. In female grasshoppers, these hormones can alter the number of eggs laid and their viability. They may affect the lifespan of the grasshoppers. The effects of plant hormones varies depending on the type of hormone and its concentration. Researchers are looking into the possibility of artificially manipulating these growth hormones to control grasshopper infestations.

INSECT **Gypsy Moth**

## DESCRIPTION

The dreaded gypsy moth caterpillar doesn't look dreadful. The mature caterpillar is about 2½ inches long. It has five pairs of blue spots and six pairs of red spots along its back. In July, it encases itself in brown shells to pupate. The adult male moth is brown and the female white. Both have feathered antennae, and their wingspans measure about 1½ inches; however, the females can barely fly. They lay eggs in masses of 400 to 500, and these masses are covered with velvety, buff-colored hairs. They can survive temperatures as low as −25°F. Only one generation occurs each year. Gypsy moths are an introduced pest that has so far infested only the eastern United States.

Gypsy moth larvae are often confused with the eastern tent caterpillar and fall webworm, both of which make silken tents in trees. Gypsy moths do not make tents.

## MOST OBVIOUS SYMPTOMS

When gypsy moths strike they strike hard. Masses of caterpillars will infest a tree and defoliate it. At first, you probably won't notice any damage, since the young larvae are quite small and feed only on the leaf edges. When they reach a length of 1 inch, they'll begin making large holes in the leaves.

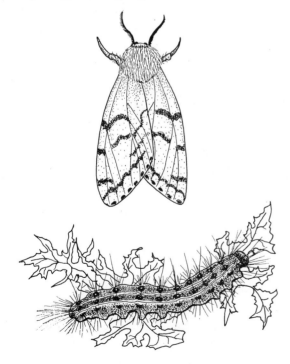

## BEST CONTROL STRATEGY

Spray trees with Bt (*Bacillus thuringiensis*) every 10 to 14 days from late April to mid-June. In June, trap caterpillars with the burlap skirts described under "Traps and Mechanical Controls," below.

## MONITORING GYPSY MOTHS

### Emergence Time

Eggs begin hatching by late April or early May. Not all the larvae emerge at the same time. The crucial control period is from late April to early June, after the larvae reach ¾ inch long and have begun to eat leaves. Gypsy moths pupate for two weeks in midsummer.

### Early Warning Devices

#### Pheromone Trap

Pheromone traps can warn of the arrival of gypsy moths in your yard. The pheromones attract the moths and then a sticky substance in the trap catches them. Place pheromone traps in the yard and around the garden two to three weeks before the expected emergence of the adult gypsy moths, usually sometime in July. You'll catch more gypsy moths if you place the traps near the tops of trees and orient them so the openings face the prevailing wind direction. These traps will not control the moths; they'll only alert you to their presence and give you an indication of the severity of the infestation.

## OPTIONS FOR CONTROLLING GYPSY MOTHS

### Traps and Mechanical Controls

#### Burlap Trap

When larvae are 1 inch long, they become night feeders and come down from the tree each morning. You can take advantage of this behavior and trap them. Wrap a piece of burlap a foot wide around the tree trunk, about chest high. Tie it at the center with heavy twine, letting the top fold over to form a skirt. Descending caterpillars will hide under the fold. In the late afternoon, put on garden gloves and sweep the caterpillars off into a container of detergent and water.

### Sticky Trap

Sticky bands around tree trunks also stop the caterpillars. Wrap a 4-inch-wide piece of cotton batting around the trunk of the tree, about chest high. Over this, tie a 6- to 12-inch-wide piece of tar paper smeared with a sticky material like Tanglefoot. Replace the band whenever needed until mid-July, at which time you should remove it. The U.S. Department of Agriculture cautions against applying any sticky substance, especially grease, tar, or other petroleum products, directly to the bark of trees; this can cause swelling and cankering.

### Destroying Egg Masses

Look for egg masses on tree trunks, on the ground, on rocks or walls, and in fact, in any sheltered spot. Scrape them off into a bucket of water and kerosene.

## Botanical Poisons

See the beginning of the chapter for more information on ryania.

### Ryania

Ryania is usually used against codling moths, but it also controls gypsy moths. Make the first application in the spring, when 75 percent of the flower petals have fallen; then follow with three sprayings, at one- to two-week intervals.

## Insect Predators and Parasites Available Commercially

Beneficial nematodes will burrow inside gypsy moth caterpillars and reproduce. Once inside, they release bacteria that kill the caterpillars. Chalcid and trichogramma wasps parasitize the eggs of gypsy moths.

# PREVENTING GYPSY MOTHS

## Fall Cleanup

Gypsy moths lay their eggs just about anywhere: on lawn furniture, stone walls, woodpiles, fences, garages, and outbuildings. In the fall, check all these spots for masses of eggs and remove and destroy any that you find by scraping them into a can of kerosene, gasoline, or water, or by burning them. Eggs, larvae, and pupae can also be found in plant debris, so a good fall cleanup will help to prevent the return of gypsy moths next year.

## Barriers

### Cotton Batting

Just wrapping cotton batting around tree trunks can stop some gypsy moths from climbing the tree to do their damage.

## Animal Predators

The more birds living and breeding in and around your garden, the fewer gypsy moth problems you'll have. Gypsy moths are part of the diet of 45 species of birds, including blue jays, chipping sparrows, crows, cuckoos, grackles, robins, starlings, towhees, and vireos. Chickadees, nuthatches, and titmice will eat any egg cases attached to the bark of trees over winter. Chipmunks, moles, shrews, squirrels, voles, white-footed mice, and other rodents eat gypsy moth caterpillars.

## Insect Predators Found in the Garden

Among the important beneficial insects that prey upon gypsy moths are assassin bugs, ground beetles, soldier beetles, tachinid flies, and several types of wasps.

## Other Preventive Steps

Maintain good growing conditions for trees. The healthier the tree, the better its chances of surviving defoliation. Fertilize, water, and prune regularly. Keep the roots healthy by not using lime or weed killers around the base of trees; they can damage shallow root systems. Never use de-icing salts nearby. Grasses tend to compete heavily with trees for water, so replace them with a less thirsty ground cover, or simply mulch with leaves or other material. Avoid compacting the soil around the base of trees with heavy equipment or paths. Diversify plant species. Replace dead or dying trees with ones that are less favored by gypsy moths, such as ash, the conifers, hickory, honey locust, maple, and tulip poplar. Consult your local nurseryman and County Extension agents on trees most compatible with your climate and soil.

# INSECT *Japanese Beetle*

## DESCRIPTION

The Japanese beetle is about ½ inch long. It is a shiny metallic green and has copper-colored wings. The grub is grayish and has a dark brown head. Two rows of spines form a V on the underside of the grub's last abdominal segment. When full grown, the grub is plump, and if it were to stretch out, it would measure ¾ to 1 inch in length; however, most of the time you'll find these chubby larvae curled in an arc-shaped position. The female beetles lay their white eggs in the soil. Adults eat foliage and fruit. They can fly a distance of up to 5 miles, and go out only in the daytime. Larvae feed on grass roots. Japanese beetles have a one- or two-year life cycle. They overwinter in the soil at the larval stage. Japanese beetles are found primarily in the eastern half of the United States, but are moving westward.

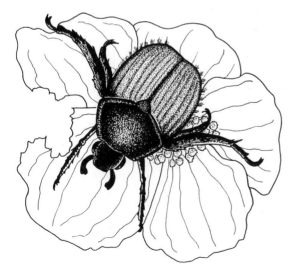

## MOST OBVIOUS SYMPTOMS

Beetles congregate in groups of a handful to hundreds on plants and flowers. They skeletonize leaves and destroy flowers. Grubs chew on turf roots. A serious infestation can create large dead patches in the lawn.

## BEST CONTROL STRATEGY

Handpick beetles from plants and drop them into a pail of soapy water. Set up pheromone beetle traps a week before expected emergence in your area, making sure traps are no closer than 50 feet from vulnerable plants. Handpick stragglers, or use pyrethrum if traps cannot handle the infestation.

Treat the soil of lawns and gardens with milky spore disease (*Bacillus popilliae*) or with beneficial nematodes.

# MONITORING JAPANESE BEETLES

## Emergence Time

After mating in late July and early August, the females lay eggs in the soil. Grubs hatch and burrow through the soil, feeding on decaying vegetation at first, then progressing to the roots of grass and other plants. They stay underground all winter. In spring and early summer, they pupate and will emerge as adults in late June or early July. The life cycle normally takes one year, but in cold, wet climates it may take two.

## Early Warning Devices

### Trap Crop

Borage is a common trap crop for Japanese beetles. White geraniums, grape vines, and zinnias, especially white or light-colored ones, can be used as trap crops to spot early infestations of Japanese beetles. Japanese beetles also love to feed on the evening primrose (*Oenothera*), which grows as a weed everywhere. Locate trap crops within 10 to 15 feet of the plants threatened by the beetles.

### Other Early Warning Devices

Japanese beetles can be monitored and trapped with a commercially available pheromone trap. The pheromone gives off an odor that attracts the beetles, which then fall into the bag. Do not locate these traps closer than 50 feet to the vulnerable plants, as not all of the beetles attracted to the devices are caught. The traps can also be used to control a beetle infestation.

# OPTIONS FOR CONTROLLING JAPANESE BEETLES

## Traps and Mechanical Controls

### Pheromone Trap

A very effective way to control Japanese beetles is with pheromone traps that lure these insects with food and sex attractants. The attractants are attached to a slick plastic bag that the beetles cannot climb. Set them up a week or so prior to the emergence of adults in late spring or early summer. Hang them about 5 feet off the ground, and never place the traps any closer than 50 feet to a vulnerable plant, since some beetles do miss the trap.

### Handpicking

Handpicking immediately makes a sizable dent in the Japanese beetle infestation. If you remove the adults as early in the season as possible, you can prevent many of them from laying eggs. Handpick beetles in the morning, when they are still covered with dew and less likely to fly. To make this task a little easier, spread a cloth under the infested plant and shake it gently. Then gather the fallen beetles and drop them into a mixture of water and detergent or kerosene.

## Botanical Poisons

See the beginning of the chapter for more information on pyrethrum and rotenone.

### Pyrethrum

Pyrethrum paralyzes Japanese beetles on contact. Its effectiveness can be increased by adding some isopropyl alcohol to the spray. Usually, two applications, three to four days apart, will control the problem.

### Rotenone

Dust plants with rotenone, or spray them with a 5 percent solution, if other controls have failed.

## Biological Controls

### Milky Spore Disease (*Bacillus Popilliae*)

Milky spore will infect larvae and kill them, but it

takes a couple years to control a population of beetles this way. Should you want to try this method, apply the granular form of milky spore to mowed areas of the lawn, using a regular fertilizer spreader. It infects grubs as soon as they start to feed. Milky spore disease remains in the soil, where it will infect the next crop of beetle grubs. It is an expensive control method. Traps are cheaper and just as effective.

## Insect Predators and Parasites Available Commercially

If grubs are a particular problem in your garden, you should consider applying beneficial nematodes to the soil. They will seek out the grubs, burrow into them, and reproduce. Nematodes release bacteria, which kill the grubs.

## PREVENTING JAPANESE BEETLES

### Animal Predators

Starlings are the only birds willing to eat the adult beetles, but robins, starlings, and other grub-eaters will eat the larvae in the spring.

### Insect Predators Found in the Garden

Assassin bugs and spring and fall tiphia wasps attack Japanese beetle larvae.

### Other Preventive Steps

Fallen fruit left rotting on the ground is an invitation to all nearby beetles, so pick up any fruit as soon as it falls.

# INSECT *Lace Bug*

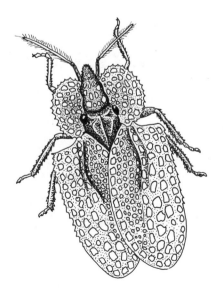

## DESCRIPTION

Lacebugs are quite appropriately named—their delicate wings resemble pieces of lace. These insects have square-shaped bodies, only about ³⁄₁₆ inch long. The nymphs are dark and spiny, and move with a strange sideways motion. Adults hibernate under the edges of the bark of trees and shrubs and emerge to lay their eggs soon after the leaves unfold. The nymphs hatch in May and begin to feed on leaves. This group of insects includes the azalea lace bug (*Stephanitis pyrioides*), the rhododendron lace bug (*S. rhododendri*), the sycamore lace bug (*Corythucha ciliata*), the chrysanthemum lace bug (*C. marmorata*), the elm lace bug (*C. ulmi*), the walnut lace bug (*C. juglandis*), the oak lace bug (*C. arcuata*), and the willow lace bug (*C. mollicula*).

## MOST OBVIOUS SYMPTOMS

Lace bugs suck sap from the undersides of leaves, causing foliage to turn pale or mottled. A reddish orange discoloration on the undersides of leaves is a good sign that your plants are indeed infested with lace bugs. The top surfaces take on a mottled appearance, much as if they had been sprinkled with white pepper. You may also find shiny spots of brown excrement on the bottom surfaces of leaves. The foliage of infested trees can drop prematurely.

In eastern states, lace bugs can do considerable damage to elms. They first infest the tender foliage in spring. The leaves become spotted and eventually turn brown and die.

## BEST CONTROL STRATEGY

You can simply crush lace bugs as you find them, or spray infested plants with insecticidal soap, making two applications one or two weeks apart. If the infestation is so serious that the soap can't control it, spray plants with nicotine sulfate or pyrethrum every seven to ten days until symptoms disappear.

INSECT # Leafhopper

## DESCRIPTION

Leafhoppers are wedge-shaped insects, ¼ to ⅓ inch long. They carry their wings in a rooflike position over their bodies, which accounts for their unusual shape. As for color, they may be green, brown, or yellow, and often have colorful markings. Leafhoppers move sideways and are very active. Their life cycles vary depending on the species; some overwinter as eggs, others as adults. Eggs are laid on the undersides of leaves. Some species spread viral diseases. Leafhoppers occur throughout the United States.

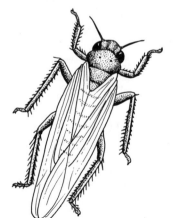

## MOST OBVIOUS SYMPTOMS

Nymphs and adults suck juices from plant leaves, buds, and stems. Foliage often appears mottled with white or yellow spots, and may drop. The plants weaken. The large amounts of honeydew excreted by leafhoppers give plants a glazed appearance. Black sooty mold may grow on this honeydew.

## BEST CONTROL STRATEGY

Spray infested plants with insecticidal soap laced with isopropyl alcohol. Add 1 tablespoon alcohol to 1 quart soap. In spring, spray young plants with insecticidal soap and seaweed extract, and spread agricultural fleece over them to keep leafhoppers away. After a month, remove the cover.

## MONITORING LEAFHOPPERS

### Emergence Time

Nymphs appear in early spring.

## OPTIONS FOR CONTROLLING LEAFHOPPERS

### Mechanical Controls

#### Handpicking
If you move quickly, you can catch leafhoppers and crush them.

### Botanical Poisons

See the beginning of the chapter for more information on pyrethrum, rotenone, and sabadilla.

#### Pyrethrum
Pyrethrum paralyzes leafhoppers, but must come in direct contact with the insects to be effective. Usually, two applications to the infested plant, three to four days apart, will be sufficient.

#### Rotenone
Dust rotenone on plants, or make a 5 percent solution and spray it.

#### Sabadilla
Sabadilla dust should be applied on the undersides of wet plants. Try to sprinkle it on the leafhoppers themselves.

### Insect Predators and Parasites Available Commercially

Green lacewings will attack leafhoppers, but they are difficult to keep in the yard. Braconid, ichneumonid, and trichogramma wasps also attack leafhoppers.

## PREVENTING LEAFHOPPERS

### Fall Cleanup

Adults like to hibernate in weeds, but dislike perennial grasses. So by keeping the winter garden clean and having an area of weed-free turf around your garden beds, you can discourage this pest. It is particularly important to get rid of thistles, plantains, and dandelions.

### Animal Predators

Chickadees, purple finches, sparrows, swallows, titmice, and wrens eat leafhoppers.

### Insect Predators Found in the Garden

Assassin bugs, big-eyed bugs, damselflies, and syrphid flies are important predators. Parasitic wasps that occur naturally are also valuable in controlling these pests.

### Other Preventive Steps

Weed control is effective in reducing egg-laying sites. It is especially important to get rid of thistles, plantains, and dandelions.

INSECT **Leafminer**

## DESCRIPTION

Leafminers are the larvae of various insects: small black flies, moths, sawflies, or beetles. Adults will usually lay eggs on the undersides of leaves. The larvae that hatch are green or black and about ⅛ inch long. Upon emerging, they tunnel into the leaves between the upper and lower surfaces and feed on the inside of leaves. Several generations develop each summer, and these pests pass the winter in a cocoon in the soil. Leafminers carry disease. Many species occur throughout North America.

## MOST OBVIOUS SYMPTOMS

White or brown tunnels or blotches can be seen through the surface of leaves that have been mined by leafminers. Often you will be able to see the brown specks of excrement left behind by the larvae, and you may see the larvae themselves. Eventually, the leaves will blister or curl, turn brown, and die.

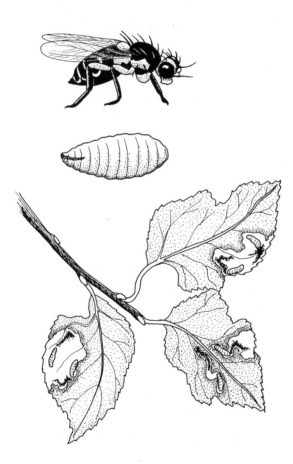

## BEST CONTROL STRATEGY

To remove leafminers from your plants, remove the infested leaves. Spray with insecticidal soap to kill any adults that might lay eggs on your plants. If leafminers are a problem year after year, consider covering vulnerable plants in spring with agricultural fleece or some other material that will prevent these pests from getting to your plants.

## MONITORING LEAFMINERS

### Emergence Time

Leafminers emerge from the soil in early spring. Egg laying continues throughout the summer as new generations mature.

## OPTIONS FOR CONTROLLING LEAFMINERS

### Natural Sprays

See the beginning of this chapter for more information on horticultural oil.

### Horticultural Oil

The newer horticultural oils, called superior horticultural oils, are lighter and less viscous (60 to 70) than traditional oils, and evaporate much more quickly from leaves and stems. They can be used during the growing season to control leafminers. Make a 2 to 3 percent solution and spray plants thoroughly. You want to spray the pests directly, because the oil works by suffocating the insects.

### Mechanical Controls

#### Handpicking

Handpick the eggs. Turn the leaves over and look for them. They are chalky white and $1/16$ to $1/8$ inch long. Three, four, or even five of them will be lined up next to each other. Scratch them off and destroy them. Flies will continue to lay eggs, so repeat this process once a week for three or four weeks. If the eggs have already hatched, the upper surface of the leaves will have grayish blisters. Cut off the blisters; it's not necessary to cut off the entire leaf. The plants will survive and grow quickly if you leave as much healthy tissue as possible. Destroy all the damaged leaf parts that you cut from the plant.

## Insect Predators and Parasites Available Commercially

Green lacewings eat leafminer eggs, and certain chalcid and braconid wasps may parasitize leafminers.

# PREVENTING LEAFMINERS

## Fall Cleanup

Leafminers overwinter in the soil and emerge in early spring; consequently, a thorough fall cleanup helps control them. Cultivate the soil around plants in late fall to expose these insects to birds and other predators. Leave the soil bare until it freezes solid, and then lay down a winter mulch. Remove weeds, especially lamb's-quarters.

## Preventive Spray Programs

The key to preventing leafminers is to try to catch the adult—whether it is a fly, a moth, or a flying beetle—before it lays its eggs on the target plant. Try to find out, within a day or two, the expected date of emergence of the adult insect; then spray vulnerable plants with insecticidal soap or horticultural oil at that time. This would be about May 1 in most parts of the country. In a cold spring, you can delay the first application a week or so. For best results, make two more applications at seven- to ten-day intervals. To control a second brood of leafminers, spray plants again about July 1 and July 10. Spray only the target plants to avoid hurting too many beneficial insects in the area. (See the beginning of the chapter for more information on the sprays mentioned.)

## Barriers

### Netting or Fleece
The best way to prevent leafminers is to screen them out. Fine screening or agricultural fleece are all effective barriers, allowing sun, air, and rain to get through while preventing leafminers from laying eggs at the plants' stems.

## Animal Predators

Chickadees, purple finches, and robins eat leafminers.

## Insect Predators Found in the Garden

Ladybugs eat the eggs of leafminers.

# INSECT *Leaf Roller*

## DESCRIPTION

Leaf rollers are the caterpillars of moths. They may be light to dark green or cream to yellow in color, and grow to a length of ⅜ inch to 1¾ inches. The adult moths are small—¼ to ½ inch long—with brown or gray wings. Often, two generations occur in a year, one in spring and the other in late summer. They pass the winter in their pupal stage in plant debris under trees. These insect pests roll leaves around themselves for protection while they are in their pupal stage. Some of the more common pests are the oblique-banded leaf roller (*Choristoneura rosaceana*), the red-banded leaf roller (*Argyrotaenia semipurpurana*), and the oak leaf roller (*Argyrotoxa semipurpurana*).

## MOST OBVIOUS SYMPTOMS

You'll probably first notice an infestation when you see that the leaves on your trees are rolled up. Leaf rollers protect themselves inside rolled leaves, which they bind with strands of silk. Once they've built little homes for themselves, they'll go out and chew holes in flower buds and leaves. These pests have a fair appetite and can skeletonize leaves, which will turn brown and drop in late summer.

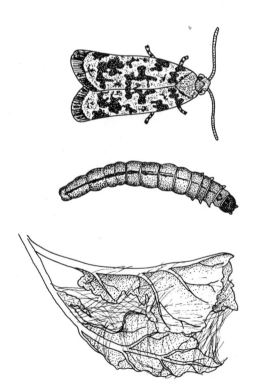

## BEST CONTROL STRATEGY

Crush leaf rollers as you find them, and spray plants with Bt (*Bacillus thuringiensis*). If leaf rollers are a common problem in your yard, spray vulnerable plants with Bt before you expect the caterpillars to begin feeding.

## MONITORING LEAF ROLLERS

### Emergence Time

Leaf rollers overwinter as pupae in garden debris, and the moths appear in spring.

## OPTIONS FOR CONTROLLING LEAF ROLLERS

### Botanical Poisons

See the beginning of the chapter for more information on pyrethrum and rotenone.

#### Pyrethrum and Rotenone
If the infestation of leaf rollers is heavy, dust plants with a mixture of equal parts of pyrethrum and rotenone powder, or make a spray with these two insecticides. Apply the mixture twice, allowing only 30 minutes between applications. The pyrethrum drives caterpillars out of hiding and the rotenone kills them.

#### Tobacco Dust
#### and Pyrethrum or Rotenone Spray
You can also try a mixture of equal parts of tobacco dust and either pyrethrum or rotenone. Using either a dust or a spray, make two applications, half an hour apart.

### Insect Predators and Parasites Available Commercially

Green lacewings and trichogramma wasps attack leaf roller eggs.

## DESCRIPTION

Leaftiers are green or pale yellow caterpillars, ⅜ to ¾ inch long. The adult moths have gray or brown wings and are about ¼ to ½ inch long.

## MOST OBVIOUS SYMPTOMS

Leaftiers attack the terminal buds of plants. They bind leaves around these buds with strands of silk to create a shelter for themselves while they feed. These leaves will become ragged, turn brown, and die.

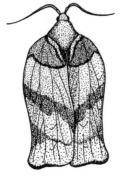

## BEST CONTROL STRATEGY

Light infestations are easily controlled simply by handpicking the caterpillars; otherwise, spray with Bt (*Bacillus thuringiensis*) every 10 to 14 days until the pests are gone. If leaftiers infest your plants year after year, start spraying with Bt before you expect the caterpillars to begin feeding.

## MONITORING LEAFTIERS

### Emergence Time

Leaftiers overwinter as partially grown larvae and resume feeding the following spring.

## OPTIONS FOR CONTROLLING LEAFTIERS

### Natural Sprays

See the beginning of the chapter for more information on garlic spray.

#### Garlic
Flower buds sprayed with a garlic solution are less appealing to most leaftiers.

### Botanical Poisons

See the beginning of the chapter for more information on pyrethrum and rotenone.

#### Tobacco Dust and Pyrethrum or Rotenone Spray
If a leaftier infestation is serious, dust plants with a mixture of equal parts of tobacco and pyrethrum or rotenone powder, or you can apply the tobacco dust and follow with a pyrethrum or rotenone spray. Make two applications 30 minutes apart. The tobacco drives the caterpillars from hiding, and the botanical poison kills them.

# Lilac Borer

## DESCRIPTION

The lilac borer is a creamy white caterpillar with a brown head. The insect measures ¾ to 1½ inches long when fully grown. These larvae remain nestled in the stems of plants for the winter. When spring arrives, the adult, a clear-winged moth, emerges and lays eggs on roughened or wounded places on the bark.

In certain areas of the Northeast, the leopard moth borer occurs more often on the lilac than the lilac borer. These larvae are pale yellowish or cream colored and marked with numerous black spots. The adult moths are white with black markings. They are sluggish creatures, fairly feeble in flight.

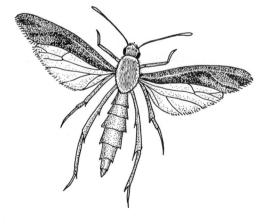

## MOST OBVIOUS SYMPTOMS

The lilac borer attacks lilac, privet, and other ornamental shrubs by tunneling under the bark and into the wood, thus girdling the stems and causing foliage to wilt. Often the branches become so weakened by the boring that they break.

Rough knotlike swellings on the trunk and limbs of shrubs, and the breaking of small branches at the point of injury, indicate the presence of the lilac borer. Sawdust hangs at the openings made by borers. Infested branches often wilt because of the destruction of the sapwood, which these larvae eat as they drill their way into the heartwood. Roughened scars on the stems mark places where borers have worked for several seasons. Sometimes the damage produced by borers opens shrubs to infection from the wood-destroying fungus *Polyporus versicolor*. This fungus appears as soft hairs of various colors.

The leopard moth borer also invades the heartwood, tunneling up and down for some distance. Its tunnel is much larger and straighter than that of the lilac borer. As they drill into shrubs, leopard moth larvae push sawdust out of their holes and onto the ground. These little piles of sawdust are a sure sign of borer activity.

## BEST CONTROL STRATEGY

To control either of these borers, examine your lilacs just before spring arrives and cut and destroy any dying or unhealthy-looking stems, which may contain borers. Since the partly grown insects pass the winter in the stems of lilacs, the infested branches should be cut out and destroyed before the pest begins working in the spring.

During the summer season, check for borers, and if you find that they have infested your plants, follow the control techniques described on page 273 for borers in general.

# INSECT *Mealybug*

## DESCRIPTION

These insects might reach ⅓ inch in length. They have flattened oval bodies covered with white waxy powder. Short soft spines protrude from their edges. Mealybugs feed on stems, branches, and leaves, and can often be found in leaf axils and other protected sites. They tend to congregate, and a group of them looks like a mass of cotton. Mealybugs do build cottony egg sacks on leaves, and they excrete honeydew, which can attract ants. Mealybugs occur primarily in eastern states. Some of the more common species are the citrus mealybug (*Planococcus citri*), the long-tailed mealybug(*Pseudococcus longispinus*), and the comstock mealybug (*Pseudococcus comstocki*).

## MOST OBVIOUS SYMPTOMS

The most obvious sign of mealybug attack is perhaps the mealybugs themselves, with their white,

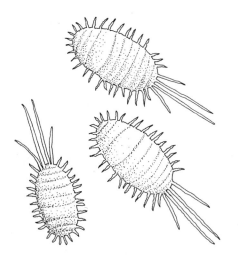

cottony appearance. They gather in masses on the stems, branches, and leaves of the plants they attack. As they suck sap from the leaves and stems, plants lose their vigor. They do not grow well and may die if the infestation is severe. You may also find ants or mold on your plants. They are attracted to the honeydew secreted by mealybugs.

## BEST CONTROL STRATEGY

Control mealybugs by spraying infested plants with the alcohol mixture described below. Heavy infestations will require that you apply insecticidal soap or pyrethrum three times at seven- to ten-day intervals.

## OPTIONS FOR CONTROLLING MEALYBUGS

### Natural Sprays

#### Alcohol

A solution made from isopropyl alcohol and oil can be successfully used to combat mealybugs. Make this mixture by combining 1 cup alcohol and ½ teaspoon horticultural oil in 1 quart water. You can substitute insecticidal soap for the oil for equally effective results. The alcohol kills the adult mealybugs, while the oil smothers any unseen young or eggs. Apply this solution every two days until mealybugs have been eradicated.

Minor infestations of mealybugs can be controlled simply by touching them with a cotton swab dipped in rubbing alcohol.

#### Water

By spraying plants forcefully with water, you can knock many mealybugs from the leaves.

## Insect Predators and Parasites Available Commercially

Green lacewings, ladybugs, and trichogramma and chalcid wasps all prey on mealybugs.

*Cryptolaemus montrouzieri*, a small gray beetle, feeds solely on mealybugs. These beneficial insects are particularly effective in greenhouses. Several releases a year give one of the surest and most economical methods of controlling these pests in the greenhouse. Release them at a rate of three to four beetles per plant. If mealybugs are infesting fruit trees, ten beetles per tree is recommended. You can purchase them from Rincon-Vitova Insectaries (see the source list at the back of the book for the address).

## PREVENTING MEALYBUGS

### Preventive Spray Programs

#### Glue

To trap mealybugs on trees and shrubs, dissolve ¼ pound yellow carpenter's glue in 1 gallon warm water, and leave it standing overnight. First test this mixture on a few leaves of the plant you want to treat. If the plant seems unharmed after a day or two, spray the mixture on twigs and leaves. When the mixture dries, it will flake off, taking the trapped bugs with it. In midseason, several applications, made seven to ten days apart, are needed to stop consecutive generations of pests.

#### Horticultural Oil

In late winter, before any leaf buds begin to open, spray dormant oil on trees and woody shrubs to smother any overwintering insects. Be certain to cover the entire surface of the tree or shrub.

## Animal Predators

Titmice, mockingbirds, and turtles all enjoy eating mealybugs.

## Insect Predators Found in the Garden

Mealybugs must watch out for the attack of syrphid flies.

---

INSECT **Midge**

## DESCRIPTION

Midges are midgets. They're lucky if they reach a length of ¹⁄₁₄ to ⅛ inch. These two-winged flies have long legs and antennae. Eggs hatch in just two days, and the larvae begin feeding at the base of flower buds or leaf stems, causing them to become distorted; the plant parts later turn brown and die. As many as 20 to 30 whitish or light orange maggots may be at work inside a single bud. Within a week, the larvae will drop to the ground and build small white cocoons in the soil. One week later, a new generation of midges will emerge. Several broods occur during each blooming season. Rose midges cause considerable damage to garden roses in the eastern states. Some other common species include the chrysanthemum gall midge (*Diarthronomyia chrysanthemi*), the violet gall midge (*Phytophaga violicola*), the rhododendron tip midge (*Giardomyia rhododendri*), the catalpa midge (*Cecidomyia*

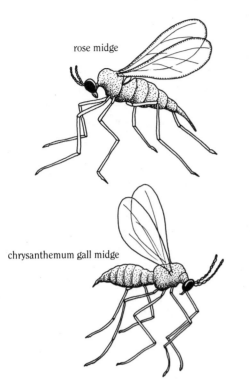

rose midge

chrysanthemum gall midge

*catalpae*), the dogwood club gall midge (*Mycodiplosis clavula*), the juniper midge (*Contarinia juniperina*), and the willow-beaked gall midge (*Mayetiola rigidae*).

## MOST OBVIOUS SYMPTOMS

The buds and foliage of midge-infested plants wilt, turn brown, and become deformed. Many species cause galls to form around their eggs and developing larvae. Infested plants are usually dwarfed, and blossoming is limited.

## BEST CONTROL STRATEGY

Handpick infested leaves and flower buds as soon as possible and destroy them. Then spray the plant with insecticidal soap. Mixing tobacco dust into the soil around the base of plants also helps to control this pest. Spray trees with dormant oil in early spring, before the leaves have popped out, to smother any overwintering pests.

# INSECT **Mite**

## DESCRIPTION

Mites are not true insects; they are relatives of spiders and belong to the arachnid family. You will barely be able to see them, because they are so small. They have four pairs of legs, and piercing-sucking mouth parts. Mites attack many kinds of plants, feeding at leaf undersides, flowers, bulbs and corms, and at the blossom ends of fruit. As they feed, they inject toxins into plant tissues, which causes discoloration and distortion.

Mites love hot, dry conditions, especially in greenhouses. The hotter it is, the more rapidly they develop from egg to adult, and the more eggs they lay. And mites can reproduce rapidly—the red spider mite will produce a new generation every two weeks if conditions are right.

Outdoor plants repeatedly sprayed with pesticides are most likely to develop bad spider mite infestations, because the sprays kill off the pests' natural enemies, such as predatory mites, green lacewings, ladybugs, and damsel bugs. Repeated spraying has also made mites immune to most of the chemical pesticides in use today. Virtually no garden plant is safe from their attack. Mites occur throughout the United States. Many species are known; some of the more common mites are the cyclamen mite (*Steneotarsonemus pallidus*), the broad mite (*Polyphagotarsonemus latus*), and the two-spotted spider mite or red spider mite (*Tetranychus telarius*).

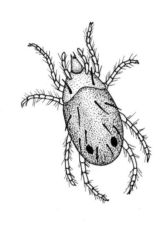

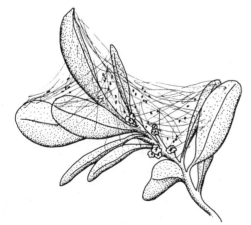

# MOST OBVIOUS SYMPTOMS

If you see white or yellow stippling or red spots on the upper surfaces of leaves, your plant is probably infested with mites. The undersides of leaves will be speckled with the tiny pellets of excrement and cast skins of mites, and you'll find the mites themselves as well. Leaves, shoots, and flowers may be swathed in fine webbing. Overall yellowing of the leaves begins along the veins and then spreads over the entire surface.

Foliage on infested trees becomes dry and copper colored, and curls slightly upward. Sometimes the mites spin webs on the leaves and twigs. Certain species cause galls to form on the leaves or on new shoots.

If you suspect one of your plants is infested with mites, look for these pests on the undersides of the leaves. A magnifying glass helps. Tap a few leaves or a small branch tip against a sheet of white paper, and look for mites crawling on the paper.

# BEST CONTROL STRATEGY

Start control measures as soon as you notice the first stippling of leaves. Spray infested plants in the early morning with a forceful spray of water to knock mites from the leaves. Repeat this for three days. If mites are still around, spray with insecticidal soap. A spray of insecticidal soap mixed with light horticultural oil works as a dormant spray against eggs and newly hatched nymphs.

# MONITORING MITES

## Emergence Time

The adult mites overwinter in plant debris below the surface of the soil and emerge in late spring. They complete their life cycle in about two weeks. Check leaf undersides weekly for mites and mite damage.

# OPTIONS FOR CONTROLLING MITES

## Natural Sprays and Dusts

See the beginning of this chapter for more information on garlic spray.

### Elemental Sulfur

Sulfur can control mites when dusted on leaf undersides, where the pests generally reside.

### Garlic

Some homeowners have reported successful control of mites by treating plants with a garlic spray.

### Lime Sulfur

Spray infested plants with a solution made from one part concentrated lime sulfur in ten parts water. Apply this sulfur spray every three to five days for two weeks, or until the mites are under control. Because lime sulfur can stain objects, do not use it on trees near white painted objects.

### Water

Mites prefer a warm, dry environment. Discourage them by misting daily with water and shading plants. This creates a cooler microclimate around plants and helps keep mite populations from exploding.

## Traps

### Glue Trap

By spraying plants with a glue solution, you can trap and kill certain small pests, such as mites. Make this solution by dissolving ¼ pound glue in 1 gallon warm water and letting it stand overnight. First test the mixture on a few leaves of the plant you want to treat. If the plant appears unharmed after a day or two, apply the mixture with a sprayer to twigs and leaves of vulnerable trees. Mites will get caught in the glue, and when the mixture dries, it will flake off, taking the trapped bugs with it. Make several applications in midseason, seven to ten days apart, to halt consecutive generations of mites.

## Botanical Poisons

See the beginning of the chapter for more information on pyrethrum, rotenone, and sabadilla.

### Pyrethrum

Pyrethrum paralyzes mites on contact. For best results, apply twice, at three- to four-day intervals.

### Rotenone

A spray of 1 percent solution will take care of most mite problems.

### Sabadilla

Apply sabadilla weekly on the undersides of the leaves of mite-infested plants.

### Triple-Plus

Triple-plus is a product that combines rotenone, pyrethrum, and ryania. When using it against mites, apply it in early June, and repeat applications two or three times at ten-day intervals.

## Insect Predators and Parasites Available Commercially

Green lacewings and ladybugs prey on mites, and certain predatory mites will attack their pest relatives. The predatory mites include *Phytoseiulus persimilis* and *Amblyseius californicus*. They, too, are tiny. They have translucent, pear-shaped bodies, and they move more quickly than pest mites. One release per season should help you control pests.

# PREVENTING MITES

## Fall Cleanup

Mites move readily from plant to plant—by themselves and by hitching rides on transplants, or even on your tools and hands. Wash your hands now and then while working with plants, and dip your tools in some rubbing alcohol to remove any stowaways. Keep the garden free of weeds, and remove all plant debris after the growing season. Promptly trim off yellowed leaves, dead wood, and spent blossoms with sharp, clean tools, and destroy them immediately.

## Spacing Plants

Mites will crawl from plant to plant where the leaves form bridges. By spreading plants out so that they don't touch each other, you will slow down the infestation of plants. If possible, move infested plants to an area away from healthy plants.

## Preventive Spray Programs

See the beginning of the chapter for more information on horticultural oil and insecticidal soap.

### Horticultural Oil
You can use traditional heavy horticultural spray oils from fall through early spring to smother any mites that might be overwintering on your trees. Only spray trees once a year, when they are leafless, and be sure to coat the entire surface of the tree.

### Insecticidal Soap and Seaweed Extract
On plants most vulnerable to mites, begin a biweekly preventive spray program using commercial insecticidal soap mixed with very dilute seaweed extract. Spray this solution on the undersides of all new growth. Make two or three applications every two weeks in the beginning of the growing season, followed by a monthly application just on those plants most vulnerable to mites. For shrubs and trees, add a light horticultural oil to this mixture for best results.

## Barriers

### Diatomaceous Earth
Spread diatomaceous earth around the base of plants, or dust the whole plant with it, beginning from the ground and moving upward to cover all stems and leaves. It will repel mites. Remember to dust the leaf undersides. Apply diatomaceous earth in late evening to prevent beneficial insects from being harmed by it.

## Insect Predators Found in the Garden

Damsel bugs, dance flies, firefly larvae, ladybugs, predatory midges, predatory thrips, ambush bugs, big-eyed bugs, and pirate bugs will help you keep mites out of the yard. Wild brambles offer a nice residence for many of these beneficial insects.

# INSECT **Nematodes**

## DESCRIPTION

Actually, nematodes aren't insects. They are microscopic wormlike organisms. They have whitish, translucent, unsegmented bodies covered by a tough cuticle. Most nematodes are innocuous, living out their lives in fresh water, or salt water, or in soil. Some are beneficial, parasitizing a long list of pest insects. A number of types are plant pests.

One of the more common pest nematodes is the root knot nematode (*Meloidogyne* spp.). It lives in the soil, and soon after hatching, the worms enter the roots of nearby plants. They inject saliva into tissues as they feed, introducing toxins and bacteria that cause plant tissues to rot. Cells at that point enlarge grotesquely, forming a gall (the root knot) around the nematodes. This gall interferes with nutrient transport and inhibits the growth of the plant.

## MOST OBVIOUS SYMPTOMS

Pest nematodes attack all plant parts—stems, leaves, buds, roots, bulbs, and corms. A few cause galls to develop on roots or leaves. Others produce leaf discoloration, stunting, or dieback. In general, plants infested with nematodes look sickly, wilted, or stunted. Their foliage turns yellow or bronze, and they decline slowly and die. If the root system has been attacked, it will develop poorly and may even decay, and if infested by the root knot nematode, it will show galls. Effects of nematode activity are most apparent in hot weather; plants will recover poorly from the heat.

## BEST CONTROL STRATEGY

If you find that your plants are infested with nematodes, add compost to the soil, which will attract beneficial fungi that will then attack the nematodes. Or, you can drench the soil with fish emulsion, which repels or kills nematodes. Provided this suits your landscape plans and design, you can turn an infested garden plot over to a thick planting of French marigolds for an entire season. The following year, you shouldn't have any problems with nematodes.

If nematodes are a recurring problem in your landscape, plant early in the season and use resistant varieties. Space plants so that the leaves do not touch. Avoid wetting foliage, since nematodes swim up the stems and enter leaves through the stomata (pores).

## MONITORING NEMATODES

Nematodes are always present in the soil. It's just that sometimes they get a little out of hand. If you suspect that nematodes are causing damage, there are a couple of tests you can use to determine if they indeed are harming your plants.

### Tests for Nematodes

Check the soil for root knot nematodes by taking some soil from the location you think might be infested. Plant cucumber seeds in a small pot of this soil. After the first true leaves appear, pull up the seedlings and carefully wash the soil away from the roots. If nematodes are present, you will see small beadlike knots on the roots.

Another test uses radishes instead of cucumbers. Collect soil samples at a depth of 3 inches below the surface from various sites in the garden. Mix these together and fill four small pots with the soil. Freeze two of the pots for 48 to 72 hours to kill any nematodes that might be present; then plant radishes in all four pots. Radishes are quite sensitive to nematodes. Examine the seedlings after six days. If the radishes grown in the soil that was frozen look much better than those in the untreated soil, your garden soil probably contains too many nematode pests.

## OPTIONS FOR CONTROLLING NEMATODES

### Natural Sprays

#### Fish Emulsion
Crops fertilized with fish emulsion suffer less nematode damage than those fertilized in other ways. Researchers suspect that some component of the fish oil may be toxic or offensive to the nematodes. A combination of fish emulsion and an extract from the yucca cactus provides even more effective control. In tests with citrus trees, a mixture of 70 percent fish emulsion and 30 percent yucca extract reduced root knot and pin nematode populations by up to 90 percent.

#### Seaweed Extract
Whether used as a foliar spray or as a soil drench, seaweed extract will reduce root knot nematode infestations of ornamental plants. Natural hormones in the seaweed, called cytokinins, help the plants increase their resistance to nematode invasion. Fewer larvae penetrate the roots, and those that do are inhibited in their development. As a side benefit, the seaweed extract produces bigger roots and stems and better yields. Mix 1 tablespoon liquid seaweed in 2 gallons water.

#### Yucca
An effective, nontoxic soil drench can be made with ordinary corn oil and an extract of the yucca plant

(the latter is available commercially as Pent-A-Vate). Researchers explain that the oil kills the nematodes while the yucca extract allows the oil to penetrate the soil and get to the pests. To make this drench, mix one part yucca extract with ten parts water. Then combine four parts of this with one part corn oil. Sprinkle it on the soil around plants and water it in with a hose.

# PREVENTING NEMATODES

## Fall Cleanup

In the fall, clear away decayed vegetation, and put a mulch of peat moss or some other organic material around plants. This helps prevent infestation of the lower leaves of plants by nematodes that overwinter in old, infested leaves.

## Soil Solarization

If a particular garden bed suffers consistently from serious nematode problems, you might want to consider digging it up and solarizing it. This technique has been effective in controlling nematodes in the warmer southern and western states. To solarize the soil, plow or till it deeply during hot weather. Soak the ground thoroughly with water and cover it with clear plastic. The hot temperatures that develop under the plastic will destroy nematodes and other harmful pests and diseases. (See chapter 8 for more details on solarization.)

## Companion Planting

If suited to your landscape, you can grow companion plants that will repel nematodes. French marigolds (*Tagetes patula*) effectively control harmful root knot nematodes. The marigolds act as a trap crop. The nematodes enter their roots, and once inside, they seem to be unable to reproduce. In addition, marigolds release a substance that suppresses nematode populations.

You can plant a nematode-infested area of the garden with nothing but marigolds. Let them grow, and then turn them under at season's end. The roots will decay in the soil. Once the plant matter has broken down, you can plant the usual crops again. The larvae that do penetrate the roots can't lay eggs. Keep weeds under control so that the impact of the marigolds is not diluted.

Roots of plants such as some mustards and grasses, rattlebox, smartweed, and wild chicory are also toxic to some nematodes. Some species of chrysanthemum (in particular, *Chrysanthemum coccineum* and *C. pyrethrum*) reduce harmful nematodes in the soil.

## Insect Predators Found in the Garden

Predatory mites and springtails do an excellent job of controlling nematodes.

## Other Preventive Steps

### Fallow Soil

If you garden in an area that has hot, dry summers, you can control nematodes easily by letting the infested area lie fallow and by withholding water during the hottest months. Turning the soil occasionally during this time exposes nematode eggs, many of which die in the sun. Of course, this all depends on whether you can tolerate an empty area in your landscape for a season.

### Garden Hygiene

Clean all tools and garden shoes that have been in contact with infested soil, or you may carry pests to healthy plants. You can make a good disinfectant solution from one part common household bleach and five parts water. Thoroughly wet the surfaces of greenhouse benches, bins, and containers with this solution. Clean soil and algae from tools with a scrub brush and soak the tools in the bleach solution overnight.

### Kelp Meal

Certain soil fungi that kill root knot nematodes are made more potent by the presence of kelp meal in the soil. These fungi become more lethal to nematodes. Add about 1 pound of meal to every 100 square feet of garden. This treatment is particularly effective if you also add compost to the soil.

### Leaf Mold Compost
Extensive research at the Connecticut Agricultural Experiment Station has shown that leaf mold composts can suppress populations of harmful nematodes. Compost releases fatty acids, similar to those used as pest-control agents, which reduce nematode populations. Rye and timothy grasses specifically have been found to release these fatty acids. Many plant leaves are toxic to nematodes, too. Laboratory tests have shown pine needles to be particularly potent. For best results, mix compost into the garden soil.

### Organic Material
Make sure the soil has plenty of organic matter, which encourages nematode predators such as springtails and carnivorous fungi. Rich soil stimulates root growth, which lessens the effect of nema-

tode damage. In addition, decomposing organic matter may generate nematode-toxic compounds. Soil amendments such as leaf mold, grass clippings, castor pomace (a by-product of castor oil production), and manure have been known to suppress nematodes under the right conditions.

## NOTES AND RESEARCH

Jerry McLaughlin, professor of pharmacognosy at Purdue University, is patenting a new insecticide derived from the pawpaw tree. He states that this new broad-spectrum botanical spray, comparable to pyrethrum in action and toxicity, is especially effective against nematodes, Mexican bean beetles, and mosquito larvae, but will not harm the environment.

Another product, a parasitic fungus (*Paecilomyces lilacinus*), is being introduced by a Philippine company, Asiatic Technologies, of Manila. This fungus parasitizes nematode eggs and adults. Its trade name is Biocon.

# INSECT *Rose Chafer*

## DESCRIPTION

Rose chafers, also called rose bugs or rose beetles, are tan-colored, long-legged beetles, about ¼ inch long. This pest can be distinguished readily from other rose-infesting beetles by its color and its sluggish movements. Rose chafers feed on other garden plants, such as peonies and hollyhocks, as well as roses. Occasionally they will make a real nuisance of themselves on grapes, elms, and other shrubs and trees. They'll feed on flowers for about four weeks, after which the creamy white, brown-headed larvae attack the roots of lawn grasses, where they can do considerable damage. Rose chafer larvae are easily mistaken for Japanese beetle grubs.

Rose chafers are most common in northeast-

ern states, but make trouble as far west as Colorado. They breed abundantly in sandy soils. Suburban homeowners rarely have problems with rose chafers, but they often infect roses that are grown near fallow fields. Cultivated crops make better neighbors for roses. Rose chafers can poison chickens and may kill them.

## MOST OBVIOUS SYMPTOMS

These pests eat heartily and leave the foliage and flowers of roses and hydrangea skeletonized. Rose chafers are particularly fond of white blossoms.

## BEST CONTROL STRATEGY

Control rose chafers by handpicking them. For the long term, introduce milky spore disease (*Bacillus popilliae*) into the soil to kill grubs.

INSECT **Rose Curculio**

## DESCRIPTION

The rose curculio looks rather peculiar. An adult is ¼ inch long, with a red body and a long black snout. The white larvae feed on seeds and flowers but drop to the ground to pupate and hibernate. Rose curculios occur throughout the United States, but are most common in northern, colder regions; North Dakota, in particular, experiences severe infestations.

## MOST OBVIOUS SYMPTOMS

Curculios chew holes in the buds of roses, and as a result, the buds often fail to open.

## BEST CONTROL STRATEGY

Control these insect pests by handpicking adults and larvae. Collect and destroy the damaged, dried buds, which might be harboring larvae. If the infestation is heavy, spray roses with rotenone or pyrethrum. Throughout the year, clean up garden debris to remove any pests that might be hiding there.

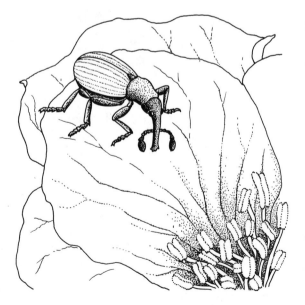

INSECT # Rose Leaf Beetle

## DESCRIPTION

Rose leaf beetles are only ⅕ inch long and resemble flea beetles, although they are not as active. They have oval-shaped bodies with a metallic green or blue sheen, and they'll arrive in your yard late in spring.

## MOST OBVIOUS SYMPTOMS

These beetles bore into flower buds and partially opened blossoms. They will also attack tender young shoots and foliage, and when abundant, they'll attack fully opened blossoms. Although it's mainly the beetles that you have to worry about, the larvae sometimes damage the roots of roses.

## BEST CONTROL STRATEGY

A light infestation is easily controlled by handpicking. Drop the beetles into a jar of water and detergent or kerosene. If beetles are too numerous to be picked off your plants, dust or spray with pyrethrum or rotenone. Further control can be achieved by treating the soil around roses with milky spore disease (*Bacillus popilliae*) or beneficial nematodes.

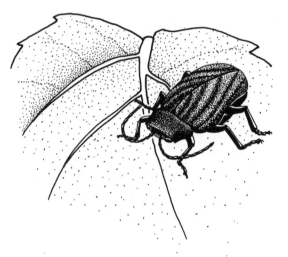

INSECT # Sawfly

## DESCRIPTION

Adult sawflies look like wasps, but have thicker midsections. They are ⅝ to 1½ inches in length and have two pairs of transparent wings. The larvae may be bluish black or olive green, and are ½ inch long.

Those sawflies most likely to infect your landscape plants are the rose slug (*Endelomyia aethiops*), the elm sawfly (*Cimbex americana*), and the violet sawfly (*Ametastegia pallipes*).

## MOST OBVIOUS SYMPTOMS

Sawflies will devour the leaves and needles of many different trees. A group can skeletonize the leaves on a plant in just one night.

## BEST CONTROL STRATEGY

Control sawflies by handpicking the larvae or by spraying infested plants with insecticidal soap, pyrethrum, or rotenone. Spray the plants thoroughly when larvae are first sighted and then watch for the second generation. Cultivate soil beneath plants to expose the pupae to weather and predator birds.

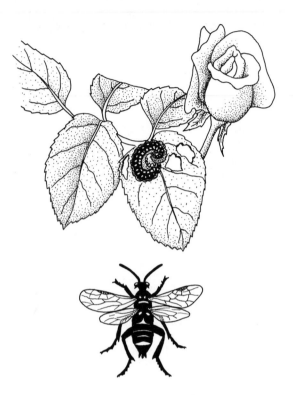

# INSECT *Scale*

## DESCRIPTION

Scale insects are related to mealybugs and aphids, although they don't look very much like either of these insects. Actually, they don't look like insects at all, but like little bumps. These insects have rounded waxy shells, which protect them while they feed. They usually gather in groups on the stems and leaves of plants. Their color may be reddish gray or brown. Some species excrete honeydew, which attracts ants and encourages the growth of sooty mold.

Under their shells, scale insects either lay eggs or bear live nymphs. These nymphs crawl to other parts of the plant and settle down to build their own shells. One to seven generations may be completed in a single year, depending on the length of the growing season.

Scale outbreaks can be triggered by pesticides used against other pests or by environmental stresses such as too much or too little water. Overuse of nitrogen fertilizer can encourage the growth of scale populations. Avoid this by using a slow-release nitrogen fertilizer.

## MOST OBVIOUS SYMPTOMS

The leaves of scale-infested plants turn yellow and may drop. The insects themselves confirm the diagnosis. Their distinct form is easy to spot, and they don't move too quickly.

## BEST CONTROL STRATEGY

If you discover scale insects before too many of them have infested your plants, simply scrape them off with your fingernail or with a cotton swab dipped in rubbing alcohol. If the pests are numerous, spray infested plants with a mixture of alcohol and insecticidal soap every three days for two weeks. In late winter, apply dormant oil to vulnerable trees and shrubs to kill any eggs or emerging larvae. But keep in mind that some plants, such as beech, maple, hickory, mountain ash, red and black oak, walnut, butternut, yew, azaleas, and broad-leaved evergreens, are sensitive to oil sprays. Do not apply heavy oils to these plants. Superior oils in dilute concentrations are probably fine, but test first.

## MONITORING SCALE INSECTS

### Emergence Time

Scale insects generally overwinter as adults or eggs on host plants. The eggs hatch in spring and larvae crawl about and begin feeding on new growth. Larvae are unprotected by the waxy scales that make adults difficult to kill, so sprays timed to coincide with the crawler stage are most effective.

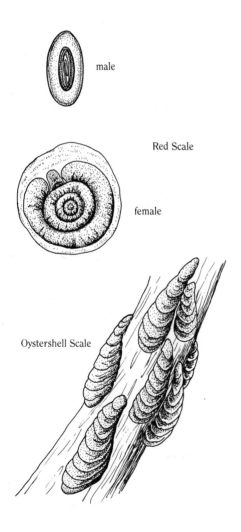

male

Red Scale

female

Oystershell Scale

## OPTIONS FOR CONTROLLING SCALE

### Natural Sprays

See the beginning of the chapter for more information on horticultural oil and insecticidal soap.

### Horticultural Oil
Light horticultural oil, also called superior horticultural spray oil, can be used during the growing season to control a scale problem. Use a 2 to 3 percent solution and be sure to spray it directly on the insects, because the oil works by suffocating them.

### Insecticidal Soap and Alcohol
Mix 1 cup isopropyl alcohol and ½ teaspoon insecticidal soap in 1 quart water and apply it to infested plants every three days for two weeks. You can substitute horticultural oil for the soap, and the spray will be equally effective.

## Botanical Poisons

See the beginning of the chapter for more information on pyrethrum.

### Pyrethrum

Pyrethrum paralyzes scale insects on contact, so you must spray it directly on the pests. By combining it with a little alcohol, you can increase its effectiveness. Two applications made three to four days apart should take care of any problem.

## Insect Predators and Parasites Available Commercially

Green lacewings, ladybugs, and various parasitic wasps will attack scale insects. The wasps *Comperiella bifasciata* and *Aphytis melinus* parasitize red scale; *Metaphycus helvolus* parasitizes black scale; *Aphytis lepidosaphes* attacks purple scale; and *Aspidiotiphagus citrinus* parasitizes hemlock scale.

## PREVENTING SCALE

### Preventive Spray Programs

See the beginning of the chapter for more information on horticultural oil.

### Horticultural Oil

Dormant oil sprays are designed to be used in the fall through early spring to smother overwintering scale insects. The heavy oils must only be used when trees are leafless, because they will damage foliage. Spray when the weather forecast indicates no rain or freezing night temperatures for at least 48 hours. The daytime temperatures should range from at least 40°F to 80°F.

These dormant oil sprays can harm certain trees and shrubs, including beech, maple, hickory, mountain ash, red and black oak, walnut, butternut, yew, azaleas, and broad-leaved evergreens. Check the information given for individual plants in Part 1 of this book to find out if a particular plant is indeed damaged by dormant oil. In most of these cases, you can use the newer horticultural oils, which are lighter.

### Lime Sulfur

Spray plants vulnerable to scale attack in late spring, before the buds open, with a solution made from one part concentrated lime sulfur in ten parts water. A combined dormant oil and lime sulfur spray applied to the trunk and branches will control scale larvae.

## Animal Predators

Chickadees and woodpeckers eat scale insects.

## Insect Predators Found in the Garden

Chalcid wasps are natural foes of scale insects.

INSECT **Slug, Snail**

## DESCRIPTION

Slugs are ugly. They are snails without shells. They have flabby, slimy bodies, usually 1 to 2 inches long, although some have been known to grow to 8 inches. Their colors vary from white to gray to yellow to brown-black. Snails and slugs are land-dwelling molluscs, related to clams and oysters. They have soft bodies covered with sticky slime, which are protected inside coiled shells. The markings on the shells vary considerably from species to species.

Slugs and snails can almost always be found in

moist, well-mulched gardens that have acidic soil. They're active at night, rasping holes with their filelike tongues in all kinds of plants. During the day, they sleep under boards or leaf litter. Slugs and snails simply love moisture and become particularly destructive in shaded gardens and during rainy spells. No matter where you live in the United States, you may have occasion to meet up with these pests.

# MOST OBVIOUS SYMPTOMS

Plants attacked by slugs suffer large ragged holes in their leaves, fruit, and stems. You may also see the slimy trails left by the creatures on the leaves or on the soil around your plants. Slugs begin feeding at the bottom of plants and work their way up. They first attack plants that have been damaged in some way, but they will eat anything.

# BEST CONTROL STRATEGY

The best way to control slugs is to set up a barrier to keep them off vulnerable plants or out of the garden. Handpicking will work if you begin early in the season, but a number of different traps also provide effective control, and by using them you won't have to handle these grotesque little creatures.

## MONITORING SLUGS AND SNAILS

### Emergence Time

Slugs and snails become active in your yard in early spring.

### Early Warning Devices

#### Slug Bar Trap

These commercial traps are small rectangular boxes that you fill with beer or slug poison and place in the garden. They are covered so the rain does not dilute the beer. You can use them to trap the first slugs of the season so that you know when they've arrived, and you can continue to catch slugs with them during the year.

#### Trap Crop

Slugs and snails are especially fond of hostas. Consider growing a few that you won't mind sacrificing to lure slugs away from other ornamentals. Collect and destroy slugs from these hostas every evening.

#### Other Early Warning Devices

Snails will crawl under upturned flower pots (clay not plastic), flat stones, or boards. Check beneath them regularly for early arrivals. If using a flower pot, place it on the north (shady side) of the plant and elevate one edge so it is easy for the animals to crawl inside. Check these traps twice a day and remove and destroy the pests.

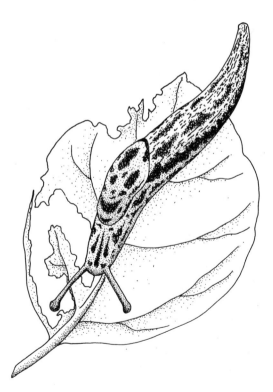

# OPTIONS FOR CONTROLLING SLUGS AND SNAILS

## Natural Sprays

See the beginning of this chapter for more information on bug juice.

### Bug Juice

If you are feeling particularly angry toward these pests, make bug juice out of them. Crush some of the slugs, mix them with water, and spray the strained liquid on infested plants. Some gardeners claim that the bug juice kills or repels the slugs.

## Traps and Mechanical Controls

### Beer Trap

Perhaps the most common and indeed one of the most effective controls for slugs and snails is the beer trap. Simply take a shallow dish, such as a pie plate, fill it with beer, and place it in the yard. Sink the pan into the soil so the slugs have easy access to the trap. Attracted by the yeast, slugs will dive in and drown. Replace the beer every few days or after a rain. Some gardeners report that 1 teaspoon baking yeast in 3 ounces water is even more effective than beer.

### Cover Trap

Anything that produces a cool, shady environment can be used as a cover trap for slugs. Lay pieces of old board, carpet, stones, plantain, or cabbage leaves in the garden, where they won't detract from the appearance of your yard. Check these cover traps twice a day and remove and destroy the pests.

### Grapefruit Rind Trap

Place hollowed halves of grapefruit open side down in the garden and check them several times a day to remove the slugs. The effectiveness of these shells lasts only two or three days. You can also use cantaloupe shells.

### Handpicking

If you don't mind grabbing their fat, slimy bodies, handpicking makes a sizable dent in the slug population right away, particularly if combined with trapping. Go out at night, armed with a flashlight and a can half full of kerosene or soapy water. Check plants, boards, mulched areas, and walkways for the slimy creatures. You can use tweezers, a pair of wooden chopsticks, or a pair of doctor's forceps if you prefer not to touch these pests with your fingers. Sprinkle table salt on slugs and snails if you want to kill them without picking them up.

# PREVENTING SLUGS AND SNAILS

## Fall Cleanup

Although you might put out cover traps during the growing season to catch these critters, pick them up in the fall so slugs and snails have trouble finding shelter for the winter.

## Preventive Spray Programs

### Horsetail

The primitive plant horsetail (*Equisitum arvense*), which grows wild throughout most of North America, contains substances that repel slugs. To make a solution from horsetail, place 1 to 2 ounces of the dried herb in a pot with a gallon of water. Bring the water to a boil and then simmer it for 20 minutes. For a little extra punch add cayenne peppers to the pot. Cool the solution and strain it; then spray it on vulnerable plants.

## Barriers

### Aluminum Sulfate

Aluminum sulfate is used to acidify soil, but research in England indicates that it also is a very effective repellent for slugs. Work it into the soil, applying about ½ pound for every 100 square feet of ground. In this quantity, it will not affect the pH of the soil very much, but will repel slugs. For quick application, you can sprinkle a small handful around the base of a vulnerable plant. Reapply the dust after a heavy rain.

### Commercial Anti-Slug Mulch

A commercial slug mulch popular in Europe contains shredded reed and tobacco plant waste. The nicotine repels slugs and the reed creates a natural barrier to block them. Do not use this mulch around plants in the nightshade family, because these plants are susceptible to mosaic virus, which is carried by tobacco. You can get good slug control by spreading it along the perimeter of a garden.

### Copper Flashing Material

Another development in the battle against slugs is the use of a strip of copper flashing material. (The commercial product is called Snail Barr.) If you have boxed raised beds, you can tack a 2-inch strip of this material around the outside, about 1 inch from the top of the bed. The reason for copper's success as a slug barrier is that it always carries a very mild electric charge, and although we can't detect it, it does give a little jolt to slugs. This product is available from Brucker Snail Barrier Company (see the source list at the back of the book for the address).

### Diatomaceous Earth

The sharp grains of diatomaceous earth will cut the soft bodies of slugs. One step on this stuff and slugs and snails will turn around and head in the other direction, so spread diatomaceous earth around any plants you want to protect. Reapply after rain.

### Eggshells

Eggshells work in the same way that diatomaceous earth does. Slugs won't wander over the sharp shells. Spread crushed eggshells thickly around plants you want to protect.

### Hardware Cloth

For gardens in boxed raised beds, tack hardware cloth with sharp points onto the outside of the box. Make sure the hardware cloth extends 2 inches above the boards. Slugs cannot crawl over this little fence.

### Sand

Although mature snails and slugs aren't bothered at all by sand, it does irritate baby slugs. Spread it around plants in spring when slugs are tiny.

### Seaweed Mulch

Slugs and snails seem to be repelled by seaweed. Rinse some well with fresh water and spread it around plants or around the outside of flower beds. And while it's protecting your garden from these pests, it adds nutrients to the soil as it decomposes.

### Sticky Band

To prevent slugs and snails from crawling up into shrubs, trees, and vines, apply a 3-inch-wide band of Tanglefoot or some other sticky substance to the trunks and stems of vulnerable plants.

### Wood Ashes

Wood ashes also act as a barrier to slugs. Sprinkle two handfuls of wood ashes around the base of each plant when plants or vines are 4 to 5 inches tall, or you can dig a trench a few inches deep and 3 to 4 inches wide around vulnerable plants and fill it with ashes. Keep ashes from contacting the plant.

## Animal Predators

Downy woodpeckers, robins, and other garden birds are happy to bite into a nice juicy slug. Some gardeners spread seed among their most vulnerable plants to encourage birds to feed there. Use cracked corn and sunflower seeds to avoid adding weeds to your flower garden.

Garter snakes are also important predators. If you mulch with black plastic, they will crawl right under it and eat up all the slugs and slug eggs. Other slug enemies include grass snakes, salamanders, shrews, toads, and turtles. Chickens don't usually care for slugs, but ducks will eat them.

## Insect Predators Found in the Garden

Black rove beetles, centipedes, firefly larvae, ground beetles, and soldier beetles all prey on slugs or slug eggs.

## Other Preventive Steps

### Prevent Nitrogen Deficiencies in Plants

Slugs prefer to eat soft, slightly rotting leaves. When plants are deficient in nitrogen, their lower leaves turn yellow and gradually decay, making them quite vulnerable to slug attack. Keep your plants well fed, and if they are beginning to look a little undernourished, give them a quick boost with manure tea.

### Eliminate Hiding Places

Slugs take up residence and breed in cool dark places such as under boards, under leafy ground covers, in weedy patches, and among rubble. If slugs are a problem in your backyard, consider removing the mulch on garden paths, the boards around raised beds, and other such potential shelters.

# INSECT *Tent Caterpillar*

## DESCRIPTION

Before you ever even see the tent caterpillar, you will see its tent. These pests build silken tents in the branches of trees and shrubs, where they reside while they feast on foliage. These pests are found throughout the United States. The eastern tent caterpillar is hairy and black with white stripes on its back. Along its sides, you'll see narrow brown and yellow lines and a row of blue spots. In the West, the caterpillar is orange-brown with blue dots on its back and sides. It will reach a length of about 2 inches. The adult moth has beige to brown wings, which span about 1¼ inches. Females lay their eggs in a ring around twigs and cover them with a shiny, hard substance. The two most common species are the eastern tent caterpillar (*Malacosoma americanum*) and the forest tent caterpillar (*M. disstria*).

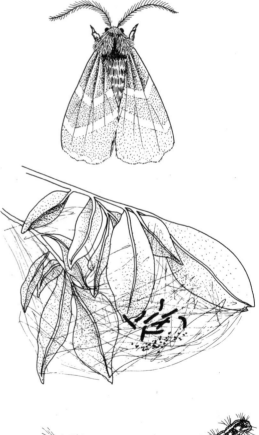

## MOST OBVIOUS SYMPTOMS

Tent caterpillars chew holes in the leaves of trees and shrubs, often skeletonizing them. In good numbers, they can defoliate a plant in only a few days.

## BEST CONTROL STRATEGY

As soon as you see tents going up in a tree or shrub, pull them down and spray your tree with Bt (*Bacil-*

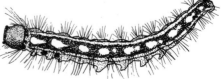

*lus thuringiensis*), reapplying it every five to seven days until the pests are gone. Spread a sticky substance such as Tanglefoot in a band around the trunk to intercept night-feeding larvae.

## MONITORING TENT CATERPILLARS

### Emergence Time

Look for the caterpillars' cocoons in late spring on tree trunks, fences, and house siding, and destroy them. Soon after hatching in the early spring, the larvae will spin their tents in trees and shrubs, from which they'll venture during the day to eat leaves and to which they'll return at night.

## OPTIONS FOR CONTROLLING TENT CATERPILLARS

### Traps and Mechanical Controls

#### Burlap Trap
You can trap the mature larvae with burlap tied around the trunk of a tree or shrub. Mature larvae will crawl down the tree to pupate and will be stopped by the burlap. Collect the caterpillars every day and destroy them.

#### Handpicking
Wearing gloves, pull the nests out of infested plants and kill the caterpillars.

### Botanical Poisons

See the beginning of the chapter for more information on pyrethrum and rotenone.

#### Pyrethrum
Pyrethrum paralyzes caterpillars on contact. It acts quickly, passing directly through the skin of the insect and disrupting its nerve centers. It must contact the insect directly to be effective. Usually, two applications to the threatened plant, three to four days apart, will successfully control a pest problem.

#### Rotenone
Rotenone can be used against tent caterpillars. A 1 percent solution will take care of most problems. Increase to 5 percent if necessary.

## PREVENTING TENT CATERPILLARS

### Animal Predators

Encourage predator birds such as Baltimore orioles, bluebirds, and chickadees.

### Insect Predators Found in the Garden

Ground beetles are excellent tent caterpillar predators, and an insect that looks like a large housefly, *Sarcophaga aldrichi,* attacks full-grown larvae. Digger wasps will attack a western species, the Rocky Mountain tent caterpillar. You can attract these and other beneficial insects by planting butterfly milkweed, dill, or coriander in your yard.

### Other Preventive Steps

In winter, search out and destroy the eggs. You'll find them in masses that surround twigs. They have a brown, varnished appearance.

 INSECT **Thrips**

## DESCRIPTION

You won't have an easy time spotting thrips, since they are only $\frac{1}{25}$ inch long; you can observe them by

shaking infested flowers over a sheet of paper. What is readily visible are their dark fecal pellets and the whitened, desiccated tissue that results from their mass feedings. The insects are very active and hop or fly away like little bits of confetti when disturbed. Adult females lay eggs on the leaves, fruit, or stems of plants. Nymphs hatch and begin feeding on the host plants. They will remain on the plant throughout adulthood. A generation of thrips is normally completed in about two weeks, and several generations occur in a year. Many species occur throughout North America. Thrips most often attack dry, stressed plants.

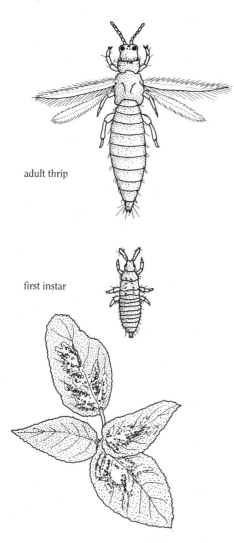

adult thrip

first instar

# MOST OBVIOUS SYMPTOMS

The chief target of thrip attack is flowers, especially white, yellow, and other light-colored blossoms. They rasp and puncture petals to feed on the juices, leaving flowers discolored and disfigured. Thrips will also feed on leaves, which become bleached and wither. Their damage to fruit scars the surfaces. New growth will be distorted. Heavy infestations destroy blossoms and leave foliage looking scorched.

# BEST CONTROL STRATEGY

Spray infested plants with insecticidal soap every three days for two weeks. Thrips prefer a dry environment, so make sure plants are adequately misted and watered.

# MONITORING THRIPS

## Emergence Time

Thrips are active in greenhouses throughout the year. Outdoors, they emerge from hibernation in the spring, and will find their way onto plants by early summer.

## Early Warning Devices

### Sticky Trap

By setting yellow sticky traps out in the landscape early in the spring, you will be able to catch the first thrips of the season and thus learn of their arrival.

# OPTIONS FOR CONTROLLING THRIPS

## Natural Sprays

See the beginning of the chapter for more information on garlic spray and horticultural oil.

### Garlic

Homemade sprays from garlic have been found to effectively repel thrips. To make the spray, mix ½ cup finely chopped garlic cloves with 1 pint water; then strain out the particles.

### Horticultural Oil

A light horticultural oil spray will smother thrips.

## Mechanical Controls

### Massaging Flowers

Try squeezing infested flowers carefully between your thumb and forefinger to kill thrips that have settled in between the petals.

## Botanical Poisons

See the beginning of the chapter for more information on avermectin, pyrethrum, and rotenone.

### Avermectin

The new avermectin insecticides such as avamectic (Avid) have been fermented from a soil-inhabiting streptomyces organism. These insecticides are very potent against thrips.

### Pyrethrum

Pyrethrum paralyzes on contact; it must actually touch the thrips to be effective.

### Rotenone

A 1 percent solution of rotenone can be used to fight thrips.

## Insect Predators and Parasites Available Commercially

Both the adults and larvae of green lacewings and ladybugs are effective thrips destroyers. Predatory mites (*Amblyseius cucumeris* and *A. mckenziei*) attack the egg and larval stages of thrips. They may require as long as two months to establish control, but they will be effective. Soil-dwelling nematodes will seek out thrips in the soil, burrow inside them, and reproduce. The nematodes release bacteria that will kill thrips.

## PREVENTING THRIPS

## Fall Cleanup

In the fall, cultivate the soil to 2 inches around your plants. Cultivate shallowly again in early spring to catch thrips that have dropped to the ground to pupate and overwinter.

If you leave gladiolus corms in the ground from year to year, they may host a population of gladiolus thrips. Dig these corms early in the fall before they are mature, and cut off the tops. The pests will be carried away in the cut portion. As a final measure, burn the tops. Preventing early infestation is necessary, since it's nearly impossible to reach the insects with sprays once they've settled in between flower petals.

In general, pick off and destroy infested buds and flowers. Don't compost them, because the insects mature there and fly back to your plants.

### Controlling Weeds

Since many kinds of weeds serve as alternate hosts for thrips, you'll want to keep them out of your garden or greenhouse; however, there is evidence that a diverse and varied natural plant community, including some weeds, supports natural thrip predators, too. Overzealous weed control near vulnerable plants may simply make those plants a better target. Keeping a few weeds in the background may not be a bad idea.

## Preventive Spray Programs

See the beginning of the chapter for more information on horticultural oil.

### Horticultural Oil

In late winter, before any leaf buds begin to open, spray dormant oil on vulnerable shrubs and trees to control thrips. Make sure the entire surface of the tree is covered.

## Barriers

### Aluminum Mulch

If you can stand them around your landscape plants,

aluminum foil and aluminum polyethylene mulches reduce the number of thrips.

### Diatomaceous Earth

Sprinkle diatomaceous earth around very small trees to create a barrier for the pest. You can also dust the whole plants, beginning from the ground and working upward. Use diatomaceous earth in the late evening or at night to minimize injury to predator insects.

### Organic Mulch

Spreading 4 to 6 inches of heavy organic mulch beneath plants keeps adult thrips from emerging in early spring. It may also prevent thrips that pupate in the soil from finding suitable pupation sites later in the season.

## Soaking Corms in Cold Storage

To fight gladiolus thrips, just before planting gladiolus corms, soak them in a solution of 1¼ tablespoons Lysol in a gallon of water. Storing corms at 40°F to 45°F also effectively eliminates remaining thrips. Generally, trouble with gladiolus thrips is much less serious when bulbs are planted early rather than late. Don't leave corms in the ground from one year to the next, particularly in an area where neighbors grow gladiolus. Dig them early in the fall, before they're mature, and cut off the tops, which harbor most of the pests.

## Insect Predators Found in the Garden

Some species of thrips are actually beneficial insects, preying upon other thrips and small insect pests. Other naturally occurring beneficials that control thrips include ground beetles, damsel bugs, minute pirate bugs, and syrphid flies.

# INSECT *Treehopper*

## DESCRIPTION

Treehoppers would make good candidates for horror movies, except that they are quite small. They look grotesquely humpbacked and have a pair of horns on their shoulders. Viewed from above, they look triangular, with a point at the rear. Treehoppers are only ¼ to ⅜ inch long. When females lay their eggs, they cut curved slits in the bark of rose twigs. These wounds open the way for rose canker and other diseases to enter a plant. The locust treehopper sucks sap and appears in three or four generations a year. As an adult, the locust treehopper is an active brown insect less than ¼ inch long. Two of the most common species are the buffalo treehopper (*Stictocephala bubalus*) and the locust treehopper (*Thelia bimaculata*).

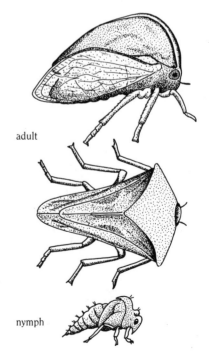

adult

nymph

## MOST OBVIOUS SYMPTOMS

Treehoppers suck sap from plants. The females do further damage when they puncture stems before depositing their eggs.

## BEST CONTROL STRATEGY

To control treehoppers, spray infested plants with pyrethrum or nicotine sulfate once a week until the pests are gone. You can also dust plants with a mixture of one part pyrethrum powder and nine parts sulfur. Apply this dust once a week. Treehoppers love alfalfa and sweet clover, so keep these weeds out of your yard.

The eggs of these insects often overwinter on the branches of roses. Destroy them by applying a light dormant oil to infested roses just before spring arrives.

# INSECT *Twig Pruner*

## DESCRIPTION

The adult twig pruner is a grayish brown beetle, about ⅝ inch long, with long antennae. The larvae do the damage, but you won't get an opportunity to see them until after they've damaged your trees: They work inside the twigs.

## MOST OBVIOUS SYMPTOMS

If, during the months of July and August, you happen to notice that an unusual number of twigs are dropping from one of your trees, suspect the twig pruner. The larvae first infest trees just under the bark; then they tunnel into twigs, where they'll remain until maturity. Adult beetles emerge the following summer. The leaves along infested twigs often become brown and dried.

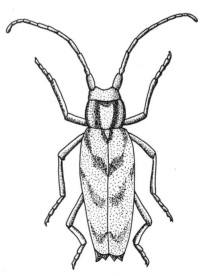

## BEST CONTROL STRATEGY

To remove these pests from your yard, gather and destroy fallen twigs.

# INSECT *Webworm*

The following information applies primarily to sod webworms, which attack lawn grasses; however, the techniques can be used to control other webworm problems as well.

## DESCRIPTION

Sod webworms grow to a length of ¾ to 1 inch. They are dull tannish brown worms with black spots along their sides and backs. Long, stiff hairs protrude from these spots. They have dark shiny brown heads. The adults are buff-colored moths with a wingspan of about an inch. They fly in the early morning or late evening in a jerky zigzag pattern, just a few feet above the lawn. The moths don't damage the lawn, but they drop eggs into the grass that, upon hatching, develop into very hungry caterpillars. These larvae hatch in six to ten days and immediately begin feeding on grass blades and building silk-lined tunnels in the thatch and debris of the lawn near the soil surface. Sod webworms are found throughout the United States.

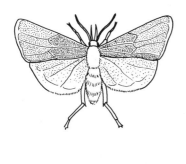

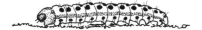

Fall webworms infest trees and shrubs. These caterpillars are pale yellow or green and measure about 1 inch in length. The adult moth has white to brown spotted wings that span 1½ inches. Like tent caterpillars, fall webworms build silken nests in trees and shrubs. You can distinguish webworm nests from those of tent caterpillars by their compact form, and they usually envelop the leaves at the ends of individual branches. Fall webworms usually strike in August or early fall.

As well as the sod webworm (*Crambus* spp.) and the fall webworm (*Hyphantria cunea*), this group includes the barberry webworm (*Omphalocera dentosa*), the pine webworm (*Tetralopa robustella*), and the garden webworm (*Loxostege rantalis*).

## MOST OBVIOUS SYMPTOMS

In late spring, if you see small dead patches, 1 to 2 inches in diameter, appearing in your lawn, you may have a problem with sod webworms. By midsummer, these will become large dead patches. Lawns will look their worst by July and August. Sod webworms cut grass blades off just above the thatch line, and they drag these blades into their silken tunnels to eat them. The grass in the damaged spots isn't actually dead, it's just been leveled to the ground.

If you suspect sod webworms, look for them in the thatch in the damaged areas of your lawn. Carefully break apart the thatch and search for their silken tubes. You also may find greenish tan pellets about the size of a pinhead; this is the excrement of the webworms.

The fall webworm builds silken nests in the branches of trees and shrubs. Inside these nests you'll see leaves skeletonized by webworms.

324

# BEST CONTROL STRATEGY

Control sod webworms by removing thatch and applying an insecticidal soap drench to the damaged areas. If this doesn't control the problem, use Bt (*Bacillus thuringiensis*). Predatory nematodes will also help you to remove these pests from your yard.

To control webworm infestations in trees and shrubs, pull down their nests and destroy them. If the larvae are small, spray plants with Bt. If you've caught them when they are mature, spray with pyrethrum or rotenone. Apply a sticky band of Tanglefoot around the trunks of infested plants to catch larvae as they crawl up trees and shrubs.

# MONITORING WEBWORMS

## Emergence Time

By the time winter arrives, the larvae will be nearly mature. They'll curl up in the soil throughout the winter and emerge in spring to resume feeding as soon as the soil temperature rises—in late April to early May.

## Bringing Sod Webworms to the Surface

In late spring or early summer, mark off two or three sections of lawn that measure 2 feet by 2 feet. Do this in damaged and undamaged areas. Then mix 2 tablespoons liquid detergent into 1 gallon water, and using a sprinkling can, pour it evenly over each area. The soap irritates the webworms. They'll crawl to the surface in 5 to 10 minutes. If the thatch layer in your lawn is thick, you may need to pour several gallons of soap solution on the test areas to be sure to saturate the thatch and reach the webworms. If you find only two or three worms for every square foot, and your lawn is healthy, these pests probably won't cause any real problems. If your lawn is stressed from compaction, lack of water, or lack of food, an infestation of even one larva per square foot will require treatment.

# OPTIONS FOR CONTROLLING WEBWORMS

## Mechanical Controls

### Removing Thatch
If the thatch on your lawn is thicker than ¾ inch, remove it. This reduces the habitat of webworms.

## Botanical Poisons

See the beginning of this chapter for more information on pyrethrum and rotenone.

### Pyrethrum
Pyrethrum paralyzes webworms on contact; it must contact the pests to work. When applying it to the lawn, soak the grass and thatch thoroughly. Usually, two applications, three to four days apart, will take care of these pests.

### Rotenone
You can substitute rotenone for pyrethrum in the above technique.

## Biological Controls

### Beauvaria Bassiana
*Beauvaria bassiana* is a fungus that attacks webworms. It does provide effective control, but you won't see results for about a year.

### Bt (*Bacillus Thuringiensis*)
Another option you have for controlling webworms is Bt. Use a foliar spray on infested trees and a drench on infested lawns. Apply Bt every 10 to 14 days until the pests are gone.

## Poultry

Chickens, if you have them or can borrow them, will clean out a webworm infestation in a matter of days.

Once they've finished the job, irrigate the lawn thoroughly.

## Insect Predators and Parasites Available Commercially

Beneficial nematodes can take care of a sod webworm infestation in about a week. When applying them to your lawn, water them into the thatch. Should damage from webworms become too extensive, consider investing in trichogramma eggs.

# PREVENTING WEBWORMS

## Preventive Spray Programs

### Insecticidal Soap Drench
You can also use insecticidal soap to control webworms. Thoroughly soak the thatch layer with it, reapplying it every two to three days if the infestation is heavy.

### Soap Drench
As described earlier, under "Bringing Sod Webworms to the Surface" on page 325, use a soap solution made from liquid detergent to bring sod webworms out in the open. Drench the damaged spots in your lawn and the adjacent areas. As soon

as the caterpillars wriggle to the surface, rake them into piles, scoop them up with a shovel, and drop them into a bucket of soapy water.

## Resistant Varieties of Plants

A number of commercially available perennial ryegrasses, such as 'Citation II', 'Commander', 'Repell', and 'Sunrise', and a few fine-bladed tall fescues, contain fungi that prevent webworms and some other insects from feeding on the grasses.

## Animal Predators

Robins and starlings can eat a lot of webworms.

## Insect Predators Found in the Garden

Braconid wasps, vespid wasps, earwigs, carabid and rove beetles, ants, and mites all attack webworms.

## Other Preventive Steps

Keep your lawn in good health with proper lawn-care techniques. Webworms prefer areas in lawns that are hot and dry during the day, often areas near driveways and patios. Prevent soil from becoming compacted and be sure your lawn gets the water it needs.

INSECT **Weevil**

# DESCRIPTION

Weevils, also called snout beetles, have long slender snouts, at the end of which are their mouth parts. Their tear-shaped black or brown bodies are covered with a hard shell, and they measure $\frac{1}{10}$ to $\frac{1}{4}$ inch in length. The adult beetles feed at night and curl up under plant debris during the day. Most species will play dead when disturbed, folding their

legs and dropping to the ground. The larvae also feed on plants. They are legless, about $\frac{1}{2}$ inch long, and white to pink in color, with brown heads.

The weevils comprise a large group of insects; about 2,500 occur in North America. You won't have to worry about all of them, though. Some of the most common include the black vine weevil (*Otiorrhyn-*

*chus sulcatus*), the Japanese weevil (*Pseudocneorhinus bifasciatus*), and the strawberry weevil (*O. ovatus*).

## MOST OBVIOUS SYMPTOMS

Adult weevils eat holes or notches in leaves; some species roll or curl them. When abundant, they can defoliate plants. The larvae carve zigzag paths into roots, fruit, or stems. Infested plants wilt and will pull out of the ground easily.

## BEST CONTROL STRATEGY

Because of their habit of dropping to the ground when startled, you can remove many weevils from infested plants by spreading a cloth beneath those plants and beating the limbs. The weevils will curl up and drop to the cloth, where you can gather them and destroy them in a jar of water and detergent or kerosene. In addition, spray infested plants weekly with a solution of pyrethrum and alcohol.

## MONITORING WEEVILS

### Emergence Times

Weevils will begin to show up in your yard in late spring—April and early May in most parts of the country.

## OPTIONS FOR CONTROLLING WEEVILS

### Traps

#### Cardboard Trap
Two or three hours after dark, when the weevils have moved up into the plant, place a strip of cardboard coated with a sticky material, such as Tanglefoot, around the trunk. The next morning, when weevils crawl down the trunk, the Tanglefoot will tangle their feet. Make sure the trap fits snugly around the trunk or the weevils will crawl underneath it.

#### Sticky Trap
A band of a sticky substance such as Tanglefoot applied around the trunk or stems of the plant will prevent weevils from climbing up for their nightly feed.

strawberry weevil

black vine weevil

## Botanical Poisons

See the beginning of the chapter for more information on rotenone and sabadilla.

### Rotenone

If you are using rotenone, a 5 percent solution will be necessary to fight weevils.

### Sabadilla

Apply sabadilla weekly on the undersides of leaves of infested plants.

## Insect Predators and Parasites Available Commercially

One of the best techniques for controlling a bad weevil infestation or preventing an attack in the first place is to introduce predatory nematodes to the garden. Release them early in the season, around planting time if possible.

## PREVENTING WEEVILS

### Fall Cleanup

Weevils will make themselves at home among any dead plants that are lying around, so keep your yard clean. They will also feed on various weeds, including morning glory, ragweed, thistle, cocklebur, and joe-pye weed. Remove these from the landscape and you'll have fewer problems with weevils.

### Animal Predators

Bluebirds, warblers, wrens, and other birds eat weevils.

### Insect Predators Found in the Garden

Spiders catch adult weevils.

INSECT **Whitefly**

## DESCRIPTION

In western states, leafhoppers are also called whiteflies. These pests are tiny, mothlike, white, winged insects. When shaken from a plant, they look like flying dandruff. The yellowish nymphs are legless, flat, and oval, and may resemble scale insects at certain stages. Females lay yellow, cone-shaped eggs on the undersides of leaves. Both nymphs and adults attack plants. Whiteflies occur throughout the United States. In the North, they are common greenhouse pests. Many generations occur in a year.

## MOST OBVIOUS SYMPTOMS

Whiteflies suck the juices from plant leaves, buds, and stems, causing serious weakening of the entire plant. The leaves will turn yellow and die, and the growth of the plant will be stunted. Honeydew produced by the whiteflies may cover fruit and foliage, and this in turn encourages the growth of sooty mold on these surfaces. Although tiny, whiteflies will be clearly visible on your plants, and therefore you will easily be able to make an accurate diagnosis if these pests have infested any of your ornamentals.

## BEST CONTROL STRATEGY

Spray infested plants with insecticidal soap as soon as you spot the problem. Apply it every two to three days for two weeks. For very serious infestations, you may have to resort to pyrethrum, but try the soap spray first.

## MONITORING WHITEFLIES

### Emergence Times

In the South, the nymphs hibernate throughout the winter and emerge in spring when air temperatures are above 65°F. In the North, whiteflies are a greenhouse pest in winter and are often brought home on infested bedding plants or nursery sets.

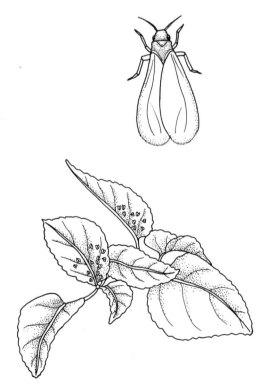

### Early Warning Devices

#### Sticky Trap
Yellow sticky traps will catch the earliest of the whiteflies in your backyard. In addition to letting you know that these pests are around, these traps help to control the infestation.

#### Trap Crop
Whiteflies will head straight for ornamental flowering tobacco if it's planted in your yard. If you can bear the thought of sacrificing them, plant a few to attract whiteflies and warn you of their arrival in your yard.

## OPTIONS FOR CONTROLLING WHITEFLIES

### Natural Sprays

See the beginning of the chapter for more information on horticultural oil.

#### Alcohol Solution
Alcohol mixed with water and superior horticultural oil can be completely effective in controlling whiteflies. Make the solution by combining 1 cup isopropyl alcohol and ½ teaspoon oil in 1 quart water. Spray plants thoroughly. Two applications, a week apart, should remove all the whiteflies. You can substitute insecticidal soap for the oil.

#### Horticultural Oil
Light horticultural oils can be used during the growing season to control pests. Make a 2 to 3 percent solution and spray it directly on the whiteflies. It works by suffocating the pests. Two applications, three to four days apart, should suffice.

#### Water
If you spray plants vigorously with water, you can knock many whiteflies from the leaves. This is best done early in the morning. Use a nozzle that will produce a fine spray of water, and be sure to spray the undersides of leaves as well as the top surfaces. Do this at least three times—three days in a row or every other day—to get the whiteflies that will hatch from eggs laid before you began spraying.

## Traps

### Sticky Trap

Yellow sticky traps will catch plenty of whiteflies, if you don't mind them hanging in and among your landscape plants. Only use them for three to four weeks; any longer and they'll trap beneficials as well.

## Botanical Poisons

See the beginning of the chapter for more information on pyrethrum and ryania.

### Pyrethrum

Pyrethrum paralyzes whiteflies on contact. Apply it directly to the whiteflies, spraying the undersides of the leaves as well as the tops. Usually, two applications made three to four days apart will successfully control the problem.

### Ryania

You can also spray infested plants with ryania. Several applications are usually needed.

## Insect Predators and Parasites Available Commercially

Green lacewings are probably the most effective insects you can buy to control whiteflies, but ladybugs and chalcid and trichogramma wasps will also attack these pests. Only use wasps, though, inside greenhouses.

## PREVENTING WHITEFLIES

### Preventive Spray Programs

See the beginning of the chapter for more information on horticultural oil and insecticidal soap.

### Horticultural Oil

In late winter, before any leaf buds begin to open, spray dormant oil on vulnerable trees to smother any overwintering pests.

### Insecticidal Soap

On plants most vulnerable to soft-bodied pests such as whiteflies, you can follow a biweekly preventive spray program using commercial insecticidal soap. Begin by spraying seedlings you start indoors, covering the undersides of leaves. Continue to spray plants every two weeks throughout the first month of the plants' lives outdoors.

### Seaweed

Spray vulnerable plants with seaweed extract in the spring. It seems that leaves coated with extract are unsuitable for whitefly reproduction. The population of insects will be reduced considerably.

## Companion Planting

If they don't detract from your landscape design, consider planting onions or chives in and around plants vulnerable to whitefly attack. Some research has shown that these alliums repel whiteflies. Gardeners often recommend nasturtiums and savory as companion plants, but no studies have shown these plants to be effective repellents.

## Animal Predators

Gnatcatchers, kinglets, phoebes, and swallows are some of the common songbirds that eat whiteflies.

INSECT # White Grub

## DESCRIPTION

White grubs look about as disgusting as their name sounds. They are the fat, whitish larvae of beetles.

Mature grubs reach a length of ¾ to 1½ inches, and have three pairs of legs. Their heads are tan, and they have large, brown-black mouth parts. White grubs characteristically curl into the shape of a C.

These pests feed on the roots of grass until the ground freezes in late fall; then they burrow down deep into the ground to stay warm. In spring, they surface to feed on grass roots. For their next course, they move on to ornamental plants. Several years pass before their life cycles are complete. White grubs frequently infest new gardens dug and built on old sod. They can be found throughout North America.

## MOST OBVIOUS SYMPTOMS

If you notice an unusual number of blackbirds, starlings, or other birds on the lawn, or if moles, skunks, or raccoons keep digging up the ground, your yard may be infested with white grubs. Damage shows up as irregular brown sections that appear burned. The sod lifts up easily in these spots. In fact, you should pick up the sod and check for grubs beneath it. They do the most damage in late spring or early fall.

Ornamental plants that have been attacked by these pests will suddenly wilt. This usually occurs in early summer.

## BEST CONTROL STRATEGY

Apply beneficial nematodes to the soil for quick control. Milky spore disease (*Bacillus popilliae*) is also effective, but complete results won't be achieved for a few years.

## MONITORING WHITE GRUBS

### Emergence Times

White grubs begin feeding on lawns in early spring, but damage won't be apparent until late spring, and sometimes you won't see any signs until early fall.

### Checking for Grubs

The best way to determine if your lawn is infested with grubs is to look for the little creatures themselves. In late May to mid-June, a little later in the far North, examine several areas of the lawn. Cut three sides of a 1-square-foot piece of sod to a depth of 4 to 5 inches, and carefully pull it up. Scrape the dirt from the roots and look for the larvae. If you find more than 15, begin control measures. In a lawn that isn't vigorous and healthy, you'll want to apply control techniques if you count 6 or more. After inspecting the roots, fold the grass back in place, tamp it, and water it in.

## OPTIONS FOR CONTROLLING WHITE GRUBS

### Biological Controls

#### Milky Spore Disease (*Bacillus Popilliae*)
For long-range effective control of grubs, milky spore disease works well. Apply it in powder form to mowed areas of the lawn. You can add it any time except

when the ground is frozen. Use approximately 20 ounces of spore dust for every 5,000 square feet of lawn. Milky spore disease remains in the soil, where it will infect the next crop of beetle grubs. The only disadvantage to using this control is that it takes three to five years to show complete results in controlling the grub population.

## Insect Predators and Parasites Available Commercially

Beneficial nematodes find their way to white grubs, burrow inside them, and reproduce. They bring in bacteria, which eventually kill the grubs. Nematodes can reduce a population of white grubs by up to 70 percent. Adequate soil moisture is essential to successful use of the nematodes, since they travel on a thin film of water through the soil, so soak the ground with ½ inch of water before applying the nematodes, and again afterward.

## PREVENTING WHITE GRUBS

### Fall Cleanup

White grubs overwinter 4 to 8 inches deep in the soil near host plants, so a little fall garden maintenance will go a long way to reducing next year's grub population. Where possible, cultivate the soil down about 2 to 4 inches to bring the grubs to the surface and expose as many as possible to predator birds.

## Animal Predators

Grackles, meadowlarks, crows, blackbirds, robins, and starlings will eat lots of grubs.

## Insect Predators Found in the Garden

Spined soldier bugs, ground beetles, wheel bugs, and the larvae of tachinid flies attack white grubs.

## NOTES AND RESEARCH

The Environmental Protection Agency is currently reviewing a new product that contains insecticidal soap and pyrethrins. This product inhibits Japanese beetles, which in turn reduces grub problems.

## INSECT Wireworm

## DESCRIPTION

Wireworms are the larvae of click beetles. They are ⅓ to 1½ inches long, dark brown to yellowish in color, jointed, hard shelled, and cylindrical. Do not confuse the larvae with millipedes, which have many pairs of legs; wireworm larvae have only three pairs directly behind the head. Wireworms chew on the underground stems, roots, and seeds of grass. They lay their eggs in the soil. Eggs, larvae, and adults overwinter in the ground. Wireworms are found throughout the United States and are especially common on land that is poorly drained or has recently been in sod. Generally, one generation occurs in a year, but certain species may require several years to mature.

## MOST OBVIOUS SYMPTOMS

Wireworms eat roots and rhizomes, causing grass to wither and die. They'll also feed on seeds.

adult click beetle

wireworm

## BEST CONTROL STRATEGY

Wireworms are easily trapped with potatoes. Simply spear pieces of potato with sticks, and bury them 2 to 4 inches in the soil, leaving a portion of the stick above ground. Set these traps 3 to 10 feet apart. The wireworms will feed on the potatoes. After a week, pull up your sticks, along with the potatoes and the wireworms inside. You can use these potato traps to determine in the first place whether the garden has wireworms.

## MONITORING WIREWORMS

### Emergence Time

Adult beetles lay eggs in the soil in the spring. The larvae hatch from the eggs the same spring and, depending on the species, will reach adulthood in two to six years.

## OPTIONS FOR CONTROLLING WIREWORMS

### Insect Predators and Parasites Available Commercially

Beneficial nematodes applied to infested soil will help control wireworms. They burrow into the larvae, carrying with them bacteria that kill the larvae.

## PREVENTING WIREWORMS

### Fall Cleanup

Adults, larvae, and pupae overwinter in soil near the host plant. Cleaning up the yard in the fall may be the most important step you take all season long. Remove any plant debris and cultivate the soil lightly around vulnerable plants.

# *Yellow Woolly Bear*

## DESCRIPTION

Yellow woolly bear caterpillars look as though they've dressed for winter with their thick yellow hairy coats. These coats have a long black stripe running down the back. Woolly bears are about 2 inches long. They attack a great number of plants. The adults are furry yellowish moths about 1½ inches wide, with white wings. Each wing has a small black spot on it.

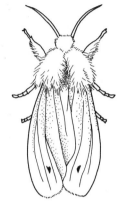

## MOST OBVIOUS SYMPTOMS

The larvae chew large holes in flowers, leaves, and tender stems. They can do considerable damage to foliage. You may find the holes they make arranged side by side across the leaves.

## BEST CONTROL STRATEGY

Control yellow woolly bears by handpicking and spraying infested plants with Bt (*Bacillus thuringiensis*).

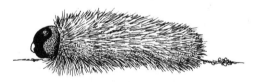

# CHAPTER 7

# *Animal Pests*

The depredations of animal pests like moles, gophers, and deer can be so discouraging that they might make you consider giving up on your property altogether. Unfortunately, there are no quick, surefire solutions to any serious animal-pest invasion. You have three basic choices in almost all cases: You can trap the pest to kill or remove it; you can set up a barrier of some kind that will effectively deny the pest access to your yard or garden; or you can put repellents on or around your plants to keep pests away from them. This chapter will focus first on the most effective control measures available for your use, and then it will address various preventive measures. The chapter ends with a pest-by-pest description of the most effective management methods.

## CONTROLLING ANIMALS

Effective animal pest control depends on three prime factors: timing, persistence, and diversity.

### Timing

In managing animal pests, good timing is crucial. Install barriers *before* you expect an animal to make its appearance, and start control measures at the very first indication of damage. Unlike most insects, animals can wipe out an entire planting or even the whole garden in a very short time if the problem is left unattended.

### Persistence

Some animals, such as squirrels and deer, are ingenious in foiling your attempts to thwart them. A single try at establishing a barrier may not do the job. You will have to keep trying until you come up with a control or combination of controls that finally outsmarts the wily marauders.

### Diversity

No single control method or preventive step is always satisfactory, even if it worked last year. Typically, a variety of strategies and devices are required, often used in combination. Placement of traps and barriers must be shifted frequently to ensure success against persistent pests.

In many cases, the only realistic option you have in controlling a pest after it has discovered your yard is trapping. Biological controls have limited effectiveness, and poisons pose hazards to the environment, pets, and children. In this section, we present control steps ranging from those with the least impact to those with greater impact on the environment.

### Traps

Most people are unhappy about having to kill any living creature, so they prefer to use what are called "live traps," which catch the animal without harming it. Once caught, the culprit is brought out to the countryside and released.

Live-trapping animal pests isn't the best control, simply because the animal might not survive in its new environment. Any given area already has an established population of wildlife, and adding a new member puts a little more demand on the available food, water, and habitats. Using barriers to prevent pests from getting to your plants in the first place is perhaps the best solution, but if it doesn't work effectively in your backyard, you may have to resort to trapping if you want to protect your landscape.

Box traps are the safest design for live-trapping garden pests. The leg-hold design and the snare design are nonspecific, and will trap and kill pets as well as pests. Also, these traps can maim an animal instead of killing it. Box traps are available for many of the most troublesome animal pests, including chipmunks, gophers, groundhogs, mice, moles, rabbits, and squirrels. (See the box, "The Best Traps for the Worst Pests," for recommended sizes.)

Of course, you can also set traps and snares that will kill animal pests, such as the mousetrap. When dealing with the prolific rodents such as gophers, mice, and moles, this is often the best method of control.

**Using Traps**

Set the trap in some sheltered area near or around where you have spotted a pest in action. Do not set the trap out in the open. Conceal it with leaves, sticks, and/or grass clippings so that it looks a bit more natural. To avoid raising the suspicion of the animals you want to catch, try not to leave your own scent on the trap any more than you have to. You can boil traps with pine cones, dried leaves, or other natural materials to mask your scent. Handle the traps and the bait with gloves—preferably rubber gloves just out of the package. Follow the directions that come with the trap to set it up correctly with bait in place. After that, check the trap every day to renew the bait and see if you have trapped the culprit. Once you have trapped the animal, consult

Box traps catch animal pests without harming them. This one traps squirrels.

---

### The Best Traps for the Worst Pests

**Chipmunks**
5″ × 5″ × 15″ box trap. Bait with peanuts or other nut meats.

**Gophers**
Standard wooden-based rat traps, a two-pronged pincher trap (called the Macabee trap), or a squeeze-type box trap. Bait with a large amount of grain, sunflower seeds, peanuts, or other nut meats.

**Groundhogs**
12″ × 12″ × 36″ box trap. Bait with nut meats or pieces of fruit.

**Mice**
5″ × 5″ × 15″ box trap, standard wooden-based mouse traps, or glue boards especially designed for mice. Bait with nut meats, dried fruit, or bacon.

**Moles**
Choker or harpoon-type trap. No bait needed.

**Rabbits**
10″ × 12″ × 30″ box trap. Bait with fresh greens, carrots, or fresh clover.

**Squirrels**
8″ × 8″ × 24″ box trap. Bait with peanuts, sunflower seeds, walnuts, almonds, oats, or melon rind.

your local County Extension agent for advice on where to take it.

## Biological Controls

Compared with the wide range of predators and parasites available for insects, there aren't many biological controls available for animal pests. While badgers eat gophers and mountain lions eat deer, people do not generally have these natural predators in their backyard. However, a couple of biological controls may already be waiting in your yard.

Many homeowners have found that animal pests tend to be less troublesome when there are dogs or cats outside much of the time. Most rabbits, for example, do not feel very comfortable eating while a dog or cat is on the prowl. Male dogs and cats will mark their territories with scent, and these boundary marks can sometimes keep rabbits from venturing onto your lawn. If you let your pets play or stay in the yard, make sure their rabies shots are up to date.

## Poisons

There are no poisons that are not in one way or another potentially dangerous to pets and children. **Do not** use poisons to control animal pests in the landscape.

# PREVENTING PEST PROBLEMS

Over the years, desperate homeowners and gardeners have resorted to a number of ingenious tactics in the battle against animal pests. Here are some of the most successful preventive measures, from fences to bars of soap.

## Barriers

If you know from past experience that one or more animal pests are likely to attack your backyard, then the best approach to controlling them is to deny them access in the first place. There are a number of techniques for preventing access, some more effective than others. If you want to use a barrier, that usually means building some kind of fence.

## Fences

Here you have a choice: You can put up a temporary fence that is designed to be movable and easily erected, or you can take the time and go to the expense of building a permanent fence to solve the pest problem once and for all. There are any number of fence designs in both categories designed to keep animals out of a garden bed or stand of shrubs, and there are just as many stories about how some of those animals, especially raccoons and deer, overcame the barrier and still entered the garden sanctuary.

Fencing off a small, garden-sized section of your property is relatively easy, or you can fence around the entire yard. Remember that various animals can jump, dig, and squeeze through small places. The size of the fence depends on which pest or pests you are trying to thwart: Make sure your fence is high enough to be effective. To keep deer out, it must be at least 7 to 8 feet high. A 3-foot fence will keep out gophers, groundhogs, and rabbits. Even if burrowing pests are not currently a problem, if you are going to the trouble of erecting a permanent fence, it is a good idea to bury at least 6 inches of it in the ground to forestall any future subterranean invasions. Finally, be sure your fence is a solid barrier—spacings between boards or other materials should be less than 2 inches. The actual design of your fence and the materials you use will ultimately depend on how much time and money you wish to spend.

## Repellents

For many years, gardeners have been trying to find substances that will repel animals from their yards and gardens. There are now on the market a number of products that promise to successfully ward off various animal pests, including birds, rabbits, raccoons, and deer. In addition, there are dozens of home remedies invented by frustrated gardeners under siege from some troublesome animal. These products work better for some gardeners than others, and no one product seems to be foolproof all of the time in all areas of the country. If you prefer not to rig a barrier, then you may wish to experiment with one or more of these repellent products; however, you must not be too confident about their effectiveness in your particular landscape.

Repellents come in two general forms—those that repel by odor and those that repel by some visual, tactile, or audible characteristic.

## Using Scent to Repel Pests

Various animal repellents are sold commercially in many garden centers and through mail-order catalogs. Big-Game Deer Repellent, Hinder, and Ro-Pel are a few examples. The success of the scent repellents is quite spotty. Some homeowners swear by them; others find they don't work at all. Dozens of home remedies have been reported in garden magazines, and several scent repellents seem to be particularly popular.

**Cat Litter.** Many gardeners find that used cat litter repels rabbits when it's sprinkled on the lawn and around ornamentals, and repels moles and gophers when it's buried. The advice is to sprinkle well-used litter around vulnerable plants, replacing it each week and after each rain. For moles and gophers, dump the litter right into the holes of the active burrows. But use caution when handling and distributing litter: Cat feces may contain toxoplasmosis parasites, which can infect humans. **Do not** use litter around edible plants.

**Hair.** Lots of homeowners report that they have kept deer away by hanging human hair from the trees around their landscape. Use mesh bags with a ⅛-inch or smaller mesh. Place at least two large handfuls of hair in each bag and hang them from the branches of trees and shrubs at a height of about 30 inches. They should be no farther than 3 feet apart. This method works best if you replace the hair every four days, which means that you really need to be friends with a barber or hairdresser to make this system work.

**Soap.** Deer are also repelled by strongly scented soap. Use bars of deodorant soap, keeping them in their wrappers so they'll last longer. String them on wires and hang them about 4 feet above the ground (deer-nose height) on the branches of the trees or shrubs to be protected. Space them no farther than 3 feet apart. Ornamenting your trees and shrubs with soap in late winter provides protection throughout this season, when hungry deer cause widespread damage to tender new shoots.

While gardeners have tried many other materials, such as ammonia, vinegar, blood meal, and manure from zoo carnivores to repel animals through noxious odors, none have been proven uniformly effective. That is why we hesitate to recommend them as repellents for animal pests.

## Using Tactile and Audio Tricks

A host of audio, visual, and tactile tricks that keep pests away have been tried and recommended. The following two techniques are frequently recommended. Though no scientific research supports their effectiveness, their popularity suggests that they might be worth a try.

**Pepper Technique.** Pepper is organic, so it doesn't harm the soil, and it's very inexpensive. Sprinkle black or hot pepper all over and around plants. It reportedly repels rabbits and squirrels. Reapply the pepper after rain.

**High-Tech Vibrations.** The Rodent-Repelling Garden Stake is a commercial device from West Germany. It is battery-powered and vibrates at 60-second intervals to repel burrowing rodents and moles over as much as ⅓ acre. Technology like this has its price, and this gadget carries a hefty price tag (over $75). It is carried by Hammacher Schlemmer (see the source list at the back of the book for the address).

These schemes just scratch the surface of the long list of home remedies for animal pests. In the rest of this chapter we will look at individual animal pests and the best prevention and control measures for each. Keep in mind that if you have neither the time nor the inclination to experiment, or lack the patience to try multiple approaches, then the most reliable control device is a trap, and the best prevention is an effective barrier.

# *Guide to Animal Pests*

People create lovely landscapes for their pleasure and enjoyment. However, a property with a lovely lawn and a variety of healthy trees, shrubs, vines, and ground covers will also, inevitably, attract pest animals. While many of these animals are appealing in nature, they are seldom welcome in the yard. As they go about raising a family, eating, and sleeping, they inadvertently damage plantings. What follows in this section are profiles of the most troublesome pests and options for controlling and preventing problems. Some of these solutions have been proven more effective than others; you'll need to try them to see how they work in *your* landscape.

## ANIMAL *Chipmunk*

Chipmunks are territorial animals. Males and females live apart rather than in communal burrows. They have a keen sense of smell and a strong sense of curiosity. In the course of gardening, your scent is transferred to plants, bulbs, or seeds that may be planted in the chipmunk's territory. The chipmunk feels its territory has been invaded; curiosity overcomes caution, and the animal digs up the plant.

### SIGNS OF CHIPMUNK DAMAGE

Plants and bulbs are dug up, especially just after they have been planted in the soil.

### BEST CONTROL STRATEGY

Traps are about the only effective control for chipmunks. Use a 5″ × 5″ × 15″ box trap, baited with peanuts or other nut meats.

## STEPS TO PREVENT CHIPMUNK DAMAGE

### Repellents

Ro-Pel repels chipmunks by odor and taste. Spray it on bulbs, seeds, and landscape plants before planting them. Be sure to wear gloves and a mask; the label warns that you should avoid skin contact and inhalation of the fumes. Ro-Pel is available from Burlington Scientific Corporation and Ringer Corporation (see the source list at the back of the book for the addresses).

### Barriers

Once any type of plant that has previously been bothered by chipmunks is in the ground, cover it with a piece of screening or fencing. Ordinary window screening or fence with a mesh of up to 1 by 2 inches will suffice. Place the screening on top of the plant, securing it with stones. The plant may be slightly flattened, but will recover in a few days. On bigger plants, place the screen flat on the ground around the base (fencing that is heavier need not be secured). The screening discourages the chipmunks from coming near the plant. Leave it in place for about a week, until your scent dissipates and the plant has established itself. Screening works over bulb beds as well.

### Antitranspirants

Recent research suggests that spraying bulbs with an antitranspirant spray (usually applied to the foliage of broad-leaved evergreens to keep them from dehydrating and wilting in winter) masks the human scent, so the chipmunk will overlook them. Commonly available antitranspirants include Wiltpruf, Pro-Tec, and VaporGard. These products are widely available in garden centers and nurseries.

# ANIMAL Deer

Deer can spell disaster for a landscape. They usually feed in the late evening or early morning, when no one is around. One or two deer can virtually destroy an ornamental or vegetable garden in one night. Far from finicky eaters, they devour almost everything found in the flower and food garden, as well as foliage and bark from trees and shrubs. Various species of deer thrive throughout the United States and Canada.

## SIGNS OF DEER DAMAGE

Deer can chew young plants to the ground. On fruit trees and other ornamental trees and shrubs, deer will eat leaves, flower buds, shoots, fruit, and even bark.

## VULNERABLE PLANTS

Deer will eat almost anything: fruits, vegetables, flowers, and foliage. On small trees, especially fruit trees, they relish the growing tips in summer and the buds in winter.

## BEST CONTROL STRATEGY

The most effective way to control deer is with a wall or fence.

## STEPS TO PREVENT DEER DAMAGE

### Barriers

A 6-foot solid wood or masonry wall will deter deer even though they could jump over it, because they are less likely to bother a yard or garden they can't see. For small areas, homeowners have had success with a double woven wire fence 8 to 10 feet tall.

Don't skimp on fence height—a wire fence *must* be that tall to be effective. If you don't care about looks or are desperate enough to try anything, a double fence of string has also been proven effective. The second fence should be 3 feet inside the first; both should have three strings and be 3 feet tall. The double fence confuses the deer and they won't try to jump. Make sure the string is easy to see.

### Repellents

Many times a particular odor repels deer. However, it *must* be kept fresh to be effective. One handy trick is to mix your repellent agent with an anti-transpirant such as Wilt-pruf, Pro-Tec, or VaporGard to give it season-long effectiveness.

#### Soap

For the orchard or any newly planted trees, string bars of deodorant soap on wire and hang them on outer tree branches about 30 inches from the ground and no farther than 3 feet apart. Leave soap wrappers on so the soap will last longer.

## Deer-Resistant Plants

A number of landscape plants aren't too palatable to deer unless they are terribly hungry. If you are troubled by deer on your property, consider growing some of these plants in your landscape. They come from lists accumulated by gardeners and landscape professionals who, over the years, have observed that these plants *tend* to be free of deer damage. That doesn't mean that the deer in your backyard might not eat them, but at least they're less likely to do so.

### Deer-resistant trees include:
California bay or Oregon myrtle (*Umbellularia californica*)
edible figs (*Ficus* spp.)
English or Persian walnut (*Juglans regia*)
hazlenut (*Corylus americana*)
hollies (*Ilex* spp.)
maples (*Acer* spp.)
oaks (*Quercus* spp.)
pines (*Pinus* spp.)
redwood (*Sequoia sempervirens*)
spruces (*Picea* spp.)
sweet gums (*Liquidambar* spp.)
tanbark oak (*Lithocarpus densiflorus*)

### Deer-resistant shrubs include:
bottle brushes (*Callistemon* spp.)
Carolina jessamine (*Gelsemium sempervirens*)
daphnes (*Daphne* spp.)
English lavender (*Lavandula angustifolia*)
Japanese barberry (*Berberis thunbergii*)
jasmine (*Jasminum officinale*)
junipers (*Juniperus* spp.)
oleander (*Nerium oleander*)
rhododendron hybrids (*Rhododendron* spp.), excluding azaleas
rockroses (*Cistus* spp.)
santolinas (*Santolina* spp.)
Scotch broom (*Cytisus scoparius*)
shrubby cinquefoil (*Potentilla fruticosa*)
spindle tree (*Euonymus japonica* 'Aureo-marginata')
sweet shrub (*Calycanthus occidentalis*)
wild lilac (*Ceanothus sanguineus* 'Blue Jean' and 'Emily Brown')

### Deer-resistant vines include:
Algerian ivy (*Hedera canariensis*)
clematis (*Clematis* spp.)
English ivy (*Hedera helix*)

### Deer-resistant ground covers include:
Aaron's beard or creeping St.-John's-wort (*Hypericum calycinum*)
blue star creeper (*Laurentia fluviatalis*)
carpet bugle (*Ajuga reptans*)
manzanita or bearberry (*Arctostaphylos uva-ursi*)
sea pink (*Armeria maritima*)
trailing African daisy (*Osteospermum fruticosum*)
vinca, myrtle or periwinkle (*Vinca major*, *V. minor*)

### Deer-resistant ferns, foliage plants, and grasses include:
chain ferns (*Woodwardia* spp.)
dusty miller (*Senecio cineraria*)
fescues (*Festuca* spp.)
lady fern (*Athyrium filix-femina*)
lamb's-ears (*Stachys byzantina*)
pampas grasses (*Cortaderia* spp.)
sword ferns (*Nephrolepis* spp.)
wire grass (*Juncus parryi*)
wood ferns (*Dryopteris* spp.)

### Eggs

Another effective control is an egg spray. Louisiana researchers found that a spray of 18 eggs in 5 gallons of water protected an acre of soybeans from deer. The deer were repelled by the smell of decomposing eggs, which in that dilution was too faint for humans to detect.

### Hair

Human hair, available from beauty parlors and barber shops, provides some protection if the deer aren't desperate for food. Use mesh bags with ⅛-inch or smaller mesh, and fill each with at least two large handfuls of hair. Hang them from outer tree branches about 30 inches from the ground and no more than 3 feet apart.

### Hot Sauce Spray

Another effective remedy is a homemade hot sauce or spray of Tabasco sauce. Mix 1 to 2 tablespoons Tabasco sauce and 2 tablespoons antitranspirant in 1 gallon water. Spray vulnerable shrubs and plants with this mixture. Be sure to respray after it rains.

### Garlic

Recent research has shown that selenium, which gives off a garlicky odor, prevents deer from eating tree shoots and seedlings. Since the selenium in garlic is the component responsible for the notorious "garlic breath," spraying a garlic solution (see chapter 6 for instructions on how to make this solution) on trees might have a similar repellent effect. Like hot sauce, it would have to be reapplied after rains. And remember, you might be repelled by your garlicky trees too! An alternative is planting a time-release garlic capsule (available at health-food stores) at the base of each tree or shrub.

### Commercial Repellents

If home remedies don't work, there are many commercial products that may be worth a try.

**Big Game Repellent (Deer Away).** This product repels by odor and is made from eggs, which repel deer as they decompose. It's a highly effective repellent. Apply it according to package directions and reapply after rains.

**Bonide Rabbit-Deer Repellent and Bulb Saver.** One taste of this stuff and rabbits and deer should walk away. Spray, brush, or dip branches. Use it for shrubs, evergreens, trees, and fruit trees. Bonide Repellent will last three to six months. It is available from Bonide Chemical Company (see the source list at the back of the book for the address).

**Chew-Not.** This product also repels by taste. Spray, brush, or dip branches in the solution. It is primarily used on fruit trees and some varieties of evergreen. Chew-Not's disadvantage is that it leaves an unattractive white residue on the plants due to its eggwhite consistency. It is available from Nott Manufacturing Company (see the source list at the back of the book for the address).

**Hinder.** This is a soap-based formulation that repels by odor. It must be reapplied after heavy rains. It comes as a spray, and is available from Uniroyal-Leffingwell Chemical Company (see the source list at the back of the book for the address).

**Ro-Pel.** Both the odor and taste of this product repel pests. Spray it on both sides of the leaves of landscape plants. Be sure to wear gloves and a mask when using it. Ro-Pel is available from Burlington Scientific Corporation and Ringer Corporation (see the source list at the back of the book for the addresses).

# ANIMAL Gopher

Gophers range in length from 6 to 12 inches. They have a thick body with small eyes and ears. Their sense of smell is excellent. They seldom are found aboveground. Once gophers arrive in your yard, they

resemble a small invasion force. One acre can feed and house 16 to 20 gophers, so it is easy to see why they can be a very serious problem. Gophers range from Indiana west to the Pacific Ocean. The most common is the pocket gopher (*Geomys bursarius*).

## SIGNS OF GOPHER DAMAGE

Gophers push soil out of their holes, creating distinctive fan- or crescent-shaped mounds on the surface of the ground. After digging a mound, they may close up the entrance hole with a soil plug. One gopher can create several mounds a day. Gopher tunnels, about 2 inches in diameter, follow no pattern, running from a few inches to 2 feet below the soil. You know you have gophers when your plants are damaged in areas where there are fan-shaped

mounds. Sometimes plants simply disappear—one morning you'll look out and find that a gopher has yanked your pansies down into its tunnel.

## VULNERABLE PLANTS

Gophers eat the underground parts of garden crops and a wide variety of roots, bulbs, tubers, grasses, and seeds. They can damage lawns, flowers, vegetables, vines, and trees. Their mounds sometimes smother small plants, and they can girdle and kill young fruit trees.

## BEST CONTROL STRATEGY

A sure way to drive this pest away is to determine the location of all the entrances to its tunnel system and then fumigate. Find a piece of hose material that can be attached to the exhaust of a power lawn mower. Stick one end of the hose into the gopher's tunnel, then seal the opening with soil. Next, drop some oil onto the inside of the hot exhaust pipe to create smoke, and attach the other end of the hose to the smoking pipe. After a few minutes, you should see smoke coming from all other entrances to the tunnel system. You may see gophers emerging as well.

Once you identify all the entrances to the tunnel system, you have several choices. You can seal them with piles of soil and continue to blow exhaust from the power mower into the tunnel, killing the inhabitants with poisonous carbon monoxide fumes, or you can put sulfur into the holes and seal all the entrances. The cheapest source of sulfur is one of the emergency highway flares that come with auto safety kits or are found in auto supply stores. Cut through an emergency flare with a sharp knife (not a saw). Dig into the runway, then pour the flare powder directly into the tunnel. Cover this hole, as well as all the exit holes that you have discovered. The more airtight the tunnel system is, the more anxious the gophers will be to leave. Once you are sure that the gophers are gone, seal the tunnels securely with soil. You'll know the gophers are gone when you no longer see fresh mounds around your property.

Another option is to place small ammonia-soaked sponges into each gopher hole and then seal them all. Gophers will abandon their burrows in a hurry. The best time to use this control is in early spring.

## OTHER OPTIONS FOR CONTROLLING GOPHERS

### Flooding

Set up traps over the openings of the gopher tunnels, then locate the main gopher burrow by probing the soil with a long screwdriver or similar probe. When the probe hits the main tunnel, it should suddenly drop about 2 inches. Once you've located the main tunnel, insert a garden hose into it. When you turn the water on, it will flow in both directions throughout the tunnel system. The gopher will try to escape by exiting from one of the mounds. It can then be trapped.

### Traps

Trapping can effectively eliminate gophers. Place standard wooden-based rat traps in shallow pits near burrow entrances. Cover the trap trigger with a thin layer of dirt and lure your victims to the traps by sprinkling grain on the dirt.

You can also trap gophers with a Macabee or other pincher trap, or with a box trap such as the Gopher Getter. You'll need two or more traps. Set them with special care. Wear gloves to prevent human scent from contaminating the devices. If you inadvertently touch the traps, you can wash them in soapy water. Open up the main burrow enough to allow you to insert two traps, one facing in each direction. The gopher will run over the trigger mechanism, regardless of the direction in which it is moving. Attach strong twine or rope between the trap and a stake driven into the ground. This prevents the rodent from pulling the trap deep into the burrow. Use a wooden board, cardboard, or other sturdy material to cover the traps, and be sure to sift dirt around the edges of the covering to exclude light. If the gopher sees light, it will push soil toward it, tripping the trap without being caught. If you don't catch any gophers within three days, pull out the traps and reset them in a new location.

## STEPS TO PREVENT GOPHER DAMAGE

### Barriers

Bulb beds and individual shrubs or trees can be protected with ½-inch-mesh wire if it is laid on the bottom and sides of the planting hole. Be sure to place the wire deep enough so that it does not restrict root growth.

Gophers occasionally feed on the bark of certain trees, particularly stone fruits such as peaches and cherries. It is wise to protect the trunks of vulnerable trees with cylinders of ½-inch galvanized hardware cloth sunk 12 inches underground and rising 12 inches above the surface.

### Repellents

#### Cat Litter

Dump several scoops of well-used cat litter right into each burrow entrance. As mentioned at the beginning of this chapter, do not use this trick in the food garden. It is an option for the flower garden and general landscape, if children won't be playing in the soil.

#### Ro-Pel

A commercial product, Ro-Pel can be used to keep gophers away. Both the odor and taste of this product repel these rodents. Spray it on both sides of the leaves of landscape plants. Be sure to wear gloves and a mask when using it. Ro-Pel is available from Burlington Scientific Corporation and Ringer Corporation (see the source list at the back of the book for the addresses).

**GoPherIt**

GoPherIt is a battery-powered sound-emitting device that you can insert into the lawn or garden. It emits sound waves every 15 seconds, and will keep gophers out of areas of up to 100 feet in diameter. The sound waves cannot be detected by humans or non-rodent pets. GoPherIt is available from Peaceful Valley Farm Supply and Ringer Corporation (see the source list at the back of the book for the addresses).

# ANIMAL Mole

Moles do not eat plants, but they do eat lots of grubs, beetles, earthworms, and other soil dwellers. Moles cause trouble because they harm the root systems of young plants when they tunnel through the soil in search of food. This damage is compounded by the fact that they can spread disease from plant to plant. In addition, other pests that are more harmful, like field mice, use mole runs. Several mole species are known; they are found throughout the United States.

## SIGNS OF MOLE DAMAGE

In their search for food, moles make an extensive network of tunnels, many of which are used only once. They are solitary animals, and it is likely that only one or two moles are responsible for all the damage to your lawn or garden. Moles are active all year long. When cold weather comes, they follow the earthworms deep into the soil below the frost line. Mole tunnels can be distinguished from gopher tunnels by the fact that they do not have the characteristic fan-shaped mound at the entrance that gopher tunnels have.

## VULNERABLE PLANTS

Lawns rich in grubs and earthworms are most likely to be riddled with molehills. Young seedlings in the early spring can be harmed by moles tunneling in search of grubs and other insects.

## BEST CONTROL STRATEGY

Traps can be effective, but you have to be persistent. The best time to trap is in early spring when the first mole ridges appear. To find out which runs are used as "travel lanes," step lightly on a small section of several tunnels so that you disturb but do not completely collapse them. Mark these sections with stones or garden stakes. In two days, note which ones are raised—those are active runs and good locations for setting a trap. You can restore the turf over unused tunnels with a lawn roller or by treading on them.

Choker traps (such as the Nash mole trap),

scissor-jawed traps (such as the Out O' Sight), and harpoon traps (such as the Victor mole trap) do catch moles when used properly. Install these traps according to instructions that come with them. They all basically work by springing when a mole sets off the trigger-pan as it attempts to raise a flattened portion of its run.

# ·OTHER OPTIONS FOR CONTROLLING MOLES

## Digging

As an alternative to trapping you can try digging out moles. Because moles may be active at any time of the day, it is often possible to see the soil ridging up as the mole moves along. Put a shovel into the soil right behind the mole, and flip the animal out into a bucket, which you can then fill with water to drown the culprit.

## Flushing

A technique that's effective when mole runs are short is to flush the little animals out with water. Just open the main run, insert a garden hose, and turn on the water. When the water spreads through the tunnels, adult moles will try to escape through other exits, where you can kill them with a shovel. If you flood the runs in spring, you will also drown the young in their nest.

# STEPS TO PREVENT MOLE DAMAGE

## Get Rid of Grubs

Beetle grubs feed on plant roots and in turn are eaten by moles. Remove the grubs and your lawn will be less attractive to moles. Kill Japanese beetle grubs in your soil with applications of *Bacillus popilliae* (commercially available as Doom and Grub Attack, among other brand names). Other beetle grubs can be controlled with parasitic nematodes (sold as Bioquest; see the source list at the back of the book for suppliers of these products).

# Repellents

## Cat Litter

You might achieve success with the strong odor of well-used cat litter. Dump several scoops of litter into the mole's burrow. A sprinkling of tobacco or red pepper into each burrow may also deter moles.

## Mole Mover II

The Mole Mover II is a battery-operated vibrating device that you set in the soil. The vibrations emanating from it supposedly drive moles away for good. For information contact Gardener's Supply Company (see the source list at the back of the book for the address).

## GoPherIt

Like the Mole Mover II, GoPherIt produces battery-powered vibrations that clear moles within a 50-foot radius. It is available from Peaceful Valley Farm Supply and Ringer Corporation (see the source list at the back of the book for the addresses).

## Windmills

Another vibration trick is to set windmills (available commercially through garden supply catalogs) in mole runs. These windmills create vibrations that seem to deter moles. A less expensive alternative is to insert a child's pinwheel into the tunnel ridge. Empty glass soda bottles work along the same principle. Set a bottle straight down into the mole run, open end up. The wind blowing across the opening of the bottle creates vibrations that spread along the mole tunnel.

## Rodent Rocks

Rodent Rocks are porous lava stones that have been soaked in an organic repellent containing onions and garlic. When the rocks are buried 6 inches deep and 2 to 4 feet apart, their odor is claimed to effectively repel moles for 4 to 12 months. Circle the lawn with rodent rocks for best effectiveness.

You can buy a package of about 60 Rodent Rocks from Gardener's Supply Company (see the source list at the back of the book for the address).

## Barriers

Moles will avoid hard, stony soil, which is difficult to dig through. You can create an effective barrier by digging a trench 2 feet deep and 6 inches wide around vulnerable areas. Fill the trench with heavy clay and stony and/or compacted soil and keep it dry. You can pave or mulch the barrier to create an attractive path around the lawn or garden.

## NATURAL PREDATORS

Cats are natural predators. They'll kill moles, but they won't eat them because of their bad taste.

## NOTES AND RESEARCH

No evidence exists to support claims that castor beans (sometimes called mole plants) keep moles away, or that daffodil bulbs or dandelions work either.

# ANIMAL *Mouse*

A number of different types of mouse may nibble on your landscape plants. The field mouse (also called the meadow vole) is chunky in build, with small ears that are almost concealed in fur. They are white underneath and gray-brown on top. The house mouse, which is less likely to damage your landscape plants, is gray all over, with large, distinct ears. The white-footed mouse and related deer mouse range over most of the continent. They have whitish underparts like the field mouse, as well as whitish legs and feet and tails over 2 inches long.

## SIGNS OF MOUSE DAMAGE

Mice are known to move into mole tunnels and use them to gain access to plant roots. They create surface trails through long grass, weeds, and brush, and can also burrow underground. They are most damaging in winter, when they gnaw the bark of young shade or fruit trees, sometimes girdling and killing the trees. Because of their tunneling habits, mice can chew bark from trunks several inches

underground, girdle trees at ground level, or reach higher branches by digging through snow. Orchardists report that voles can kill scores of fruit trees in an orchard during a single winter. Tree-girdling usually occurs between October and April. Mice may also overwinter in the mulch placed around strawberries or perennial flowers, where they chew on the roots. They are generally active all year round.

## VULNERABLE PLANTS

Roots of vegetable and flower plants in the garden are fair game for mice. These rodents also gnaw on roots of young trees and shrubs, as well as on bark buried under the snow during the winter months.

## BEST CONTROL STRATEGY

The traditional mousetrap still works. The most effective way to reduce mice through trapping is to buy a large number of snap-traps and plan a one- or two-night massacre. Buying a few traps to catch mice over a long period of time does not work as well. Bait the traps with a tiny dab of peanut butter or bacon, or a 50/50 mix of peanut butter and uncooked oatmeal. A good technique is to bait the traps for two or three nights without setting them. Then when you finally do set the traps, you'll catch the mice by surprise.

A steel drum with bait inside makes a very simple homemade mousetrap. The mice scramble into the standing drum, and once they are inside, they can't climb out. You'll have caught them red-handed.

## OTHER OPTIONS FOR CONTROLLING MICE

### Glue Board

Besides the basic mousetrap, there is also a product on the market called a glue board. This is a sheet of extremely sticky material that literally stops mice in their tracks when they try to run across it. Once you've caught a mouse, dispose of both the glue board and the pest. J. T. Eaton & Company carries glue board traps (see the source list at the back of the book for the address).

### Vitamin D Bait

A vitamin D-pelleted bait causes a calcium imbalance in the mouse's blood. Mice stop feeding after eating the pellets and die in two to four days. This bait is toxic only to rodents. It is available from Necessary Trading Company and Natural Gardening Research Center (see the source list at the back of the book for the addresses).

## STEPS TO PREVENT MOUSE DAMAGE

### Ro-Pel

Mice do not like the taste of Ro-Pel. Spray it on both sides of the leaves of landscape plants. Be sure to wear gloves and a mask when using it. Ro-Pel is available from Burlington Scientific Corporation and Ringer Corporation (see the source list at the back of the book for the addresses).

### Barriers

#### Plastic Guards

Commercial plastic wrap-around guards placed around the base of trees will prevent mice from chewing on bark, but these guards must be installed each fall and removed each spring. If they are left on year-round, the trunks become more vulnerable to borer attack and the bark remains tender and slow to harden off.

#### Hardware Cloth

Galvanized hardware cloth makes a durable mouse-proof guard that can be left on all year. Buy ¼-inch mesh in a 24-inch width. Cut the hardware cloth wide enough to completely encircle the tree. If you plan to leave it on year-round, allow plenty of room for the trunk to expand as it grows. Make a cylinder around the trunk, fastening the edges securely. Bury the cylinder at least 2 inches deep to keep mice from digging under it. Make sure the top of the cylinder extends above the snow line.

## Other Options

Good sanitation is one way to discourage mice from visiting your yard. Clean up all possible food sources, such as vegetables left in the garden at season's end and fallen apples, crabapples, or other fruit. Be sure to use rodent-proof containers of metal or glass to store seeds and birdseed, and keep bird-seed swept up.

Always pull mulch away from the base of young shade and fruit trees in the winter. Don't mulch perennials or strawberries until the ground freezes hard. Putting mulch down early invites the mice to set up housekeeping and gives them easy access to roots in unfrozen soil.

Keep an area of at least 3 feet clear around trees, removing tall grass, weeds, and shrubby growth. Mice do not like to come out in the open and will hesitate to cross that bare space to gnaw on the trees.

## NATURAL PREDATORS

Any owls and snakes on your property will help keep the population of mice under control. Of course, one of the best rodent controls known is the house cat.

## ANIMAL *Rabbit*

Rabbits have shown themselves to be extremely adaptable to human environments. Cottontails are active mainly from dusk until midmorning and spend the warmer part of the day in shaded areas. They may hide under thick shrubs or beneath garden sheds. The Eastern cottontail is the species usually found nibbling in the yard and garden, but various species of rabbit are found throughout the United States and Canada.

## SIGNS OF RABBIT DAMAGE

Herbaceous plants, especially young ones, will be nibbled down to the base. In winter, rabbits remove a considerable amount of bark from young trees, and they chew the new shoots.

## VULNERABLE PLANTS

Rabbits' favorite foods include carrots, geraniums, grasses, lettuce, marigolds, peas, strawberries, tulip shoots, raspberry canes, weeds, and the bark of young shrubs and trees, particularly euonymus, honey locust, and sumac. They especially relish young bean growth and the bark of young fruit trees (apple trees are the all-time favorite). Rabbits don't like corn, cucumbers, or squash, and will only eat evergreen bark if they're really desperate.

## BEST CONTROL STRATEGY

Trapping is the most effective way to control rabbits. Commercial box traps measuring 10″ × 12″ × 30″

are recommended. Rabbits are more likely to enter a dark trap than one that's well lighted, so put a tarpaulin over the trap.

# STEPS TO PREVENT RABBIT DAMAGE

## Barriers

Ordinary chicken-wire fence can rabbit-proof the flower garden, but it isn't very attractive. Bury the fence 6 inches into the soil and extend it at least 2 feet aboveground. Make sure the holes in the mesh are smaller than 2 inches—1 to 1½ inches is ideal.

## Tree Guards

### Commercial Wrap and Alternatives

Tree guards are an essential piece of equipment in the war against rabbits. When preparing newly planted trees or an orchard for the winter, wrap the lower portion of trunks with commercial tree wrap, burlap, aluminum foil, or a piece of metal window screen. The wrapping should be 2 feet above the height of the deepest expected snow cover—rabbits can walk on top of the snow. In winter, tramp down the snow around your trees so rabbits can't chew on low limbs. Remove protective wrappings each spring to prevent the trunks from becoming tender and to avoid attracting borers.

### Wire Guards

You can put wire guards around individual plants, shrubs, or trees if you have the time and patience to make them. Make a cylinder around each plant with hardware cloth, attaching it to stakes to keep it upright. Make the guards higher than 18 inches so a rabbit can't stand up on its hind legs to reach its lunch. If you use wire around tree trunks, extend it 2 feet above the projected snow depth.

## Repellents

Repellents may help you reduce rabbit damage. As mentioned in the beginning of the chapter, these vary in effectiveness. In the case of rabbit control, taste repellents are often more effective than scent repellents.

### Scent Repellents

You can choose from a wide range of scent repellents to keep rabbits away from your plants. Rabbits tend to avoid anything that smells of blood. Sprinkling dried blood meal on the soil around vulnerable plants may keep rabbits away, but you'll have to reapply it after each rain.

Some gardeners have reported that vinegar wards off rabbits. Save a few corn cobs after a meal and cut the cobs in half. Soak them in vinegar for 5 minutes, then scatter them throughout the flower or vegetable garden. Two weeks later, soak them again in the same vinegar. You can keep reusing this vinegar; just keep it in its own labeled bottle.

Other rabbit repellents reported effective by some homeowners include lion and tiger manure (sold by some zoos as ZooDoo); a solution of cow manure and water applied as a spray; onions interplanted among crops; fish tankage and bonemeal; and soybeans planted adjacent to the garden. Sprinkle or place repellents immediately around the target plants.

### Taste Repellents

You can purchase commercial taste repellents or make one at home. During the growing season, discourage rabbits by spraying nicotine sulfate on your garden. Prepare the spray by mixing ½ teaspoon 40 percent nicotine sulfate in 1 quart water. An even easier repellent to use is black or hot pepper. Simply sprinkle it all over and around plants.

Ro-Pel is a taste repellent. It can be dusted on plants, or you can follow the package instructions to make a spray. Ro-Pel is available from Burlington Scientific Corporation and Ringer Corporation (see the source list at the back of the book for the addresses).

A combination antitranspirant and pest repellent is Bonide Rabbit-Deer Repellent & Bulb Saver, available from Bonide Chemical Company (see the source list at the back of the book for the address). The branches of shrubs, evergreens, trees, roses, fruit trees, ornamentals, and nursery stock should be sprayed or brushed with or dipped into this product. The effect will last three to six months.

### Visual Repellents

Inflatable or cast plastic snakes and owls look lifelike and are readily available from most mail-order garden catalogs. These pseudo-predators will frighten rabbits away from the tree or garden area they're placed in. Move them every few days so the rabbits won't catch on.

## Eliminate Daytime Cover

One way to reduce the rabbit population in the yard is to remove brush piles, one of their favorite daytime resting places. Clear out overgrown walls, fences, and ditches. Lack of cover will discourage rabbits from hanging around. Anything you can do to eliminate sanctuaries will help solve the rabbit problem; however, if you live next to a wooded area, there may be too many hiding places to deal with in this manner. Fortunately, nearby big trees may help, since they will encourage predators such as owls and hawks.

ANIMAL **Squirrel**

Eight species of squirrel live in the United States. The most common are the eastern gray squirrel and the fox squirrel, which can make nuisances of themselves at bird feeders and cause occasional problems in the landscape.

## SIGNS OF SQUIRREL DAMAGE

Squirrels eat crocuses and other bulbs. They often make holes in the lawn or garden as they search for nuts buried earlier in the season.

## VULNERABLE PLANTS

Squirrels eat nuts (including green and ripe walnuts and almonds), fruits (such as oranges, apples, and avocados), buds, bulbs, and bark. They love birdseed.

## BEST CONTROL STRATEGY

You can catch a squirrel in a medium-sized box trap baited with fruit, nuts, or peanut butter.

## STEPS TO PREVENT SQUIRREL DAMAGE

### Scent Repellents

Ro-Pel, a commercial product, smells and tastes awful to squirrels. Soak bulbs in Ro-Pel before planting them, and squirrels will leave them alone. This repellent is available from Burlington Scientific Corporation and Ringer Research (see the source list at the back of the book for the addresses).

### Sticky Repellents

The Squirrel, also commercially available, is a sheet of paper coated with gel. The unpleasant sensation of gel on their feet discourages squirrels from encroaching on the protected area. This paper is available from J. T. Eaton & Company (see the source list at the back of the book for the address).

### Squirrel Baffles

To keep squirrels out of bird feeders, put a baffle on the pole beneath the bird feeder or on the wire it's strung on. Baffles are available from the same companies that sell bird feeders and supplies. You can also make your own from stovepipe.

# CHAPTER 8

# *Diseases*

**I**f you're like most homeowners, you fight disease backwards. You'll encounter a disease problem on your property, then seek out control measures. Only after the crisis has passed will you think in terms of prevention. Whether you approach disease control with a "prevention first" attitude or wait until something goes wrong, this chapter will help you identify and solve your problems. It offers information on the general types of disease that threaten landscape plants, and discusses backyard management of plant disease, including controls and preventive tactics. Since there is very little variation in treatment techniques between the specific diseases within each type of disease—all fungal diseases respond well to the same techniques, for example—there are no individual disease entries. For more specific treatments, refer to the plant entries in Part 1, Plant Problems.

Unfortunately, there are fewer tools for fighting disease in the landscape than there are for use against insect and animal pests—that's why prevention is so important. Often, by the time a disease makes its presence known, it's too late to save infected plants. You have little choice but to consign sick plants to the trash. However, the removal of infected plants does serve as an important control of disease in your landscape as a whole.

Luckily, there are some cases where this all-or-nothing approach is unnecessary. A number of fungal diseases cause spots or some yellowing, but they are not lethal to the plant or seriously detrimental

to the performance of that plant in the landscape. So don't panic at first sight of a single yellow leaf on your azalea bush. Look at the general vigor of the plant. If it looks otherwise healthy, wait for a few days or even weeks to see if in fact you have a serious problem. A fungal disease occurs slowly. If your plants are deteriorating very rapidly (within a few days), it is more likely a sign of a viral or bacterial disease, and in that case the infected plants should be removed and destroyed immediately.

## CONTROLLING DISEASE

The first step in controlling diseases in the landscape is to spot and identify them. Look for symptoms. Examine your plants for changes in their general appearance. Many, if not most, of the symptoms you will find on your plants are caused by insects rather than disease. By reading the descriptions given for disease and insect pest problems in this book, and with some experience, you will learn to distinguish insect damage from disease damage. (See chapter 6 to familiarize yourself with the symptoms of insect problems.)

Once you've decided that the problem is caused by a disease rather than an insect pest, you will need to determine the exact disease that has infected your plants. Unfortunately, not every disease exhibits a distinctive pattern of symptoms. Many symptoms can be caused by more than one disease. (See the box, Symptoms of Disease, on page 358.)

357

## Symptoms of Disease

1. Chlorosis (yellowing) of leaves.
   All leaves.
   Youngest leaves only.
   Older leaves only.
   Leaf edges.
   Between leaf veins.
   Round spots, all leaves.
   Irregular spots, all leaves.
   Small dots, all leaves.
   Mosaic patterns, all leaves.
2. Dead or brownish areas on leaves.
   Leaf edges or tips.
   Spots or sections, all leaves.
   Edge and inner sections, all leaves.
3. Water-soaked or greasy appearance.
4. Premature defoliation.
5. Wilting plant.
6. Abnormal plant growth.
7. Rotten spots on leaves or fruit.
8. Plant dies mysteriously.

Plant diseases can be divided into five broad categories: environmental disorders and fungal, bacterial, viral, and nematode-caused diseases. It's not always easy to decide which category your plant problem falls under, though, not only because many symptoms are characteristic of several diseases, but also because a plant may have more than one disease at the same time. Nevertheless, some problems are more common than others, and homeowners learn to diagnose disease problems from their experience of what has happened in their yard in previous years. Although there is some overlap, each type of disease can be recognized by a general set of symptoms.

There are a number of good books for identifying diseases: *Rodale's Garden Insect, Disease, and Weed Identification Guide,* Cynthia Westcott's *Plant Disease Handbook,* Time-Life's *Pests and Diseases,* and Pascal Pirone's *Diseases and Pests of Ornamental Plants* are particularly easy to use.

If you have just begun to work with a yard and garden, you will find that most of your disease problems will actually be disorders caused by environmental conditions (watering, feeding, location, and so forth) rather than true diseases. The most common true-disease problems will be fungal diseases. Bacterial, viral, and nematode-caused diseases occur less often.

## ENVIRONMENTAL DISORDERS

The environment surrounding a plant above and below the ground is crucial to its health. Disruptions or changes in environmental conditions can cause disorders in otherwise healthy plants. Above the surface of the soil, the vagaries of wind, rain, light, air temperature, and humidity cause such problems as dieback, leaf scorch, and sunscald. Environmental conditions below the surface of the soil, such as the tilth of the soil, nutrient deficiencies or excesses, moisture content, soil temperature, and an inappropriate pH, cause other disorders. (See chapter 9 for more information on soil problems.) Environmental disorders can weaken a plant and lead to real pathogenic disease. For example, anthracnose and powdery mildew are fungal diseases encouraged by hot, dry summer weather.

The causes of environmental ailments most frequently fall into one of five categories: soil deficiency, which includes pH problems and basic mineral imbalances; improper watering; problems with light intensity, which can be caused by inadequate hardening off as well as by putting a plant in the wrong place; improper fertilization, which involves the quantity of and balance of nutrients you add to the existing environment; or some kind of physical damage to the bark or the roots. (See chapter 10 for information on watering and fertilizing.)

Of the five groups of plant diseases, environmental disorders are the easiest to correct once they have been properly diagnosed. Getting a proper diagnosis, however, takes some skill and experience. Any of the symptoms listed in the box, Symptoms of Disease, on the preceding page may be the result of a disorder; however, the most common are general weakening of the whole plant or some color change in the leaves, such as yellowing or reddening.

## Symptoms and Causes of Disorders

The following list of symptoms and causes will help you identify the environmental problems in your landscape.

### Chlorosis

Chlorosis is the yellowing of leaves. Its appearance on your plant differs, depending on the type of problem your plant has.

**On All Leaves.** This may be caused by a lack of nutrients, extremely bright light, or high temperatures.

**On Youngest Leaves.** A lack of iron or manganese, or insufficient light, may cause yellowing of the youngest leaves.

**On Older Leaves.** Chlorosis on the older leaves may only mean the soil lacks nitrogen or potassium, or it may need aeration.

**On Leaf Edges.** This is often a sign of a deficiency in both magnesium and potassium.

**Between Leaf Veins.** This may indicate a deficiency in iron or manganese, or there may be sulfur dioxide in the air.

**As Irregular Spots.** Cold water can cause irregular yellow spots on leaves.

**As Mosaic Pattern.** Cold water can cause a mosaic pattern of yellow spots on leaves.

### Dead Areas on Leaves

Environmental disorders are often signaled by the rotting of areas on leaves.

**On Leaf Edges or Tips.** This could indicate a potassium deficiency, boron excess, fluoride excess, excessive heat or cold, or insufficient water.

**As Spots or Sections.** Cold water can cause dead spots or sections on leaves.

**On Edges and Inner Sections.** This may be caused by too much light, cool temperatures, or cold water.

**With Water-Soaked or Greasy Appearance.** Excessive heat or cold or cold water on the foliage may produce this effect.

## Winter Environmental Disorders in Trees and Shrubs

Your landscape plants face a number of environmental problems in the cold-weather areas of the country, including winter injury, sunscald, and tipburn. It may not be possible to escape some winter damage, but there are ways of reducing risks.

### Winter Injury

Winter injury occurs to many landscape plants during subfreezing temperatures, especially when the water in the soil is frozen, making it unavailable to the roots. Plants continue to transpire, especially if it is sunny and windy. When more water evaporates during transpiration than the plant can absorb, desiccation occurs. Desiccation is the excessive drying up of leaves, followed by twigs, roots, and so forth, and it can be very harmful—even fatal—to the plant. Winter injury is more common on broad-leaved evergreens such as azaleas than it is on conifers, which have less leaf surface for evaporation, or deciduous plants, which don't hold their leaves through winter. Preventive measures include watering the plants well before the ground freezes and whenever it thaws; spraying the leaves with an antitranspirant such as Cloud Cover, VaporGard, or Wilt-pruf; mulching; and protecting the plants with burlap or windscreens from drying winds and bright sun while the ground is frozen. When using an antitranspirant, remember to reapply it several times throughout the winter. (See chapter 10 for more details about winter protection of landscape plants.)

### Sunscald

Sunscald may sound like something that happens in hot weather, but it is a cold-weather problem, occurring in winter and early spring. It is particularly noticeable on young trees planted where daytime heat is high, such as beside a wall that reflects the sun's heat. Tender bark on a southern surface warms much more than on a northern surface. The temperature of dark-colored bark is raised considerably by the sun's rays, but if a chilling breeze comes along or a cloud suddenly covers the sun, the mercury falls rapidly. The sudden change makes the plant cells rupture, causing the bark to split open. Bacteria or insects may enter the splits and cause further damage. Sunscald on trees can be prevented by wrapping the trunks with a commercially available tree wrap or with burlap or agricultural fleece. Some homeowners guard against early-spring sunscald by spraying the bark on the south side of the young trees with white latex paint in the fall. The light color reflects the sun's rays and prevents sudden temperature changes.

### Tipburn

Tipburn, or windburn, is a result of drying by the sun or wind. It usually appears on the western or southwestern side of an evergreen shrub. Although the damage occurs in the winter, there may be no sign of trouble until spring. Then the tips of leaves or needles turn brown, and in severe cases whole leaves or the ends of affected branches die. To prevent tipburn, water well in the fall and apply a heavy mulch. Protect vulnerable shrubs with a windbreak of stakes and burlap, or shelter them with a pile of brush. (See chapter 10 for more information about winter protection.)

### Winter Dieback

Winter dieback is the equivalent of tipburn in deciduous plants. It is a particular problem with shallow-rooted plants such as young trees and deciduous shrubs. As with tipburn, the damage may not become noticeable until spring. Branch tips that were healthy in the fall will appear dead. To check the extent of the damage, scrape away a small patch of bark on the affected twig. If the twig is alive, the underbark will be bright green. If it is dead, it will be black. Fall watering and good mulch will prevent dieback.

## Control of Deficiency Disorders

Nutritional disorders can usually be quickly remedied by applying the appropriate foliar spray to a weakening plant, then correcting the soil deficiency that caused the problem. However, you can also take long-term measures to control environmental problems without ever pinpointing the specific cause. Simply follow these steps:

1. Make sure the soil is healthy, with the proper pH level, nutrient balance, and drainage, and sufficient water-holding capacity for the plants you're growing.

2. Make sure the plant gets the right amount of water.

3. Make sure the plant gets the right amount of fertilizer.

For example, if you spread an inch of compost on the soil under your shrubs and throughout the garden every year, you will be correcting many of the soil deficiencies most commonly found in the new landscape. If you spray your plants once or twice a season with a kelp extract, your plants will get the necessary micronutrients, even if there are some deficiencies in the soil. If you make sure that the plants get a consistent level of water (about 1 inch a week), you eliminate over- or underwatering. And finally, if you add an appropriate amount of slow-acting organic fertilizer (roughly 1 cup per 25 square feet of yard or garden) once a season, you will eliminate most nutritional problems. So even though it may be difficult to identify the specific environmental cause of a problem, these easy steps will help to remedy and prevent the current problem and any potential environmental disorders.

## Tree and Shrub Wounds

Trees and larger shrubs are vulnerable to damaging wounds to their bark and roots, caused by both man and nature. Some damage is normal, and if the wound is treated promptly and correctly, only scars will remain on the plant. If left untreated, wounds can be attacked by pest insects and disease, which can eventually cause the death of the tree or shrub.

## Symptoms and Causes of Wounds

Wounds can be caused by storms, high winds, insects, and animals. Man does his share of harm with lawn mowers, automobiles, nails, fence staples, and grass trimmers. Every time you prune a tree or shrub, you are creating a wound on that plant. A tree wound includes any injury that damages living tissue, including the bark. The larger the injured area, the more vulnerable the plant becomes to insect and disease invasion.

## Control of Wound Problems

Trees and shrubs have active defenses against wounds, and if conditions are good, can prevent most wounds from getting worse all by themselves. Usually the tree or shrub will produce a callus growth over the wound, closing it to insects and disease. (Note, however, that a tree wound *never* heals; it just seals.) More important, a healthy tree will wall off the area behind the wound with a barrier of resistant wood.

The usual approach to treating a wound is to paint it with a pruning paint sold at the local garden center or nursery. Definitive research by pruning experts has shown that tree paint or sealant of any kind, far from helping wounds, can actually encourage decay. So prune properly, leaving the branch collar unharmed rather than flush-cutting, and hold the paint. Keep the tree healthy with a good feeding program and make sure it has enough water. It may take three years, but the wound will callus over without decaying.

Bark injury—say, knocking off a strip of healthy bark with a lawn mower—requires emergency treatment. Speed is the critical factor in treating bark injuries. If you act promptly, you can nail the detached bark back in place. Wrap 2 inches of moist spagnum moss over the bark after you reattach it, then cover the moss with white polyethylene to prevent moisture loss. Remove the moss and plastic after two weeks; hopefully, the bark will have reattached itself.

# FUNGAL DISEASE

Disease fungi are microscopic plants that take nourishment from the plants on which they live—in other words, they are parasites. Fungal diseases exhibit a number of distinctive symptoms, often indicated by their names. Downy mildew and powdery mildew create pale patches on the leaves of the plants. Rusts can be identified by their rusty color on leaves. Leaf spot causes round, yellow spots on the leaves that darken over time. Many fungal diseases can be controlled or even eliminated by proper yard care. When you spot a problem in a plant, rule out possible environmental problems before looking for a fungal cause.

## Symptoms of Fungal Disease

The following symptoms may indicate a fungal disease of some kind:

- Pale patches on leaves
- Chlorosis (yellowing of leaves), specifically round spots or irregular yellow-green spots that darken with time
- Dead spots or sections on leaves
- Water-soaked or greasy sections on leaves or stems
- Rust-colored spots
- Sudden death of small seedlings

Fungal disease tends to spread over the entire plant somewhat slowly, occurring over weeks rather than days, whereas problems caused by viruses or bacteria spread quite quickly. However, this does not mean you should wait to confirm that you have a fungal problem, because organic fungicides are not very effective in controlling a disease if it is well established in the plant.

## Control of Fungal Disease

Treatment of fungal disease varies, depending on the specific disease. In some cases, you should simply remove the affected leaves. However, in most cases, you should leave the plant alone and begin some control strategy using fungicidal sprays or dusts. Discussions of diseases in the chapters dealing with individual plants offer specific control steps, but in general, once you've decided your plant has a fungal disease, such as rust or black spot, it often can be arrested by the application of an appropriate organic fungicide.

### How to Use Organic Fungicides

Fungicides are much less effective once a disease has become well established, so for best results apply them early in the season—even before there is evidence of plant damage, if a particular disease has consistently been a problem in your yard. This means, of course, that you must remember when a fungal disease struck a particular plant or shrub last year so you can anticipate its arrival at about the same time this year. Generally, you should repeat fungicide treatments every week or ten days throughout the growing season to prevent a fungal disease from developing or to keep it controlled.

Remember, whether you use a dust or a spray, only those parts of the plant that are actually coated with the fungicide are protected; that is why some kind of "sticker" material should be included in any spray mixture. Problems on individual plants can be handled with a fungicide sold in its own applicator bottle. If you have many infected plants or larger plants, you may need to use about ½ to 1 gallon of spray. For the more mature shrubs and large trees, up to 2 gallons may be necessary for complete coverage. In that case, it is better to purchase the concentrated form of fungicide and mix it with water yourself. For very large shade trees, you will probably not be able to reach most of the leaves. For serious disease problems on large trees, seek professional help from an arborist.

The organic fungicides listed below are safe to use in the landscape, but handle them with respect. Wash your hands thoroughly after using these materials, and thoroughly wash before eating any fruit or vegetables that may have been sprayed with these products.

A single organic fungicide will not control all fungal diseases. Fortunately, your landscape will not experience large numbers of different fungal diseases. All homeowners should have a sulfur-based fungicide on their shelf, since it does control several fungal problems. You can add other products to your store as they become necessary.

### Types of Organic Fungicide

Although there are many powerful fungicides on the market that will control most fungal diseases, only a few are considered totally safe to the environment and are recommended here for safe application in the home ecosystem.

**Antitranspirants.** Researchers at Texas Tech University, in Lubbock, found that antitranspirants sprayed on zinnias kept these highly susceptible plants free of powdery mildew—in fact, the antitranspirant worked better than a chemical fungicide. The plants were sprayed with antitranspirant five times during the growing season. The researchers concluded that antitranspirants controlled the mildew because the antitranspirant film on the leaves repelled the fungus organism, and it also prevented the coat of water necessary to the fungus's development from forming. An added benefit was increased vigor and flowering, due to increased water and nutrient content in the plant cells. Antitranspirants are available under a number of brand names, including Cloud Cover, VaporGard, and Wilt-pruf.

**Baking Soda.** Japanese researchers found that baking soda (sodium bicarbonate) controls powdery mildew and other mildews when sprayed on plants at weekly intervals at a concentration of 1 level teaspoonful per 2 quarts water. Not only did the soda prevent fungal spores from germinating and stop the development of the disease, but it even appeared to help the plants repair fungus-damaged tissue.

**Bordeaux Mixture.** This fungicide is a mixture of salts of copper and hydrated lime and has a very low level of toxicity. It works by burning the spores of fungal disease. Do not mix it with other materials, except oil. When combined with Bt (*Bacillus* *thuringiensis*), it makes the Bt ineffective. Do not use Bordeaux mixture during cool, wet weather or it will damage plants. It can be used to control anthracnose, black rot, fire blight, leaf spot, and other fungal diseases. Wherever Bordeaux mixture is recommended you may safely substitute one of the fixed-copper fungicides (see below). Bordeaux mixture is corrosive to iron and steel.

**Fixed-Copper Compounds.** The fixed-copper compounds, such as basic copper sulfate, copper oxychloride, and cuprous oxide, effectively control various fungal and bacterial diseases. These compounds are sold under various trade names and should be used only as directed on the labels. Do not use them during cool, wet weather or they may damage the plants. They help to control anthracnose, bacterial spot, downy mildew, early blight, late blight, leaf spot, powdery mildew, and other fungal diseases.

Among the fixed-copper fungicides on the market are Basic Copper Sulfate, Basi-Cop, Bonide, C-O-C-S, Copper 53 Fungicide, Coprantol, Kocide 101, Microcop, Miller 658, T B-C-S 53, Tribasic Copper Sulfate, and Top Cop.

**Fungicidal Soap Spray.** Safer has developed a fungicidal soap made from sulfur in a soap base. It is applied as a spray. Simply follow the package directions for application. It is available in a ready-to-use form, Garden Fungicide, and a concentrate called Safer Fungicide Concentrate. The Necessary Trading Company offers both products (see the source list at the back of the book for the address).

**Garlic.** Garlic's antiseptic properties make it an effective control for mildews and other fungi. Apply it as a spray to landscape plants. To prepare a solution, chop up enough garlic cloves to fill ½ cup. Mix the garlic with 1 pint water and leave it to steep for a few minutes; then strain out the chopped cloves.

**Lime Sulfur.** A fungicide that is somewhat caustic and works by burning the germinating fungal spores, lime sulfur helps to control cedar-apple rust, leaf spot, powdery mildew, scab, and other fungal diseases. To use it, make a dilution of 1 part lime sulfur to 50 parts water. Spray plants right after a rain, before the leaves dry. Lime sulfur is also available as a dust. Neither the spray nor the dust should be used when temperatures climb above 80°F. Do not spray shrubs or trees when they are in blossom. Lime sulfur will stain buildings, walls, and trellises.

**Sulfur.** Sulfur is one of the best natural fungicides available, and it has a very low toxicity. Applied to the surface of leaves, ground sulfur rock will prevent the germination of certain fungal spores that fall on a treated leaf. Sulfur is also available in liquid form, combined with a soap-base material as the carrier. The liquid sticks to the undersides of leaves better than the powder.

Sulfur fungicides, such as Ortho's Flotox, will help control the following fungal diseases, among others: anthracnose, cedar-apple and other rusts, leaf spot, and powdery mildew.

**Water.** Experiments at Laredo Junior College, in Texas, showed that spraying plants daily with a garden hose equipped with a spray nozzle provided effective control against powdery mildew. Protection was as great as that provided by a chemical fungicide, and the fungicide had an added drawback: When treatment was discontinued, the fungicide-treated plants quickly succumbed to fungal disease, while water-sprayed plants displayed more resistance.

## Preventing Fungal Disease

As they say, the best defense is a strong offense. Fungal disease may be hard to get rid of, so the best control is to prevent infection of your plants in the first place. There are a number of practices you can follow that will enable you to do this.

### Resistant Varieties
The best way to prevent fungal disease in your yard and garden is to use varieties of plants that have been bred to be resistant to or tolerant of specific diseases. (Resistant varieties have a strong ability to withstand or repel a disease; tolerant varieties can survive and produce flowers and/or fruit in spite of infection.) Resistant and tolerant varieties are not

always available, but when they are, try the plant to see how you like it. These varieties are something of an event in the plant world, and are almost always called out in catalogs, so they're easy to spot. Examples include 'Rose Pinwheel' zinnia, 'Bonica' rose, 'Peachblush' and 'Red Carpet' lilies, and 'American Liberty' elm. Some varieties, like 'Gold Rush' and 'Prelude' lilies, are notoriously susceptible to certain fungal diseases and should be avoided if those diseases are problems in your landscape.

## Mulching

Most fungal spores are spread by the wind and by rain bouncing them up onto plants from the soil. Using mulch around your shrubs and in your gardens prevents this by acting as a barrier. Use drip irrigation to avoid the splashing of water that occurs with overhead watering. If you must use a sprinkler, water before noon so the sun will dry off the moisture on the leaves, eliminating the moist environment the spores need to multiply. Do not work in your garden in humid, rainy weather or when your plants are wet, or you may become a "Typhoid Larry," carrying spores from plant to plant.

## Proper Spacing

If fungal disease is a serious problem in your area, and especially if you live in a hot, humid climate, provide maximum spacing between the plants in your landscape to encourage good air circulation around them. Fungal disease thrives in hot, damp areas with poor air circulation. The better the air circulation, the faster the plants will dry after a rain or after overhead watering. This rule also applies to shrubs and trees. If fungal disease is a problem with those plants, they should be pruned so that the tree canopy is open enough to allow light and air to reach the interior of the tree. Don't prune during April, May, or June, when plants tend to be wet and fungi are trying to gain a foothold.

## Fall Cleanup

Critical to preventing any serious fungal disease is a very thorough yard and garden cleanup in the fall, which reduces the overwintering sites for fungal spores. Conscientiously rake up leaves of infected plants and dispose of them. Resist the urge to compost these leaves.

## Sulfur

Use sulfur in two-week intervals as a preventive method during periods when you expect fungal infections to occur. Do not apply it when air temperatures are over 80°F, as it can damage leaves at high temperatures.

## Solarization

Solarization of the soil is a technique that has proven effective in reducing fungal disease in the landscape. (See page 368 for a description of the procedures for solarizing your soil.) If you're starting a flower bed in a site that you know is troubled with fungal disease, this technique can give the soil a fresh start.

## Keeping Tools Clean

It is always wise, if fungal disease is a problem anywhere in your yard or garden, to keep your tools clean. Some homeowners keep handy a covered 5-gallon pail with a common household bleach solution made of one part bleach to four parts water, or a copper fungicide solution mixed according to the directions on the container. Dip shovels, rakes, and hoes in either of these solutions after working in the yard and garden around vulnerable or infected plants. Pruning tools should be disinfected after each cut to avoid spreading disease. After disinfecting your tools, coat them with oil to keep them from rusting.

# BACTERIAL DISEASE

The bacteria that attack landscape plants are carried to those plants in flowing or splashing water or in transported soil. They can enter a plant through wounds or through the tiny natural openings in the epidermis. Once inside, bacteria travel short distances in the sap of the plant.

## Symptoms of Bacterial Disease

Disease bacteria are microscopic organisms that cause trouble when they live in landscape plants. Pathogenic bacteria operate in a number of harmful ways. The bacteria that cause rots release an enzyme that dissolves cell walls in leaves, stems, and tubers. Wilts are caused by bacteria that block a plant's vascular system. Crown gall occurs when bacteria invade through plant wounds or bruises, then exude substances that promote abnormal growth in the host plant. The following symptoms may indicate a bacterial disease of some kind:

- Rotted leaves, stems, branches, or tubers, sometimes accompanied by an offensive smell
- Wilted leaves
- Large, irregularly shaped galls near the soil line on roots or stems

## Control of Bacterial Disease

Bacterial disease cannot be cured. *All the infected plants must be removed immediately and put in the trash, even if they have only slight symptoms of bacterial disease.* Do not place diseased plants in your compost pile, even if you maintain an active pile that heats up.

## Preventing Bacterial Disease

Prevent the spread of a bacterial disease by cleaning your pruning tools after cutting a diseased plant. There are a number of disinfectants used by professional landscape gardeners. Isopropyl alcohol is an excellent disinfectant for grafting and pruning tools. Use it between cuts to prevent the spread of plant disease. Some professionals use a bleach solution made up of one part common household bleach and four parts water. After disinfecting your tools, coat them with oil to prevent rusting. Wash your hands after handling infected plants, not because they are dangerous to you, but because your unwashed hands could transmit the disease to healthy plants.

# VIRAL DISEASE

Viruses are basically protein packets with DNA or RNA inside. They are parasites, multiplying inside their hosts or, if no host is available, lying inactive—but viable—in dead plant material for up to 50 years while waiting for a new victim.

Viruses are spread from plant to plant in a number of ways. Insects, especially aphids, leafhoppers, mealybugs, and whiteflies, often carry them. Aphids are the worst offenders; the green peach aphid can carry more than 50 different plant viruses. Viruses can also be carried on your hands and on garden tools. Smokers can transmit a mosaic virus from their cigarettes. Cuttings taken from infected stock plants will result in infected progeny, and viruses also can be carried by seeds.

## Symptoms of Viral Disease

The following symptoms may indicate a viral disease:

- Poor plant performance, characterized by small, stunted foliage or small, off-color blossoms
- Sudden death of a plant
- Chlorosis (yellowing of leaves), specifically irregular yellow spots on leaves, often accompanied by leaf curling or excessive branching
- Mosaic yellow-and-green mottling pattern on leaves, stems, or even blossoms
- Dead areas on leaves
- Puckered, rolled, or extremely narrow ("shoestring") leaves

## Control of Viral Disease

Viral disease cannot be cured. Remove and destroy the infected plants—remember, dead plant matter left in the garden continues to harbor disease. As with bacterial disease, *remove all infected plants, even if symptoms are mild.* Do not place diseased plants in your compost pile, and clean your hands and tools with a bleach solution made up of one part household bleach to four parts water. If a plant you want to grow is prone to a particular virus, buy certified disease-free seed or stock when available, and grow resistant varieties when available.

# NEMATODES

Nematodes are tiny parasitic worms that feed on and reproduce in plants. Although they are actually pests and are dealt with in chapter 6, the problems they cause are included in the disease chapter because their symptoms are like those caused by disease, and the symptoms continue for the life of the plant, as do those of the pathogenic diseases. Nematodes also carry many viral diseases. And like viruses, they can remain dormant in the soil—some species for up to 30 years.

Generally, it is difficult to diagnose nematode damage just by looking at the plant. Very often the only sign of a nematode problem is weakened plants that don't look healthy and vigorous. An exception is the root knot nematode, which forms galls or swellings on plant roots. Put nematodes at the bottom of your list of suspects when you are trying to identify a disease. If no other explanation seems to fit, check the possibility that your plants have nematodes. (See chapter 6 for more information on controlling nematodes.)

# GENERAL DISEASE PREVENTION PRACTICES

Because they often work fast and are difficult to control, the best way to fight plant diseases is to prevent them from getting a foothold in the first place. Fortunately, prevention is easier than fighting a plant disease that is established in your landscape. A few simple yard and garden maintenance steps will go a long way toward prevention. For example, simply by spreading compost, using seaweed extract sprays, and watering properly, you can significantly reduce the incidence of environmental disorders. Using mulch reduces the spread of fungal and bacterial disease that is often transported to the plant by rain splashing up from the soil. Viral disease can often be prevented by controlling insect pests such as aphids, which are disease carriers. These and many other general yard-care practices can keep your landscape almost disease-free.

## Landscape Management Practices

The best approach to yard-wide disease prevention is to follow basic yard-care practices that help prevent *all* disease. You might think building healthy soil with compost or adding mulch around your plants is simply extra effort, but such practices expend less energy than trying to combat a disease once it has taken hold in the landscape. In addition, many of these landscape management practices prevent other potential problems—soil deficiencies, pest infestations, and poor drainage. Remember, a healthy landscape is your strongest ally in disease prevention. Vigorous plants can withstand many diseases on their own.

---

## *Steps for Disease Prevention*

1. Build healthy soil.
2. Use compost.
3. Use resistant varieties.
4. Use a foliar spray.
5. Use mulch.
6. Eliminate the method of transmission.
7. Water plants before noon.
8. Keep tools clean.
9. Clean up the landscape in fall (see chapter 6 for information on fall cleanup practices).
10. Solarize the soil (see page 368 for information on soil solarization).
11. Use drip irrigation to prevent fungal disease.
12. To avoid spreading fungal disease, don't work with plants when they are wet.

## Build Healthy Soil

Soil that has a minimum content of 5 percent organic matter (more than 10 percent is even better), has a pH of around 6.5, contains at least five earthworms per cubic foot, and gets an annual 1-inch layer of compost will fight disease as effectively as any other tool or technique. A healthy soil maintains a balance between beneficial bacteria, fungi, and other microorganisms and those pathogens that can cause disease if allowed to multiply. The most common disease viruses, bacteria, and fungal spores in your neighborhood are usually present in the soil. However, beneficial microorganisms can keep those diseases under control as long as the soil is healthy. (See chapter 9 for more information on soil management.)

## Use Compost

Compost benefits the garden in many ways, and one of the benefits it offers is disease control. Recent research by Safer Agro-Chem, in Wellesley, Massachusetts, has shown that compost produces certain fatty acids that are toxic to fungal disease and to certain bacterial diseases of plants. Decomposing rye and timothy grasses, for example, release fatty acids that control parasitic nematodes.

Research by the Ohio Agricultural Research and Development Center has shown that compost, especially the kind that is made by simply piling up compost materials and leaving them to decompose, suppresses harmful root-invading fungi, which can cause such diseases as root rot and damping-off. Certain beneficial bacteria, for example, are present in compost. These bacterial allies produce substances called siderophores, which tie up iron, depriving harmful organisms of this necessary element. Beneficial fungi found in compost, particularly species of *Trichoderma* and *Pythium,* are antagonistic to pathogenic fungi. For example, they will attack rhizoctonia root rot fungi and some water mold fungi. The more of these beneficial bacteria and fungi present in the soil, the fewer disease problems.

Compost produced by chopping and turning the materials in your compost pile, with its high temperatures, has less disease-suppressive ability than a low-temperature compost made without turning, because beneficial microorganisms are killed by the high heat. "Seeding" high-temperature compost with small amounts of mature compost made at moderate temperatures around 80°F restores its ability to fight disease-causing organisms. (See chapter 9 for more information about compost.)

## Use a Foliar Spray

A number of natural fungicides made from sulfur suspended in liquid soaps are available commercially. Use them to prevent as well as control disease. When mixed with a seaweed extract, these fungicides can be especially effective in stopping fungal disease cold. Use this type of mixture as a preventive spray every two weeks during the early part of the growing season on those plants and shrubs that are vulnerable to fungal disease. (Roses are good candidates for this treatment.) Wait at least four days after applying any pesticide spray before using these fungicides to avoid a conflict between the two products.

## Use Mulch

Organic mulches also can help in the fight against disease. For example, research is beginning to suggest that organic mulches such as chopped leaves may mitigate the harmful effects of certain soil fungi and nematodes by creating a chemical environment that either repels those disease-carriers or kills them outright. (See chapter 10 for more information about mulch and mulching systems.)

## Eliminate the Method of Transmission

If you know your landscape plantings are vulnerable to certain diseases, or if you simply want to take all possible measures to prevent disease in your yard and garden, consider the ways in which disease is transmitted to plants and remove those means of transmission.

Virtually all of the fungal diseases are transmitted by the movement of microscopic spores that travel to the plant by wind or water. Water splashing up from the ground during rains or overhead watering commonly carries fungal disease up to the plant from the ground. One way to prevent this is to spread black plastic or geotextile mulch over the soil early in the season, even before the soil thaws from the winter freeze. Most fungal spores do not emerge from the soil until air temperatures are in the 70s. If you have black plastic or geotextile mulch in place on your flower beds and around your shrubs by mid-spring, you prevent spores from bouncing up onto the plants. Unfortunately, this trick won't work on established perennial flower beds or beds that have spring bulbs in them, since these plants begin emerging early.

Using drip irrigation to water your landscape, instead of an overhead sprinkler or hose, is another way to eliminate the splashing of water that carries spores and bacteria with it. A drip irrigation system laid under the black plastic mulch provides constant soil moisture while reducing fungal disease problems. Drip systems for the entire yard may be too expensive, but you might consider using a drip system in flower beds, shrub borders, or other parts of the yard that are particularly vulnerable to fungal disease problems.

Finally, don't handle plants that are wet. Handling wet plants can transfer pathogens from plant to plant.

## Water Plants before Noon
One of the easiest ways to reduce the incidence of plant disease, especially bacterial and fungal disease, is to water your yard in the morning. This allows plants to dry thoroughly before nightfall, denying these types of disease the moist, damp conditions they thrive in.

## Keep Tools Clean
If disease is a problem in your landscape, it is especially important to keep your gardening tools cleaner and more sterile than you normally might. Hoes, rakes, shovels, trowels, and other tools can carry fungal spores, bacteria, and viruses and spread those pathogens to other plants in your yard. Keep a 5-gallon pail containing bleach solution (one part household bleach to four parts water) handy. Then,

as a matter of routine, you can dip your tools in the solution to disinfect them after you've scraped off the soil.

## Clean Up the Garden in Fall
Fall cleanup is one of the most important steps you can take to reduce both insect and disease problems in your landscape. It is essential that all debris from infected plants be removed from the yard and garden and placed in the trash. Other organic material, weeds, fallen leaves, and even compost should be removed and composted. Diseases overwinter on plant residues, so even healthy annual plants left in the garden beds provide a good environment for diseases that might be carried into the garden by air, water, insects, or animals. (See chapter 6 for a detailed discussion about fall cleanup of the landscape.)

## Solarize the Soil
In the past, it was assumed that if certain disease pathogens, such as verticillium wilt and fusarium wilt, were present in the soil, they would remain there, and you would always have problems with those diseases. Over the past ten years, a technique called solarization has been developed that may solve many yard and garden disease problems. Solarization was developed in Israel, and has since been tested at universities across the United States. It is a process that produces very high levels of heat and humidity in the soil. This process pasteurizes the soil, destroying harmful bacteria, fungi, some nematodes, virtually every type of insect larva, and the store of weed seeds near the soil surface. Solarization is an effective control for a number of chronic disease problems found in the landscape.

An unexpected and unexplained bonus of solarization is that it also enhances the soil's ability to grow especially robust and healthy plants. Plants perform splendidly in beds that have been solarized. Solarization destroys harmful organisms, but it seems that certain beneficial organisms are not harmed. Jim DeVay, chairman of the plant pathology department at the University of California at Davis, says,

"While many fungi, bacteria, and other pathogens are killed, certain fungi that play an important role in utilization of plant nutrients and crop development withstand the heat and survive."

Solarization only works on a new bed, that is, one that has no plants growing in it. The best time to solarize soil is during July and August, when temperatures are highest and days are sunny. The procedure for solarizing all or part of a bed is fairly straightforward. Simply follow these steps:

1. Loosen up the top foot or so of soil with a fork, U-bar digger, or tiller.

2. Water the soil heavily so that it is soaking wet—wetter than if you were simply watering your plants. Then let the bed sit overnight.

3. The next day, cover the bed, or part of the bed, with 3- to 6-mil clear plastic film. Do not use black plastic, which will not produce the desired greenhouse effect.

4. Seal the plastic film along all edges with soil, and keep the bed tightly covered for four to six weeks.

It is likely to rain during the four- to six-week solarization period, leaving puddles on the plastic. Take a broom and sweep the puddles away: They reduce the effect of sunlight striking the film. Do not punch holes in the plastic to drain the water, because that will let the heat escape.

After the solarization process is finished, you can plant anything you want in that area right away. Try not to disturb the soil very much when you put in the new plants. The weed seeds near the surface have been killed, but the seeds 4 or more inches down could still germinate if brought to the surface.

PART 3

# *Landscape Management*

# CHAPTER 9

# *Managing the Environment*

**M**any landscape and garden problems could be avoided if homeowners took a plant's-eye view of the environment. Shrubs, trees, vines, and ground covers need light, water, air, nutrients, and warmth in order to grow and develop. Just how adequately the landscape supplies these needs for each plant depends on the microclimate—the local climatic conditions of a specific site. Sunlight, soil texture and richness, air circulation, temperature range, and other factors interact to create the microclimate. A shrub in an open field has growing conditions different from those of a shrub surrounded by trees or located next to a garage. Conditions in the area near a wall are likely to be quite different from those at the edge of the property. The microclimate in a particular spot even changes with time. It varies from season to season and even changes throughout a single day. To keep your landscape plants looking and feeling their best, you must take into account the microclimate around them and adjust the growing conditions as best you can to suit their desires.

## SUNLIGHT

Light, of course, is critical to plant growth. When deciding what plants to grow and where to grow them, you must carefully consider how sunlight falls around your yard. Remember, trees are leafless in early spring, and what seems like a lovely sunny space for a shrub may be a shaded one in summer and fall. Your home also casts shadows on the landscape, and exactly where they fall depends on the time of the year and the time of day.

Once you've evaluated the availability of sunlight in your landscape, you must consider the light requirements of the plants themselves and then match the right plant to the right place in your yard. A plant that needs full sun will become stunted, pale, and leggy in a shady location. Its blossoms will look poor, and it will be more vulnerable to insects and disease. On the other hand, a plant that prefers shade will become bleached and stunted under full sun. It, too, will be more susceptible to insects and disease.

## Full Sun

A plant that requires full sun needs unfiltered, uninterrupted sunlight from sunrise to at least 3:00 P.M. Morning sun is better than late afternoon sun because it warms the plants faster.

## Partial Sun

Plants preferring partial sun need five or six hours of direct sunlight, with shade or filtered sun the rest of the day. Most flowering shrubs prefer these conditions.

## Partial Shade

One might assume that partial shade and partial sun mean the same thing, but they don't. Plants that like partial shade belong in an area that gets dappled sun all day long, or dappled sun interrupted for up to four hours by either direct sun or full shade. Partial shade also refers to conditions under tall trees, the branches of which form a high canopy over the garden and filter the sunlight. This is also referred to as indirect light.

## Full Shade

Yes, some plants actually thrive in full shade. This is solid, sunless shade such as that provided by a building or a dense overhang of foliage. When locating plants next to a structure that provides such dense shade, remember that if the structure is very light in color, it will reflect sunlight and heat onto your plants and may damage them in the middle of the summer. These conditions might encourage bulbs and shrubs to bloom early in the spring.

## SOIL TEMPERATURE

While we are all aware of the impact air temperature has on plants, it's easy to overlook the effects of soil temperature on plant growth. The temperature of the soil directly influences the activity of microlife, which is responsible for making nutrients available to plants. Microlife will not become active until the temperature reaches 40°F to 45°F. For example, the bacteria needed to make nitrogen available to plant roots do not become active until the soil temperature is about 40°F, and they don't reach the height of their activity until the temperature climbs to 80°F. Of course, temperatures that are too high

have an adverse effect. Plant growth and microlife activity slow down at 85°F or higher.

So, your growing season does not really start with the last spring frost and end with the first fall frost. It starts when the soil temperature reaches 45°F and ends when the soil temperature drops down again to 45°F. Little correlation exists between air and soil temperature. It might be a balmy spring day, but if the soil temperature isn't warm enough, there's no point in sowing your seeds or planting your seedlings. To determine the temperature, use a standard soil thermometer, which you can purchase at your local hardware store or garden center, or through a mail-order garden catalog.

## AIR TEMPERATURE

Air temperatures that are too low or too high also can cause problems. High air temperatures promote excessive moisture loss and possible wilting. Frosts cause irrevocable damage to plant tissue. At low temperatures, the liquid in plant cells freezes, causing the cells to expand and burst.

To protect plants from frost damage, cover them with a protective material or device. Agricultural fleece works well. A relatively new landscape product for homeowners, fleece is a very lightweight material (0.6 ounce per square yard) made of soft polypropylene or spunbonded polyester. It lets in 75 to 80 percent of outside light. Air and water pass through it, so no special ventilation or openings are required. This material does not break down under the ultraviolet rays of the sun. It will not rot, shrink, or sag in wet weather. With careful removal and storage, it can be used for at least two seasons.

When you expect freezing temperatures to hit, simply drape some fleece over young, tender plants and small shrubs. Weight it down along the edges with rocks or soil to keep it from flapping in the wind and to keep insects from getting inside. Agricultural fleece protects plants at temperatures as low as 28°F in the spring and 25°F in the fall; however, leaves touching the material may suffer minor frost damage.

# WIND AND AIR CIRCULATION

Wind is no friend of the landscape gardener. It wreaks havoc on shrubs and trees, breaking branches and tearing leaves. Together with the sun, wind can severely desiccate or dehydrate plants. In the spring, harsh winds can stunt seedlings and prevent vines or roses from attaching themselves to a trellis.

When choosing a site for new plants, pick one that is sheltered from the wind. If your most protected spot still is visited by harsh winds occasionally, or if you simply live in a windy location, you may need to take extra measures to protect your landscape plants, especially during winter.

## Windbreaks

Traditionally, homeowners shielded their landscapes from wind by growing shrub or tree barriers. Now, instead of waiting years for a natural windbreak to grow, you can buy a special netting. Made of tightly knitted polyethylene threads, you simply attach it to any kind of fence post and build a wind fence for protection. You can purchase the material in widths of 3½ or 6 feet and lengths of either 25 or 50 feet.

Set up the wind fence perpendicular to the direction of the prevailing wind. It can be off perpendicular as much as 20 degrees and still be helpful. You can run this fabric fence right along the edge of the vulnerable area or set it back as much as 10 feet from the plants.

It is better to slow or filter the wind rather than trying to block it completely. A natural windbreak of pines is better than a stone wall, since the wind comes faster over and around the wall than it does through the trees. Wind netting acts like pines; it reduces wind speed by 60 percent, so that a 20-mile-per-hour gust passing through it becomes a mere 8-mile-per-hour breeze.

A windbreak protects an area six to ten times the height times the length of the material. Therefore, a 25-foot netting that is 3½ feet tall can protect a 500- to 900-square-foot area, and a 50-foot netting that is 3½ feet tall can protect a 1,000- to 1,750-square-foot area. A 3½-foot-high fence is good

Although a natural windbreak of pines looks more decorative in the landscape, you may need to set up a wind fence to protect plants in a windy site while your living fence grows.

for areas with few tall plants. If you have several tall plants that need protecting, use the 6-foot fences.

## Antitranspirant Sprays

You can also protect your shrubs and ornamental plants from harsh wind by spraying them with an antitranspirant. These sprays, also called antidesiccants, are organic, biodegradable materials that form a clear, flexible film over the surface of the plant. This film holds in moisture, which would otherwise evaporate quickly in high winds. It does not interfere with plant growth.

Antitranspirant sprays are used most often to protect small shrubs and evergreen trees, including azaleas, rhododendrons, and arborvitae. Apply them in late fall while the air temperature is above 40°F. Use an antitranspirant just before transplanting bushes and small trees; it will help the plant retain moisture and recover from the shock of transplanting.

Antitranspirant sprays help prevent plants from losing water to the drying winds of winter.

# SOIL

Soil not only supports plants but provides the food and water necessary for their growth. Both the structure and composition of the soil affect how much water and how many nutrients your plants get. Before you plant any flowers, foliage plants, or shrubs, evaluate the quality of the soil. If improvements need to be made, make them. Once plants are in the ground, soil improvement is much more difficult.

## Soil Structure

The looser the garden soil is, the better it drains, and the more readily the root system can spread.

## Soil Compaction

Pressure from equipment and foot traffic compacts the soil in your garden. Water and oxygen cannot easily penetrate compacted soil to reach the roots of your plants. In addition, the lack of water and oxygen prevents organic matter from decomposing properly. It doesn't take much compaction to affect plant growth. Research by Al Trouse of the U.S. Department of Agriculture's National Tillage Machinery Laboratory shows that normal, everyday compaction can reduce plant growth by at least 10 percent.

To correct a compaction problem, double-dig the soil and add lots of organic matter. Adding organic material to the surface doesn't help at all if the soil underneath is hard.

## Soil Drainage

The health of plants in the yard and garden depends on the soil's ability to quickly drain away excess water. If water fills all the pores in the soil, oxygen cannot get to the plants and they drown. Very few plants tolerate boggy soil conditions.

If you notice that puddles remain in your lawn or garden long after a rainstorm has ended or after the snow has melted, your soil may be draining poorly. To be sure, perform this drainage test:

1. Dig a hole in the garden about the size of a gallon jug.

2. Fill the hole with water and let it drain.

3. As soon as the water has drained, immediately fill it again and keep track of how much time it takes to drain. If it takes more than eight hours to drain, you have a drainage problem that needs attention.

To solve the problem, work lots of organic material into the top 24 inches of the soil. You can also move your plants to a better site, or get professional advice on laying a drainage system.

## Poor Water Retention

While good drainage is essential, you also need to check your soil to be sure it can hold water. For example, a sandy soil has excellent drainage, but it cannot hold water long enough for the roots to absorb it. If you have to water your plants every few days, your soil is too porous. Here again, adding organic matter can correct the situation.

## Soil Composition

The health of your plants depends not only on the physical structure of the soil but also the contents of the soil. A good soil for landscape gardening includes almost 25 percent water and 25 percent air. Minerals, organic matter, and microorganisms make up the rest. All these elements are essential resources for growing healthy plants.

### The Ideal Soil

The ideal soil for your landscape is fertile, loose, friable, and rich in organic material. Soil containing minerals, a good population of microorganisms, and at least 5 percent organic matter is the perfect environment for growing healthy plants, trees, and shrubs.

Plants do not get their food from the soil. They make their own food (protein and carbohydrate) using air, water, sunlight, and nutrients from the soil. Plants need nitrogen, phosphorus, potassium, calcium, magnesium, and sulfur in large quantities. Minor nutrients, such as cobalt and sodium, are required in much smaller doses.

All these nutrients are important; however, what is equally important is that they are available to the plant in certain balanced amounts. This requirement is further complicated by the fact that the pH level of the soil (acid or alkaline) affects the plants' ability to absorb certain of these critical nutrients. Therefore, problems can arise from having a surplus or a deficiency of a certain nutrient, or from having an improper pH level that chemically locks up certain nutrients, making them unavailable for use by the plant.

Much of a plant's needs are met from the minerals in the soil, but nearly all of the nitrogen and sulfur and more than one-third of the phosphorus are supplied by organic matter. This organic material must decompose so that sufficient quantities of nitrogen, phosphorus, potassium, calcium, magnesium, and other plant nutrients are in a form useful to your plants. This is where microorganisms help out. Their activity determines the amount of nutrients available each day to the plant's roots.

So, the objective of the landscape gardener is to develop soil that not only has lots of organic material, but an active microlife that constantly breaks down that organic matter to meet the needs of all your ornamental plants.

### Taking a Soil Test

With a little practice, the home gardener can see and feel soil structure, but overall fertility is more difficult to determine. If you are remodeling your landscape, planting a lawn for the first time, or if your garden doesn't seem to be as vigorous as you expected despite constant care, have a soil test done.

You can purchase soil-test kits commercially, but you can get a more thorough and accurate report from the County Extension Service (CES) in your area. You'll find the address listed in the telephone book under state or local government offices. You can purchase one of these CES soil-test packets from your local agent for only a few dollars. The packet will contain a plastic or cloth bag, a pre-addressed envelope, and a questionnaire about your property. Be sure to take your soil sample properly so it will accurately represent the soil in your lawn and garden. Follow the directions that come with the packet.

The soil-test report will tell you whether the levels of nitrogen, phosphorus, and potassium in your soil are low, medium, high, or excessive. Ornamental plants do best in soils that contain medium to high levels of these important elements. The soil analysis also will report your soil's pH level and will indicate the levels of critical minerals like calcium and magnesium. Finally, most reports will indicate the percentage of organic material found in your soil.

### Soil pH

Soil pH is a measure of the acidity or alkalinity of your soil. The pH scale goes from 0 (very acid) to 14 (very alkaline). A moderate pH level provides the

TABLE 4.

## Lab Report for a Fertile Soil

| Soil Component | Amount of Component (lb/100 sq ft) |
|---|---|
| Nitrate nitrogen | 1.114 |
| Phosphorus | 0.36 |
| Potassium | 0.8 |
| Magnesium | 0.64 |
| Organic matter | 1 in. |
| pH | 6.0 to 6.5 |

best environment for the soil-dwelling microorganisms that make nutrients, especially nitrogen, available to plants. If soil pH is too low or too high, nutrients needed by plants to make food will not dissolve quickly and may turn into insoluble forms that the plant cannot use. For best plant growth, you should try to keep the landscape's pH between 6 and 7, a slightly acidic level. Many soils naturally fall within this range, but some need to be corrected. See the individual plant entries in chapters 1 to 5 for specific pH preferences.

### Taking a pH Reading

If you want to check just the pH of your soil without having to take an entire soil test, use the commercially available plastic strips with pH-sensitive dyes or a meter that measures the soil's pH from electrodes inserted into the soil. The strips are almost as accurate as the meters and cost a lot less.

To use the strip, make a slurry of your soil and some distilled water in a clean dish. This mixture should have a consistency like molasses. Slide the mixture slowly off a spoon or spatula and let it stand for an hour or so. If it has thickened too much, add a little more water to get it to the right consistency again. Place the pH strip directly into the slurry and leave it there for at least 1 full minute—6 minutes produces the most accurate results. Remove the strip and rinse it with distilled water. You can then

## Acid-Loving Plants Adjust pH Themselves

Research is finding that plants that prefer acid soils somehow are able to increase the acidity around them when an inch of compost is added to the landscape or garden every year.

A recent study was done by the University of Connecticut's department of agriculture on a property that had soil with a nearly neutral pH. The homeowner had planted some rhododendrons and azaleas many years previously without taking any special steps to prepare the soil for these acid-loving plants. For years, this homeowner had put 1 inch of compost around each plant annually (compost is almost always nearly neutral in pH). When a researcher took soil samples, he found that the soil around the rhododendrons and azaleas was acidic, and the rest of the property was still neutral. Scientists haven't figured out how, but the plants seem to have created their own acidic environment.

It is still a good idea to add lots of peat moss or other acidic material to a neutral soil when planting an acid-loving plant such as rhododendron. This helps the plant get off to a good start. But after that you needn't worry about the pH of the soil as long as you add compost every year.

match its color to a chart that comes with the pH kit. Each color represents a different pH level.

### Correcting an Acid Soil

When soil pH is below 6, certain nutrients do not dissolve well and cannot be absorbed by most plants, except acid-loving plants such as holly and azaleas. Nitrogen, phosphorus, and other major nutrients are locked into more complex compounds that do not readily break down to release these nutrients. Without these elements, plants have trouble producing food. If your soil is too acid, you need to add limestone, wood ashes, or organic material to raise the pH. Once the pH level rises and stabilizes between

6 and 7, locked-up nitrogen and phosphorus will gradually unbond and become available for uptake by the roots of the plants.

**Limestone.** Adding limestone to the lawn and garden reduces the acidity and improves soil structure and fertility. Limestone comes in several forms. Hydrate of lime acts fast but tends to leach away quickly. Ground limestone dissolves more slowly and is available to plants over a longer period. It comes in two forms: calcic and dolomitic. Choose the dolomitic type, since it contains magnesium as well as calcium, both necessary nutrients. Because ground limestone breaks down very slowly in the soil, apply it to the lawn and garden in the fall. This assures that it will benefit your plants in the spring. (See table 5 to find out how much limestone you need to add to your soil.)

Lime not only raises pH levels, but also increases the bacterial activity in the soil, thereby speeding up the decomposition of organic matter. Consequently, if you add lime but not organic material to your soil, you will only get the best results in the first season. In subsequent years, productivity will fall unless you also add some organic material.

**Wood Ashes.** In place of limestone, you can use wood ashes to reduce soil acidity; however, they are stronger and fast-acting, so use them with caution. Ashes contain 20 to 50 percent calcium carbonate (a form of lime). The highest percentages are in the hardwoods, especially the young trees. Wood ashes also contain two of the basic components of a complete fertilizer, 3 to 7 percent potassium carbonate (potash) and 8 to 20 percent phosphorus pentoxide

TABLE 5.

## Adding Lime to a Loam Soil

| Change in pH | Amount of Lime (lb/100 sq ft) |
|---|---|
| From 4.0 to 6.5 | 16.1 |
| From 5.0 to 6.5 | 10.6 |
| From 6.0 to 6.5 | 4.1 |

TABLE 6.

## Adding Wood Ashes to a Loam Soil

| Change in pH | Amount of Wood Ashes (lb/100 sq ft) |
|---|---|
| From 4.0 to 6.5 | 15 |
| From 5.0 to 6.5 | 10 |
| From 6.0 to 6.5 | 5 |

(phosphorus). In addition, they contain the trace elements sodium, magnesium, iron, copper, zinc, manganese, boron, silicon, and sulfur.

Because wood ashes are twice as high in acid-neutralizing power as ground limestone, use them sparingly. Do not apply them year after year without measuring soil pH every season. You may spread the wood ashes on the soil at any time of the year, although late winter or early spring are the best times.

Mixed with water, wood ashes produce lye, which burns plants; therefore, don't spread them near germinating seeds and seedlings. In general, spread about 5 to 15 pounds of ashes on every 100 square feet of soil, depending on the acidity. Add less to sandy soils and more to clay soils. (See table 6 for details on the amounts of wood ashes required to correct acid soils.)

**Organic Matter.** Organic matter in the form of well-rotted manure, compost, or other material has a stabilizing effect on soil pH: It can raise the pH of an acid soil or lower the pH of an alkaline soil. Adding organic matter to the soil is a good long-term solution to any problem with pH. As a matter of routine, add about 1 inch of compost to your plant beds and under your shrubs every year.

### Correcting an Alkaline Soil

A pH reading of over 7 indicates an alkaline soil. By adding gypsum (calcium sulfate), aluminum sulfate, powdered sulfur, or organic matter, you can bring the pH to a neutral level more acceptable to most plants.

TABLE 7.

## Adding Sulfur to a Loam Soil

| Change in pH | Amount of Sulfur (lb/100 sq ft) |
|---|---|
| From 9.0 to 6.5 | 5 to 6 |
| From 8.0 to 6.5 | 2 to 3 |
| From 7.5 to 6.5 | 1 to 1½ |

**Aluminum Sulfate.** To lower the pH of your soil from 8 to 7, apply 1 pound of aluminum sulfate to every 20 square feet of ground. If you want to lower the pH from 8 to 6, apply 1 pound over every 11 square feet. You'll find additional information about application of aluminum sulfate on the package.

**Powdered Sulfur.** Powdered sulfur is another quick remedy for alkaline soils. (See table 7 for application rates.)

**Organic Matter.** As discussed earlier for acid soils, adding organic matter to the soil brings its pH into balance. If your soil is too alkaline, add 2 to 3 inches of compost to bring the soil down to a neutral pH. Once the soil has reached that pH level, adding about an inch of well-rotted compost or manure to the soil every spring should keep the pH in balance.

## IMPROVING SOIL

Adding compost to the soil offers several benefits and creates a rich, healthy microclimate around your landscape plants. Properly made compost looks just like the dark, almost black material you find in the forest under the layer of leaves on the forest floor. It looks and feels much like a potting soil mix you might buy from your local gardening store, and it has little odor.

### Making Compost

Good compost requires four elements: carbon-containing materials (such as straw or dried leaves), nitrogen-containing materials (such as fresh grass clippings or kitchen garbage), oxygen, and moisture.

Making compost is a very simple process. Simply gather a pile of organic material and let it sit in a corner of your yard for a few years. This method does produce compost, but it takes a long time. The active method requires that you chop the materials before adding them to the pile; then, a few times during the year, turn or mix the pile to encourage rapid decomposition.

Woody plant materials, such as wood chips, pine cones, and brush, take a long time to decompose even when shredded. Consider composting them separately.

Never include any meat, bones, or grease in your compost pile, because they will attract rodents and give the compost pile a bad smell. A compost pile should not smell bad. If it does, you may have added too much nitrogen or green material or allowed the pile to get too wet. A compost pile requires much more carbon material (such as straw, leaves, and other dried organic material) than nitrogen material (such as grass clippings, fresh-picked weeds, and kitchen garbage). Many gardening books recommend a carbon-to-nitrogen ratio of about 30 to 1. My experience indicates that you can cut down that ratio to even 10 to 1 if you turn the pile frequently. If the pile smells bad, add more carbon material. If the pile is not heating up, add more nitrogen material. You can tell if your pile is working well by sticking your fist about a foot into it. If the material feels warm, the pile is decomposing nicely.

Although water is necessary for the decomposition process, you can have too much of a good thing. The material in the pile should feel damp, like a sponge that has been thoroughly soaked and then wrung out, but not moist. Once you have built your compost pile, cover it to keep the rain from soaking it, cooling it down, and leaching away its nutrients.

### Speeding Up the Process

There are three tricks that will speed up the composting process:

TABLE 8.

## Common Composting Materials

| Carbon Materials | Nitrogen Materials |
| --- | --- |
| Aged sawdust | Fresh grass clippings |
| Dry leaves | Kitchen scraps |
| Seaweed | Manure |
| Straw | Weeds and garden waste |

1. Put your compost materials through a shredder or chop them with a rotary lawn mower first. They will decompose much faster than unchopped material.

2. Turn the pile every four to six days. By mixing the material, you bring more oxygen into the pile, which serves as fuel for the microorganisms that are actually breaking down the organic materials.

3. Add a composting catalyst to the pile. This catalyst is usually a powder containing billions of bacteria. It is available in some garden centers and nurseries, or you can order it through the mail from Ringer Corporation and Necessary Trading Company, among others (see the source list at the back of the book for addresses). Use this to get a new pile going rather than as ongoing fuel for the composting process. Follow the package instructions for details on application.

To really speed things up, shred material as you build the pile, and then shred the material in the pile every five or six days. In addition, use compost to get things going. Such a process should give you finished compost in about three weeks. Normally, if you don't shred the material and you turn the pile once a month, you will have finished compost in three to four months.

## Applying Compost

Compost can be added to the soil in a number of different ways. You can add a 1-inch layer to each garden bed in spring and work it into the soil by hand or with a rotary tiller, or you can simply leave the layer on top of the soil. Worms and microorganisms will move your compost down into the soil. For a quick boost to landscape plants, spread some in a circle around each plant. Do this once a year and you will see an improvement in the general health of your landscape every year.

## Conditioning the Soil with Compost

Compost improves soil in a number of ways. It can alleviate drainage problems, correct pH, and enrich infertile soils.

If your compost is made of leaves and grass, it contains about 0.8 to 1 percent nitrogen and will yield enough nitrogen for an average garden when applied at a rate of about 0.6 pounds for 100 square feet. This means that a 1-inch layer of this compost each spring supplies your garden with the nutrients it needs.

If you have a lawn area of 200 square feet, you will need about 120 gallons of compost to cover that area with a 1-inch layer. This adds up to about 17 cubic feet of compost. You can get this amount of compost from a pile that starts out being about 4 feet high and 3 to 4 feet across. Most ornamental plants, including trees and shrubs, require about ½ pound to 1 pound of nitrogen per 100 square feet.

Compost can be used as a side-dressing for plants, though its contribution as a fertilizer is so slow that this is rarely practical. Nevertheless, a couple of handfuls of compost sprinkled around each plant early in the season will provide a continuous, though modest, source of nutrients for the whole season.

## Reducing Watering Needs with Compost

Compost benefits clayey soils by opening them up so water can drain. It has the opposite effect on sandy soils. Compost has tremendous water storage capabilities and can be mixed into sandy soils to prevent moisture from just passing by the roots of

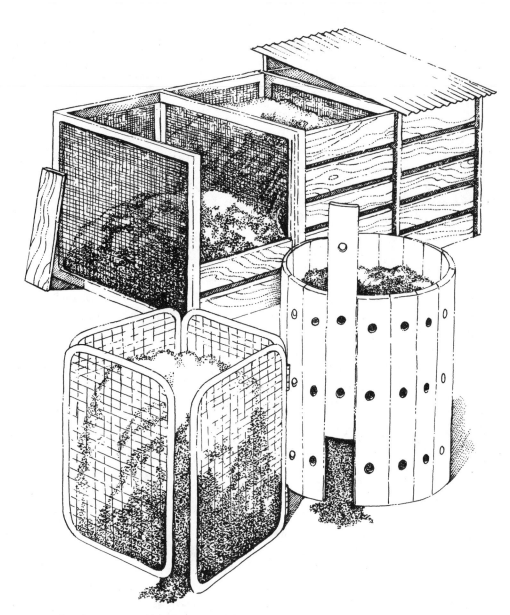

You can construct a compost bin from any of a variety of materials and in the shape and size that best suits your needs and space.

plants. A layer of compost on the surface of your garden beds will help soak up water rather than letting it puddle and run off, washing away nutrients and eroding the soil. As the humus content of your soil increases, its ability to hold water increases. Boosting your soil's humus content from 2 to 5 percent can quadruple its water-holding capacity.

## Using Compost to Ward Off Insects and Disease

When fighting pests and disease in the landscape, you probably think of Bt (*Bacillus thuringiensis*), rotenone, and copper fungicides rather than compost. Although compost isn't a major pest control, it does offer some protection. It contains certain fatty acids that are toxic to fungal and bacterial disease. As for fighting insect pests, studies have shown that leaves, especially pine needles, contain substances that suppress harmful nematodes. Although these relationships are still very much under study, research may well uncover more about the disease-prevention benefits of compost.

## Using Compost to Reduce Weed Problems

The weed-reducing abilities of compost lie in the high temperatures of this organic matter. If you make compost via the active method, your pile will heat up to temperatures around 150°F—hot enough to kill most annual weed seeds that are in the pile. Spread a 1-inch layer of finished compost over your garden beds and you can prevent germination of most new annual weed seeds residing in the top inch of the soil.

# CHAPTER 10

# Managing
# the Landscape

**O**nce you have readied the foundation of your landscape, improved the soil fertility and structure, corrected pH, and so forth, you can turn your attention to the care of the trees, shrubs, flowers, and other plants that make up your beautiful backyard. The techniques described here are easy and effective yard-care practices, which will keep your landscape healthy and looking great year after year, without a whole lot of effort.

## WATERING THE LANDSCAPE

Each type of landscape plant has different watering needs. While a 100-foot oak tree rarely needs watering, a newly seeded lawn might need water every day for two weeks. Generally speaking, small plants, annuals, and lawns require a constant supply of water throughout the growing season; small trees and shrubs require watering only during a drought.

Understanding how water penetrates the soil and how it is absorbed by plants will help you to practice more efficient watering techniques. Gravity pulls water down into the soil. When water meets individual soil particles, it forms a thin layer around each particle. Soil holds back a certain amount of water against the force of gravity. This is called the soil's field capacity, and it varies with the texture and structure of the soil.

Plant roots use the power of suction to take water away from soil particles until the water film is so thin that no more water can be sucked up by the plant. It is a regular war of the worlds down there, with soil and roots fighting for droplets of water. The landscape gardener must make sure there is always enough water to satisfy the needs of the root systems but not so much water that oxygen is denied to those same roots.

Water is lost to the environment through evaporation from the soil surface and through transpiration. The amount of water lost depends on the temperature of the air and soil, the amount of humidity in the air, the amount of wind, whether it is cloudy or sunny, and whether the plant is mulched.

## Deciding to Water

A plant reacts very simply to too little or too much water—it just stops growing. Actually, once you see that a plant has started to wilt, it has already stopped growing for a day or more. Wilting that occurs during the heat of a midsummer day is common and temporary; don't be alarmed by it. However, wilting that extends beyond the heat of day, especially if it occurs in the morning, is a signal that the plant is suffering a serious water shortage. Therefore, try to anticipate a plant's water needs before its growth even slows down, much less stops. The trick to successful watering is to keep the water supply as consistent as possible.

The symptoms of overwatering are very much like those of underwatering—pale foliage and wilting. So how do you distinguish them? Simply check the soil around the plant. If it is moist or wet, your plants are receiving too much water, and if it is dry, they aren't receiving enough.

Keeping track of rainfall helps you avoid overwatering or underwatering your landscape. The best way to do that is to mount a rain gauge someplace in or around your property. A convenient place is just outside your back door. On a rainy day, you can check it from inside the house without getting wet.

A rain gauge is a plastic calibrated tube available at garden centers. Use it only when the temperature is well above freezing. In early spring and late fall, watch for possible overnight freezes; most gauges crack when frozen.

If you don't have a rain gauge, a coffee can or similar container will work as well. For quick and accurate measurements, mark a plastic straw in inches and fractions. After it rains, insert the straw to the bottom of the can, put your thumb over the top end of the straw, and withdraw it to read the depth of the rainfall. Remember to empty the can after each rainfall.

Keep track of the rainfall on a weekly basis. If, after a few days, less than ½ inch of rain has fallen, you should think about watering, particularly the annuals, new transplants, and lawn. You don't have to keep precise records on paper. Just keeping rough track in your head is all that is needed to use this easy system.

## Deciding How Much to Water

Most homeowners tend to overlook their ornamental shrubs and plants when they think about watering. A common reason is that during July and August, when plants in the landscape usually need the most watering, homeowners find other demands on their time, such as vacations. Without consistent watering, these plants, and lawns too, go through a dry/wet/dry cycle that stops and starts their growth over and over again. This stop/start routine seriously reduces the plants' productivity. Of course, overwatering the lawn or garden causes just as much harm as underwatering. If the soil gets saturated, it has less space for that critical element, oxygen; and again, plant growth suffers.

A general rule of thumb is to be sure your landscape receives about 1 inch of water a week from rain and/or from watering systems. This standard may be too much water for some properties and too little for others. Garden beds with lots of compost and mulch lose little or no water from evaporation. The weekly needs of these beds will be something less than 1 inch a week, probably between ½ inch and ¾ inch, depending on the season. Those in very sandy soils containing little organic matter and unprotected by mulch may need 2 inches of water a week. An inch of water puts ½ gallon of water on each square foot of your garden. Likewise, ½ inch will then put ¼ gallon or 1 quart of water on each square foot. To get 1 inch a week on a 200-square-foot garden bed, you need about 100 gallons of water, less any rain that falls.

So, how often and how long should you water? If it does not rain, you may need to water your garden beds and lawn two or three times a week for about 20 minutes. That means putting about 1 quart of water on each square foot of garden space, resulting in about ½ gallon of water a week, less evaporation and runoff. It's a good idea to spread the watering over the week rather than dousing tender plants once a week during a dry period. Remember, for small plants consistency is more important than quantity. You do not want the plants to experience dry periods, then wet periods, then dry periods, over and over again.

The objective of regular watering is to replace the moisture that is lost through transpiration so that moisture levels remain more or less constant. We know that water loss begins at the top of the soil and works its way down. We also know that a plant's root system is generally as deep in the soil as the plant is tall. Research on watering has indicated that 1 inch of water penetrates 24 inches in sandy soil, 16 inches in loamy soil, and 11 inches in clay soil. So when you water by drip irrigation for just 20 minutes, you still may be sending water down fairly deep, because the water will seep down toward that soil needing replenishment.

The guideline of watering for 20 minutes, two or three times a week (depending on rainfall), should not be followed blindly throughout the entire season. In the summer months, during very hot periods with little rain or breeze, you may need to increase watering to a half hour or more two or three times a week. Feel the ground under the mulch to check. It should always feel moist. It should never feel dry.

In the fall, you can probably cut back watering to only 10 or 15 minutes twice a week, since plant transpiration slows down as the days get shorter and growth slows.

Master gardeners, who know which plants need extra water at certain times in their life cycles, use this approach to watering as a base. Individual water supplements to certain plants can easily be done by hand. For most of us, a simple watering program will keep the plants in the landscape looking better than they ever have in the past.

## How to Water

Most people water their lawns and gardens from above, using an oscillating sprinkler or a hand-held hose or watering can of some sort. This has several disadvantages. In the first place, it takes a considerable amount of time. Also, when you water this way, you lose about 30 percent of the water to evaporation and runoff. That means that you must add at least 30 percent more water than you would otherwise. If your garden is mulched, you will also use more water with the overhead method because water must penetrate the mulch before it reaches the soil and some will be absorbed by the mulch itself.

Overhead watering causes another, more serious problem. It encourages disease among your landscape plants. Fungi like moist conditions and may find the wet leaves of your plants very enticing. Of course, leaves do get wet when it rains, but if you can avoid wetting the leaves every time you water, you will definitely reduce the chances of disease infecting your landscape plants.

If you do use overhead watering methods, use the following techniques for best results. First, always water deeply so that the soil is moistened at least 12 inches down. Apply about 1 inch of water a week, preferably in three sessions. If possible, water in the morning, so foliage has a chance to dry. This minimizes disease problems. And last, avoid watering at midday because too much water will be lost to evaporation.

These overhead watering techniques will get the job done, but if you desire a more efficient, effective, and time-saving method, you should give serious consideration to installing a drip irrigation system.

## Using Drip Irrigation

Drip irrigation systems offer a number of important benefits to the yard and garden. First, a drip system uses much less water than the traditional sprinkler. You can assume that you will save at least 30 percent, and in some cases 50 percent, of the water you would use with other methods of watering, such as sprinklers. Water from a drip system has no chance to evaporate or run off, because it is completely absorbed by the soil.

Drip irrigation saves time. You can water your garden in 10 seconds, the time it takes to turn on the system. And with a timer, watering takes no time at all, since it is completely automated. Set the timer for 20 minutes, and it automatically turns the water on and off. If you are not sure how much water your drip irrigation system releases in 20 minutes, simply place a coffee can under it while it runs and time how long it takes the coffee can to fill up; then compute how much would have been released in 20 minutes. A 1-pound coffee can holds 1 quart of water. You can use this same technique to determine how long it takes an aboveground sprinkler system to release 1 inch of water on the lawn or garden bed.

Research has demonstrated that drip irrigation systems, especially those used in conjunction with mulch, increase the productivity of your landscape. Plants bloom earlier, grow more vigorously, and produce larger blossoms. Because the water never touches plant leaves, the chances of moisture-related disease occurring are reduced.

In addition, drip systems have a cooling effect on the soil and will keep temperatures down during the hottest months of summer, providing more favorable conditions for plant growth.

Finally, a drip irrigation system reduces the problem of soil compaction. Soil that becomes very saturated with water loses its structure and becomes compacted. Since drip irrigation systems release water so slowly, compaction does not become a problem.

Initially, drip irrigation costs more than a watering can, and installation requires a little effort, but a top-quality system will last for decades with very little maintenance.

# FEEDING THE LANDSCAPE

Taking good care of your soil, as discussed in chapter 9, goes a long way toward keeping landscape plants lush and healthy. Once you've conditioned the soil with compost and corrected any imbalances in mineral content or pH, you need only a little fertilizer during the growing season to keep plants looking their best. Actually, most plants in your landscape, including the grass in your lawn, will grow very well with just one application of fertilizer each year. Do not try to increase your garden's productivity by simply adding more and more fertilizer. Excessive fertilizing can cause as much or more harm to the lawn and garden as adding none at all.

You can choose from a number of different organic fertilizers, depending on the needs of your backyard. They all provide nutrients in varying degrees, but they differ in cost, availability, method of application, and duration of effectiveness.

A drip irrigation system in your garden beds releases water slowly and regularly so that your plants have a consistent supply of moisture.

## Commercial Organic Fertilizers

Most commercial organic fertilizers come in a form that provides one of the three primary plant nutrients

—nitrogen, phosphorus, or potassium. They usually come in a dry granular form that can be sprinkled directly onto the lawn or garden soil. They act slowly to provide nutrients over a period of years.

### Nitrogen Fertilizers
Blood meal and cottonseed meal are good sources of nitrogen, and they release it slowly to the garden. They tend to be expensive and are perhaps best for small beds or to side-dress plants and shrubs that need lots of nitrogen. Manure and compost are also good sources of nitrogen.

### Phosphorus Fertilizers
Commercial phosphorus fertilizers come in two forms, slow acting and quick acting. For the main feeding of the landscape, slow-acting fertilizers such as rock phosphate do the job. Work 2½ pounds of rock phosphate into every 100 square feet of soil each fall to provide all the phosphorus your plants need. If one of your landscape plants has an immediate deficiency in phosphorus, spray with diluted fish emulsion for a quick solution. Plants can easily absorb the needed phosphorus from the liquid spray through their leaves.

### Potassium Fertilizers
Like phosphorus, commercial potassium fertilizers come in slow-acting and quick-acting forms. The slow-acting potassium fertilizers include granite dust and greensand. Mix 2½ pounds of either of these powders into every 100 square feet of soil every fall, and your landscape shouldn't ever be in need of potassium. If one of your plants exhibits signs of a potassium deficiency, you can immediately remedy the problem by spraying the plant with dilute fish emulsion. Another solution is to spread wood ashes around the base of the plant.

### Compost
Compost is most often used to improve the overall condition of the soil. Information on making it and using it for this purpose can be found in chapter 9. In addition, though, homemade compost is a perfectly good general-purpose fertilizer, containing some nitrogen, phosphorus, and potassium as well as almost the entire range of micronutrients. Its phosphorus content is low though, so add rock phosphate directly to your garden, or mix it into your compost pile.

Many homeowners use compost as a side-dressing during the growing season. Landscape plants do grow more vigorously if you occasionally spread a few handfuls of compost around the base of the plants.

## When and How Much to Fertilize

Assuming you have made any general soil improvements to your landscape and the soil is reasonably fertile, you can simply follow a three-step fertilizing routine to keep your landscape plants healthy and lush.

1. Give plants, trees, and shrubs their "main meal" (see below) for the entire season in the fall or early spring.

2. During the growing season, give them occasional "snacks" to boost them under the extra stress of summer sun.

3. Finally, give them some "vitamins" once a month throughout the season to help them get maximum benefit from soil nutrients.

### Main Meal
One main feeding each year gives landscape plants, including large trees, what they need to thrive. Supplemental feedings do benefit plants, but this main meal is really all that's needed to keep plants healthy and productive all season long. You can choose from several types of fertilizers for this single application. (See table 9 for the amounts needed.)

### Snacks
Although one main feeding is all your plants need, if you want your trees, shrubs, and other landscape plants to look their best, give them occasional snacks throughout the growing season. Snacks are very dilute applications of fertilizer that give plants a boost. You can apply them as often as every month or as little as once or twice during the growing season. If you decide on the latter, apply the fertilizer in late spring and again in midsummer.

TABLE 9.

## Main Meal

Make sure your garden receives the following amounts of nutrients for optimum production. These quantities are based on a 100-square-foot garden. If you are combining various sources of nutrients to fertilize your garden, use one source of each nutrient in the amount given below.

| Nutrient | Source | Application |
|---|---|---|
| Nitrogen | Compost (spring) | 1 in.; 9 cu ft; 3 bushel baskets |
| | Dehydrated manure (spring) | 20 lb |
| | Dried chicken manure (spring) | 10 lb |
| | Aged cow or horse manure, undried (spring) | 40 lb |
| Phosphorus | Rock phosphate (fall) | 2.5 lb; about 1 coffee can full |
| Potassium | Granite dust (fall) | 2.5 lb; about 1 coffee can full |
| | Greensand (fall) | 2.5 lb; about 1 coffee can full |

If you are using dry fertilizer, work it lightly into the soil around the plant. A more efficient and effective means of supplying a snack is in liquid form. Whether you apply the liquid fertilizer as a foliar spray over the entire plant or pour it into the soil as a drench, the plants will absorb the nutrients 20 to 30 times faster than they will from dry fertilizer. Make the liquid very dilute so you are sure not to harm the plants. In most cases, a dilution of 1 tablespoon fertilizer to 1 gallon water is safe and effective. At that dilution you can give your plants snacks every month or as frequently as every two weeks without harming them. You can add a tablespoon of seaweed extract to the liquid fertilizer two or three times during the season to satisfy the vitamin needs of your plants. Use fish emulsion; it contains a broader spectrum of micronutrients than many other liquid fertilizers commonly used. (For more information on vitamins for your plants, see the facing page.)

If you use any liquid fertilizer as a drench (pouring it directly into the soil), rather than as a foliar spray, apply it right after a rain or immediately after you have watered the garden. The fertilizer will spread more evenly in the moist soil and will be more readily accessible to roots. Although a liquid fertilizer is quickly absorbed by the roots of plants, there is still some loss, because some nutrients leach down past the roots.

For that reason, applying liquid fertilizer as a foliar spray has become an increasingly popular method of giving supplements to plants, because the plant gets 100 percent of the nutrient value of the fertilizer. The best time for foliar fertilizing is in the early morning on a cloudy, humid day. If you spray in the evening, the leaves of your plants will remain wet overnight, and this could create disease problems. Adding a surfactant to the fertilizer helps it stick to the leaves and improves absorption.

As for the sprayer, never use one that was once

used to apply pesticides or fungicides. It is almost impossible to remove 100 percent of any residue from the tank, hose, and nozzle, and even a tiny bit can damage tender landscape plants. Set the sprayer to as fine a spray as possible.

## Vitamins

The final touch in fertilizing is to give all your landscape plants a dose of seaweed extract three or four times a year. Seaweed extract is sold as a liquid or powder concentrate of one or more varieties of kelp. It works much like a vitamin pill works for people. It doesn't offer much to feed on, but it enhances a plant's general health and condition. It helps the plant absorb nutrients more effectively from the soil, and it makes the fertilizer you use work better. Seaweed also makes plants much more resistant to drought and disease, and in some cases increases a plant's insect resistance. It is a very valuable amendment.

Seaweed is totally safe and provides some 60 trace elements that plants need in very small quantities. It contains growth-promoting hormones, does not leach, and has a slow release rate. It is a great source of vitamins and beneficial enzymes for plants. Its carbohydrates help plants absorb otherwise unavailable trace elements. Spraying plants with seaweed extract stimulates leaf bacteria thought to increase the rate of photosynthesis.

If the seaweed is applied directly to the soil, rather than onto the plants, it stimulates soil bacteria. This in turn increases the fertility of the soil through humus formation, aeration, and moisture retention. In this improved bacterial environment, nitrogen-fixing bacteria will be stimulated to fix more elements from plant residues and soil minerals.

A good general application rate for the powdered form, sold as kelp meal, is 1 pound of kelp meal per 100 square feet of garden applied each spring. You can also divide this into three or four portions and apply it once a month for the first four months of the growing season. If you use the liquid form, apply the spray once a month for the first four or five months of the growing season.

You can also use fresh seaweed. Thoroughly rinse it to get rid of the salt and either spread it around your shrubs and plants as mulch, or compost it. Seaweed decays quickly because it contains little cellulose. Furthermore, there's no need to worry about introducing weed seeds to your garden beds with seaweed mulch.

# RECOGNIZING SIGNS OF NUTRIENT IMBALANCES

If you take measures to maintain a high overall quality of soil and if you fertilize regularly, your plants should be happy and healthy. However, sometimes nutrient deficiencies or excesses do occur. The best way to identify a possible soil deficiency is to observe the plants and shrubs in your yard. They usually signal their distress over a lack of some mineral or nutrient through their foliage. Usually a plant suffering from some deficiency grows more slowly and produces small blossoms. As the deficiency worsens, these subtle signs give way to more serious symptoms distinctive to each nutrient, and the plants become susceptible to pests and disease. However, the symptoms are not always textbook-consistent and may be caused by more than one element shortage. Nutrient excesses result in improper growth of the plant. Consider them as a problem after you've ruled out the possibility of a pest or disease problem. Following are discussions of the three major nutrients—nitrogen, phosphorus, and potassium—along with details on how to correct an imbalance of those nutrients.

## Nitrogen

Nitrogen is essential to all stages of plant growth, and it must be readily available throughout the season. Since this nutrient is rapidly depleted from the soil, it must be replaced almost continuously by adding manure, blood meal, fish emulsion, or other fertilizers to the soil. The amount of nitrogen needed varies with the type of plant, ranging from low (less than 0.1 pound for every 100 square feet), to medium (0.1 pound to 0.3 pounds for every 100 square feet), to high (0.3 or more pounds for every 100 square feet). In a normal landscape, you should try to maintain a medium level of nitrogen, or 0.1 to 0.3 pounds for every 100 square feet, for your plants.

### Correcting a Deficiency

Signs of a nitrogen deficiency include very slow growth, stunting, and leaves that are smaller than normal. The leaves turn pale, beginning at the tips. Eventually, the whole leaf will turn yellow. Lower leaves are affected first. In severe deficiencies, the underside of the stems and leaves turn bluish purple. The plants become spindly and drop older leaves. The blossoms are small and highly colored when open.

Because nitrogen is so soluble, nitrogen deficiencies are common in very light or sandy soils, where more leaching occurs. It can occur also in soils with a high organic content when soil temperatures are around 40°F.

If you suspect a nitrogen deficiency, immediately spray plants with diluted fish emulsion or some other liquid fertilizer. Add a 1-inch layer of compost or aged manure to the soil, and continue to spray plants weekly with liquid fertilizer until symptoms disappear.

### Managing an Excess

Some homeowners, in their enthusiasm to feed their plants, apply too much fertilizer. The result is a plant with far too much lush, green foliage and no blossoms. This problem often occurs with lawn grass in the spring. Plants growing too fast from having too much nitrogen are more likely to suffer from the drought and heat of summer, making them more vulnerable to pests and disease.

Once you've applied the fertilizer, there's no turning back. All you can do is stop fertilizing immediately. Rain and watering will carry away the excess over time.

## Phosphorus

Phosphorus increases the rate of plant maturity, and it strengthens stems. It helps a plant build resistance to pests and disease, and it is necessary

### TABLE 10.

## Nitrogen Sources

The following are quick-acting nitrogen sources, which are either applied directly to the soil or applied to the leaves as a foliar spray.

| Source | Application |
| --- | --- |
| Fish emulsion | Apply weekly |
| Manure tea | Apply weekly |

The following are long-term slow-release nitrogen sources, which are sprinkled around each plant.

| Source | Application |
| --- | --- |
| Blood meal, dried (12-3-0) | Once in spring |
| Compost | Once in spring |
| Cottonseed meal (7-2-2) | Once in spring |
| Manure, aged (0.5-0.1-0.4) | Once in spring |
| Manure, dried (1.3-0.9-0.8) | Once in spring |
| Soybean meal (6-0-0) | Once in spring |

for proper fruiting, flowering, seed formation, and root branching.

### Correcting a Deficiency

A deficiency of phosphorus can show up as a reddish purple color on all the plant leaves, especially the undersides, and in the veins and stems. The young leaves will be unusually small and dark in color. As they mature, they become mottled and may turn bronze. A deficiency in phosphorus impairs metabolism, so the plant may produce very thin stems. A plant that produces lush green foliage but no flowers also may be suffering from a phosphorus deficiency.

A phosphorus deficiency is more likely to occur in acid soils than in alkaline ones. Sometimes it is a temporary condition caused by cold, wet soils. Phosphorus is less soluble in cold soil, and the acids that break it free from other elements need heat to function. In addition, phosphorus uptake can be enhanced by soil microbes, and unless the temperature and moisture content are hospitable, the microbes won't develop. A temporary deficiency is most likely to occur in early spring when soil is cold and wet and the small plant roots have less ability to absorb this nutrient.

If you suspect a phosphorus deficiency, apply a foliar spray of fish emulsion. The plant or shrub can immediately absorb the phosphorus through its leaves. Apply a dilute solution each week until the symptoms disappear. Wood ashes are very soluble and contain some phosphorus, so a light mulching around suffering plants may also help eliminate the symptoms. Adding lots of compost makes conditions favorable for microorganisms, which help make phosphorus available to plants. Over the long term, build up the soil's phosphorus by adding rock phosphate powder to the soil in the fall.

### Managing an Excess

Too much phosphorus can bind up trace elements such as iron, manganese, and zinc, making those nutrients unavailable to your plants. Excess phosphorus occurs only occasionally, and you probably won't detect it except through a soil test.

Little can be done to lower the phosphorus level of your soil. Do not add any phosphorus-rich amendments to the soil for at least two to three years. Instead, work nitrogen- and potassium-rich

TABLE 11.

## Phosphorus Sources

The following are quick-acting phosphorus sources, which are either applied directly to the soil or applied to the leaves as a foliar spray.

| Source | Application |
| --- | --- |
| Fish emulsion | Apply weekly |

The following are long-term slow-release phosphorus sources, which are sprinkled around each plant.

| Source | Application |
| --- | --- |
| Manure, dried (1.3-0.9-0.8) | Once in fall |
| Rock phosphate (0-31-0) | Once in fall |

materials into the soil to neutralize the excess phosphorus.

## Potassium

Plants need potassium, or potash, to form sugars, starches, and proteins. Potassium promotes the action of certain enzymes and boosts the cold-hardiness of many plants. It enhances the color of some plants and is necessary for the development of root systems.

### Correcting a Deficiency

You can see if a plant needs potassium by looking at the leaves, starting at the bottom of the plant. As potassium moves through the plant, it travels from the lower, older leaves to the upper, younger ones. When there is a shortage of potassium in the soil, the lower leaves turn gray-green, often with yellowing or mottling along the margins. Eventually they turn brown and take on a scorched appearance. In some cases, a potassium deficiency shows up in different symptoms, such as bronze coloring of the leaves and curling and drying of leaf margins. Symptoms may become more severe late in the growing season as the only potassium available moves to the developing blossoms. A plant suffering from a potassium deficiency shows poor resistance to disease, heat, and cold. Its blossoms may be misshapen and small.

Potassium leaches out of very light soils. It is most likely to be deficient in the upper layers of soil, since plants remove it from these levels. The quick solution to a potassium deficiency is to spray plants with fish emulsion. Apply it weekly until the symptoms disappear. A side-dressing of wood ashes also can help a plant recover from a deficiency.

For a long-term solution to a potassium deficiency, add greensand, granite dust, seaweed, or animal manure to the soil. Hardwood ashes, a source of potash, can be applied at any time of the year. Since the nutrients in wood ashes leach quickly, store them in a dry location, or simply layer them in the compost pile as you would ground limestone, for best results.

### Managing an Excess

An excess of potassium is more difficult to diagnose, but too much of this element results in stunted

TABLE 12.

## Potassium Sources

The following are quick-acting potassium sources, which are either applied directly to the soil or applied to the leaves as a foliar spray.

| Source | Application |
| --- | --- |
| Fish emulsion | Apply weekly |

The following are long-term slow-release potassium sources, which are sprinkled around each plant.

| Source | Application |
| --- | --- |
| Cow manure, dried (1.3-0.9-0.8) | Once in fall |
| Granite dust (0-0-5) | Once in fall |
| Greensand (0-1.5-5) | Once in fall |
| Wood ashes (varies) | Once in fall |

growth of a plant. If the levels of potassium in the soil are too high, do not add wood ashes, manure, or any other potassium-rich amendment to the soil for at least two to three years. Instead, add nitrogen and phosphorus amendments to help balance the excess potassium; then grow lots of plants to take up that potassium from the soil.

## MULCH IN THE LANDSCAPE

Mulch provides numerous services and is one of the most important tools available to the property owner. It can be used all around the landscape for all kinds of plantings. Most gardeners use it to cut down on watering and weeding tasks, but it offers other benefits as well. Mulch reduces soil compaction and stabilizes soil temperatures. It even works to control insects and disease. Mulch comes in many different forms, and your particular purpose for using it determines which form you choose. The best mulches are easy to lay down and require little maintenance during the growing season.

## Conserving Water with Mulch

Mulch can be used to conserve soil moisture. It protects soil from the drying effects of sun and wind. A good layer of organic mulch reduces the rate of evaporation from the soil by as much as 50 percent, depending on the amount and kind of material that is used. Mulch may spell the difference between your plants surviving a drought in the middle of August or burning up.

## Controlling Weeds with Mulch

Probably the most popular use of mulch is as a weed-control measure. A thick layer of organic mulch (at least 2 inches, preferably 4) will prevent most annual weeds from growing. Those few that do get through are easily pulled, because the soil under the mulch, if it has been properly prepared, never gets hard and compacted. A good mulch virtually eliminates the onerous task of weeding the landscape.

## Fighting Insects and Disease with Mulch

Yes, mulch even contributes to insect and disease control. For example, a thick straw mulch discourages adult beetles from laying eggs at the base of plants.

Unfortunately, organic mulch encourages slugs. They like to escape the heat of a summer day and crawl into the cool, dark environment provided by bark, leaves, and other organic matter. If you have problems with slugs, don't let that deter you from using mulch, because its benefits far outweigh that one liability, and many simple, effective controls can take care of a slug problem. Slugs become most active when air temperatures are between 60°F and 70°F. They simply loll about when the temperature rises above 80°F. Consequently, if you live in heavy slug country, you might apply your mulch a little later in the season and take it off in the early fall to minimize serious slug damage. (See chapter 6 for more information on slug control.)

Mulch helps reduce disease problems, too. Fungal disease often spreads to plants from the soil as splashing water bounces the spores off the hard ground onto plant foliage. Mulch prevents this from occurring.

In addition, some research suggests that certain organic materials, such as leaves or bark from specific trees, may produce a chemical reaction in the soil when used as a mulch. Some of these reactions might be harmful to the plant; others, however, are definitely beneficial and may reduce the harmful effects of certain soil fungi and nematodes.

## Protecting the Soil with Mulch

Rain can leach nutrients down into the soil to depths where they can't be reached by the roots of landscape plants. This reduces the fertility of the soil and can affect the health and vigor of your plants. Because mulch slows down the rate at which rain enters the soil, it gives the soil a chance to absorb the water; valuable water doesn't drain off the surface or flow rapidly down into the subsoil past the roots, taking all the soil's nutrients with it.

Heavy organic mulch also reduces soil compaction. Bare soil tends to become compacted over time from the beating of the rain and the drying out of the soil particles in the blazing sun. Mulch protects the surface of the soil from the impact of rain and sun and lessens compaction. Less compaction means healthier roots and a more active population of beneficial microorganisms below the surface of the soil.

In fact, mulch encourages microorganisms to work nearer the surface of the soil by keeping the soil there moist and friable. Furthermore, the mulch itself gradually decomposes, providing an ongoing nutrient supplement to your plants. Some gardeners worry about the fact that the decomposing mulch ties up nitrogen in the top few inches of the soil; however, the amount of nitrogen lost is usually insignificant compared to the total nitrogen available in a healthy soil.

Finally, mulch protects soil through the winter by stabilizing soil temperatures. It won't keep the soil from freezing, but it will prevent heaving. Mulch also keeps beneficial microorganisms thriving through these cold months.

## Kinds of Mulch

The best mulch for a landscape will be easy to work with, allow air to pass through it, be relatively windproof, hold some moisture, and look attractive. What more could you want? The following materials are those most popular for landscape use. Some materials are easier to come by than others, and some have advantages over others. However, any mulch is better than no mulch at all!

### Aged Sawdust

Sawdust should be aged in an exposed pile for at least a year before you use it. Fresh sawdust leaches nitrogen from the top few inches of your soil, which will have to be replaced if you want healthy plants.

### Chopped Leaves

Leaves make an attractive mulch after you chop them, and they must be chopped, since whole leaves will mat and prevent water from getting into the soil. They will cool the soil 10°F to 18°F during the heat of the summer.

There are many ways to chop leaves. The easiest way is with a shredder designed specifically for handling leaves. Be careful when using one; some shredders work well with dry leaves but jam when leaves are wet. You can also use a rotary lawn mower to shred leaves. Chop them as you mow the lawn, controlling the pattern of mowing so that you are always blowing the leaves and grass into the middle of the lawn. This way the leaves go through the mower several times and become well shredded. Some people have had success shredding leaves with a snow blower set in slow-slow drive. Or, you can put leaves in a large garbage can and use a lawn trimmer to chop them. This shreds dry leaves very finely but doesn't work too well with wet leaves.

### Compost

If you have a large compost pile, you can take some of the partially decomposed compost and lay that down around plants as mulch. This accomplishes several things at the same time. It feeds, weeds, warms, and protects the plants in your landscape.

### Geotextile Mulch

A number of new synthetic fabrics made of polyester, nylon, or polypropylene have been developed for use as mulch. Unlike plastic mulches, these geotextiles let water and air into the soil. They are tough enough to last for several seasons, even with lots of holes cut in them. Geotextiles work well around small trees, shrubs, and especially rose bushes. You can lay the fabric in the spring and then cover it with a more attractive organic mulch for a terrific weed control system that still offers all the other benefits of organic mulch.

### Grass Clippings

Grass clippings make an excellent organic mulch. Spread them in a 1-inch layer. A thicker layer would cause the clippings to decompose and become putrid. They must be dry to serve as an effective mulch. Be sure never to use grass clippings that have herbicide residue on them, or you may harm your tender ornamental plants.

### Peat Moss

Peat is another popular organic mulch; however, it tends to dry out. A serious drought can cause it to form a dry crust that actually repels water instead of absorbing it.

### Pine Needles

Pine needles make an attractive mulch and seem to help in controlling several harmful soil fungi, including fusarium. They do tend to make soil more acidic, so don't use them in an area of your yard that needs a near-neutral pH. You can use them, though, around acid-loving plants such as rhododendrons and azaleas.

### Seaweed

Seaweed, eelgrass, and other marine plants make a practical, effective mulch, where they are available, but they don't look very attractive around plants. They contain higher levels of trace minerals than other organic matter. Be sure the salt level of this material is safe. Wet some and taste it with your tongue. If you taste any salt, don't use it. Rather, throw it in the compost pile or leave it to stand in the rain for several months before you use it.

### Shredded Bark

Shredded bark or wood chips must be spread in a thick layer around shrubs and trees to be effective as a weed control. You can use shredded pine bark, nugget pine bark, or wood chips. The shredded pine bark has the nicest appearance, since it looks very natural. Nugget pine bark costs the most, but it has the advantage of being available in many different sizes. Wood chips are the least expensive of the three.

### Stones

Stones are a fine mulch around shrubs and trees. Like all good mulches, they discourage weeds, protect the plants' roots, retain moisture, and encourage essential soil aeration. They also hold midday heat and release it gradually during the cool night. Some stone mulches are made from 8-inch or 9-inch flat stones set closely together, at least an inch from the tree's trunk. You can also angle the stones so that rain water runs down to the roots. Stone mulches protect dwarf trees from the power mower and provide favorable conditions for soil bacteria and earthworms.

## CONTROLLING WEEDS

Weeds must be removed from the landscape. They compete with plants for nutrients and water, becoming more aggressive as they mature. In addition, weeds harbor insect pests and can host disease. Even dead weeds cause trouble. Their hollow stems become winter rooming houses for harmful insect pests that will emerge the next year to attack your trees, shrubs, and other ornamental plants. Certain plant diseases overwinter on weeds and will be ready to infect your plants in the spring.

## Identifying Weeds

To best control weeds, it helps to know which ones are growing in your yard. If you can't find them in a weed or plant identification guide, ask your local County Extension Service, which is always concerned about reducing the population of noxious weeds in the area. Annual weeds and perennial weeds present different kinds of problems, so you need to know which is which before you can begin to effectively control the weeds in your landscape.

## Annual Weeds

Most weeds that you see in the landscape are annuals. They seem to survive all abuse during the growing season, yet do eventually die at the end of the season. If you allow them to, they will spread thousands of seeds over your yard to guarantee their return next year. Annual weeds are prolific. A single plant can produce enormous numbers of seeds. For example, a single chickweed will produce 15,000 seeds, shepherd's purse puts out 40,000 seeds, and good old lamb's-quarters is right up there with 70,000 seeds. All of these seeds lie in the soil, just waiting for the light and water they need to germinate. As you might guess, the key to controlling annual weeds is to control their seeding activity.

### Controlling Annual Weeds

To reduce if not eliminate annual weeds in the landscape, you want either to break the reproductive cycle of the weeds already on your property or keep new weeds from getting into the yard in the first place.

The best way to control annual weeds is to prevent them from emerging by cultivating the soil and then mulching the garden beds and around shrubs and trees. Lightly turn over the top 2 inches of soil in your garden beds 10 to 14 days before setting out plants in the spring. Most of the annual weed seeds that are on or near the surface of the soil will sprout within two weeks. Once they have, rake the soil lightly to destroy the tender young plants. Rake or hoe to a very shallow depth so that you wipe out the weed seedlings without bringing more weed seeds to the surface. Weed seeds require light to germinate. Those too deep in the soil to germinate may remain viable for many years and are just waiting for you to bring them to the surface.

Now you can plant your seeds or your annual flower sets, which will get a much better start with less competition from the annual weeds. Ten days after planting, cultivate the garden again around your new plants, still working at a very shallow level.

Those three cultivations should keep the annual weeds from getting a foothold. Occasional hand pulling should be all that's needed to keep them down. Mulching at this time will eliminate even this task.

If you don't use mulch in your garden or around your shrubs, an effective way to break the reproductive cycle of annual weeds is to pull or cultivate those that do appear as soon as possible, before they have a chance to set seed and spread it through the garden. Try to get rid of annual weeds within the first three weeks of their growth. If you pull a few weeds each time you are in the yard, weed pulling never becomes an overwhelming task. This system of early pulling works in the lawn as well, but only if your lawn harbors a relatively small percentage of weeds. Weeds are easiest to uproot right after a rain, when the soil is damp. Try very hard to pull up the roots, rather than just breaking off the stems.

In general, if you are able to pull up all the annual weeds that do appear, you will have only about half as many weeds the next year, and half again the third year. Eventually, you will reach the point where weeds are a very minor issue in your landscape. It typically takes homeowners five to seven years of weeding to eliminate most of the annual weeds. If you mulch, too, annual weeds may be virtually gone in just two to three years.

## Perennial Weeds

Although the possibility of vast numbers of annual weeds popping up all over the garden seems intimidating, it's the perennial weeds that can cause the most serious problems in the lawn and garden, and they need very direct attention. Perennial weeds are tough plants that often grow right through a heavy mulch. To control perennials, you must con-

*(continued on page 402)*

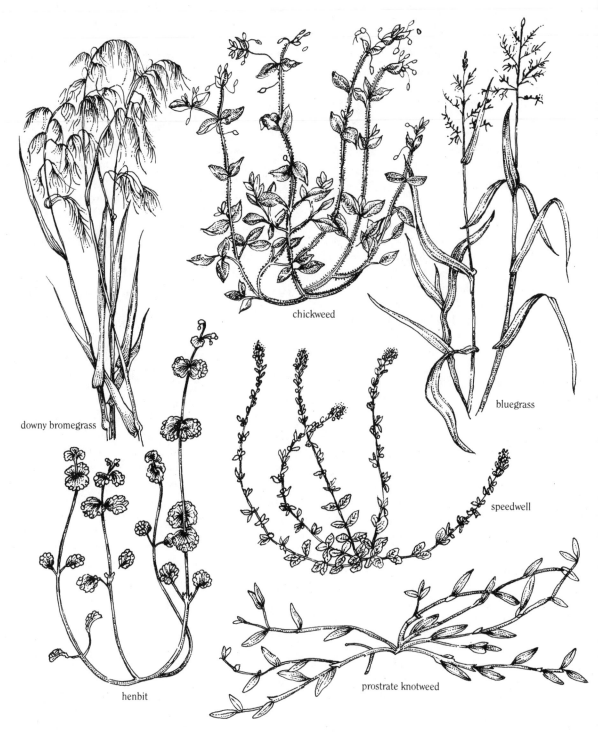

chickweed

bluegrass

downy bromegrass

speedwell

henbit

prostrate knotweed

Annual weeds

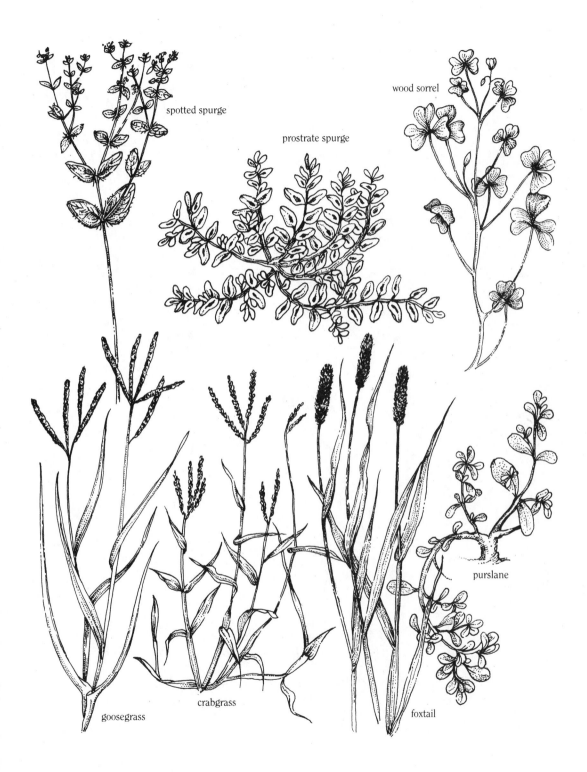

spotted spurge

prostrate spurge

wood sorrel

goosegrass

crabgrass

foxtail

purslane

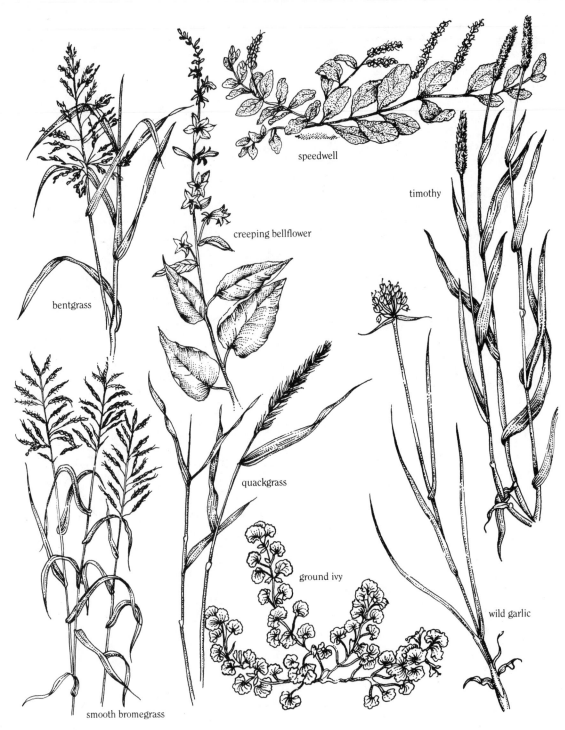

speedwell

timothy

creeping bellflower

bentgrass

quackgrass

ground ivy

wild garlic

smooth bromegrass

Perennial weeds

plantain

nimble weed

bermudagrass

mouse-ear chickweed

yellow nutsedge

tall fescue

zoysia

trol their roots, but they tend to have amazing root systems, which make them extremely difficult to eliminate. Leafy spurge, for example, has roots that grow 4 to 8 feet deep. Canada thistle's roots may penetrate to depths of 20 feet! It's no wonder that these plants are so very difficult to pull up completely. And in most cases, if you leave just a little bit of the root in the ground, the weed will regenerate and appear again. And don't think you can divide and conquer: If your rotary tiller happens to chop one of these roots into many small pieces, it's like cloning; you will have propagated that villain and created a much more serious weed problem for yourself.

### Controlling Perennial Weeds

Controlling perennial weeds requires diligence and determination. Hand pulling these weeds is not as simple as plucking tender annuals from the soil. You need to catch every plant soon after it emerges from the soil. A weeding tool is extremely valuable for this task, because with it you can cut the roots down 4 to 5 inches. By doing this, you have completely cut off the weed's access to sunlight. After cutting the same plant down a few times, it will eventually die. If you leave just a few portions of a perennial weed near the soil surface, you will continue to be plagued by the plant. Only if you are particularly persistent will you succeed in beating back perennial weeds by pulling.

Fortunately, there is one widely available herbicide called SharpShooter. It is made of soap-based fatty acids, which dry out plants quickly. Treated weeds lose their moisture in a matter of a few minutes and die within hours. This herbicide is safe to use. It breaks down on the plant and does not harm the environment.

## Fall and Spring Cleanup

In the discussion on controlling insects in chapter 6, you are encouraged to do everything you can to attract birds to your landscape, and you are strongly urged to rigorously clean your yard and garden after the annuals have died in the fall. These insect control practices also reduce weed problems. You should do everything you can to prevent annual weeds from going to seed. Those few weeds that do go to seed attract seed-eating birds, which keep the weeds somewhat under control. When you cultivate around plants in the fall to expose the overwintering larvae of pest insects, you are also bringing many of the hidden weed seeds to the surface to germinate. A light raking and subsequent winter chill will reduce their numbers further next spring.

## Mulch to Control Weeds

Perhaps the best way to solve a weed problem is to use mulch during all or at least part of the growing season. Mulch does a number of good things for your garden, and controlling weeds is one of them. A layer of mulch over the surface of the growing bed prevents annual weeds from getting a chance to even germinate. Those few weeds that do pop up through the mulch are easily pulled by hand.

## Begin with a Weedless Flower Garden

If you are going to create a new garden plot, eliminate all the weeds before you plant one ornamental, and you will have practically solved weed problems before they've even begun. To clear an area of weeds, you can cover the site for a full year, or you can solarize the soil during a six- to ten-week period in the summer.

### Covering the Plot

A simple method for clearing an area for a new garden bed requires nothing more than covering the site heavily with mulch. Blanket the area with a thick layer of overlapped newspapers and top that with several inches of bark or sawdust mulch; then leave it fallow for a whole year. This will eliminate virtually all of your toughest perennial and annual weeds. It is truly a simple technique, but it takes a long time.

### Solarizing the Soil

A second method for eliminating weeds from a patch of the landscape uses the energy of the sun. Solarizing the soil not only kills weed seeds but destroys disease spores as well, and it works quickly.

In midsummer, when temperatures are hottest, soak the area with water and cover it with clear plastic. After a few days of continuous summer sunlight, the soil temperature begins to soar, reaching 140°F at the surface and as high as 100°F 18 inches down. This heat creates nearly 100 percent humidity in the water-soaked soil. During a four- to six-week period, the high heat and humidity pasteurize the soil, destroying many of the weed seeds near the surface. (See chapter 8 for precise, step-by-step instructions on solarizing a garden plot.)

The solarization process does not work uniformly for all weeds, but that is not a serious drawback. Research has shown that after 40 summer days under clear plastic, dayflower seeds, for example, were killed to a depth of a little over 4 inches, while sedges and barnyard grass seeds were killed to a depth of only 1½ inches; however, it took just three weeks to kill goosegrass seeds to a depth of 2 inches.

# WINTERIZING SHRUBS AND TREES

In northern parts of the United States and in Canada, some trees, especially young ones, and many shrubs suffer damage from winter weather conditions. Broad-leaved evergreen shrubs such as rhododendrons and azaleas are particularly vulnerable to winter damage. During warm spells in winter, the still-frozen roots of trees and shrubs cannot replace moisture lost through the leaves. As a result, plants become desiccated and may suffer winterkill or winter injury. Winterkill usually shows up in the spring. Some of the leaves may turn brown around the edges, the bark may start to split, and an entire branch may die. In some cases, the whole plant dies. To protect vulnerable evergreen shrubs and trees from the harshness of winter, follow the steps below:

1. Water before the ground freezes.
2. Spray with an antitranspirant.
3. Shield the exposed plants.
4. Renew the antitranspirant spray.
5. Apply mulch.
6. Remove snow.
7. Shear hedges.

## Water before the Ground Freezes

The single most important thing you can do to protect shrubs and small trees from winter damage is to give them a good watering before the ground freezes, usually in October or November. Water twice, two weeks apart, starting about a month before you expect the freeze. Soak the soil around your trees and shrubs to a depth of 18 inches to 2 feet.

## Spray with an Antitranspirant

Antitranspirants form a protective coating over the foliage of plants, which reduces the rate of moisture loss by up to 80 percent. Although this coating acts as a sealant to keep moisture from readily escaping, it is still porous enough to allow the exchange of gases between the air and the plant. Spray your plants with antitranspirants when the air temperature is above 40°F and before the ground freezes hard. You can find antitranspirants in garden supply centers or mail-order catalogs as ready-to-use sprays or in concentrated forms that must be mixed with water for spraying.

Most antitranspirants won't be effective throughout the winter, so spray your trees and shrubs again after February 1. Wait for a sunny day when the air temperature is above 40°F and spray all your vulnerable shrubs and trees again.

## Shield the Exposed Plants

If winds are a problem in your area, you may want to build a wind fence to protect trees and shrubs and other ornamental plants from cruel winter blasts. Burlap is a good material to wrap around plants to protect them from breakage, windburn, bright sun, and salt that might splash up from nearby roads in winter. You can also use it to protect tender blossom buds on forsythias, azaleas, and magnolias.

Make a wind screen simply by nailing some burlap to wooden stakes. Placed around your landscape plants, it will break the force of the wind without blocking essential air flow. Although burlap breathes somewhat, leave openings at the top and bottom for air circulation. (See chapter 9 for a discussion about wind and windbreaks.) If you don't have burlap, agricultural fleece makes a good substitute. Never cover plants with plastic, though; it might suffocate your plants when the weather turns warmer.

To protect upright evergreens such as juniper and arborvitae from ice damage and snow breakage, simply tie up the branches, just as Christmas trees are wrapped, with heavy string, rope, or tapes.

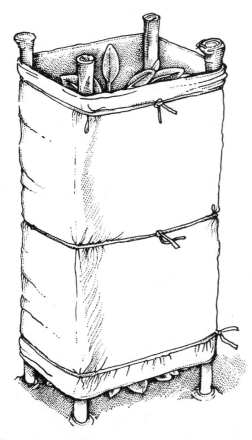

To protect shrubs against the harsh drying winds of winter, set stakes around your plants and wrap them with burlap.

## Apply Winter Mulch

If you thought mulch offered several benefits during the growing season, you'll find it is also important to the care and health of your plants throughout the winter season, so place some winter mulch around your vulnerable trees and shrubs. It limits the heaving of newly planted nursery stock during thaws. It keeps the ground from freezing too hard, allowing roots to absorb some moisture throughout the winter so that the plants are not as likely to dehydrate. And as an extra benefit, it prevents the soil from warming up rapidly in the spring. When the soil warms too rapidly, shrubs and trees bloom too early, and blossoms may be damaged by a late spring frost.

Lay a 2- to 6-inch layer of organic mulch around your plants at about the same time you apply the antitranspirant spray as described earlier. Spread the mulch so it covers the area from the trunk out to the drip line, the circle covered by the outermost branches, since feeder roots often extend some distance from the trunk of the tree or shrub.

## Remove Snow

If snow accumulates on your shrubs and small trees, remove it carefully. To lighten the weight on brittle branches, brush the snow upward, away from yourself, rather than in a downward motion. This reduces the risk of breaking any small limbs.

## Shear Hedges for Winter

If you live in an area that gets a fair amount of snow each year, do not let your hedges get too wide (more than 3 feet) or they may experience winter damage. One trick is to shear the tops into a rounded or pointed shape rather than a flat one, so heavy loads of snow can easily slide off without crushing the hedges.

If you follow all these simple but important practices, your yard and garden will look great year after year, and you'll enjoy hours of pleasure in your beautiful landscape.

# Sources for Equipment and Supplies

A major source of information for this section came from *Gardening by Mail 2,* by Barbara J. Barton, Tusker Press, 1987

## ANIMAL REPELLENTS AND TRAPS

Agrilite
P.O. Box 12
93853 River Rd.
Junction City, OR 97448

Alternative
3439 E. 86th St., Suite 259D
Indianapolis, IN 46240

Bonide Chemical Co.
2 Wurz Ave.
Yorkville, NY 13495

Bountiful Gardens
5798 Ridgewood Rd.
Willits, CA 95490

Brookstone Co.
127 Vose Farm Rd.
Peterborough, NH 03458

Burlington Scientific Corp.
91 Carolyn Blvd.
Farmingdale, NY 11735

W. Atlee Burpee Co.
300 Park Ave.
Warminster, PA 18974

D. V. Burrell Seed Growers Co.
P.O. Box 150
Rocky Ford, CO 81067

Charley's Greenhouse Supply
1569 Memorial Hwy.
Mt. Vernon, WA 98273

Clapper Co.
1121 Washington St.
Newton, MA 02165

Dalen Products
11110 Gilbert Dr.
Knoxville, TN 37932-3099

Down to Earth Distributors
850 W. 2nd St.
Eugene, OR 97402

Dramm Co.
P.O. Box 1960
Manitowoc, WI 54221-1960

Earlee
2002 Hwy. 62
Jeffersonville, IN 47130

J. T. Eaton & Co.
1393 E. Highland Rd.
Twinsburg, OH 44807

Evans BioControl
895 Interlocken Pkwy. Unit A
Broomfield, CO 80020

Gardener's Supply Co.
128 Intervale Rd.
Burlington, VT 05401

Gardens Alive!
5100 Schenley Place
Lawrenceburg, IN 47025

Great Lakes IPM
10220 Church Rd. N.E.
Vestaburg, MI 48891

Green Earth Organics
9422 144th St. E.
Puyallup, WA 98373

Hammacher Schlemmer
618 N. Michigan Ave.
Chicago, IL 60611

Harmony Farm Supply
P.O. Box 451
Graton, CA 95444

Hartmann's Plantation
310 60th St.
P.O. Box E
Grand Junction, MI 49056

Hydro-Gardens of Denver
P.O. Box 9707
Colorado Springs, CO 80932

InterNet
2730 Nevada Ave. N.
Minneapolis, MN 55427

Ken-Bar
24 Gould St.
Reading, MA 01867

Kenco Chemical & Mfg. Corp.
8461 Bay Pine Rd.
Suite 1
Jacksonville, FL 32216

Kilgore Seed Co.
1400 W. First St.
Sanford, FL 32771

Lakeland Nursery Sales
340 Poplar St.
Hanover, PA 17331

Orol Ledden & Sons
Center & Atlantic Aves.
P.O. Box 7
Sewell, NJ 08080-0007

A. M. Leonard
P.O. Box 816
Piqua, OH 45356

Liberty Seed Co.
128 First Dr. S.E.
P.O. Box 806
New Philadelphia, OH 44663

Mellinger's
2310 W. South Range Rd.
North Lima, OH 44452-9731

Modern Farm
1825 Big Horn Ave.
Cody, WY 82414

BCS Mosa
P.O. Box 1739
Matthews, NC 28106

Natural Garden Co.
27 Rutherford Ave.
San Anselmo, CA 94960

Natural Gardening Research
  Center
Hwy. 48
P.O. Box 149
Sunman, IN 47041

Nature's Control
P.O. Box 35
Medford, OR 97501

Necessary Trading Co.
703 Salem Ave.
New Castle, VA 24127

North Star Evergreens
P.O. Box 253
Park Rapids, MN 56470

Nott Manufacturing Co.
Pleasant Valley, NY 12569

Ohio Earth Food
13737 Duquette Ave. N.E.
Hartville, OH 44632

Organic Pest Management
P.O. Box 55267
Seattle, WA 98155

Peaceful Valley Farm Supply
  Co.
11173 Peaceful Valley Rd.
Nevada City, CA 95959

Plow and Hearth
560 Main St.
Madison, VA 22727

Pony Creek Nursery
Tilleda, WI 54978

Ringer Corp.
9959 Valley View Rd.
Minneapolis, MN 55344

Rodco Products Co.
P.O. Box 944
2565 16th Ave.
Columbus, NE 68601

Safe-N-Sound
P.O. Box 153
116 Main St.
Garrison, IA 52229

Seabright Enterprises
4026 Harlan St.
Emeryville, CA 94608

Stark Bros.
Hwy. 54 W.
Louisiana, MO 63353-0010

Tregunno Seeds
126 Catherine St. N.
Hamilton, Ontario L8R 1J4

Uniroyal-Leffingwell
  Chemical Co.
111-T S. Barry
Brey, CA 92621

Vesey's Seeds
P.O. Box 9000
Charlottestown, Prince
  Edward Island C1A 8K6

Waushara Gardens
Plainfield, WI 54966


## BENEFICIAL INSECTS AND DISEASES

Agrilite
P.O. Box 12
93853 River Rd.
Junction City, OR 97448

Alternative
3439 E. 86th St., Suite 259D
Indianapolis, IN 46240

Bio-Control Co.
P.O. Box 247
Cedar Ridge, CA 95924

BioLogic
418 Briar Ln.
Chambersburg, PA 17201

Bio-Resources
P.O. Box 902
Santa Paula, CA 93060

Bountiful Gardens
5798 Ridgewood Rd.
Willits, CA 95490

W. Atlee Burpee Co.
300 Park Ave.
Warminster, PA 18974

Colorado Insectary
Box 3266
Durango, CO 81301

Down to Earth Distributors
850 W. 2nd St.
Eugene, OR 97402

Evans BioControl
895 Interlocken Pkwy. Unit A
Broomfield, CO 80020

Foothill Agricultural Research
510 W. Chase Dr.
Corona, CA 91720

Fountain Sierra Bug Co.
P.O. Box 114
Rough & Ready, CA 95975

Green Earth Organics
9422 144th St. E.
Puyallup, WA 98373

Harmony Farm Supply
P.O. Box 451
Graton, CA 95444

Hydro-Gardens of Denver
P.O. Box 9707
Colorado Springs, CO 80932

I.F.M.
333B Ohme Garden Rd.
Wenatchee, WA 98801

Lakeland Nursery Sales
340 Poplar St.
Hanover, PA 17331

Mellinger's
2310 W. South Range Rd.
North Lima, OH 44452-9731

Natural Gardening Co.
27 Rutherford Ave.
San Anselmo, CA 94960

Natural Gardening Research
  Center
Hwy. 48
P.O. Box 149
Sunman, IN 47041

Nature's Control
P.O. Box 35
Medford, OR 97501

Necessary Trading Co.
684 Salem Ave.
New Castle, VA 24127

North Star Evergreens
P.O. Box 253
Park Rapids, MN 56470

Organic Pest Management
P.O. Box 55267
Seattle, WA 98155

Peaceful Valley Farm Supply
  Co.
11173 Peaceful Valley Rd.
Nevada City, CA 95959

Plow and Hearth
560 Main St.
Madison, VA 22727

Pony Creek Nursery
Tilleda, WI 54978

Reuter Laboratories
8450 Natural Wy.
Manassas Park, VA 22111

Richter's
P.O. Box 26
Goodwood, Ontario L0C 1A0

Rincon-Vitova Insectaries
P.O. Box 95
Oak View, CA 93022

Ringer Corp.
9959 Valley View Rd.
Minneapolis, MN 55344

Clyde Robin Seed Company
P.O. Box 2855
Castro Valley, CA 94546

Rocky Mountain Insectary
P.O. Box 152
Palisade, CO 81526

Smith & Hawken
25 Corte Madera
Mill Valley, CA 94941

Spalding Laboratories
760 Printz Rd.
Arroyo Grande, CA 93420

Unique Insect Control
5504 Sperry Dr.
Sacramento, CA 95621

West Coast Ladybug Sales
P.O. Box 903
Gridley, CA 95948


## COMPOSTING EQUIPMENT

Amerind-MasKissic
P.O. Box 111
Parker Ford, PA 19457

Bonide Chemical Co.
2 Wurz Ave.
Yorkville, NY 13495

Brookstone Co.
127 Vose Farm Rd.
Peterborough, NH 04358

W. Atlee Burpee Co.
300 Park Ave.
Warminster, PA 18974

Charley's Greenhouse Supply
1569 Memorial Hwy.
Mt. Vernon, WA 98273

Composting Fast-Easy
709 W. Stonecrest Circle
St. Joseph, MO 64508

Dalen Products
11110 Gilbert Dr.
Knoxville, TN 37932-3099

Earlee
2002 Hwy. 62
Jeffersonville, IN 47130

Gardener's Supply Co.
128 Intervale Rd.
Burlington, VT 05401

Garden Way Mfg. Co.
102nd St. & Ninth Ave.
Troy, NY 12180

Green Earth Organics
9422 144th St. E.
Puyallup, WA 98373

Greener Thumb
109 E. 20th St.
Littlefield, TX 79339

Harmony Farm Supply
P.O. Box 451
Graton, CA 95444

Kemp Co.
160 Koser Rd.
Lititz, PA 17543

Kinsman Co.
River Rd.
Point Pleasant, PA 18950

Orol Ledden & Sons
Center & Atlantic Aves.
P.O. Box 7
Sewell, NJ 08080-0007

A. M. Leonard
P.O. Box 816
Piqua, OH 45356

Liberty Seed Co.
128 First Dr. S.E.
P.O. Box 806
New Philadelphia, OH 44663

McDermott Garden Products
P.O. Box 129
1300 S. Grand Ave.
Charles City, IA 50616

Mantis Mfg. Corp.
1458 County Line Rd.
Huntingdon Valley, PA 19006

Mellinger's
2310 W. South Range Rd.
North Lima, OH 44452-9731

Modern Farm
1825 Big Horn Ave.
Cody, WY 82414

Natural Gardening Co.
27 Rutherford Ave.
San Anselmo, CA 94960

Necessary Trading Co.
684 Salem Ave.
New Castle, VA 24127

Nitron Industries
P.O. Box 400
Fayetteville, AR 72702

North Star Evergreens
P.O. Box 253
Park Rapids, MN 56470

Peaceful Valley Farm Supply
Co.
11173 Peaceful Valley Rd.
Nevada City, CA 95959

Plow and Hearth
560 Main St.
Madison, VA 22727

Richter's
P.O. Box 26
Goodwood, Ontario L0C 1A0

Ringer Corp.
9959 Valley View Rd.
Minneapolis, MN 55344

Rodco Products Co.
P.O. Box 944
2565 16th Ave.
Columbus, NE 68601

Scotchmen
R.D. 1
Pottstown, PA 19464

Smith & Hawken
25 Corte Madera
Mill Valley, CA 94941

Stark Bros.
Hwy. 54 W.
Louisiana, MO 63353-0010

Tregunno Seeds
126 Catherine St. N.
Hamilton, Ontario L8R 1J4

## DRIP IRRIGATION SYSTEMS AND DEVICES

Agrilite
P.O. Box 12
93853 River Rd.
Junction City, OR 97448

Aquatic Irrigation Systems
619 E. Gutierrez
Santa Barbara, CA 93103

Aquatic Systems
1900 N. 25th Dr.
Phoenix, AZ 85009

Brookstone Co.
127 Vose Farm Rd.
Peterborough, NH 03458

W. Atlee Burpee Co.
300 Park Ave.
Warminster, PA 18974

Charley's Greenhouse Supply
1569 Memorial Hwy.
Mt. Vernon, WA 98273

Clapper Co.
1121 Washington St.
Newton, MA 02165

Dalen Products
11110 Gilbert Dr.
Knoxville, TN 37932-3099

Dramm Co.
P.O. Box 1960
Manitowoc, WI 54221-1960

Drip Irrigation Garden
16216 Raymer St.
Van Nuys, CA 91406

Full Circle Garden Products
P.O. Box 6
Redway, CA 95560

Gardena
6031 Culligan Way
Minnetonka, MN 55345

Gardener's Supply Co.
128 Intervale Rd.
Burlington, VT 05401

Harmony Farm Supply
P.O. Box 451
Graton, CA 95444

Hartmann's Plantation
P.O. Box E
Grand Junction, MI 49056

Hydro-Gardens of Denver
P.O. Box 9707
Colorado Springs, CO 80932

Hyponex Co.
P.O. Box 4300
Copley, OH 44321

International Irrigation
Systems
L.P.O. Box 160
Niagara Falls, NY 14304

Lakeland Nursery Sales
340 Poplar St.
Hanover, PA 17331

Orol Ledden & Sons
Center & Atlantic Aves.
P.O. Box 7
Sewell, NJ 08080-0007

A. M. Leonard
P.O. Box 816
Piqua, OH 45356

Liberty Seed Co.
128 First Dr. S.E.
P.O. Box 816
New Philadelphia, OH 44663

Mantis Mfg. Corp.
1458 County Line Rd.
Huntingdon Valley, PA 19006

Mellinger's
2310 W. South Range Rd.
North Lima, OH 44452-9731

Misti-Maid
5500 Boscell Commons
P.O. Box 4607
Fremont, CA 94538

Necessary Trading Co.
684 Salem Ave.
New Castle, VA 24127

OFE International
P.O. Box 164402
Miami, FL 33116

Pacific Products
P.O. Box F
El Cajon, CA 92022

Peaceful Valley Farm Supply
Co.
11173 Peaceful Valley Rd.
Nevada City, CA 95959

Raindrip
P.O. Box 2173
21305 Itasca St.
Chatsworth, CA 91313-2173

Rain Matic Corp.
1227 S. 22nd St.
Omaha, NE 61803

Richdel
P.O. Drawer A
Carson City, NV 89702

Rodco Products
P.O. Box 944
2565 16th Ave.
Columbus, NE 68601

Smith & Hawken
25 Corte Madera
Mill Valley, CA 94941

Stark Bros.
Hwy. 54 W.
Louisiana, MO 63353-0010

Submatic Irrigation Systems
P.O. Box 246
Lubbock, TX 79408

Trickle Soak Systems
P.O. Box 38
Santee, CA 92071

Urban Farmer
2833 Vicente St.
San Francisco, CA 94116

Vesey's Seeds
P.O. Box 9000
Charlottestown, Prince
Edward Island C1A 8K6

Wade Mfg. Co.
1025 S.W. Allen Blvd.
Beaverton, OR 97005

## EARTHWORMS

Beatrice Farms
Dawson, GA 31742

Bountiful Gardens
5798 Ridgewood Rd.
Willits, CA 95490

W. Atlee Burpee Co.
300 Park Ave.
Warminster, PA 18974

Cape Cod Worm Farm
30 Center Ave.
Buzzards Bay, MA 02532

Carter Fishworm Farm
Plains, GA 31780

Harmony Farm Supply
P.O. Box 451
Graton, CA 95444

Nature's Control
P.O. Box 35
Medford, OR 97501

Necessary Trading Co.
684 Salem Ave.
New Castle, VA 24127

Organic Pest Management
P.O. Box 55267
Seattle, WA 98155

Richter's
P.O. Box 26
Goodwood, Ontario L0C 1A0

Rodco Products
P.O. Box 944
2565 16th Ave.
Columbus, NE 68601

Unique Insect Control
5504 Sperry Dr.
Citrus Heights, CA 95621

## FUNGICIDES

Agrilite
P.O. Box 12
93853 River Rd.
Junction City, OR 97448

Bonide Chemical Co.
2 Wurz Ave.
Yorkville, NY 13495

W. Atlee Burpee Co.
300 Park Ave.
Warminster, PA 18974

D. V. Burrell Seed Growers Co.
P.O. Box 150
Rocky Ford, CO 81067

Charley's Greenhouse Supply
1569 Memorial Hwy.
Mt. Vernon, WA 98273

Clapper Co.
1121 Washington St.
Newton, MA 02165

Earlee
2002 Hwy. 62
Jeffersonville, IN 47130

Full Circle Garden Products
P.O. Box 6
Redway, CA 95560

Gardener's Supply Co.
128 Intervale Rd.
Burlington, VT 05401

Green Earth Organics
9422 144th St. E.
Puyallup, WA 98373

Harmony Farm Supply
P.O. Box 451
Graton, CA 95444

Hartmann's Plantation
310 60th St.
P.O. Box E
Grand Junction, MI 49056

Kilgore Seed Co.
1400 W. First St.
Sanford, FL 32771

Orol Ledden & Sons
Center & Atlantic Aves.
P.O. Box 7
Sewell, NJ 08080-0007

Liberty Seed Co.
128 First Dr. S.E.
P.O. Box 806
New Philadelphia, OH 44663

Mellinger's
2310 W. South Range Rd.
North Lima, OH 44452-9731

Natural Gardening Co.
27 Rutherford Ave.
San Anselmo, CA 94960

Natural Gardening Research
  Center
Hwy. 48
P.O. Box 149
Sunman, IN 47041

Necessary Trading Co.
684 Salem Ave.
New Castle, VA 24127

North Country Organics
P.O. Box 107
Newbury, VT 05051

North Star Evergreens
P.O. Box 253
Park Rapids, MN 56470

OFE International
P.O. Box 164402
Miami, FL 33116

Ohio Earth Foods
13737 Duquette Ave. N.E.
Hartville, OH 44632

Organic Pest Management
P.O. Box 55267
Seattle, WA 98155

Pacific Products
P.O. Box F
El Cajon, CA 92022

Pony Creek Nursery
Tilleda, WI 54978

Richter's
P.O. Box 26
Goodwood, Ontario L0C 1A0

Ringer Corp.
9959 Valley View Rd.
Minneapolis, MN 55344

Stark Bros.
Hwy. 54 W.
Louisiana, MO 63353-0010

Tregunno Seeds
126 Catherine St. N.
Hamilton, Ontario L8R 1J4

Urban Farmer
2833 Vicente St.
San Francisco, CA 94116

Vesey's Seeds
P.O. Box 9000
Charlottestown, Prince
  Edward Island C1A 8K6

## INSECT CONTROLS AND TRAPS

Agrilite
P.O. Box 12
93853 River Rd.
Junction City, OR 97448

Agri-Systems International
125 W. 7th St.
Windgap, PA 18091

Alternative
3439 E. 86th St., Suite 259D
Indianapolis, IN 46240

BioLogic
418 Briar Ln.
Chambersburg, PA 17201

Bonide Chemical Co.
2 Wurz Ave.
Yorkville, NY 13495

Bountiful Gardens
5798 Ridgewood Rd.
Willits, CA 95490

Bramen Co.
P.O. Box 70
Salem, MA 01970-0070

Brookstone Co.
127 Vose Farm Rd.
Peterborough, NH 03458

Brucker Snail Barrier Co.
9363 Wilshire Blvd.
Beverly Hills, CA 90210

W. Atlee Burpee Co.
300 Park Ave.
Warminster, PA 18974

D. V. Burrell Seed Growers Co.
P.O. Box 150
Rocky Ford, CO 81067

Charley's Greenhouse Supply
1569 Memorial Hwy.
Mt. Vernon, WA 98273

Clapper Co.
1121 Washington St.
Newton, MA 02165

Colorado Insectary
Box 3266
Durango, CO 81301

Concept Membrane
P.O. Box 6059
Bend, OR 97708

Dalen Products
11110 Gilbert Dr.
Knoxville, TN 37932-3099

Down to Earth Distributors
850 W. 2nd St.
Eugene, OR 97402

Dramm Co.
P.O. Box 1960
Manitowoc, WI 54221-1960

Earlee
2002 Hwy. 62
Jeffersonville, IN 47130

Evans BioControl Co.
895 Interlocken Pkwy. Unit A
Broomfield, CO 80020

Foothill Agricultural Research
510 W. Chase Dr.
Corona, CA 91720

Full Circle Garden Products
P.O. Box 6
Redway, CA 95560

Gardener's Supply Co.
128 Intervale Rd.
Burlington, VT 05401

Garden Way Mfg. Co.
102nd St. & Ninth Ave.
Troy, NY 12180

Great Lakes IPM
10220 Church Rd. N.E.
Vestaburg, MI 48891

Green Earth Organics
9422 144th St. E.
Puyallup, WA 98373

Greener Thumb
109 E. 20th St.
Littlefield, TX 79339

Harmony Farm Supply
P.O. Box 451
Graton, CA 95444

Hercon Labs
200B Corporate Ct.
Plainfield, NJ 07080

Hydro-Gardens of Denver
P.O. Box 9707
Colorado Springs, CO 80932

Hyponex Co.
P.O. Box 4300
Copley, OH 44321

I.F.M.
333B Ohme Garden Rd.
Wenatchee, WA 98801

Insects
10505 N. College Ave.
Indianapolis, IN 46280

Ken-Bar
24 Gould St.
Reading, MA 01867

Kenco Chemical & Mfg. Corp.
8461 Bay Pine Rd.
Suite 1
Jacksonville, FL 32216

Kilgore Seed Co.
1400 W. First St.
Sanford, FL 32771

Lakeland Nursery Sales
340 Poplar St.
Hanover, PA 17331

Orol Ledden & Sons
Center & Atlantic Aves.
P.O. Box 7
Sewell, NJ 08080-0007

A. M. Leonard
P.O. Box 816
Piqua, OH 45356

Liberty Seed Co.
128 First Dr. S.E.
P.O. Box 806
New Philadelphia, OH 44663

Mantis Mfg. Corp.
1458 County Line Rd.
Huntingdon Valley, PA 19006

Mellinger's
2310 W. South Range Rd.
North Lima, OH 44452-9731

Modern Farm
1825 Big Horn Ave.
Cody, WY 82414

Natural Gardening Co.
27 Rutherford Ave.
San Anselmo, CA 94960

Natural Gardening Research
Center
Hwy. 48
P.O. Box 149
Sunman, IN 47041

Nature's Control
P.O. Box 35
Medford, OR 97501

Necessary Trading Co.
684 Salem Ave.
New Castle, VA 24127

North Country Organics
P.O. Box 107
Newbury, VT 05051

North Star Evergreens
P.O. Box 253
Park Rapids, MN 56470

OFE International
P.O. Box 164402
Miami, FL 33116

Ohio Earth Food
13737 Duquette Ave. N.E.
Hartville, OH 44632

Organic Pest Management
P.O. Box 55267
Seattle, WA 98155

Pacific Products
P.O. Box F
El Cajon, CA 92022

Peaceful Valley Farm Supply
Co.
11173 Peaceful Valley Rd.
Nevada City, CA 95959

Plow and Hearth
560 Main St.
Madison, VA 22727

Raintree Nursery
391 Butts Rd.
Morton, WA 98356

Reuter Laboratories
8450 Natural Wy.
Manassas Park, VA 22111

Richter's
P.O. Box 26
Goodwood, Ontario L0C 1A0

Ringer Corp.
9959 Valley View Rd.
Minneapolis, MN 55344

Seabright Enterprises
4026 Harlan St.
Emeryville, CA 94608

Southern Exposure Seed
Exchange
P.O. Box 158
North Garden, VA 22959

Spalding Laboratories
760 Printz Rd.
Arroyo Grande, CA 93420

Stark Bros.
Hwy. 54 W.
Louisiana, MO 63353-0010

Tregunno Seeds
126 Catherine St. N.
Hamilton, Ontario L8R 1J4

Unique Insect Control
5504 Sperry Dr.
Citrus Heights, CA 95621

Urban Farmer
2833 Vicente St.
San Francisco, CA 94116

Vesey's Seeds
P.O. Box 9000
Charlottestown, Prince
Edward Island C1A 8K6

Whitmire Research
Laboratories
3568 Tree Court Industrial
Blvd.
St. Louis, MO 63122

Zoecon Industries
12200 Denton Dr.
Dallas, TX 75234

## LAWN PRODUCTS

Necessary Trading Co.
684 Salem Ave.
New Castle, VA 24127

Sudbury Lawn & Garden
Products
P.O. Box 34820
Phoenix, AZ 85067

## LIQUID ORGANIC FERTILIZERS

Agri-Systems International
125 7th St.
Windgap, PA 18091

Bonide Chemical Co.
2 Wurz Ave.
Yorkville, NY 13495

Bountiful Gardens
5798 Ridgewood Rd.
Willits, CA 95490

Bramen Co.
P.O. Box 70
Salem, MA 01970-0070

W. Atlee Burpee Co.
300 Park Ave.
Warminster, PA 18974

D. V. Burrell Seed Growers Co.
P.O. Box 150
Rocky Ford, CO 81067

Charley's Greenhouse Supply
1569 Memorial Hwy.
Mt. Vernon, WA 98273

Clapper Co.
1121 Washington St.
Newton, MA 02165

CompuGarden
725 Richmond Ave.
Silver Spring, MD 20910

Down to Earth Distributors
850 W. 2nd St.
Eugene, OR 97402

Earlee
2002 Hwy. 62
Jeffersonville, IN 47130

Full Circle Garden Products
P.O. Box 6
Redway, CA 95560

Gardener's Supply Co.
128 Intervale Rd.
Burlington, VT 05401

Green Earth Organics
9422 144th St. E.
Puyallup, WA 98373

Harmony Farm Supply
P.O. Box 451
Graton, CA 95444

Hartmann's Plantation
310 60th St.
P.O. Box E
Grand Junction, MI 49056

Hyponex Co.
P.O. Box 4300
Copley, OH 44321

Kilgore Seed Co.
1400 W. First St.
Sanford, FL 32771

Lakeland Nursery Sales
340 Poplar St.
Hanover, PA 17331

Liberty Seed Co.
128 First Dr. S.E.
P.O. Box 806
New Philadelphia, OH 44663

Mantis Mfg. Corp.
1458 County Line Rd.
Huntingdon Valley, PA 19006

Mellinger's
2310 W. South Range Rd.
North Lima, OH 44452-9731

Natural Gardening Co.
27 Rutherford Ave.
San Anselmo, CA 94960

Natural Gardening Research
Center
Hwy. 48
P.O. Box 149
Sunman, IN 47041

Necessary Trading Co.
684 Salem Ave.
New Castle, VA 24127

North American Kelp
Cross St.
Waldoboro, ME 04572

North Country Organics
P.O. Box 107
Newbury, VT 05051

North Star Evergreens
P.O. Box 253
Park Rapids, MN 56470

OFE International
P.O. Box 164402
Miami, FL 33116

Ohio Earth Food
13737 Duquette Ave. N.E.
Hartville, OH 44632

Organic Pest Management
P.O. Box 55267
Seattle, WA 98155

Peaceful Valley Farm Supply
Co.
11173 Peaceful Valley Rd.
Nevada City, CA 95959

Pony Creek Nursery
Tilleda, WI 54978

Richter's
P.O. Box 26
Goodwood, Ontario L0C 1A0

Tregunno Seeds
126 Catherine St. N.
Hamilton, Ontario L8R 1J4

Trickle Soak Systems
P.O. Box 38
Santee, CA 92071

Otis S. Twilley Seed Co.
P.O. Box 65
Trevose, PA 19047

Urban Farmer
2833 Vicente St.
San Francisco, CA 94116

Vesey's Seeds
P.O. Box 9000
Charlottestown, Prince
    Edward Island C1A 8K6

## METERS AND INSTRUMENTS

Agrilite
P.O. Box 12
93853 River Rd.
Junction City, OR 97448

Brookstone Co.
127 Vose Farm Rd.
Peterborough, NH 03458

W. Atlee Burpee Co.
300 Park Ave.
Warminster, PA 18974

D. V. Burrell Seed Growers Co.
P.O. Box 150
Rocky Ford, CO 81067

Charley's Greenhouse Supply
1569 Memorial Hwy.
Mt. Vernon, WA 98273

Clapper Co.
1121 Washington St.
Newton, MA 02165

Earlee
2002 Hwy. 62
Jeffersonville, IN 47130

Environmental Concepts
710 N.W. 57th St.
Ft. Lauderdale, FL 33309

Full Circle Garden Products
P.O. Box 6
Redway, CA 95560

Gardener's Supply Co.
128 Intervale Rd.
Burlington, VT 05401

Green Earth Organics
9422 144th St. E.
Puyallup, WA 98373

Harlane Company
266 Orangeburgh Rd.
Old Tappan, NJ 07675

Harmony Farm Supply
P.O. Box 451
Graton, CA 95444

Hartmann's Plantation
310 60th St.
P.O. Box E
Grand Junction, MI 49056

Hydro-Gardens of Denver
P.O. Box 9707
Colorado Springs, CO 80301

Indoor Gardening Supplies
P.O. Box 40567
Detroit, MI 48240

International Irrigation
Systems
L.P.O. Box 160
Niagara Falls, NY 14304

Lakeland Nursery Sales
340 Poplar St.
Hanover, PA 17331

Orol Ledden & Sons
Center & Atlantic Aves.
P.O. Box 7
Sewell, NJ 08080-0007

A. M. Leonard
P.O. Box 816
Piqua, OH 45356

Liberty Seed Co.
128 First Dr. S.E.
P.O. Box 806
New Philadelphia, OH 44663

Mellinger's
2310 W. South Range Rd.
North Lima, OH 44452-9731

Modern Farm
1825 Big Horn Ave.
Cody, WY 82414

Necessary Trading Co.
684 Salem Ave.
New Castle, VA 24127

OFE International
P.O. Box 164402
Miami, FL 33116

Ohio Earth Food
13737 Duquette Ave. N.E.
Hartville, OH 44632

Organic Pest Management
P.O. Box 55267
Seattle, WA 98155

Ozark Handle & Hardware
P.O. Box 426
Eureka Springs, AR 72632

Peaceful Valley Farm Supply
Co.
11173 Peaceful Valley Rd.
Nevada City, CA 95959

Plow and Hearth
560 Main St.
Madison, VA 22727

Ringer Corp.
9959 Valley View Rd.
Minneapolis, MN 55344

Rodco Products Co.
P.O. Box 944
2565 16th Ave.
Columbus, NE 68601

Science Associates
P.O. Box 230
Princeton, NJ 08542

Stark Bros.
Hwy. 54 W.
Louisiana, MO 63353-0010

Trade-Wind Instruments
1076 Lorraine St.
Enumclaw, WA 98022

Tregunno Seeds
126 Catherine St. N.
Hamilton, Ontario L8R 1J4

Otis S. Twilley Seed Co.
P.O. Box 65
Trevose, PA 19047

Urban Farmer
2833 Vicente St.
San Francisco, CA 94116

Wade Mfg. Co.
1025 S.W. Allen Blvd.
Beaverton, OR 97005

## ROW COVERS AND SHADING MATERIALS

Bountiful Gardens
5798 Ridgewood Rd.
Willits, CA 95490

Brookstone Co.
127 Vose Farm Rd.
Peterborough, NH 03458

W. Atlee Burpee Co.
300 Park Ave.
Warminster, PA 18974

Charley's Greenhouse Supply
1569 Memorial Hwy.
Mt. Vernon, WA 98273

Dalen Products
11110 Gilbert Dr.
Knoxville, TN 37932

Drip Irrigation Garden
16216 Raymer St.
Van Nuys, CA 91406

Earlee
2002 Hwy. 62
Jeffersonville, IN 47130

Gardener's Supply Co.
128 Intervale Rd.
Burlington, VT 05401

Green Earth Organics
9422 144th St. E.
Puyallup, WA 98373

Green Garden
P.O. Box 351
Somerset, PA 15501

Harmony Farm Supply
P.O. Box 451
Graton, CA 95444

Hydro-Gardens of Denver
P.O. Box 9707
Colorado Springs, CO 80932

Ken-Bar
24 Gould St.
Reading, MA 01867

Orol Ledden & Sons
Center & Atlantic Aves.
P.O. Box 7
Sewell, NJ 08080-0007

A. M. Leonard
P.O. Box 816
Piqua, OH 45356

Liberty Seed Co.
128 First Dr. S.E.
P.O. Box 806
New Philadelphia, OH 44663

Mantis Mfg. Corp.
1458 County Line Rd.
Huntingdon Valley, PA 19006

Mellinger's
2310 W. South Range Rd.
North Lima, OH 44452-9731

Modern Farm
1825 Big Horn Ave.
Cody, WY 82414

Necessary Trading Co.
684 Salem Ave.
New Castle, VA 24127

OFE International
P.O. Box 164402
Miami, FL 33116

Peaceful Valley Farm Supply
Co.
11173 Peaceful Valley Rd.
Nevada City, CA 95959

Ringer Corp.
9959 Valley View Rd.
Minneapolis, MN 55344

Smith & Hawken
25 Corte Madera
Mill Valley, CA 94941

Otis S. Twilley Seed Co.
P.O. Box 65
Trevose, PA 19047

Vesey's Seeds
P.O. Box 9000
Charlottestown, Prince
Edward Island C1A 8K6

## SPRAYERS

Alternative
3439 E. 86th St., Suite 259D
Indianapolis, IN 46240

Amerind-MasKissic
P.O. Box 111
Parker Ford, PA 19457

Brookstone Co.
127 Vose Farm Rd.
Peterborough, NH 03458

W. Atlee Burpee Co.
300 Park Ave.
Warminster, PA 18974

D. V. Burrell Seed Growers Co.
P.O. Box 150
Rocky Ford, CO 81067

Charley's Greenhouse Supply
1569 Memorial Hwy.
Mt. Vernon, WA 98273

Clapper Co.
1121 Washington St.
Newton, MA 02165

Down to Earth Distributors
850 W. 2nd St.
Eugene, OR 97402

Dramm Co.
P.O. Box 1960
Manitowoc, WI 54221-1960

Drip Irrigation Garden
16216 Raymer St.
Van Nuys, CA 91406

Earlee
2002 Hwy. 62
Jeffersonville, IN 47130

Gardena
6031 Culligan Way
Minnetonka, MN 55345

Gardener's Supply Co.
128 Intervale Rd.
Burlington, VT 05401

Garden Way Mfg. Co.
102nd St. & Ninth Ave.
Troy, NY 12180

Green Earth Organics
9422 144th St. E.
Puyallup, WA 98373

Green Garden
P.O. Box 351
Somerset, PA 15501

Greenleaf Technologies
P.O. Box 12726
Memphis, Tn 38182

Harmony Farm Supply
P.O. Box 451
Graton, CA 95444

H. D. Hudson Mfg. Co.
500 N. Michigan Ave.
Chicago, IL 60611

Insects
10505 N. College Ave.
Indianapolis, IN 46280

Kinsman Co.
River Rd.
Point Pleasant, PA 18950

Lakeland Nursery Sales
340 Poplar St.
Hanover, PA 17331

Orol Ledden & Sons
Center & Atlantic Aves.
P.O. Box 7
Sewell, NJ 08080-0007

A. M. Leonard
P.O. Box 816
Piqua, OH 45356

Liberty Seed Co.
128 First Dr. S.E.
P.O. Box 806
New Philadelphia, OH 44663

Mantis Mfg. Corp.
1458 County Line Rd.
Huntingdon Valley, PA 19006

Mellinger's
2310 W. South Range Rd.
North Lima, OH 44452-9731

BCS Mosa
P.O. Box 1739
Matthews, NC 28106

Natural Gardening Co.
27 Rutherford Ave.
San Anselmo, CA 94960

Necessary Trading Co.
684 Salem Ave.
New Castle, VA 24127

North Star Evergreens
P.O. Box 253
Park Rapids, MN 56470

OFE International
P.O. Box 164402
Miami, FL 33116

Ohio Earth Food
13737 Duquette Ave. N.E.
Hartville, OH 44632

Organic Pest Management
P.O. Box 55267
Seattle, WA 98155

Peaceful Valley Farm Supply
  Co.
11173 Peaceful Valley Rd.
Nevada City, CA 95959

PeCo Inc.
P.O. Box 1197
100 Airport Rd.
Arden, NC 28704

Plow and Hearth
560 Main St.
Madison, VA 22727

Pony Creek Nursery
Tilleda, WI 54978

Raindrip
P.O. Box 2173
21305 Itasca St.
Chatsworth, CA 91313-2173

Richdel
P.O. Drawer A
Carson City, NV 89702

Richter's
P.O. Box 26
Goodwood, Ontario L0C 1A0

Ringer Corp.
9959 Valley View Rd.
Minneapolis, MN 55344

Scotchmen
R.D. 1
Pottstown, PA 19464

Smith & Hawken
25 Corte Madera
Mill Valley, CA 94941

Stark Bros.
Hwy. 54 W.
Louisiana, MO 63353-0010

Tregunno Seeds
126 Catherine St. N.
Hamilton, Ontario L8R 1J4

Otis S. Twilley Seed Co.
P.O. Box 65
Trevose, PA 19047

Urban Farmer
2833 Vicente St.
San Francisco, CA 94116

Vesey's Seeds
P.O. Box 9000
Charlottestown, Prince
  Edward Island C1A 8K6

# *Recommended Reading*

Books     Ball, Jeff. *The Self-Sufficient Suburban Garden.* Emmaus, Pa.: Rodale
Press, 1983.

————. *Jeff Ball's 60-Minute Garden.* Emmaus, Pa.: Rodale Press, 1985.

Barton, Barbara. *Gardening by Mail 2.* Sebastopol, Calif.: Tusker Press, 1987.

Bilderback, Diane, and Dorothy Patent. *Backyard Fruits and Berries.* Emmaus,
Pa.: Rodale Press, 1984.

Bubel, Nancy. *The Seed-Starter's Handbook.* Emmaus, Pa.: Rodale Press, 1978.

Carr, Anna. *Rodale's Color Handbook of Garden Insects.* Emmaus, Pa.: Rodale
Press, 1979.

————. *Good Neighbors: Companion Planting for Gardeners.* Emmaus, Pa.:
Rodale Press, 1985.

Cravens, Richard H. *Pests and Diseases.* Alexandria, Va.: Time-Life Books, 1977.

Creasy, Rosalind. *The Complete Book of Edible Landscaping.* San Francisco:
Sierra Club Books, 1982.

Davis, Brian. *The Gardener's Illustrated Encyclopedia of Trees and Shrubs.*
Emmaus, Pa.: Rodale Press, 1987.

Dirr, Michael A. *A Manual of Woody Landscape Plants,* 3rd ed. Champaign, Ill.:
Stipes Publishing Co., 1983.

Felt, E. P. *Plant Galls and Gall Makers.* New York: Hafner Publishing Co., 1965.

Fryer, Lee. *The Bio-Gardener's Bible.* Radnor, Pa.: Chilton, 1982.

Harris, Richard W. *Arboriculture*. Englewood Cliffs, N.J.: Prentice-Hall, 1983.

Hill, Lewis. *Pruning Simplified*. Emmaus, Pa.: Rodale Press, 1979.

Hirshberg, Gary, and Tracy Calvan, eds. The New Alchemy Institute Staff. *Gardening for All Seasons*. Andover, Mass.: Brick House Publishing, 1983.

Kourik, Robert. *Designing and Maintaining Your Edible Landscape Naturally*. Santa Rosa, Calif.: Metamorphic Press, 1986.

Logsdon, Gene. *Organic Orcharding*. Emmaus, Pa.: Rodale Press, 1981.

———. *Wildlife in Your Garden*. Emmaus, Pa.: Rodale Press, 1983.

MacNab, A. A. et al. *Identifying Diseases of Vegetables*. University Park, Pa.: Pennsylvania State University, 1983.

Minnich, Jerry. *The Earthworm Book*. Emmaus, Pa.: Rodale Press, 1977.

Minnich, Jerry, and Marjorie Hunt. *The Rodale Guide to Composting*. Emmaus, Pa.: Rodale Press, 1979.

The National Gardening Association. *Gardening*. Reading, Mass.: Addison-Wesley Co., 1986.

Phillips, Roger. *Trees of North America and Europe*. New York: Random House, 1978.

Pirone, Pascal P. *Diseases and Pests of Ornamental Plants*. New York: Ronald Press Co., 1970.

———. *Tree Maintenance*. New York: Oxford University Press, 1978.

Schultz, Warren. *The Chemical-Free Lawn*. Emmaus, Pa.: Rodale Press, 1989.

Sinclair, Wayne A., Howard H. Lyon, and Warren T. Johnson. *Diseases of Trees and Shrubs*. Ithaca, N.Y.: Cornell University Press, 1987.

Smith, Miranda, and Anna Carr. *Rodale's Garden Insect, Disease, and Weed Identification Guide*. Emmaus, Pa.: Rodale Press, 1988.

Taylor's Guide Staff. *Taylor's Guide to Ground Covers, Vines and Grasses*. Boston: Houghton Mifflin, 1987.

———. *Taylor's Guide to Trees*. Boston: Houghton Mifflin, 1988.

Wescott, Cynthia. *The Gardener's Bug Book.* Garden City, N.Y.: Doubleday & Co., 1973.

Wyman, Donald. *Wyman's Gardening Encyclopedia.* New York: Macmillan Publishing Co., 1986.

Yepsen, Roger B., Jr. *The Encyclopedia of Natural Insect and Disease Control.* Emmaus, Pa.: Rodale Press, 1984.

**Magazines**    *Avant Gardener,* P.O. Box 489, New York, NY 10028

*Common Sense Pest Control Quarterly,* Bio-Integral Resource Center (BIRC), P.O. Box 7414, Berkeley, CA 94707

*Fine Gardening,* Taunton Press, Box 355, 63 South Main Street, Newtown, CT 06470

*The Green Scene,* Pennsylvania Horticultural Society, 325 Walnut Street, Philadelphia, PA 19106

*Horticulture,* Horticulture Partners, 20 Park Plaza, Suite 1220, Boston, MA 02116

*Hort Ideas,* Route 1, Gravel Switch, KY 40328

*IPM Practitioner,* Bio-Integral Resource Center (BIRC), P.O. Box 7414, Berkeley, CA 94707

*National Gardening,* National Gardening Association, Depot Square, Peterborough, NH 03458

*Rodale's Organic Gardening,* Rodale Press, 33 East Minor Street, Emmaus, PA 18098

# Hardiness Zone Map

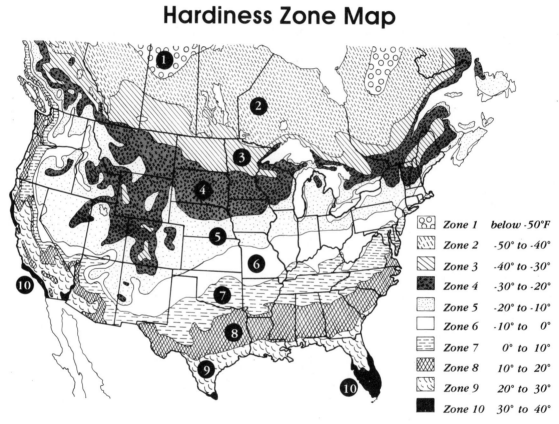

| | Zone 1 | below -50°F |
|---|---|---|
| | Zone 2 | -50° to -40° |
| | Zone 3 | -40° to -30° |
| | Zone 4 | -30° to -20° |
| | Zone 5 | -20° to -10° |
| | Zone 6 | -10° to 0° |
| | Zone 7 | 0° to 10° |
| | Zone 8 | 10° to 20° |
| | Zone 9 | 20° to 30° |
| | Zone 10 | 30° to 40° |

Average Minimum Temperatures for Each Zone

# *Index*

Page references in *italic* indicate tables.

Rodale Press, Inc., publishes RODALE'S ORGANIC GARDENING,
the all-time favorite gardening magazine.
For information on how to order your subscription,
write to RODALE'S ORGANIC GARDENING, Emmaus, PA 18098.